Oracle9*i* Developer: Developing Web Applications with Forms Builder

John Adolph Palinski

Australia • Canada • Mexico • Singapore • Spain • United Kingdom • United States

Oracle9*i* Developer: Developing Web Applications with Forms Builder

By John Adolph Palinski

Senior Vice President, Publisher:
Kristen Duerr

Executive Editor:
Jennifer Locke

Acquisitions Editor:
Bill Larkin

Product Manager:
Tricia Boyle

Development Editor:
Betsey Henkels

Associate Product Manager:
Janet Aras

Editorial Assistant:
Christy Urban

Senior Product Marketing Manager:
Jason Sakos

Production Editor:
Megan Belanger/Brooke Booth

Cover Designer:
Rakefet Kenaan

Compositor:
GEX Publishing Services

Manufacturing Coordinator:
Laura Burns

Printed in Canada

1 2 3 4 5 6 7 8 9 WC 06 05 04 03

For more information, contact Course Technology, 25 Thomson Place, Boston, Massachusetts, 02210.

Or find us on the World Wide Web at: www.course.com

ISBN 0-619-15911-1

BRIEF

Contents

TABLE OF Contents

CHAPTER FOUR
Formatting the Form Using the Layout Editor 143

CHAPTER FIVE
Controlling Form Behavior and Format Using Properties, Property Classes, and the Property Palette 207

CHAPTER NINE
Adding Menus, Popup Menus, Alerts, Timers, and Hierarchical Tree Items to Forms 463

CHAPTER TEN
Using SQL in Data Blocks, Debugging, and Creating Calendars 529

Preface

This book is a detailed guide to learning and using the Oracle9*i* Forms Builder, which is the latest version of Oracle's main rapid application development (RAD) tool. With Oracle9*i* Forms Builder, you can develop Web forms deployable in Oracle9*i*AS. This book also supports developers using Oracle6*i* Form Builder—the latest version of the tool that Oracle has developed to run in the client-server environment. Throughout the book, a distinctive 6*i* icon identifies explanations and exercises related to Oracle6*i*. The techniques demonstrated in the book are essential to a developer creating robust business-class applications for either Web or client-server environments.

Intended Audience

This book is intended to support individuals in application development courses covering the use of Oracle9*i* Forms Builder. It is also intended to support individuals who are preparing for Oracle certification in the Application Developer track.

Prior knowledge of general relational database terminology and concepts is required. In addition, the reader should have a basic knowledge of SQL (Structured Query Language). While it is preferable that the reader know Oracle9*i* SQL, the reader's experience using SQL on other databases, such as SQLServer, is acceptable. The reader should be able to write SQL commands for querying, inserting, updating, and deleting data in relational tables.

It is also highly recommended that the reader have some knowledge of Oracle's development language, PL/SQL. The reader should understand the basic code blocks and PL/SQL constructs. The reader should also understand how to create and use stored procedures such as functions, procedures, and packages.

Oracle Certification

This book helps readers prepare for Oracle9*i* Forms Developer certification. At the time of publication, the Oracle9*i* Forms Developer exam objectives were not available. When they become available, a mapping grid will be posted to our Web site. You can then view the objectives and see where each is covered in this text. To access this information, go to *www.course.com* and search for this book by title or author. More information about Oracle certification tracks, specific exams, and registration is available at *www.oracle.com/education/certification*.

The Approach

This book presents concepts and exercises that teach you to be a competent Oracle Forms developer. The concepts and practices are presented within the structure of the system development life cycle. The first chapter reacquaints the reader with relational database design theory, entity relationship diagrams, data schema diagrams, and data flow diagrams. The reader is shown how to identify applications and the database that supports the applications. From this point, you learn to operate a basic form and to create increasingly powerful forms. Throughout the book, the reader is presented with development principles useful with any system development work. For example, each chapter presents formatting tips for the development of forms that operators can use easily and efficiently in an actual working environment.

An important component of the book is the ongoing case project, which allows the reader to not only practice the skills learned in each chapter but also reinforces the use of Forms Builder in relation to the system development life cycle. As a simplified version of a budgeting system for a construction company, the case project builds chapter by chapter. The first chapter presents a data flow diagram of the budgeting process and an entity relationship diagram of the database. The reader is asked to study these diagrams and determine the applications to be built. In subsequent chapters, the case project requires the reader to add components to the system based on the concepts learned in the chapter. In the last chapter, the reader returns to the system development life cycle by performing a system test on the budgeting application using the data flow diagram processes from the first chapter. The case project is designed to expose the reader to an actual system development project using Oracle9*i* Forms Builder.

Overview of This Book

The material in this book helps students to achieve the following objectives:

- Understand key components of the Oracle9*i* Forms Builder tools and architecture
- Operate a form and understand its default behavior
- Create a form using the Data Block and Layout wizard
- Understand the key components of a form, menu, and object library
- Use properties and the Property Palette to control the behavior and look of your forms
- Use the Layout Editor to format forms
- Understand when triggers fire and how to execute PL/SQL code scripts when the triggers fire
- Use common triggers and built-ins to enhance the operability of your forms
- Add radio group buttons, check boxes, list items, hierarchical tree items, and list-of-values to your forms

- Replace the default Select, Insert, Update, and Delete statements generated by the form with your own statements
- Call other forms and reports from your form
- Use Oracle's object technology in the form
- Debug a form using the message built-in and Forms Builder's Debug Console
- Create bean areas in your form that use JavaBeans and use Java classes wrapped in PL/SQL with a trigger

Chapter 1 describes how to understand and document system requirements consisting of the database and applications. **Chapter 2** introduces you to the Forms Builder integrated development environment, and shows you how to create a simple form, execute the form, perform complex searches on the form, and modify database records. **Chapter 3** shows you how to use the Object Navigator to locate and create form components, how to create a detail data block that is synchronized with a record on a master data block, and what the components of the form are. **Chapter 4** shows how to use the Layout Editor to format the form. **Chapter 5** introduces the Property Palette, property classes, object groups, and object libraries. **Chapter 6** discusses triggers, trigger events, built-in subprograms, and the PL/SQL Editor, which is used to add PL/SQL and built-ins to the trigger. **Chapter 7** describes the various types of items that can be displayed on your form (for example, radio group buttons, check boxes, list items, and images) and how to create and launch a LOV (list-of-values). **Chapter 8** discusses the various types of canvases and shows how to display them. This chapter also covers how to create toolbars, dialog boxes, and how to call other forms. **Chapter 9** covers popup menus, events, timers, calendars, and hierarchical items. The chapter also discusses how to use a menu to bind your applications into a system. **Chapter 10** defines how to replace the SQL in your forms and how to debug the form. **Chapter 11** shows how to employ both Oracle object technology and Java in your form. It also covers techniques for using your form on the Web.

The five appendices at the end of the book contain information on the following: installing the Oracle9*i* Personal edition; Property Definitions; System Variable Definitions; Triggers; and Built-in Subprograms. In addition, a comprehensive Glossary at the back of the book defines terms used throughout the text.

Features

To enhance students' learning experience, each chapter in this book includes the following elements:

- **Chapter Objectives:** Each chapter begins with a list of the concepts to be mastered. This list is a quick overview of chapter contents as well as a useful study aid.

- **Methodology:** As new commands are presented in each chapter, the syntax of the command is presented and then an example illustrates the command in the context of a business operation. This methodology shows the student not only *how* the command is used but also *when* and *why* it is used. The step-by-step instructions in each chapter enable the student to work through the examples in this textbook, engendering a hands-on environment in which the student reinforces his or her knowledge of chapter material.

Tip: This feature, designated by the *Tip* icon, provides extra information about how to solve a problem, a timesaving shortcut, or recommendations for certain real-world situations.

Note: These explanations, designated by the *Note* icon, provide further information about concepts or syntax structures.

Caution: This icon indicates concepts or steps that often cause difficulty. Each caution anticipates a potential mistake and provides methods for avoiding the same problem in the future.

Oracle6*i* Form Builder: Although this book is primarily geared to Oracle9*i* Forms Builder, it supplies information so that readers using Oracle6*i* Form Builder can study and learn successfully. To that end, the "6*i*" icon is used to denote instances throughout the text where important pieces of information about Oracle6*i* Form Builder are provided. In particular, the icon points out instances in which a certain task or series of steps differs if the reader is using version 6*i* rather than 9*i*.

- **Chapter Summaries:** Each chapter is followed by a summary of chapter concepts in bulleted form. These summaries are a helpful recap of chapter contents.
- **Review Questions:** End-of-chapter assessment begins with a set of approximately 15 review questions that reinforce the main ideas introduced in each chapter. These questions ensure that students have mastered the concepts and understand the information presented.
- **Exam Review Questions:** Five certification-type questions are included to prepare students for the type of questions that can be expected on a certification exam, as well as to measure the students' level of understanding.
- **Hands-on Assignments:** Along with conceptual explanations and examples, each chapter provides approximately five hands-on assignments related to the chapter's contents. These assignments simulate practical experience. In some cases, the assignments are based on tables or other structures created using a script provided with the book that the student runs just before working on these assignments.

- **Great State Electric Budgeting System Case Project:** Each chapter contains one installment of the case project. The case project is designed to build within the context of the system development life cycle and result in a budgeting system typical of one used by an actual construction company. This case is designed to help students apply what they have learned to real-world situations. The case installments give students the opportunity to actually understand and perform the tasks needed to design and build an Oracle Forms system, much as one would do in an actual business situation.

Teaching Tools

The following supplemental materials are available when this book is used in a classroom setting. All Teaching Tools available with this book are provided to the instructor on a single CD-ROM.

- **Electronic Instructor's Manual:** The Instructor's Manual that accompanies this textbook includes the following elements:
  - Additional instructional material to assist in class preparation, including suggestions for lecture topics
  - Answers to end of chapter Review Questions, Exam Review Questions, and Hands-on Assignments (when applicable)
- **ExamView®:** This objective-based test generator lets the instructor create paper, LAN, or Web-based tests from test banks designed specifically for this Course Technology text. Instructors can use the QuickTest Wizard to create tests in fewer than five minutes by taking advantage of Course Technology's question banks—or create customized exams.
- **PowerPoint Presentations:** Microsoft PowerPoint slides are included for each chapter. Instructors might use the slides in three ways: As teaching aids during classroom presentations, as printed handouts for classroom distribution, or as network-accessible resources for chapter review. Instructors can add their own slides for additional topics introduced to the class.
- **Data Files.** These include the completed source code files to the various practice sections found in the chapter and listing files containing PL/SQL and SQL scripts that can be copied into the forms. The data files are provided through the Course Technology Web site at *www.course.com*, and are also available on the Teaching Tools CD-ROM. Additional script files needed for specific chapters are also available through the Web site.

- **Solution Files.** Solutions to the end of chapter material are provided on the Teaching Tools CD-ROM. The solution files also contain a partially completed budgeting application that represents the work that was to take place up to and including the respective chapter's installment. Solutions may also be found on the Course Technology Web site at *www.course.com*. The solutions are password protected.

Dedication and Acknowledgments

I would like to dedicate this book to my father, Adolph Palinski. He was a member of the Greatest Generation and I have always been very proud of his services during the war. During WWII he was in the Coast Guard working on a sub-chaser looking for U-boats off the Atlantic seaboard. As a very little boy every evening I would stand on the corner waiting for him to come home from work. He would stop, pick me up, and drive me around the block before parking the car in the garage. My father died in 1967, and I miss him more every day that passes. When the time is right, I hope that he picks me up on the corner in his company car and takes me to the place he and the rest of my family will be.

There are a number of people that I would like to acknowledge. The first is my Developmental Editor, Betsey Henkels. She has worked with me every step of this book. She has been extremely patient with me, but more importantly she has helped to develop a very good book and has been fun to work with. I would also like to thank my Product Manager, Tricia Boyle. She kept us on schedule and provided many suggestions to help produce an excellent product. I would also like to thank my agent, Neil Salkind, and Bill Larkin, Acquisition Editor, for giving me a chance.

Another person I would like to thank is my co-worker and friend, Roger Garfoot. Roger is a premier Java developer, and his expertise was vitally needed to complete the Bean area discussion in Chapter 11.

Finally, I would like to thank my wife Linda. She has been next to me for the past year offering encouragement while I was writing this book. I couldn't have done it without her support and love.

Our team of reviewers also provided extremely helpful suggestions, feedback, and insight into the development of this textbook. They are as follows: Douglas Bock, Southern Illinois University; Gary Hackbarth, Iowa State University; Donna Lohn, Lakeland Community College; and Mark Smith, Trident Technical College.

Read This Before You Begin

To the User

Data Files

This book has numerous practice sections and abundant end-of-chapter material. The practice sections are designed so that you will not need data files. Except for Chapter 9, the practice sections in each chapter consist of developing a new form from scratch. Each practice section builds on the previous chapter practice section or asks you to create a new form. Thus, if you are able to accomplish the practice exercise you do not need to use the data files, except in one or two specific instances. The four different types of files provided for this book are listed below:

- The FMB files are Forms Builder source code files saved after the practice exercise has been completed. The purpose of these files is three-fold:
  1. To allow you to operate the form and see the effect of the practice before you begin to modify your own form.
  2. To allow you to review the completed form if you do not fully understand the practice instructions.
  3. To give you a form that can be used for subsequent practices if you cannot complete a practice or choose not to. Because this text covers both versions, you have been supplied with Forms modules for both Oracle9*i* Forms Builder and Oracle6*i* Form Builder.
- Two TIF image files have been included. One contains the data flow diagram used in Figure 1-14, which is a copy of the data flow diagram used in the Great State Electric Budgeting case project. A second TIF file is included so that you have an image to display in one of the chapter practice sections.
- Listing files: For practices that require more than six or seven lines of code, a TXT file is included so that you do not have to type the code. However, you are encouraged to type the scripts rather than copying them to help you learn the SQL language, which is very important to Forms Builder and Oracle.
- Java files: Chapter 11 has two Java files – a **.jar** file containing an actual JavaBean and a Java file that contains a wrapper.

Your instructor will provide you with the data files, or you can obtain them electronically from the Course Technology Web site by accessing *www.course.com* and then searching for this book's title. It is highly recommended that you work through all the practices, assignments, and case study segments to reinforce your learning.

The script files for Chapters 1-11 are found in the **Data** folder under their respective chapter folders (**Chapter09**, **Chapter10**, etc.) on your data disk and have the file names that correspond with the instructions in the chapter. If the computer in your school lab—or your own computer—has the Oracle9*i* Database and Oracle9*i* Forms Builder (or Oracle6*i* Form Builder) software installed, you can work through the chapter practice sections, examples, and complete the Hands-on Assignments and ongoing Case Project segments. All examples in this book were performed using the Oracle9*i* Database and Oracle9*i* Forms Builder. However, almost everything presented in this book can also be accomplished with an Oracle8*i* Database and Oracle6*i* Form Builder. You have also been supplied with Oracle6*i* Form Builder modules. In several cases, practices could *only* be performed using version 6*i* or 9*i*. In those cases, you were not provided the alternative version (that is, only files for the version that works were provided). These instances are indicated in the chapters.

Using Your Own Computer

To use your own computer to work through the chapter examples and to complete the Hands-on Assignments and Case Project, you need the following:

- **Hardware:** A computer capable of using the Microsoft Windows NT, 2000 Professional, or XP Professional operating system. You should have at least 256 MB of RAM and between 2.75 GB and 4.75 GB of hard disk space available before installing the software.
- **Software:**
  - Oracle9*i* Release 2 Enterprise Edition, or, at a minimum, Oracle9*i* Release 2 Personal Edition
  - Oracle9*i* Forms Developer is included in the back of this book

  As mentioned previously, if you are using Oracle6*i* Form Builder, you can work through most of the material in the book as well.
- **Data files:** You can get the data files from your instructor, or you can obtain the data files electronically by accessing the Course Technology Web site at *www.course.com* and then searching for this book's title.

Visit Our World Wide Web Site

Additional materials designed especially for you might be available on the World Wide Web. To check for these materials, go to *www.course.com* periodically and search this site for more details.

TO THE INSTRUCTOR

To complete some of the chapters in this book, your students may need access to a set of data files. These files are included in the Instructor's Resource Kit. They may also be obtained electronically by accessing the Course Technology Web site at *www.course.com* and then searching for this book's title.

Solution files are also available for this book. The solution files consist primarily of the form modules for each of the chapter assignments. These files reflect the form after the assignment was completed. In many cases, the assignments were constructed so that you would use the form module from the previous assignment. You have also been supplied with the budgeting application for the Great State Electric Budgeting System Case Project. This is an application that is to be built in 11 installments. You have been provided with the forms module that reflects the work to be completed in each chapter. The completed application exists in Chapter 11. You have also been provided versions of the application in both Oracle9*i* Forms Builder and Oracle6*i* Form Builder.

The material in this book was tested once using the Microsoft Windows 2000 Professional operating system with Oracle9*i* Release 2 Enterprise Edition and using the Microsoft Windows XP Professional operating system with Oracle9*i* Personal Edition, Release 2 (9.2.0.1.0). The material was also tested using both Oracle9*i* Forms Builder and Oracle6*i* Form Builder.

Oracle9*i* Software

The Course Technology Kit for Oracle9*i* Software contains the database software necessary to perform all the tasks shown in this textbook. The software included in the kit can be used with Microsoft Windows NT, 2000, or XP operating systems. Please contact your Course Technology Sales Representative, or visit *www.course.com*, for information about purchasing this CD Kit. Detailed installation, configuration, and logon information are provided at *www.course.com/cdkit* on the Web page for this title.

When you install the Oracle9*i* software, you will be prompted to supply the database name for the default administrative user accounts. Make certain that you record the names and passwords of the accounts, because you may need to log into the database with one of these administrative accounts in later chapters. After you install Oracle9*i*, you will be required to enter a user name and password to access the software. One default user name created during the installation process is "scott". The default password for the user name is "tiger". If you have installed the Personal Edition of Oracle9*i*, you will not need to enter a Connect String during the login process. As previously mentioned, full instructions for installing and logging into Oracle9*i*, Release 2, are provided on the Web site for this textbook at *www.course.com*.

Course Technology Data Files

You are granted a license to copy the data files to any computer or computer network used by individuals who have purchased this book.

CHAPTER

1

IDENTIFYING THE APPLICATIONS AND THE DATABASE SCHEMA

In this chapter you will:

- Learn how Oracle Forms Builder is integrated into the system development life cycle
- Use data flow diagrams to identify applications, processes, and the data needed for the processes
- Use entity relationship diagrams to initiate the design of the database schema
- Use the data schema diagram to identify the database properties
- Learn how Forms Builder uses the Oracle9*i* database

A developer usually follows a methodology when designing and building a computer system. Without a methodology, the developer can flounder and produce an incomplete system. If, by chance, the developer finishes a product without using a methodology, the product might not meet user requirements.

This chapter briefly reviews the system development life cycle and explains how Oracle's Forms Builder tool set fits within this life cycle. Before you begin learning how to use Forms Builder, it is important that you become aware of powerful tools that can help you develop effective forms. This chapter discusses several of the tools that you can use to identify the information you need to begin developing forms.

In the Case Project at the end of each chapter, you are presented with the Great State Budgeting System, which comprises a series of applications that you build piece by piece throughout the book for practice with Forms Builder. At the end of this chapter, you are asked to identify the forms needed for the system and the data processed by each form. To develop an Oracle Forms system, a wide range of skills is needed, and each chapter in this book builds up your skills.

To help you get an idea of the flow of subjects in this book, each chapter begins with a roadmap showing the topics previously covered, the topics in the current chapter, and future topics. Figure 1-1 is the initial roadmap.

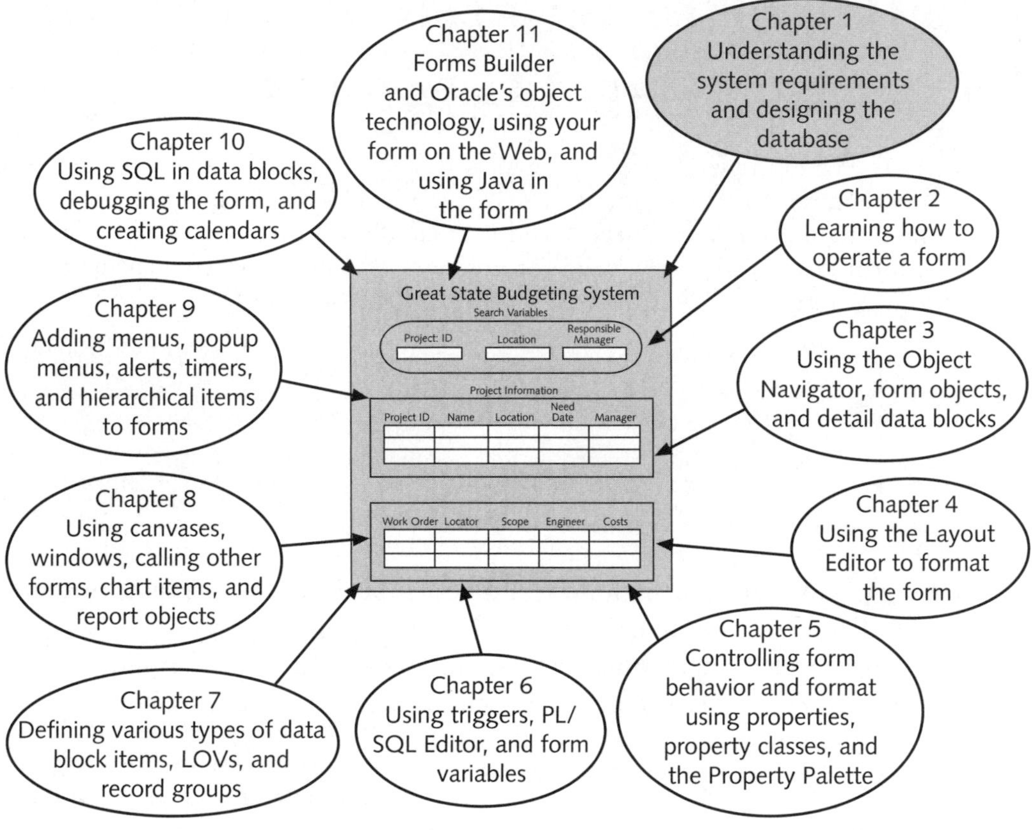

Figure 1-1 Roadmap

INTEGRATION OF ORACLE FORMS BUILDER INTO THE SYSTEM DEVELOPMENT LIFE CYCLE (SDLC)

System development projects go through a series of phases, starting with project identification and ending with implementation and system use. These phases are called the system development life cycle and are outlined below:

- Project identification and selection
- Project initiation and planning
- Analysis
- Logical design

- Physical design
- Implementation
- Maintenance

This list of phases represents the traditional approach to system development. A subset of the SDLC, called **rapid application development (RAD)**, is often used to eliminate some traditional tasks and thereby speed up the implementation of the system.

Forms Builder can be used to support both the traditional SDLC methodology and RAD. For example, during the physical design phase of a project, the analyst confirms user requirements. One part of these requirements is the design of the forms used within the system. **Forms** are the mechanisms that allow a user to interact with the database. A form enables the user to add records to the database, modify existing records, delete records, retrieve records from the database, and view records.

Using a RAD approach, the developer can confirm requirements by showing the user a **prototype**, which is an early facsimile of the final product. The purpose of the prototype is to give users a sample of the physical characteristics of the application they will use when the system is implemented. Prototypes are especially important in the RAD approach. With the RAD approach, developers and users create, analyze, and modify prototypes in a series of iterations until the design is approved. With the refinement of the prototype in each iteration, the prototype moves closer to its final form. The RAD approach allows the physical design and implementation phases to be combined to reduce the overall implementation time.

Oracle's Forms Builder is a RAD tool that supports the iterative prototyping of forms. Forms Builder contains a wizard that allows you to easily and quickly identify attributes that are to appear on the form. Forms Builder has another wizard that allows you to give the form a basic format. The Forms Builder Layout Editor can then be used to refine the form. Another important feature of Forms Builder is that the wizard generates the code needed to retrieve records to the form, and it inserts, updates, and deletes records as well. In essence, a developer can easily create and give the user a basic working prototype within thirty minutes and thereby significantly help the analyst during the physical design phase of the project.

Forms Builder also supports the use of Oracle's Designer 9*i* computer-aided software engineering (CASE) tools. The **CASE** tools offer the developer a formal methodology of design and development. They also offer the developer a wide array of tools used to document requirements and design the final application. Several of these tools are discussed in this chapter.

Designer 9*i* is a code generator and creates a Forms Builder design module as the last step of the design process. Forms Builder is then used to finalize the application behavior and generate the executable code. The executable code is then tested and placed into production. Figure 1-2 illustrates the various SDLC phases and shows when Designer 9*i* and Forms Builder 9*i* are used.

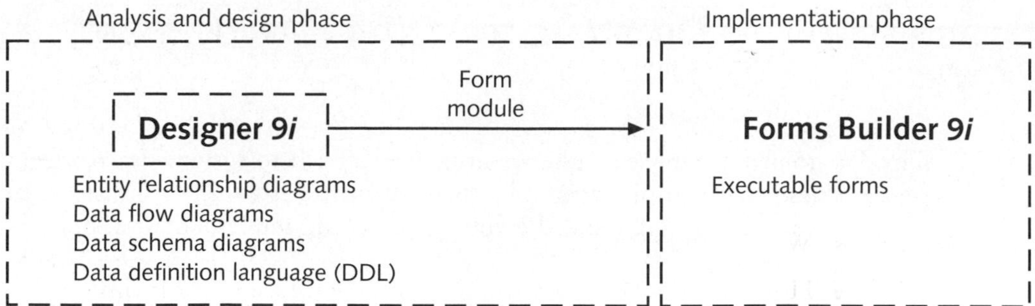

Figure 1-2 Designer and Forms Builder within the SDLC phases

If developers choose a methodology that does not use the CASE design tools, they can still use Forms Builder. To work with Forms Builder without CASE, developers simply create and implement the Oracle **database schema**, which comprises the tables that model the system entities. Then developing Forms Builder modules begins. Regardless of the approach, developers need to gather the following information before creating the forms:

- Database schema or design
- List of forms to be created
- Guidelines on how the forms are to be used to add, update, delete, and view data
- Database schema attributes to be used on the form
- Form-processing logic

It is possible for the developer to determine these requirements intuitively, but this approach is not reliable. It is safest to use several traditional tools to determine the design. These tools are:

- **Data flow diagram (DFD)**: displays the flow of data through a system
- **Entity relationship diagram (ERD)**: groups and relates sets of attributes that were identified on the data flow diagram
- **Database schema diagram (DSD)**: depicts the final database schema

The following sections of the chapter give you a brief overview of these tools. The tools help you identify the information needed to set up the Oracle database and begin developing forms. At the completion of this chapter, you may not be an expert with the tools, but you will have an idea of the information and tasks that must be completed before using Forms Builder effectively. You are then presented with the analysis materials that help you understand the requirements for the Case Project: the Great State Budgeting System.

Using Data Flow Diagrams to Identify Applications, Processes, and Data

A data flow diagram is the first tool that an analyst uses to document the results of the information-gathering effort completed during the analysis phase of the SDLC. This section describes the following:

- What a data flow diagram depicts
- How data flow diagrams support the identification of forms
- How graphic symbols are used in data flow diagrams

Scoping Out the Big Picture

Data flow diagrams are useful at the start of a project to pose and answer basic questions about the system to be developed. Before outlining the questions that data flow diagrams answer, it is useful to define a few key terms: **Data** is a fact with meaning and is stored and created in a system. For example, the name John is a fact. When combined with the fact Palinski, it gains specific meaning—the name of a person. Systems and databases store sets of related facts. An **entity** is an item about which data is kept. The entity consists of a variety of facts that describe it. A **process** creates, transforms, or uses data.

Data flow diagrams answer these questions:

- How is data brought into the target system?
- What are the system's processes?
- What data is needed by a process?
- Where does the process data come from?
- Where does the data transformed by the process go?
- Where does data rest within the system?
- What entities supply data to the system?
- What entities receive data from the system?

Identifying Forms Needed

Data flow diagrams help the form developer identify the forms to be developed and the data needed by each form. Any process on the data flow diagram that requires interaction with the user requires a form. Other processes will probably require a **PL/SQL** (Oracle's proprietary programming language) code block or stored procedures. A **code block** is a series of PL/SQL statements. **Stored procedures** are code blocks that have names and are stored in the database. The data flow diagram also identifies the data needed for the process and the data that leaves the process.

Data flow diagrams are one of the tools that can be developed in Oracle's Designer 9*i*. However, the data flow diagram can be developed by a variety of other tools, or even drawn by hand. For large and complex systems, it is most effective, however, to use a CASE tool such as Designer 9*i*. Each automated tool and textbook has a slightly different version of the diagram, but each employs the same concepts and is basically the same.

Diagram Symbols

Figure 1-3 shows the four symbols that are used in data flow diagrams, as listed here:

- **External entity (EE1)**: This symbol represents something outside the system that sends data into the system or receives data from the system. External entities are called **sources** and **sinks**, depending on whether they send or receive data from the system.
- **Process (EP1)**: This symbol represents work done by the system to store, modify, or move data. All forms are associated to one or more processes.
- **Flow (Data Flow)**: This symbol represents the data that flows into or out of a process.
- **Data store (DS)**: This symbol represents data at rest. The attributes associated with these stores will be the basis of the data model used in the system.

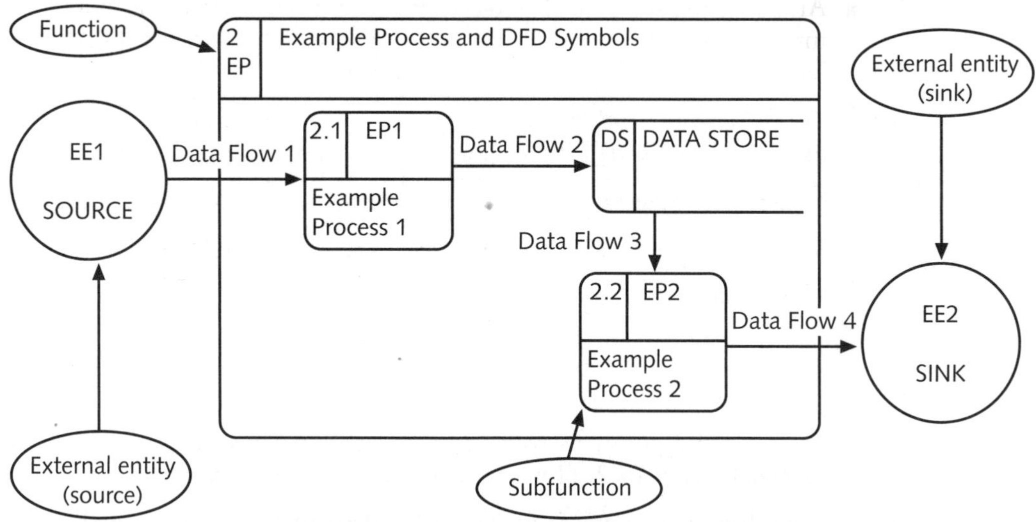

Figure 1-3 Example data flow diagram displaying four symbols

Figure 1-3 illustrates the four data flow diagram symbols. The depicted symbols are based on Oracle Designer 9*i*. The following points may help you understand the diagram:

- The scope of the overall system is represented by the symbol labeled EP. Designer 9*i* calls this symbol a function, which is really another name for a process. All functions or processes have a unique number. This function is number 2.

- Systems are generally decomposed into subprocesses. Decomposition allows the developer to concentrate and understand more granual parts of the system. The symbols EP1 and EP2 are also function (or process) symbols. They represent the decomposition of function EP or 2. The sum of EP1 and EP2 functionality is the same as the functionality for EP. These function symbols are numbered 2.1 and 2.2. The numbers indicate that the functions are subfunctions 1 and 2 of function 2. Function 2.1 and 2.2 may also be decomposed to a finer granularity. Decomposing function 2.1 into three subfunctions would result in functions with numbers 2.1.1, 2.1.2, and 2.1.3. The number of the latter function indicates that it is subfunction 3 for subfunction 1 of function 2. This numbering scheme allows a developer to break down system functionality and retain easy-to-understand linkages between functions that are represented on numerous diagrams.
- External entities are represented by ovals or circles with the symbols EE1 and EE2. The symbols are outside function 2, because they are external to the system. Symbol EE1 can also be called a source, because it is sending data into the system. Symbol EE2 receives data from the system. Another name for this object is sink.
- Data stores are represented by an open rectangle with a rounded end and the symbol DS.
- Arrows represent data flows. Data flows represent attributes that are going into or leaving a process, data store, or external entity. All data going into or leaving a process must be associated to a data flow.

Figure 1-3 does not represent an actual system but does illustrate how to read a data flow diagram. The following list describes the actions represented in the diagram:

- External entity EE1 sends data, represented by flow Data Flow 1, into the system.
- Function 2.1 receives the data represented by Data Flow 1. The function performs work on the incoming data and sends a set of data represented by Data Flow 2 to data store DS.
- Function 2.2 retrieves data from data store DS. This data is represented by Data Flow 3.
- Function 2.2 performs work on the data and sends data out of the system to external entity EE2. This data is represented by Data Flow 4.

Among other functions, data flow diagrams identify the forms and the data used or produced by the form. Analyzing a data flow diagram's processes provides this information, because a form is always associated to a process. Any process that requires human interaction requires a form. Processes receiving or sending data to external entities probably require a form, especially if the process records the incoming data in the database. The majority of the data enters a system through some type of online transaction. This transaction could be a bar scan, a sale logged by a supermarket scanner, a form operated on a workstation, a form on the Web, or a form on a personal digital assistant. When you review the data flow diagram to determine the processes that require human interaction, the forms that are needed become evident. Processes that do not require a form are either a PL/SQL procedure or a process that creates a report using a tool, such as Oracle Reports Builder.

In the case of the data flow diagram shown in Figure 1-3, process 2.1 probably requires a form, because it receives data from external entity EE1. Process 2.2 may also require a form. This depends on several things:

- Is the external entity EE2 a human or is it another system or external data store?
- If external entity EE2 is a human, does Data Flow 4 represent a report?
- If external entity EE2 is a human and Data Flow 4 is not a report, a form is needed.

The next task is to identify the data needed by the form. Data needs are determined by analyzing the data flows of the process. When analyzing the data flows, you can use the following principles to determine the data:

- Forms used to receive data from an external entity must contain input areas for each of the data elements represented by an incoming data flow.
- Data received from a data store is displayed on the form if it is used for supplemental information or is to be modified. A description of a code value is an example of this type of data.
- Data received from a data store that is used only for processing or calculations may not appear on the form.
- Data sent from a process that did not come into the process through a data flow is a calculated value. This data may or may not be displayed, but the form needs to have processes that create this data for the outgoing flows.

Through analyzing the data flow diagram, you have identified the forms and the data needed by the forms. The next task is to design or identify the database schema that stores the data while it is in the system. This is done using entity relationship diagrams, which are covered in the next section.

USING ENTITY RELATIONSHIP DIAGRAMS TO INITIATE THE DESIGN OF THE DATABASE SCHEMA

An **entity relationship diagram** is an analysis tool that is used to group related data. In the previous section, you saw that data flows in data flow diagrams identify the data needed or produced by a process. The data flow only indicates the needed elements and does not indicate how data is stored in the database.

Data flow diagrams also contain data stores that represent data at rest. A data store can be used to identify the stored data elements, but it does not identify the database structure or how the data is grouped. The database schema specifications are initially determined by the preparation of an entity relationship diagram. The developer can then use this tool to understand and begin the database design. It is important to have a good database design, because the database is the foundation of any system.

This section describes the following:

- Symbols used in entity relationship diagrams
- Properties of identifiers and primary keys
- Relationships between entities
- Documenting the attributes that describe an entity

Understanding the Entity Relationship Diagram Symbology

Entity relationship diagrams identify entities and their relationships to each other. An entity is something about which data is kept. Entities are real-world objects, such as cars, the moon, students, or courses. Each occurrence of an entity is called an **instance**. An example of an instance of the entity "STUDENT" is my son, Matthew. Databases store entity attributes. These **attributes** describe or model the entity. Examples of attributes for my son, Matthew, are his name, social security number, enrollment date, GPA, and courses taken.

Database design begins with the process of associating the data flow elements to the entity they model. A typical system database is composed of the following three types of entities:

- **Regular entities** (such as a university, student, or course): A regular entity can exist without the existence of another entity. The existence of a student or course does not rely on any other entity.
- **Weak entities** (such as a student parking ticket): Weak entities require the existence of another entity. A parking ticket cannot be issued to a student unless the student instance exists.
- **Associative entities** or **gerunds** (such as the courses taken by a student): These types of entities associate instances of several entities. They may also have data elements associated to them. The COURSES TAKEN entity is an example of an associative entity. It is a linkage between a student and the courses offered. The COURSES TAKEN entity is related to both the STUDENT and COURSES TAKEN entities. Examples of attributes associated to the associative entity, COURSES TAKEN, include STUDENT_ID, COURSE_ID, and GRADE.

A form often contains a mixture of data from regular, weak, and associative entities. The regular entities display data attributes that are unique to the entity instance. The weak and associative entities supply repeating sets of data for every occurrence of the regular entity. Forms Builder displays the regular entities in a form component called **master**

data block. Forms Builder displays the weak and associative entities in a component called **detail data block**. By analyzing the entity relationship diagram, developers determine which entities to display on the form and the type of data block to use.

Determining Identifiers and Primary Keys

Each entity must have one or more attributes whose values make that entity instance unique from any other entity instance. These attributes are called **identifiers**. Examples of identifiers are student IDs, social security numbers, or vehicle identification numbers. Identifiers are also called **primary keys**. An attribute is an identifier if it has these properties:

- The identifier or primary key value is unique across all entity instances.
- The identifier value or primary key does not change throughout the life of the entity.
- The instance identifier or primary key always contains a value. This property is called **NOT NULL**, which means not blank.

Regular entities should have an identifier or primary key composed of a single attribute. Weak entities normally have primary keys composed of two attributes. One of these attributes is the identifier attribute of the parent entity. This attribute is called a **foreign key** and is needed to associate the weak entity instance to an instance of its regular entity parent. Associative entities require the primary key attribute from each of the entities that it associates as part of its own primary key. Primary keys that comprise two or more attributes are called **composite keys**.

As a form developer, you must be able to identify the primary and foreign keys. Forms Builder creates code using these values to ensure that the records in detail data blocks pertain to the same master data block instance. Analyzing an entity relationship diagram enables you to identify the primary and foreign keys before creating master and detail data blocks in Forms Builder.

Understanding Entity Relationships

Entities can be related to each other and even to themselves, and these relationships are important, because they are the paths to the database attributes. Relational databases, such as Oracle, are composed of related tables. Entities become tables as the design moves from logical to physical stages. Desired attributes are almost always contained in multiple tables. As a developer, you will have to locate and access these attributes from the various tables. You will need to know if entities are related and the keys that relate the attributes.

STUDENT	COURSES TAKEN	COURSES OFFERED
STUDENT_ID	STUDENT_ID	OFFERING_ID
NAME	OFFERING_ID	COURSE_ID
ENROLLMENT_DATE	GRADE	LOCATION

Figure 1-4 Entities and attributes

Figure 1-4 illustrates the importance of relationships. Assume that your database has the three entities depicted in the figure: STUDENT, COURSES TAKEN, and COURSES OFFERED. A student can and probably does take courses. There is a relationship between the entities STUDENT and COURSES TAKEN. The regular entity, COURSES OFFERED, is also related to the associative entity, COURSES TAKEN. The three entities are related through the COURSES TAKEN entity.

If the information needed by the developer consists of the student name, course location, and the grade, the information must come from all three entities. An entity relationship diagram depicting the entities and relationships confirms that it is possible to retrieve this information. A line is displayed between the related entities. The developer can also determine the primary and foreign keys. Looking at Figure 1-4, you should be able to see that a STUDENT instance can be related to the COURSES TAKEN entity by common STUDENT_ID values. The COURSES OFFERED entity is related to the COURSES TAKEN entity by common OFFERING_IDs. Thus, all of the desired attributes can be accessed by relating an instance in the STUDENT entity to instances in the COURSES TAKEN entity and these related instances to instances in the COURSES OFFERED entity.

Understanding entity relationships also helps you to design more effective applications. Databases often contain descriptive tables. These tables are used to describe codes or other nondescriptive values, such as a course number. These kinds of tables support the list of values or pick lists that you create on your forms. For example, the COURSES TAKEN data requires the user to enter an OFFERING_ID. It is much easier to enter this value if the user can pick out the OFFERING_ID from a list that contains the course name and course number. Related entities can always be used as the source of values for the list of values and pick lists on a form, and following the relationships in an entity relationship drawing helps you to identify these opportunities.

Relationship Types

Entity relationship diagrams show three basic types of relationships:

- **Unary**: The entity is related to itself. An instance of a course that requires a prerequisite is an example of this relationship. Because the prerequisite is another COURSE instance, the entity's relationship is to itself. This type of relationship means that one of the attributes is a foreign key related to a primary key value in another instance.
- **Binary**: The entity is related to one other entity. This most common type of relationship means one of the entities contains a foreign key that relates it to the other entity.
- **N-ary**: Multiple entities are related to each other.

A line drawn between the entities symbolizes the relationship. In addition, text is placed at either end of the relationship to describe how the entities are related. Figure 1-5 illustrates several entities in unary and binary relationships. The figure was created in Designer 9*i* and is representative of this tool's symbols.

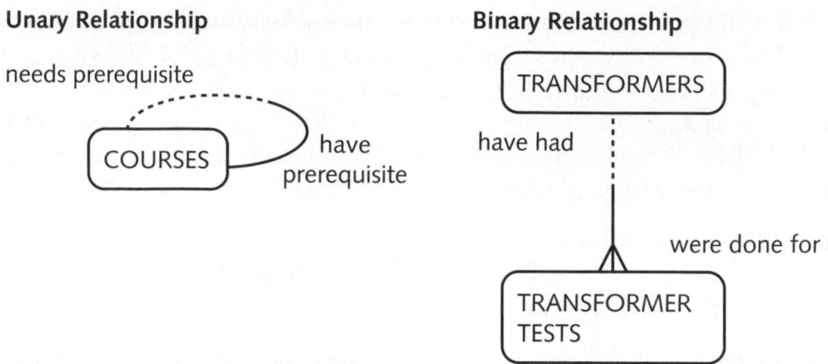

Figure 1-5 Oracle Designer depictions of unary and binary relationships

Cardinality and Ordinality

Relationships contain two important properties called cardinality and ordinality. **Cardinality** identifies the number of instances that a related entity can have. For example, a student can take many different courses. The cardinality of the STUDENT entity to the COURSES TAKEN entity is many. Cardinality is a property that exists on both sides of the relationship. You have seen the cardinality identified from the STUDENT to the COURSES TAKEN entities. The cardinality from the COURSES TAKEN (by a student) entity to the STUDENT is one. A specific course can only be taken once by a student; the student cannot enroll in the same course twice.

Understanding the cardinality of a relationship is important to the form developer, because cardinality determines which of the entities will be used in a master data block and which will be in the detail data block. Master data block is a Forms Builder term that indicates the parent or controlling set of records. The entity with a cardinality of one, such as STUDENT, is the master data block in a form. The entity with a cardinality of many is the detail data block. Detail data blocks normally display multiple instances of a related entity for each occurrence of the parent entity in the master data block. The COURSES TAKEN entity is in the detail data block, and multiple instances of the entity are likely to be displayed for each STUDENT instance.

The second relationship property, **ordinality**, describes whether the related instance is mandatory. For example, can a COURSES TAKEN entity instance exist without a related STUDENT instance? The answer is no. You must have a STUDENT instance before you can have a COURSES TAKEN instance. Thus the ordinality property is mandatory. Ordinality also exists on both sides of the relationship. A STUDENT entity instance can exist without a COURSES TAKEN instance, as is the case if the student hasn't registered yet. Thus the ordinality of this relationship is optional.

Cardinality and ordinality can be represented in the entity relationship diagram by several methods of textual and graphical notation. Figure 1-6 illustrates the various graphical notations used by Designer 9*i* and described as follows:

- **One**: a single line
- **Many**: a crow's-foot or three lines
- **Mandatory**: solid lines
- **Optional**: dashed lines

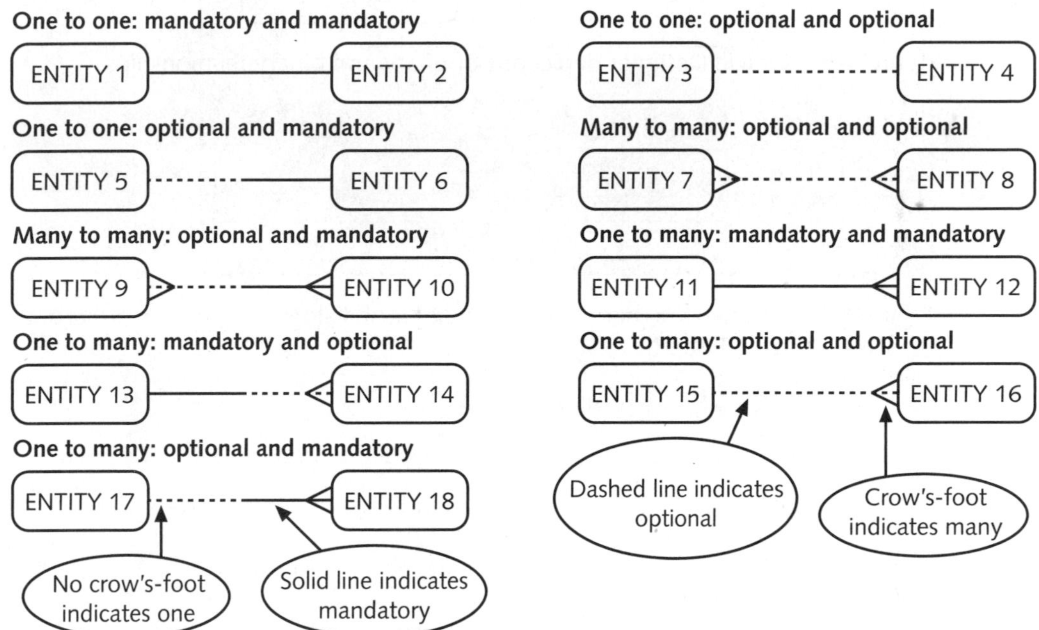

Figure 1-6 Oracle Designer relationship symbols

Entity Attributes and Properties

An entity relationship diagram is the first tool to use when designing a database, because the entity relationship drawing groups attributes. The attributes describe or model an entity. As part of the process, the developer must document these attributes and their characteristics. Figure 1-7 depicts a Designer 9*i* dialog box that contains attributes for an entity in a typical system, a transformer. A transformer is an electrical device that changes electrical voltage. The figure illustrates the Designer 9*i* dialog box that is used to record the attributes. Properties that are identified in this dialog box are representative of those that you would document in any entity relationship diagram.

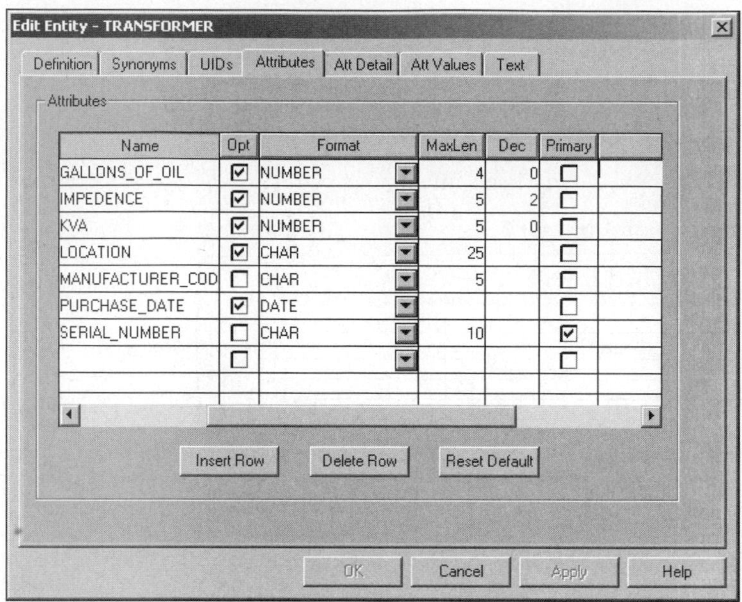

Figure 1-7 Oracle Designer relationship diagram dialog box used for entry of attributes and properties

The properties depicted in Figure 1-7 are:

- **Name**: This is the name of the entity attribute.
- **Optional (Opt)**: This property indicates whether a value must always exist in the attribute. Attributes that must always contain a value are considered NOT NULL. As a form developer, you must ensure that this property is respected and enforced.
- **Format**: This property describes how the attribute is stored in the database. Example formats are CHAR, VARCHAR2, DATE, or NUMBER.
- **MaxLen**: This property sets the size of the attribute.
- **Dec**: This is the number of decimal positions.
- **Primary**: This attribute is part of the primary key.

Properties that pertain to domains are also important to form developers. These properties specify the types of values that can be placed into the form data item. Figure 1-8 displays a second panel of the dialog box for the KVA transformer item. It is used to record the following properties:

- **Value**: the lowest value that can be placed in this attribute
- **High Value**: the maximum value that can be placed in this attribute

- **Abbreviation**: a shortened version of the attribute name
- **Meaning**: a description of the attribute

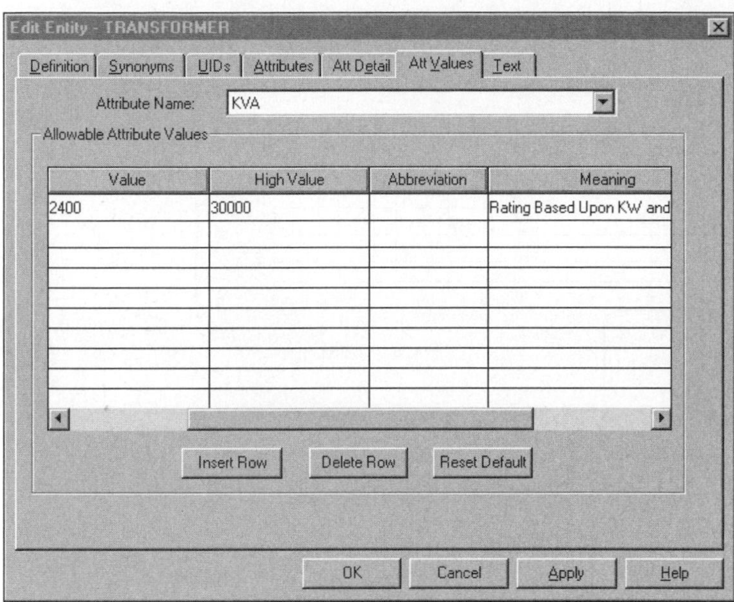

Figure 1-8 Oracle Designer entity relationship diagram dialog box used for entry of range values

To create a form, you must know the entity characteristics shown in Figures 1-7 and 1-8. Forms contain text items that display the entity attributes. The developer must know the data type and length of the attribute, because the text item must have the same properties. The developer must also ensure that proper values are entered into the text item. This requires information about the range, which can be determined from the entity relationship diagram. If you are using Designer 9*i* to create these items, this information is transferred to the database schema and to the Forms Builder form. If you are not using Designer 9*i*, this information must be identified, incorporated into the database schema, and then transferred to Forms Builder.

Figure 1-9 depicts a completed entity relationship diagram for TRANSFORMER and TRANSFORMER_TEST entities. The diagram was prepared in Designer 9*i*. The entities are related in a one-to-many relationship that is either mandatory or optional. The following are descriptions of the symbols that are shown in the diagram and are associated with the attributes:

- **#**: an attribute that is the identifier (or primary key)
- *****: a value that is mandatory for the attribute
- **O**: a value that is optional for the attribute

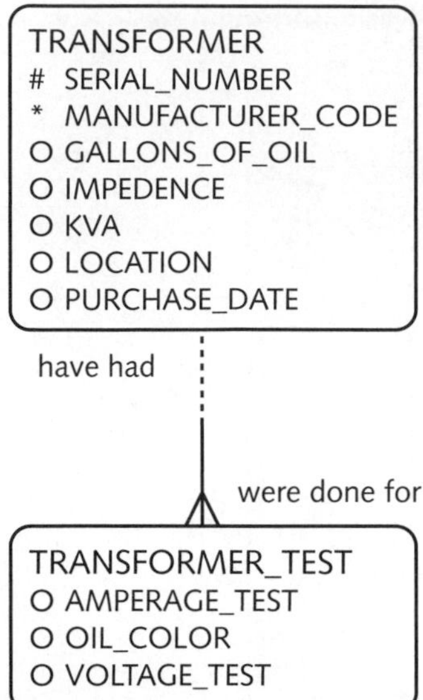

Figure 1-9 Entity relationship diagram of the TRANSFORMER and TRANSFORMER_TEST entities

You may have noticed that the foreign key (SERIAL_NUMBER) attribute is not shown in the TRANSFORMER_TEST entity. Foreign keys are not shown on entity relationship diagrams, and this is one of the reasons why this is not the preferred tool. The preferred tool is the data schema diagram discussed later in the chapter.

Associating Entities and Attributes to a Data Flow

The processes of a data flow diagram identify a system form, and the data flows identify the data that is needed by that form. The form's data attributes are stored in an Oracle table. This table is related to an entity in the entity relationship diagram. You should associate data flows with entities in the analysis phase, so that you can identify the proper tables to use when in Forms Builder. Designer 9*i* has a data flow diagram dialog box that associates entities (and attributes) to a particular data flow. This dialog is illustrated in Figure 1-10.

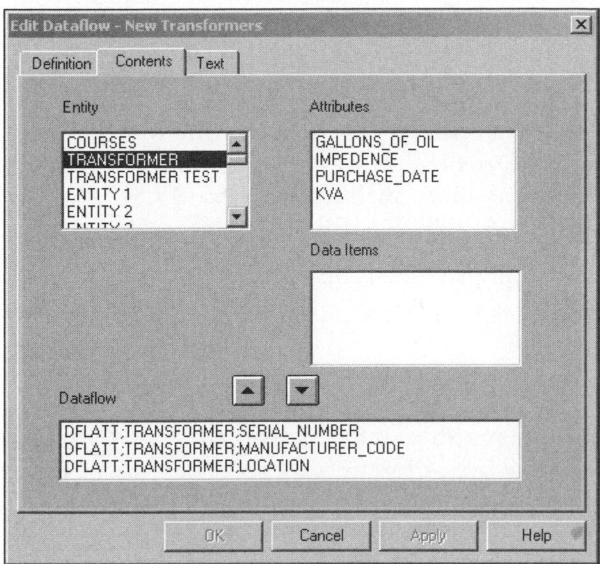

Figure 1-10 Oracle Designer dialog box used to associate entities and attributes to a data flow

Designer 9*i* Entity Relationship Diagram Dialog Box Used for Entry of Attributes and Properties

Some entity relationship diagrams may not correspond exactly to the database schema, because the entities have not been **normalized**. Normalization is a process used to design an efficient and flexible database. If you develop the entity relationship diagram in Designer 9*i*, it will conform fairly closely to the database schema, because Designer 9*i* pushes the developer to normalize the entities. If you are using a different tool or preparing the entity relationship drawing on paper, exercises called relational modeling and normalization may need to be applied to the entities before the database objects can be created. The result of this application is an efficient relational database schema that can be used to create the Oracle database. The developer or database administrator can then create the database objects from the schema.

Because Designer 9*i* entity relationship diagrams are closely related to the database schema, it is important to perform the normalization during the creation of the entity relationship drawing, since Designer 9*i* takes the entities and relationships and designs the schema. It also writes the **data definition language (DDL)** commands used to create the database objects. After Designer 9*i* creates the database schema, a data schema diagram is available to the developer. It turns the entities and attributes into tables and columns. **Tables** are the objects that physically store data in the database. **Columns** identify the particular values stored in the table. The data schema diagram is the best tool available for understanding the tables in a database and is more valuable than the entity relationship diagram in the following ways:

- The data schema diagram shows foreign keys; entity relationship drawings do not. Foreign keys are implied by the relationships. The primary key of the parent entity is a foreign key in the child entity.
- The relationship description contains the name of the foreign key constraint placed on the parent table. A **foreign key constraint** is a database feature that ensures weak entity instances, such as TRANSFORMER_TEST, will not exist without a related TRANSFORMER entity instance.
- The data schema diagram displays the actual database column names. The names used in the entity relationship diagram may not relate exactly to the column name.
- The data schema diagram displays the attribute format.

Figure 1-11 illustrates a data schema diagram based on the TRANSFORMER and TRANSFORMER_TEST entities. This diagram was generated using Designer 9*i* and can be used to create the tables that compose the database. It is also the most effective tool available for understanding the database for which you will create forms.

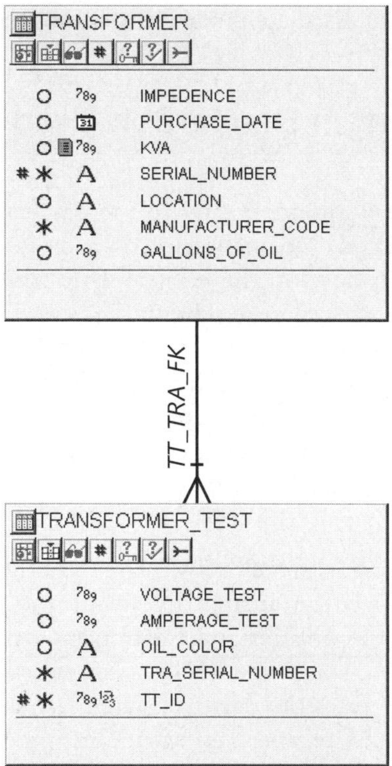

Figure 1-11 Oracle Designer data schema diagram of the TRANSFORMER and TRANSFORMER_TEST tables

How Forms Builder Uses Oracle 9*i* Database

After understanding, designing, and creating the Oracle database, you are ready to begin using Forms Builder. Forms Builder is tightly integrated with the Oracle database. You have seen that data flow diagrams identify the forms, entities, and attributes that appear on the form. The entity relationship diagram or the data schema diagram indicates the relationships between entities. The relationship and data characteristic information is passed to Forms Builder through its wizards. This means that the form developer does not have to specify the data properties. Forms Builder determines this information from the database by performing the following tasks:

- Gives all form items their names based upon the database table
- Sets the data type and length of all data items based on the database table
- Ensures any text item related to a NOT NULL constrained column always contains a value by setting a form text item property to "Required"
- Identifies matching primary and foreign key columns when creating master and detail data blocks

As you will see in the next chapter, simply by specifying the tables and columns that appear on the form, you give the form a great deal of functionality. This gives the developer a significant head start on the development of a system.

Where You Are and Where You're Going

This chapter briefly reviewed the system development life cycle and explained how Oracle's Forms Builder tool set fits within this life cycle. It also showed you how data flow diagrams are used to identify applications, processes, and the data. You were introduced to entity relationship diagrams and to the data schema diagrams. You finish this chapter understanding generally how Forms Builder uses the Oracle9*i* database.

The next chapter begins the coverage of Forms Builder itself by introducing you to the Forms Builder products that are used to build and execute a form. You also learn how to use wizards to create a simple form. The last part of the chapter shows you how to retrieve records into the form and perform data manipulation language (DML) operations.

Chapter Summary

- Forms Builder supports the system development life cycle and allows the developer to prototype forms during the analysis phase. Forms Builder also creates the final system forms during the implementation phase.
- Forms Builder is used to complete and implement the design produced in Oracle's Designer 9*i* CASE tools.

- Data flow diagrams can be used to understand the movement and processing of data in a system.
- Data flow diagrams contain four symbols: external entity, data store, process, and data flow.
- Forms and the data that is needed on a form are identified by analyzing a data flow diagram.
- Entity relationship diagrams are tools that enable the developer to aggregate common data items and determine relationships between the common sets of data.
- Entity relationship diagrams have three types of entities: regular, weak, and associative. A regular entity can exist on its own. A weak entity must have a parent entity instance. An associative entity describes the relationship between two entities.
- Entity relationship diagrams have three basic types of relationships: unary, binary, and N-ary.
- Relationships have two sets of properties: cardinality and ordinality. Cardinality describes the number of related entity instances. Ordinality identifies whether a related instance is mandatory or optional.
- Normalized entities on an entity relationship diagram can be used to create the database objects.
- A database schema diagram is used to understand the actual tables.

REVIEW QUESTIONS

1. Match the following terms that have appeared in this chapter with their descriptions:

a. Source	________________	Data at rest
b. Data flow	________________	A relationship between one entity and one other entity
c. Data schema diagram	________________	A value that exists in another table as a primary key value
d. Sink	________________	Displays constraint names
e. Crow's-foot	________________	Dashed lines
f. Unary relationship	________________	An external entity that sends input to a system
g. Binary relationship	________________	A relationship that exists with the same entity
h. Constraint	________________	Solid lines
i. Primary key	________________	A database tool that is used to ensure referential integrity

j. Foreign key	______________	An external entity that receives the output of a system
k. Entity relationship diagram	______________	A symbol that represents a cardinality relationship property of many instances
l. Data store	______________	Identifies the data needed on a form
m. Optional relationship symbol	______________	An attribute whose value makes the instance unique from any other instance
n. Mandatory relationship symbol	______________	Does not show foreign key attributes

2. Why would a developer want to use Forms Builder during the analysis phase of the system development life cycle?
3. How are Forms Builder and Designer 9*i* related?
4. How are Forms Builder and the Oracle database related?
5. Explain how a data flow diagram can be used to identify the forms needed in a system.
6. Explain the purpose of an entity relationship diagram.
7. Explain how data flow diagrams and entity relationship diagrams are related.
8. Explain the advantages or disadvantages of a many-to-many relationship.
9. Which tool would the developer use to identify the data elements that belong on a form?
10. Which tool is most helpful for understanding the database structure? Why?

Case Project: Great State Electric Budgeting System

Great State Electric (Great State) is a leading Midwest utility. It supplies electricity to approximately 250,000 customers. The company has its own generating plants. The utility also has a transmission system that allows the company to move the electricity to substations where it can then be distributed to businesses and residences. As the Great State service area expands, the utility adds new facilities to serve the new customers.

The utility also spends a great deal of money upgrading its distribution system. Facilities that are old or do not have adequate capacity are upgraded. Every year in July, a construction budget must be prepared, submitted, and approved by senior management and the board of directors. The existing budgeting system is prepared using Microsoft Excel. The system is difficult to use, because projects must be copied from one spreadsheet to another. You have been hired to develop a new budgeting system using Oracle Forms Builder.

The Process

Figure 1-12 is a data flow diagram for the proposed budgeting system. The following bullets describe the processes:

- Construction projects are identified by the Planning (P) source. Planning is responsible for analyzing future growth and monitoring existing facilities. Identified projects will be entered into the system by Planning personnel.
- Planning sends the data represented by data flow Project Scope into the system. The data in this flow consists of PROJECT entity attributes. Two important data items in this flow are the Need Date and the Department. The Need Date identifies the date when the construction work is to be completed. The DEPARTMENT value depends on the type of work. Each project that is placed in the system is assigned to one of three engineering departments: Transmission, Substation, or Distribution. Transmission designs the transmission facilities that move the electricity from the generating plant to the substation. The Substation department designs the substation facilities. These facilities transform or reduce the voltage of the electricity, so that it can be distributed to the customer. The Distribution department designs the circuitry that moves the electricity from the substation to the customer.
- Process 1.1 receives data flow Project Scope and places the data into the PROJECTS data store.
- When the project is created, Planning assigns it to an engineering department. The manager of the assigned department reviews the project (Process 1.2). The manager then assigns the project to an engineer (Process 1.2). The engineer is responsible for creating a project estimate. The assignment information is then sent to the PROJECTS data store using data flow Budget Estimate Assignments.
- In the next step of the process, the engineer identifies the project he is responsible for and creates an estimate. The estimating process begins with the division of the project work into work orders. Each work order covers a different part of the project and has its own bill-of-material and costs. The division (work breakdown) of the project is primarily based on the craft people involved in the work. Cement masons cannot perform electrical work. To illustrate, the construction of a substation requires work orders for the building, the equipment foundations, and the electrical equipment. Each of these work breakdowns receives its own work order. Each work order can then be further subdivided into tasks. A task represents a specific job that is to be performed. Each task is assigned to a construction department, assigned a cost account, and estimated. This work is represented by Process 1.3. The outputs of the process are sent to the WORK ORDERS data store. The data is represented by data flow labeled "Work Breakdown Structure and Costs."
- Process 1.4 represents the review of the work order estimates by an engineering supervisor. The flows into and out of the process are represented by data flows: Estimates, Approvals, and Rejections.

- Process 1.5 represents the review of the entire project by management. The approval is then sent to the PROJECTS data store.
- Process 1.6 represents the process that creates the budget. This consists of a report sent to the Budgeting (B) source.

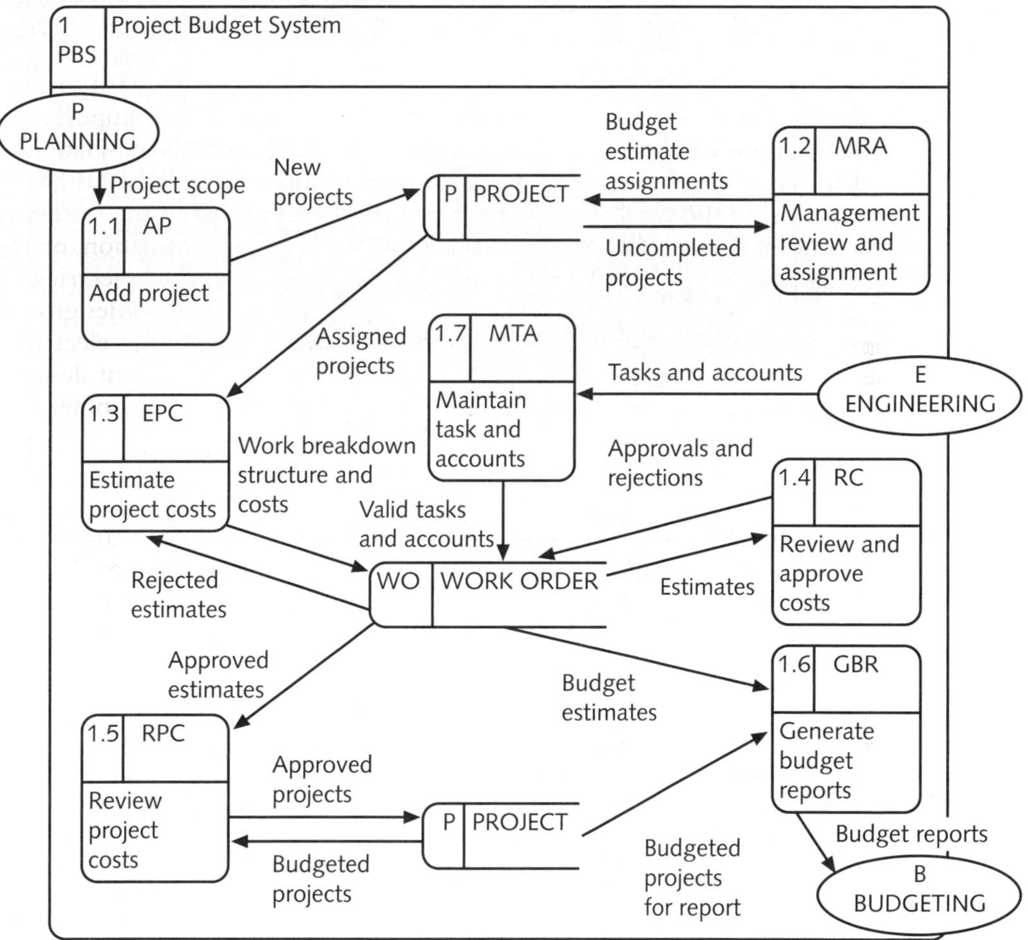

Figure 1-12 Great State Budgeting System data flow diagram

The Data

Figure 1-13 depicts an entity relationship diagram for the Great State Budgeting System. This diagram lists the various entities and attributes in the system.

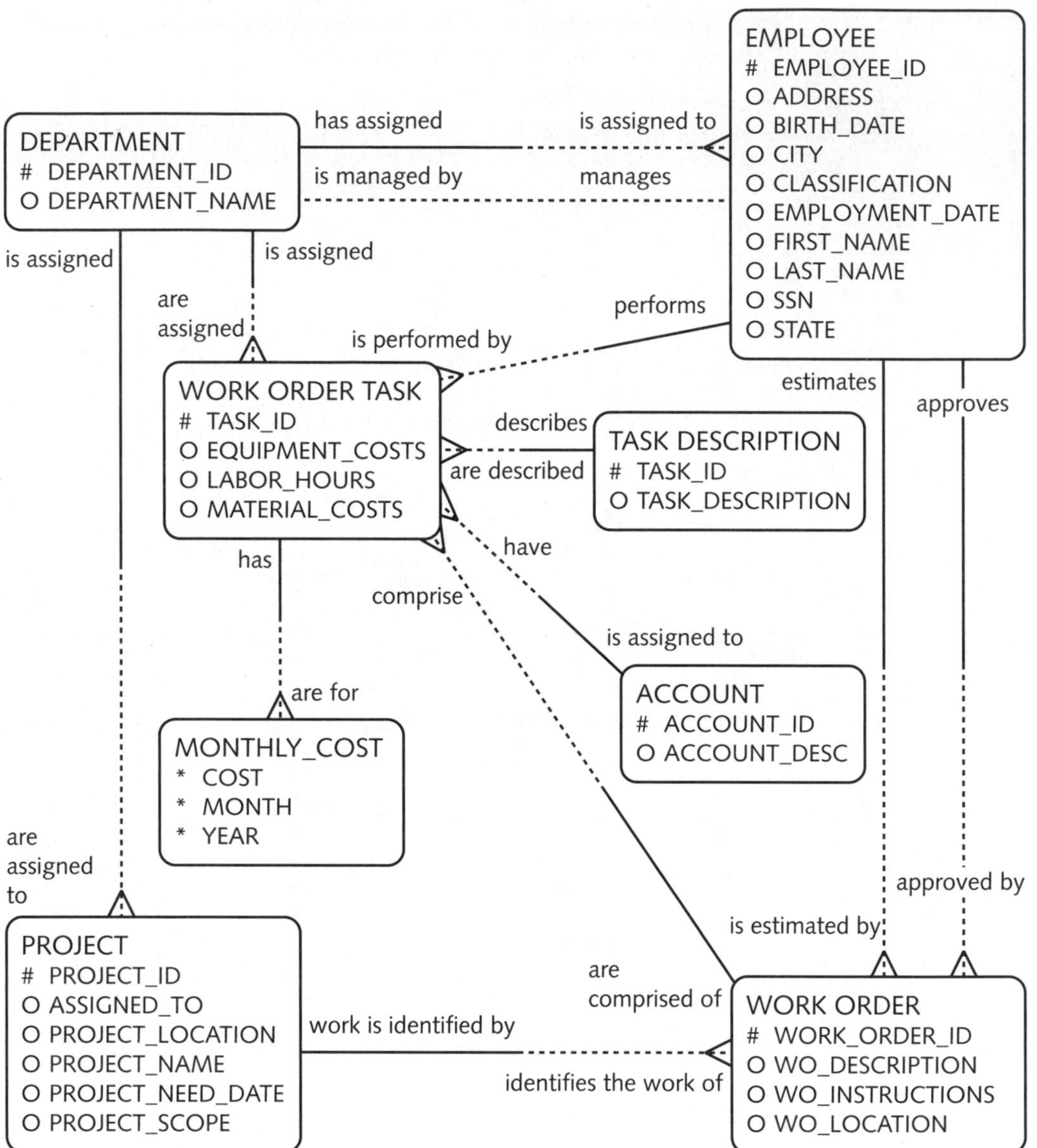

Figure 1-13 Great State Budgeting System entity relationship diagram

Table 1-1 depicts the project data flows and the entities that comprise the flow.

Table 1-1 Data flows and entities

Data flow	Entity
Project scope	None
New projects	PROJECT
Uncompleted projects	PROJECT
Budget estimate assignments	PROJECT
Assigned projects	PROJECT
Work breakdown structure and costs	WORK ORDER WORK ORDER TASK MONTHLY_COST
Rejected estimates	WORK ORDER WORK ORDER TASK MONTHLY_COST
Estimates	WORK ORDER WORK ORDER TASK MONTHLY_COST
Approvals and rejections	WORK ORDER
Approved estimates	WORK ORDER WORK ORDER TASK MONTHLY_COST
Budgeted projects	PROJECT
Approved projects	PROJECT
Budgeted projects for report	PROJECT
Budget estimates	WORK ORDER WORK ORDER TASK MONTHLY_COST ACCOUNT
Budget reports	None
Tasks and accounts	TASKS ACCOUNTS
Valid tasks and accounts	TASKS ACCOUNTS

Tables

Figure 1-14 is the data schema diagram for the budgeting database. It displays the tables, columns, column properties, and the table constraints.

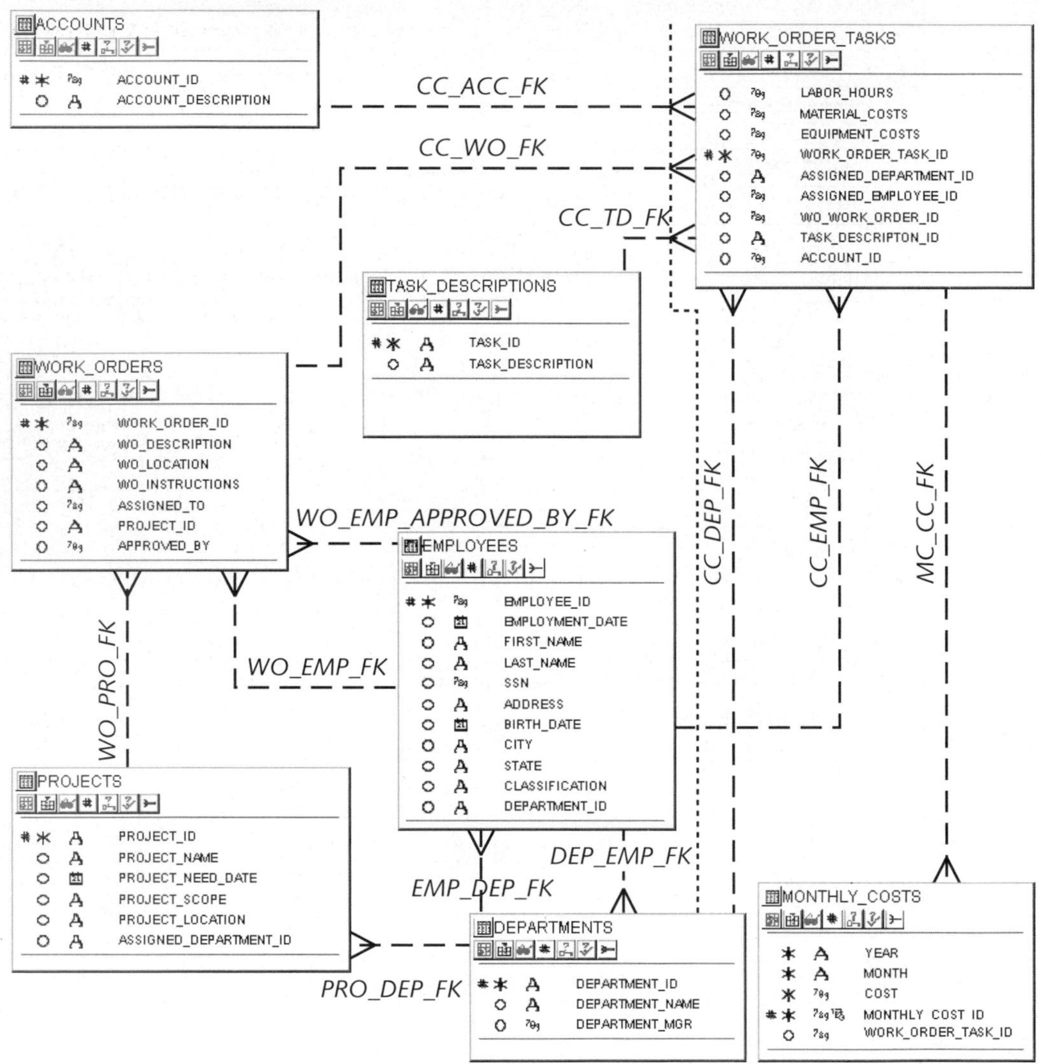

Figure 1-14 Great State Budgeting System data schema diagram

The following tables describe the system's table columns and their characteristics.

Table 1-2 PROJECTS table columns and characteristics

Column name	Data type	Nulls allowed	Primary key	Foreign key
PROJECT_ID	VARCHAR2(10)	No	Yes	
PROJECT_NAME	VARCHAR2(60)	No		
PROJECT_NEED_DATE	DATE	Yes		
PROJECT_SCOPE	VARCHAR2(2000)	Yes		
PROJECT_LOCATION	VARCHAR2(200)	Yes		
ASSIGNED_DEPARTMENT_ID	CHAR(3)	Yes		DEPARTMENTS
ASSIGNED_TO	NUMBER(5,0)	Yes		EMPLOYEES

Table 1-3 WORK_ORDERS table columns and characteristics

Column name	Data type	Nulls allowed	Primary key	Foreign key
WORK_ORDER_ID	NUMBER(5,0)	No	Yes	
WO_DESCRIPTION	VARCHAR2(100)	No		
WO_LOCATION	VARCHAR2(200)	Yes		
WO_INSTRUCTIONS	VARCHAR2(2000)	Yes		
APPROVED_BY	NUMBER(5,0)	Yes		EMPLOYEES
ASSIGNED_TO	NUMBER(5,0)	Yes		EMPLOYEES
PROJECT_ID	VARCHAR2(10)	No		PROJECTS

Table 1-4 DEPARTMENTS table columns and characteristics

Column name	Data type	Nulls allowed	Primary key	Foreign key
DEPARTMENT_ID	CHAR(3)	No	Yes	
DEPARTMENT_NAME	VARCHAR2(20)	No		
DEPARTMENT_MGR	NUMBER(5,0)	Yes		EMPLOYEES

Table 1-5 EMPLOYEES table columns and characteristics

Column name	Data type	Nulls allowed	Primary key	Foreign key
EMPLOYEE_ID	NUMBER(5,0)	No	Yes	
EMPLOYMENT_DATE	DATE	No		
FIRST_NAME	VARCHAR2(10)	No		
LAST_NAME	VARCHAR2(20)	No		
SSN	NUMBER(9,0)	Yes		
ADDRESS	VARCHAR2(25)	Yes		
BIRTH_DATE	DATE	Yes		
CITY	VARCHAR2(15)	Yes		
STATE	VARCHAR2(2)	Yes		
CLASSIFICATION	VARCHAR2(20)	Yes		
DEPARTMENT_ID	CHAR(3)	No		DEPARTMENTS

Table 1-6 WORK_ORDER_TASKS table columns and characteristics

Column name	Data type	Nulls allowed	Primary key	Foreign key
WORK_ORDER_TASK_ID	NUMBER(5,0)	No	Yes	
ASSIGNED_DEPARTMENT_ID	CHAR(3)	No		DEPARTMENTS
ASSIGNED_EMPLOYEE_ID	NUMBER(5,0)	Yes		EMPLOYEES
WO_WORK_ORDER_ID	NUMBER(5,0)	No		WORK_ORDERS
TASK_DESCRIPTION_ID	CHAR(5)	No		TASK_DESCRIPTIONS
ACCOUNT_ID	NUMBER(5,2)	No		ACCOUNTS
LABOR_HOURS	NUMBER(5,0)	Yes		
MATERIAL_COSTS	NUMBER(7,0)	Yes		
EQUIPMENT_COSTS	NUMBER(7,0)	Yes		

Table 1-7 TASK_DESCRIPTIONS table columns and characteristics

Column name	Data type	Nulls allowed	Primary key	Foreign key
TASK_ID	CHAR(5)	No	Yes	
TASK_DESCRIPTION	VARCHAR2(25)	Yes		

Table 1-8 ACCOUNTS table columns and characteristics

Column name	Data type	Nulls allowed	Primary key	Foreign key
ACCOUNT_ID	NUMBER(5,2)	No	Yes	
ACCOUNT_DESCRIPTION	VARCHAR2(25)	No		

Table 1-9 MONTHLY_COSTS table columns and characteristics

Column name	Data type	Nulls allowed	Primary key	Foreign key
MONTHLY_COST_ID	NUMBER(5,0)	No	Yes	
WORK_ORDER_TASK_ID	NUMBER(5,0)	No		WORK_ORDER_TASKS
YEAR	CHAR(4)	No		
MONTH	VARCHAR2(8)	No		
COST	NUMBER(7)	No		

Your Work

Now that you have an idea of the processes, data, and tables involved in the Great State Budgeting System, it's time to get down to work.

1. Use the data schema diagram from Figure 1-14 to create the data definition language commands needed for the budgeting system. A more readable diagram, **Fig0114.tif**, is available in the **Chapter.01 folder** on your student disk. You may compare your commands against the commands depicted in the Case Project for Chapter 2. You will also find the budgeting system database scripts in the Chapter.02 student disk.
2. Use the data flow diagram from Figure 1-12 to identify the locations in the system where a form is needed.
3. Identify the entities or tables that will appear on the various forms.

This case study is continued at the end of Chapter 2.

CHAPTER

2

INTRODUCTION TO ORACLE'S FORMS BUILDER 9*i*

In this chapter you will:

- Compare Forms Builder to other forms development tools
- Learn about the major Developer 9*i* Forms Builder tools
- Launch Forms Builder and connect to Oracle
- Practice using the main Forms Builder integrated design environment (IDE) tools: Object Navigator, Layout Editor, Property Palette, and PL/SQL Editor
- Create a simple form using the Data Block and Layout Wizards
- Compile and save a form module
- Launch a form using Oracle Forms Builder runtime engines
- Learn about the form operating modes and how to determine which mode the form is in
- Filter records from the database using the form data items
- Use the form function keys

Chapter 1 explained how Oracle's Forms Builder tool set fits within the systems development life cycle. The next stage in this exploration of developing Internet applications is to understand the tool set, Oracle's Developer 9*i*. By reading this book's roadmap (see Figure 2-1), you can see that this chapter is primarily about learning how to operate the form. The chapter explains why many experts consider Forms Builder the best tool in the industry for developing client-server applications. This chapter also introduces you to the various Forms Builder tools. You then move on to opening Forms Builder and actually creating a basic form that displays employee information. The chapter demonstrates how to add, update, delete, and view records using a form. It also discusses how to perform a variety of other tasks using the function keys. The chapter also covers a topic important for your success in building forms—how a form operates by default. You need this knowledge to mold the behavior of forms.

As you read through the procedures in this and subsequent chapters, be aware that you are expected to actually work through the steps only when they are called *practice sessions*. Of course, much of the end-of-chapter material is also designed for hands-on work.

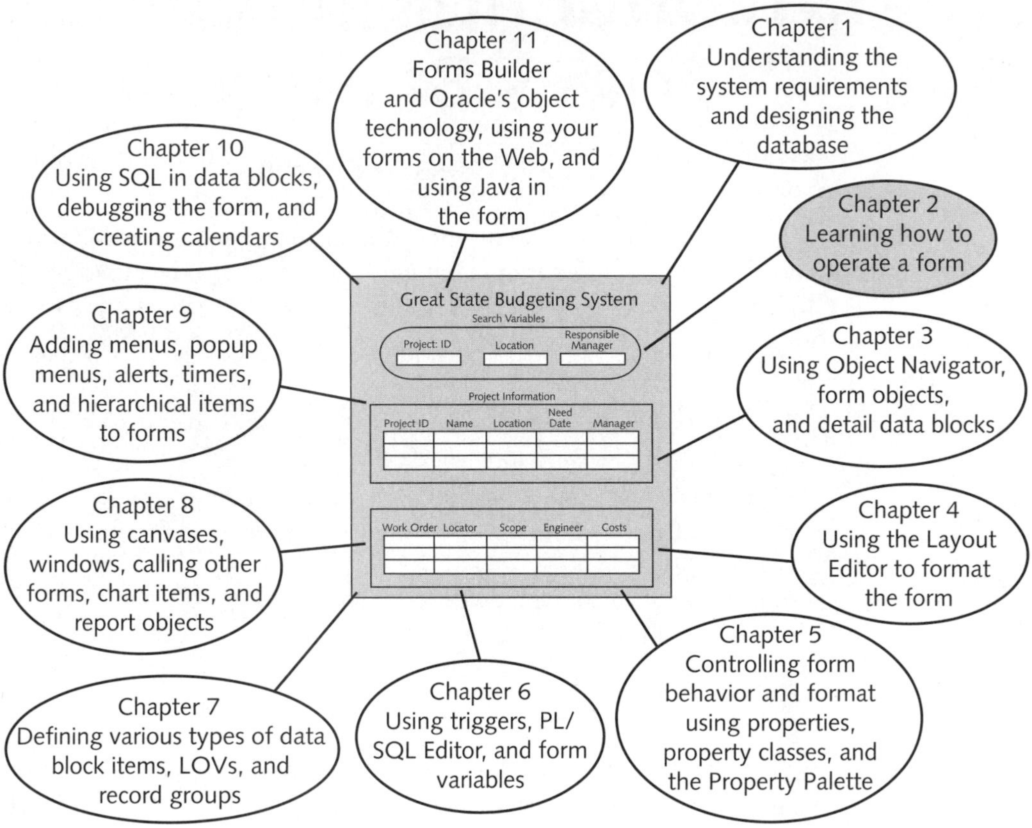

Chapter 11
Forms Builder and Oracle's object technology, using your forms on the Web, and using Java in the form

Chapter 1
Understanding the system requirements and designing the database

Chapter 10
Using SQL in data blocks, debugging the form, and creating calendars

Chapter 2
Learning how to operate a form

Great State Budgeting System
Search Variables
Project: ID | Location | Responsible Manager
Project Information
Project ID | Name | Location | Need Date | Manager
Work Order | Locator | Scope | Engineer | Costs

Chapter 9
Adding menus, popup menus, alerts, timers, and hierarchical items to forms

Chapter 3
Using Object Navigator, form objects, and detail data blocks

Chapter 8
Using canvases, windows, calling other forms, chart items, and report objects

Chapter 4
Using the Layout Editor to format the form

Chapter 5
Controlling form behavior and format using properties, property classes, and the Property Palette

Chapter 6
Using triggers, PL/SQL Editor, and form variables

Chapter 7
Defining various types of data block items, LOVs, and record groups

Figure 2-1 Roadmap

Comparing Forms Builder to Similar Tools

You can use a variety of tools and languages to develop Web applications, including several supplied by Oracle. You can develop Web applications using a simple text editor, such as Notepad, combined with Hypertext Markup Language (HTML), and supplement the HTML with JavaScript or Perl scripts. As a developer, you can also use the Java language to create an applet or even a Java Server Page. If Microsoft is your preferred flavor, you can create Active Server Pages using Visual Basic and .NET products. You may prefer to use Macromedia ColdFusion, a tool that does an excellent job of displaying dynamic data produced from a query. This book covers the Oracle9*i* Forms Developer tool set, and specifically Forms Builder, which is the development tool in the tool set.

With so many Web application development tools to choose from, why use Oracle's Forms Builder?

The vast majority of the applications you encounter on the Web are relatively simple, stateless HTML, in which the user enters a few values and submits the data to the server. The server then sends back another HTML page that contains the results of the submittal. These applications are considered simple because every time the Web display is refreshed, the server must send a completely new page to be displayed. Many Web users have slow dial-up service and are not satisfied with the response time needed for complex applications. Server pages and servlets are popular because they perform the business logic on the server and return only the content.

These simple applications work well when the customer base is outside the corporate network and the user is performing a simple task, such as ordering a product. Typical Web applications, however, pale against the applications currently used in the workplace. These workplace applications are developed on a client-server paradigm and often function at high levels of sophistication. With such systems, users can produce dynamic lists of values, have their entered values validated, work in multiple windows simultaneously, view on-line help, and perform a variety of other tasks. The client-server environment is mature and powerful, and the typical Internet application is not nearly as powerful as a client-server application.

The industry move from client-server applications to Web applications was not spurred by the power of the Web browser environment; rather, it was due to the difficulty of configuring many client units. In a client-server environment, technicians must visit each workstation on the network to configure the workstation or to install software. This is a time-consuming and expensive process. Even though the process has improved in recent years with products that allow technicians to access workstations remotely, it is still costly.

A number of years ago, Larry Ellison, Chairman and CEO of Oracle Corporation, began discussing the benefits of Web applications. Executing applications from a Web browser would eliminate the need for a technician to "touch" each workstation, thus saving considerable expense, and the user would need only a Web browser because a server would supply everything else. This schema was named "thin client" because the workstations required very limited software. The thin client schema also led to the practice of running applications on everyone's workstation rather than only on workstations maintained by technicians. For the first time in history, an application developed for a Web browser could be used on millions of workstations worldwide. No wonder everyone wants to move to the Web.

However, we still face one problem—typical Web applications are not as robust as client-server applications. The typical Web business application requires a different tool—an applet.

An applet is an application that runs inside a Web browser, and several applets can operate simultaneously inside the browser. The use of applets allows a developer to build Web-enabled applications that strongly resemble Windows client-server applications. This eliminates the need for someone to "touch" the end-user computers. Many experts consider Oracle's Forms Builder the best industry tool for developing client-server applications, as well as the best tool for developing the applets needed for Web-enabled business applications.

You might wonder why all Web applications are not sophisticated applets. The main reason is the network. Sophisticated Web applets are large and require a fast network. The typical Internet user does not like the download time required for these applications. Web applets are, therefore, best suited for users attached to corporate networks. Many experts believe that Forms Builder will be used primarily for intranet applications; that is, applications used within corporate networks. Corporate users are generally not affected by network speed and require the robustness that Forms Builder provides.

Applets can also be created using other tools and languages, such as the popular language Java. Oracle has an excellent tool called JDeveloper that allows developers to create client-server applications, Java Server Pages, applets, and a variety of other objects using the Java language. Java is a powerful language, but it is third generation. It is easier to develop applications using Forms Builder, a fourth-generation tool that makes the developer highly productive. In addition, Oracle's PL/SQL is an easy language to learn.

To summarize, Forms Builder is an ideal tool for developing corporate applications because it is the industry's best tool for developing these types of applets. Using Forms Builder, you can become a highly productive developer, and your productivity can be an important factor for your employer.

Introducing Major Forms Builder 9*i* Tools

Forms Builder has been Oracle's main form development product for more than 15 years. During this time, Forms Builder applications were used in a mainframe, character-based environment; a client-server environment; and now in the Web environment. Developer 9*i* uses three different components:

- An **integrated design environment (IDE)** called **Forms Builder** develops forms. This tool places the desired design components into a binary file with a file extension of **.fmb**. The binary form file cannot be executed until it is turned into machine code.
- Forms Builder contains a second tool called **Forms Compiler** that creates a compiled (machine language) file based on the form binary file. This file has an extension of **.fmx**. It is more common, however, to compile the file within the Forms Builder tool.

- A runtime engine called **Forms Server** executes the compiled **.fmx** files in a Web environment. Forms Server is a middleware product that receives requests from a Web browser and dishes up a Java applet based on the form to the browser. Forms Server is normally called from a Web browser, but it can also be called from a tool in the Forms Builder IDE. You will use this tool to launch the forms that you create using this book.

If you are using Developer 6*i* and the form is used in the client-server paradigm, the form is launched using Forms Runtime. Forms Runtime is available as a Form Builder 6*i* menu option or executed from Form Builder. Form Builder 6*i* can use the same **.fmx** form file as both a client-server and Web application.

Three products are needed, because each performs a different task. The **.fmb** file that is in the Forms Builder IDE contains settings and parameters that pertain to displaying the various components within the tool. It is formatted so that Forms Builder can read the file. Forms Compiler turns the Forms Builder binary file into machine code, a file that is readable by the engine (Forms Server or Forms Runtime) that executes the compiled version. Figure 2-2 illustrates the relationship among the three tools.

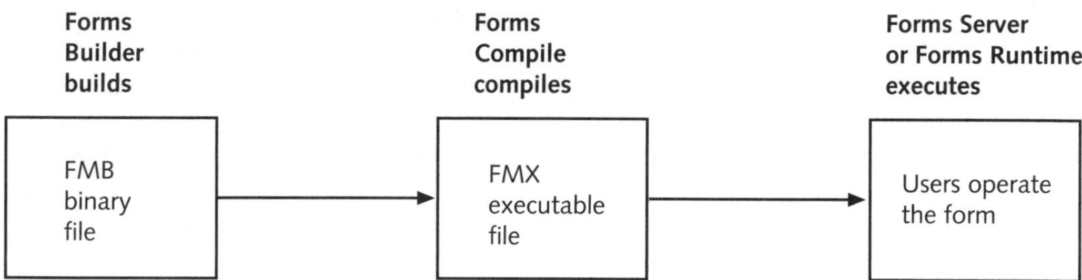

Figure 2-2 Forms Builder tool relationships and flow

Client-Server and Web Architecture

You might wonder about all of the talk of client-server environments. After all, this is a book about building Internet applications. Oracle's intended direction is to use the Web to eliminate dependency on an operating system, such as Windows. Applications developed using Forms Builder 9*i* can only be executed using the Web architecture. In the last section, I mentioned that Form Builder 6*i* builds both client-server and Web applications. Why discuss client-server and Form Builder 6*i*?

The reason for Form Builder 6*i* coverage is that a version of Form Builder has been Oracle's core development tool for many years. Thousands of Form Builder client-server applications have been developed, deployed, and are still being operated. Probably more client-server Form Builder applications exist than Internet applications. It will be years before companies move their existing systems to the Web. In fact, Oracle has announced it will support Form Builder 6*i* until 2008, so you will probably encounter it.

The product versions are very similar. The main differences are the look of the Forms Builder IDE and that Forms Builder 9*i* applications cannot be executed in the client-server environment. The figures in this book are based on Forms Builder 9*i*; however, whenever the products differ, the Form Builder 6*i* feature is described. You will find out that Form Builder 6*i* has a few features that do not exist in Forms Builder 9*i* because of the immaturity of the Web environment. The Web is not as robust as the client-server environment. However, you will find that there are actually few differences and that you can move between Form Builder 6*i* and Forms Builder 9*i* seamlessly.

One handy feature of Form Builder 6*i* is that the development of client-server and Internet applications is virtually the same. In fact, you can execute the same **.fmx** executable file in the client-server environment and on the Web. Some minor formatting differences exist, but the main difference is in deployment.

The **client-server** environment is characterized by software located on the operator's workstation. This software is designed to work with an operating system (for example, Windows), and it coordinates the file server and the database server. This software communicates with servers on a network to return the executable **.fmx** file and to make database requests. Forms Builder executable form files used in the **client-server** environment are deployed in directories accessible to the user. These files can be on the client or on a workstation connected to the client. The user executes the form by running the Forms Runtime executable **ifrun60.exe**. The executable is issued on a command line, in a shortcut, or using the Forms Runtime menu option. The following is an example of a SHORTCUT command.

```
ifrun60 c:\form_module.fmx scott/tiger
```

The first parameter calls the Forms Runtime executable. The second parameter is the executed form module followed by the Oracle ID. The last two parameters are optional. Forms Builder prompts you for these values. When the operating system encounters this command, it performs the following functions:

- Locates and executes the **ifrun60.exe** file
- Locates the target **.fmx** file on the workstation or a connected server and returns the file to the client
- Executes the form

Figure 2-3 illustrates the mechanics of using a form in the client-server environment.

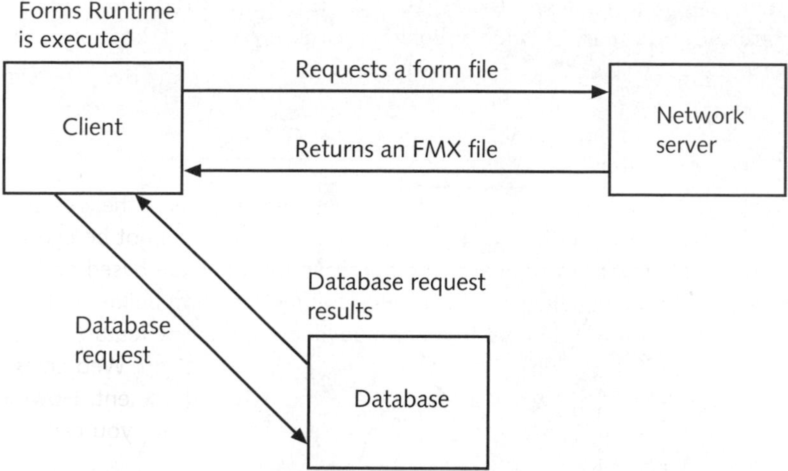

Figure 2-3 Client-server Forms Builder architecture

Web applications differ from client-server applications in that they rely on a Web browser and a Web server rather than an operating system. The Web server controls coordination rather than the client. When using a form on the Web, the executable file is registered with the Web server. The Oracle Web server is called Oracle9*i*AS, and Forms Server is one of its components.

To execute the Web form, a user requests a URL in his Web browser as shown in Figure 2-4. The URL points to an application registered within Forms Server. A listener on the Web server catches this URL request and passes it to Forms Server. The Forms Server locates and executes the **.fmx** file. It changes the **.fmx** file into a Java applet and sends it to the Web browser. To execute a form in a Web browser, the client unit must have an applet called JInitiator. When an Oracle form is executed through the Web, the Web server storing the form sends the JInitiator applet to the client's Web browser (if it does not already exist on the client). **JInitiator** is a generic applet, which is downloaded once to the client. It is actually a plug-in that ensures the Web browser can interact with Forms Server. It is also used to paint the form within the browser, validate data, and communicate with Forms Server. Forms Server reads and executes the **.fmx** file. Forms Server communicates with the database and with the applet on the Web browser.

For the most part, the form looks and operates in the same way in both the client-server and Web environments.

Launching Forms Builder's Integrated Development Environment

To launch Forms Builder, you select the Forms Builder option on the Windows Start menu. This tool is often found on an Oracle tool palette located on the taskbar. Figure 2-5 depicts a typical palette.

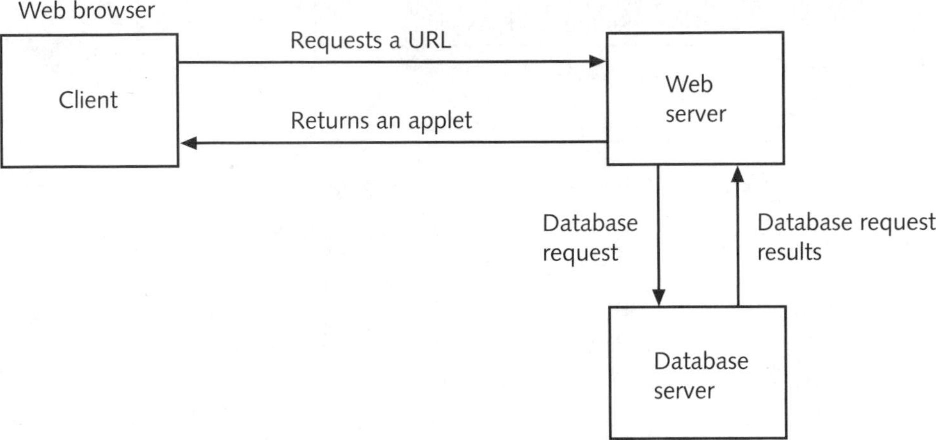

Figure 2-4 Web Forms Builder architecture

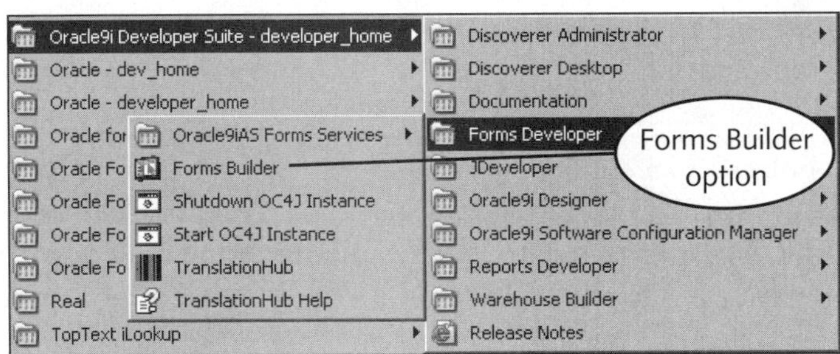

Figure 2-5 Windows Start menu displaying various Developer 9*i* tools

If for some reason you cannot locate this file on the menu, the Forms Builder executable is called **ifbld90.exe** and is located in the **Bin** subdirectory of the Oracle home directory. The home directory is generally called **Oracle**. If you cannot locate the file, try using the Find tool on your PC.

Launching Forms Builder opens the Welcome to the Forms Builder dialog box (see Figure 2-6). This dialog box is always displayed on the launch unless the Display at startup option is cleared. This dialog box can be used to start several processes, such as creating a new data block, running a form, or running a quick tour of Forms Builder. Later, you will probably deactivate this dialog box, but the tour or cue cards may be useful initially.

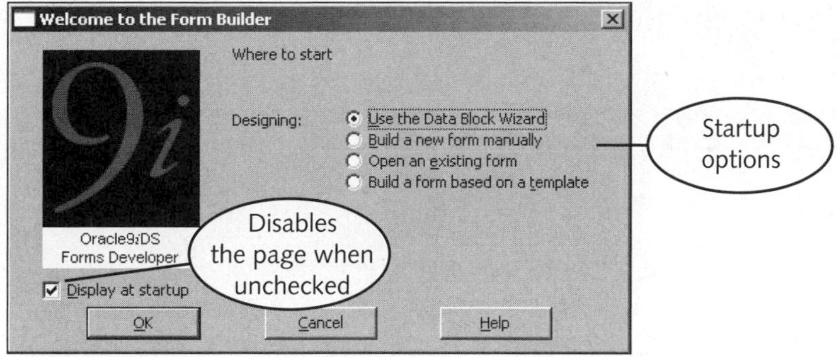

Figure 2-6 Welcome to the Forms Builder dialog box

As you increase your knowledge of Oracle, you will begin looking for shortcuts to the tools you need and will want to start your session from the main screen (Figure 2-7) rather than use a Welcome wizard. The main screen displays the Object Navigator, the heart of Forms Builder. **Object Navigator** is a Forms Builder tool that displays the various form components, as well as other form modules, menu modules, and database objects. This tool enables you to select various form objects for modification. It also allows you to add and delete form components. When Forms Builder is launched, the Object Navigator, as depicted in Figure 2-7, displays one blank module. A **module** is another name for the form binary file that contains the application components.

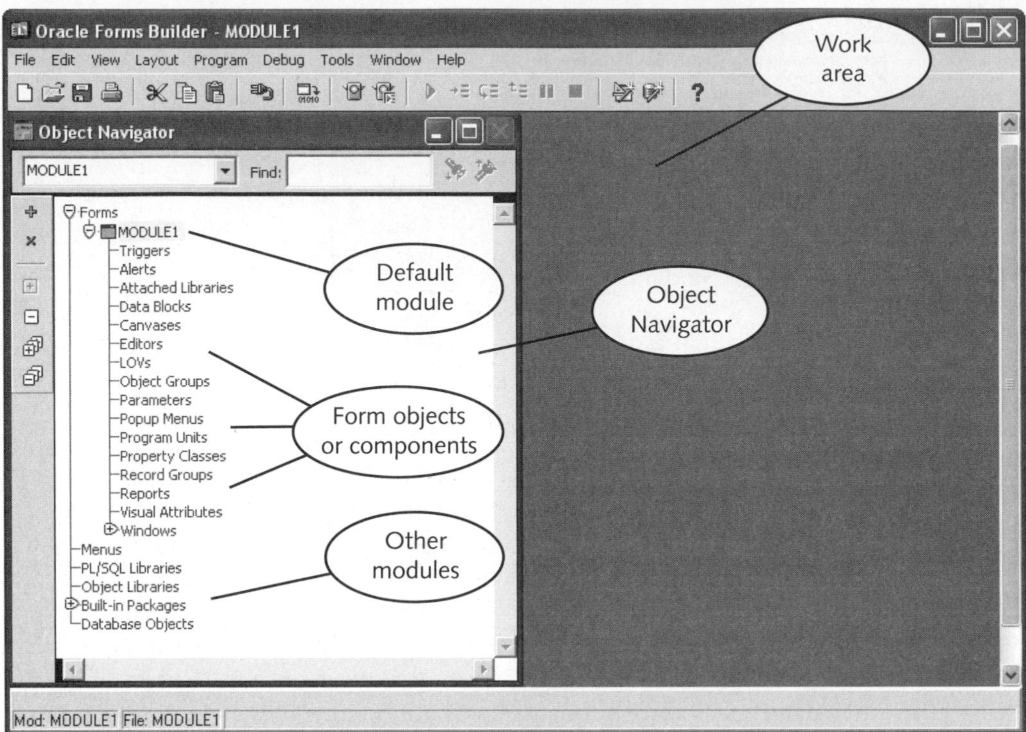

Figure 2-7 Forms Builder work area displaying the Object Navigator and one blank form module

Logging on to the Oracle Database

When starting a Forms Builder session, first connect to the Oracle database. The database furnishes much of the information you need to develop the form. It supplies Forms Builder with the names of tables and columns and each column's data type, length, and prompt properties. It also supplies constraint information that is used to set required (NOT NULL) properties and range properties.

There are several methods of connecting to Oracle. In fact, you can use Forms Builder for many tasks without connecting to the database. However, Oracle attempts to log you on to the database whenever Forms Builder needs some information from the database. This attempt can occur when you are using a wizard or compiling a PL/SQL script. When Forms Builder attempts to log you on to the database, it displays a modal dialog box (Figure 2-8) requesting you to enter the following:

- For User Name, enter the Oracle account name or ID.
- For Password, enter the password that corresponds to the user name.
- For Database, enter a set of characters called a **host** or **connect string**. These characters are a code that tells Oracle on which network server the desired Oracle instance resides.

Figure 2-8 Oracle database Connect dialog box

Normally, a developer connects to Oracle when starting a Forms Builder session by performing one of the following functions:

- From the menu, click **File/Connect**.
- Press the **Control** and **J** keys. These are IDE hot keys that perform the same function as the File/Connect menu selection.

For your first practice session, launch Forms Builder and connect to the Oracle database by performing these steps:

1. Locate and select the Forms Builder option on the Start menu.
2. If the Welcome to the Forms Builder dialog box opens, click the **Cancel** button.
3. When you are in the main work area, log on to Oracle by selecting the **File/Connect** menu option.
4. Enter your Oracle ID information into the Connect dialog box. This generally consists of the Oracle ID, password, and connect string. If you are using an Oracle database that is installed on your PC, the default ID is scott/tiger and a connect string is needed. This ID contains the tables that will be used in the examples throughout this book. However, your instructor may want you to use a different ID.
5. Click the **Connect** button. The dialog box disappears when you are connected.

Forms Builder IDE Tools: Object Navigator, Layout Editor, Property Palette, and PL/SQL Editor

Forms Builder has tools that you will use to build forms: Object Navigator, Layout Editor, Property Palette, and PL/SQL Editor. In Figure 2-7, you saw the Object Navigator, which locates and navigates to any form component. Double-clicking any object in the Object Navigator causes Forms Builder to display the selected object within the appropriate Forms Builder tool. The Object Navigator can also be used to create, delete, copy, and rename form components. It will be discussed in greater detail in Chapter 3.

The **Property Palette** is a Forms Builder tool used to define special characteristics of the form's components. Each component has a different set of **properties**. Examples of component properties include case restriction, length of value, data type, or prompt value. Properties can be used to substantially control a form's behavior. Double-clicking an object in the Object Navigator generally opens the Property Palette tool. Figure 2-9 depicts the Property Palette for a text item. The Property Palette will be discussed in greater detail in Chapter 5.

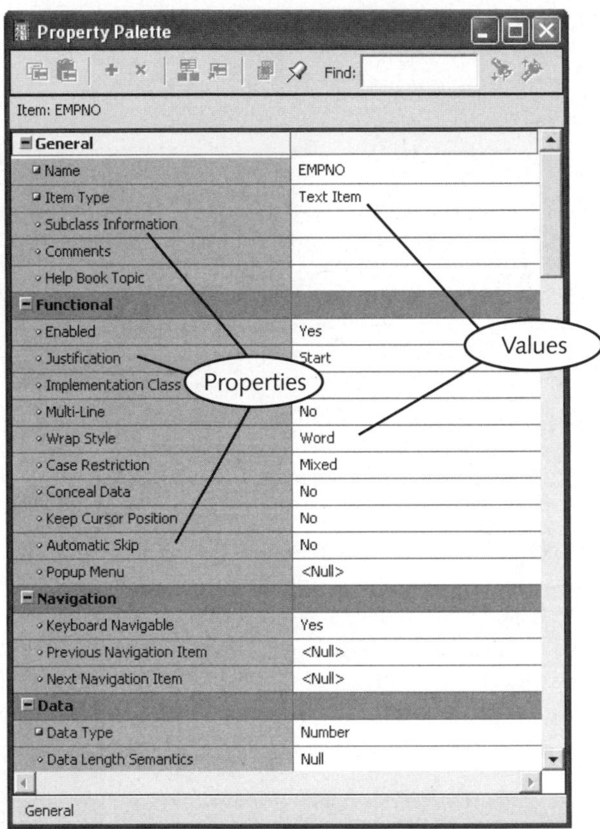

Figure 2-9 Property Palette for the EMPNO text item

The **Layout Editor** tool of Forms Builder tool paints the form. This tool allows you to move and arrange form objects, set font and fill colors, add components to the form, and add a boilerplate. Double-clicking any graphic component in the Object Navigator causes the Layout Editor to display a canvas that contains the graphic objects. Figure 2-10 depicts this tool, which will be discussed in greater detail in Chapter 4.

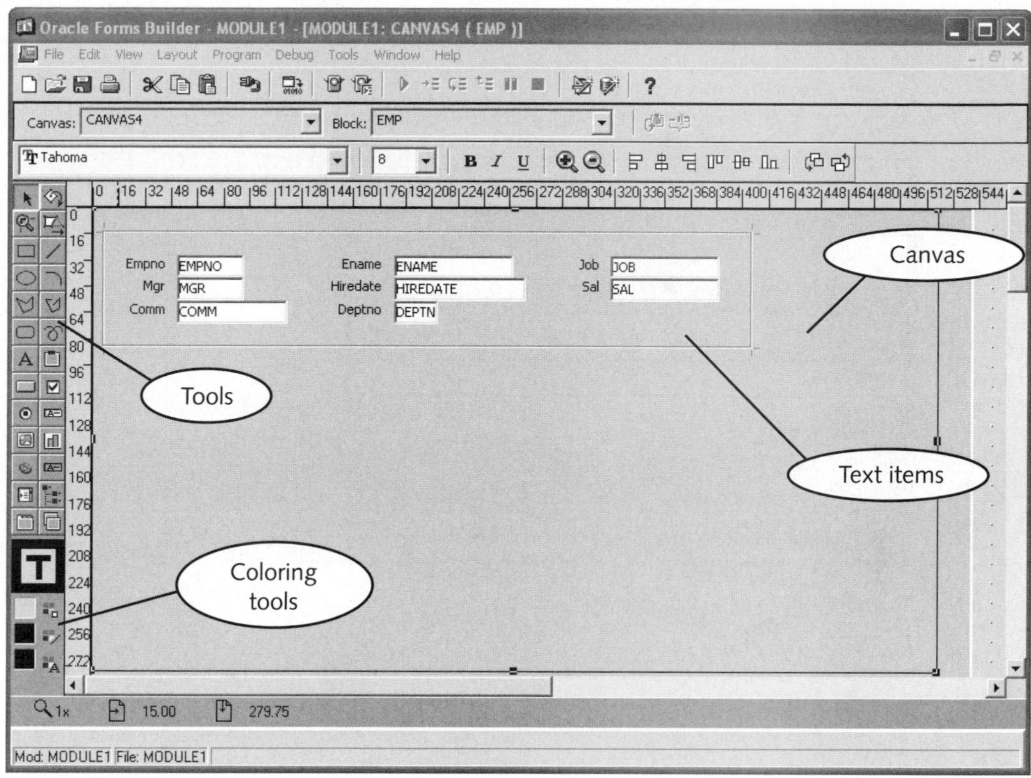

Figure 2-10 Layout Editor displaying a form's graphic components

The last major Forms Builder tool is the **PL/SQL Editor**, which is used to write the PL/SQL scripts needed by a form. These PL/SQL scripts are placed in triggers associated to a form object or into **program units** that are embedded in the triggers. A **trigger** is PL/SQL code block whose execution is based on a form event, such as double-clicking a form object, navigating to another text item, or pressing an F key. Program units are PL/SQL scripts that are named and stored within a form or in a database. Figure 2-11 depicts the PL/SQL Editor, which will be discussed in Chapter 6 along with triggers.

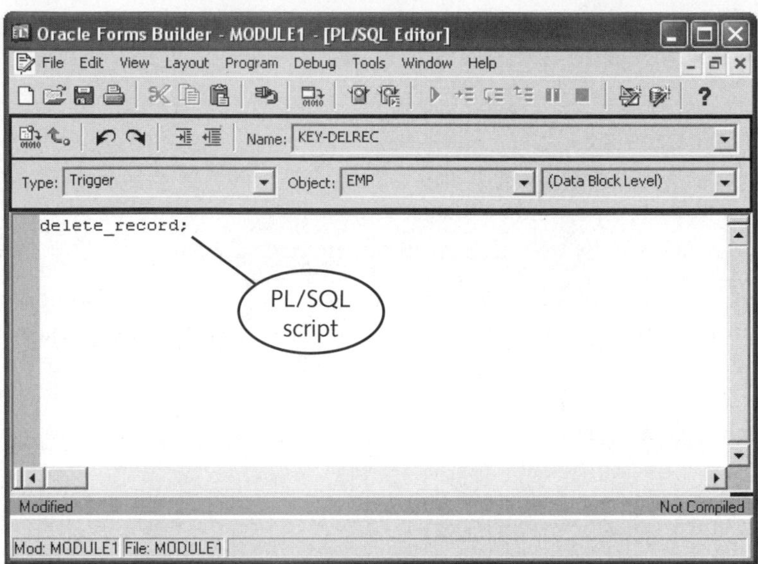

Figure 2-11 PL/SQL Editor

As you become proficient with Forms Builder, you will find yourself moving between the four tools just described. You can open any of the four tools by double-clicking objects in the Object Navigator or by selecting the tool on the Tools menu palette. One of the best ways to launch the tools is by using the F keys as follows:

- **F2**: Layout Editor
- **F3**: Object Navigator
- **F4**: Property Palette
- **F11**: PL/SQL Editor

Forms Builder also synchronizes selected objects across all the tools. For example, pressing the F4 key when an object is selected in Layout Editor causes the Property Palette for the selected object to be displayed.

Creating a Simple Form Using the Data Block and Layout Wizards

Forms are composed of a variety of objects, but each form must have the following three components:

- **Data Block**: This is the form object that contains data elements. The data block is usually closely related to a database table or view. The data block elements receive database values for display, update, or deletion. Data blocks also receive information that has been input for insertion into the database. Data blocks generate dynamic **structured query language (SQL)** and **data manipulation language (DML)** statements (INSERT, UPDATE, and DELETE) that interact with the database.

- **Canvas**: This is the form object that is shown to the user and is displayed in the Layout Editor. All displayed form components must be placed on a canvas to be displayed. Canvases also contain graphic symbols and a boilerplate.
- **Window**: This is a form object that displays the canvas.

These three components can be created manually using the Object Navigator, but it is much more common to use the Data Block and Layout Wizards, especially for newly created forms.

Creating a Form Module

The first task in creating a form is to create a form module. A **form module** is a binary file that holds the form components. To determine whether a form module has been brought into the Forms Builder session, you must display the Object Navigator. The Object Navigator displays a hierarchical list of parent and child objects. For example, if you return to Figure 2-7, you see six objects (or parent nodes) on the left side of the Object Navigator: FORMS, MENUS, PL/SQL LIBRARIES, OBJECT LIBRARIES, BUILT-IN PACKAGES, and DATABASE OBJECTS. Under the FORMS object is a node called MODULE1. This is one instance of the FORMS parent object and is a child node. The Object Navigator allows you to have multiple child nodes. Under the MODULE1 node are additional child nodes: TRIGGERS, ALERTS, ATTACHED LIBRARIES, DATA BLOCKS, and so on. These are form objects or components that make up a form. The Object Navigator lays out all available objects in this hierarchy of parent and child objects (or nodes).

If a form module exists, you see the name of the form as a FORMS object child node, as shown in Figure 2-7. Under the FORMS node is a child node called MODULE1. This is a newly created form module ready for modification. The form module is named MODULE1 by default. Forms Builder generates a new default name whenever a new module is created, and the default name changes to the name of the file when the module is saved.

The Object Navigator can contain multiple form modules. Selecting any form module child node causes that form module to be the current module. Existing form modules can be brought into Forms Builder in two ways:

- Using the File/New menu option to create a new form module
- Using the File/Open menu option to retrieve an existing module from the file system

Using the Data Block Wizard to Create a Data Block

Now that you have seen a form module created, you are ready to create the first of the three mandatory objects listed previously: the data block. Use the Data Block Wizard to create new data blocks and modify them. The wizard can be launched in three ways:

- Use the Tools/Data Block Wizard menu option.
- Click the **DATA BLOCKS** node in the Object Navigator. Click the **Create** tool on the left toolbar. The icon for this tool has a green plus sign. This option causes a dialog box to open. You are prompted to either launch the Data Block Wizard or to build it manually.
- Use the Welcome to the Forms Builder dialog box by clicking the **Use the Data Block Wizard** radio button.

As stated earlier, the Data Block Wizard can be used to create a new data block and modify an existing block. If you selected an existing block in the Object Navigator, the Data Block Wizard displays information about this data block. If you want to create a new data block, be sure that an existing data block is not selected. Forms generally contain several data blocks. After creating the first data block, it is very easy to attempt to create a second data block while the original is still selected. If you launch the Data Block Wizard with a data block selected, the wizard modifies the currently selected data block and *eliminates* the settings that you have established. This is a common error for novice developers. They launch the Data Block Wizard while a data block is selected. When they are finished, the components of the first data block are gone, leaving them mystified. If you want to create a new data block, be sure that a non-data block form module object is selected before launching the Data Block Wizard. This causes Forms Builder to create a new data block.

The Data Block Wizard consists of a series of modal dialog boxes or pages that allow you to set a number of data block properties or specifications. The Welcome to the Data Block Wizard page (not illustrated) appears first. There is a Display this page next time check box in the lower-left corner of the page. Clicking this box to clear the checkmark prevents this dialog box from appearing. Each of the wizard pages has Back and Next buttons that allow you to move between the wizard pages. Clicking the Next button on the Data Block Wizard page opens the first important wizard page.

Setting the Block's Data Source Type

The next Data Block Wizard page, the Type page shown in Figure 2-12, is used to enter the data block's data source type. This dialog box has two radio buttons: Table or View, and Stored Procedure. Selecting the Table or View option sets up the data block to use an Oracle table or view. A table is a database object that stores records. **Views** are stored

SELECT statements that create and return a result set or derived table. Stored procedures are named PL/SQL scripts that reside in the database. They can be used in conjunction with a Ref Cursor and used as a data source. The latter is an advanced topic and will be discussed later. The Table or View option is the more common option and is used in this example.

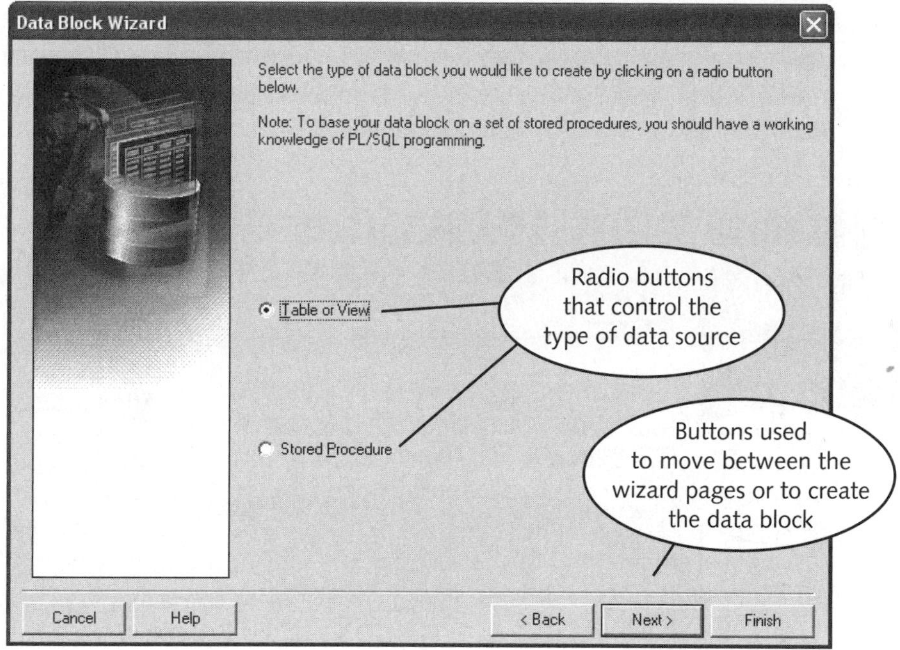

Figure 2-12 Type wizard page

Setting the Data Source with the Table Page

The next wizard page, shown in Figure 2-13, is used to set the data source. This page does not appear unless you are logged on to Oracle. If you were not previously logged on, you are prompted to log on to Oracle before the page appears. Note the following features of the wizard page shown in Figure 2-13:

- **Table or view**: Text item used to document the name of the data source table or view.
- **Browse**: Button that launches the Tables dialog box used to search and identify tables and views for the Table or View text item.
- **Refresh**: Button that populates the Available Columns list box. Use this button only if a database change occurs while the wizard is open.

- **Enforce data integrity**: Check box that causes Forms Builder to add the target table's database constraints to the data block item properties.
- **Available Columns**: List box displaying columns available for the data block.
- **Database Items**: List box displaying columns that will be placed in the data block.
- **Move buttons**: Four buttons that appear between the list boxes. They are used to add and remove columns from the list boxes. Single-arrow tools move only the selected columns; double-arrow tools move the entire contents of the list box.

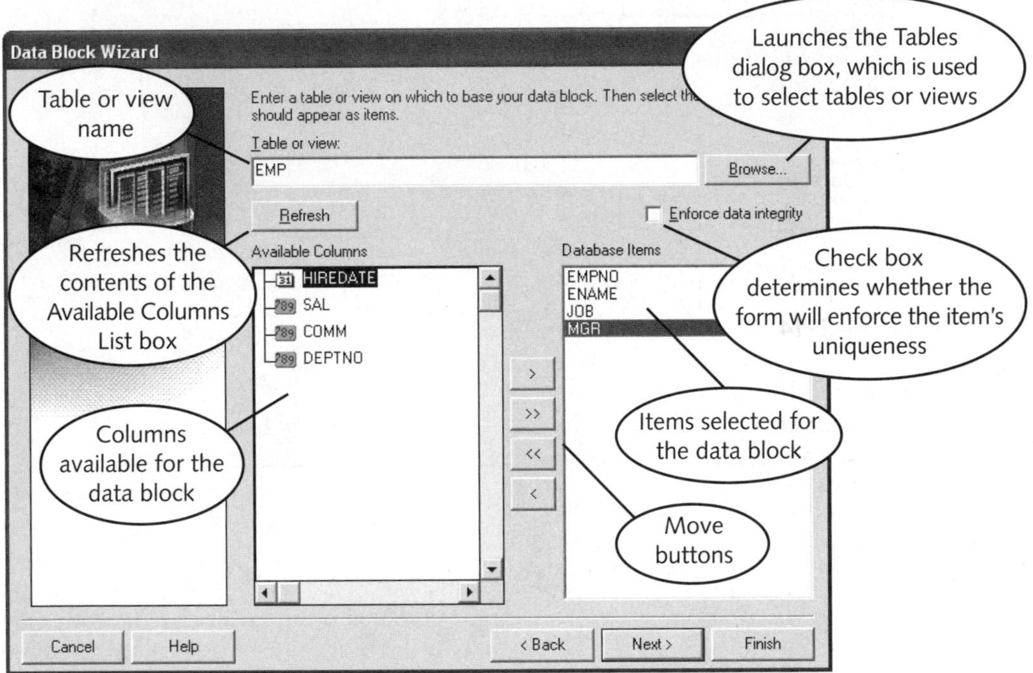

Figure 2-13 Table page of the Data Block Wizard

Double-clicking any list box column moves it to another list box. The Delete key can also be used to remove columns from the Database Items list box. The EMP table has been identified as the data source, and several columns have been selected for the data block. This book uses the EMP and DEPT tables in all examples, and these tables are supplied as sample tables in all Oracle installations.

It is not necessary to place all available columns into the data block; however, any table column that contains a NOT NULL constraint must be selected to perform DML operations without errors.

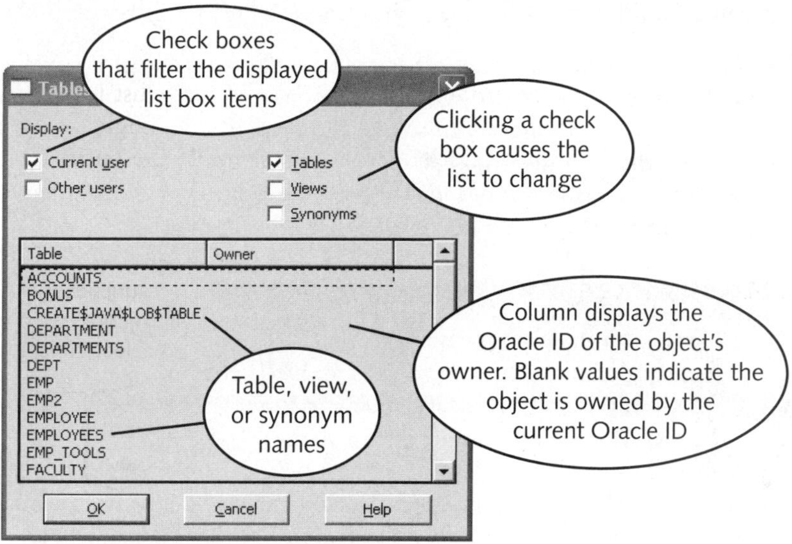

Figure 2-14 Tables dialog box used to identify the data source

Figure 2-14 depicts the Tables dialog box used to search the database for the data source. Clicking any list box object on the Tables dialog box and clicking the OK button populates text items on the Data Block Wizard Table page. The selected table name will appear in the wizard Table or View text item. In addition the wizard page, Available Columns list box, will be populated with the selected table's columns. The Tables dialog box is a common Oracle tool. Oracle is a distributed database, and the target data can be located on a variety of Oracle installations. The dialog box aids you in searching the various installations and in locating the appropriate data source. Note the following dialog box characteristics:

- **Display**: A series of check boxes used to filter the database objects.
- **Current user**: Allows objects owned by you, the developer, to appear in the list.
- **Other users**: Allows objects on which you have been granted privileges to appear.
- **Tables**: Allows database tables to appear.
- **Views**: Allows views to appear.
- **Synonyms**: Allows synonym names to appear. A **synonym** is another name for a database object.

- **Database object list box**: Displays the results of a database search based on the values in the Display check boxes. The list box has two components: TABLE and OWNER. TABLE contains the name of the object. OWNER lists the Oracle ID that owns the object. Blank values indicate the current user owns the object.

The dialog box can be resized by placing your cursor over any of the dialog box's outer edges. A black two-way arrow appears. Click and hold the left mouse button while moving the cursor. This same procedure works for most Forms Builder dialog boxes. You can change the width of the TABLE object list by placing the cursor over the line between the TABLE and OWNER headers. Click and hold the left mouse button while moving the cursor.

Congratulations Page

The Data Block Name and the Congratulations pages (Figure 2-15) are the last two Data Block wizard pages. By default, the data block is named after its data source. For example, a data block based on the EMP table is called EMP by default. The Data Block Name page allows you to give the data block a custom name.

This page does not exist in Form Builder 6*i*. You can give a data block a custom name only by using the Object Navigator. The Congratulations page informs you that you created or are about to create the data block and the data block items. It contains two radio buttons. The first creates the data block and launches the Layout Wizard that is used to place the data items on a canvas. The second option simply creates the data block. You can use the Layout Wizard later to format the block. It is fairly standard to select the first option.

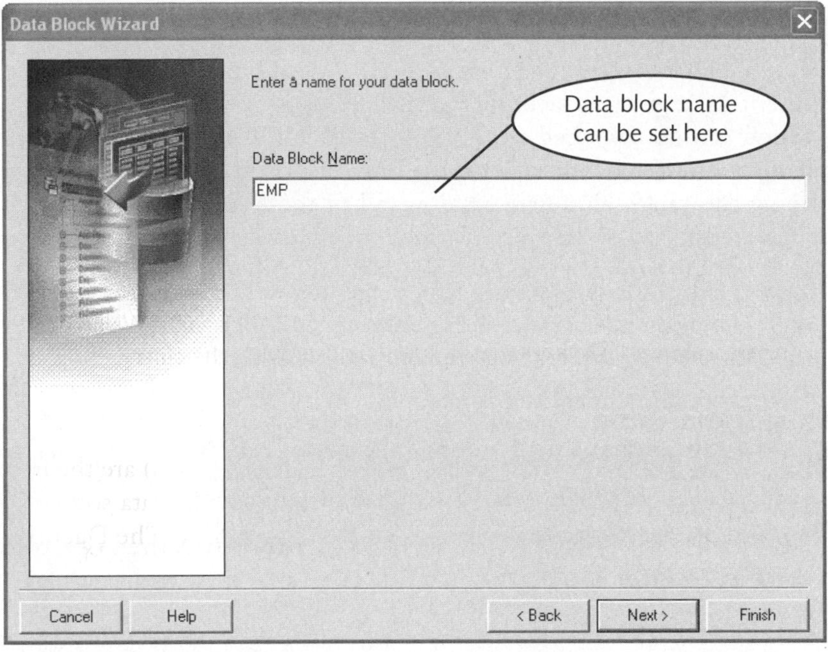

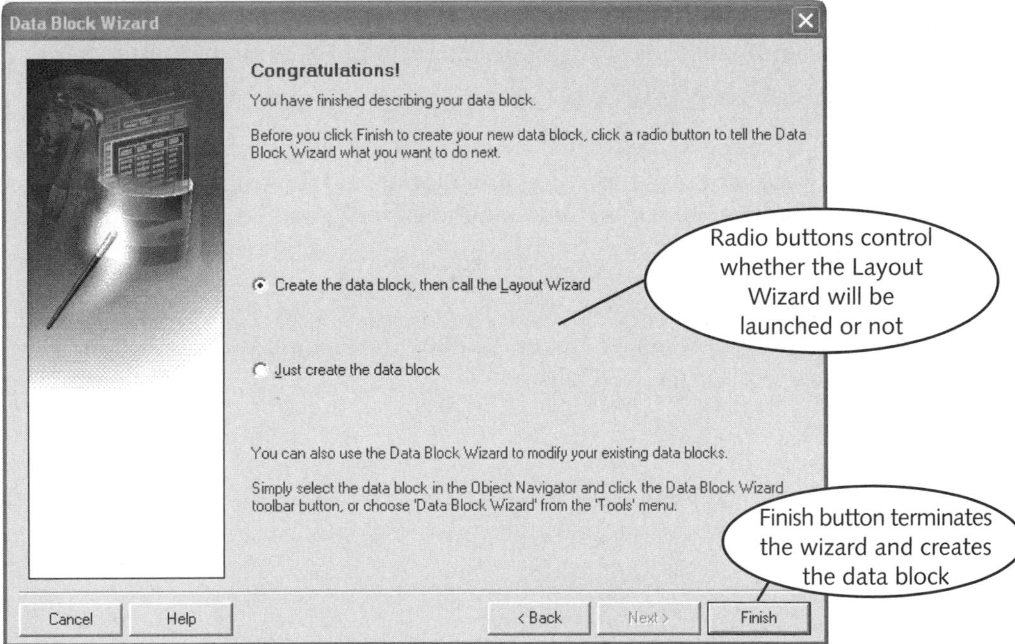

Figure 2-15 Data Block Name and Congratulations wizard pages

Using the Layout Wizard to Place Data Block Items on a Canvas

After the data block is created along with the data block items associated to table columns, the items must be placed on a canvas. This is generally done using the Layout Wizard, which can be launched from the Data Block Wizard Congratulations page or from a menu option. Data block items are only displayed by placing them on a canvas and displaying the canvas within a window. All of these items can be created manually using the Create tool in the Object Navigator. It is easier and quicker, however, to use the Layout Wizard to associate the data block items with a canvas. As a form developer, you use the Layout Editor for the following tasks:

- Create a canvas for the form if one has not been created.
- Create additional canvases if needed.
- Create **tab pages**, which are special types of canvases that overlay each other.
- Associate a data block item to a canvas or tab page.
- Set the data item's prompt or label text. A **prompt** is the boilerplate text that describes a form item.
- Set the data item's width.
- Set the basic data layout.
- Set the data display properties, including the number of records displayed.

Setting these properties goes a long way toward formatting your form. The Layout Wizard is launched by either of these methods:

- Choosing the Create the data block, and then call the Layout Wizard option on the Data Block Wizard Congratulations page
- Clicking Tools/Layout Wizard on the menu

The first Layout Wizard page (Figure 2-16) is the Welcome page. This panel does not serve any real purpose and can be disabled by clicking the Display this page next time check box to clear the checkmark.

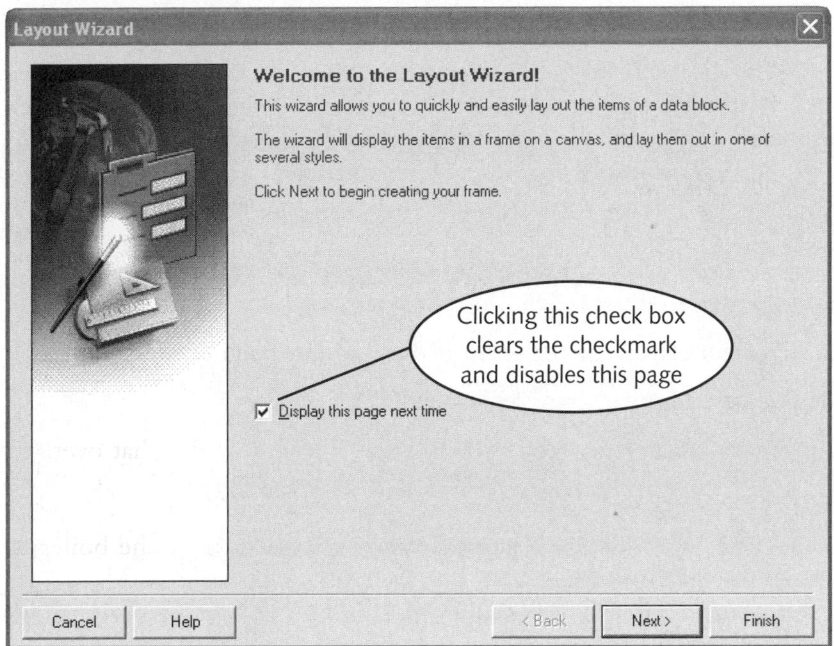

Figure 2-16 Layout Wizard Welcome page

Setting the Canvas

The Canvas wizard page is the first page of importance. It identifies the canvas that is associated to the data block items. This can be a new canvas as depicted in Figure 2-17 or an existing canvas (a canvas can display multiple data blocks). The Canvas wizard page is also used to determine the type of canvas. Five types are available: content, stacked, vertical toolbar, horizontal toolbar, and tab. Content is the basic form canvas and is the default. All forms must have at least one content canvas as discussed in greater detail in Chapter 4. Note the following Canvas wizard page features:

- **Canvas**: A pull-down list of New Canvas option and all previously created canvases. You must choose a canvas on which to place the data block items.
- **Type**: A pull-down list of canvas types.
- **Tab Page**: A pull-down list of new tab page options and all existing tab pages. The values in this list pertain to the selected canvas, and the list box is active only if the canvas is a tab canvas.

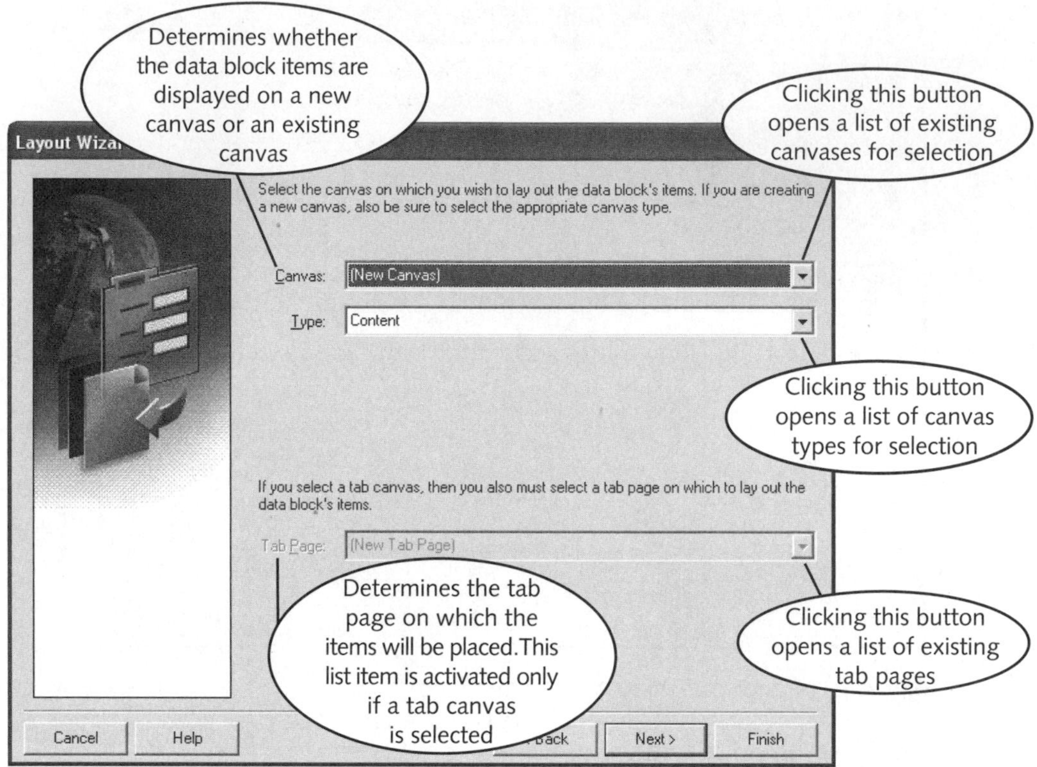

Figure 2-17 Canvas wizard page

Identifying Data Block Items for Display

The Data Block wizard page (Figure 2-18) follows the Canvas wizard page and is used to set two data block item properties: Canvas and Visible. The properties are not displayed on the page, but moving an item from the Available Items list to the Displayed Items list sets the property values. The following describes what occurs by moving an item to the Displayed Items list:

- **Canvas**: An item property that associates the item to the canvas. If this item has a NULL value it does not appear. If a Canvas property contains a canvas name, it appears on the named canvas. Moving an item to the Displayed Items list sets the Canvas property to the canvas identified on the Canvas page.
- **Visible**: An item property that determines whether the item appears when the form is executed. If this value is NO, the item appears in the Layout Editor (if the Canvas property is set to a canvas) but not when the form is executed. A value of YES causes the item to appear. Moving an item to the Displayed Items list sets this property to YES.

Other characteristics of the page include:

- **Data Block**: Pull-down list that displays the form's data blocks. This setting determines the data block supplying the items.
- **Available Items**: List box displaying data block items available for display. These items will conform to the selected data block.
- **Displayed Items**: List box displaying data block items that will be displayed.
- **Item Type**: Pull-down list that sets the selected item's type. The default is Text Item. Examples of other types are Display Item, Check Box, and Pop List.
- **View**: Pull-down list used with a radio group item to set up radio buttons.

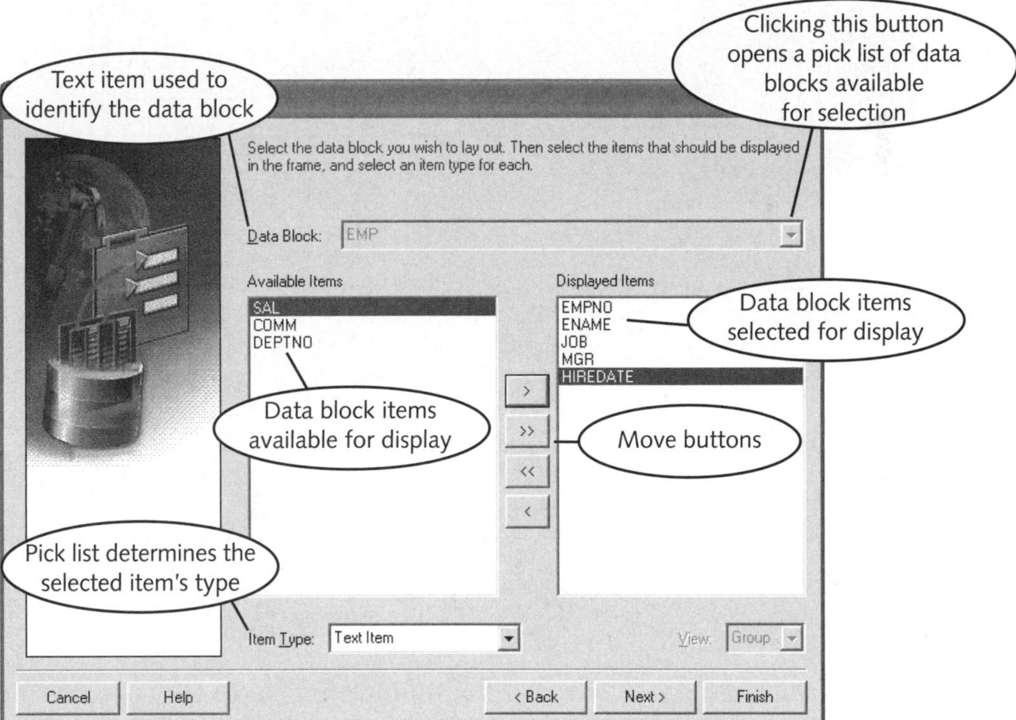

Figure 2-18 Data Block wizard page

Setting the Item Prompt and Width

The Items wizard page (Figure 2-19) sets prompt text, as well as the width and height of the displayed data items. **Prompt text** is the boilerplate that describes the data item and appears adjacent to an item on the canvas. The default prompt text is based on the database column names. Underscores and special characters contained in the column name are stripped out of the name, leaving the default. The width, height, and prompt text values are data item properties and can be reset using the Property Palette. The Items wizard page contains a single list box composed of four values per row:

- **Name**: Data block item names. This value cannot be changed.
- **Prompt**: Data item's prompt text. This value can be changed.
- **Width**: Data item's width. This value can be changed.
- **Height**: Data item's height. This value can be changed.

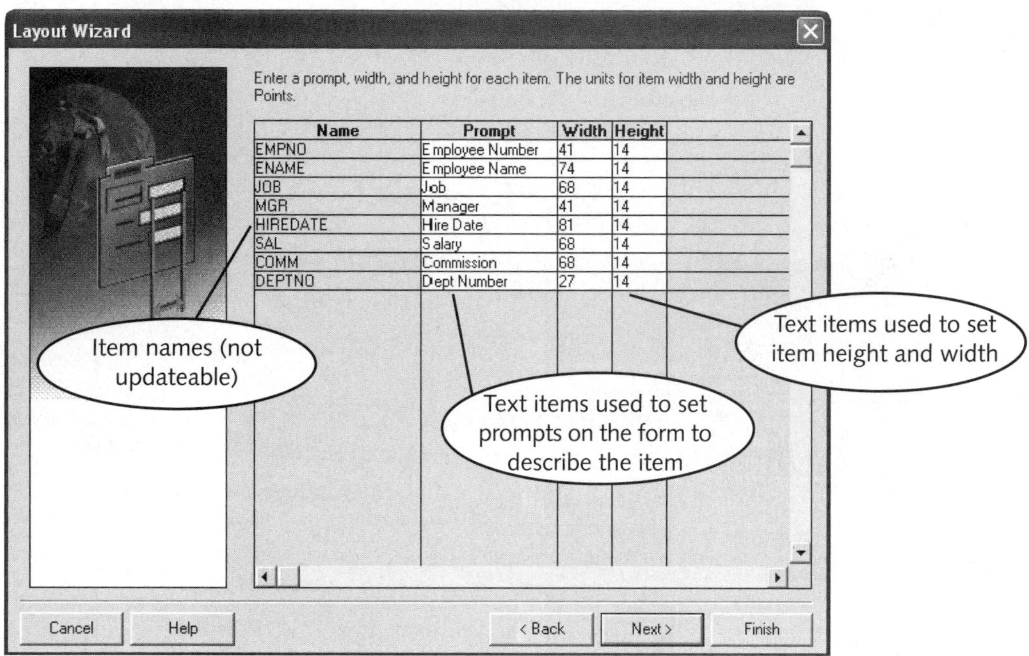

Figure 2-19 Items wizard page

Setting the Style

The Style wizard page (Figure 2-20) determines the initial layout of the displayed data items. The page consists of two style setting radio buttons: Form and Tabular. With a form style, a record's items are displayed in a number of rows. This style works best when the form is a regular entity instance. With a tabular style, a number of records are displayed in a series of columns. Each row in the layout is a database record. This style works best when the form is to display multiple rows. Data entity attributes in a one-to-many relationship are often displayed on canvases that have a combination of form and tabular styles. The data from the parent entity (for example, TRANSFORMER) is viewed in form layout, and the data from the child entity (for example, TRANSFORMER_TEST) is viewed in the tabular style. Forms Builder calls this a **master-detail layout**.

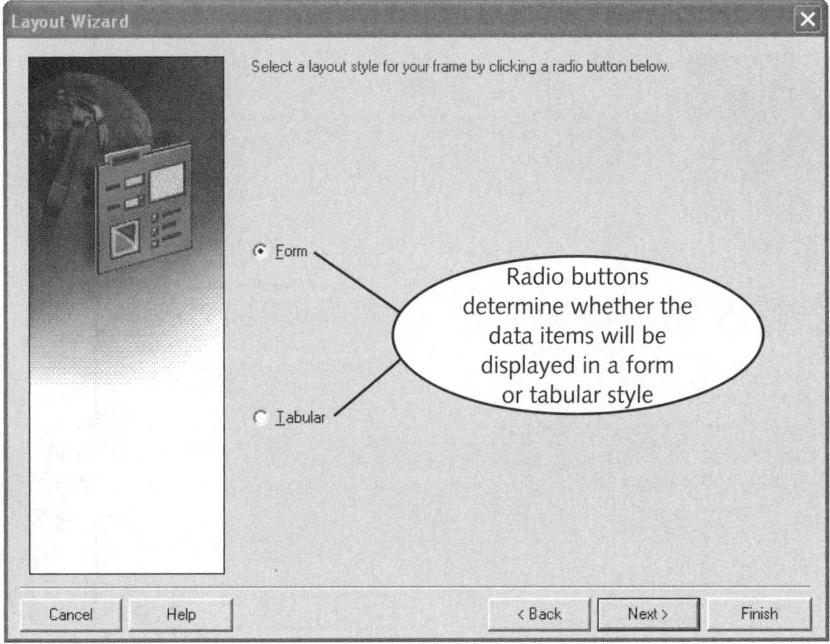

Figure 2-20 Style wizard page

Setting the Number of Rows, Frame Title, Distance Between Records, and the Scrollbar

The next to last Layout Wizard page (Figure 2-21) is the Rows page, which is used to set two data block properties: Records Displayed and Scrollbar. The defaults for these properties are 1 and NO, meaning only one data block record is displayed, and the canvas does not have a scrollbar for the data block's records. You generally use these settings on form style layouts. Tabular style layouts generally display multiple records. To display multiple records, set the Records Displayed option to a value greater than 1. It is very handy to have a scrollbar for tabular style layouts. Click the Display Scrollbar check box to display a scrollbar on the canvas.

The Rows page is also used to set frame properties. **Frames** are canvas child objects used to format sets of attributes and are discussed in greater detail in Chapter 4. However, for now you should understand that the Frame Title and Distance Between Records properties can be set on this wizard page. The Frame Title property is a boilerplate that describes the displayed items. The Distance Between Records property causes space to appear between successive rows of records.

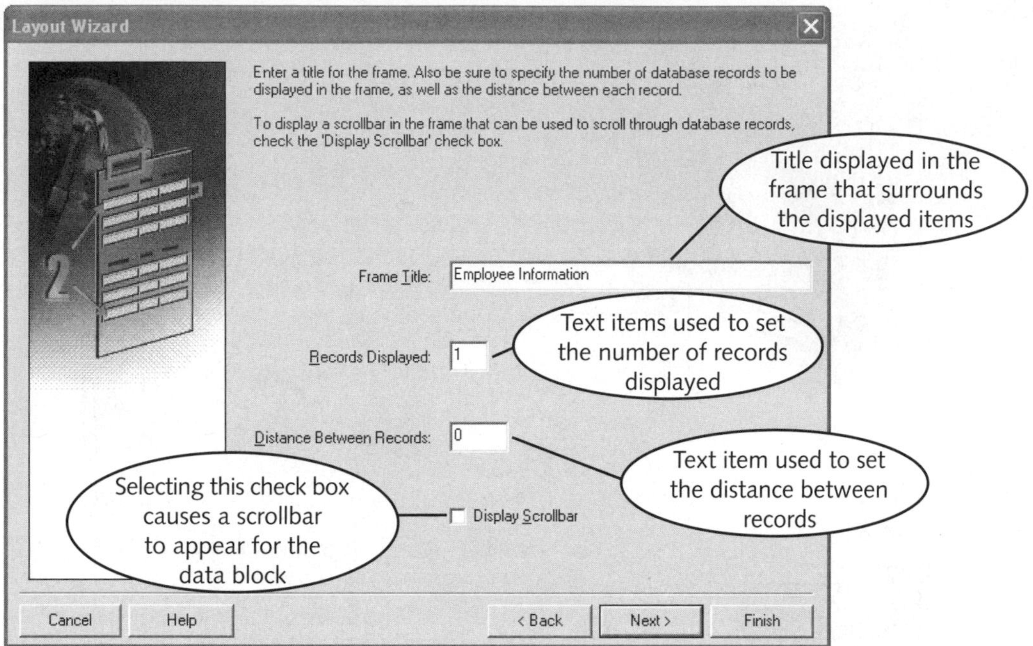

Figure 2-21 Rows wizard page

Completing the Layout and Viewing the Form Objects

The Congratulations page (Figure 2-22) is the last page of the Layout Wizard. Clicking the Finish button causes a number of form objects to be created and properties set. You can move backwards through the wizard checking the settings before clicking the Finish button, and each of the pages has a Finish button, so you can finish creating the layout on any wizard page.

After completing the tasks in the Data Block and Layout Wizards, you have developed all of the form objects needed to execute the form in client-server or Web environments. The form now has the following powerful capabilities:

- Records can be added to the database.
- Database records can be modified.
- Records can be deleted from the database.
- Records can be retrieved from the database.
- Extremely complex queries can be executed against the database.

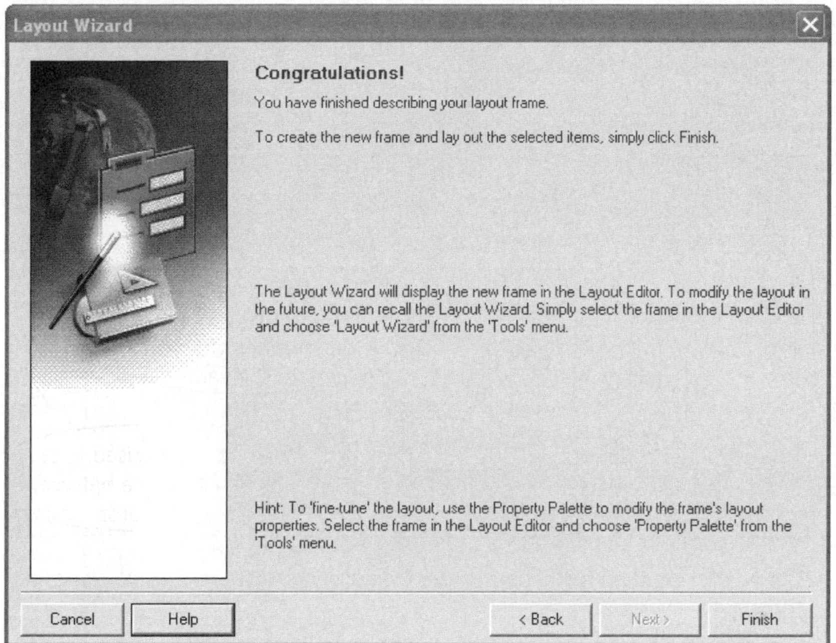

Figure 2-22 Congratulations wizard page

The default capabilities listed previously are discussed in the following sections of this chapter. Figure 2-23 illustrates the form that was created using the settings in the previous figures. The form is displayed in the Layout Editor. Notice that the data block items are located in several rows, as is the form style. To the left of the Layout Editor is the Object Navigator displaying the various form objects that are listed here:

- The data block is named EMP. The default name of data blocks is the name of the data source. The data source is the table EMP, which was set on the Table page (Figure 2-13).
- Data items include EMPNO, ENAME, JOB, MGR, HIREDATE, SAL, COMM, and DEPTNO. The default names of form items correspond to their database names.
- CANVAS4 is used to display the data items. This default name can be changed.
- FRAME5 is used to group the data items. This default name can be changed.

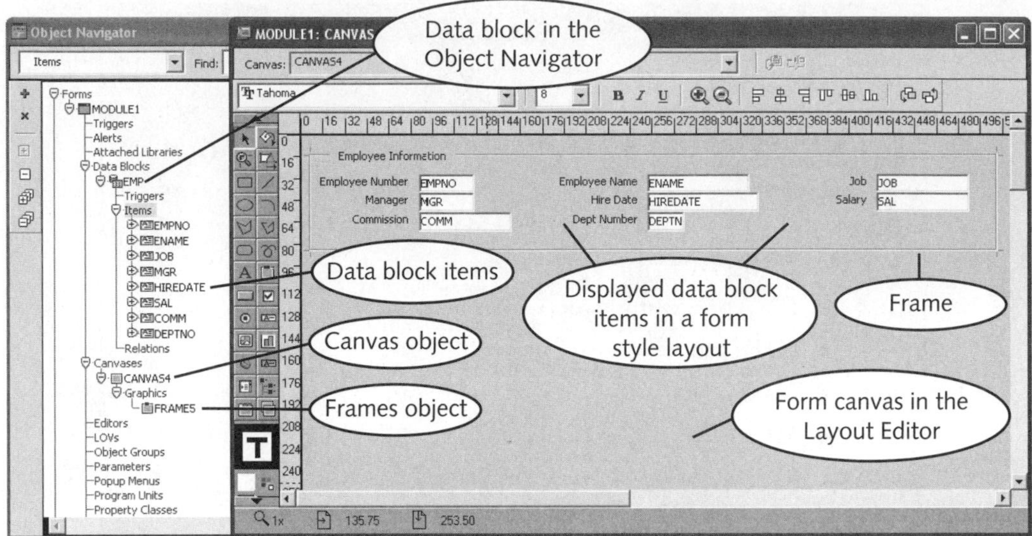

Figure 2-23 Newly created form layout and objects after the objects have been deselected

For practice, create the form module that was illustrated in Figures 2-12 through Figure 2-22 by working through the steps that follow. This practice session demonstrates steps needed to create and format a data block.

1. Create a new form module by selecting the **Object Navigator Forms** object and clicking the **Create** tool. You may also use the **File/New** menu option.
2. Launch the Data Block Wizard by selecting the Object Navigator Data Blocks object node and clicking the **Create** tool. A New Data Block dialog box opens. Select the **Use the Data Block Wizard** option. You can also select the **Tools/Data Block Wizard** menu selection. Click the **OK** button to launch the Data Block Wizard or to create the data block with no specifications.
3. If the Welcome page appears, click the **Next** button.
4. On the Type page, select the **Table or View** radio button (Figure 2-12). Click **Next**.
5. On the Table page, click **Browse** to open the Tables dialog box (Figure 2-14). Locate the EMP table. Click **EMP** to select the table. Click **OK** to close the Tables dialog box.
6. On the Data Block Name page, accept the default name. Click **Next**.
7. Move all the items in the Available Columns list to the Database Items list (Figure 2-13). Click **Next**.
8. On the Congratulations page (Figure 2-15), select the **Create the data block, then call the Layout Wizard** radio button. Click the **Finish** button to launch the Layout Wizard.

9. If the Layout Wizard Welcome page (Figure 2-16) appears, click **Next**.
10. On the Canvas page (Figure 2-17), accept the defaults. Click **Next**.
11. On the Data Block page (Figure 2-18), move all items from the Available Items list to the Displayed Items list. Click **Next**.
12. On the Items page (Figure 2-19), set the Prompt names as follows and click **Next**:
    - **EMPNO**: Employee Number
    - **ENAME**: Employee Name
    - **JOB**: Job
    - **MGR**: Manager
    - **HIREDATE**: Hire Date
    - **SAL**: Salary
    - **COMM**: Commission
    - **DEPTNO**: Department Number
13. On the Style page (Figure 2-20), click the **Form** radio button and click **Next**.
14. On the Rows page (Figure 2-21), enter the following settings and click **Next**:
    - **Frame Title**: Employee Information
    - **Records Displayed**: 1
    - **Distance Between Records**: 0
    - Do not select the Display Scrollbar check box
15. On the Congratulations page (Figure 2-22) click the **Finish** button.
16. Forms Builder now creates the canvas and window. The Layout Wizard closes, and your form should look similar to Figure 2-23.
17. Save the module as PRACTICE0201.FMB by selecting the **File/Save** menu option and entering the name and file location.

COMPILING AND SAVING THE FORM MODULES

In the last section, you created a basic form using the Data Block and Layout Wizards. This section shows you how to compile and save the form modules. After creating the form modules, they must be converted to machine code by compiling the module. This is generally done within Forms Builder, but an external product called Forms Compiler can be used. Forms Compiler is generally not used when you are developing the form, because its main purpose is to compile existing forms after a product upgrade. Using Forms Builder, a form file can be compiled in these three ways:

- Click the Program/Compile Module menu option.
- Press the Control+T (Ctrl+T) hot keys.
- Execute the form within Forms Builder using the preference option that automatically compiles the form before executing it.

Compiling the form does more than simply create a file of machine code. The compilation procedure checks for problems, including whether the PL/SQL code is syntactically correct, whether referenced variables exist, and whether visible items appear within the canvas height and width parameters. In fact, it is somewhat common to identify errors during this process, and you must correct these problems before the form can be compiled.

Compiling the form creates an executable file with a file extension of **.fmx**; however, it does not save the binary **.fmb** file. It is possible to have an executable file but no source code for the file. In order to save the binary file, you must save the file. This is done in one of two ways:

- Click the **File/Save As** or **File/Save** menu options.
- Click the **Save** tool on the toolbar.

LAUNCHING A FORM USING ORACLE FORMS BUILDER RUNTIME ENGINES

After you have developed and compiled a form, you can run it. Forms are executed by sending a URL request to Forms Server (or launching Forms Runtime for **client-server** applications). Forms Builder contains a tool that enables you to launch the form from within the IDE so that you can run and test the form while you are developing it. Forms Builder 9*i* only allows you to execute the form as a Web application.

Form Builder 6*i* allows you to execute the form as both a Web application and a client-server application.

Before you can execute the Web form using Forms Builder 9*i*, you must start a listener. The **listener** works in conjunction with an internal Forms Builder 9*i* Web server. When the listener identifies a request from a Web browser, it notifies the Forms Server of the 9*i* Web server. Forms Server then serves up the requested form application and sends it to the Web browser. If you are executing a form for the first time on your PC, the JInitiator applet is downloaded. The Start OC4J Instance Start Taskbar option, shown in Figure 2-24, is used to start the listener. It opens a Start OC4J Instance window (Figure 2-24) that launches the listener. This window does not close, so you should minimize it.

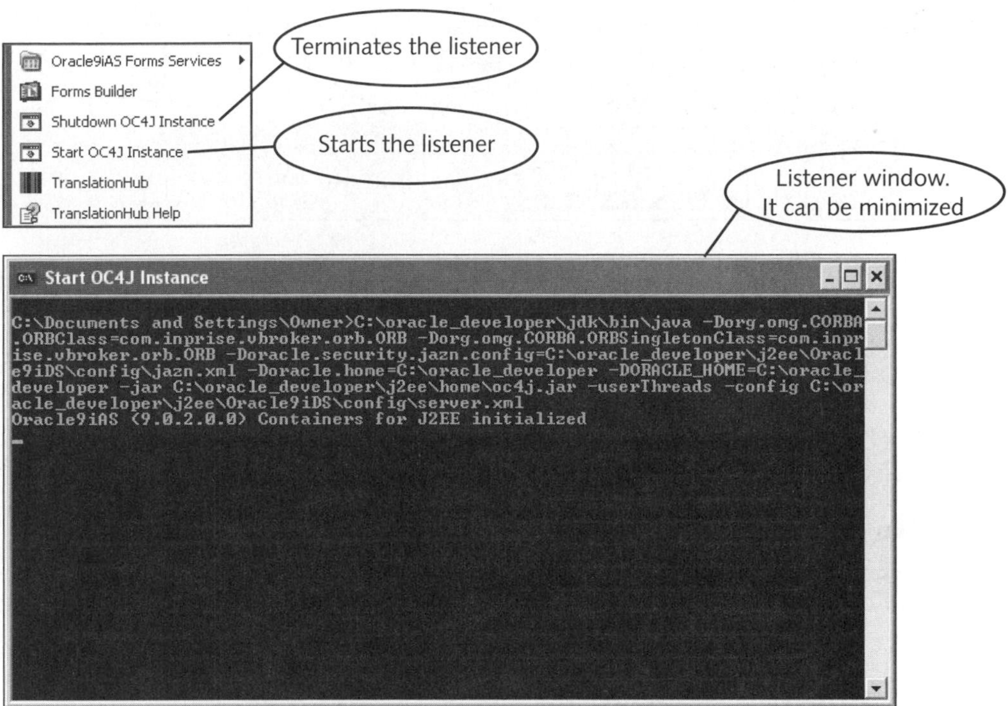

Figure 2-24 Start OC4J Start taskbar option and the OC4J Instance window

Practice launching the form from within Forms Builder by following these steps:

1. Use the Object Navigator or the Layout Editor to select any of the target form's components. Selecting a component causes that form to be set as the current form, and Forms Builder always executes the current form. Be sure that the listener is started before launching the form. If it does not exist on your workstation, Forms Builder downloads JInitiator the first time you launch a form.

2. Click the **Run Form** tool on the horizontal toolbar or select the **Program/ Run Form** menu selection. The Run Form tool is illustrated in Figure 2-25.

By default, the Oracle form takes up only a portion of the Web browser window. If your form is larger than the portion allotted to the Oracle form, you will not be able to see the entire form. If part of your form is cut off, you can correct this problem by modifying the WIDTH and HEIGHT settings in the **FORMSWEB.CFG**, which is generally located in the **C:\ORA9i\FORMS90\SERVER** directory. This is a text file, which can be edited using Editpad or Notepad. This book uses a WIDTH of 1000 and a HEIGHT of 600. The recommended values can vary based on the resolution of your workstation.

Figure 2-25 Horizontal toolbar and the Run form tools

If you are using Form Builder 6*i*, you do not have to start a listener but can simply select either the Run Form Client-Server or the Run Form Web tools located on the Object Navigator horizontal toolbar, as shown in Figure 2-26.

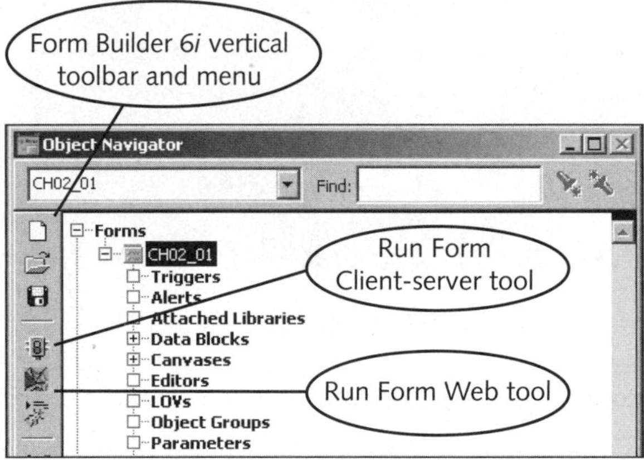

Figure 2-26 Form Builder 6*i* Object Navigator toolbar and the form runtime tools

Form Operating Modes and Determining Which Mode a Form Is In

An Oracle form has a large amount of functionality built into it by default. It is very important for you to understand the default behavior, because it will be your task as a developer to enhance or eliminate portions of this behavior. Oracle forms and all other computer forms have three basic operating modes:

- The form prompts the user for values that determine which records are to be displayed.
- The form displays the records retrieved for viewing or updating.
- The form allows the user to add new records.

An Oracle form is not different. An Oracle form also has three **modes**, as follows:

- **NORMAL**: The data block can be used to enter new records or to update and delete displayed records.
- **ENTER QUERY**: The data block prompts the user to enter values that are used to identify the displayed records.
- **QUERY**: The data block retrieves records for the form.

These modes do not pertain to the form itself; they indicate the mode of a data block on the form. A form can contain multiple data blocks, and each data block can be in a different mode. The first thing you must learn is how to distinguish which mode the data is in, and this is sometimes very confusing.

Understanding the NORMAL Mode

Data blocks that are in the NORMAL mode can be used to add records or to update records. This may sound strange, since it seems illogical to be able to add and update at the same time; however, it is true. A data block in the NORMAL mode always has at least one record in which the user can add a new record, and this is true even if the data block is displaying existing records.

Figure 2-27 illustrates this feature. The figure depicts an executed Web form, which contains the same EMP data block that was used in the last practice session. The form uses a tabular style containing multiple records rather than a form style layout. A query was executed on the data block returning records. The data block is in the NORMAL mode. The displayed EMP table records can be updated by placing the cursor in any of the text items and entering the data. A new record can be added by placing the cursor in the row immediately following the last EMP record and entering the data. Thus, the data block can be used to update existing values and add new ones at the same time.

You can always add records to a data block that is in the NORMAL mode. If the form is displaying one record in a form style layout or 20 records in a tabular layout, you can press the Down arrow key to move the cursor to the next record. Data blocks, whether form or tabular style, contain all the records returned by a query. Forms Builder always adds a row that can be used to insert records after the last record in the data block result set. Pressing the Down arrow key scrolls you through the record set, until the blank row is displayed. Using the form style can sometimes be confusing. This style is used when one record of the

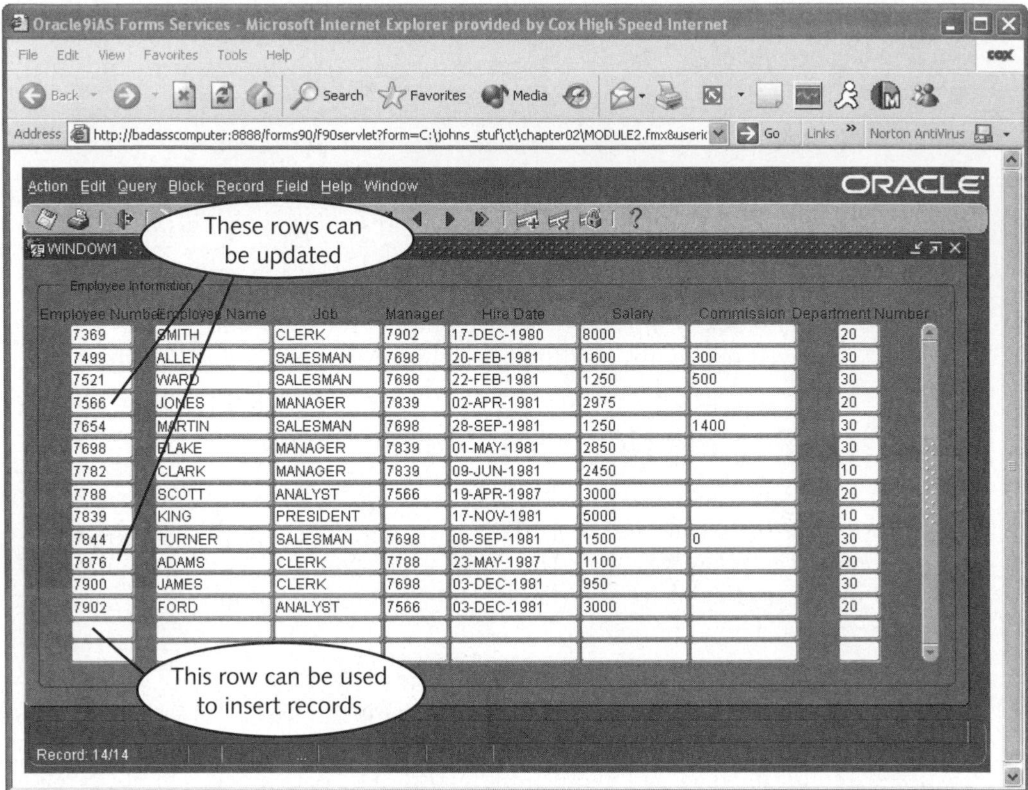

Figure 2-27 Executed tabular style form displaying records for update and a record that can be used to insert records

result set is displayed. It does not mean that the query that retrieved the record brought back only one record, but means that the style permits the display of one record at a time. If the operator presses the Down arrow key, additional records in the result set are returned. The operator can scroll forward and backward through the result set. The best way to understand this concept is to practice. In this practice session, you create a new form using the Data Block and Layout Wizards. This will be a tabular form based upon the EMP table. You then run the form, execute a query, scroll through the records, add a new record to the data block, and save the changes. To accomplish these functions, perform the following steps:

"FRM-90928 Positional parameter after key on command line" is a common error message seen by a novice Forms Builder developer. This error message is displayed in the Web browser when the executed form module has never been saved. To eliminate this error, save the form module.

1. Open Forms Builder and create a new form module on the Object Navigator.

2. Add a data block to the form using the steps on pages 60 and 61 with the following exceptions:
   - Step 13: The style is to be tabular.
   - Step 14: Set the Records Displayed to 15. Check the Display Scrollbar check box.
3. When you are finished, save the form as **PRACTICE0202.FMB**.
4. Click the **Run Form** tool. Forms Builder compiles and executes your form.
5. When the form is first displayed (Figure 2-28), no data appears. The displayed data block is in the NORMAL mode. You may enter values into the displayed text items if you choose; however, do not do so at this time.
6. Execute a query by pressing the **Control+F11 keys** (**F8** for client-server). These are hot keys that cause Forms Builder to create and execute a SELECT statement. The results of the SELECT statement are returned to the data block.

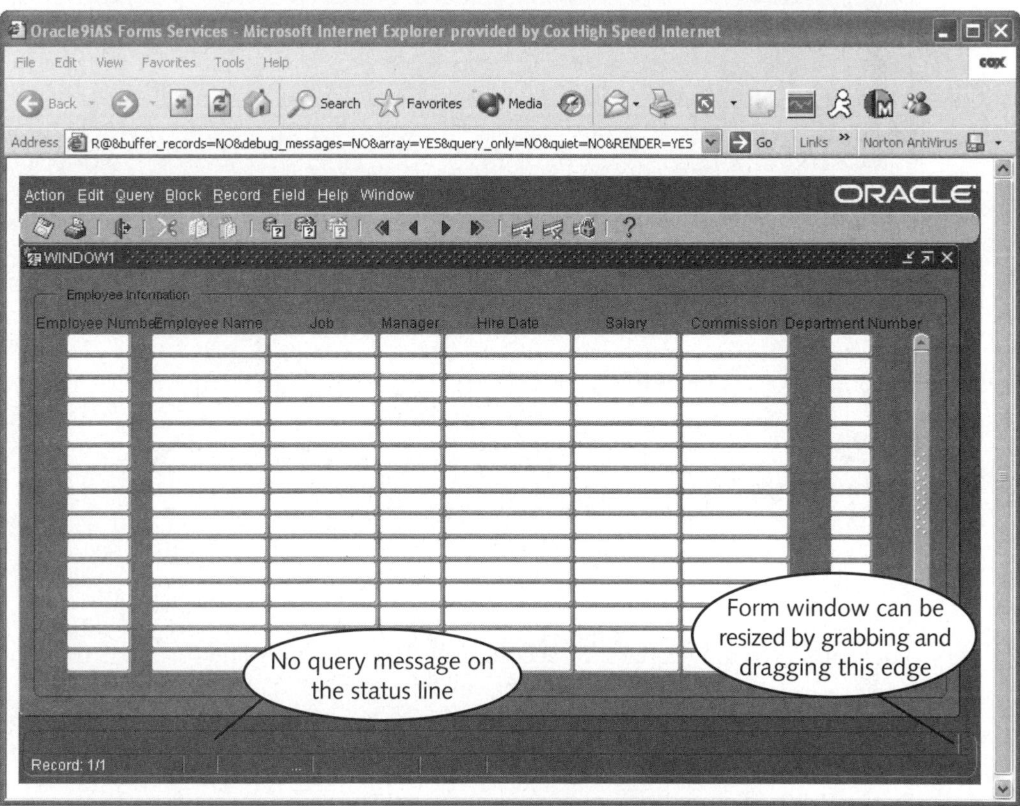

Figure 2-28 Newly executed and resized form in the NORMAL mode

7. Figure 2-29 illustrates the form after the query returns records. The form was in the QUERY mode while it retrieved records to the data block. It is now in the NORMAL mode as shown.

8. The form displays a number of records, because it is a tabular style that displays multiple records. In some cases, the query could return more records than can be displayed by the form. This is especially true for a form in the form style. You can view the additional records by pressing the Down arrow key. This causes the form to display the next result set record. The Up arrow key causes the form to display the previous record.
9. Press the **Down** arrow key repeatedly until you have scrolled through the entire result set and a blank record is displayed. Enter your name into the Employee Name text item and a numeric value into the Employee Number text item. Save the record by pressing the **Control+S** key (**F10** for client-server). Press the **Down** arrow key to make another blank record appear. Forms Builder always adds a blank record at the end of the result set.
10. Close the form by closing the Web browser.

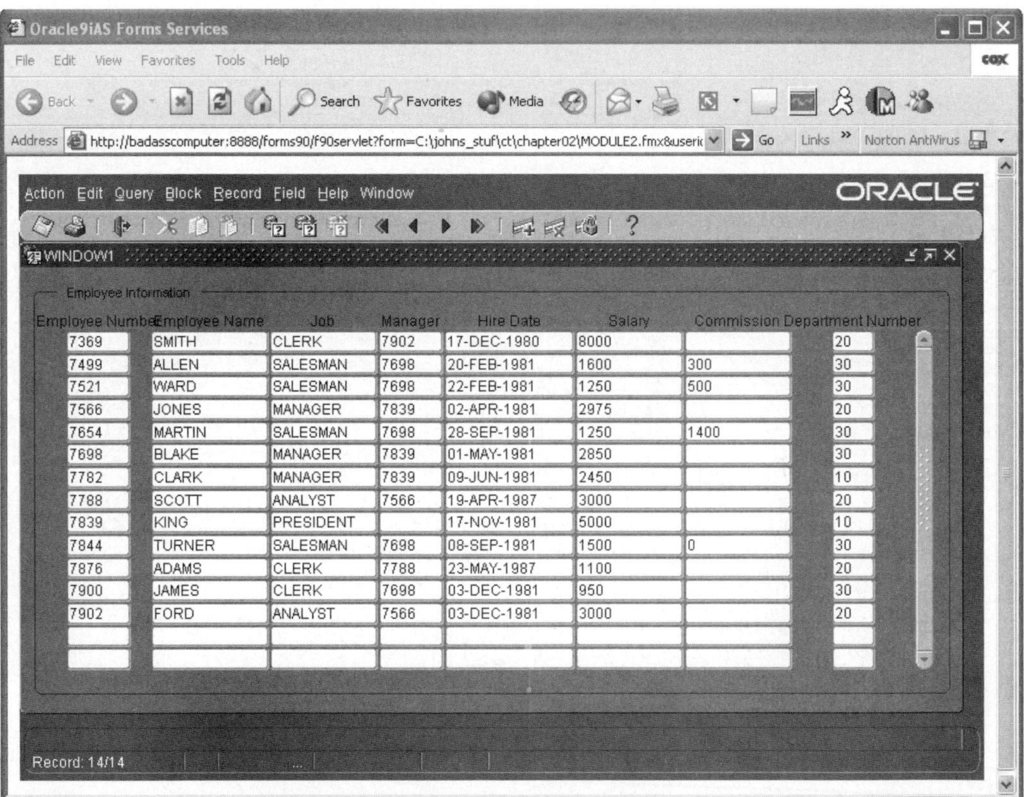

Figure 2-29 Form after a query was executed

When your result set is large and you want to avoid scrolling through the result set to find the blank record, you can add a blank record at the current data block record location by performing one of the following operations:

- Select the **Record/Insert** menu option from the default menu.

- Click the **Insert Record** tool on the default toolbar.
- Click the appropriate function or hot key. (Function keys are discussed later in this chapter.)

Understanding the ENTER QUERY and QUERY Modes

The data block is in the ENTER QUERY mode when it is prompting the user to enter a value. There is one specific identifier for this mode. In the lower-left corner (see Figure 2-30) in the form status line is the following message: "Enter a query; press Ctrl+F11 to execute, F4 to cancel."

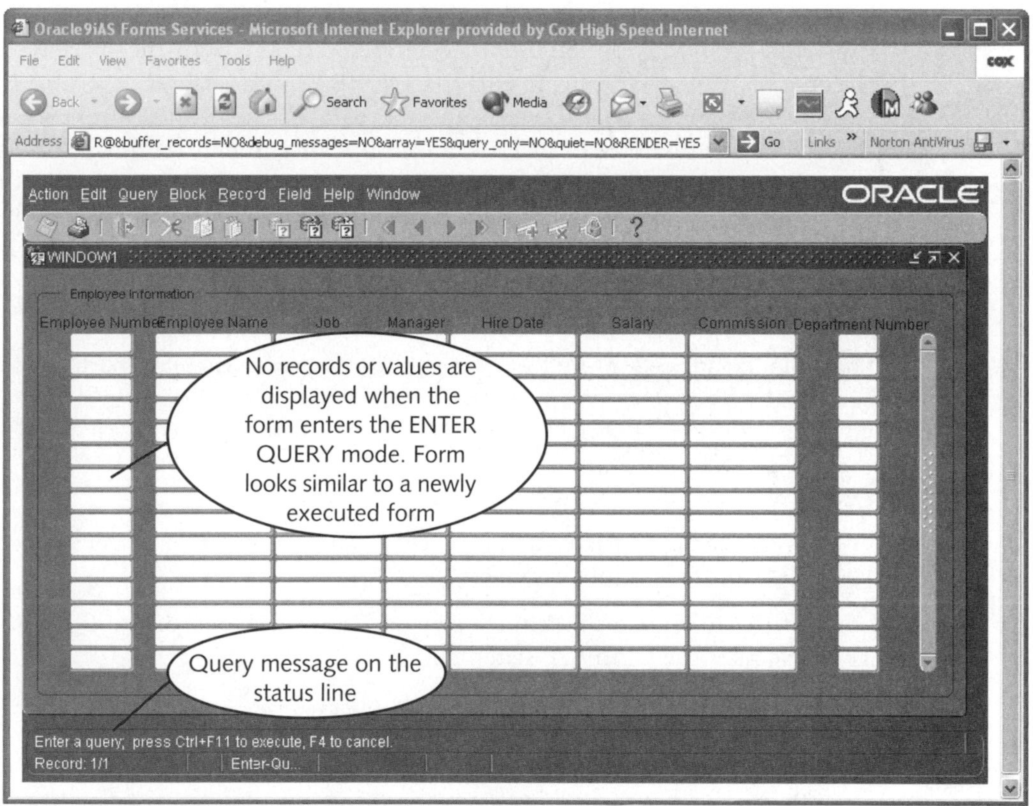

Figure 2-30 Example form in the ENTER QUERY mode

It is extremely common to mistake the ENTER QUERY mode for the NORMAL mode with no data block records displayed. When a data block (or form) is first displayed (see Figure 2-28), it is placed in the NORMAL mode with no records displayed. It looks virtually identical to the form when it is in the ENTER QUERY mode (Figure 2-30) if the values had not been entered, except for the message at the bottom-left of the form. It is a common operator error to mistake the two modes, enter a row of values, and then try to save the values. Forms Builder issues an error message, because you cannot save records in the ENTER QUERY mode. Users get upset because they have entered a row of data that will shortly be lost. It is very important to know the current mode, and the message at the bottom of the screen is the only indication of the difference between the modes when this condition exists.

The purpose of the ENTER QUERY mode is to develop the SELECT statement WHERE clause. WHERE clauses identify specific records that are to be retrieved from the database. SELECT statements are SQL commands that instruct the Oracle database to locate and retrieve records. Forms Builder creates dynamic SELECT statements based on the values or arguments entered in the ENTER QUERY mode.

The QUERY mode occurs after the user has entered the WHERE CLAUSE arguments into the data block row and attempts to retrieve records from the database that match the arguments. Placing the form into the QUERY mode causes a SELECT statement to be generated and executed by placing the data block into the QUERY mode. The SELECT statement will create WHERE CLAUSE arguments for any value entered into the data block. The data block then passes the SELECT statement to Oracle. Oracle generates the result set and passes it back to the data block. Oracle returns all records that match the WHERE CLAUSE arguments or no records at all. If the user chooses not to enter WHERE CLAUSE arguments, the SELECT statement will not contain a WHERE CLAUSE, and all of the data source's records will be returned.

The data block is placed in the ENTER QUERY mode when you perform one of these procedures:

- Click the **Query/Enter** menu option.
- Click the **Enter Query** tool on the default tool bar.
- Press the appropriate function key: **F7** in the client-server environment and **F11** in the Web environment.

Use one of the following procedures to place the data block in the QUERY mode in which it executes the SELECT statement:

- Click the **Query/Execute** menu option.
- Click the **Execute Query** tool on the default toolbar.
- Press the appropriate function key: **F8** in the client-server environment and **Control+F11** in the Web environment.

The QUERY mode lasts only as long as the SELECT statement is working. When the result set is returned, the form is placed in one of two modes:

- If it returns records, the data block is in the NORMAL mode.
- If it does not return records, the data block is placed in the ENTER QUERY mode with the following message: "FRM-40301: Query caused no records to be retrieved. Re-enter." This message is prompting for different WHERE CLAUSE arguments.

Changing Modes

Users commonly move between various data block and record modes using the techniques shown in Table 2-1.

Table 2-1 Form and data block operating techniques

Current mode	Characteristic of the current mode	Next mode or procedure	Technique
NORMAL mode: no records displayed	Data block is empty of all records and no ENTER QUERY message appears	Insert new record	Add values to the first row of the data block.
NORMAL mode: records displayed	Data block displays records	Insert new record	1. Scroll to the end of the record set. 2. Select the **Record/ Insert** menu option from the default menu. 3. Click the **Insert Record** tool on the default toolbar. 4. Press the appropriate function key: **F8** for client-server and **Control+F11** for Web.
NORMAL mode: records displayed	Data block displays records	Update an existing record	Place the cursor on a displayed value and modify.
NORMAL mode: records displayed	Data block displays records	Delete an existing record	Place the cursor on any value on the target row and perform one of the following: 1. Select the **Record/ Remove** menu selection. 2. Click the **Remove Record** tool on the toolbar. 3. Press the appropriate function key: **Shift+F6** for client-server and **Control+Up** for Web.
NORMAL mode	No records are displayed and the query message is not displayed or records are displayed in the data block	Permanently save the changes (Oracle does not save records until a commit command is issued)	1. Select the **Action/ Save** menu option. 2. Click the **Save** tool on the toolbar. 3. Press the appropriate function key: **F10** for client-server and **Control+S** for Web.

Table 2-1 Form and data block operating techniques (continued)

Current mode	Characteristic of the current mode	Next mode or procedure	Technique
NORMAL mode	No records are displayed and the query message is not displayed or records are displayed in the data block	Placing the data block in the ENTER QUERY mode.	1. Select the **Query/ Enter** menu selection. 2. Click the **ENTER QUERY** tool on the toolbar. 3. Press the appropriate function key: **F7** for client-server and **F11** for Web.
NORMAL mode	No records are displayed and the query message is not displayed or records are displayed in the data block	Closing the form (you can only close the form when the data blocks are in the NORMAL mode)	1. Select the **Action/ Exit** menu selection. 2. Click the **Exit** tool on the toolbar. 3. Press the appropriate function key: **Control+q** for client-server and **F4** for Web.
ENTER QUERY mode	Either of the two query messages are displayed	QUERY mode (executing the query and placing the data block in the Normal mode)	1. Select the **Query/ Execute** menu selection. 2. Click the **Execute Query** tool on the toolbar. 3. Press the appropriate function key: **F8** for client-server and **Control+F11** for Web.
QUERY mode	No records are displayed and the query message is not displayed or records are displayed in the data block	Normal mode with no records displayed	1. Select the **Query/ Cancel** menu selection. 2. Click the **Cancel Query** tool on the toolbar. 3. Press the appropriate function key: **Control+q** for client-server and **F4** for Web. 4. Click the **Windows Close** tool in the upper-right corner of the window.

Table 2-1 references a number of toolbar tools, which are shown in Figure 2-31.

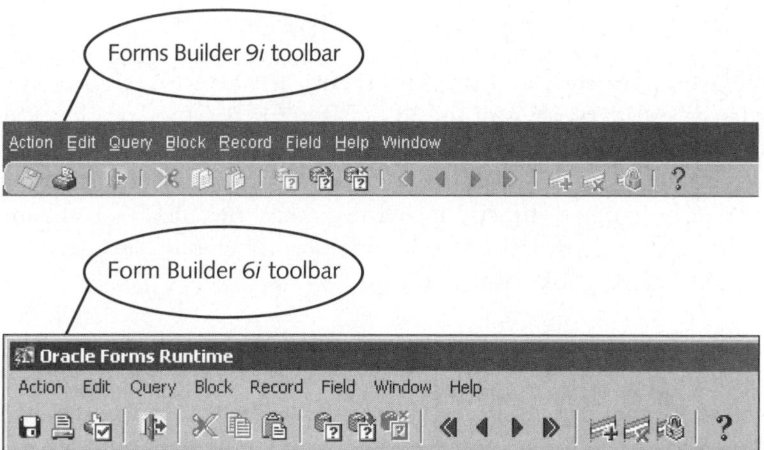

Figure 2-31 Default Forms Builder 9*i* Web form and Form Builder 6*i* client-server toolbars

Filtering Records from the Database Using a Form

Now that you know how to execute a query and return records to the data block, it is time to learn how to enter arguments for the query's WHERE clause. The most clever part of an Oracle form is its ability to accept sophisticated search arguments. Each item in the data block can become an argument in the WHERE clause of the SELECT statement issued by the data block. It is possible to enter a value of WARD and a value of S% into the form. When the query was executed, the form created the following WHERE clause and added it to the issued SELECT statement:

```
Where ename = 'WARD'
 And job like 'S%'
```

The result of the form action was to retrieve employee records that had an employee name (ENAME) FIRST_NAME value of WARD and a job that started with the character S. Any form item that contains a value is added to the WHERE clause, and any item that has a blank or NULL value is omitted. Thus, if you want to return all records, do not place any arguments into the form.

An Oracle form also allows you to employ all of the operators and functions that are available in Oracle9*i* SQL. You can enter operators such as: <, >, !=, NOT, LIKE, or IN. You can also employ any of Oracle9*i*'s array of functions such as: SUBSTR, MONTHS_BETWEEN, TO_NUMBER, SOUNDEX, LENGTH, or UPPER. In fact, you can even enter a SELECT statement as a value. The form will use this as a subquery or a correlated query in its issued SELECT statement. If entering values into a text item is not convenient, or the data source table has columns not contained in the data block, you can launch an editor that allows you to write a longer argument and additional conditions. You can use the And and Or keywords to create complex search criteria as needed and perform these types of complex searches within minutes of starting your first form.

Using Operators in a Form's Search Values

In previous discussion, it was noted that arguments can be entered directly into a displayed item when the data block is in the ENTER QUERY mode. When this happens, Oracle uses an equal sign (=) as the evaluation operator. Sometimes it would be handy to use a different evaluation operator, but this is a problem. If the argument "> 'M'" (greater than M) were entered directly into a text item, the SELECT statement would not recognize the greater than sign (>) as an operator. It would consider it a value. The WHERE CLAUSE would look similar to this:

```
Where ename = '> 'C''
```

The query will probably not return a value. The # symbol mechanism is needed to tell the form that the inputted value contains an operator. When you enter this symbol as the first character of the value, Oracle treats the following expression as WHERE clause conditions rather than literal values. For example, to retrieve all employee records with an employee name (ENAME) value greater than or equal to M, enter the following into the LAST_NAME text item: # >= 'M'. This creates the following WHERE clause (the results are seen in Figure 2-32):

```
Where ename>= 'M'
```

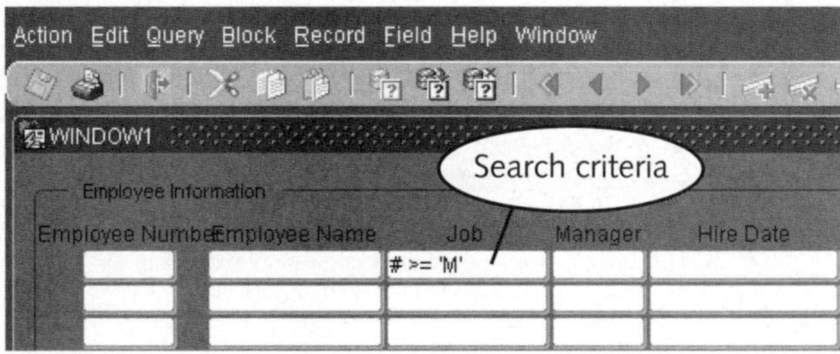

Figure 2-32 Example form showing the entry of #>= 'M' as search criteria after the QUERY_LENGTH property was increased

Each item in the data block has two length properties: Maximum Length and Query Length. Maximum Length is the maximum number of characters that you can enter into an item when the item is in the NORMAL mode. This value is set by default to the length of the related column in the database. The Query Length property is set to the same length by default. This length generally does not accommodate entering lengthy conditions, such as sub-selects or multiple arguments. Changing the maximum length is not advisable, because you receive database errors when you try to add values larger than the database setting to the table. However, if you set the Query Length property to 400 on every form you create, you can enter all the sophisticated conditions you need.

For practice, perform a query on the practice form by following these steps:

1. Execute the form.
2. Place the form into the ENTER QUERY mode by pressing the **F11** key (**F7** for client-server).
3. Enter **WARD** into the Employee Name text item.
4. Enter **S%** into the Job text item.
5. Place the form into the QUERY mode by pressing the **Control+F11** keys (**F8** for client-server).
6. Place the form into the ENTER QUERY mode again by pressing the **F11** key (**F7** for the client-server).
7. Enter **#>='C'** in the Job text item.
8. Place the form into the QUERY mode by pressing the **Control+F11** keys (**F8** for the client-server).
9. Close the form.

Using the Text Items Editor

Entering the values directly into the text item can be cumbersome. Even though the query length is long, the viewing width of the text item will not match this length. The user will not be able to see the entire condition. Forms Builder's Text Items Editor (see Figure 2-33) can be called to enter sophisticated search arguments. This can be easier to use than entering search arguments into a text item, because you can see the entire expression. To launch the editor, place your cursor into any of the data block items while it is in the ENTER QUERY mode and perform one of the following steps:

- Click the **Edit/Edit** menu option.
- Press the appropriate function key: **Control+E** for both client-server and Web.

Figure 2-33 illustrates the editor for the Job item. The condition expression starts with the symbol # followed immediately by the condition operator and an argument. This is necessary because the form initially adds the entered text as an operator and argument for the item used to launch the editor. In the case of Figure 2-33, it is the Job item. Following this condition, you can enter whatever additional conditions you deem necessary. In the case of Figure 2-33 there are two conditions.

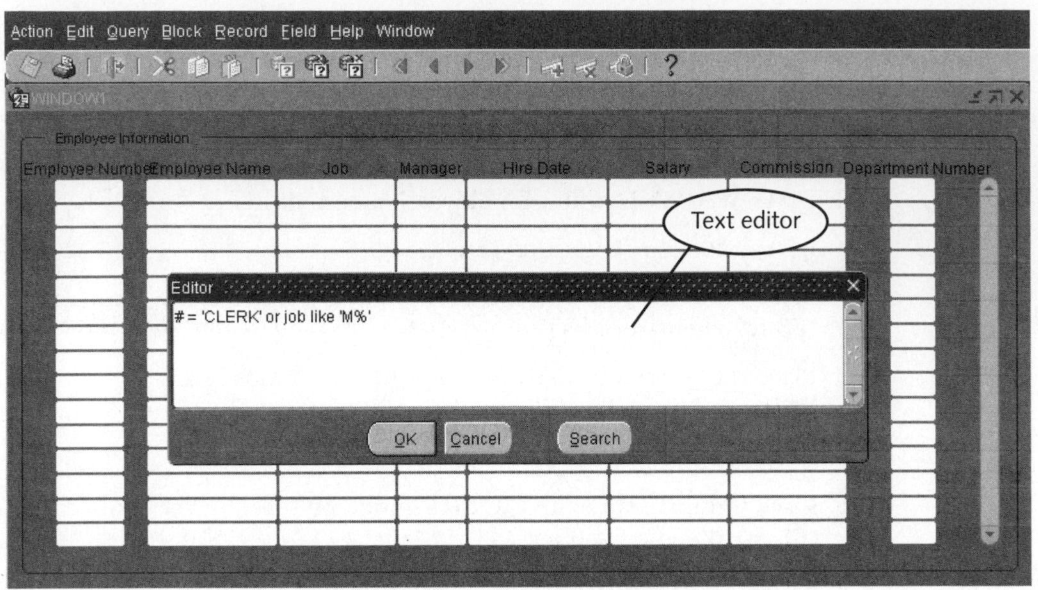

Figure 2-33 Text item editor containing complex search criteria

Using the Query/Where Dialog Box

An Oracle form has one other tool that you can use to filter the records, the Query/Where dialog box (Figure 2-34). It is used to write the entire SELECT statement WHERE CLAUSE. This tool is launched by:

- Placing an ampersand (&) into any of the text items, and
- Executing the query

Figure 2-34 depicts the Query/Where dialog box. In this example, you are trying to determine the employee most recently hired. This requires knowledge of the first hire date (HIREDATE), which is produced by the subquery. Clicking the OK button causes the form to populate the data block WHERE CLAUSE property with the Query/Where text and execute the query.

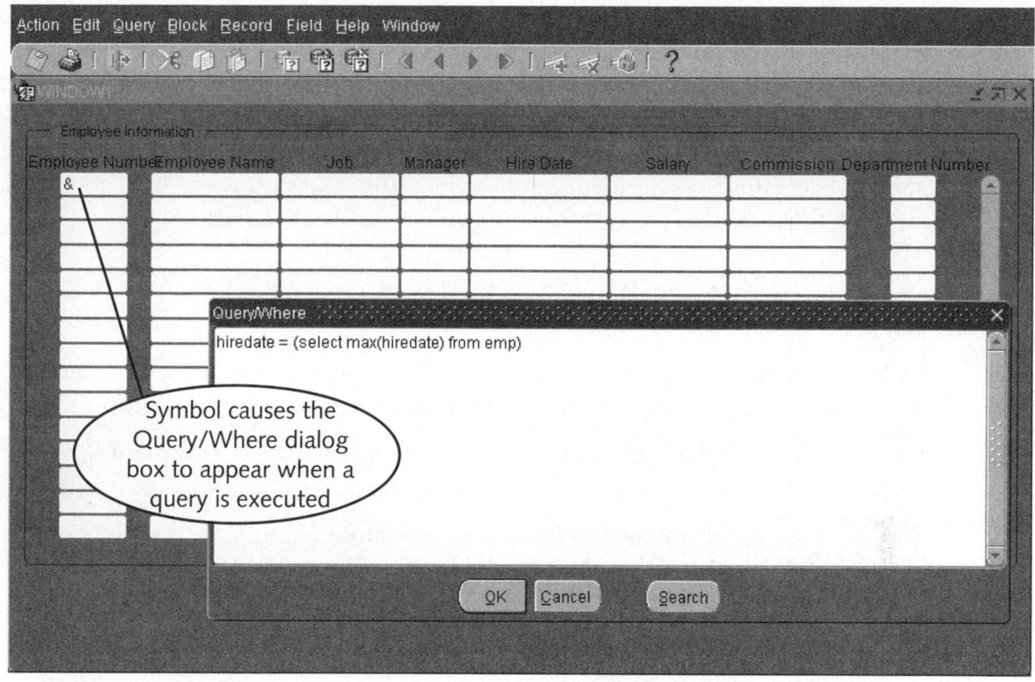

Figure 2-34 Using the Query/Where dialog box to determine the most recently hired employee

Function Keys

Throughout this chapter, there have been numerous references to function keys. **Function keys** are hot keys that perform a variety of functions. Using function keys is easier than using menu selections and toolbars. You can operate a form more quickly by pressing a key or key combination than by dragging the mouse to a menu option or tool.

The function keys that have been referenced perform tasks such as executing a query, saving records, or displaying an editor. They also do a number of other helpful things such as duplicating records, showing database errors, and counting the returned records. A form can display a list of function keys for you. The client-server and Forms runtime environments use different keys to perform similar tasks. To display the list, perform one of the following:

- Select the **Help/Keys** menu selection.
- Press the appropriate function key: **Control+F1** for client-server and **Control+K** for the Web. When performing this action on the Web, be sure that the Web form is your active form by clicking somewhere inside the form.

Where You Are and Where You're Going

In this chapter, you learned to create a form module and to create and format a data block using the Data Block Wizard. You have also learned how to query and update records. In the next chapter, you will learn how to use the Object Navigator to locate, select, delete, and create form components. You will also learn how to add data blocks to your form.

Chapter Summary

- Forms Builder is an integrated design environment that is used to design Oracle forms. It uses binary files called modules that have a file extension of **.fmb**.
- Forms can be executed when the binary source code is compiled. The compiled file has an extension of **.fmx**.
- The same form executable file can be executed using Oracle's client-server runtime engine, Forms Runtime, and the Web runtime engine Forms Server.
- Forms Runtime looks for the executable file within the server's files structure, whereas the Forms Server contacts the Oracle9*i* Web server, where the application has been registered.
- Developers must log on to the Oracle database to use many of the Forms Builder tools.
- Forms Builder has four main tools: the Object Navigator locates and creates form objects; the Layout Editor formats the display; the Property Palette controls a form's behavior; and the PL/SQL Editor enters form instructions.
- Forms Builder uses Oracle's PL/SQL language in triggers and program units.
- There are three primary form components: the data block that relates form items with the database; the canvas that displays form items; and the window that displays the canvas.
- The first step in creating a form is to create a form module.
- The Data Block and Layout Wizards can be used to create an initial data block, canvas, and window.
- The Data Block Wizard contains the following settings pages: the Type page identifies the data source type; and the Table page identifies the actual data source and the columns that will be contained on the form.
- The Layout Wizard contains the following settings pages: the Canvas page identifies the type of canvas; the Data Block page associates data block items to a canvas; the Items page sets item prompt text and lengths; the Style page sets the basic layout style; and the Rows page determines how many rows will be displayed.

- A form can be launched and used immediately after completing the Layout Wizard.
- A form has three operating modes: NORMAL, ENTER QUERY, and QUERY. The NORMAL mode is used to view, add, modify, and delete records. The ENTER QUERY mode is used to enter selection criteria. The QUERY mode is used to retrieve database records.
- The NORMAL mode is identified by the displayed records and the lack of an ENTER QUERY message in the lower-left corner of the form.
- When a form is in the NORMAL mode, the last data block record can be used to add records. The user can always scroll to this record.
- The ENTER QUERY mode is identified by one of two ENTER QUERY messages displayed in the lower-left corner of the form.
- A form has the capability of documenting extremely complex search criteria. All items displayed on the form can be used as arguments.
- Items that contain NULL values are not used as arguments.
- A user can employ operators and functions as arguments by placing the pound symbol (#) as the first character of the argument.
- For each form item, an editor is available to enter long argument values.
- A Query/Where dialog box is available to write the entire SELECT statement WHERE clause.

Review Questions

1. Match the following terms with their description:

a. Data block	________________	Form object that displays form components
b. Function keys	________________	Form object that displays the canvas
c. Canvas	________________	Form tool used to modify the physical attributes
d. NORMAL mode	________________	Form tool used to enter and validate PL/SQL
e. Object Navigator	________________	The Layout Wizard page used to identify the data block associated to the canvas
f. Window	________________	Symbol entered into a text item that causes the form to treat the entered value as a condition rather than an argument

g. **.fmx**	____________	Form dialog box used to enter WHERE clause conditions
h. Layout Editor	____________	A form object that interacts with the database
i. ENTER QUERY mode	____________	Form binary code file used by the IDE environment
j. **.fmb**	____________	The Data Block Wizard page used to identify the table or view associated to the data block
k. PL/SQL Editor	____________	Symbol entered into a text item that causes the Query/Where dialog box to be displayed
l. Data Block page	____________	Hot keys that perform a variety of form tasks such as executing a query
m. Table page	____________	Forms Builder tool used to identify, create, and delete form objects
n. #	____________	Operating mode used to view and modify database records
o. Query/Where dialog box	____________	Operating mode used to enter search arguments
p. &	____________	Form executable file extension
q. :"FRM-40301: Query caused no records to be retrieved. Re-enter."	____________	The message returned when the query cannot find records that match the search arguments

2. Explain the difference between the QUERY, ENTER QUERY, and NORMAL modes.
3. Explain how to tell the difference between a data block in the NORMAL mode that is not displaying any records and a data block in the ENTER QUERY mode.
4. Explain the purpose of function keys and why they should be used.
5. How do you delete a record?
6. Explain the purpose of a data block, canvas, and a window.
7. You have a form in the ENTER QUERY mode. How do you place the form into the NORMAL mode?
8. How can you enter a long expression into a text item as a search argument?

Exam Review Questions

1. You are creating a new layout using the Layout Wizard. Which two statements are true?
   a. You can update the item prompts.
   b. You can set the item height, width, and font properties.
   c. You can add the form window title.
   d. You can set the number of records to be displayed.
2. You have just created a data block using the Data Block Wizard and launched the Layout Wizard. Which object can be created by the Layout Wizard?
   a. Canvas
   b. Data block
   c. Window
   d. Data items
3. You need to create a query to retrieve employees who were hired between January 1, 1975 and December 31, 1999. Where can you enter this search criteria?
   a. Enter Query dialog box
   b. Query Wizard
   c. Query/Where dialog box
   d. QUERY data block window
4. You need to create a query that retrieves records for a specific employee. Which operation mode allows you to enter selection criteria?
   a. NORMAL
   b. FETCH RECORDS
   c. EXECUTE QUERY
   d. ENTER QUERY
5. You have just launched the EMPLOYEES form to enter new employee information. Which operation mode should you use to insert, update, and delete records?
   a. QUERY WHERE
   b. NORMAL
   c. Execute query
   d. ENTER QUERY

HANDS-ON ASSIGNMENTS

1. Launch Forms Builder and create a new empty form module. Develop and save a form similar to the practice form, except that the form is in tabular style displaying multiple records by performing the following steps:
   a. Launch Forms Builder and log on to the database using the File/Connect menu option.
   b. Add a new form module to the Object Navigator. Click the **FORMS** object node and click the **Create** tool.
   c. Create a new data block based on the EMP table. Select the **Tools/Data Block Wizard** menu option.
   d. On the Type page, select the **Table or View** option. Click **Next**.
   e. On the Table page, click **Browse**. The Tables dialog box opens. Locate and select the **EMP** table. Click **OK**. This closes the dialog box and populates the Table or View text item. Move all of the columns from the Available Columns list to the Database Items list. Click **Next**.
   f. On the Data Block Name page, accept the default block name and click **Next**. Note that this page is not available in Form Builder 6*i*.
   g. On the Congratulations page, select the **Create the data block, then call the Layout Wizard** setting. Click **Finish**.
   h. On the Layout Wizard Canvas page, select the default settings. Click **Next**.
   i. On the Data Block page, move all items from the Available Items list to the Displayed Items list. Click **Next**.
   j. On the Items page, set the following Prompt values and click **Next**:
      - **EMPNO**: Employee Number
      - **ENAME**: Employee Name
      - **JOB**: Job
      - **MGR**: Manager
      - **HIREDATE**: Hire Date
      - **SAL**: Salary
      - **COMM**: Commission
      - **DEPTNO**: Department Number
   k. On the Style page, select the **Tabular** option and click **Next**.
   l. On the Rows page, enter the following values and click **Next**:
      - **Frame Title**: Employee Information
      - **Records Displayed**: 12

- **Distance Between Records**: 0
- Click the Display Scrollbar check box

m. Click **Finish**.

n. Save the form as **Ch02ex01.fmb** by selecting the File/Save menu option or clicking the Save tool.

2. To launch form **Ch02ex01.fmb**, perform the following steps:

   a. Select form **Ch02ex01** in the Object Navigator. Click the **Run Form** tool or the **Program/Run Form** menu option.

   b. Place the form into the ENTER QUERY mode by pressing the **F11** (or **F7**) function key.

   c. Execute a query without entering a search value by pressing **Control+F11** or **F8** function keys.

   d. Scroll to a blank record, and populate the record. Save the record using the **Control+S** (or **F10)** function keys.

   e. Place the form into the ENTER QUERY mode using the form menu.

   f. Enter the Employee Number value you added in Step d into the Employee Number text item.

   g. Execute a query using the Query menu.

   h. Delete the record you created in Step d.

   i. Identify and display all of the employees with a JOB value of SALESMAN. Remember that Oracle is case sensitive.

   j. Identify and display all of the employees who have an "I" in their last names.

   k. Identify all employees who are managers and have an "O" in their last names.

   l. Identify all employees who have a last name starting with a character alphabetically less than or equal to "M."

   m. Identify and display the most recently hired employee.

   n. Exit the form.

You should receive a prompt asking if you want to save the changes. In Step d, you deleted a record whose change was never committed. Oracle always prompts for unsaved changes before closing the form. Select the **Yes** button.

3. In this exercise you modify a value and cause a database error. You then use the function keys to identify the error.

   a. Launch form module **Ch02ex01.fmb**.

   b. Place the form into the ENTER QUERY mode and execute the query. Scroll through the list of employees until you reach the insert record. Scroll back several records.

c. Change the EMPNO item value to **7369**. This value exists on another record and will cause a database error.

d. Save the record by pressing the **Control+S** keys (or **F10** in the client-server mode).

e. A database error occurs. Use the function keys to display the errors. Use the Help facility to identify these keys.

f. Close the session by pressing the **Exit** menu option. You will be prompted on whether you want to save the record. Click the **NO** button.

Case Project: Great State Electric Budgeting System

In the Chapter 1 Case Project, you were asked to create the database for the project based on the data schema diagram portrayed in Figure 1-12. The first section of this Case Project shows you the results of your work for Case Project 1.

Results for Case Project 1

The following listing shows the data definition language statements used to create the database. Please note that this listing can be found in the Chapter 2 folder on your student disk.

Listing 2-1 Budget database DDL

```
create table task_descriptions
 (task_id            char(5) primary key,
 task_description   varchar2(25));

create table accounts
 (account_id            number(5,2) primary key,
  account_description varchar2(25) not null);

create table departments
(department_id         char(3) primary key,
 department_name       varchar2(30) not null,
 department_mgr        number(5,0));

create table employees
 (employee_id           number(5,0) primary key,
  employment_date       date not null,
  first_name            varchar2(10) not null,
  last_name             varchar2(20) not null,
  ssn                   number(9,0),
  address               varchar2(25),
  birth_date            date,
  city                  varchar2(15),
```

```
  state                     varchar2(2),
  classification            varchar2(20),
  department_id             char(3) references departments);
create table projects
(project_id                 varchar2(10) primary key,
 project_name               varchar2(60) not null,
 project_need_date          date,
 project_scope              varchar2(2000),
 project_location           varchar2(200),
 assigned_department_id         char(3) references departments,
 assigned_to                  number(5,0) references employ-
ees);

create table work_orders
(work_order_id              number(5,0) primary key,
 wo_description             varchar2(100) not null,
 wo_location                varchar2(200),
wo_instructions            varchar2(2000),
 Approved_by              number(5,0) references employees,
 Assigned_to              number(5,0) references employees,
 Project_id              varchar2(10) references projects);

create table work_order_tasks
 (work_order_task_id                number(5,0) primary key,
  assigned_department_id   char(3) not null references dep
artments,
  assigned_employee_id  number(5,0) references employees,
  wo_work_order_id    number(5,0) not null references work
_orders,
  task_description_id              char(5) not null
references task_descriptions,
  account_id     number(5,2) not null references accounts,
  labor_hours               number(5,0),
  material_costs            number(7,0),
  equipment_costs           number(7,0));

create table monthly_costs
(monthly_cost_id            number(5,0) primary key,
 work_order_task_id         number(5,0) references work_order_
tasks,
 year                       char(4) not null,
 month                      varchar2(8) not null,
 cost                       number(7) not null);
```

The second task from the previous chapter's Case Project is to review the Figure 1-12 data flow diagram and determine all of the places in the system where a form is needed. Table 2-2 details the processes or functions that can be identified from the data flow diagram. The third task is to determine the entities or tables that will be required for each of the forms. Table 2-2 also identifies these items.

Table 2-2 Budgeting processes that require forms

Process number	Function description	Entities
1.1	Add project to database and assign to a department	PROJECTS EMPLOYEES
1.2	Review the project and assign it to an engineer	PROJECTS EMPLOYEES DEPARTMENTS
1.3a	Identify assigned projects	PROJECTS DEPARTMENTS
1.3b	Divide the project into work orders	PROJECTS WORK_ORDERS
1.3c	Divide the work order into a series of tasks	WORK_ORDERS WORK_ORDER_TASKS TASK_DESCRIPTIONS
1.3d	Estimate the work order and monthly costs	WORK_ORDERS WORK_ORDER_TASKS TASK_DESCRIPTIONS MONTHLY_COSTS ACCOUNTS
1.4	Review and approve work order estimates	WORK_ORDERS WORK_ORDER_TASKS TASK_DESCRIPTIONS MONTHLY_COST ACCOUNTS DEPARTMENTS EMPLOYEES
1.5	Review project costs	PROJECTS WORK_ORDERS WORK_ORDER_TASKS DEPARTMENTS EMPLOYEES
1.6	Maintain accounts	ACCOUNTS
1.7	Maintain task descriptions	TASK_DESCRIPTIONS
1.8	Maintain employees	EMPLOYEES

The next task in the system development life cycle process is to identify the number of form modules or applications that will be needed. Generally speaking, if different processes require the same tables, they are candidates for the same form module. The process of identifying the applications is really more art than science, in that you need to visualize the applications and how they work together.

The software engineer for this project determined the budgeting system should consist of one Web form with eight canvases. This form will take longer to download to the Web browser than a series of form modules, but the engineer believes the user will frequently move between the different canvases. By downloading all the canvases once, the overall application performance will improve by eliminating the need to download the same form repeatedly. Table 2-3 contains the canvases, canvas types, windows, data block source items, the DML operations supported by the data block, and the DFD process supported by the canvas.

Table 2-3 Budget module components

Supported process	Canvas name	Canvas type	Window	Data block source type and data blocks	Supported DML operations
1.1	PROJECT_ ADD	Stacked	Add_ projects	PROJECTS	Insert
1.2 1.3b 1.5	MAIN	Tab (Projects tab page)	Main	QUERY_FROM clause (PROJECT_ DATA) WORK_ ORDERS Control block (PROJ_SEARCH_ CRITERIA)	Update/Delete/ Select Insert/Update/ Delete/Select None
1.3a 1.3b 1.3c 1.4	MAIN	Tab (WORK_ ORDERS tab page)	Main	Control_block (WO_SEARCH_ CRITERIA)	None Insert/Update/
				WORK_ORDER_ TASKS	Delete/Select
				MONTHLY_COST	Insert/Update/ Delete/Select
				QUERY_FROM clause (WORK_ORDER_ DATA)	Update/Delete/ Select
1.3b	WO_ INSTRUC-TIONS	Stacked	Wo_ instructions	QUERY_FROM clause (WO_INSTRUCTIONS)	Update
1.6	MAIN	Tab (ACCOUNTS page)	Main	ACCOUNTS	Insert/Update/ Delete/Select
1.7	MAIN	Tab (TASK_ DESCRIP-TION page)	Main	TASK_DESCRIPTIONS	Insert/Update/ Delete/Select
1.8	MAIN	Tab (EMPLO-YEES page)	Main	EMPLOYEES	Insert/Update/ Delete/Select

After reviewing Table 2-3, you should understand that the system will consist of the following:

- One tab canvas called MAIN
- Five main tab pages called PROJECTS, WORK_ORDERS, ACCOUNTS, TASK_DESCRIPTIONS, and EMPLOYEES
- Two stacked canvases called WO_INSTRUCTIONS and PROJECT_ADD

These eight canvases will display all of the system's data items and will support all of the business processes identified in the systems data flow diagram (Figure 1-12).

MAIN Tab Canvas and the PROJECTS Tab Page

The primary system canvas will be the MAIN canvas. This canvas is a tab canvas consisting of five tab pages. A canvas is a form object that displays data items. A tab canvas is a series of overlaying pages with tabs. Each of the pages is a canvas that shows data items. The user clicks on the desired page tab to move between the pages. This type of canvas was chosen because the entire application is to be downloaded at one time to the Web browser. The first form, screen, or canvas displayed by the system will be the MAIN tab canvas and the PROJECTS tab page. The main tab page is displayed in the main window.

The application displayed on the PROJECTS tab page will be a directory. This is a special style application fully detailed in a later chapter. In brief, it has a form module data block, called a **control block**, that is not related to any data source. Some of the tab page forms in this system use the control blocks to enter search values.

Besides the control block, this canvas will contain two data blocks that are related to a data source. The first data block displays multiple project records. The data source will be a QUERY FROM clause that is essentially an inline view (or SELECT statement) that resides within the form. This data block will support update and delete operations on the PROJECTS table.

The third data block on the PROJECTS tab page will display work orders for the selected project. This block will be coordinated with the PROJECTS block, so that it always displays the correct work orders. The WORK_ORDERS table is the data source for this block. The user will be able to insert, update, and delete records from this block.

To better understand the project, examine Figure 2-35, which depicts the completed PROJECTS tab page. A developer does not have the advantage you have of seeing the final product before building a system. The developer can only envision what the final product will look like in his or her head or use a hand-drawn image.

PROJECT_ADD Stacked Canvas

Figure 2-36 shows a stacked canvas, which is used solely to add projects. Stacked canvases can overlay other canvases. This canvas (form) will be used as a popup dialog box for adding a project. This canvas will have its own window and will overlay a portion of the MAIN canvas. The user will be able to move the window around the work area but will not be able to update, delete, or query PROJECTS information from this form.

Figure 2-36 depicts the completed PROJECT_ADD stacked canvas within the Add New Projects window.

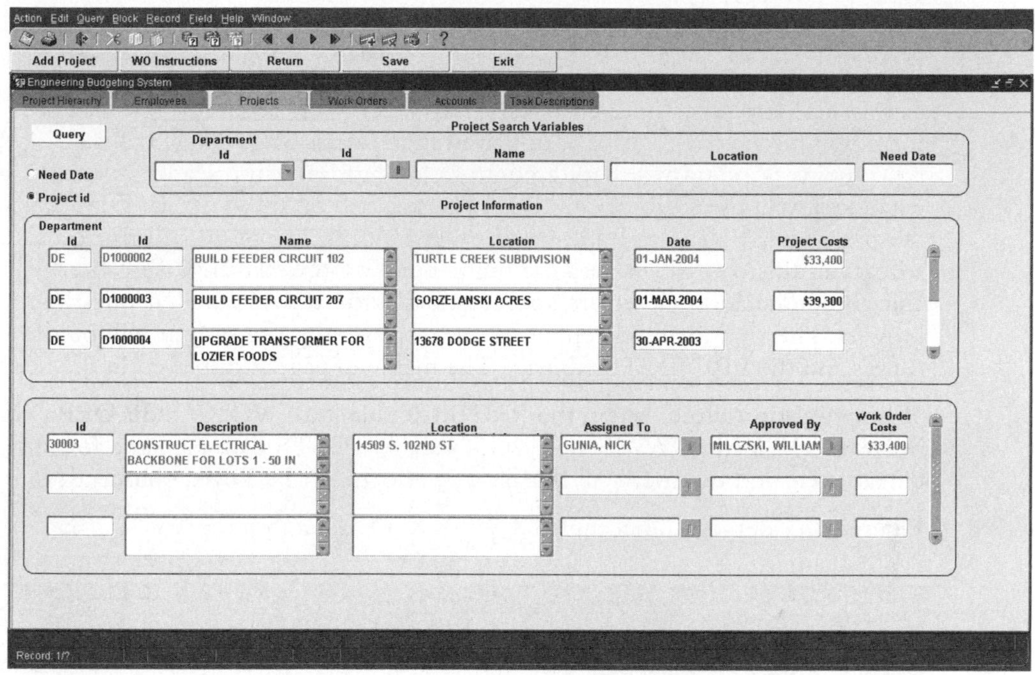

Figure 2-35 PROJECTS tab page used to assign engineers, create work orders, and review project costs

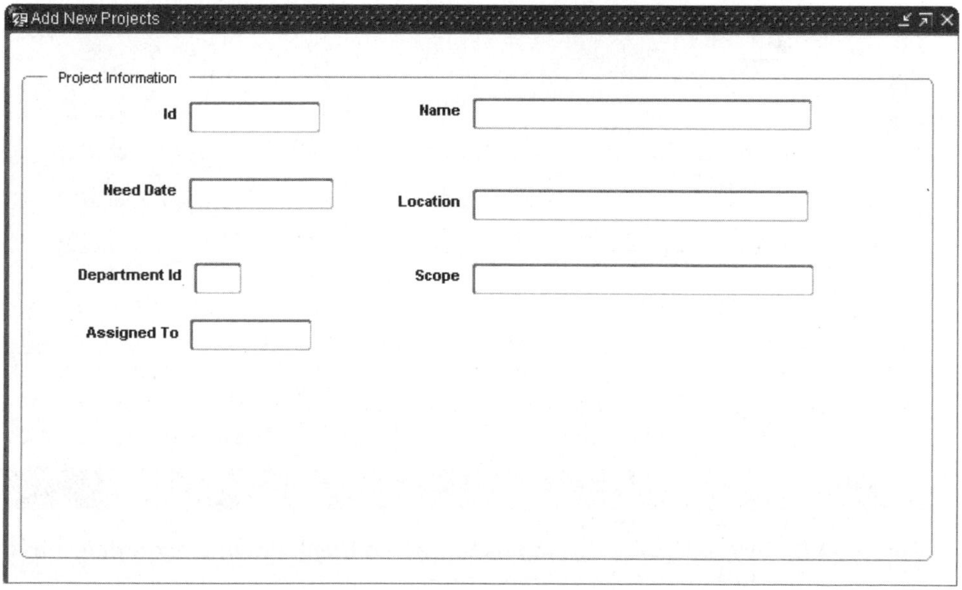

Add New Projects

Project Information

Id

Name

Need Date

Location

Department Id

Scope

Assigned To

Figure 2-36 PROJECT_ADD form used to add projects to the database

WORK_ORDERS Tab Page

This tab page will be the most complicated in the system. The purpose of this tab page canvas is to break the scope of work into a series of tasks and estimate the costs. This form will be a second tab page displayed in the main window. It will also be a directory type application and will have a control block for entering search criteria. The primary data block will use a QUERY FROM clause based on the WORK_ORDERS table. The tab page will display multiple work order records. The user will not be able to insert records in this data block, because this is done on the PROJECTS tab page, but will be able to update and delete work order information.

This tab page will also have data blocks for work order tasks and monthly costs, because this is the form on which engineers will make estimates. The records in these data blocks will be coordinated with the currently selected WORK_ORDER record. The WORK_ORDER_TASKS and MONTHLY_COSTS data blocks will use tables as the data source, and the user will be able to perform all the DML functions.

Figure 2-37 depicts the completed WORK_ORDERS tab page.

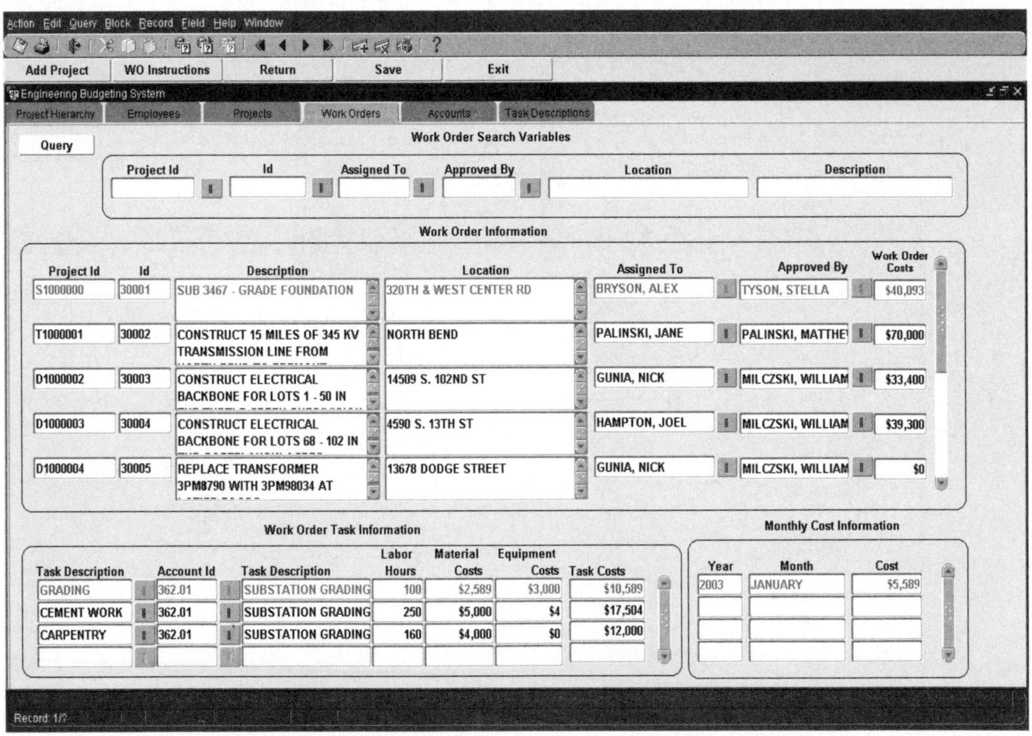

Figure 2-37 WORK_ORDERS tab page used to break down work orders into multiple tasks and estimate the monthly costs

WO_INSTRUCTIONS Canvas

The WO_INSTRUCTIONS canvas will be used to enter detailed instructions and location information. The information in these data block items is too lengthy to appear on a tabular style form that is used on the WORK_ORDERS tab page. This canvas will display unique information about the work order in a form style. The stacked canvas will be displayed in its own window. The user will be able to update work order values on this canvas. Figure 2-38 illustrates the completed WO_INSTRUCTIONS form.

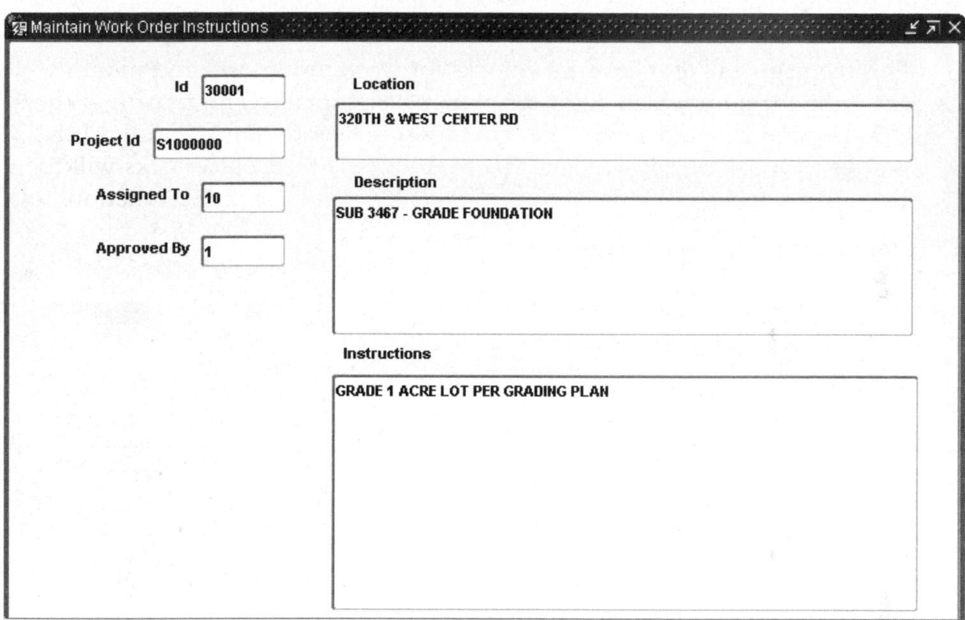

Figure 2-38 WO_INSTRUCTIONS stacked canvas used to enter work instructions and location information

ACCOUNTS, TASK_DESCRIPTIONS, and the EMPLOYEES Tab Pages

The ACCOUNTS, TASK_DESCRIPTIONS, and the EMPLOYEES tab pages are used to maintain subsidiary information needed by the system. Each of these tab page canvases will be a page on the MAIN tab canvas. The data blocks will be based on the ACCOUNTS, TASK _DESCRIPTIONS, and the EMPLOYEES tables. The user will be able to perform the full range of DML functions on these tab pages. Figures 2-39 through 2-42 illustrate the completed forms.

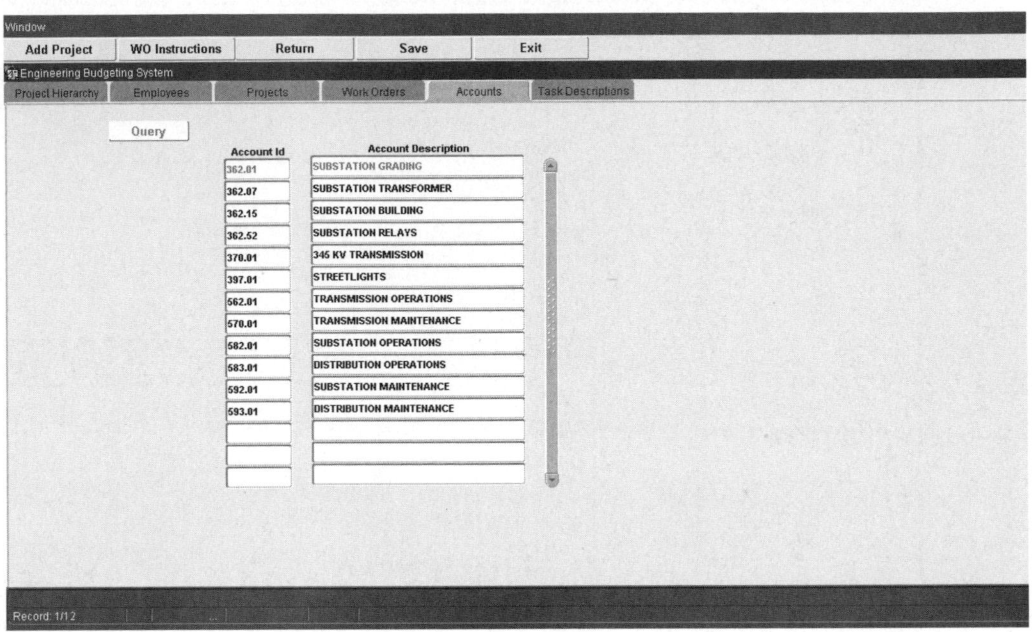

Figure 2-39 ACCOUNTS tab page used to maintain account information

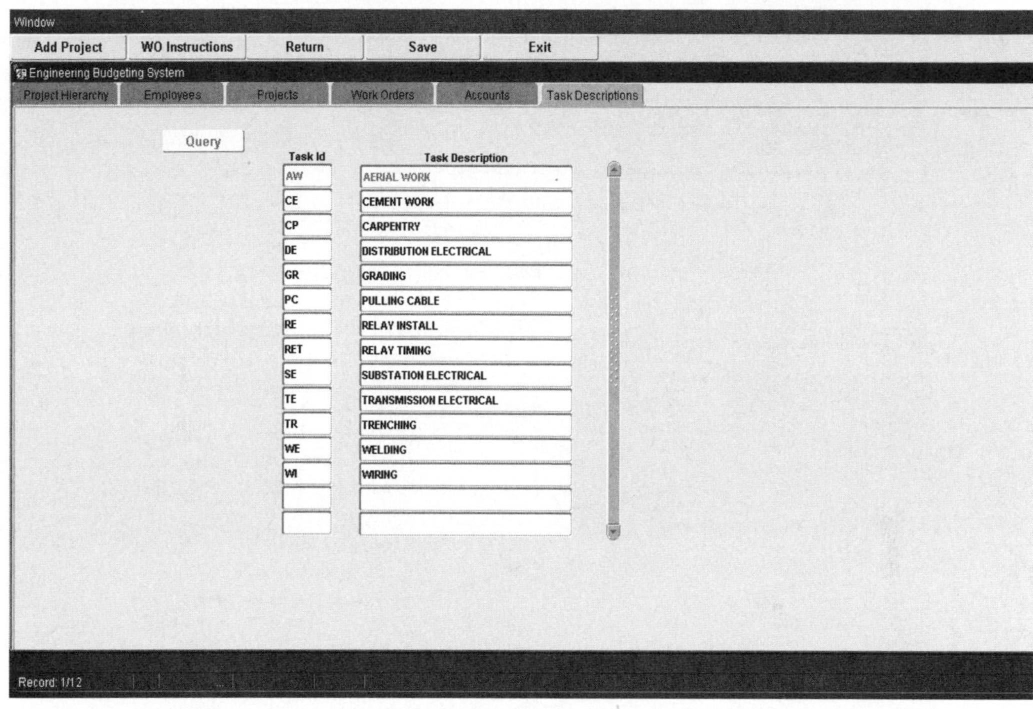

Figure 2-40 TASK_DESCRIPTIONS tab page used to maintain task descriptions

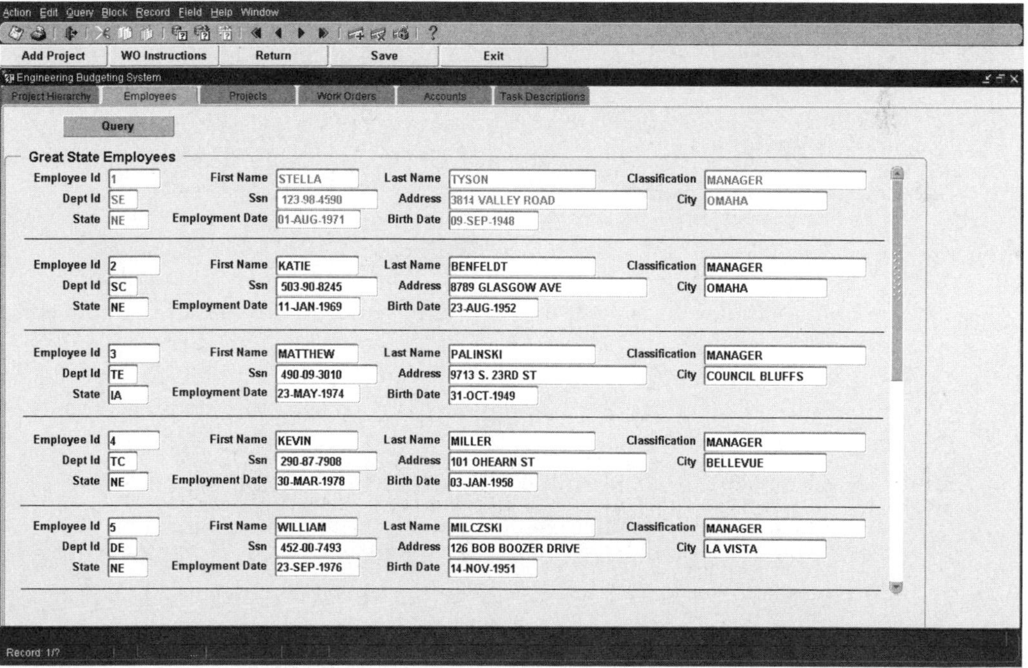

Figure 2-41 EMPLOYEES tab page used to maintain employee information

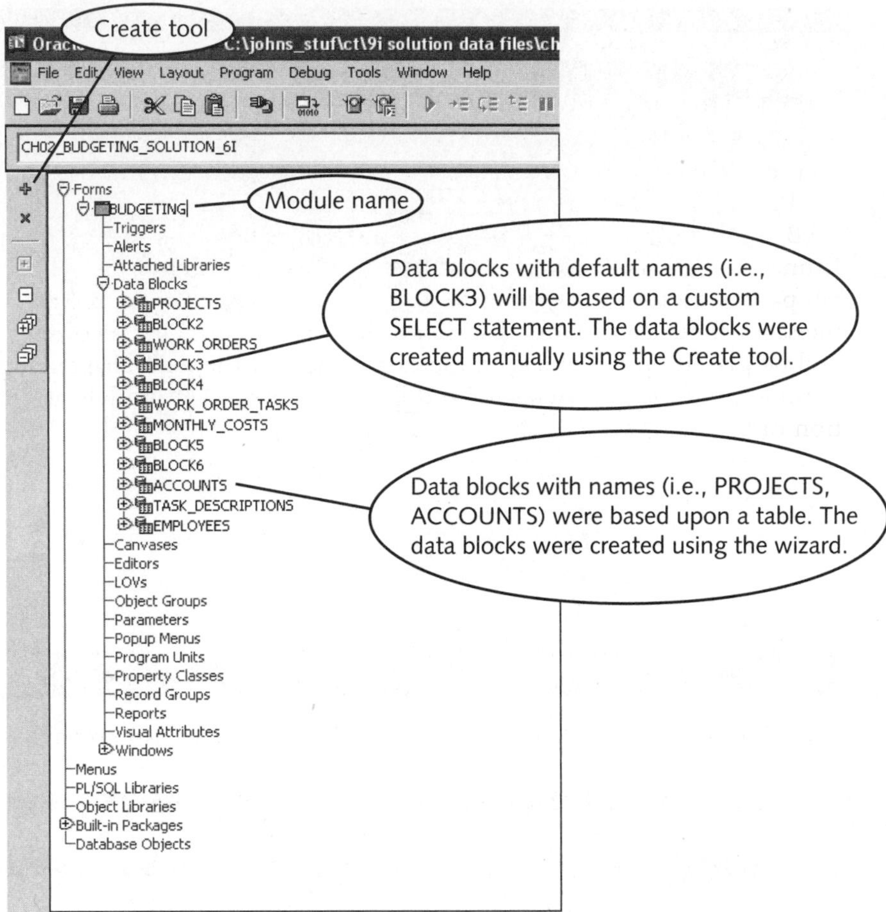

Figure 2-42 Object Navigator and BUDGETING form after adding the control and data blocks

Your Work

As a new form developer, you may not fully understand some of the concepts mentioned previously. The following chapters will elaborate on many of the concepts in far greater detail. However, you do need to begin developing the system. You should have enough Forms Builder skills to complete this Case Project for this chapter. Develop the following components:

1. Create and save a form module called BUDGETING.
2. Create all of the Table 2-3 data blocks. The control blocks (PROJ_SEARCH_CRITERIA and WO_SEARCH_CRITERIA) and the data blocks based on a QUERY FROM clause (PROJECT_DATA, WORK_ORDER _DATA, and WO_INSTRUCTIONS) should be created manually. This means you should not use the Data Block Wizard to create these

blocks. Don't worry about naming these canvases at this time; you will learn this in the next chapter. You may use the Data Block Wizard to create the remainder of the data blocks (PROJECTS, WORK_ORDERS, WORK_ORDER_TASKS, MONTHLY_COSTS, TASK_DESCRIPTIONS, ACCOUNTS, and EMPLOYEES). These tables will be based on a table and will receive the table's name by default. Use the Layout Wizard to create the EMPLOYEES tab page. When creating this layout, be sure to specify a TAB_CANVAS and a new tab page. The tab page should display 20 records. Launch the application and test it. The form should display the EMPLOYEES tab page, which you may operate. You may encounter Forms Builder warning messages about data blocks that do not have any items. This is correct, and items will be placed on the blocks in the case project of the next chapter. Figure 2-42 illustrates the Object Navigator and the budgeting form module at the completion of this work.

CHAPTER

3

USING THE OBJECT NAVIGATOR, FORM OBJECTS, AND DETAIL DATA BLOCKS

In this chapter you will:

- Learn the importance of the Object Navigator and how to use it
- Learn definitions of form objects
- Be exposed to the types of files used by Forms Builder
- Create and use detail data blocks
- Use control blocks
- Create a data block using a FROM clause query as the data source

Looking at the roadmap (Figure 3-1), you can see that the purpose of this chapter is to understand the Object Navigator. The Object Navigator is the central Forms Builder tool for adding, deleting, and locating form objects. In addition, this chapter introduces you to numerous form terms, which refer to objects in the Object Navigator. Many of these objects are discussed in greater detail in later sections of the book. This chapter covers the modules or types of files that are opened in the Object Navigator, the various Object Navigator tools, and the form components that are listed in the Object Navigator hierarchy. These components include:

- Triggers or PL/SQL scripts used by the form (discussed in Chapter 6)
- Alerts, which are modal dialog boxes that display messages (discussed in Chapter 9)
- Attached libraries of PL/SQL code that can be used by the form (discussed in Chapter 6)
- Data blocks used by the form to issue Select, Update, Delete, and Insert statements (discussed in Chapters 2 and 3)

- Relationships used to coordinate records from parent and child tables (discussed in this chapter)
- Canvases used to display form items (discussed in Chapters 4 and 8)
- Editors associated to an item that are used to enter lengthy values (discussed in Chapter 9)
- Lists of values (LOVs) that dynamically produce value lists used as item values (discussed in Chapter 7)
- Object groups that hold form components that can be copied into other forms (discussed in Chapter 5)
- Parameters that are used to transfer values (discussed in Chapter 6)
- Popup menus displayed by right-clicking the mouse (discussed in Chapter 9)
- Program units that are named PL/SQL scripts defined within the form (discussed in Chapter 6)
- Property classes used to set form object characteristics such as font, height, or width (discussed in Chapter 4)
- Record groups that return dynamic or static values to form objects (discussed in Chapter 7)
- Reports that can be launched from the form (discussed in Chapter 8)
- Visual attributes that control how form items appear (discussed in Chapter 4)
- Windows that display canvases (discussed in Chapter 8)
- Menu modules attached to a form that can be used to perform tasks, such as calling another form (discussed in Chapter 9)
- PL/SQL libraries that can be attached to the form (discussed in Chapter 6)
- Object libraries that consist of form components that can be copied into a form (discussed in Chapter 4)
- Built-in packages developed by Oracle for your use
- Database objects such as tables, views, or stored procedures (discussed in Chapter 10)

The chapter discusses the creation of detail blocks that are related and synchronized to a master block, a common form feature. Finally, the chapter introduces you to the data block FROM clause query property.

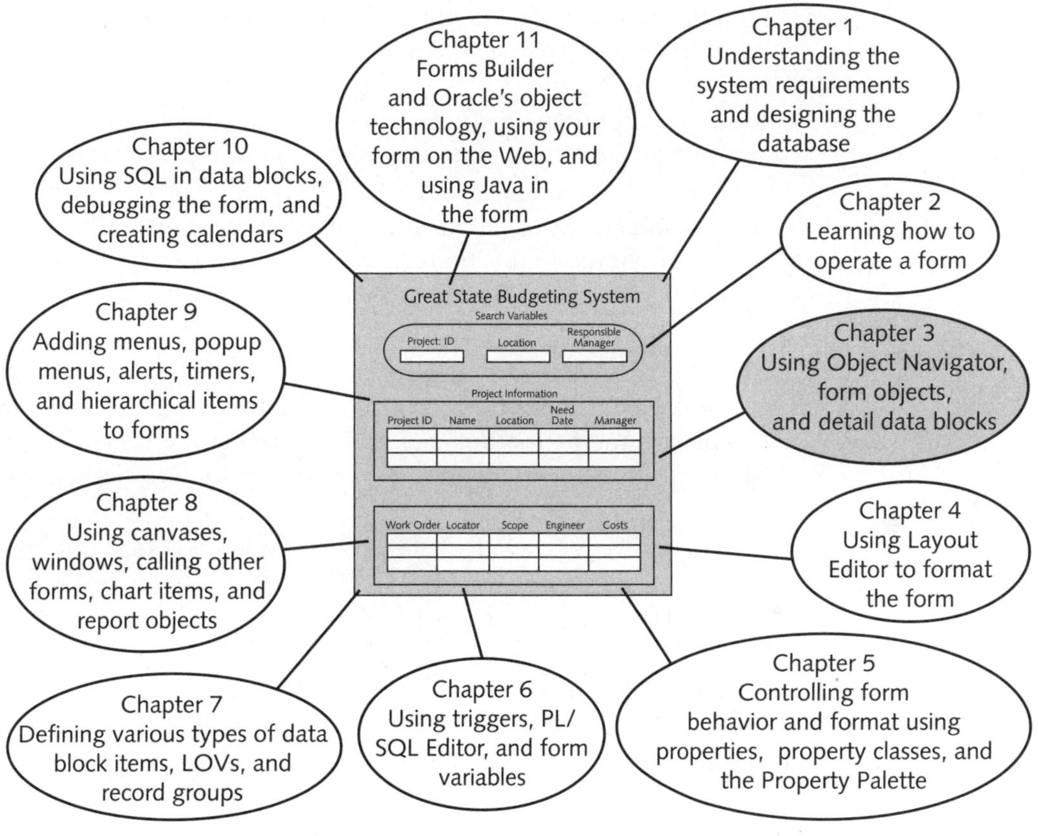

Figure 3-1 Roadmap

IMPORTANCE OF THE OBJECT NAVIGATOR AND ITS USE

The Object Navigator is the central Forms Builder tool. It lists every form component. If you want to modify an object on the form, you simply locate and highlight the object in the Object Navigator and double-click its icon. Forms Builder then opens the appropriate editor for the selected object. The Object Navigator is also commonly used to add, delete, and rename form components.

The Object Navigator is a hierarchy of objects. At the highest level are binary files that reside on the server. Whenever a file is opened or created, the object is listed under the appropriate parent object. The file objects and their functions are:

- **Forms**: Form modules or applications used to view, modify, and delete data.
- **Menus**: Menu modules or applications containing paths to the various system applications. Menu modules cannot be executed by themselves; they must be attached to form modules.
- **PL/SQL libraries**: Modules containing various PL/SQL procedures. Libraries of procedures can be shared between form modules.

- **Object libraries**: Modules containing form components that can be copied into a form module. These are effective tools for standardizing form components.
- **Built-in packages**: A series of procedures developed by Oracle. These procedures perform a variety of functions, such as sending messages or debugging procedures.
- **Database objects**: Database objects available to the user. All database objects such as tables, views, or functions accessible to the user are displayed. These are excellent tools for reviewing metadata.

Object Navigator Toolbar

On the left side of the Object Navigator is a vertical toolbar that can perform a variety of tasks. You can determine the tool functionality by placing the cursor over the tool to make a ToolTip description appear. Figure 3-2 depicts the Object Navigator toolbar.

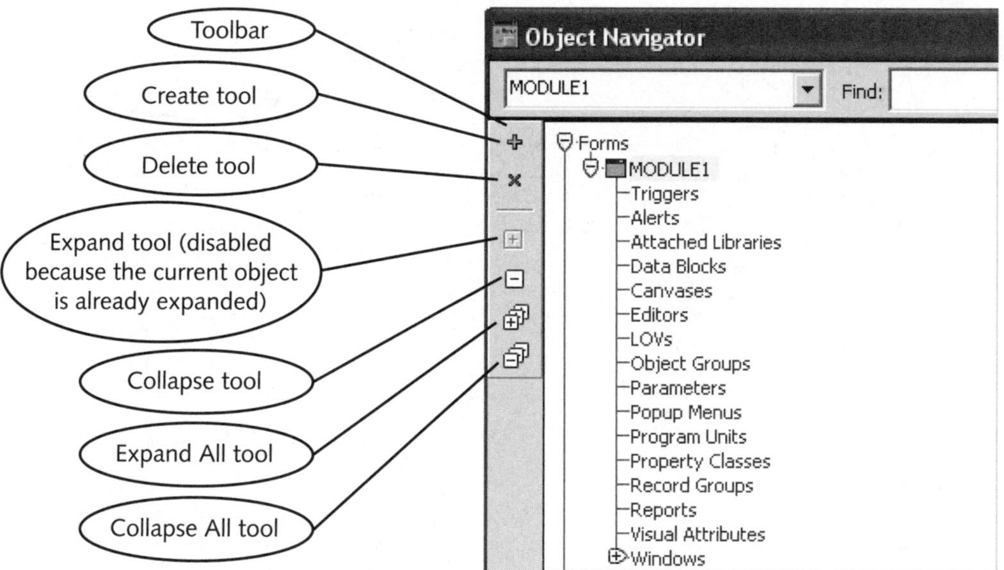

Figure 3-2 Object Navigator toolbar

Expanding and Collapsing the Object Navigator Hierarchy

Each of the form file objects can have numerous child objects, and a complex form can have one hundred or more objects. This is further complicated by the fact that it is common to have several form modules open at the same time. Needless to say, it can be difficult to read and locate items in the Object Navigator. Fortunately, the Object

Navigator has the ability to expand and collapse objects. When an object is expanded, its child objects can be seen, and when an object is collapsed, the child objects are hidden. This allows you to hide child objects when they are of no interest and bring them into view when they are.

You can determine whether an object is expanded, collapsed, or has child objects by the node prefix. The prefix uses the following symbols (see Figure 3-3):

- **No symbol prefix**: Object does not have a child object. Notice the Triggers, LOVs, or Popup Menus node in Figure 3-3.
- **Plus sign in prefix**: Object has child objects and the object is collapsed.
- **Negative sign in prefix**: Object has child objects and the object is expanded.

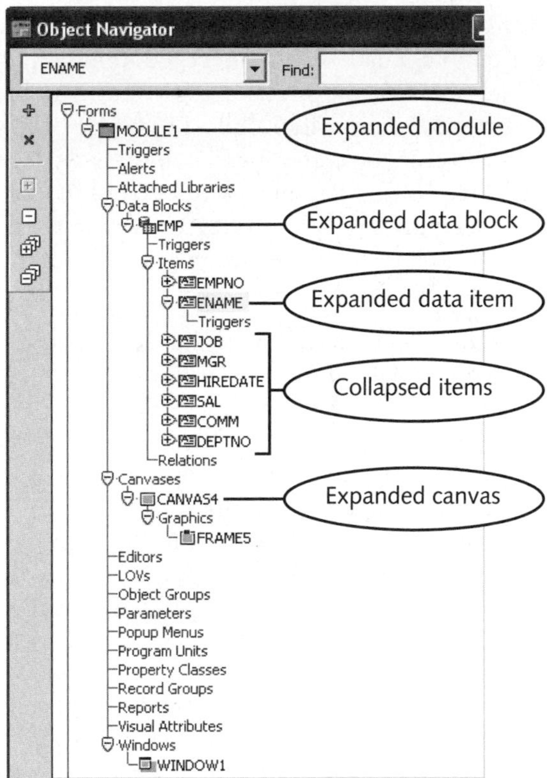

Figure 3-3 Object Navigator displaying expanded and collapsed objects

To expand a highlighted object, perform one of the following actions:

- Click the plus-sign prefix.
- Click the Expand tool on the Object Navigator vertical toolbar.

- Click the Expand All tool on the Object Navigator vertical toolbar.
- Select the View/Expand menu option.
- Select the View/Expand All menu option.

To collapse a highlighted object, perform one of the following actions:

- Click the negative-sign prefix.
- Click the Collapse tool on the Object Navigator vertical toolbar.
- Click the Collapse All tool on the Object Navigator vertical toolbar.
- Select the View/Collapse menu option.
- Select the View/Collapse All menu option.

The Expand and Expand All tools function differently. Objects can contain a number of different types of child nodes. For example, a data block object has items as child objects, and it also has triggers as child objects. Using the Expand tool on a data block object causes the first line child object to appear. The initial child objects are the Items and Triggers nodes. The actual items and triggers do not appear, because they are two levels below the data block. The Expand All tool differs from the Expand tool in that it expands all objects below the highlighted object, regardless of the level. Using the Expand All tool on the data block causes the Items and Triggers nodes to appear, as well as the actual items and triggers.

The Collapse and Collapse All tools work somewhat similarly to the Expand and Expand All tools. The Collapse tool hides all child objects. However, it does not collapse all nodes below the selected node. For example, if you expand a data block to see its items and the item triggers, collapsing the data block object hides all of the objects. Re-expanding the data block object causes the expanded items to reappear, just as they were before the collapse. The items and item trigger objects reappear, because they were never collapsed. In contrast, the Collapse All tool collapses all objects below the highlighted objects. In this example of using the Collapse All tool, when the data block is re-expanded, only the item and trigger nodes are shown. The items must be expanded in order to see the actual items.

It is common to have a variety of different objects expanded during a working session, and collapsing object paths can become tedious. To collapse all objects and clean up the hierarchy, you can highlight the form object and use the Collapse All tool. This quickly cleans up the hierarchy.

You will often need to locate or identify a form object. Rather than drilling down each path to a trigger or object, highlight the form module and use the Expand All tool to expand all objects. You can then quickly scroll through the complete object list to find the desired trigger or object.

As practice in the use of the Expand and Collapse tools, perform the following steps:

1. Create a form based on the EMP data block. The data block style should be Form.
2. Open the **Object Navigator** and locate the form module. It has a default name starting with MODULE.
3. Select and highlight the newly created form module object. Click the **Expand All** tool.
4. Collapse all the objects by clicking the **Collapse All** tool.
5. Expand the module by clicking the **plus sign** to the left of the module.
6. Select the **Data Blocks** node. Click the **plus sign** expanding the node. The EMP data block should appear.
7. Select the **EMP** data block and click the **plus sign** to expand the node. Notice that the Triggers node has an open box. This signifies it does not have child objects.
8. Select the **Items** node and click the **plus sign** to expand the node. This causes the EMP data block's items to appear.
9. Double-click the icon to the left of the ENAME (EMPLOYEE NAME) item. This causes the item's Property Palette to appear.
10. Close the Property Palette by clicking the window's **Close** tool.
11. In the Object Navigator, locate and expand the Canvases node. Double-click the icon to the left of the canvas object. It should have a default name beginning with "CANVAS". This opens the Layout Editor displaying the canvas.
12. Save the form for later practice.

Object Navigator Object Symbols and Toolbar

Each Object Navigator item type has its own graphic symbol or icon. This symbol is displayed to the left of the object's name. You will soon learn to identify object types by their symbols. The only other way to determine the object type is by opening the object's Property Palette, a time-consuming task. The graphic symbol is most important for data block items, because a data block item can be one of 15 different types. For example, **display items** and **text items** appear exactly the same in the Layout Editor. The difference between the two is that a text item value can be modified, while a display item cannot. The display item and text item symbols are boxes displaying the characters "ABC". The symbols differ in that the display item symbol is darkened. Figure 3-4 illustrates a data block containing several different item type symbols.

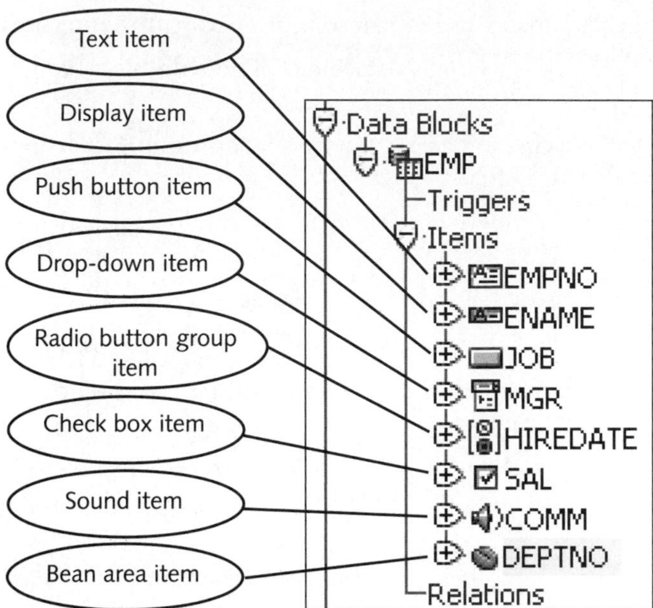

Figure 3-4 Examples of item type symbols

Object Navigator Techniques

There are a variety of Object Navigator techniques that help you work efficiently. The following list describes them:

- **Adding an object**: You can add a new object by selecting any object and using the Create tool (green plus sign).
- **Bookmarking**: You can mark selected objects for quick return. This is done by highlighting an object and selecting the Edit/Add Bookmark option. The Edit/Go To Bookmark option moves you directly to the bookmark. Previous bookmarks are replaced when a new one is set.
- **Changing names**: You can change the name of any form object by clicking the object twice. Be sure to pause between clicks to differentiate from double-clicking. This technique causes the object name to turn into a text item, which allows you to modify the value. You can also change the object's name by double-clicking any object icon and opening its Property Palette.
- **Copying**: You can copy any object by pressing the Control+C keys, using the Copy toolbar tool, or selecting the Edit/Copy menu option. This places the object in the Windows Clipboard.

- **Cutting**: You can cut any object by pressing the Control+X keys, using the Cut toolbar tool, or selecting the Edit/Cut menu option. This removes the object from the Object Navigator and places it in the Windows Clipboard.
- **Deleting an object**: You can delete an object by selecting any object and using the Delete tool (red x), pressing the Delete keyboard key, or selecting the Edit/Clear menu option.
- **Duplicating**: You can duplicate a highlighted object by selecting the Edit/Duplicate menu option or by pressing the Control+D keys.
- **Moving**: You can move an object between similar form objects in the same form or between similar objects in different form modules. Click the object, hold down the left mouse button, and drag the object to the new location.
- **Making multiple selections**: Multiple objects can be selected for any of the previous actions. If the items are adjacent, highlight one of the end objects, then hold down the Shift key while highlighting the opposite end object. This highlights the entire set of objects between the two selected objects. To select disparate objects, hold down the Control key while highlighting the objects. If, at some point, you select an object without holding the Shift or Control keys, all of the previously selected objects are unhighlighted.
- **Navigating**: Right-clicking the mouse on any object causes a popup menu to appear. The menu has options to cut, copy, paste, and call the various Forms Builder editors, wizards, and other tools.
- **Pasting**: You can paste an object residing in the Windows Clipboard into a form by pressing the Control+V keys, using the Paste toolbar tool, or selecting the Edit/Paste menu option.
- **Searching**: You can search on a word using Object Navigator tools. The following section describes this technique.

Searching with the Object Navigator

The Object Navigator can contain a large quantity of objects. Sometimes you may want to search based on a name rather than by scanning the hierarchy. The Object Navigator has a search tool called Fast Search located at the top-right corner of the tool that can perform the search (see Figure 3-5). The Fast Search tool has the following characteristics:

- You can begin a search by entering a value in the Find text box. Object Navigator immediately seeks the first object that matches the characters.
- The two search tools (flashlight icons) are used to perform forward and backward hierarchy searches. These tools are used when the first search fails to locate the needed item. Searches begin from the currently selected node object in one direction. When the end of the hierarchy is reached, the search is terminated. The search tools can be used to continue the search in the opposite direction.

- The wild card character (*) can be used to represent one or many characters. This is used when spelling may be ambiguous.
- The left pick list always displays the currently selected object and contains any previously selected objects. You can return to a previously selected object by clicking any object in the pick list.

Figure 3-5 illustrates the use of the Fast Search tool. The characters " EMP" were entered into the search text item. Forms Builder identified and highlighted the first occurrence of these characters.

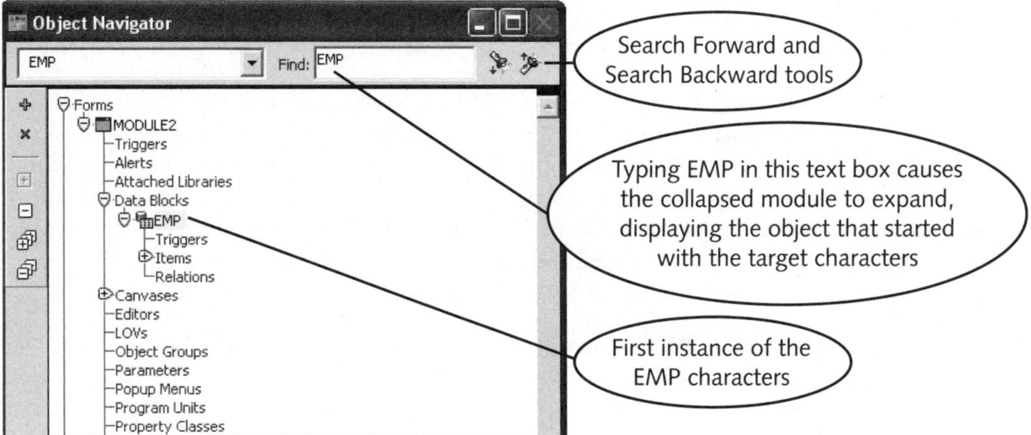

Figure 3-5 Using the Fast Search tool

Moving Objects

One of the more common Object Navigator functions is to move objects between forms or between data blocks. When you create objects in the Layout Editor, Forms Builder sometimes places the object in the incorrect data block, so you must move the object. Another common use is when you want to copy objects from another module. Object components are often exactly the same or very similar in different forms. If you don't want to use and maintain an object library, you can drag or move selected objects to other forms. This, in effect, copies the components to the new form module.

As you drag the selected objects (if you have used the multiple select technique), Forms Builder changes the cursor to a Stop symbol as you move the cursor over objects not compatible with the selected objects (see Figure 3-6). An example would be moving a selected data block item over an Alerts object. As you move over an object over a valid parent object, the cursor changes to an open box symbol. The objects are moved when you release the mouse button. Forms Builder keeps the original object names unless they exist in the list. In this event, Forms Builder creates default names that begin with the object name (i.e., CANVAS1, CANVAS2).

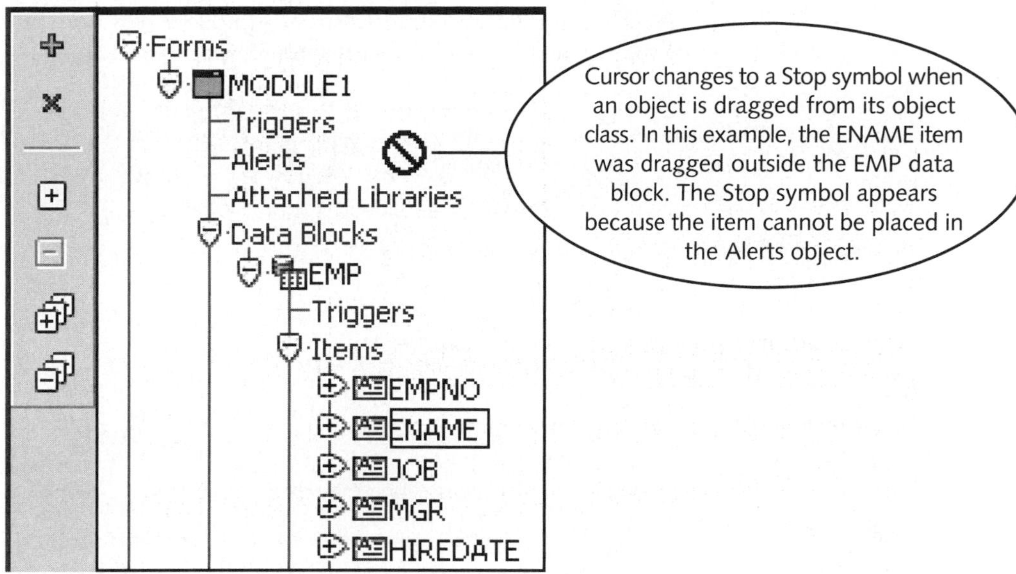

Figure 3-6 The Stop symbol displayed during an object move

The default tab order of a data block's items and the default order of the canvas display are determined by their position in the Object Navigator. It is common to use the moving technique discussed previously to set the proper table and canvas display order.

When you move objects between form modules, Form Builder displays a Forms dialog box (Figure 3-7) before copying the objects. This dialog box prompts you on whether the copied objects should be subclassed. A **subclass** is a set of objects that are linked to similar objects in another form. The subclass allows you to modify an object in one form and have the related object modified in another form. To effect the changes in linked forms, you must recompile all the forms using the subclassed objects. Objects are often used repeatedly on different forms, but it is difficult to find an effective way to track the subclasses and linked forms.

For practice, perform the following steps, which have just been described. Be sure the listener has been started.

1. Use the form created in the previous practice session. Be sure that the form was saved. Execute the form and perform a query. Tab through the displayed items noticing the tab order. Close the form.
2. Open the **Object Navigator** and rearrange the EMP data block items. The top item should be DEPTNO followed by COMM, SAL, HIREDATE, MGR, JOB, ENAME, and EMPNO. Execute the form and tab through the items noticing the new tab order. Close the form.

3. Grab the **CANVAS** object and drag it out of the Canvases node. Notice the Stop symbol that appears as you move it over different nodes.

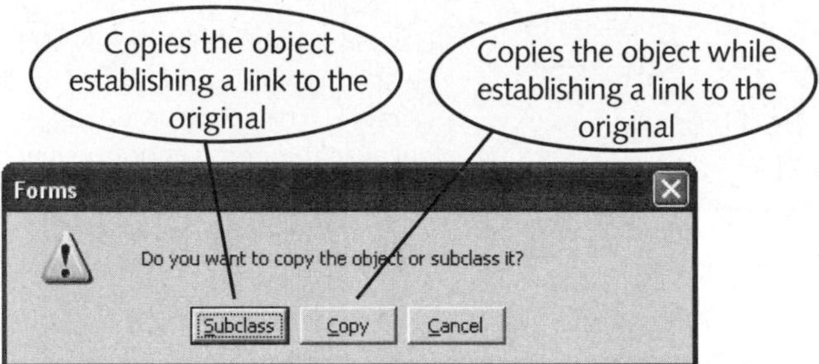

Figure 3-7 Forms dialog box prompting whether to create subclassed objects

4. Create a new blank form module by selecting the **Forms** node and clicking the **Create** tool.
5. In the original module, select the **EMP** data block. Drag this item to the Data Blocks node in the new module. Click the **Copy** button in the displayed Forms dialog box.
6. In the original module, select the default canvas. Drag this item to the Canvases node in the new module. Click the **Copy** button in the displayed Forms dialog box.
7. In the original module, select the default window. Drag this item to the Windows node in the new module. Click the **Copy** button in the displayed Forms dialog box.
8. You have now copied the new form components into the new form. Save the form and execute it. Close the form.
9. Select the **Forms** node and click the **Collapse All** button.
10. Locate the **Find** text box. Enter "EM" into the item. The hierarchy should expand displaying the EMP data block item.
11. Expand the **EMP** data block. Expand the **EMP/Items** node. Select the **COMM**. Click the **Delete** button. A Delete confirmation alert will appear. Click the **Yes** button and you have deleted the item.

Changing the Object Navigator View

The Object Navigator displays form objects in two different manners. The more common view used in the previous figures is the Ownership view. The Ownership view hierarchy lists all the form objects beginning with the highest-level object. The second is the VISUAL view that lists only displayed form objects. These objects consist of the form's visual attributes, windows, canvases, items, and frames. The VISUAL view hierarchy of objects resembles the hierarchy in which the items are displayed. At the top level is the WINDOW object that is needed to display a canvas. A canvas is needed to display data block items. You can change the view types using the Ownership View view or the Visual View view menu selections. Figure 3-8 illustrates a form module in the VISUAL view.

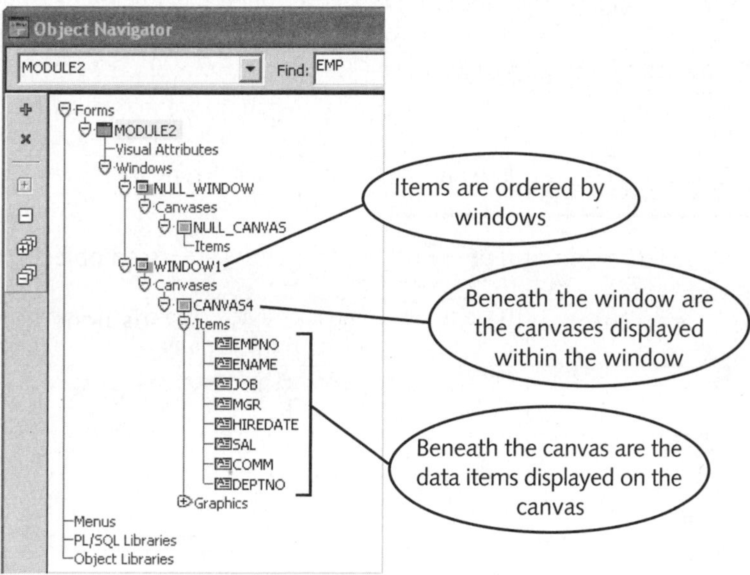

Figure 3-8 Forms module in the VISUAL view

DEFINITIONS OF VARIOUS FORM OBJECTS

There are a variety of form objects. Table 3-1 offers a brief description of the objects and the hierarchy or path used to locate the objects. Later chapters in the book describe how to employ these objects in your form, but first you must know how to locate the object.

Table 3-1 Form object descriptions

Parent object	Object type	Description
Form	Alerts	A called modal dialog box used to notify the user of a specific event.
Form	Attached Libraries	PL/SQL library that is compiled as part of the form.
Form	Canvases	A graphic area that is viewed by the user. All displayed objects appear on a canvas.
Form	Data Blocks	An object that relates form data with the database. Data blocks display values and interact with Oracle.
Form	Editors	Editors used within the form for the entry of values.

Table 3-1 Form object descriptions (continued)

Parent object	Object type	Description
Form	LOVS	A called dialog box that displays a dynamically produced list of values.
Form	Object Groups	A set of form objects used within the form inherited from an object library.
Form	Parameters	Variables that receive or are required at form startup.
Form	Popup Menus	A function menu attached to a form item or canvas that is launched using the right mouse button.
Form	Program Units	PL/SQL named procedures that reside in the form.
Form	Property Classes	A set of properties used to format various common items.
Form	Record Groups	A SELECT statement or static value that is listed and used to populate a LOV.
Form	Reports	Reports Builder modules that can be called by the form. These modules are based on the contents of a form data block.
Form	Triggers	PL/SQL code that is executed as the result of a form event.
Form	Visual Attributes	A set of formatting property values that can be assigned to another form object.
Form	Windows	The form object that displays the canvas.
Canvas	Graphics	Various form graphics symbols that appear on the canvas. These symbols can consist of rectangles, arcs, or text. The most commonly accessed Graphics child object is a frame.
Graphics	Frame	A graphic tool used to format a set of data block items.
Data Blocks	Items	An object that holds a value. Examples are text items, radio buttons, or check boxes.
Data Blocks	Triggers	PL/SQL code that is executed as the result of a data block event.
Data Blocks	Relations	A set of properties that control the behavior between master and detail data blocks.
Items	Triggers	PL/SQL code that is executed as the result of an item event.
Item (Radio Group)	Radio Buttons	Objects that correspond to the various options available in the radio group.

Types of Files Used by Forms Builder

Files can be brought into Forms Builder in several ways. To create a new file, highlight the file type object in the Object Navigator and perform one of the following:

- Click the New Module tool on the toolbar.
- Select the File/New menu selection.

To open an existing file within Forms Builder, perform one of the following:

- Click the Open tool on the toolbar.
- Select the File/Open menu option.

There are a variety of file types that are used by Forms Builder as described in Table 3-2.

Table 3-2 Developer 9*i* file types

File extension	Description
.fmb	Form binary file used in Forms Builder
.fmt	Text version of a form binary file
.fmx	Form executable file used by the runtime engines
.mmb	Menu binary file used in Forms Builder
.mmt	Text version of a menu binary file
.mmx	Menu executable file used with the form executable file
.olb	Object library binary file used in Forms Builder
.olt	Text version of an object library
.pld	Text version of a PL/SQL library
.pll	PL/SQL library binary file used in Forms Builder
.plx	PL/SQL library executable file
.rdf	Report binary file used in Reports Builder
.rep	Report executable file that can be launched from a form

Table 3-2 contains several text file versions of files. Text files are almost never used; however, Oracle provides the capability to produce the files. These files are readable versions of the binary files. In early versions of Forms Builder, it was common to create a text version of the binary file for editing. It was sometimes easier to edit this file than to use the Forms Builder integrated developer environment (IDE). This has changed over the years, and now Oracle does not support editing of the text file. However, the conversion functionality remains. To convert binary to text and text to binary, use the Files/Convert menu option. This option launches the Convert dialog box depicted in Figure 3-9.

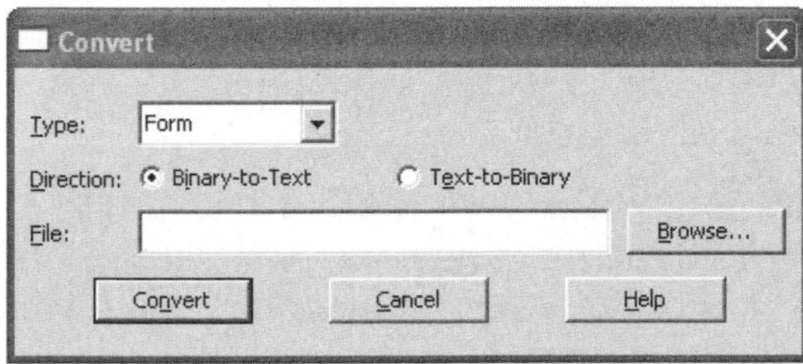

Figure 3-9 The Convert dialog box

Creating and Using Detail Data Blocks

Relational data is stored in a series of related tables. The tables are often related through a series of one-to-many relationships, as shown in the example depicted in Figure 3-10. The example is a construction project, which is composed of many work orders. The work orders divide the project into a finer detail. Work orders can be further decomposed by identifying their individual tasks. This series of one-to-many relationships form a grandparent, parent, and child relationship. Grandparents are created first, then the parents, and finally the children. Forms seldom contain only one table.

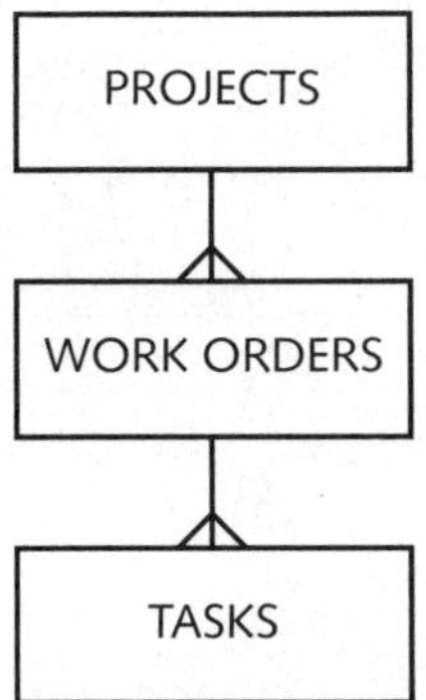

Figure 3-10 Schema depicting the relationship between PROJECTS, WORK ORDERS, and TASKS

The majority of the forms require the data from multiple data sources. Using our example, an engineer would want to see in one form the project description and location, the work orders for the project, and the tasks for each work order. This requires a form that has a data block for each of the tables (PROJECTS, WORK ORDERS, and TASKS). The PROJECTS data block displays information about a specific project, the WORK ORDERS data block displays information that pertains to the selected project in the PROJECTS data block, and the TASKS data block displays the tasks that correspond to the selected work order in the WORK ORDERS data block.

Figure 3-11 illustrates one of the forms from the Case Project that depicts the need for multiple forms. The form has WORK_ORDERS, TASKS, and MONTHLY_COSTS data blocks that are synchronized. Records in a child data block such as TASKS must always be related to a selected work order. This synchronization is a complex coding problem, but fortunately Forms Builder makes it easy for us.

Forms Builder holds child records in detail data blocks, so named because they offer more detailed information about the regular or parent entity. Referring back to ERD concepts discussed in Chapter 1, detail data blocks are used for weak entities, entities that cannot exist on their own. In our example, a work order cannot exist without a project, and a task cannot exist without a work order. Related Forms Builder data blocks are called master-detail data blocks.

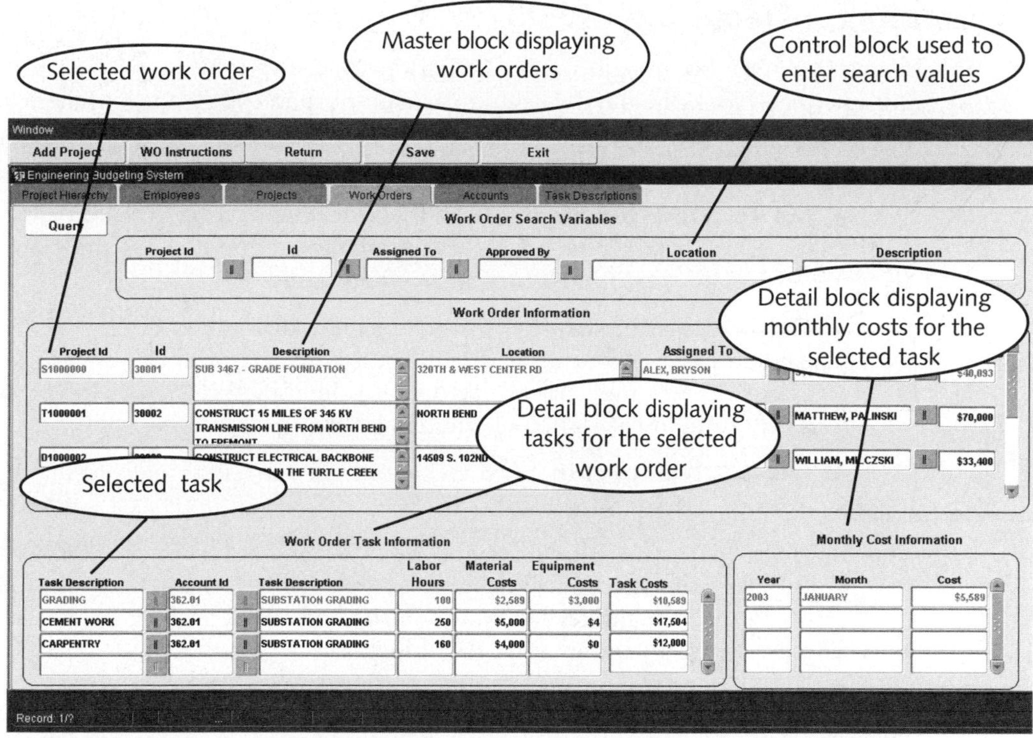

Figure 3-11 Case Project form depicting multiple data blocks

Master-detail data blocks are generally created using the Data Block Wizard. The wizard populates data block properties and creates data block triggers (PL/SQL code) that ensure the detail data block displays records for the selected parent record. It is far easier to set this up using the wizard than without. It is sometimes necessary to create a detail data block manually, but this is exceedingly rare.

It is highly possible to have multiple detail blocks for a master block. This is likely to occur if multiple relationships exist for the entity. For example, an employee can have eyeglass purchases and tool purchases. Each of these is a different relationship and has different data blocks. An entity relationship drawing (or data schema diagram) is an excellent tool to identify candidate detail data blocks.

Creating a Detail Data Block

Forms Builder adds an additional page to the Data Block Wizard when the second of multiple data blocks is added to the form. The purpose of this page, called the Master-detail page (see Figure 3-12), is to identify the primary and foreign key fields in each of the data sources. This page has the following characteristics:

- **Master Data Blocks list box**: Identifies the data block(s) selected as a master data block(s). This list box may initially be populated if the detail data block data source has a foreign key constraint.
- **Create Relationship button**: Launches a dialog box displaying the form's data blocks. This button is used if the Master Data Blocks list box is not populated. The desired master data block is identified in this dialog box. To select a block, highlight the block and click OK.
- **Delete Relationship button**: Deletes the currently selected master block from the Master Data Blocks list box.
- **Auto-join data blocks check box**: When this box is checked, Forms Builder scans the Oracle database to determine form data blocks that are candidates for the master block. When the box is unchecked, Forms Builder displays all the form's existing data blocks.

The following items are not displayed on the Master-detail page unless a master data block has been selected:

- **Detail Item drop-down list**: Lists the detail data block data source columns. This drop-down list is used to identify and select the relationship's foreign key column.
- **Master Item drop-down list**: Lists the master data block data source columns. This drop-down list is used to identify and select the relationship's primary key column.
- **Join Condition list box**: Displays the join condition that is created for the master-detail data blocks. This box cannot be modified. If the conditions are not correct, they must be deleted using the Delete Relationship button.

If the proper join items are not displayed in the Detail Item and Master Item pick lists, always select the item from the Detail Item pick list first. This causes Oracle to review any foreign key constraints and properly populate the other boxes.

Data sources that have composite keys, which are multiple-column primary keys, require multiple join conditions. You can create multiple conditions by selecting the Create Relationship button. After properly creating the JOIN conditions, Forms Builder can develop the form components that keep the blocks in synchronization.

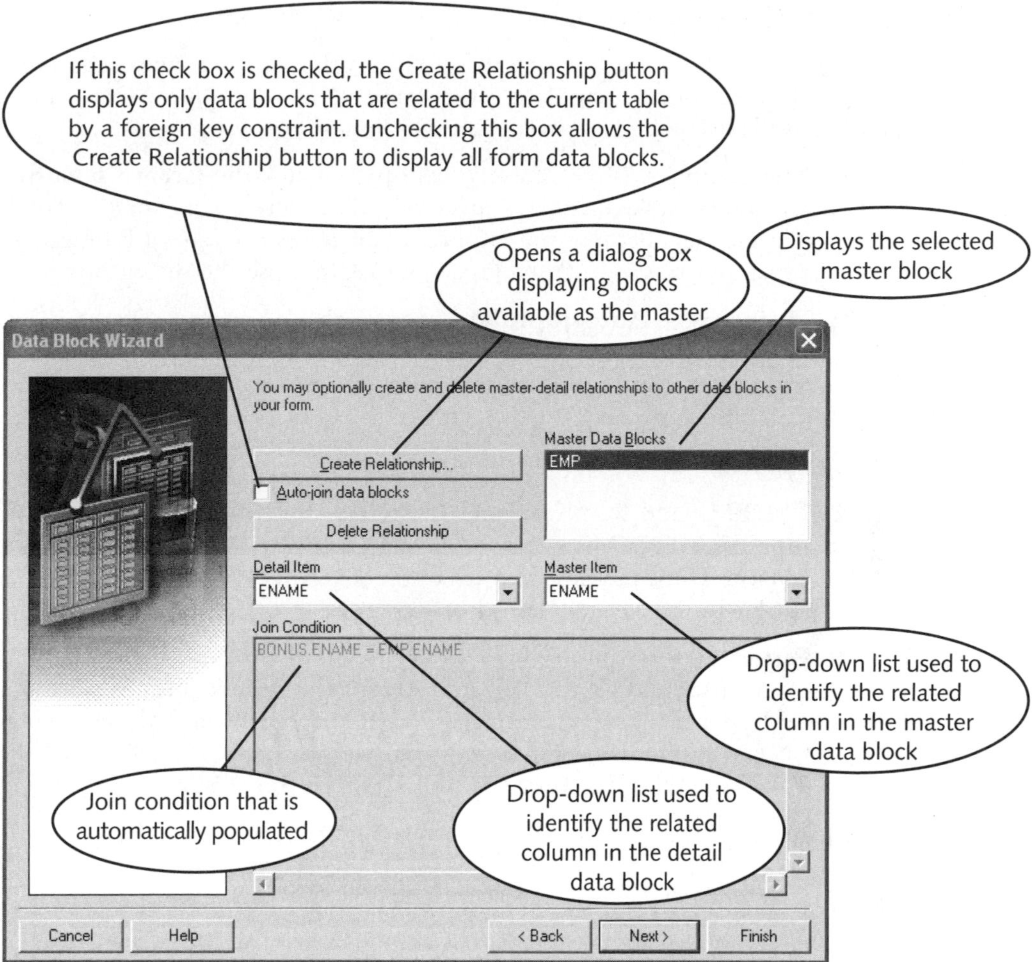

Figure 3-12 Master-detail wizard page using default Oracle tables

As practice, perform the following steps to add the BONUS table as a detail data block to your practice form. BONUS is a default table provided by Oracle. It does not contain any values but can be used to illustrate the creation of a detail block.

1. Open the previously created form in the Object Navigator.
2. Launch the Data Block Wizard. Be sure an existing data block (EMP) was not selected when the wizard was launched. If it was, you will be updating the existing block rather than creating a new one.

3. On the Type page, select the **Table or View** option.
4. On the Table page, enter BONUS into the Table or view text item. Click the **Refresh** button populating the Available Columns list. Move all of the Available Columns rows to the Database Items list.
5. The next page is the Master-detail page. Click the **Create Relationship** button. A message appears specifying that there are no master data blocks. This appears because the BONUS table does not have a Foreign Key constraint to the EMP table. Click **OK** to close the dialog box.
6. Uncheck the **Auto-join data blocks** check box and click the **Create Relationship** button. The Relation Type dialog box opens. Select the **Based on a join condition** option and click **OK**. A dialog displaying the EMP data block appears.
7. Select the **EMP** data block and click **OK**.
8. The EMP and BONUS tables are related by common ENAME values. You should see ENAME displayed in the Detail Item drop-down list. Open the **Master Item** pick list and select the **ENAME** column. ENAME should appear in the Master Item drop-down list.
9. Perform the remaining steps to create and format the data block using the Data Block and Layout Wizards. Accept the default settings on the remainder of the Data Block Wizard pages. In the Layout Wizard, do not select the ENAME column, because it is displayed in the master block. Select the **Tabular style**, **five records**, and **Display Scrollbar**.
10. After creating the form, save and launch the form. Notice the detail data block.
11. Retrieve a record in the master block. Enter values in the corresponding detail block.
12. Save the records. Perform another query to determine whether the records are displayed when the target master record is displayed.
13. Save the form.

How Forms Builder Keeps Master-Detail Data Blocks Synchronized

A developer does not normally have to modify the PL/SQL triggers or other components that are created for the master-detail blocks. However, it is wise to understand how they operate together. You may occasionally wish to modify the default behavior. Table 3-3 details the various master-detail objects and settings.

Table 3-3 Master-detail data block components

Object type	Name	Description
Item	Copy From property	The master data block's related item name is placed in this detail data block item. This ensures that the detail block always displays the records for the selected master data block record, because its primary key value is automatically copied into this detail block item. When a query is executed, this value limits the returned records to those matching the master data block record.
Form trigger	On-Clear-Details	PL/SQL program that executes whenever a new record is selected in the master data block. It executes an Oracle executable called Clear_all_master_details. This executable or built-in subprogram removes all records from the detail block. It does not save the records; it merely removes them from display, leaving them in memory.
Master data block trigger	On-Populate-Details	PL/SQL program that fires as a result of the execution of an On-Clear-Details trigger. This trigger executes a query on the detail data block based on the new value in the related item's Copy From property.
Master data block trigger	On-Check-Delete-Master	PL/SQL program that fires if there is an attempt to delete a record on the master data block and the master data block relation's Delete Record Behavior property is set to "Non-Isolated." The trigger attempts to delete the related record in the detail data block.
Master data block relations	Generated	Contains several properties that affect the coordination between the master and detail data blocks. Relations are discussed in greater detail in the next section.

Relations

Relations is a master data block object that controls the coordination between the master and detail data blocks. The Data Block Wizard normally creates relations, but they can be created manually. Relations properties determine whether a master record can be deleted if related detail records exist, whether the related detail records should be deleted along with the master record, and whether the detail block should be populated immediately following the selection of a new master record. Three properties control these operations:

- **Delete Record Behavior:** Determines how the deletion of master records affects the detail records. Options are: CASCADING, which causes the detailed records to be deleted along with the master record; ISOLATED, which allows the master record to be deleted without the deletion of the detail records; and NON-ISOLATED, which is the default setting that prevents master record deletion if existing detail records exist.

- **Deferred:** Along with the Automatic Query property, determines when the detail block is populated after a change of selected master records. Options are YES and NO.
- **Automatic Query:** Determines whether the detail block is populated before navigation to the block. Options are YES and NO.

The Deferred and Automatic Query properties work together. Table 3-4 describes how they affect form behavior.

Table 3-4 Deferred and Automatic Query relation property actions

Deferred property value	Automatic Query property value	Action
YES	YES	Forms Builder retrieves detail records when the user navigates to the data block.
YES	NO	Forms Builder retrieves detail records when the user navigates to the data block and executes a query.
NO	YES	Forms Builder retrieves the records immediately.
NO	NO	Forms Builder fetches the detail records immediately.

The Relations object has the following additional properties:

- **Relation Type**: Indicates the link between the two data blocks is a JOIN, which is the default, or an object ref pointer. The values are JOIN and REF. Setting a value of REF indicates that a REF column in a block points to data in another block.
- **Detail Block**: The name of the related detail block.
- **Join Condition**: The condition that describes the relationship.
- **Prevent Masterless Operation**: Prevents records from being inserted into the detail block, if a master record does not exist.

After reviewing the various Relations properties, you may wonder if they supercede the foreign key constraints that may exist in the database. The answer is no. The relation's properties should emulate the database constraints. If they don't, Oracle returns a database error and voids the transaction. For example, if you try to insert a detail record into a table that has a foreign key constraint, Oracle returns an error message if a parent record does not exist, regardless of the Prevent Masterless Operation property.

Even though you almost never have to worry about Relations properties, Oracle always includes questions about their behavior on the certification exam. You should be knowledgeable about this subject before taking the test.

Coordination Type Toggle

In the previous section, Table 3-4 outlined the Deferred and Automatic Query Relations properties. For optimal performance, these properties can be modified from the default in order to reduce the number of records returned. However, there may be times when the operator may want to change the original properties at runtime. For instance, suppose the operator is scrolling through a set of master records, but does not want to see the detail records for each master displayed. The Deferred and Automatic Query properties can be set to YES and NO, respectively. This combination of properties would require the operator to navigate to the detail block and execute a query.

In some cases, the operator may want to override the properties and populate detail records without having to execute queries. Changing data block coordination requires a **coordination-type-toggle** trigger. This is a trigger that sets the Deferred and Automatic Query properties at runtime. This trigger requires the use of an Oracle-developed built-in subprogram called Set_relation_property. This built-in is available for use within a form.

The following command can be placed inside the form to change the properties. The command sets the Automatic Query property to YES for the named relation. The relations property name value is the name displayed in the Object Navigator. The same command can be used for the Deferred property.

```
Set_relation_property ('relation_name',
                        autoquery,
                        Property_true);
```

Relation properties can also be tested using the Get_relation_property built-in. Using this property enables you to determine the current state of the properties. If you know the current state, you can toggle to the other value. The following is an example of a script that can be used in a trigger to toggle the Automatic Query property on and off.

```
If get_relation_property('relation_name', autoquery) =
              'FALSE' then
       set_relation_property ('relation_name',
                              autoquery,
                              property_true);
  else
       set_relation_property ('relation_name',
                              autoquery,
                              property_false);
  end if;
```

You should note that the Get_relation_property and Set_relation_property built-ins are not unique to Relations. All other form objects have similar Get and Set type built-ins that allow you to modify properties dynamically. This will be discussed in greater depth in later chapters.

Control Blocks and Their Use

Data blocks that are not associated with a data source are called **control blocks**. They are very important form components, because they are used to hold form values. A form often has values that must be retained throughout its life or scope. These values can be the current date, user ID, passwords, or any other value that is not associated to a database table. These values are stored or assigned to control block form items.

Control blocks are used to store values rather than data blocks, because they are static. This means the mode cannot be changed and the block cannot issue any SQL statement. If a value were stored in a data block, it would be cleared every time the data block was placed in the Enter Query mode. The first task Forms Builder performs when placing a data block in the Enter Query mode is to issue a CLEAR_BLOCK command that flushes the data block of all existing values. Thus, you cannot retain values in a data block.

Control block values generally contain values that are not displayed on a canvas, but this is not always true. A custom form style called a **Directory** that is discussed later in this book uses a control block to store search values. In Chapter 2, you saw that search values are entered directly into data block items. When the query returns records to the data block, the search values are overwritten. The user may not remember the original search values or has to re-enter the search value if the original values did not provide the proper filtering. In many cases, it is preferable to enter the search values into a control box and use data item Copy From properties to assign the data item a value from an item on the control block. When the records are displayed, the original search values continue to be displayed in the control block. The user can view the original search values and only has to make small modifications rather than having to re-enter all of the search variables. Several of the Case Project forms have this feature.

A control block can be created by selecting the data block's object node and clicking the Create tool.

Creating a Data Block with a FROM Clause Query as the Data Source

Normally, a data block is based on a table. However, sometimes it is advantageous to change the data source to a FROM clause query. These advantages are discussed in greater detail in Chapter 10. A FROM clause query is a SELECT statement that resides as a data block property. When Forms Builder creates the form's SQL, it uses the FROM clause query rather than developing it from the data block's columns.

Data blocks often contain descriptive items not existing in the source table. Normalization causes descriptive fields such as task descriptions or account descriptions to be moved to a table of their own. Yet these values are needed with their child tables to better understand the information. For example, the Case Project budgeting database schema depicted in Figure 3-13 has a WORK_ORDER_TASKS table. This table contains several foreign keys. It contains foreign keys to the TASK_DESCRIPTIONS and ACCOUNTS tables. The descriptions of these items are needed along with the values of the WORK_ORDER_TASKS records to make each record more meaningful.

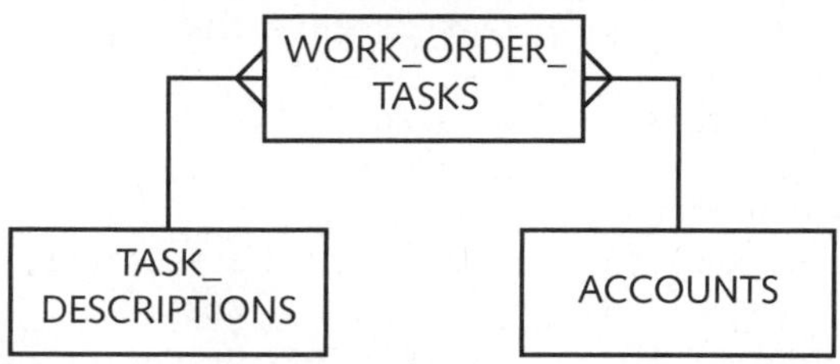

Figure 3-13 Budgeting database schema

Look at Listing 3-1. It contains two SELECT statements. The first statement creates a result set of the records in the WORK_ORDER_TASKS table. It is exactly the data that would be viewed in a data block based on the table. The records are not very intuitive and require specialized knowledge of the department ID and account codes. The second SELECT statement joins the WORK_ORDER_TASKS, TASK_DESCRIPTIONS, and ACCOUNTS tables. The codes are replaced by their descriptions. This makes each row much more meaningful to the common user.

Listing 3-1 Two SELECT statements

```
SQL> select wo_work_order_id, work_order_task_id,
assigned_department_id DEP_ID,
  2     task_description_id, account_id
  3     from work_order_tasks wot
  4   order by 1, 2;

WO_WORK_ORDER_ID WORK_ORDER_TASK_ID DEP TASK_ ACCOUNT_ID
---------------- ------------------ --- ----- ----------
           30001                  1 SC  GR        362.01
           30001                  2 SC  CE        362.01
           30001                  3 SC  CP        362.01
           30002                  8 TC  TE        370.01
           30003                 10 DC  DE        583.01
           30004                 11 DC  DE        583.01
           30006                  4 SC  CE        362.15
           30006                  5 SC  CP        362.15
           30007                  6 SC  CE        362.07
           30007                  7 SC  CP        362.07
           30009                  9 TC  TE        370.01
11 rows selected.
```

```
SQL> select wo_work_order_id, work_order_task_id, department_name,
      task_description, account_id
      from work_order_tasks wot, task_descriptions td, departments dep
      where wot.task_description_id = td.task_id
       and assigned_department_id = department_id
    order by 1, 2;

WO_WO WORK DEPARTMENT_NAME                TASK_DESCRIPTION          ACCOUN
----- ---- ---------------                ----------------          ------
30001    1 SUBSTATION CONSTRUCTION        GRADING                   362.01
30001    2 SUBSTATION CONSTRUCTION        CEMENT WORK               362.01
30001    3 SUBSTATION CONSTRUCTION        CARPENTRY                 362.01
30002    8 TRANSMISSION CONSTRUCTION      TRANSMISSION ELECTRICAL   370.01
30003   10 DISTRIBUTION CONSTRUCTION      DISTRIBUTION ELECTRICAL   583.01
30004   11 DISTRIBUTION CONSTRUCTION      DISTRIBUTION ELECTRICAL   583.01
30006    4 SUBSTATION CONSTRUCTION        CEMENT WORK               362.15
30006    5 SUBSTATION CONSTRUCTION        CARPENTRY                 362.15
30007    6 SUBSTATION CONSTRUCTION        CEMENT WORK               362.07
30007    7 SUBSTATION CONSTRUCTION        CARPENTRY                 362.07
30009    9 TRANSMISSION CONSTRUCTION      TRANSMISSION ELECTRICAL   370.01
11 rows selected.
SQL>
```

It should be apparent that the second result set is preferable in the data block. In order to bring descriptive values into the data blocks, one of three techniques can be used. The first technique is to add display items not associated to the data source table to the block. A Post-Query trigger populates the items by executing a PL/SQL script once for each record retrieved by the data block. The trigger selects the descriptive values from the database, based on the foreign key values in the data block record. This is a common technique, and it allows the developer to avoid having to create data manipulation language (DML) statements for the data block. The problem with this technique is that the data block needs to execute the Post-Query trigger many times. Each time the trigger is executed, a database query is performed degrading performance. A second problem is that the user cannot use the display items populated by the Post-Query trigger to filter records, because the display items are not related to the data source and are not in the data block.

A second possibility is to use a view, which may also enhance performance. Creating a tuned complex SQL statement substantially reduces the work Oracle must do to retrieve the result set, in comparison with using the Post-Query trigger method. Because all of the values in the data block are returned by the view, the descriptive items can be used to enter search criteria. A disadvantage of a view is that the developer must create the DML statements used by the data block. This task isn't extremely difficult and consists of creating On-Lock, On-Update, On-Insert, and On-Delete triggers that contain the various DML statements.

A FROM clause query is a SELECT statement that replaces the default clause that was based on the data block items. Default data block SELECT statements are composed of any data block item associated to the database. Items are associated to the database by setting the item's database item property to YES. A FROM clause query is actually indistinguishable from using a view. The FROM clause query is preferred, however, because it resides in the form rather than in the database. If the database view, which is totally separate from the form, is deleted, moved, or has the permissions revoked, the form is disabled. Placing the SELECT statement in the form rather than in the database as a view eliminates many of these problems. It also keeps your database clean and uncluttered by database views that are simply used by a form.

The FROM clause query techniques do have some disadvantages. The Data Block Wizard cannot be used to create the data block. The data block, its items, and all the needed properties must be set manually. This can take a great deal of work. However, once the data block is set up, the Layout Wizard can be used to complete the formatting.

To practice creating a FROM clause query, perform the following steps:

1. Manually create a data block.
2. Open the **Property Palette** for the newly created data block. Double-click the data block icon in the Object Navigator or select the data block node and press the **F4** key.
3. If necessary, locate the **Database Data Block** property and set the value to **YES**.
4. Locate the **Query Data Source Type** property and set the value to **FROM clause query**.
5. Locate and highlight the **Query Data Source Name** property. A button appears on the right side of the property text item. Clicking this button launches the Query Data Source Name dialog box used to enter the SELECT statement.
6. Enter the following script in the Query Data Source Name dialog box. Before closing the dialog box, copy the Select statement and test it in SQL*Plus to ensure it is accurate:

```
select dname department_name,
       count(*) number_of_employees,
       sum(nvl(sal,0)) total_salary,
       avg(nvl(sal,0))average_salary
from dept, emp
where dept.deptno = emp.deptno(+)
group by dname
```

7. Create a data block item using the Create tool for the DEPARTMENT_NAME, NUMBER_OF_EMPLOYEES, TOTAL_SALARY, and AVERAGE_SALARY columns.
8. Name each data block item. It is preferable to give the data block item the same name as its associated database item. This saves you the task of setting the item's Column Name property.

9. Modify the Data Type, Maximum Length, Database Item, Column Name, and Query Length properties. The Data Type and Maximum Length properties should be set to the same settings as the related database items. The Column Name property should be set to the name of its associated FROM clause query column, unless the item has the same name as the database item. The Query Length property must be at least the same size as Maximum Length. However, it can be larger, which is preferred.

Figure 3-14 illustrates the Query Data Source Name dialog box and the data block Property Palette. The SELECT statement is recorded in this dialog box. It is accepted and inserted in the property by clicking the OK button. Forms Builder does not validate this statement, and it is very possible to enter an invalid SQL statement. If you enter a syntactically incorrect statement, you are notified when you operate the form and attempt to execute a query. Oracle returns a database error that you can view by launching the Display Error dialog box.

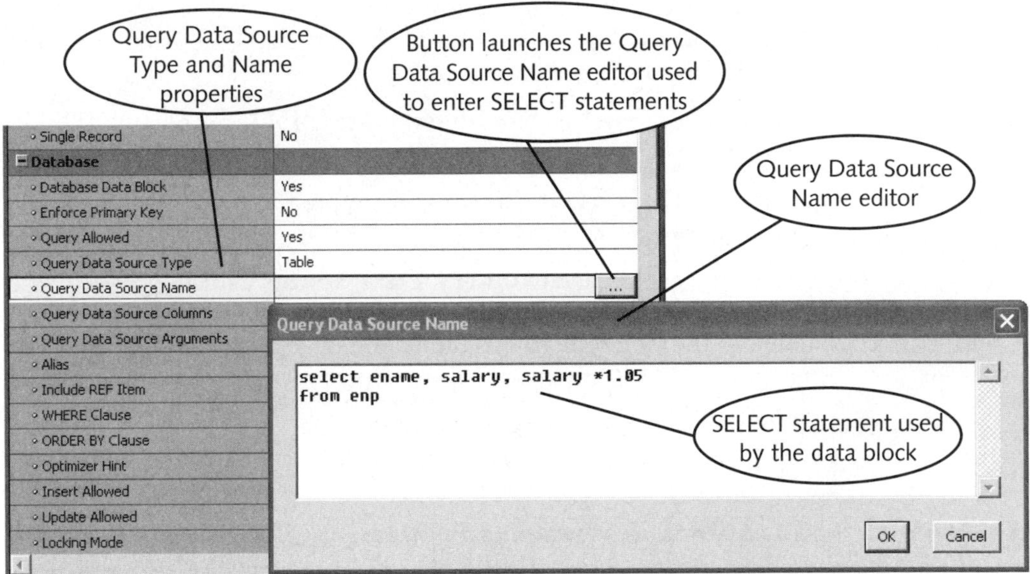

Figure 3-14 Query Data Source Name dialog box

Do not type the FROM clause query SELECT statement directly into the Query Data Source Name dialog box. Ensure that the SELECT statement is syntactically correct and returns the proper result set. Write the statement in an external editor such as Notepad, and execute the statement in SQL*Plus. Another available tool is Toad, a product that can be downloaded from Quest Software. Either method ensures that your SELECT statement is correct and saves debugging time.

FROM clause queries are discussed in greater detail in Chapter 10. They are only mentioned here because it will be necessary for you to populate the Query Data Source Type and Query Data Source Name properties.

WHERE YOU ARE AND WHERE YOU'RE GOING

In this chapter, you learned how to use the Object Navigator, which is the core Forms Builder tool. You learned how to bring objects into the Navigator, how to expand and collapse nodes, and how to create and copy objects. In the next chapter, you learn how to operate the Layout Editor to format the form. You will learn how to arrange data items, place graphics in a form, resize items, and a host of other formatting tasks.

CHAPTER SUMMARY

- The Object Navigator is the core of Forms Builder. It lists every form object in a hierarchy and allows you to rapidly locate any object.
- File objects such as form and menu objects are the highest in the objects hierarchy.
- Each of the file objects contains a variety of child and grandchild objects. For instance, a form module has data block objects as its children, and data block objects have data items as their children.
- Each object has an icon on its left that identifies the object type.
- Developers use Expand and Collapse tools to see hidden children objects or to hide objects.
- The Object Navigator can be used to add and remove form objects, copy objects between forms, and move objects.
- The Object Navigator also has tools that allow the developer to locate objects by a word search.
- Objects can be moved by selecting the object and dragging it to a new location.
- Multiple objects can be selected by holding down the Shift or Control key while selecting the objects.
- A data block item can be changed into a variety of types such as a sound, text item, display item, radio group, check box, or list item.
- Forms often have related data blocks that show tables related in a one-to-many relationship. The detail block often uses a tabular multirecord layout.
- Detail blocks are most often created using the Master-detail page of the Data Block Wizard.
- Detail blocks are coordinated with a master block by a series of triggers and the detail block Copy From property.

- Relations is a data block child object that contains properties that determine block coordination. The properties determine whether master block records can be deleted before the detail block records, whether deleting the master record also deletes the child records, and whether the child record must be deleted individually before the master record can be deleted. Properties also exist that determine when the detail block is populated with records.
- Control blocks are data blocks that are not related to a data source. They cannot be placed into the Enter Query or Execute Query modes and are used to hold form variables.
- Data block records often contain descriptive values from other tables. In order to bring these values into the block, the developer must use a Post-Query trigger, a view, or a FROM clause query.
- FROM clause queries are excellent tools, because they do not clutter the database and do not rely on database actions.
- A view can be used with the Data Block Wizard, but data blocks based on a FROM clause query must be created manually.

Review Questions

1. Match the following terms that have appeared in this chapter with their descriptions:

a. **.fmt**	________	Symbol indicating all child objects are displayed
b. Automatic Query property	________	Object Navigator tool that expands all child objects beneath the target object
c. Subclassed object	________	Menu binary source code file extension
d. Negative sign in the Object Navigator	________	Suppresses the detail data block re-query operation until the user navigates into the data block
e. Relations	________	Object Navigator object that has database child objects and can be used to identify tables, columns, and stored procedures
f. Copy From property	________	Form text file extension
g. Expand All tool	________	Indicates the selected object cannot be copied into the object
h. Object library	________	Form block not associated to a data source

i. Delete Record Behavior property	______________	Item property that copies a value automatically from another form item
j. Plus sign in the Object Navigator	______________	Causes a query to be executed on the detail data block as a result of changing current master block records
k. **.mmb**	______________	Form object linked to a similar item in another form
l. Fast Search tool	______________	Reports Builder compiled file extension
m. Control block	______________	Relations property that determines how master and detail data blocks coordinate record deletions
n. Cursor turns into a Stop symbol	______________	Forms Builder object that contains form components that can be reused in a form
o. Database Objects node	______________	Object Navigator tool used to identify an object based on spelling
p. **.rep**	______________	Symbol indicating an object has hidden child objects
q. Deferred property	______________	Form object that determines whether a master record can be deleted without deleting the detail records

2. Why is the Object Navigator considered the central Forms Builder tool?
3. Explain three different ways of opening a form object's Property Palette from the Object Navigator.
4. Identify situations in which the Expand, Expand All, Collapse, and Collapse All tools should be used.
5. You are not sure a data block item's data type property is correct. This item is related to a database column. Using Forms Builder, how can you determine whether the data type is correct?
6. Explain two ways of changing an object's name.
7. Explain two ways of selecting multiple objects in the Object Navigator.
8. You have created a PL/SQL procedure that is executed from several different places within the form. You don't want multiple copies of the same procedure. What form object allows you to write one procedure for use in multiple triggers?
9. Without looking at a data item's Property Palette, how can you determine the item type?

10. Which form object would you use to store form objects that you want to reuse?
11. What are the pros and cons of subclassing an object?
12. What design tool can you use to determine candidates for master-detail blocks? How can you tell if the tables work in this type of layout?
13. You have just created a relationship on the Master-detail page of the wizard. You noticed that the relationship is incorrect. How can you correct this?
14. How does the Auto-join data blocks check box of the Master-detail page affect the page?
15. Why is it best to store nondatabase form variables in a regular data block?
16. What is the most common layout style for a detail data block? Why?
17. What is the purpose of a Relations object?
18. Which Relations property prevents the detail block from executing a query until the user navigates into the block?
19. Why is it inadvisable to delete a master record without first deleting the children? Which Relations property prevents this from occurring?
20. Why can't you execute a query on a control block?
21. Discuss the pros and cons of populating descriptive items using a post-query trigger, view, or FROM clause query.

Exam Review Questions

1. You are developing a form that has four different tables connected through primary and foreign key relations. When users access one of these tables, they need the information from the other tables. How should this form be developed?
   a. Create four form modules. Each module will access one of the tables. The other modules will be displayed by clicking a button.
   b. Place all four tables in two different master-detail forms. Each form will have the ability to call the other form when buttons are clicked.
   c. Place the four data blocks in a single form and connect the data blocks through master-detail relationships.
   d. Create a data block for each table and display them in a single form.
2. Which Forms tool would you use to design and save the definition of a form?
   a. Forms Compiler
   b. Forms Runtime
   c. Forms Builder
   d. Project Builder

3. You created a form that has an EMP master block and two detail blocks, BONUS and COMMISSION. You have deleted the COMMISSION data block and want to delete everything associated to it. What else must you delete?
   a. You must delete the relation that existed between the COMMISSION and EMP data blocks.
   b. You must delete all coordinating triggers that are associated with the COMMISSION and EMP data blocks.
   c. You must delete the Frame graphic object associated to the COMMISSION data block.
   d. No action is necessary. Forms Builder will remove any object created by default when the detail block is deleted.
4. What type of block does not contain database columns?
   a. Master
   b. Detail
   c. Control
   d. Default
5. You have created a new form displaying the DEPT and EMP records in a master-detail relationship. You performed a query on the master block, but the records in the detail block do not appear. What could be wrong?
   a. The EMP data block's Relations Automatic Query property is set to NO.
   b. The DEPT data block's Relations Automatic Query property is set to NO.
   c. The EMP data block's Relations Isolated property is set to NO.
   d. The DEPT data block's Relations Isolated property is set to NO.

HANDS-ON ASSIGNMENTS

1. In this assignment, you practice creating and operating a master-detail data block form. Using the default Oracle database tables DEPT and EMP, create a master-detail form by following these steps:
   a. Create a new form module.
   b. Use the Data Block and Layout Wizards to create a data block using DEPT as the data source. Choose all the selections on the Available Columns Data Block Wizard page and the Available Items Layout Wizard pages pick lists. The form style is FORM, and only ONE record is to be displayed, because this is the master block.
   c. Use the Data Block and Layout Wizards to create a data block using EMP as the data source. Choose all the selections on the Available Columns Data Block Wizard page and the Available Items Layout Wizard pages pick lists. The form style is TABULAR, TEN records should be displayed, and the data block should have a scrollbar. This is the detail block.

   d. Launch the form in the Web environment.
   e. Execute a query without entering any search values.
   f. Scroll through the various departments and create a new department. Create at least three new employee records for this department. Commit the new records.
   g. Save the form as **ch03ex01.fmb**.
   h. Execute a query that retrieves the SALES department employees. Give each of the employees a 10% raise.

2. The purpose of this assignment is to give you practice in loading modules, locating items within the module, expanding objects, and collapsing objects. Load form module **ch03ex01.fmb**.
   a. Highlight the **Forms** object. Use the Fast Search tool to locate the EMP data block.
   b. Highlight the form module object. Press the **Collapse All** tool.
   c. Use the Expand tool to locate the JOB data item in the EMP data block.
   d. Open the **Property Palette** for the JOB data item by double-clicking the icon to its left.
   e. Expand the canvas object. Change the name of the canvas to **DEPARTMENTS**.
   f. Change the names of the two frame objects (canvas child items) to **DEPARTMENTS** and **EMPLOYEES**. Perform this task by opening the object's Property Palette by double-clicking the icon or pressing the F4 key.
   g. Save the form module as **ch03ex02.fmb**.

3. The purpose of this assignment is to demonstrate the differences between the Ownership view and the Visual view. Using form module **ch03ex02.fmb**, perform the following:
   a. Using the Object Navigator, select any form object.
   b. Select the **View/Visual View** menu option. How did this change the view? Can you locate any triggers?
   c. Select the **View/Ownership View** menu option. Click the **View/Show PL/SQL only** menu option. Expand the various form objects. What form components are now missing? Be sure to click the View/Show PL/SQL only menu option to return the display to its original state.

4. This assignment demonstrates the copying of objects between forms.
   a. Create a new blank form module.
   b. Drag (copy) the **DEPT** data block from the **ch03ex02.fmb** module into the new one.
   c. Drag (copy) the **Departments** canvas into the new module.

d. Expand the DEPARTMENTS canvas object and its child Graphics object displaying the frame object. Delete the frames using the **Delete** key. You will have to confirm the deletion.

e. Drag the **Windows** object into the new module.

f. Expand the new module's **Dept** data block and delete the **Triggers** and **Relations** objects.

g. Save the form as **ch03ex04.fmb**. Execute and operate the form.

5. This assignment demonstrates the effect of subclassing an object.

   a. Create a new form module.

   b. Drag all objects from form **ch03ex04.fmb** into the new module.

   c. When you copy the **DEPT** data block, be sure to use the Subclass option rather than the Copy function. A red arrow appears on the icon indicating this is an inherited object.

   d. Save the form as **ch03ex05.fmb**.

   e. Operate the new form to ensure that it is working.

   f. Open form **ch3ex04.fmb**. Locate the **DEPT** data block. Open the object's Property Palette by double-clicking the icon or by highlighting the object and pressing the **F4** key.

   g. Change the Dept data block's Number of Records Displayed property to **4**.

   h. Save and operate this form. How many records are not displayed? Close the form.

   i. Operate form **ch3ex05.fmb**. How many records are displayed in this form? What caused the number of records displayed in this form to change?

6. This assignment demonstrates the effect of the various Relations object Delete Record Behavior property values.

   a. Execute the form **ch03ex02.fmb**.

   b. In assignment 1, step f, you created department and employee records. Display these records in your form. Delete the department record. What was the message you received? Why did you get the message?

   c. Delete an employee record? What happened? Why were you able to delete the record?

   d. Close the form and locate the DEPT data block Relations object. Open the Property Palette for this object by double-clicking the object's icon or selecting the object and pressing the **F4** key.

   e. Change the Delete Record Behavior property to **Isolated**. Execute the form and locate the department you created in assignment 1.

f. Delete the department record. What happened? Why were you able to delete the record?

g. Commit the changes. Were you able to save them? What was the error message? Use your function keys to display the database error. What does the error message mean?

h. Repeat step 6d.

i. Change the Delete Record Behavior property to **CASCADING**. Execute the form and locate the department you created in assignment 3.

j. Delete the department record. What happened? Why were you able to delete the record?

k. Commit the changes. Were you able to save them? Why can you now save the records?

7. This assignment demonstrates the effects of a Relations object's Automatic Query and Deferred properties.

   a. Execute the form you used in assignment 2, **ch03ex02.fmb**. Execute a query and scroll through the records. Close the form.

   b. Change the DEPT data block Relations object's Deferred property to **YES** and the Automatic Query property to **NO**.

   c. Execute the form and perform a query. How do the results differ from the results seen in step a? Why?

   d. Place your cursor into the detail block. Execute a query. What happened?

   e. Close the form. Change the DEPT data block Relations object's Automatic Query property to **YES**.

   f. Execute the form and perform a query. Place your cursor into the detail block. How did your form react as compared to step d?

   g. Close the form.

   h. Change the DEPT data block Relations object's Deferred property to **YES**.

CASE PROJECT: GREAT STATE ELECTRIC BUDGETING SYSTEM

At the completion of this portion of the Case Project, you should have created the following:

- A form module called **Budgeting.fmx**.
- Seven data blocks. The blocks should be based on the following tables: PROJECTS, WORK_ORDERS, WORK_ORDER_TASKS, MONTHLY_COSTS, ACCOUNTS, TASK_DESCRIPTIONS, and EMPLOYEES. The data blocks should have the same names as the corresponding tables.

- Five control blocks. These blocks were manually created and have not been named.
- One tab canvas with a default name that displays the EMPLOYEES data block.
- One tab page with a default name.
- One frame object.

In this portion of the Case Project you perform the following tasks:

- Change the manually created data blocks so that they conform to Table 2-10.
- Add SELECT statements to the PROJECT_DATA, WORK_ORDER_DATA, and the WO_INSTRUCTIONS blocks changing them from control blocks to data blocks.
- Create relationships between the master and detail data blocks as follows: relate PROJECT_DATA to WORK_ORDERS and relate WORK_ORDER_DATA to WORK_ORDER_TASKS and to MONTHLY_COSTS. Once the relationships are made, the form is ready for the formatting processes that occur in the next portion of the Case Project.

The budgeting form has several different types of data blocks. Review Table 2-10 to observe the following:

- The PROJECTS, ACCOUNTS, TASK_DESCRIPTIONS, and EMPLOYEES data blocks have their own, individual stacked canvas or tab pages. No other data blocks share their canvas or tab pages. This indicates that these data blocks are displayed independently of any other data block and are not to be associated in master-detail relationships. This is true, because the intent of the PROJECT_ADD stacked canvas is solely to add projects, and the purpose of the ACCOUNTS, TASK_DESCRIPTIONS, and EMPLOYEES tab pages is to maintain descriptive information.
- The remainder of the data blocks are displayed on two different tab pages: PROJECTS and WORK_ORDERS. Each of these tab canvases has a control block and two or more data blocks that are related in master-detail relationships.

The PROJECTS and WORK_ORDERS tab pages will be Directory-style forms, which are very user-friendly (or conceptually clear) and remove some of the complexity of the default Oracle form. This style has a control block for entering search values. The control block is used because the selection values remain visible and can be easily modified for additional queries.

The control block is linked to the master data block using the Copy From properties on data block items. This property causes control block values to be copied into the master block automatically every time a query is launched. Thus, values entered into the control block are used to filter records on the master block. The master blocks on each tab page form have detail blocks that display related child records. The WORK_ORDERS tab pages even have grandchild data blocks. Figure 3-15 illustrates the completed WORK_ORDERS tab page.

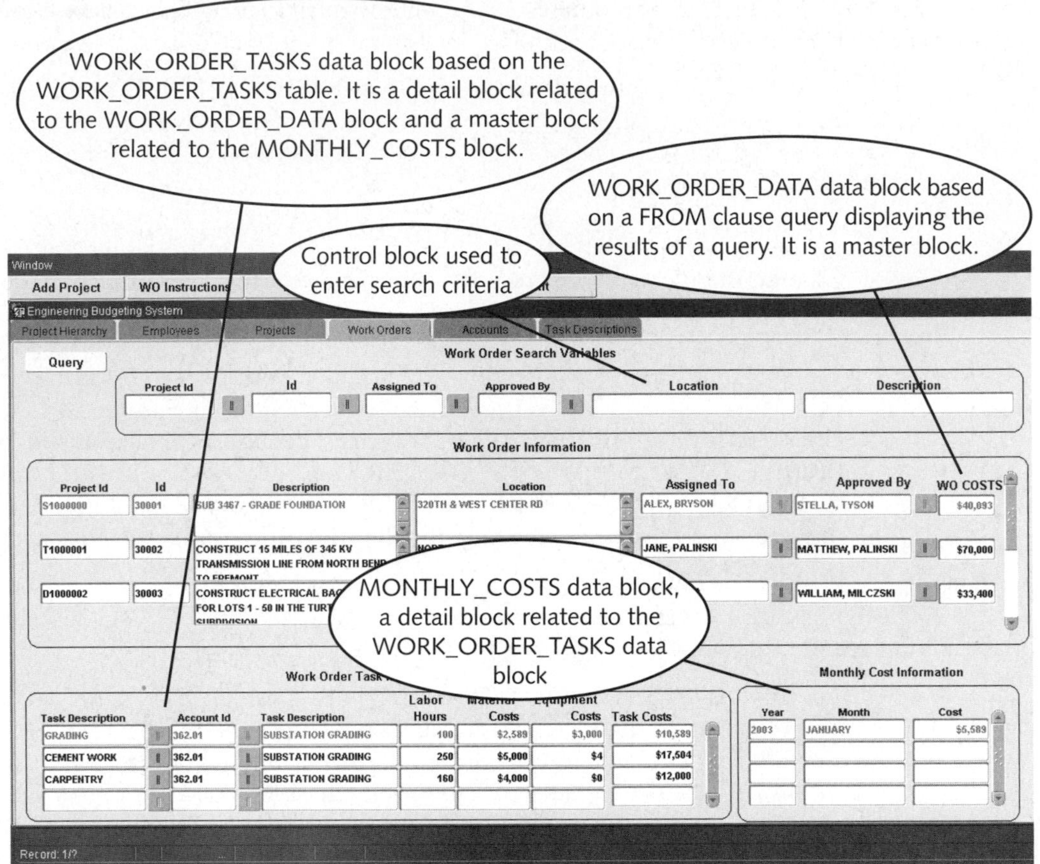

Figure 3-15 Completed WORK_ORDERS tab page illustrating a Directory form

PROJECTS Canvas Characteristics

The PROJECTS canvas master data block (PROJECT_DATA) is based on a FROM clause query. A FROM clause query is used for the PROJECT_DATA data block for two reasons: 1. The PROJECTS table is being used as the data source for the PROJECTS data block that is displayed on the PROJECTS_ADD stacked canvas; and 2. It is not advisable to have two data blocks in the same application using the same table as a data source, because concurrency problems may occur and aggravate the user.

More importantly, the project data master data block records contain information not found in the PROJECTS table. This information consists of the actual employee names and the summarized project estimated costs. This additional information could have been brought into the form by executing SELECT statements against the WORK_ ORDERS and EMPLOYEES tables each time a record is retrieved. However, the

PROJECT_ DATA data block could potentially retrieve a large number of projects, and the performance requirements caused by issuing additional SELECT statements would probably be prohibitive.

In addition, some of the descriptive items will be needed to filter records. For instance, the user may want to see projects above a certain dollar range. You cannot use COSTS as an argument unless it is placed in the SELECT statement. Thus, basing the data block on a complex SELECT statement increases performance requirements and enhances search capabilities. The SELECT statement used in the data block joins the PROJECTS table to the DEPARTMENTS table. This join allows the data block to relate a project to a specific department. The PROJECTS table is also joined to the WORK_ORDERS table. The WORK_ORDERS table is joined to the WORK_ORDER_TASKS table. This allows the project to be related to the various work order cost components. The ERD depicted in Figure 1-13 or the data schema diagram in Figure 1-14 can be used to validate these relationships. Listing 3-2 contains the SELECT statement that should be used in the PROJECTS data query FROM clause property.

3

Listing 3-2 SELECT statement that should be used in the Project_data Query Data Source Name property

```
select projects.project_id, project_name, project_scope,
       project_location, project_need_date,
       projects.assigned_department_id,
       department_name, projects.assigned_to,
       nvl(sum(labor_hours),0) labor_hours,
       sum(nvl(labor_hours,0)*50 + nvl(material_costs,0)
        + nvl(equipment_costs, 0)) total_costs
from projects, departments, work_orders, work_order_tasks
where projects.assigned_department_id = departments.department_id(+)
 and projects.project_id = work_orders.project_id(+)
 and work_orders.work_order_id = work_order_tasks.wo_work_order_id(+)
group by projects.project_id, project_name, project_scope,
       project_location, project_need_date, projects.assigned_department_id,
       department_name, projects.assigned_to
```

The PROJECTS tab page will have one additional data block, which is a detail data block using the WORK_ORDERS table. The users will create their work orders on this data block. Each record in this block will display the estimated work order costs, because the user will want to see how the total project costs are broken down. This value does not exist in the WORK_ORDERS table. The block will have display items that will contain the rolled-up costs. A Post-Query trigger will compute the costs, because performance is not a consideration. The PROJECTS master data block has the potential to display thousands of projects. However, the WORK_ORDERS data block will only display the work orders for the selected project, which is a small number.

The control block on the PROJECTS tab page contains duplicates of the important PROJECT_DATA data block items. These are the items that the user is most likely to employ to filter records. The proper items can be determined from your user interviews during the analysis phase of the SDLC. In this Case Project, the PROJECT_DATA items that should be added to the control block are:

- **PROJECT_ID**: Allows the user to retrieve a specific project and its associated work orders.
- **PROJECT_NAME**: Allows the user to retrieve projects with common name values. This field enables users to locate related projects by common names.
- **PROJECT_LOCATION**: Allows the user to retrieve projects for a specific location. This is another method of identifying common projects.
- **PROJECT_NEED_DATE**: Allows the user to retrieve projects needed within a specific time range. This is a useful search for identifying rush work.
- **DEPARTMENT**: Allows the user to retrieve projects assigned to a specific department.
- **TOTAL_COSTS**: Allows the user to retrieve projects within a specific estimated cost range. This search helps the user identify important projects.

WORK_ORDERS Tab Page Characteristics

The WORK_ORDERS tab page is another Directory-style form. This tab page is used to break down the work order into tasks and prorate the current year's costs over a series of months. The Great State accountants will use these values to determine the needed cash flow. Thus, the form will have a series of master-detail data blocks. The WORK_ORDER_DATA data block using a FROM clause query will be the first (or grandfather) master data block. The WORK_ORDER_TASKS data block will be a detail block to the WORK_ORDER_DATA data block. It will display the tasks for the selected work order. This data block will also be a (parent) master data block for the MONTHLY_COSTS data block.

Listing 3-3 displays the SELECT statement for the WORK_ORDER_DATA data block FROM clause query.

Listing 3-3 SELECT statement to enter into the WORK_ORDER_DATA data block data Query Data Source Name property

```
select project_id, work_order_id, wo_description, wo_location,
       approved_by, assigned_to, wo_instructions,
       nvl(sum(labor_hours),0) labor_hours,
       sum((nvl(labor_hours,0)*50 )+ nvl(material_costs,0)
          + nvl(equipment_costs,0))  total_costs
from work_orders,work_order_tasks
where work_orders.work_order_id = work_order_tasks.wo_work_order_id(+)
group by project_id, work_order_id, wo_description, wo_location,
         approved_by, assigned_to, wo_instructions
```

The control block for this tab page has items similar to those used in the WORK_ORDER_DATA data block. The items will be used to filter the result set displayed by the data block. The following list outlines the control block fields and what they allow the user to do:

- **PROJECT_ID**: Retrieve works orders, work order tasks, and monthly costs for a specific project.
- **WORK_ORDER_ID**: Retrieve a specific work order.
- **WORK_ORDER_DESCRIPTION**: Retrieve work orders based on the description. This is a useful search when the user does not know the project ID or work order ID, and it is also useful in identifying related work orders.
- **WORK_ORDER_LOCATION**: Retrieve work orders based on the location. This is a useful search when the user does not know the project ID or work order ID and is also useful for identifying related work orders.
- **APPROVED_BY**: Retrieve work orders approved by a specific employee.
- **ASSIGNED_TO**: Retrieve work orders assigned to a specific employee. This is a useful search for identifying an employee's work load.
- **TOTAL_COSTS**: Identify work orders within a specific cost range. This is a primary factor in the work order importance.

Your Work

1. Change the name of one of the default control blocks to **PROJ_SEARCH_CRITERIA**. This block will be used on the PROJECTS tab page.
2. Add the search items to the newly named PROJ_SEARCH_CRITERIA control block. These items can be copied from the PROJECTS data block: **PROJECT_ID**, **PROJECT_NAME**, **PROJECT_LOCATION**, **PROJECT_SCOPE**, **PROJECT_NEED_DATE**, **ASSIGNED_DEPARTMENT_ID**, and **ASSIGNED_TO**. After the copy procedure, the Object Navigator should look like Figure 3-16.

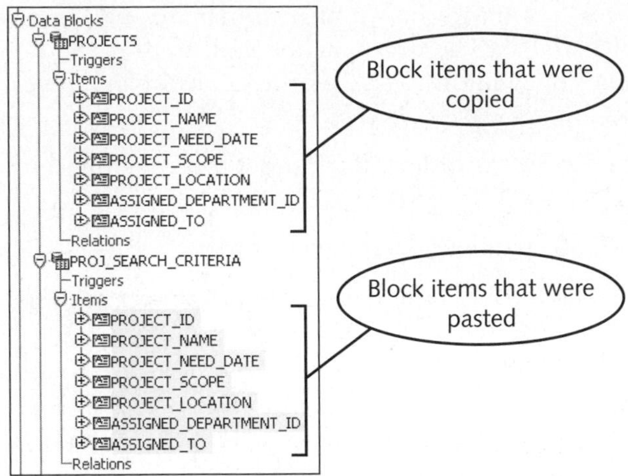

Figure 3-16 Object Navigator after copying items into the PROJ_SEARCH_CRITERIA control block

3. Change the name of one of the default control blocks to **PROJECT_DATA**. This data block will use a FROM query clause as a data source. Use the Listing 3-3 SELECT statement as the data source. To add the SELECT statement, perform the following:
   a. Type the Listing 3-2 SELECT statement into a text editor, such as Notepad or WordPad (or use the supplied data file).
   b. Copy the **SELECT** statement and execute it in SQL*Plus.
   c. Repeat steps a and b until the SELECT statement works.
   d. Select the **PROJECT_DATA** data block in the Object Navigator.
   e. Open the Property Palette for this object by pressing the **F4** key.
   f. Locate the Database Data Block property and set it to **YES**.
   g. Locate the Query Data Source Type property. Open the pick list, and change the property setting to **From clause query**.
   h. Locate the Query Data Source Name property. Open the Query Data Source Name dialog box by clicking the button in the property value text item.
   i. Paste the tested **SELECT** statement into the Query Data Source Name dialog box. Click the **OK** button. Figure 3-17 depicts the Property Palette and the dialog box as they appear before the OK button is clicked.

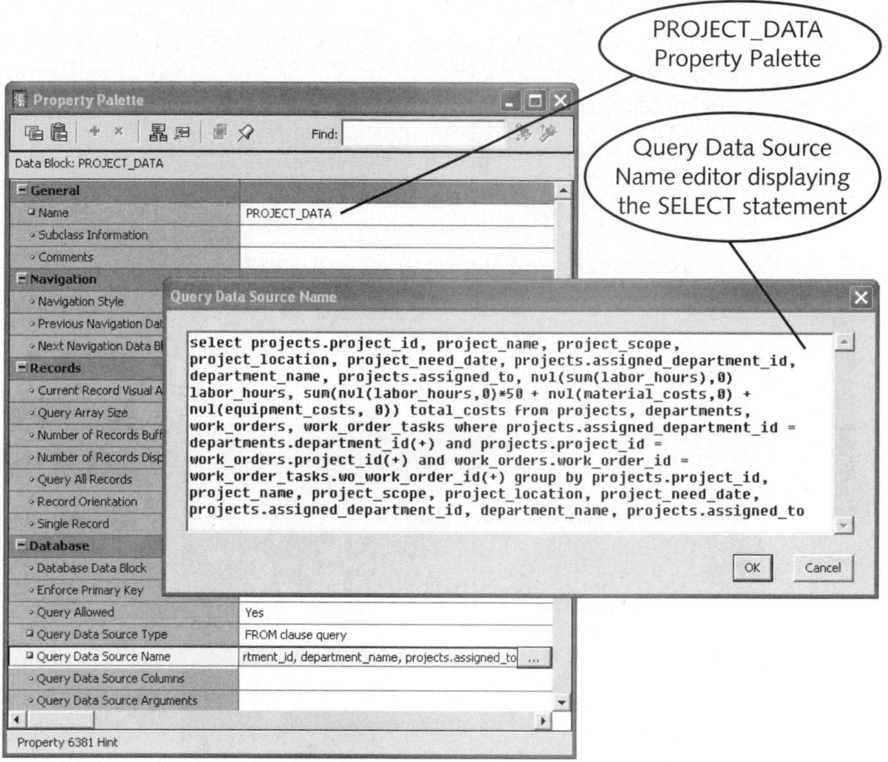

Figure 3-17 Query Data Source Name dialog box after the SELECT statement was pasted in

4. Add items to the PROJECT_DATA data block. Copy all data items in the PROJECTS data block and paste them into the PROJECT_DATA data block.
5. Highlight the **PROJECT_ID** data item in the PROJECT_DATA data block Open the item's Property Palette by pressing the **F4** key and locate the PRIMARY_KEY property. If this property is not set to **YES,** set it. This is necessary because Forms Builder requires one item in a data block to be a primary key.
6. Change the name of one of the remaining default control blocks to **WO_SEARCH_CRITERIA**. This block will be used on the WORK_ORDERS tab page.
7. Add the search items to the WO_SEARCH_CRITERIA control block. These items can be copied from the WORK_ORDERS data block. Select and copy the following items: **PROJECT_ID**, **WORK_ORDER_ID**, **WO_DESCRIPTION**, **WO_LOCATION**, **APPROVED_BY**, and **ASSIGNED_TO**. Paste the copied items into the **WO_SEARCH_CRITERIA** data block.

8. Change the name of another remaining default control block to **WORK_ORDER_DATA**. This data block will be based on a FROM clause query. Use the Listing 3-3 SELECT statement as the data source. To add the SELECT statement, perform the following:
   a. Type the Listing 3-3 SELECT statement into a text editor, such as Notepad or WordPad or use the supplied data file.
   b. Copy the **SELECT** statement and execute it in SQL*Plus.
   c. Repeat the procedure in steps a and b until the SELECT statement works.
   d. Select the **WORK_ORDER_DATA** data block in the Object Navigator.
   e. Open the Property Palette for this object by pressing the **F4** key.
   f. Locate the **Database Data Block** property and set it to **YES**.
   g. Locate the Query Data Source Type property. Open the pick list, and change the property setting to **FROM clause Query**.
   h. Locate the Query Data Source Name property. Open the Query Data Source Name dialog box by clicking the button in the property value text item.
   i. Paste the tested **SELECT** statement into the Query Data Source Name dialog. Click **OK**.
9. Add items to the WORK_ORDER_DATA data block. Copy all the items from the WORK_ORDERS data block, and paste them into the WORK_ORDER_DATA data block.
10. Highlight the **WORK_ORDER_ID** item in the WORK_ORDER_DATA data block. Open the item's Property Palette by double-clicking the icon to the left or pressing **F4**. Locate the Primary Key property and, if it is not already set, set it to **YES**.
11. Change the name of the last default control block to **WO_INSTRUCTIONS**. This data block will also be based on a SELECT statement.
12. To add the SELECT statement, perform the following:
    a. Select the **WO_INSTRUCTIONS** data block in the Object Navigator.
    b. Open the Property Palette for this object by pressing the **F4** key.
    c. Locate the Database Data Block property and set it to **YES**.
    d. Locate the Query Data Source Type property. Open the drop-down list, and change the property setting to **FROM clause query**.
    e. Locate the Query Data Source Name property. Type "**Select * from work_orders**" into the property. Click **OK**.
13. Add the items to the WO_INSTRUCTIONS data block. Copy all of the WORK_ORDERS data block items and paste them into the WO_INSTRUCTIONS data block.

14. Highlight the **WORK_ORDER_ID** item in WO_INSTRUCTIONS. Open the item's Property Palette, and locate the Primary Key property. If it is not set to **YES**, set it.

15. Associate and create a relationship between the PROJECT_DATA and the WORK_ORDERS data blocks. PROJECT_DATA will be the master block and WORK_ORDERS the detail data block. You should use the Data Block Wizard to perform this task. Select the WORK_ORDERS data block in the Object Navigator, and launch the Data Block Wizard. The data blocks are related by common PROJECT_ID values. Initially a column other than PROJECT_ID will probably display. Open the Detail Item drop-down list and select the PROJECT_ID item. This should populate the Master Item text box with the PROJECT_ID and record the proper join condition. Figure 3-18 illustrates the Master-detail page after the two blocks have been related. (Note: you will have to uncheck the Auto-join data blocks check box because the PROJECT_DATA data block is based on a SELECT statement.)

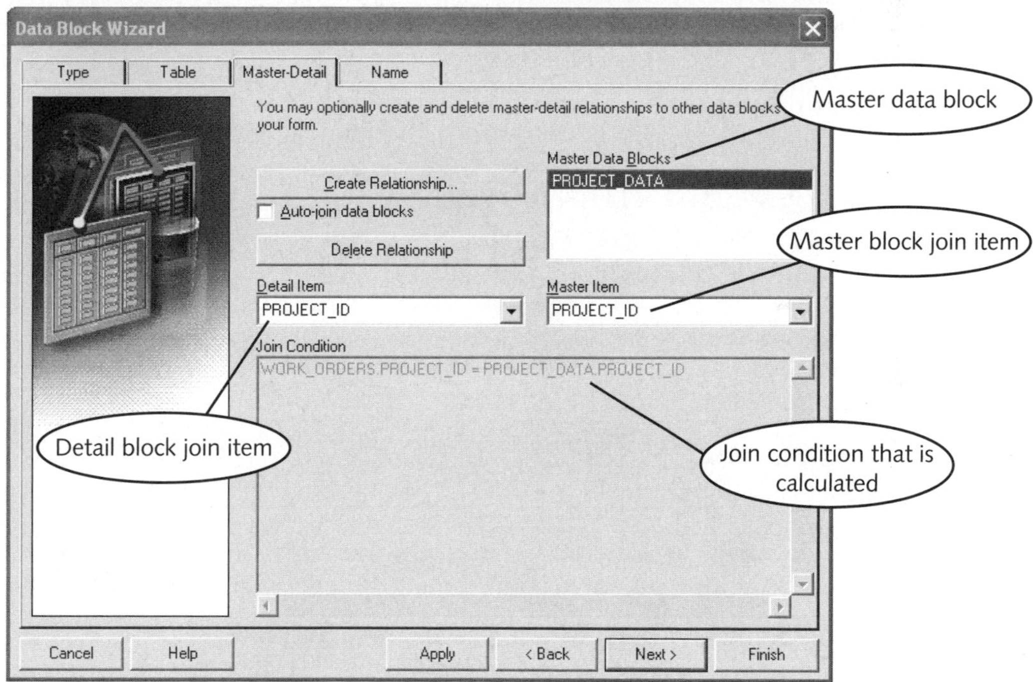

Figure 3-18 Master-Detail wizard page depicting the PROJECT_DATA and WORK_ORDERS data blocks

16. Associate the WORK_ORDER_DATA and the WORK_ORDER_TASKS data blocks. WORK_ORDER_DATA will be the master block and WORK_ORDER_TASKS the detail data block. The data blocks are related by common WORK_ORDER_ID. Select the **WORK_ORDER_TASKS** data block and launch the Data Block Wizard to set the relationship. The data blocks are related by WO_WORK_ORDER_ID and WO_WORK_ORDER_ID.

You must uncheck the Auto-join data blocks check box.

17. Associate and create a relationship between the WORK_ORDER_TASKS and the MONTHLY_COSTS data blocks. WORK_ORDER_TASKS will be the master block and MONTHLY_COSTS the detail data block. Select the **MONTHLY_COSTS** data block and launch the Data Block Wizard. The data blocks are related by common WORK_ORDER_TASK_ID items.
18. Arrange the data blocks in the following order:

    PROJ_SEARCH_CRITERIA

    PROJECT_DATA

    WORK_ORDERS

    WO_SEARCH_CRITERIA

    WORK_ORDER_DATA

    WORK_ORDER_TASKS

    MONTHLY_COSTS

    PROJECTS

    WO_INSTRUCTIONS

    ACCOUNTS

    TASK_DESCRIPTIONS

    EMPLOYEES
19. Execute and operate the form. It should compile without errors. You should be able to view employee information.

CHAPTER

4

FORMATTING THE FORM USING THE LAYOUT EDITOR

In this chapter you will:

- Learn design concepts
- Learn the relationships between the Web browser window, the canvas, and the form window
- Learn about frames and use them to format data block items
- Operate the Layout Editor
- Add and overlay graphic objects
- Learn the purpose of the Format and Layout Editor toolbars
- Learn the purpose of the Layout Editor menu formatting options
- Learn the purpose of the ruler, rule guides, grid, snap-to-grid, and layout options
- Color form components using the fill, line, and text color tools

Looking at the book roadmap in Figure 4-1, you can see that this chapter is about using the Layout Editor, the second major Forms Builder tool, to format the form. Because this chapter focuses on form formatting, it opens with a brief discussion of good form design concepts and then covers how windows and canvases are related. Windows and canvases are used to present the form to the operator, and this chapter describes their properties. Frames are child canvas objects that are used to format data block items, and this chapter describes how to format frame items using frame properties. The Layout Wizard can be used to set various canvas properties and format the data block items. A major portion of the chapter covers the Layout Editor, which is a form-painting tool that allows you to easily design a form layout. This chapter also explains the various tools and options that can be used to change item properties. By the end of this chapter, you should be able to design a well laid-out presentation for your data.

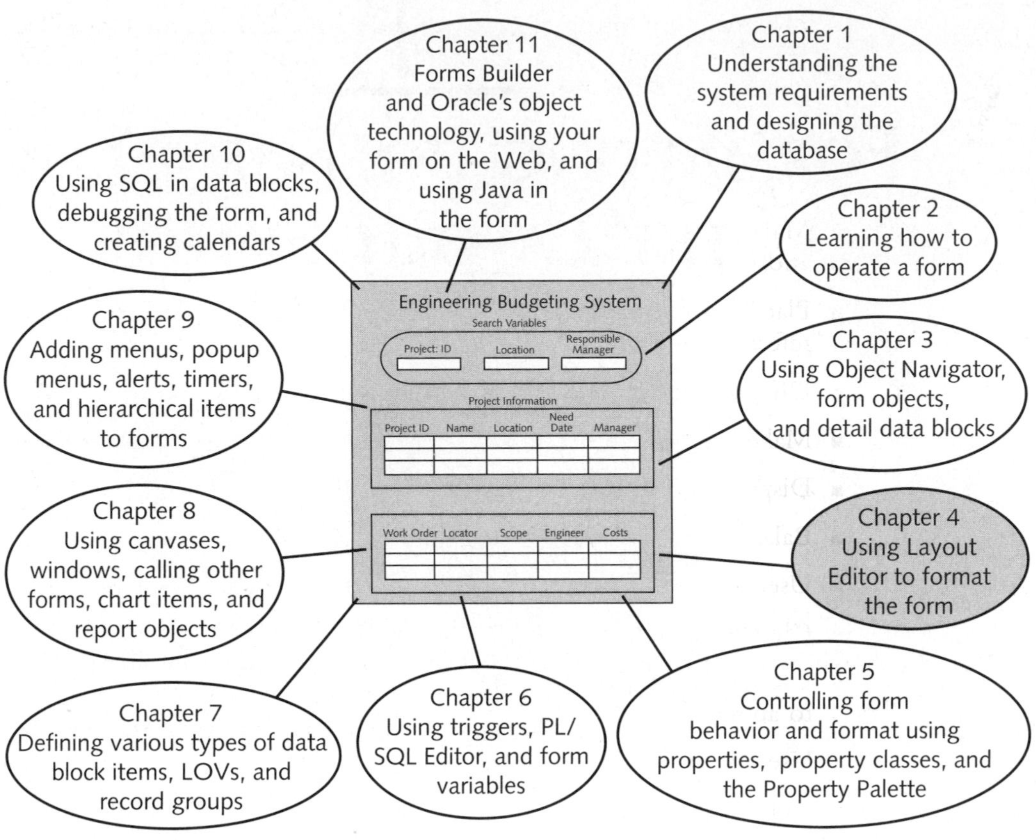

Figure 4-1 Roadmap

Design Concepts

This chapter describes the various form layout tools in the Layout Editor. Before learning how to use these tools, it is important to understand the basics of good design concepts. Concentrate on making your forms clear rather than impressive to the user. The following are some general form guidelines you may want to consider for your form design:

- Give each form a title that describes the purpose of the form. Window objects contain a Delete window property that can be used to set the title that is displayed on the window. It is a good practice to always populate this property with a descriptive form name.
- Provide instructions on how to operate the form. You may even consider placing these instructions on the form using the Layout Editor's Text tool.

- Use zones and boxes to organize the information in the forms. The Layout Editor has frames and graphic tools that can draw rectangles and lines that will help you organize your information.
- Place administrative information at the bottom of the form.
- Organize tabs from left to right within a specific zone.
- Make sure the user understands how to navigate between zones, items, and forms.
- Place a date on your form. Users often capture the form on paper as a reference and will use the date as a timestamp.
- Use section headings, column headings, and labels.
- Make sure your prompt values are the same for a specific item across all forms.
- Display code descriptions rather than the code.
- Balance the placement of the information on the form.
- Use adequate spacing and distance.
- Clearly show where the user is within a process.
- Use highlighting and bold colors sparingly and only to draw the user's attention to appropriate objects, such as errors and warnings.
- Use color to promote an understanding of a display.
- Cool colors such as green or light blue are pleasing to the eye. Hot colors such as red and yellow are not. Try to employ the cooler, calming colors.
- Use mixed case rather than all capitals when possible; it is easier to read.
- Left-justify character values and right-justify numeric data.
- Use double-spacing for text when possible.
- Use at least two spaces between columns.
- Display similar information vertically in multiple columns.

Relationships Between the Web Browser Window, the Canvas, and the Form Window

Data items are placed on a canvas that is displayed by a window. In fact, unless you have a data block on a canvas, the form closes without ever operating. A **canvas** is exactly what its name implies. It is a form object for displaying text items, radio buttons, prompts, rectangles, images, sounds, and a wide variety of other form objects. Just as a painter puts a vision of the world on a canvas, the developer puts his vision of a system interface on the form by using an electronic canvas.

A window is the user's mechanism for looking at the canvas. The function of a form window is similar to the function of a window in your house. When you first look out the window you can see a portion of the world. Part of the world is also obscured because of the size of the window. It's not possible to see the entire world through a window. Even though a canvas has a finite size, the canvas can be larger (or smaller) than the window. When a canvas is larger than the window, the window has scroll bars, so that the user can move the canvas within the window, just as you would look out your window. The difference is that you reposition yourself by walking to a corner of a room or toward the window instead of moving the canvas with a scroll bar.

A form window is not the same as a window displayed on the Windows desktop. It is a window that is displayed inside the Forms Builder runtime engine. Forms Server sends the form to an applet that displays the form window inside the Web browser. The form window operates like any other window, except that it operates inside a Web browser or Forms runtime window if it is a client-server application, as you can see in Figure 4-2. This figure displays two different Oracle form applications, each in its own windows inside the Web browser. Also notice that the Web browser is actually a window displayed by the Windows operating system.

The Oracle form window can be maximized, minimized, moved, or resized. In Figure 4-2, you can see that both of the Oracle form windows are in a different mode. One of the windows is minimized and appears near the bottom of the Web browser. It does not appear at the bottom of the Windows desktop (on the taskbar) as a normal Windows application would. If you minimize the Web browser, a symbol will appear at the bottom of the desktop, but the symbol represents the Web browser, not the Oracle form window. Oracle form applications only appear in a window inside another window.

In addition to the minimized form, Figure 4-2 illustrates a second window that is displayed in its normal size. This window can be resized, moved, and maximized. A maximized window is not shown because it would take all of the space defined within the Web browser for the Oracle applications, and you would not be able to see the minimized and normal windows.

The windows in Oracle Forms and Microsoft Windows operate in the same way. The windows have three modes:

- **Normal**: The window takes up only a portion of the entire Web browser space.
- **Maximized**: The window takes up the entire available space.
- **Minimized**: The window is not displayed, but a minimized symbol appears.

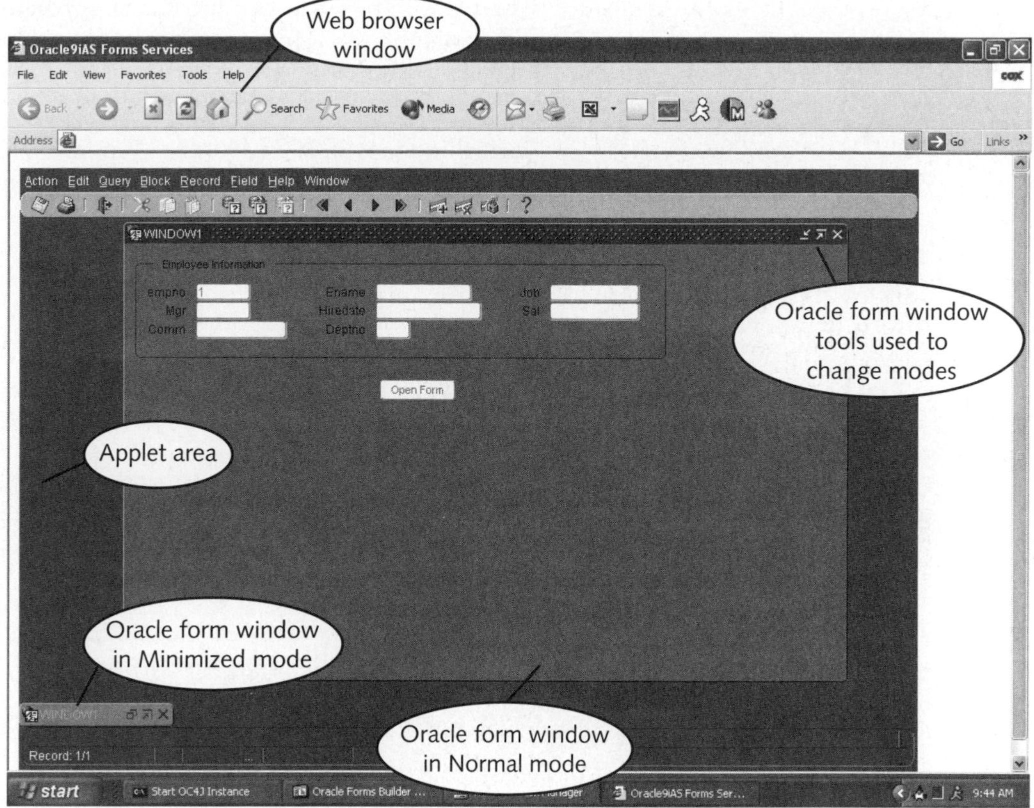

Figure 4-2 Displaying minimized and normal sized Oracle form windows in a maximized Web browser window

By default, the Web browser window and the Oracle form window in the Web browser are displayed in the Normal mode. This means that the Oracle form window takes up a portion of the Web browser. The window can be maximized to display more of the canvas. However, the maximization must be done manually or programmatically. The following are some window characteristics that result from sizing the different windows:

- Maximizing the Web browser causes more space to be displayed within the browser window, but it does not increase the size of the form window. The form window simply occupies a smaller portion of the browser.
- Maximizing the form window takes up all of the allotted space in the Web browser window. If the canvas is larger than the Web browser window, the browser window does not display all of the canvas.

- If the canvas is smaller than the Web browser window in either the Normal mode or Maximized mode, maximizing the Form window causes the entire Web browser window to be covered by the canvas. Boilerplate or data items are not enlarged. Blank canvas areas are displayed in the window.
- If the form window in Normal mode is smaller than the Web browser window, the browser window displays blank space. This is very common for newly created applications.

Figures 4-3 through Figure 4-5 illustrate the Web browser and Oracle form windows in various combinations of Normal and Maximized modes.

- Figure 4-3 illustrates the Web browser and an Oracle form in Normal mode, a mode in which the windows can be moved around and resized, and the window does not cover the underlying object.

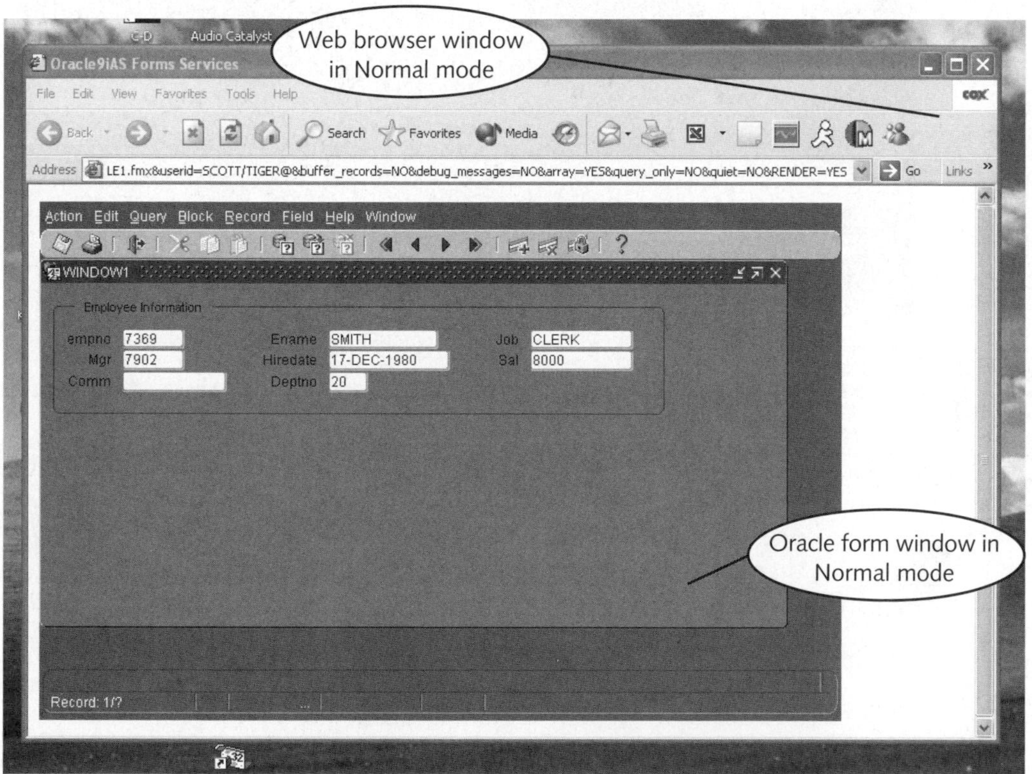

Figure 4-3 Web browser window and a form window in Normal mode

- Figure 4-4 illustrates the Web browser in the maximized mode and Oracle form in the Normal mode. Notice that the Web browser takes up the entire screen. You cannot see the Windows desktop, and the Web browser window cannot be moved or resized. The Oracle form, however, is in the Normal mode. It can be moved and resized within the Web browser.

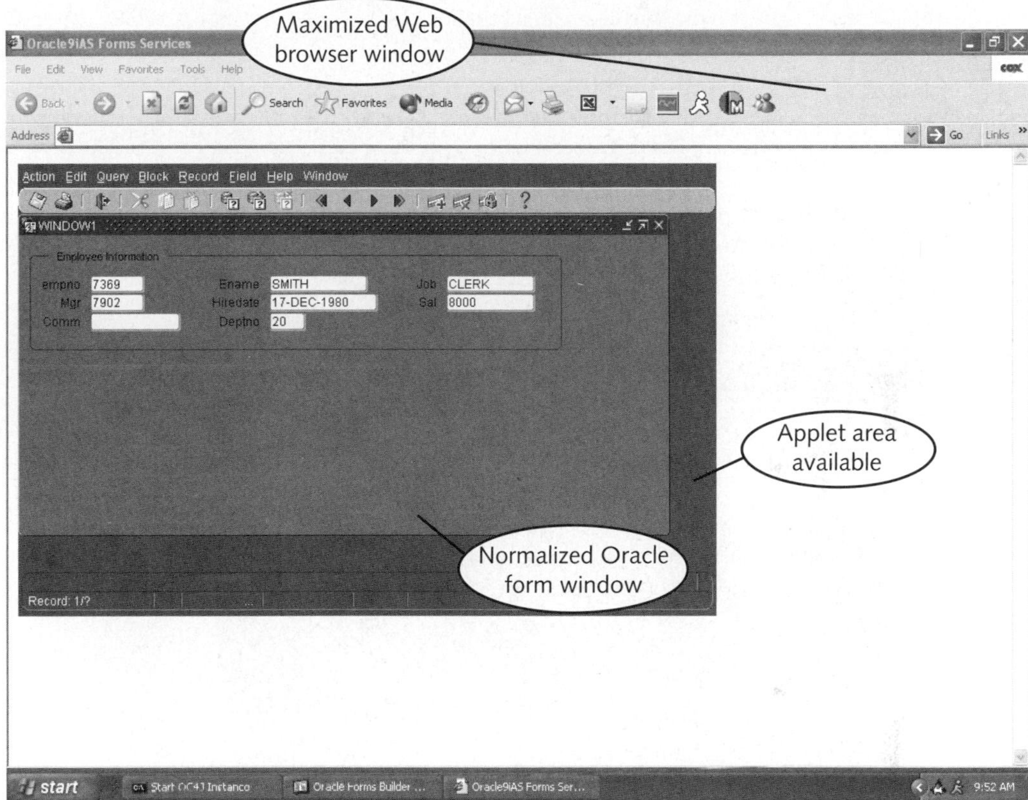

Figure 4-4 Web browser window in Maximized mode and a form window in Normal mode

- Figure 4-5 illustrates both the Web browser and form windows in the Maximized mode. The Web browser window covers the entire screen, and the form window covers the entire Web browser window. Neither window can be moved or resized unless they are placed in the Normal mode.

One of your first tasks as a developer is to determine the amount of space that is available within the Web browser window when it is maximized. This depends somewhat on the screen resolution. The higher the resolution, the more space available. You must determine the normal resolution of your target users' screens to determine the size of the Web browser window. The Web browser window is sized by trial and error as follows:

1. Create a window and canvas of a specific height and width. (Setting the height and width will be discussed shortly.)
2. Execute the form.

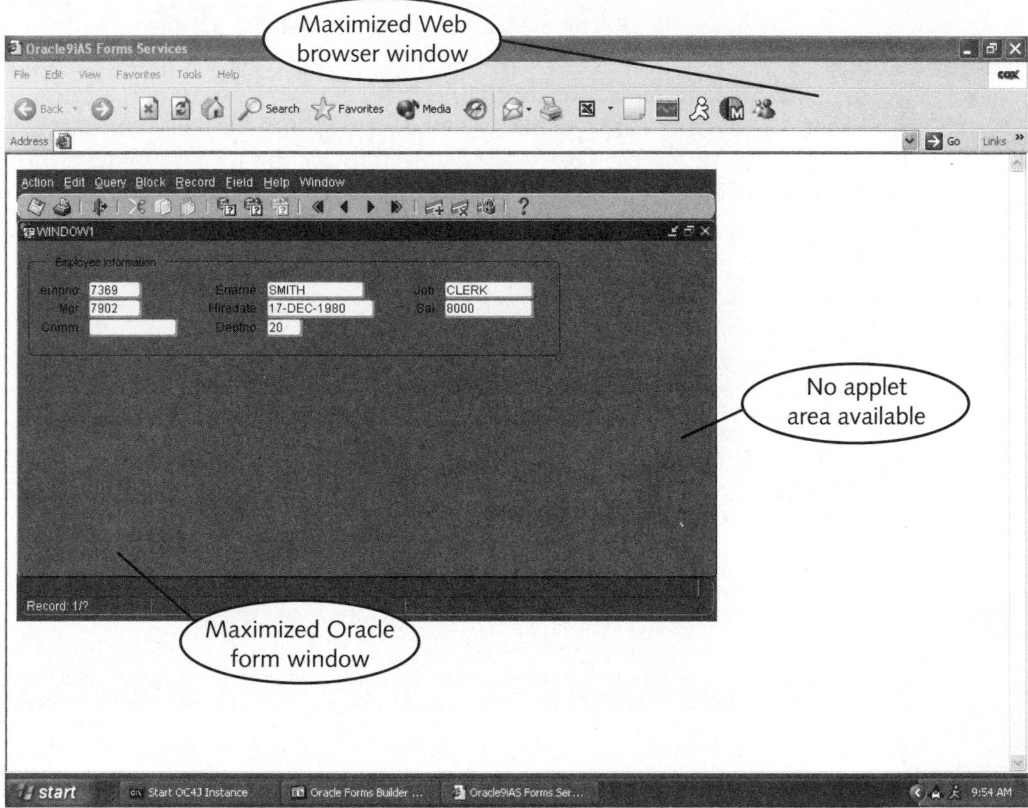

Figure 4-5 Web browser window and a form window in Maximized mode

3. Maximize the Web browser window and the Oracle form window within the Web browser. If the canvas covers the entire form window and scroll bars appear in the window, the canvas is too large. If the canvas does not fill the entire window, it is too small. If either of these conditions is true, repeat Step 1 with different settings. If the canvas appears within the form window without any window scroll bars, the height and width of the canvas is the maximum size you have available. Remember these size guidelines for use in future forms.

You should perform the same procedure for the Web browser in the Normal mode. When this is done, you will know how much canvas real estate you have available within the window. If your form does not have a large number of displayed data block items, graphics, and boilerplate, you can choose to initially display your form and the Web browser in the Normal mode leaving a portion of the desktop open to your view. If you have a large number of objects, you may need to use the entire screen. In this case, you must maximize the form and Web browser windows. You have a variety of options from which to choose, but you cannot begin designing the form until you know the height and width values for the Normal and Maximized window modes.

There are two other settings that control how much of the form can be seen in the Web browser. Figure 4-6 illustrates these settings. The Web browser is maximized in the figure. Notice that only a portion of the Web browser window is occupied by the form. The applet that displays the form determines the area occupied. This area cannot be resized. The size must be set before the Web browser displays the Oracle applet that displays the form. The height and width of this area is set in the **formsweb.cfg** file. This file is used by the applet sent by the Form Server to control the area within the browser that can be used by the form. It is best to set the **formsweb.cfg** height and width settings to cover the maximized size of the Web browser window.

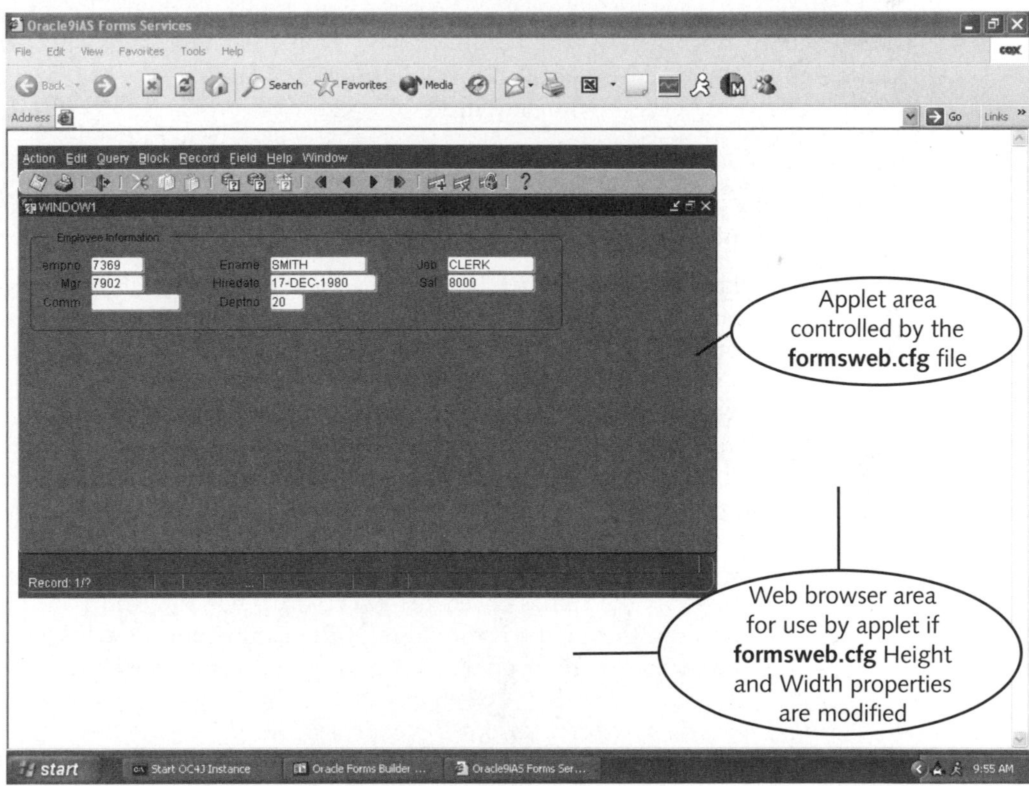

Figure 4-6 Maximized Web browser window illustrating the size of the applet area

To reiterate, when designing the form, you must identify and set the following:

- Determine the height and width of the canvas.
- Set the height and width of the window to the size you have determined.
- Identify the height and width of the form window when it is displayed in the Normal mode. If the canvas is larger than this size, your form must be displayed in the Maximized mode. It is poor design to force a user to maximize a new window to see the form contents. If the canvas is larger than the Normal mode form window, it should be maximized when the form is opened. This can be done with the Set_window_property built-in.
- Set the **formweb.cfg** height and width settings to be equal to or larger than the size of the canvas and form window.

The original form canvas and window created by the Layout Wizard is probably smaller than the Web browser window. Forms Builder bases the canvas Height and Width properties on the number of data items it places on the canvas. This probably doesn't match the way you want the canvas to be displayed in the form window. To get the form canvas and window to cover the entire Web browser, you must set their Height and Width properties. The form canvas and form window each has independent size properties, because Forms Builder does not force the developer to make them the same size, even though the Layout Wizard originally makes the sizes the same.

The canvas and form window Height and Width properties can be set two ways:

1. Open a property palette (discussed in detail in the next chapter) for the Canvas and Window objects. Locate and modify the Height and Width properties.
2. Open the Layout Editor (see Figure 4-7), click and hold the bottom-right corner of the canvas or view, and drag to the proper size. The view is a rectangle that represents the window to which the canvas is assigned. Changing the view changes the Width and Height properties of the window.

Object libraries contain reusable form components. After you determine the height and width of the canvas and window, these objects can be brought into an object library and reused on other forms. This enables you to avoid the task of sizing canvases and windows. This topic will be covered in greater depth in Chapter 5.

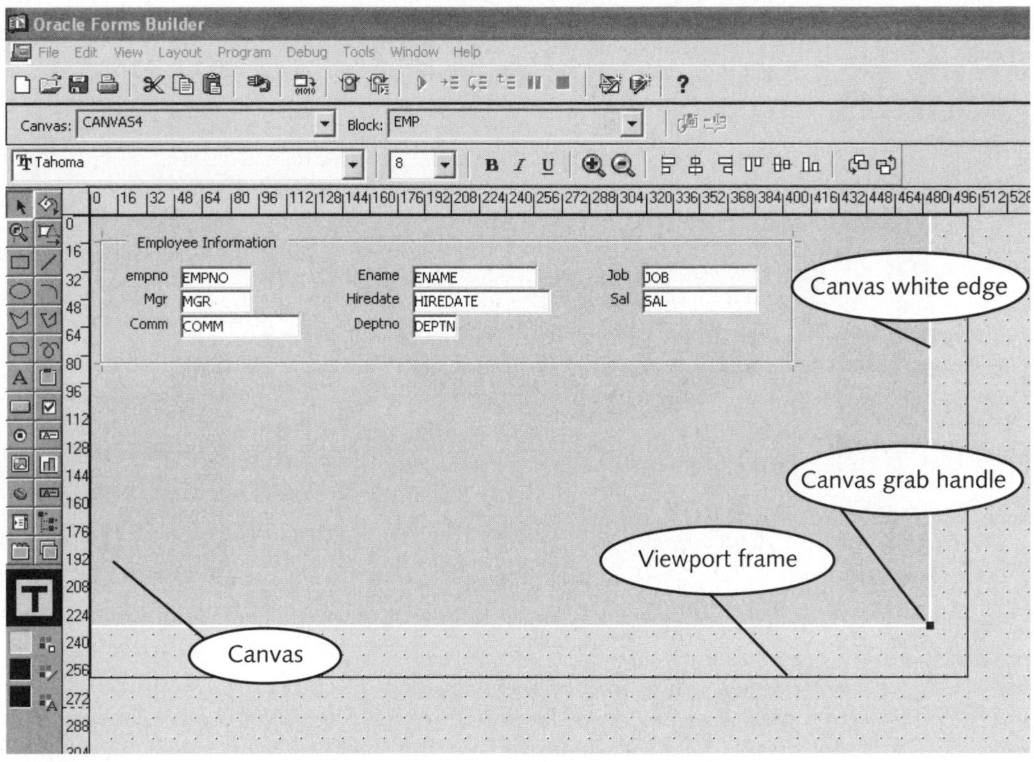

Figure 4-7 Layout Editor displaying a canvas and a view

4

USING FRAMES TO FORMAT DATA BLOCK ITEMS

A **frame** is a canvas child object that can be used to format a data block's items. It is depicted on the canvas as a rectangular box surrounding a data block's items. The shape of the frame determines the positioning of the items in the frame. You can change the position of the items by clicking or selecting the frame and dragging it. Because a frame is an object, it is has a legion of formatting properties, including the following:

- Text or boilerplate displayed within the frame
- Color and width of the frame
- Foreground and background colors of the items within the frame
- Distance Between Records that controls the space between the arrangement
- Layout Style (Form or Tabular) that controls the arrangement of the block's items
- Top Prompt Alignment that aligns prompts displayed above the item
- Number Of Records Displayed that controls the number of records appearing within the frame

Figure 4-8 illustrates a data block based on the EMP table (one of your practice tables). A default frame with grab handles surrounds the data block items. The **grab handles** can be used to change the size of the frame causing the layout of the items in the data block to change.

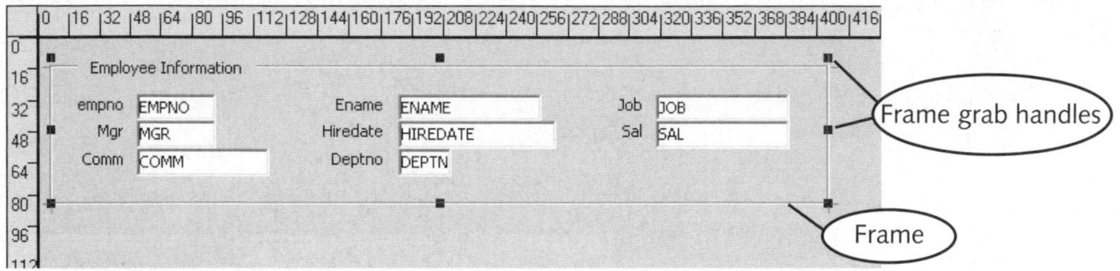

Figure 4-8 Default frame and frame grab handles in Layout Editor

You can create frames using the Layout Wizard or the Frame tool in the Layout Editor, but you use the Property Palette to change the frame properties. Appendix B contains descriptions of the various frame properties, and you should review the list. The properties offer a number of options for formatting the data items. There are two benefits to using the frame properties to format data block items:

- Setting a frame property ensures that all common components have the same format. For instance, the Start Prompt Alignment option ensures that all item prompts begin in the same location. This is very difficult to achieve by setting each item separately.
- A great deal of formatting work can be avoided by using frame properties rather than dragging or formatting each frame object.

Frames have two properties that can cause some consternation to the new developer. The Shrinkwrap property causes frame objects to collapse into the smallest area. If you try to modify the layout, Forms Builder does not accept the changes and continues to collapse the objects. Setting the property to NO prevents this from happening.

A second property that can be troublesome is the Update Layout property. It determines when the frame objects are updated. The Update Layout property offers three options: AUTOMATICALLY, MANUALLY, and LOCKED. The default property, AUTOMATICALLY, causes the frame to accept the changes immediately. The second option is MANUALLY. This property causes Forms Builder to delay the modification until the Update Layout tool in the Layout Editor toolbar is clicked. The last option is LOCKED. This option prevents the frame layout from changing as a result of setting a frame property.

Figure 4-9 illustrates the EMP data block shown in Figure 4-8. Notice the difference caused by changing the frame properties:

- **Frame Alignment**: Changed from Column to Start
- **Vertical Margin**: Changed from 14 to 60
- **Start Prompt Offset**: Changed from 7 to 60

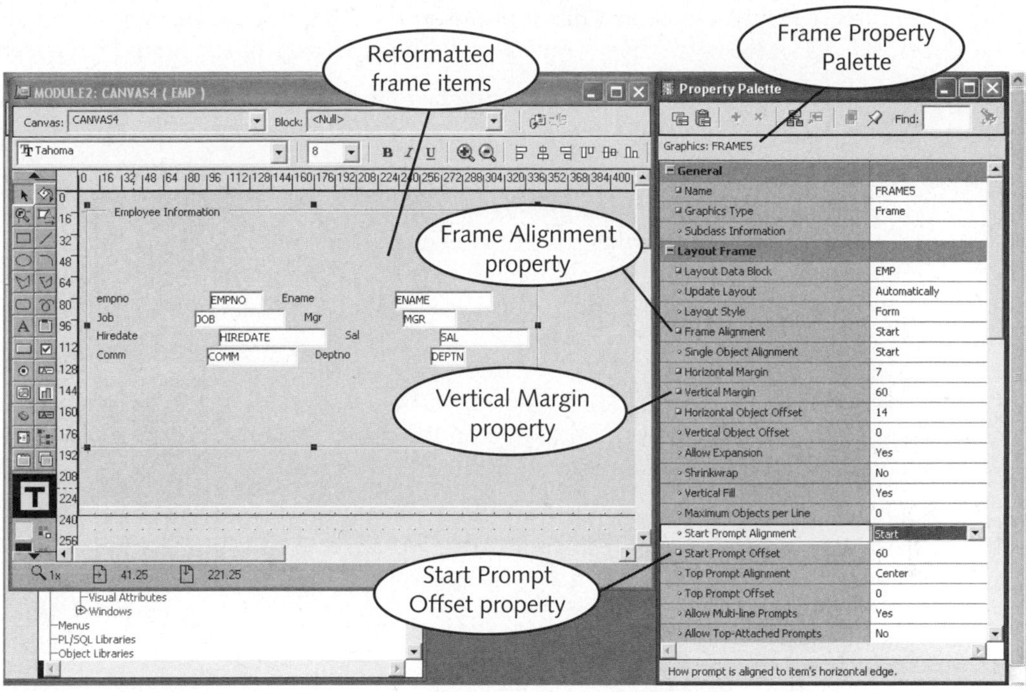

Figure 4-9 Data items depicted in Figure 4-8 after resetting frame properties

It is not mandatory to enclose a data block's items with a frame. Many developers simply delete the frame object, because the Shrinkwrap property can be a problem. However, a frame can facilitate setting prompts and other item properties, especially if the data items have common formats. Frames can save you formatting time by automatically formatting all of the data block items at one time. This is especially true for prompts. It can be very time consuming to move the prompts manually. After setting the frame properties, you should set the Update Layout property to Locked. This prevents inadvertent changes from occurring. You can also delete the frame object at this time; however, if you do, you can no longer use the frame properties to update the data block items. Setting the Update Layout property is your best option.

To practice working with a frame, perform the following steps:

1. Open the Object Navigator and create a new form module.
2. Add a data block to the form using the Data Block Wizard and the Layout Wizard. The data block should have the following settings:

   Table: EMP

   Style: FORM

   Frame Title: Employee Information

3. Open the Layout Editor by pressing the **F2** key. Notice the frame around the data items.
4. If the frame has grab handles, click anywhere within the form to deselect the frame. The grab handles disappear when the frame is not selected.
5. The frame should have greater width than height. Click an edge of the frame causing the grab handles to appear. Place your insertion point over the grab handle at the bottom-right corner of the frame. Hold the Left Mouse button down and drag the grab handle down to the left so that the height is greater than the width. Notice that all of the enclosed data items shift.
6. Select a frame grab handle and return the frame to its original size.
7. Place your insertion point over a frame edge. Hold the Left Mouse button down and drag the frame to another location on the canvas without resizing the frame. Notice that all of the items are moved along with the frame.
8. Open the Object Navigator and expand the Canvas object to locate the Frame object. Select the **Frame object** and press the **F4** key to open its Property Palette.
9. Locate the following properties and reset their values:

   Frame Alignment: Change from Column to **Start**.

   Vertical Margin: Change from 10 to **60**.

   Start Prompt Offset: Change from 7 to **60**.
10. Open the Layout Editor by pressing the **F2** key. Notice the effect of the property changes.
11. Open the Property Palette for the frame and modify other properties to see the effect.
12. Save the form for later practice.

OPERATING THE LAYOUT EDITOR

The Layout Editor is one of Forms Builder's main design tools. It displays canvases, form window views, data block items, boilerplate, and graphics in a special painting environment. This environment allows you to graphically create and set the properties of all displayed objects through the Layout Editor rather than in the Property Palette. It is important to remember that whenever you perform a procedure in the Layout Editor, you are actually setting a property. You can also accomplish the same formatting by opening each item's Property Palette. However, this is time consuming, and the Layout Editor is far more effective at setting formatting properties than manually changing each individual property. There may be times, though, when it is preferable to set an item property on the Property Palette rather than on the Layout Editor.

The Layout Editor makes it possible to drag items and text into position, add data items, set font characteristics, arrange and size items, and set colors. The Layout Editor can be launched in three ways:

- Double-click the left icon of any Object Navigator graphic item.
- Press the F2 key.
- Select the Tools/Layout Editor menu selection.

Layout Editor Components

The Layout Editor has a number of components. The first of these is the work area (see Figure 4-10) where the formatting occurs. At the base of the work area is an underlying **grid**. The grid consists of a series of equally spaced points that can be used as a guide in arranging items. The grid covers the entire work area. Grids will be discussed in more detail later in this chapter.

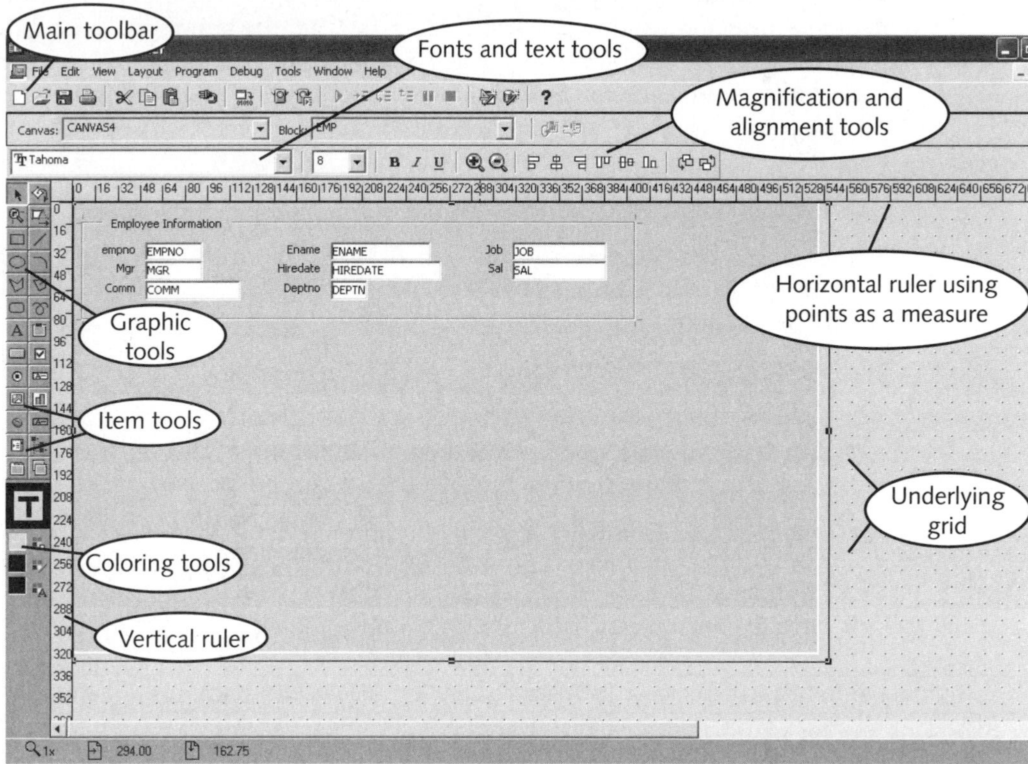

Figure 4-10 Layout Editor

The canvas is displayed above the grid. Initially the canvas is a gray rectangle with white borders on the left and bottom edges. Displayed objects such as boilerplate text and data items are displayed on top of the canvas. Form items can only be placed on the canvas, so if they are placed in the work area outside the canvas, the form does not compile. The last work area component is the view. A **view** represents the window in relationship to the canvas.

On the left side of the Layout Editor is the tool palette. The palette contains tools for adding graphic features such as rectangles, text, data items, buttons, images, and sounds. The tool palette also has three tools for coloring form objects. At the top of the Layout Editor is a toolbar used to set font characteristics, arrange selected items, and layer graphic items. Above this toolbar is another toolbar with standard tools for saving and opening files and a pull-down menu with additional options. Together, the work area, tool palette, toolbars, and menu offer you a wide variety of tools to format your forms.

Sizing the Canvas and Window

It is possible to size the canvas and window directly in the Layout Editor rather than entering height and width property values. A view represents the area of the window. When the canvas and window are first created, they are the same size. The top-left corner of both the canvas and view are located in the top-left corner of the work area at position 0,0. The default canvas and view sizes will probably not suit your design, and you will have to resize the view and canvas.

Before you can resize the canvas, you should select and resize the view. Because the view overlays the canvas edge, you cannot select the canvas until you increase the size of the view.

Both the canvas and window can be resized by grabbing their bottom-right corners. Looking at the Layout Editor, the view is a thin black frame that has no fill. To change the view (or window) size:

1. Select the view by clicking any portion of the black frame (see Figure 4-7). Grab handles appear when the view frame is selected.
2. Place the insertion point over a grab handle, hold the Left Mouse button down, and drag the view frame.

The middle view grab handles only allow you to resize the frame horizontally or vertically. The corner grab handles allow you to resize both horizontally and vertically.

Canvases are identified by the white right and bottom edges. To change the canvas size you would follow these steps:

1. Select the canvas by clicking any portion of the white frame. One grab handle appears at the lower-right corner of the canvas (see Figure 4-7).
2. Place the insertion point over the grab handle, hold the left mouse button down, and drag the handle.

As practice, perform the following steps to open the previous practice form module and resize the canvas and view:

1. Open the form module in the Object Navigator.
2. Run the form and notice the size of the window and the canvas. Close the form.
3. Open the Layout Editor by pressing the **F2** key.
4. Select the Viewport frame. This may require several tries. When drag handles appear, drag the Viewport frame away from the canvas.
5. Select the canvas by clicking the bottom-right corner. A black grab handle appears. Grab this handle and resize the canvas. Be sure to make the canvas smaller than the view frame.
6. Run the form and see if the canvas and window sizes have changed.
7. Repeat steps 5 and 6. This time make the canvas bigger than the view.
8. Save the form for later practice.

Moving, Arranging, and Sizing Items

Any item on the canvas can be moved to another location by selecting the object and dragging it to the new location. Text and display items actually consist of two components: the prompt and the item. When you move an item, the prompt is moved along with it. The prompt retains the same relative position to the item after it is moved. This makes sense because moving the item does not modify the item's prompt position properties. The prompt can be repositioned by selecting the prompt and dragging it to the new location. Repositioning the prompt changes the item's prompt offset properties but not the item's position property. Thus, as the item is moved around the canvas, the prompt retains the same position relative to the item.

Multiple items can be selected by holding down the Shift key while selecting items. It is then possible to move the entire set of selected items. It is also possible to micro-move selected items by using the arrow keys. When small changes are needed, you will find these keys easier to use than dragging with a mouse.

A good form design concept is to align the left edge of the form items. It is also preferable to right-justify the prompts for these items. Figure 4-11 illustrates this type of design.

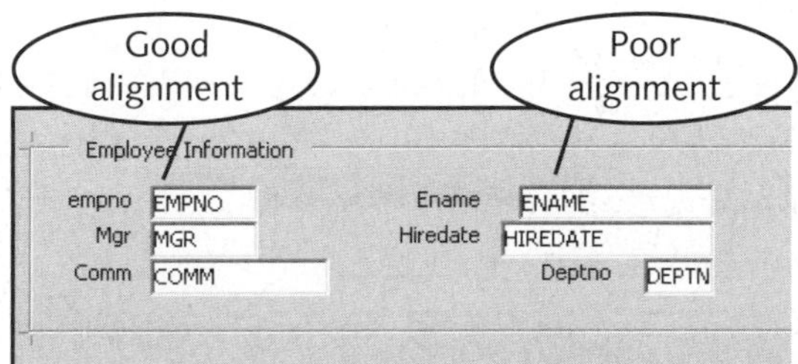

Figure 4-11 Aligned text items and prompts

Forms Builder has two excellent tools for aligning selected items. These are the alignment tools on the Layout Editor toolbar and the Layout/Align Components menu selection discussed in the following sections.

Alignment Toolbar

The Layout Editor toolbar has six alignment tools, which are used to align two or more selected items including their prompts. Figure 4-12 illustrates the tools, which are described as follows:

- **Align Left**: Aligns the left edge of all selected items. This is a common alignment for text items.
- **Align Center horizontally**: Determines the horizontal middle point of all selected items and aligns the selected items to this point.
- **Align Right**: Aligns the right edge of all selected items. This is a common alignment for prompts.
- **Align Top**: Aligns the top edge of all selected items. This tool is commonly used to align items on a row.
- **Align Center vertically**: Determines the vertical middle point of all selected items and aligns the items to this point. If the selected items are in a columnar layout, all the items are moved to one point.
- **Align Bottom**: Aligns the bottom edge of all selected items. This tool is also commonly used to align items on a row.

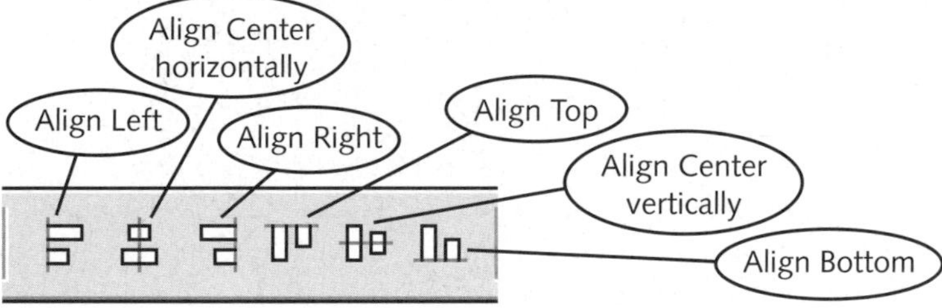

Figure 4-12 Alignment tools

The following list presents a formatting sequence for using the tools of the toolbar. These steps are used for data blocks in a Form style. The data items are initially laid out in multiple columns. The initial practice form layout is a good example of this placement:

1. Use the drag method to roughly align all items.
2. Select all of the items in the left-most column. Align the left edges using the Align Left tool.
3. Select all of the prompts for the column items that are furthest to the left. Align the right edges using the Align Right tool. This right-justifies the column prompts that are furthest to the left.

4. Select all of the items in the top row. Use either the Align Top or Align Bottom tool to align the row.
5. Repeat Step 4 for each row.
6. Repeat steps 2 and 3 for each column of items.
7. Micro-adjust any items using the arrow keys.

Items can be selected *en masse* by using the Selection tool on the left toolbar. Place the insertion point at one corner of the target items. Hold the left mouse button and drag the insertion point to the opposite corner. A box appears in the Layout Editor. When you release the mouse button, all items in this box are selected. You can then select additional items by holding down the Shift key and clicking the items. You can also deselect items by holding down the Shift key and clicking selected items.

As practice, format the form that you used in the previous practice session by performing the following steps:

1. Open the Layout Editor for the practice form.
2. Resize the frame so that the EMP data block items are listed in two columns.
3. Select one of the items and drag to another location. Move it back to its previous location. Notice that the prompt stays in its position relative to the item.
4. Select one of the prompts and drag it to the left of the item. Notice that the item stays in its original location.
5. Select multiple items and move them around the canvas returning them to their original location.
6. Use the formatting sequence described previously to align all of the items.
7. Save the form for later practice.

The Layout /Align Components Menu Option

Selecting the Layout/Align Components menu option launches the Align Objects dialog box shown in Figure 4-13. This dialog box has the same alignment settings as the toolbar, plus several additional settings. The dialog box has additional settings used to distribute or stack the selected items both vertically and horizontally.

The Distribute option evenly spaces the selected objects. For example, if five items are selected and the Horizontally Distribute option is selected, Forms Builder shifts the items so that equal space is placed between each object. The two end items remain in the same place, but the inner three are moved. The same thing happens if the Vertically Distribute option is selected. The difference is that the end items will be the top-most and bottom-most items. You should be aware that it makes no difference for the tool if the items are on a single row or column, because the tool looks at all selected items and arranges them.

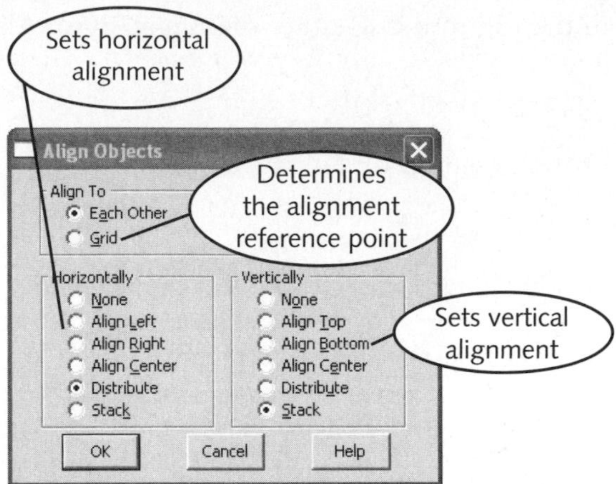

Figure 4-13 Align Objects dialog box

The Stack option places the items adjacent to each other. It shifts all of the selected items together until they are aligned with no space between them. The Horizontally Stack option causes the right or left item edges to abut, and the Vertically Stack option causes the top or bottom edges to abut. Figure 4-14 illustrates the use of several different alignments of the same items:

- Horizontal left align/vertical distribute
- Horizontal left align/vertical stack
- Horizontal right align/vertical stack
- Horizontal stack/vertical bottom align
- Horizontal distribute/vertical bottom align

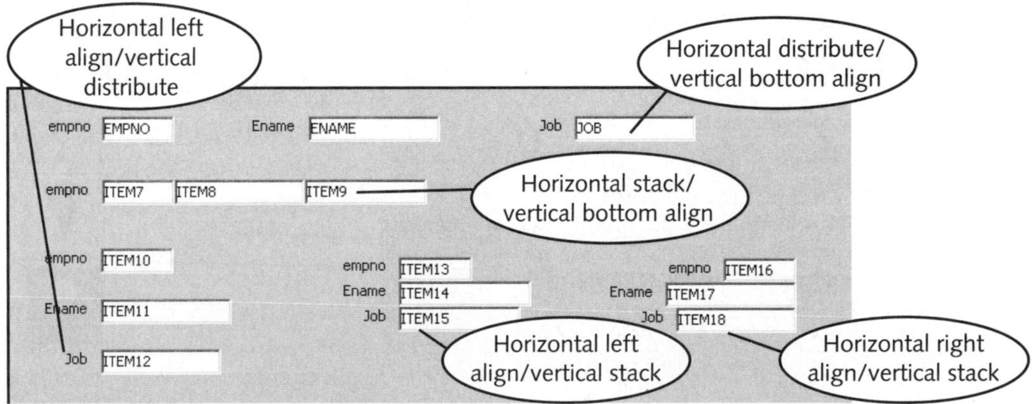

Figure 4-14 Various alignments

The Align Objects dialog box has three groupings of radio button settings. The horizontal and vertical settings are evident, but the Align To settings may not be. The Align To setting controls the overall alignment. You can align the objects to each other, which is the default and preferred method, or you can align the selected items to the grid points that underlie the work area. You can also choose to align the objects to the nearest grid point. If you select the Horizontally Distribute option using the Align To grid setting, the end points jump to the nearest grid point and then distribute the items. This option is a throwback to character-based development and isn't used much anymore.

It is common to have an extra item selected or to select the wrong option. When this occurs, the object aligns far differently than you expect. To avoid the frustration of trying to realign items, click the Edit/Undo menu item or press the Control+Z keys. Forms Builder reverts to the previous layout. This is one of the few places in Forms Builder that you can undo a task.

Sizing Items

Sizing objects in the Layout Editor is easy. Selecting the item causes grab handles to appear around the item, which you can select and drag to change the size of the object. This technique works very well when changing the width of an item. If a text item is a little wider than it should be, no one will notice. However, your users will notice that the height of an item is not the same as other form items, even if it is only one point size different. Unless there is a special reason for a difference, you should ensure that all text items are the same height. For this reason, it is preferable to use a method other than dragging for changing the height. It is much better to use the Size Objects dialog box (see Figure 4-15).

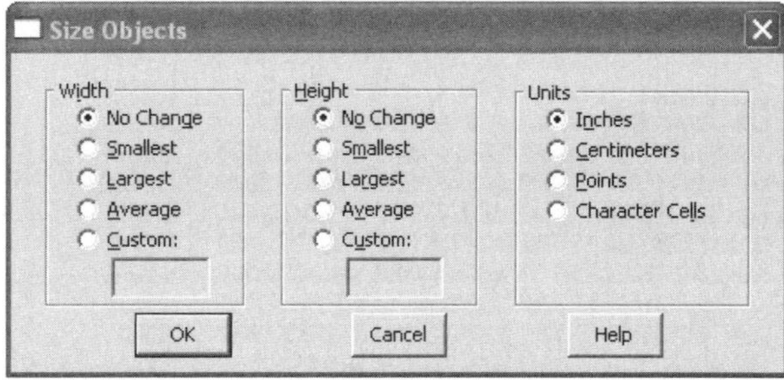

Figure 4-15 Size Objects dialog box

The Size Objects dialog box is similar to the Align Objects dialog box in that it contains three groups of radio button options: Width, Height, and Units. Width and Height each have five radio buttons that perform the following functions:

- **No Change**: Does not modify the width or height.
- **Smallest**: Sets the width or height equal to the smallest selected item.
- **Largest**: Sets the width or height equal to the largest selected item.

- **Average**: Sets the average height or width of all selected items to the average of the items.
- **Custom**: Allows you to set the value. Selecting this option activates the text box in each of the groups. You can then enter a custom value. This value is based on the Units Selected option. Setting a value of 1 using the inches unit sets the items equal to one inch.

The third group of radio button options is Units. Units control the overall width and height settings you have chosen for your text boxes. You can choose inches, centimeters, points, or character cells. Points are the number of resolution points on the screen. The greater the resolution, the more points seen. A character cell is a unit of measure used primarily in character-based mainframe applications. When using character cells, a form consists of a specific number of cells, generally 24 rows of 80 cells. Each character on the form must fall into one of the cells. This unit is not a recommended unit of measure.

Whether you use inches, centimeters, points, or character cells, Forms Builder translates the property setting to points, which is the default setting.

As practice, perform the following steps:

1. Open the practice form you have been using in this chapter.
2. Open the Layout Editor and select the **MGR** and **JOB** items.
3. Select the **Layout/Size Components** menu selection, which opens the Size Objects dialog box.
4. Click the **Width/Largest** radio button.
5. Click **OK**. This causes the MGR and JOB items to have the same width.
6. Save the form for later practice.

Selecting and Grouping Objects

As you format and arrange objects and items on the canvas, you will continually select the items using several methods as follows:

- Place the insertion point over the object and click the left mouse button.
- Hold the Shift key while selecting additional objects.
- Use the Selection tool to create a box around a set of objects.
- Use the Edit/Select All tool to select all Layout Editor objects.

Regardless of the technique that you employ, as soon as you select another object without holding down the Shift key, all previously selected objects are deselected. This may be an accident or, more likely, you want to work on other objects. As you work on a form layout, you often have to repeatedly select the same groups of items. It can be time consuming to continually select the same objects. The Layout/Group Operations menu option can alleviate this problem.

The Layout/Group Operations/Group menu option essentially places all currently selected items into a group. The grab handles disappear from the individual items, and a set of grab handles is displayed around the group. This is illustrated in Figure 4-16. The figure depicts a set of items that have been individually selected and a set of items that have been grouped.

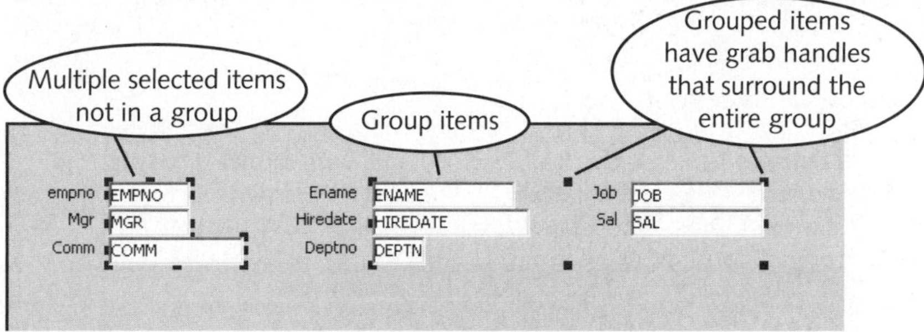

Figure 4-16 Ungrouped and grouped objects

The advantage of grouped items is that all of the items are selected when you select any of the group objects. This prevents you from having to perform continuous multi-select procedures. Other grouping techniques include:

- **Adding an item to an existing group**: Select the group. Select the new item(s) while holding the Shift key down. From the menu, select **Layout/Group Operations/Add to Group**.
- **Removing an item from an existing group**: Select the group. Select the target item within the group. The group grab handles disappear and grab handles appear around the item. From the menu, select **Layout/Group Operations/Remove from Group**.

As practice, perform the following steps:

1. Open the practice form with which you have been working in this chapter, and display the canvas in the Layout Editor.
2. Select the **MGR**, **COMM**, and **EMPNO** items.
3. From the menu, select **Layout/Group Operations/Group**. Notice that the item grab handles disappear and a large grab handle is placed over all three items.
4. Select any of the three items and drag it to a new location. Notice that the other items are also moved.
5. Ungroup the items by selecting **Layout/Group Operations/Ungroup** from the menu.
6. Save the form for later practice.

Switching Canvases and Moving Items to Different Blocks

The Layout Editor has two pick lists at the top of the screen called Canvas and Block. These lists always display the current canvas and block properties for the currently selected object. Figure 4-17 illustrates a master-detail layout with the HIREDATE item selected. The canvas and block properties are displayed in the pick lists.

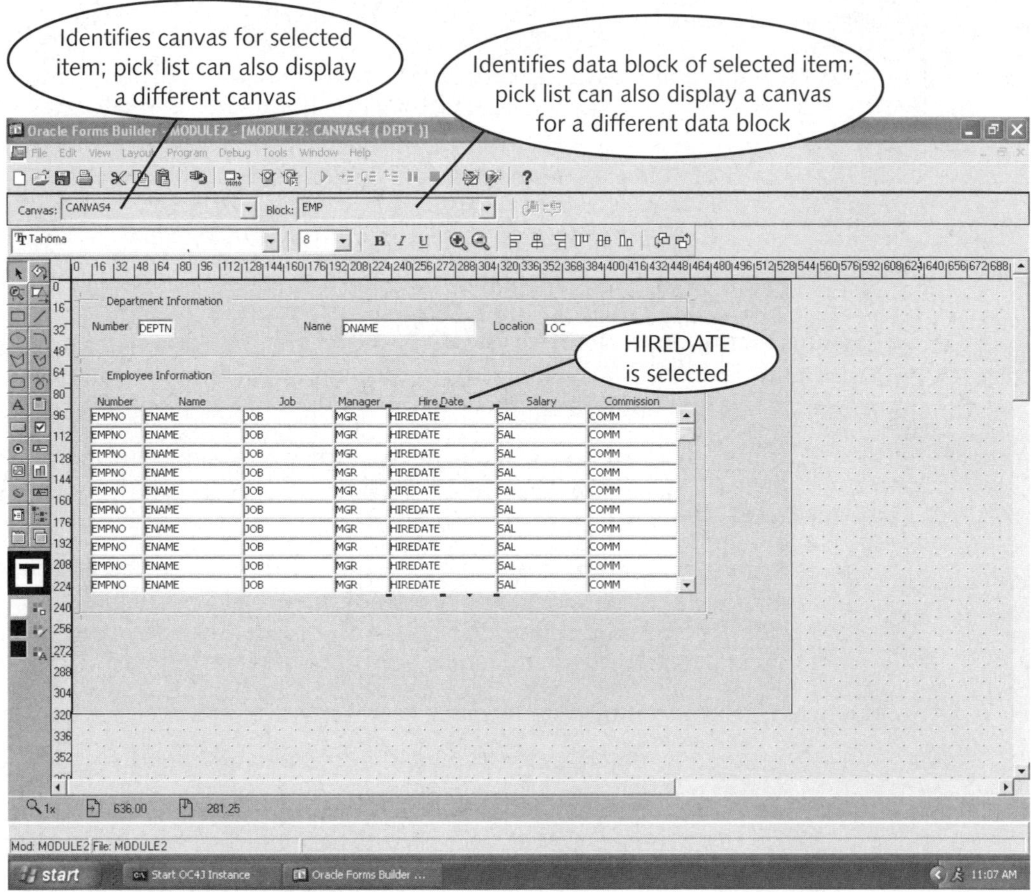

Figure 4-17 Canvas and Block drop-down lists displaying currently selected items

To switch canvases: Open the Canvas Pick List and select the desired canvas.

Forms Builder has several types of canvases. The most common canvas is a content canvas. This is a base canvas, and Forms Builder can display a single content canvas at a time. However, Forms Builder has a second type of canvas called a stacked canvas. This type of canvas can overlay a portion of a content canvas. Stacked canvases are used as dialog boxes that float above the content canvas or as a device to temporarily cover part of the content canvas.

You can select the stacked canvas using the drop-down list and work on it just as any other canvas. However, it is usually necessary to display the stacked canvas in the Layout Editor on top of the content canvas. This is especially true if you intend the stacked canvas to cover a portion of the content canvas rather than appear as a floating dialog box canvas. It requires extra steps to overlay a content canvas with a stacked canvas.

To overlay a canvas with a stacked canvas, you must use the View/Stacked Views menu option. This option is not enabled unless the Layout Editor is displaying a content canvas. The option opens the Stacked/Tab Canvases modal dialog box. This dialog box displays the available stacked or tab canvases that can overlay the current content canvas. When the dialog box initially opens, the displayed stacked or tab canvas is highlighted as illustrated in Figure 4-18. In this example, CANVAS9 (rectangle with the horizontal lines) is highlighted and is displayed. CANVAS10 is not highlighted and is not displayed.

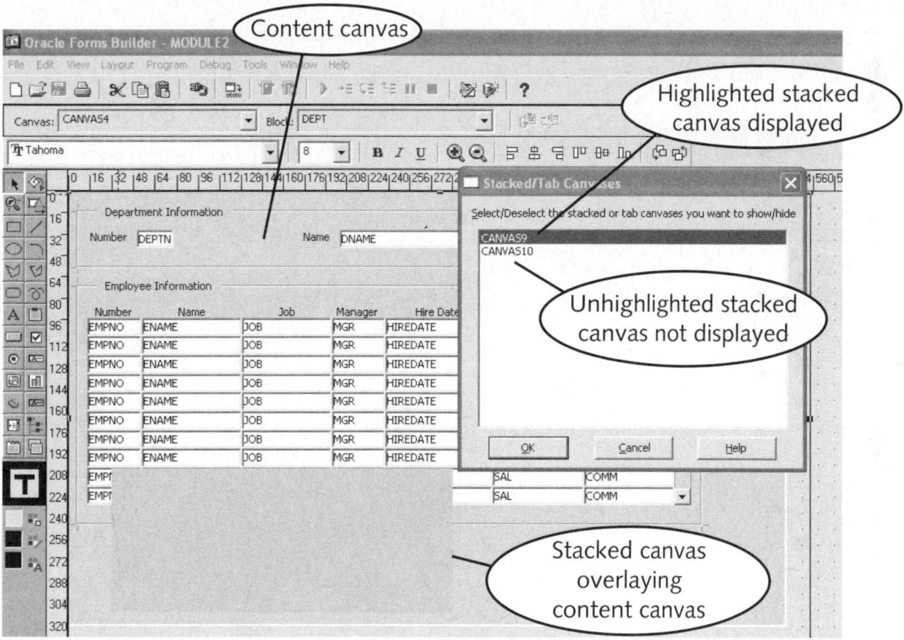

Figure 4-18 Stacked/Tab Canvases dialog box

The following operating procedures apply to the Stacked/Tab Canvases dialog box when a single canvas is displayed:

- To display the stacked canvas, highlight the canvas and click **OK**.
- To hide the stacked canvas, deselect the canvas by holding down the Control key and clicking the canvas. Click **OK**.

When multiple canvases are displayed in the Layout Editor, selecting a canvas deselects any other canvases. To select multiple canvases, use the Shift key while making selections to prevent deselection from occurring.

When displaying an individual canvas in the Layout Editor, the top-left corner of the canvas is always placed in the top-left corner at position (0,0) of the Layout Editor. This does not mean the canvas is displayed in that position in the window or that the stacked canvas is displayed in that position on the content canvas. Stacked canvases have the following two properties that determine where they are displayed in relation to the underlying content canvas:

- **Viewport X Position**: Determines the X position of the stacked canvas (or how much to the right) in relation to the X coordinate of the content canvas' top-left corner.
- **Viewport Y Position**: Determines the Y position of the stacked canvas (or how much from the top) in relation to the Y coordinate of the content canvas' top-left corner.

To illustrate, Figure 4-19 depicts a content canvas, a stacked canvas, and the stacked canvas' property palette. Notice the Viewport X Position and Viewport Y Position property values. These properties place the stacked canvas at the bottom of the underlying content canvas.

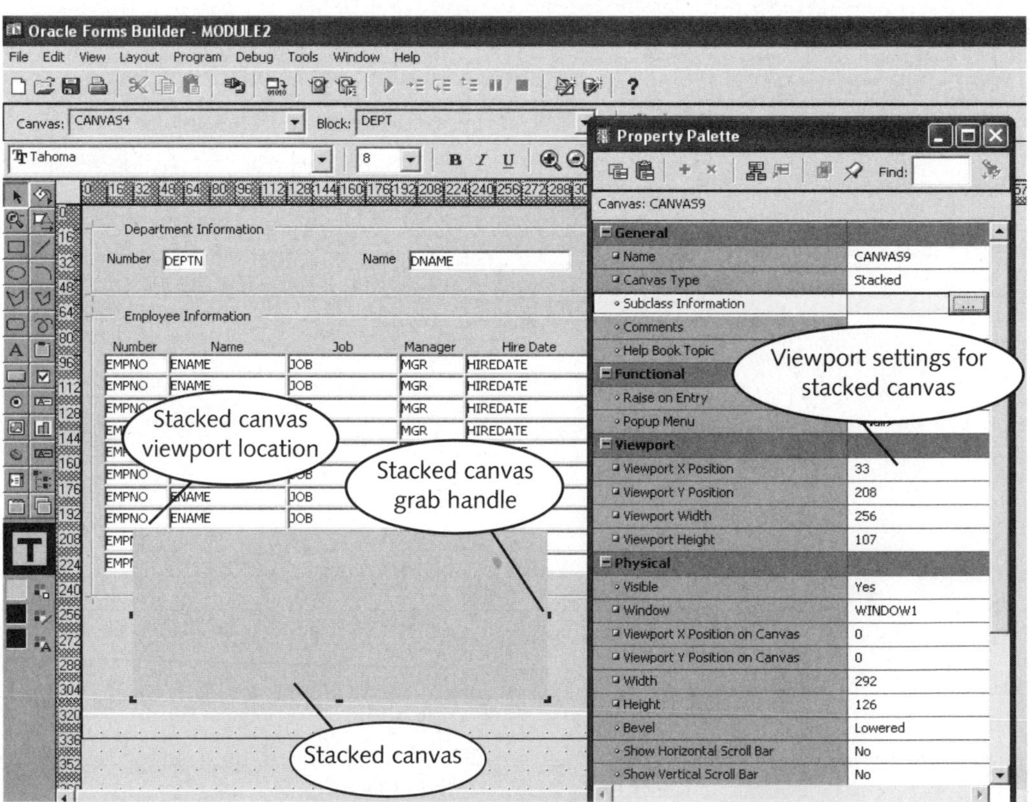

Figure 4-19 Stacked canvas overlaying a content canvas showing viewports

The stacked canvas Viewport X Position and Viewport Y Position properties can be set in the Property Palette for the canvas. You can also set the properties by dragging the overlying stacked canvas to its relative position on the content canvas. The stacked canvas can be selected, dragged, and resized. Selecting the canvas causes grab handles to appear, which can be used to drag and resize.

It is sometimes difficult to move the stacked canvases; this forces you to click a grab handle several times. This is a problem with Forms Builder. Do not get frustrated. Just keep trying until you can move the stacked canvas. Generally, the top-middle drag handle works best when repositioning the stacked canvas. You can also open the Property Palette for the canvas and adjust the Viewport properties.

When you create and add a data block item, such as a text item, display item, or check box, to a canvas using the Layout Editor tools, Forms Builder does not always place it in the proper data block. If it is not placed in the proper data block, the item will not be populated when Forms Builder returns records to the form. In addition, the SQL generated by the data block in which it was placed will be in error, because the data block item name is placed in the SQL statement generated by the data block. This name will not correspond to the data source columns and will produce an "Invalid Column Name" error. For this reason, when you create a data block item in the Layout Editor, you must manually move the item to the proper data block. In the last chapter, you saw that the Object Navigator is often used to drag an item into the proper data block. It is also possible to use the Layout Editor to perform this same function.

To change a displayed item's data block property, perform the following steps:

1. Select the item(s).
2. Select a new data block using the Layout Editor's Block Pick List. This assigns the data block item to the selected data block.

Canvases, data block items, graphics, boilerplates, or any other graphic objects can also be deleted by selecting the object in the Object Navigator and clicking the Delete key or the Delete tool. Many of the items can also be deleted in the Layout Editor using the Delete key and tool. However, a canvas can only be deleted from the Object Navigator.

Adding and Overlaying Graphic Objects

It is important to design systems and the forms they include so that the forms are conceptually clear. This means that the user should be able to easily understand how to operate the form. One technique to make your form understandable is to group common items, such as addresses or employee-specific information. Enclosing groups of items within a rectangle makes it visually clear to the user that the items belong together. Other techniques for grouping items include drawing lines to indicate commonality of data items, adding text for instructions, and adding other graphic symbols. The Layout Editor has a series of graphic tools (see Figure 4-20) used to create and maintain these objects.

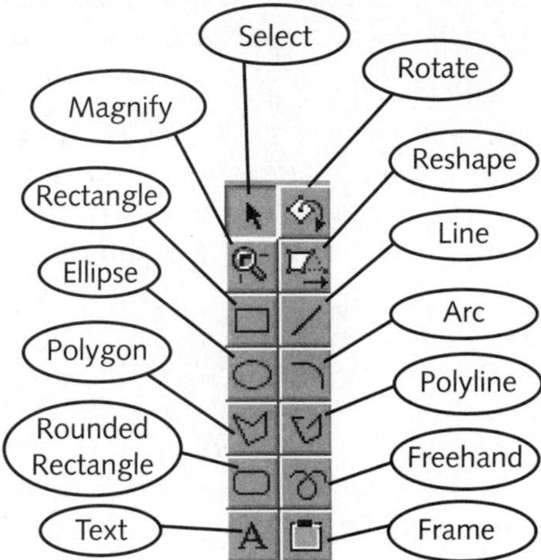

Figure 4-20 Layout Editor graphic tools

Use the Layout Editor graphic tools, shown in Figure 4-20, as described in the following list. As the tools are described, you may wish to test them on the chapter's practice form. To do so, open the Object Navigator and select the Canvas object. Click the **Create** tool creating a new canvas. Double-click this canvas in the Object Navigator. The Layout Editor displays the canvas. You may delete the canvas when you are finished.

- **Select**: Selects or makes current a Layout Editor item.
- **Magnify**: Makes items appear larger. Select the tool and then click an area in the Layout Editor. You can also use the F9 key or the View/Zoom In menu selection. The F10 key and the View/Zoom Out menu selection reverse the magnification.
- **Rectangle**: Creates a rectangular object. Select the tool, click on the canvas while holding down the left mouse button, and then size and shape the object.
- **Ellipse**: Creates an elliptical object. Select the tool, click on the canvas while holding down the left mouse button, and then size and shape the object.
- **Polygon**: Creates a polygon object (e.g., triangle or pentagon as shown in Figure 4-21). Select the tool and click on the canvas. Move the insertion point to the next vertex and click the left mouse button. Continue selecting vertex points until you are ready to add the last vertex. Double-clicking the last vertex causes Forms Builder to add the vertex and close the polygon.

- **Rounded Rectangle**: Creates a rectangle with rounded corners. Select the tool, click on the canvas while holding down the left mouse button, and then size and shape the object.
- **Text**: Adds boilerplate text. All text in Figure 4-21 was added using this tool. Select the tool and click on the canvas. A text box opens with a blinking insertion point. Add the text to the box. Press **Enter** to add text to a subsequent line. Click an area outside the tool to complete the procedure.
- **Rotate**: Changes the orientation of a graphic item. To rotate a graphic component, select the item, click the **Rotate** tool, place the insertion point over the item's grab handle, hold the left mouse button down, and drag (rotate) the item to the desired orientation.
- **Reshape**: Changes the shape of an existing graphic object. Select the item and click the tool. The grab handles shrink to the edges of the item. Grab a handle and reshape the item.
- **Line**: Creates a line. Select the tool, click on the canvas while holding down the left mouse button, and drag the insertion point.
- **Arc**: Creates an arc object as shown in Figure 4-21. Select the tool, click on the canvas while holding down the left mouse button, and drag the insertion point.
- **Polyline**: Creates a line that contains one or more vertexes. Select the tool and click on the canvas. Locate and click the various vertices. The line is completed by double-clicking.
- **Freehand**: Draws a freehand line as shown in Figure 4-21. Select the tool and click on the canvas. Hold down the left mouse button and drag the insertion point. A line is drawn under the insertion point until the left mouse button is released.
- **Frame**: Adds a frame to the layout as shown in Figure 4-21. This is the same type of frame that is associated to a data block.

By default, graphic objects added to the canvas overlay any existing canvas object including data items. It is generally necessary to stack or arrange form objects, as illustrated in Figure 4-21. On the right side of the figure is a rectangle that overlies an oval. Both of these objects are then overlain by a polygon. The overlay can be reversed as illustrated by the stacked objects below those just described: the oval overlies the rectangle and the polygon. Forms Builder has both Layout menu selections and the following toolbar tools that allow you to stack items on the canvas:

- **Bring to Front**: Brings the selected object to the top of the stack.
- **Send to Back**: Sends the selected object to the bottom of the stack.

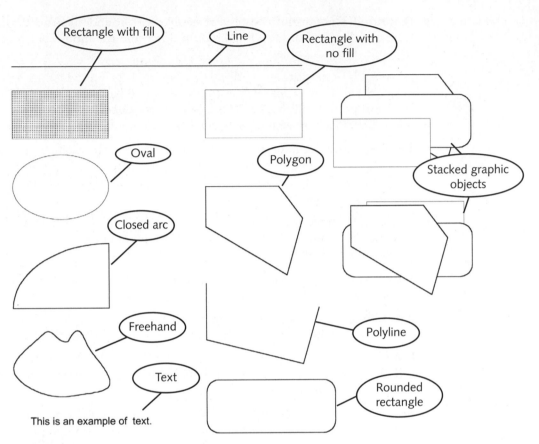

Figure 4-21 Various graphic objects

The Layout menu selections are:

- **Bring to Front**: Brings the selected object to the top of the stack.
- **Send to Back**: Sends the selected object to the bottom of the stack.
- **Move Forward**: Brings the selected object one layer toward the top of the stack.
- **Move Backward**: Sends the select object one layer toward the bottom of the stack.

Note: The Oracle 9*i* Layout menu is called the Format menu in Oracle 6*i*.

Forms Builder and Layout Editor Toolbars

So far you have learned to work with the following formatting tools: the Layout Editor, with its two toolbars located above the Layout Editor window, and the alignment tools. In addition, there are a variety of other tools that are of interest. This section describes the various tools beginning with the main Forms Builder and Layout Editor toolbars that are shown in Figure 4-22. The Forms Builder toolbar tools are:

- **New Module**: Creates a new, blank form module.
- **Open**: Launches the Open dialog box used to retrieve a file into Forms Builder.
- **Save**: Saves the currently selected file.
- **Print**: Prints the contents of the Layout Editor.
- **Cut**: Removes the currently selected object(s) and sends them to the Clipboard.
- **Copy**: Sends a copy of the currently selected object(s) to the Clipboard.
- **Paste**: Places the contents of the Clipboard onto the canvas.
- **Connect to Database**: Opens the Connect dialog box, which is used to connect to the Oracle database.
- **Compile Module**: Compiles the currently selected form module.
- **Run Form**: Executes the form using the Web runtime engine.
- **Run Form Debug**: Executes the form in the debug mode.
- **Go**: Form debugging tool that causes Forms Builder to begin executing statements.
- **Step Into**: Form debugging tool that causes Forms Builder to execute the steps in a called procedure.
- **Step Over**: Form debugging tool that causes Forms Builder to skip the steps in a called procedure.
- **Step Out**: Form debugging tool that causes Forms Builder to leave a called procedure and return to the next step in the calling PL/SQL code block.
- **Pause**: Form debugging tool that halts form execution.
- **Stop**: Form debugging tool that stops debugging.
- **Data Block Wizard**: Starts the Data Block Wizard.
- **Layout Wizard**: Starts the Layout Wizard.
- **Help**: Starts the Forms Builder Help utility.

The Layout Editor tools are:

- **Canvas Pick List**: Pick list displaying the currently selected item's canvas property (discussed in an earlier section).
- **Block Pick List**: Pick list displaying the currently selected item's data block property (discussed in an earlier section).

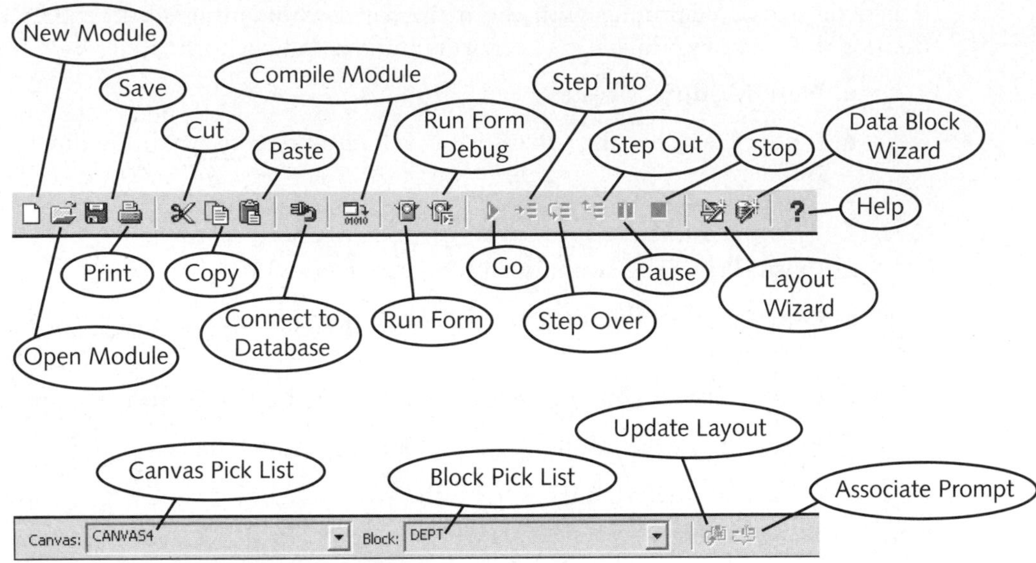

Figure 4-22 Forms Builder and Layout Editor toolbars

- **Update Layout**: Modifies the contents of a frame that has the Update Layout property set to Manually.
- **Associate prompt**: Associates selected text to a selected item.

On the far right of the Layout Editor toolbar is the Associate Prompt tool. This tool is used to populate an item's Prompt property. Normally the prompt is set using the Items page of the Layout Wizard. The Layout Editor has tools for adding each of the item types to the canvas. When you add an item to the layout using the Layout Editor item tools, the data item prompt is not populated. The text item will be displayed with no prompt, and therefore the form operator will not understand the purpose of the text item. This is why the Layout Editor has a tool that associates text, which is added to the layout using the Text tool, to an item as a prompt. To associate text to an item as a prompt, perform the following steps:

1. Select the target text and data block items. Use the shift key to avoid deselecting an item.
2. Click the **Associate Prompt** tool. If the data block item already has a prompt, an alert appears warning that you are about to replace an existing prompt.

Figure 4-23 illustrates the association of text to the prompt. A text item was added to the canvas using the Text Item tool, and prompt text was added to the canvas using the Text tool. The new item and text are selected. Clicking the Associate Prompt tool associates the two.

When the Layout Editor is displayed, a Format toolbar is displayed beneath the Form Builder IDE toolbar. This toolbar has five important tools: Font, Size, Bold, Italics, and Underline, as shown in Figure 4-24. These tools are used to format any text that is displayed on the canvas. To format text, select the target items and click the appropriate tool.

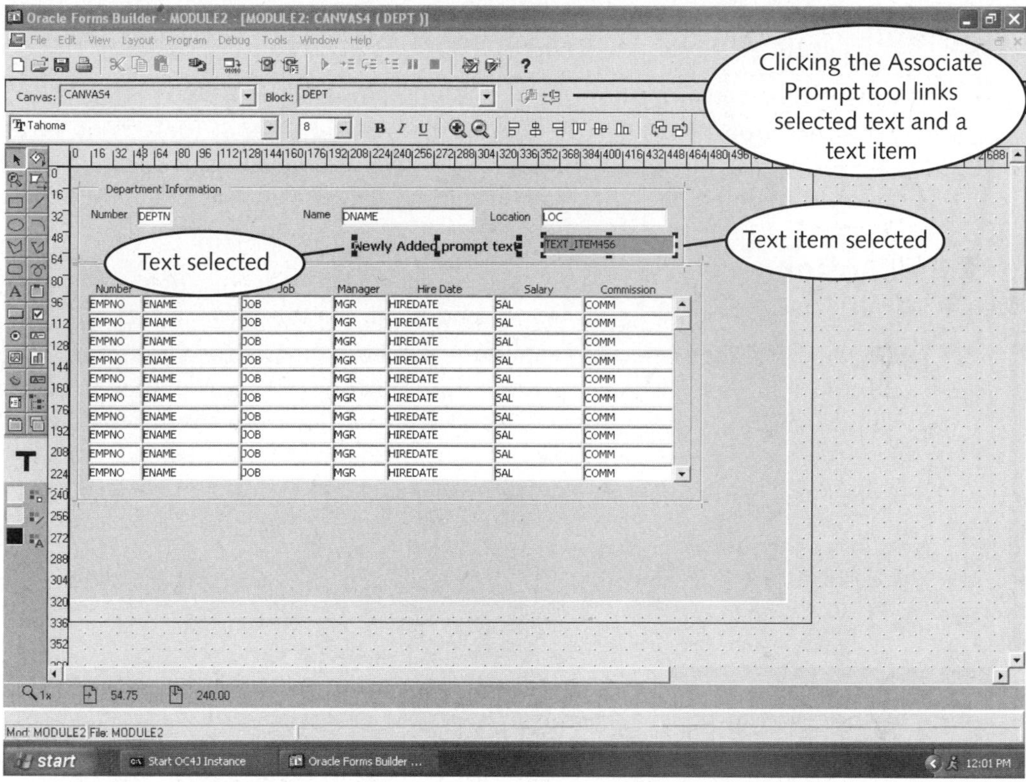

Figure 4-23 Using the Associate Prompt tool to link a newly entered text item and text

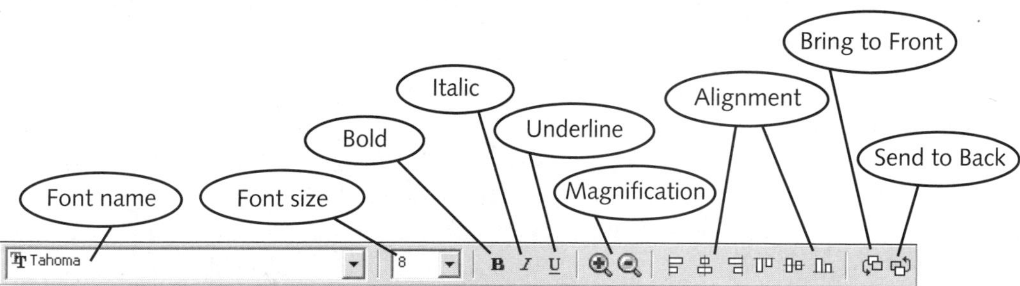

Figure 4-24 Format and Alignment toolbar

It is best not to use an overly fancy font. The font can appear to be clever and sophisticated, but in all likelihood it will be hard for the user to read. MS Sans Serif, size 8 (or 10), bold is a fairly good choice for a font. If you need a smaller font, Small Fonts is a wise choice.

Layout Editor Menu Formatting Options

There is one remaining set of Layout Editor tools that have not been described, the Layout menu options. These options consist of three sets of tools: Font, Line, and Text. The Line and Text tools do not have a corresponding toolbar, but they are located on the Layout menu along with graphic and layout settings that will be discussed shortly.

Font Options

The first Layout menu option displays the Font dialog box depicted in Figure 4-25. This dialog box has the same font options as the Format toolbar. The options allow you to set the font, font style, and size. Only the Strikeout option is unique to the dialog box. This option draws a line through the selected text. The main advantage of using the dialog box is the Sample window visible in Figure 4-25. This window allows you to see a sample of the text with the options you've chosen.

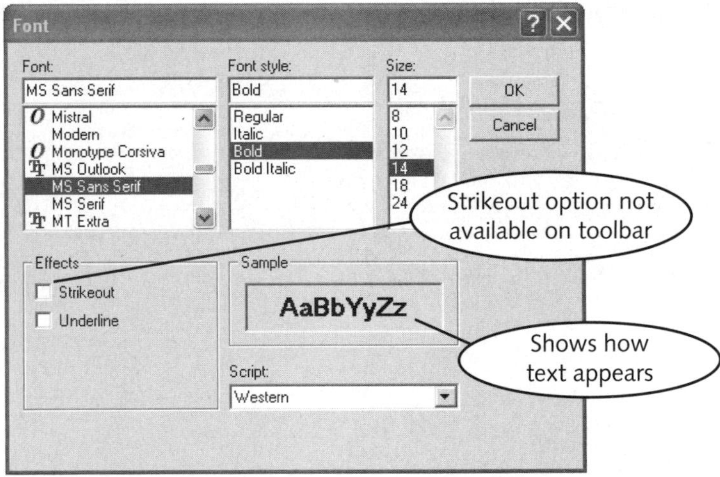

Figure 4-25 Font dialog box

Justify Option

The Layout/Justify menu option is used to justify the text. Text can consist of prompts, item values, or a multiline boilerplate. Figure 4-26 illustrates five text menu items, each using a different justification. They are described here:

- **Left-justified**: Places the first text character on the left side. This option is best used for character values.

- **Center-justified**: Aligns the text so that equal space exists on both sides of the value.
- **Right-justified**: Aligns the text so that the last character is adjacent to the right side of the text area. This style is appropriate for numbers.
- **Start-justified**: Aligns the text with the starting edge of the text area. The starting edge is determined by the item's Reading Order property. Text is right-justified if the Reading Order property is right-to-left. It is left-justified if the Reading Order property is left-to-right.
- **End-justified**: Aligns the text with the ending edge of the text area. This edge is determined by the item's Reading Order property. Text is right-justified if the property is left-to-right and left-justified if the property is right-to-left.

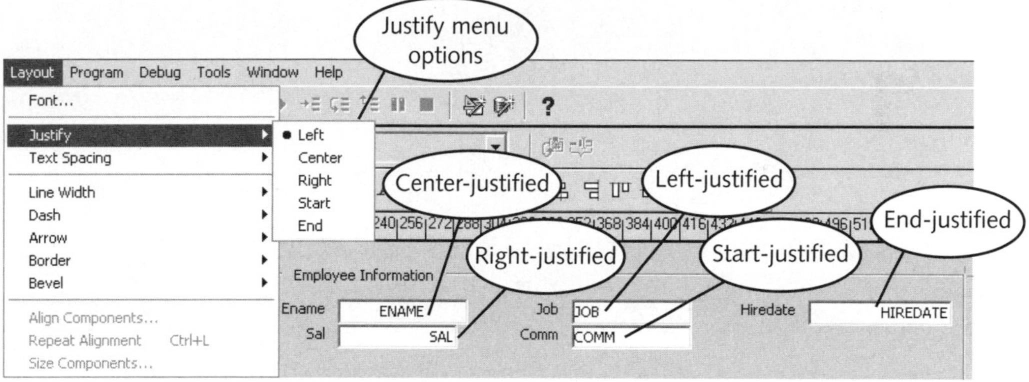

Figure 4-26 Examples of text justification

As practice, perform the following steps:

1. Open the practice form and display the canvas in the Layout Editor.
2. Select the **ENAME** item.
3. Select the **Layout/Justify/Right** option. Notice that this will right-justify the value in the ENAME text item. It will also appear right-justified when the form is executed.
4. Save the form for later practice.

Text Spacing Options

The Layout/Text Spacing option opens a submenu that allows you to set spacing that is used on multiline text such as a paragraph. There are four options: Single (the default), 1 ½, Double, and Custom. Selecting the Custom option opens the dialog box depicted in Figure 4-27. This dialog box allows you to choose various point settings.

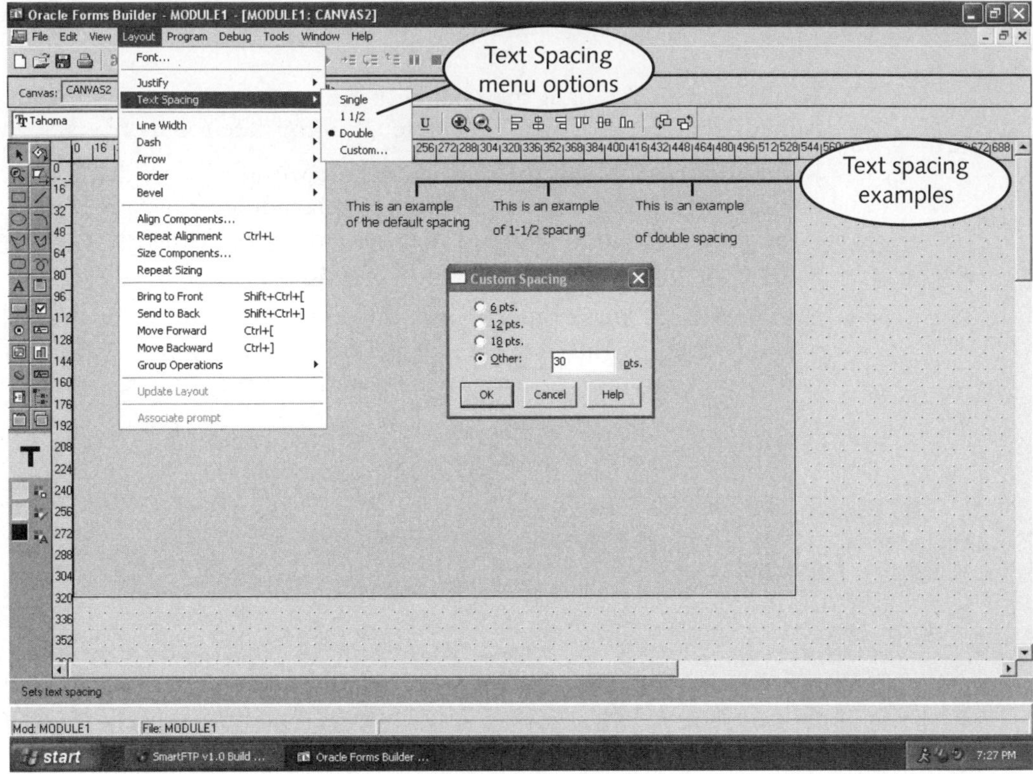

Figure 4-27 Layout/Text Spacing menu options, Custom Spacing dialog box, and text spacing examples

Line, Text Item, and Frame Format Options

The Layout menu (Format menu in Oracle 6*i*) has three tools that enable you to format a line, as shown in Figure 4-28. The Layout menu also controls some of the lines that are drawn to format graphic objects. The options are described here:

- **Line Width Palette**: Opens a palette of various line width options. This palette can be used on all graphic objects to increase the line width. The custom option at the bottom of the palette launches the Custom Line Width dialog box used to enter custom sizes in point, centimeter, or inch units.
- **Dashed Line Palette**: Opens a palette of various dashed line types. This tool can only be used on a line.
- **Arrow Palette**: Opens a palette of various arrow tips. This tool is used to add an arrow tip at the end of a line.
- **Border Palette**: Opens a palette of options that can turn off an object's top, bottom, left, and right borders.

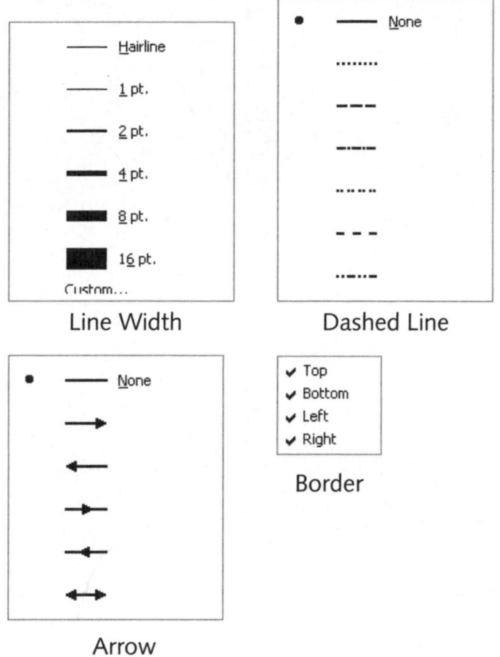

Figure 4-28 Line Width, Dashed Line, Arrow, and Border palettes

The Layout menu has settings that control the bevel of text boxes and display items. **Bevel** is contrasting white and black edges that make the text box item appear to be raised, lowered, inset, or outset from the canvas. Figure 4-29 illustrates the various bevel styles.

The last Layout menu option is Border. Border removes borders on frames or rectangular graphic objects. The Border options can be used to remove any or all of the four frame edges.

Graphics Options

The Edit menu has a Graphics Options submenu (see Figure 4-30) that contains a variety of graphic options that open a number of dialog boxes. These dialog boxes control graphic features such as the degree of corner rounding for rounded rectangles, the types of line edges, and the point of origin of the graphic object. Using these options gives a customized style to the graphic design of a form.

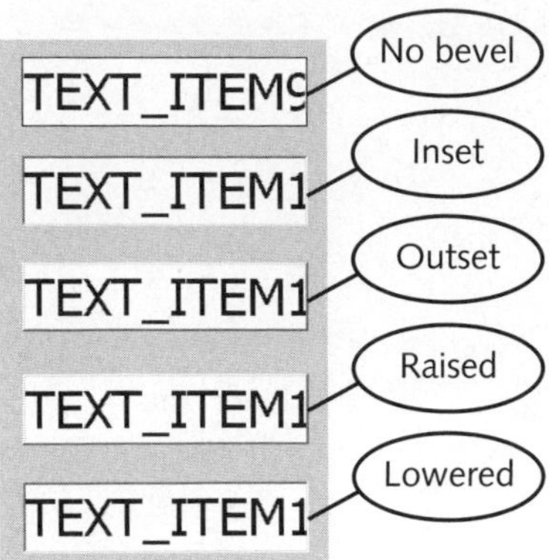

Figure 4-29 Bevel styles

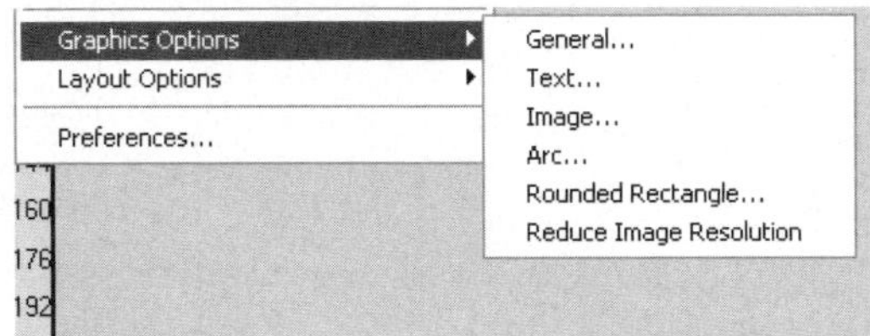

Figure 4-30 Graphics Options submenu

General Graphics Option

The General graphics option opens the General Drawing Options dialog box shown in Figure 4-31. This dialog box has three types of settings:

- **Cap Style**: This setting determines the end of the point of the graphic object. The options are Butt (straight edge on the end of the object), Round (rounded edge), and Projecting.
- **Object Creation**: This setting determines how the graphic object will be drawn. The options are Draw from Corner and Draw from Center. If you choose Draw from Center, a plus (+) is placed in the center of all Layout Editor graphic tools.
- **Join Style**: This setting determines the type of corner on rectangular objects. The options are Round (rounded edge), Bevel (shaved edge), and Mitre (squared).

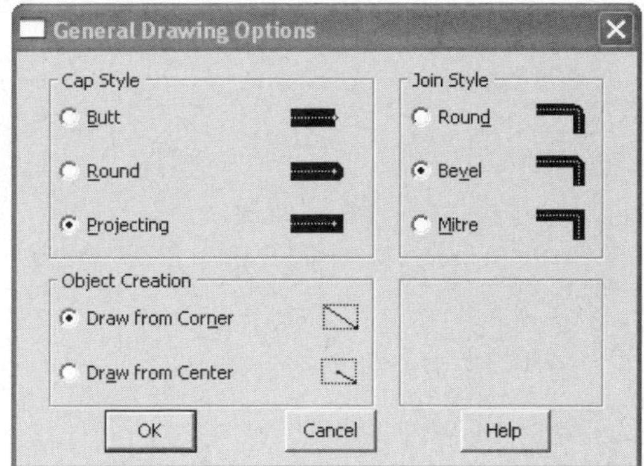

Figure 4-31 General Drawing Options dialog box

The second Graphics Options menu selection, Text, is used to set the default position of the text. The tools on this option control the placement of the text in relationship to their origin after the text has been placed on the canvas. The origin is the location of the first character (or the location of the insertion point) when the text is added. For example, when the Horizontal Origin At Right option is chosen, it places the entered text to the right of the insertion point. This positioning and the Text Drawing Options dialog box are illustrated in Figure 4-32. This dialog box contains three sets of settings:

1. **Horizontal Origin**: Determines how text is aligned horizontally. The options are At Left, At Center, and At Right.
2. **General Options**:
   - **Scalable Fonts**: Determines whether the text in a text object is scaled proportionally to the object itself when it is resized.
   - **Invisible Text**: Determines when the displayed text will be visible or hidden.
   - **Fixed Bounding Box**: Allows a text box to be sized independently of the text it contains. When this item is unchecked, the box size can only be changed to fit the text.
   - **Wraparound**: Determines whether text is wrapped to the next line in order to fit within the text box. This option is only available if the Fixed Bounding Box option is selected.
   - **Scalable Bounding Box**: Determines whether the bounding text box can be resized. This option is only available if the Fixed Bounding Box is selected.
3. **Vertical Origin**: Determines how text is aligned vertically. The options are At Top, At Center, and At Bottom.

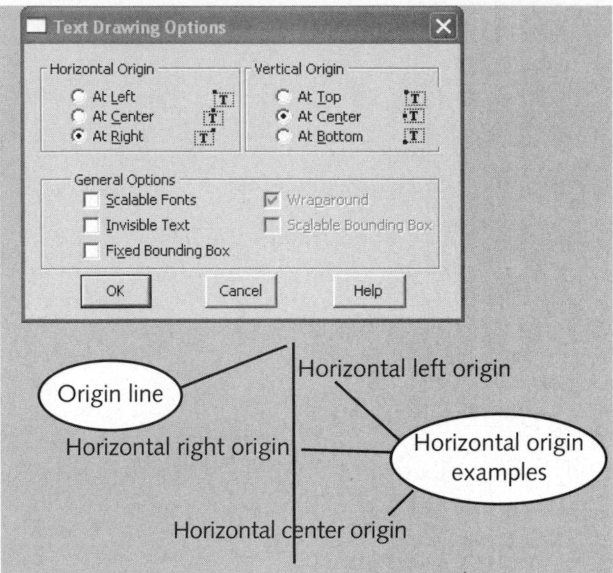

Figure 4-32 Text Drawing Options dialog box and examples of horizontal positioning

The third Graphics Options menu selection, Image, is used for images. It opens the Image Drawing Options dialog box (see Figure 4-33) that displays these sets of options:

- **Image Quality**: Controls the quality of an imported image. The higher the quality setting, the better the image. Higher settings also result in slower response time.
- **Image Dither**: Controls image dither. With **dithering**, Forms Builder simulates and substitutes colors that appear in the image but are not in the color palette. If the option is not selected, Forms Builder substitutes a color rather than creating a match. A dithered image looks better but results in slower response time.

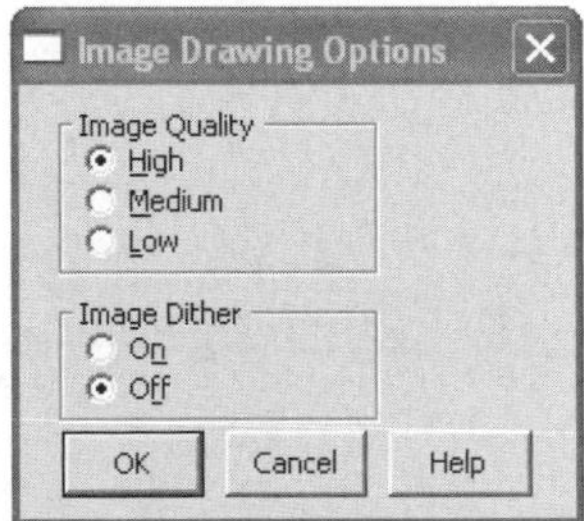

Figure 4-33 Image Drawing Options dialog box

The fourth Graphics Options menu selection, Arc, controls the default arc object properties (see Figure 4-34). Two sets of options are available, as follows:

- **Arc Fill**: Determines how the fill is drawn. The Pie option causes the fill to be rendered from the center point of the circle described by the arc. The Chord option is used if the fill is to be rendered within a line segment between the arc's two end points.
- **Arc Closure**: Determines how arcs are drawn. The Closed option is used if the arc border is to be rendered on the entire perimeter of the arc object's fill area. If the Open option is selected, the end points are not closed.

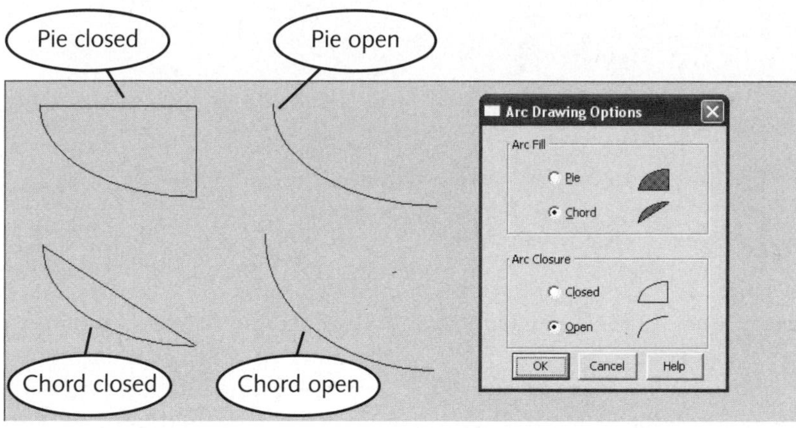

Figure 4-34 Arc Drawing Options dialog box

The next Graphics Options menu selection opens the Rounded Rectangle Drawing Options dialog box (see Figure 4-35). This dialog box controls the amount of rounding on the corners of the rectangle. There are two sets of options, as follows:

- **Corner Radius**: Text boxes that are used to specify the amount of rounding on the corners of rectangular objects. The larger the amount, the greater the rounding. Both vertical and horizontal settings can be entered. Figure 4-35 illustrates two rounded rectangles. One has vertical and horizontal settings of 2 and the other settings of 10.
- **Units**: Identifies the unit of measure.

The last Graphics Options menu selection, Reduce Image Resolution, is used to reduce the quality of an image, which increases response time.

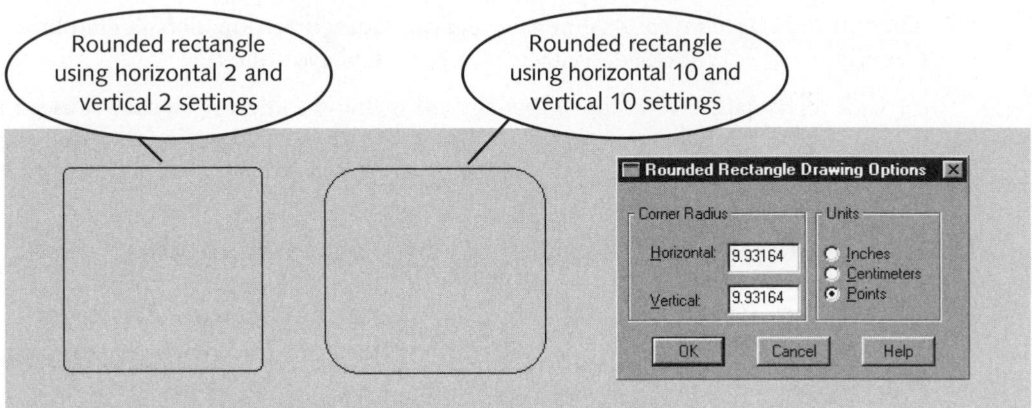

Figure 4-35 Rounded Rectangle Drawing Options dialog box and examples of rounded rectangles

Ruler, Ruler Guides, Grid, Snap-To-Grid, and Layout Options

The Layout Editor has two tools that can be used to orient and align objects. These tools are the ruler and the grid. The Layout Editor left and top edges contain a measuring tool called the **ruler** (see Figure 4-36). The top ruler measures the horizontal distance from the origin in the top-left corner of the work area. The left ruler measures the vertical distance from the same point. Each ruler can be represented in one of four units of measure: points, inches, centimeters, and character cells. The unit of measure can be changed using the Edit/Layout Options/Ruler menu selection.

Points is the default unit of measure. As you move the insertion point in the work area, two different sets of information are displayed:

- At bottom of the work area, Forms Builder displays the unit of magnification, as well as the current X and Y coordinates of the insertion point. The coordinates can aid in placing an object in the proper location.
- Both the horizontal and vertical rulers display a dashed line indicating the current X and Y coordinates.

Rule guides are other Layout Editor tools that are used to align objects. Rule guides are horizontal and vertical lines that appear in the work area. These lines can be used as an alignment base for placing objects. To add a rule guide, you would follow these steps:

1. Grab the black edge of the horizontal or vertical ruler.
2. Hold down the Left Mouse button and drag the insertion point into the work area. A dotted black line appears as a rule guide.
3. Release the mouse button when you are finished.

The rule guides can be reselected and moved to other locations. In addition, you can place as many rule guides as you need. To remove a rule guide, follow these steps:

1. Place your insertion point over the rule guide and hold down the Left Mouse button.
2. Move the insertion point perpendicular to the rule guide. When the insertion point is off of the work area, release the mouse button.

Figure 4-36 illustrates the horizontal and vertical rulers, rule guides, magnification, position, and the coordinate indicators.

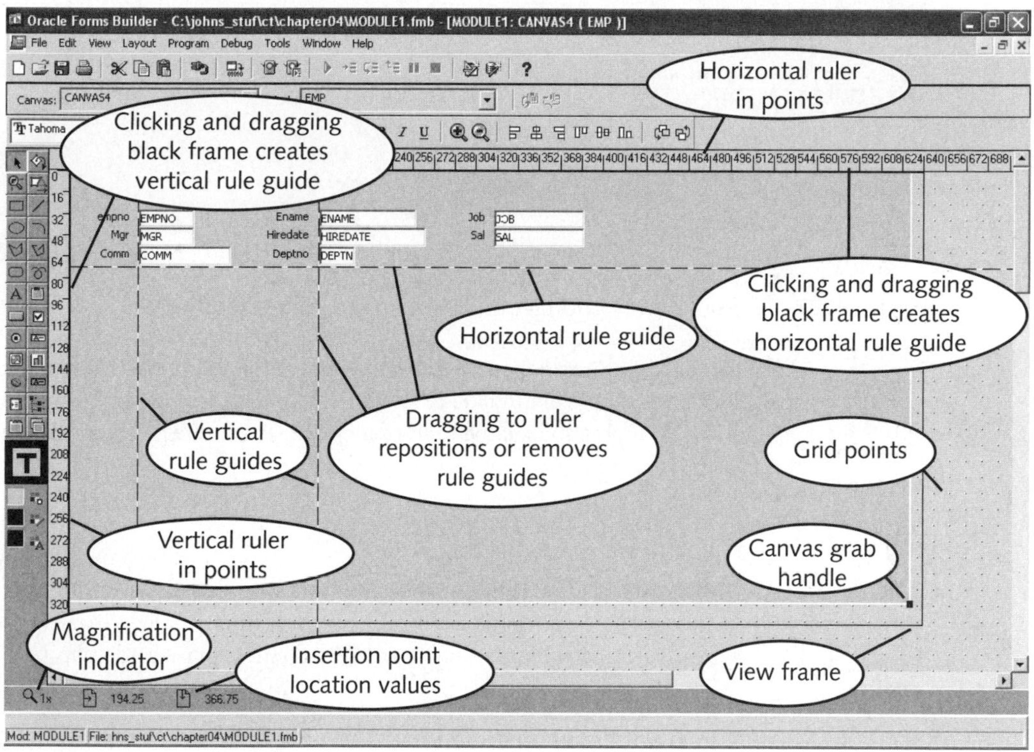

Figure 4-36 Layout Editor containing rule guides, ruler, magnification, and coordinate indicators

Grids

The grid is an alignment tool that consists of a set of equally distant points. The points are used to align objects. When using the grid tool, it is best to hide the canvas, which is simply a colored layer underlying objects. This allows you to see your canvas objects in relation to the grid points. Unchecking the View/Show Canvas menu option hides the canvas.

The View/Snap to Grid option is used in conjunction with the grid. This option causes the top-left corner of the selected object to move to a grid point or a spot halfway between grid points. When this option is used, you will notice that the object jumps as it is dragged. Snap-to-grids allows for easy initial placement of objects. However, it can be frustrating, because the grid point may not be the exact position desired. If the position is wrong, turn off the View/Snap to Grid option and use the alignment or other tools. The View/Snap to Grid option toggles on and off using the View/Snap to Grid menu option.

Figure 4-37 depicts the Layout Editor work area displaying the grid. One text item is snapped to a grid point and the other to a midpoint.

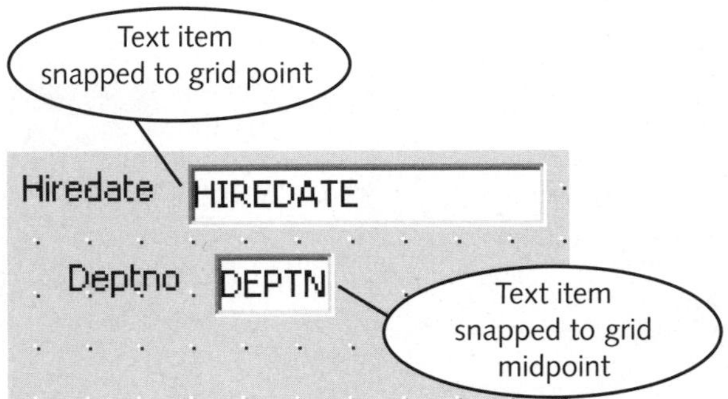

Figure 4-37 Layout Editor grid layout illustrating snapped text items

The View menu has a variety of settings that affect the items displayed in the Layout Editor. It is possible to hide or show the canvas, view, grid, rulers, and ruler guides. You can also hide the toolbar and status bars, effectively increasing the size of the work area.

Layout Options

The Layout Options of the Edit menu allow you to open two different dialog boxes, Ruler Settings and Layout Settings. The Ruler Settings dialog box (as shown in Figure 4-38) has a number of options that control the ruler, grid, and snap to grid. These options are as follows:

- **Units**: Determines the measurement units displayed on the ruler.
- **Grid Spacing**: Determines the space between the grid points. The spacing is based on the selected units. If the radio buttons do not contain the desired spacing, the Other radio button and accompanying text item can be used to enter a custom value.
- **Number of Snap Points Per Grid Spacing**: Determines the number of snap points that will exist between grid points. The default is 2.
- **Character Cell Size**: This setting was used with old installations of Forms Builder. In this environment, a form was divided into a series of cells. The cells were arranged in 24 rows and 80 columns. This setting determines the height and width of the cells. This option is used when the unit of measurement is character cells.

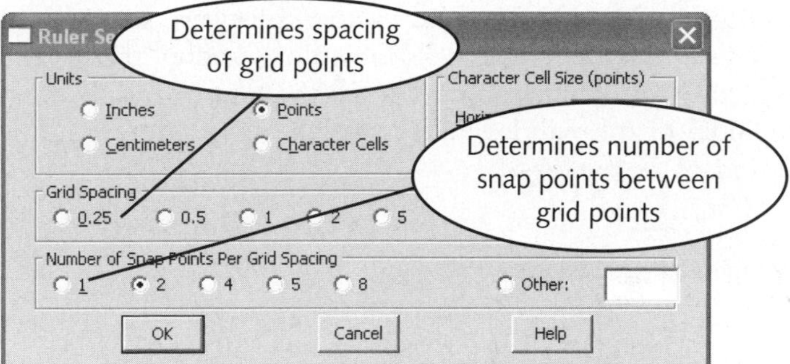

Figure 4-38 Ruler Settings dialog box

The Layout Settings dialog box is used to set the size of the work area. The work area is the maximum space in which you can develop a canvas and can be much larger than the Layout Editor window, even though this is not recommended. The dialog box has both vertical and horizontal work area settings based on the selected unit of measure.

The Layout Settings dialog box also has settings for page direction. These settings are used when the layout is printed using the Print Window command. If your canvas is larger than a printed page, it must be printed on multiple pages. The Page Direction option determines whether the pages will be printed top-to-bottom and left-to-right, or left-to-right and top-to-bottom. Figure 4-39 illustrates the Layout Settings dialog box.

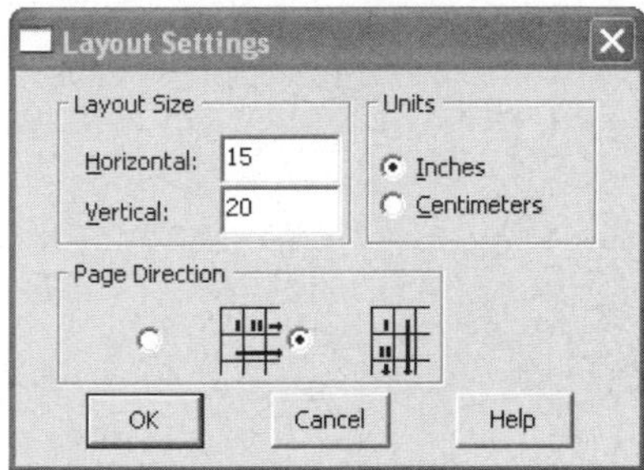

Figure 4-39 Layout Settings dialog box

Coloring Your Components Using the Fill, Line, and Text Color Tools

The vertical toolbar has three tools that are used to color objects such as canvases, frames, graphic items, and data items. All objects have three different color components: the line that is the edge of the object, the fill that is the inside of the object, and text that is displayed inside the object. The Layout Editor has three corresponding tools that are used to set the color properties for any selected item(s). These tools are called Fill Color, Line Color, and Text Color.

The tools are adjacent to a color window. This window displays the color component of the currently selected item. Above these tools is a color window that shows the color components overlaying each other. The outer color is the line color. The next is the fill color. The T in the middle of the window represents the text color. Figure 4-40 illustrates the color tools and color windows.

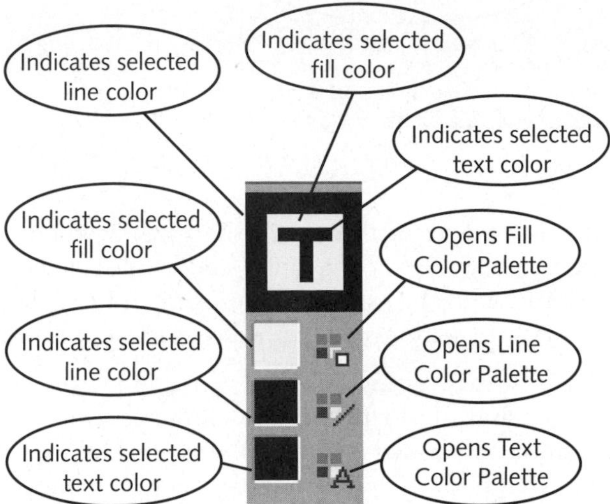

Figure 4-40 Color tools and windows

Clicking any of the tools causes the Fill Color Palette to appear (see Figures 4-41 and 4-42) with its series of color boxes that represent the various color options. Items are colored by selecting the desired color. The selected color box appears raised. The color palettes can be left open by selecting the Tear Off Palette option that appears at the bottom of the palette. This option changes the palette from a menu into a dialog box. The box can then be moved around in the work area.

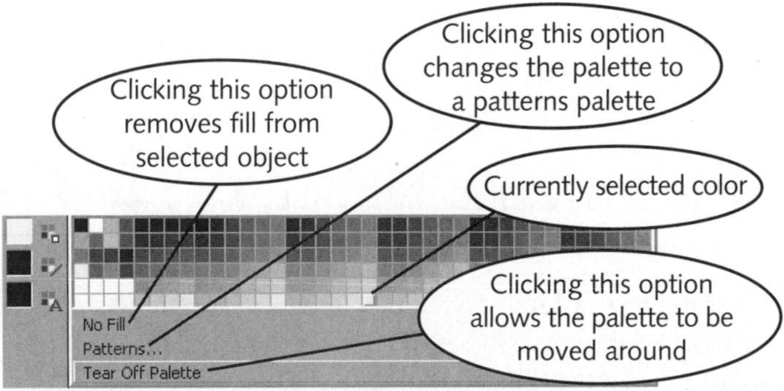

Figure 4-41 Fill Color Palette

The Fill Color and Line Color palettes have a Patterns option that is also located at the bottom of the palette. Clicking this option causes the color palette to change into a pattern palette. This palette has three different components. The top 90% displays the various available patterns. At the bottom are two color pick lists, which control the foreground and background pattern colors. To change either of these components, click the pick list and select the desired component.

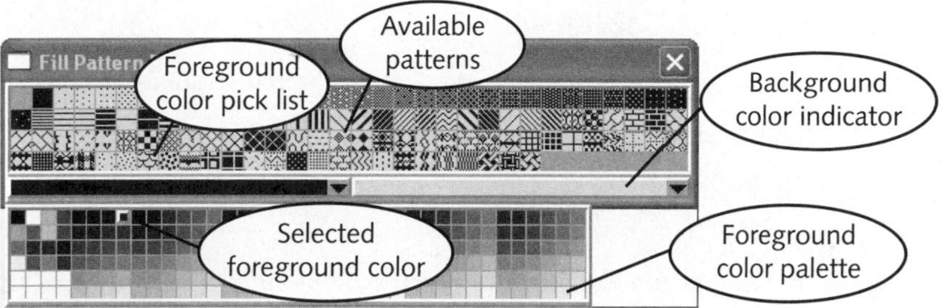

Figure 4-42 Fill Color Palette displaying available patterns

For practice using colors, perform the following steps:

1. Open the practice form used in this chapter and display the canvas in the Layout Editor.
2. Select the bottom-right corner of the canvas. Be sure it is not the view frame. You may want to shut off the view frame by unchecking View/Show View menu option.
3. With the canvas selected, click the **Fill Color** tool. This displays the color palette. Select a color on the palette to color the canvas.
4. Select the **ENAME** item on the canvas.
5. Open the Fill Color tool and select a **yellow** color.
6. Open the Line Color tool and select a **red** color.
7. Open the Text Color tool and select a **blue** color.
8. Notice that the Color toolbar indicator matches the colors you used on the item.
9. Save the form if you wish.

WHERE YOU ARE AND WHERE YOU'RE GOING

In this chapter, you were presented with a variety of formatting tools residing in the Layout Editor. They allow you to format anything that appears on the canvas. You have also seen how to size the canvas and its window. In the next chapter, you will learn how to use the Property Palette, the third of the Forms Builder tools. Every form object except the PL/SQL code has properties. The next chapter will show you how to use this tool to control the form behavior and format.

Chapter Summary

- Data items must be placed on a canvas in order to be displayed. Because a form canvas shares some characteristics of an artist's canvas, you must have a visual image of a form and place the vision on the canvas.
- A form window is not a Microsoft window; it is a window that is displayed inside the Web browser window. The form window can be minimized, closed, placed into the Normal mode, moved, or resized.
- By default, the form window is displayed in the Normal mode.
- Proper canvas height and width can only be determined by trial and error.
- A frame is a canvas child object that is used to standardize data block item display properties.
- Frames can be created using the Layout Wizard or using the Frame tool in the Layout Editor, but the frame properties are changed with the Property Palette.
- The Shrinkwrap property causes the frame objects to collapse into the smallest possible area.
- The Update Layout property determines when the frame objects will be updated.
- The Layout Editor displays canvases and form window views in an environment that contains a wealth of formatting and coloring tools.
- The Layout Editor makes it possible to drag items and text into position, add data items, set font characteristics, arrange and size items, and set colors.
- The Layout Editor has a work area that is used to format the form.
- The grid is a series of equidistant points that cover the work area. The canvas is placed over the grid.
- A view is a black frame within the work area that represents the existing window view of the canvas.
- Views and canvases can be resized by selecting their bottom-right corners and dragging to the desired size.
- Items and graphic objects can be placed on the canvas. They can also be moved and resized by selecting the object and dragging the grab handles.
- Multiple items can be selected by holding down the Shift key while selecting the items.
- The alignment tools on the toolbar and the Layout/Align Components menu options can be used to position items.
- The Layout/Size Components menu options can be used to size all selected objects.
- Items can be grouped to avoid having to continually reselect them.

- The Layout Editor has pick lists that can be used to display different canvases and to change the data block of selected items.
- Stacked canvases can overlay a content canvas by using the View/Stacked Views canvas menu selection.
- Forms Builder has a variety of graphic objects that can be placed on the canvas. These objects can overlay each other and can be properly stacked using toolbar tools and menu selections.
- The Layout Editor has a variety of tools for justifying text, changing the size of a line, and controlling the layout.
- The Layout Editor has horizontal and vertical rulers that can be displayed in different measurement units.
- Rule guides can overlay the work area. They are used to align form objects.
- The Snap to Grid option causes data items to automatically move to a specific grid point.
- Form objects have three color components: fill, line, and text. Each of these components has a tool that can be used to set the properties.

Review Questions

1. Match the following terms that have appeared in this chapter with their descriptions:

a. Normal mode	________	Causes all of the data block items enclosed within the frame to move to the smallest area possible.
b. Fill Color	________	The color of the outside edge of a selected object.
c. View	________	Allows you to overlay a stacked canvas on a content canvas within the Layout Editor.
d. Maximize mode	________	The default window size.
e. Rule guides	________	Six Layout Editor tools used to align selected objects.
f. F2 key	________	Graphic identifier displayed when an item is selected. It is used to resize and move the object.
g. Frame	________	A tool used to avoid having to continually reselect objects.
h. Send to Front	________	Layout Editor object used to identify the window's viewing area.

i. Shrinkwrap property	________________	Displays the Layout Editor.
j. Minimized mode	________________	A series of equidistant points overlaying the work area.
k. Groups	________________	Causes the selected object to move to the bottom of an object stack.
l. Line color	________________	Vertical or horizontal lines used to align objects.
m. Snap-to-Grid	________________	The color that is displayed within an object.
n. Grab handle	________________	Option that causes a selected object to always be placed at the nearest point.
o. Stacked/Tab Canvases dialog box	________________	The window covers the entire screen.
p. Format toolbar alignment tools	________________	Used to stack or distribute selected objects.
q. Send to Back	________________	A canvas child object used to format a data block's prompts.
r. Arrange/Align Object menu selection	________________	The window is hidden, only displaying an icon.
s. Grid	________________	Setting that determines when the layout will be modified.
t. Work area	________________	Tool that moves the selected object to the top of an object stack.
u. Update Layout property	________________	The Layout Editor space that can be used to modify a canvas.

2. You have just created a default layout for your data block and your prompts are to the left of the item. How can you make them appear above the item?
3. You are having trouble aligning your objects and have decided to use the grid. What do you need to do in order to begin using the grid?
4. You are attempting to move several items in the Layout Editor, and they keep moving to different locations. What could the problem be?
5. You have added several new text items to your screen. The size (height) does not match the other items on the screen. Explain how to make the sizes the same.
6. You just got off the phone with a user who has criticized an application you had developed. As you design a new application for the user, what colors can you use to make him slightly calmer?

7. How do you change the color of the canvas?
8. You have just launched a new default form. When viewing it, you notice that initially only half of the canvas is displayed. Several of the items are hidden until you maximize the window. How can you solve this so that the user sees all the form items when the application is launched?
9. You have drawn a rounded rectangle around a series of data items, but you don't like the line thickness or the color. How can you make the line thicker and change its color?

10. You have executed a new form and have noticed that all of the numbers are displayed on the left. How do you right-justify the numbers?
11. You have just inherited a form from another developer. The developer had a degree in fine arts from a prestigious art institute and has used the following fonts: Sage, Quark Neon, and Penchant. Do you think these fonts are appropriate for a business application? If not, can you identify three or four fonts that are more suitable?
12. You have just created a control block and want to add several data items to the block. These data items will match existing fields in another block. How can you use the Layout Editor to create the items and place them in the proper data block?
13. Your form has a frame around a series of data items. You want to keep the frame and the frame title, but you do not want the left, right, and bottom frame components. How can you get rid of these components and keep the frame title?
14. Your form has a scrollbar. You would like to add some color and patterning to the scrollbar. How can you change the scrollbar to appear in a yellow brick format?
15. You have added six graphic items to a form. These graphic objects partially overlay each other. How do you perform the following?
    a. Move the top object currently at position 6 to position 4.
    b. Move the object at position 3 to position 6.
    c. Move the object at position 5 to position 1.
    d. Move the object at position 2 to position 5.
16. You are performing some intensive form modifications and continually select the same items. How can you avoid having to continually reselect each item? How can you add an item to the group after it is created? How can you remove an item?
17. You have just created a default form style layout, and the items are scattered around the layout. Describe a methodology for placing the items in rows and columns.
18. You have created a stacked canvas. This canvas will display several employee attributes that are appropriate for management personnel to see. The attributes will display when management personnel view the form but will not display when union employees view the form. You are designing the content canvas and want to see how the canvas will appear when the stacked canvas is displayed. How can you display this canvas over the content canvas within the Layout Editor? How do you move the stacked canvas to its proper location?

EXAM REVIEW QUESTIONS

1. As you modify a frame property, the layout immediately reflects the change. Which property was set to ensure the automatic layout update?
   a. Update Frame
   b. Data Block Layout Update
   c. Update Layout
   d. Frame Layout
2. Which property would you use to set the style of a data block's items in a frame?
   a. Record Orientation
   b. Layout Style
   c. Layout Data Block
   d. Data Block Layout
3. You are adding a company boilerplate to the form module. Which form object is used to display the graphic object?
   a. Window
   b. Canvas
   c. Frame
   d. Data Block
4. Which property determines the size of the font in points?
   a. Font Size
   b. Font Width
   c. Font Weight
   d. Font Height
5. You created an EQUIPMENT_COSTS text item. The item must appear on the right side of the text item. On which Layout menu palette would you find the tool?
   a. Alignment
   b. Position
   c. Justification
   d. Border

HANDS-ON ASSIGNMENTS

1. In this assignment, you create a new form module and a data block based on the EMP table. You then format the data block items using frame properties:
   a. Create a new form module. Add a data block based on the EMP table using the Data Block Wizard and the Layout Wizard. The style should be FORM.
   b. After the data block is created, modify the frame properties to re-create the layout shown in Figure 4-43. To open the frame's Property Palette, select the frame in the Layout Editor and double-click the **Left Mouse button** or press the **F4** key.
   c. Save the form module as **ch04ex01.fmb**.

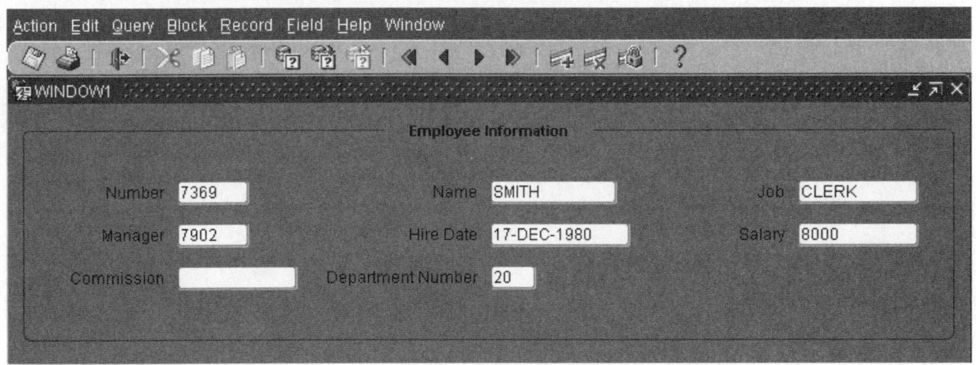

Figure 4-43 Formatted layout using frame properties

2. In this assignment, you create and overlay graphic objects, copy the graphic objects, and change their arrangement.
   a. Open form module **ch04ex01.fmb**.
   b. Open the Object Navigator and select the **Canvas Object** node. Create a new canvas by clicking the **Create** tool.
   c. Display the newly created canvas in the Layout Editor. Select the canvas in the Object Navigator and press the **F2** key.
   d. Figure 4-44 has two sets of stacked graphic objects. Create and arrange the set of graphic objects shown on the left side of Figure 4-44. Be sure to use the Group tool to keep the text and graphic objects together.
   e. Copy and paste the object you created in Step d.
   f. Reformat the objects of Step e to look like those displayed in Figure 4-44 on the right.
   g. Save the form module as **ch04ex02.fmb**.

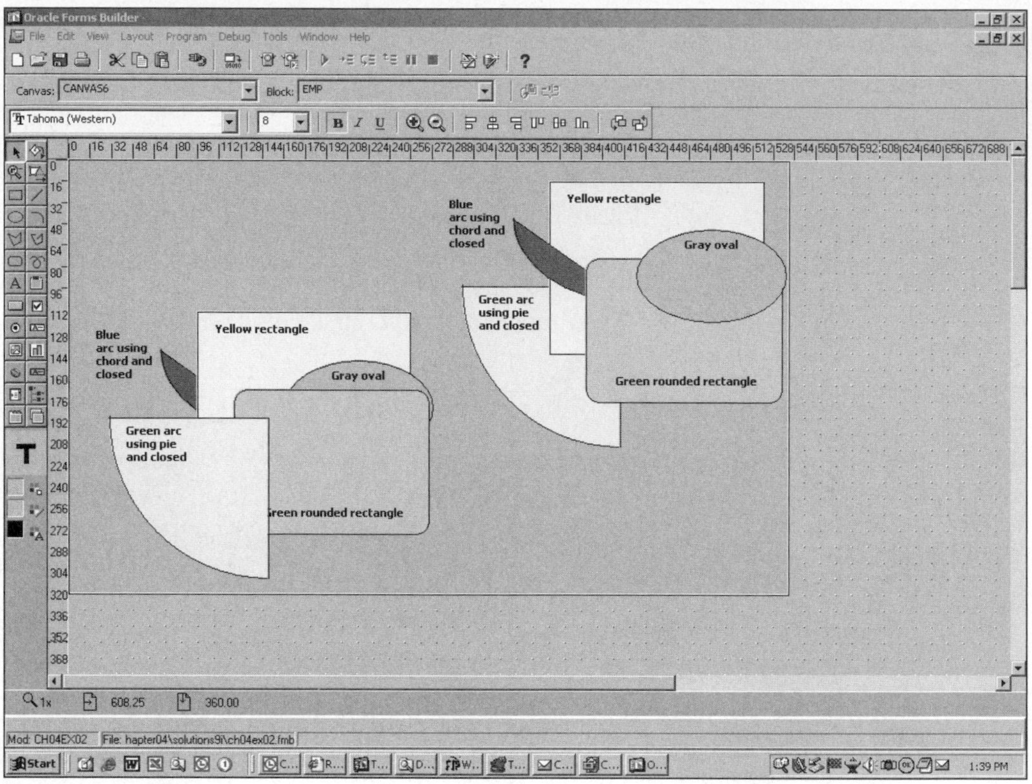

Figure 4-44 Graphic object stacks

3. In this assignment, you create a new form module and data block based on the EMP table. You then delete the frame and format the data block using the alignment tools. Perform the following steps:
   a. Create a new form module.
   b. Using the Data Block Wizard, create a data block based on the EMP table.
   c. Launch the Layout Wizard and place the data block items on a canvas. Do not set any prompt values on the Layout Wizard Items page. The form style should be FORM.
   d. Open the Object Navigator and delete the Frame object.
   e. Open the Layout Editor and format the canvas to look like Figure 4-45.
   f. Save the form as **ch0403.fmb**.

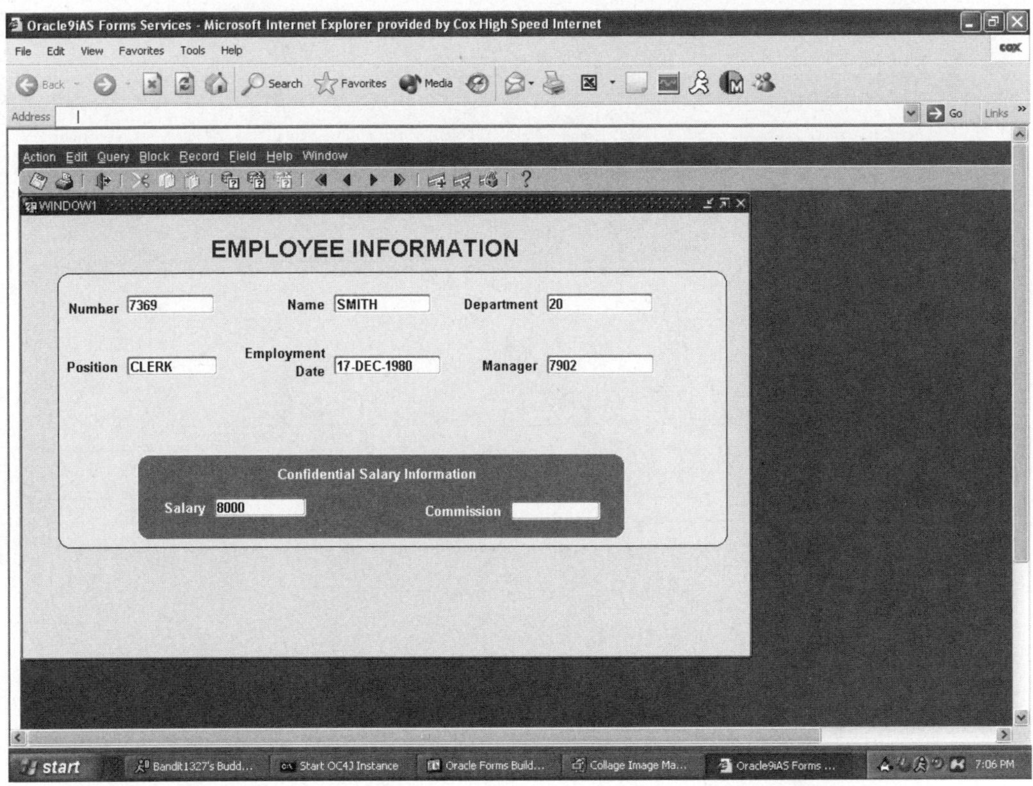

Figure 4-45 Example form layout

4. In this assignment, you create a master-detail form based on the DEPT and EMP tables and then format the items in the Layout Editor.
   a. Create a new form module in the Layout Editor.
   b. Create a block using the Data Block Wizard and the Layout Wizard. The block should use the DEPT table as the data source. The style should be FORM with only one record displayed.
   c. Create a detail block using the Data Block Wizard and the Layout Wizard. The block should use the EMP table as the data source. The style should be TABULAR and display 10 records.
   d. Use the Layout Editor to format the canvas to look like Figure 4-46.
   e. Save the form as **ch04ex04.fmb**. Launch the form and review your modifications.

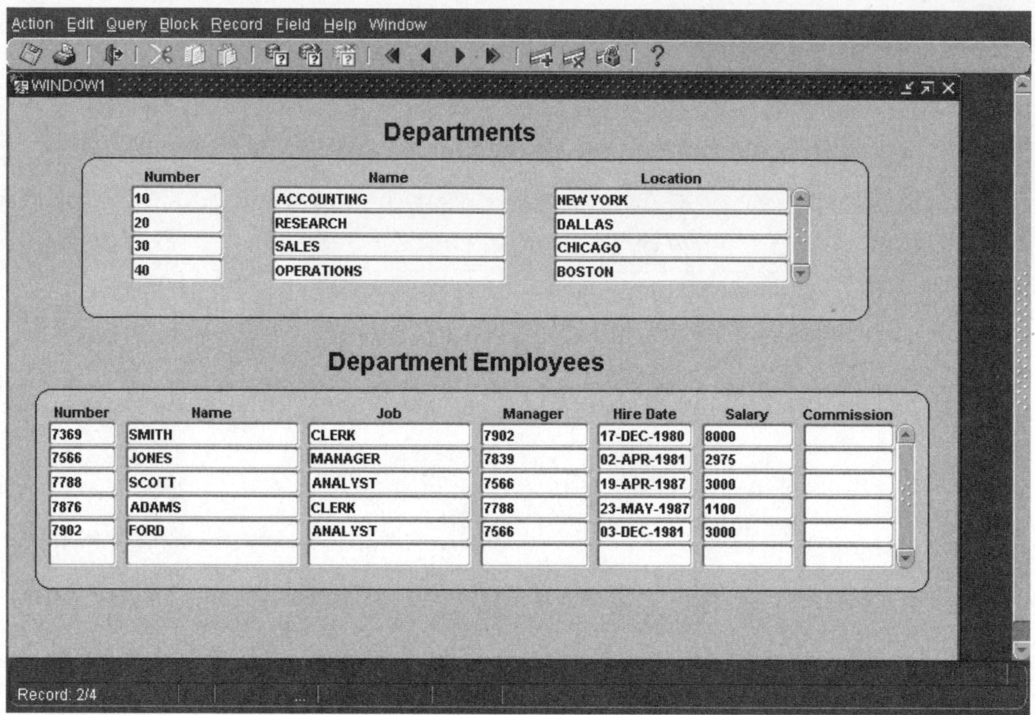

Figure 4-46 Master-detail form

CASE PROJECT: GREAT STATE ELECTRIC BUDGETING SYSTEM

At the end of the Case Project in Chapter 3, you had created but not formatted or placed the following data blocks on a canvas:

- **PROJECTS**: Will be placed on the PROJECT_ADD stacked canvas.
- **PROJ_SEARCH_CRITERIA**: Control block to be placed on the PROJECTS tab page. The tab page will be a child of the MAIN tab canvas.
- **PROJECT_DATA**: Displays project information on the PROJECTS tab page. The tab page will be a child of the MAIN tab canvas.
- **WORK_ORDERS**: Displays work order information on the PROJECTS tab page. The tab page will be a child of the MAIN tab canvas.
- **WO_SEARCH_CRITERIA**: Control block to be placed on the WORK_ORDERS tab page. The tab page will be a child of the MAIN tab canvas.
- **WORK_ORDER_DATA**: Displays work order information on the WORK_ORDERS tab page. The tab page will be a child of the MAIN tab canvas.

- **WORK_ORDER_TASKS**: Displays work order tasks on the WORK_ORDERS tab page. The tab page will be a child of the MAIN tab canvas.
- **MONTHLY_COSTS:** Displays work order task monthly costs on the WORK_ORDERS tab page. The tab page will be a child of the MAIN tab canvas.
- **WO_INSTRUCTIONS**: Will be placed on the WO_INSTRUCTIONS stacked canvas.
- **ACCOUNTS**: Will be placed on an ACCOUNTS tab page.
- **TASK_DESCRIPTIONS**: Will be placed on the TASK_DESCRIPTIONS tab page. The tab page will be a child of the MAIN tab canvas.

This Case Project installment is lengthy. In this project, you use the Layout Wizard to associate each of the above data blocks with the appropriate stacked canvas, tab canvas, and tab page. You then rename items and perform minor formatting. When you finish the project, you can execute the form and see the main system forms. The layouts used are the basic defaults, but you can begin adding important tools to the forms in future chapters.

Your Work

1. Open the Object Navigator and select the one canvas item. This canvas is the form's tab canvas. Change the name to **MAIN**.
2. Expand the **MAIN** canvas to expose the tab page used to display the EMPLOYEES data block. It should be the only tab page listed. Change the name of the tab page to **EMPLOYEES**.
3. Select the **EMPLOYEES** tab page and press the **F4** key. This opens the Property Palette of the objects. Locate the LABEL property. Change the value to **EMPLOYEES**. This changes the name on the tab.
4. Use the Layout Wizard to place the **PROJECTS** data block on a new stacked canvas. Select the **PROJECTS** data block in the Object Navigator and launch the Layout Wizard. Make the following selections and settings:
   - **Canvas**: NEW CANVAS
   - **Type**: STACKED
   - **Selection**: All available items
   - **Width and Height**: On the Prompt page, set the PROJECT_NAME, PROJECT_SCOPE, and PROJECT_LOCATION width and height values to **70** and **50**, respectively. These values are large to ensure that the canvas width is not expanded.
   - **Style**: FORM
   - **Frame Title**: PROJECT INFORMATION
   - **Records Displayed**: 1

5. Locate the new canvas in the Object Navigator and change the name to **PROJECT_ADD**.
6. Open the **PROJECT_ADD** canvas in the Layout Editor. Format the canvas as you like. Figure 4-47 illustrates a typical format.

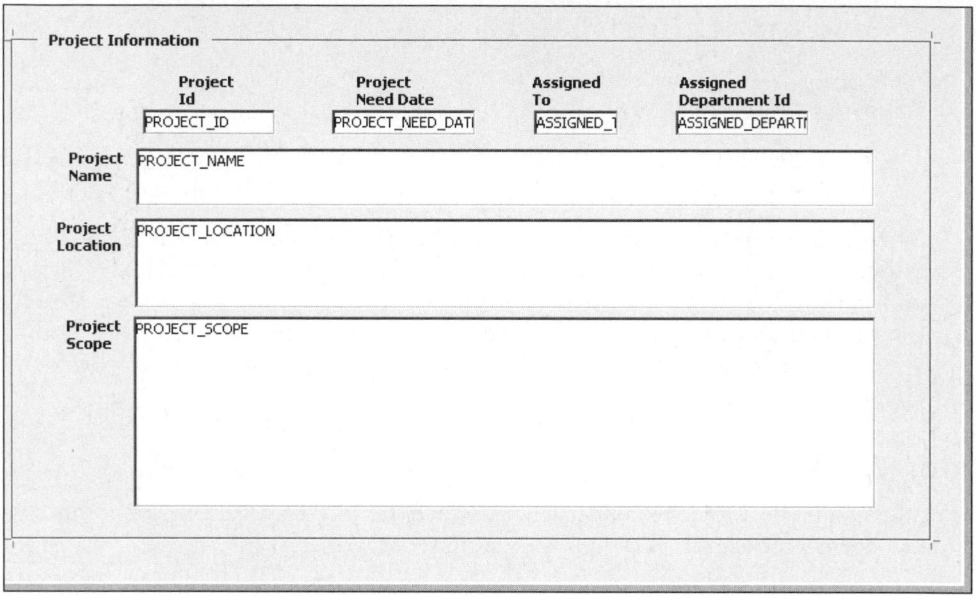

Figure 4-47 PROJECT_ADD stacked canvas

7. Use the Layout Wizard to place the PROJ_SEARCH_CRITERIA on a new tab page. Use the following selections and settings:
   - **Canvas**: MAIN
   - **Tab Page**: NEW TAB PAGE
   - **Display**: All available items
   - **Width**: Change the Width of PROJECT_NAME and PROJECT_LOCATION to **90**
   - **Style**: TABULAR
   - **Frame Title**: PROJECT SEARCH VARIABLES
   - **Records Displayed**: 1
8. Locate the newly created tab page in the Object Navigator. Change the name to **PROJECTS**. Format the data block to resemble Figure 4-48.

If you execute this form, the PROJ_SEARCH_CRITERIA data block and the newly created tab page appear, because it is the first listed data block.

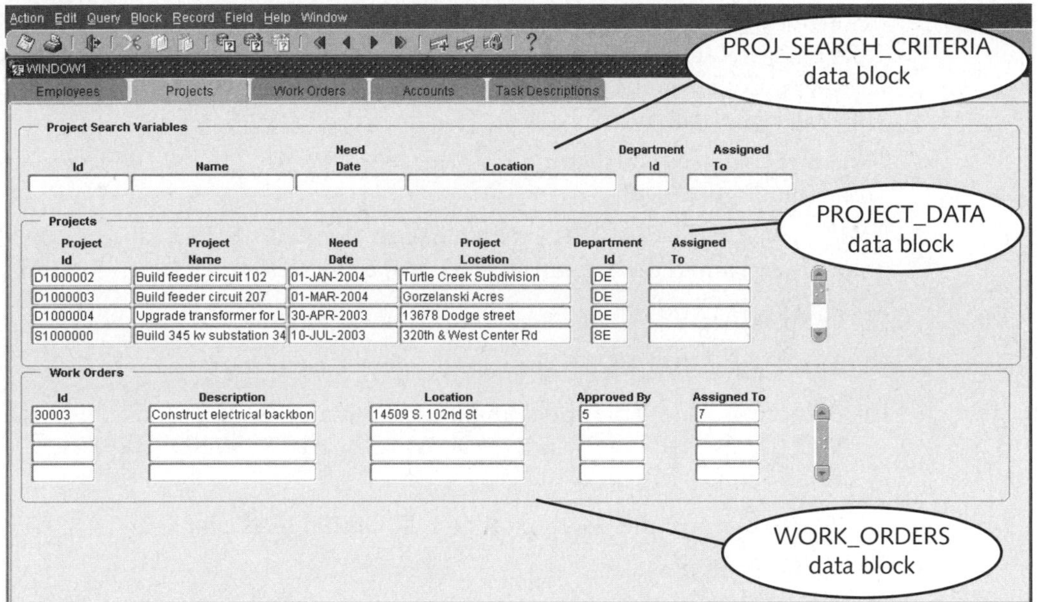

Figure 4-48 PROJECTS tab page with default settings

9. Select the newly created tab page and press the **F4** key. This opens the object's Property Palette. Locate the Label property. To change the name that is displayed on the tab, change the value to **PROJECTS**.
10. Use the Layout Wizard to place the PROJECT_DATA data block on the PROJECTS tab page. Use the following selections and settings:
    - **Canvas**: MAIN
    - **Tab Page**: PROJECTS (be sure to set this correctly)
    - **Selection**: Select the following available items: PROJECT_ID, PROJECT_NAME, PROJECT_NEED_DATE, PROJECT_LOCATION, ASSIGNED_TO, and ASSIGNED_DEPARTMENT_ID
    - **Width**: Change the width of PROJECT_NAME and PROJECT_LOCATION to **90**
    - **Style**: TABULAR
    - **Frame Title**: PROJECTS

- **Records Displayed**: 4
- **Scroll bar**: Check the Display Scrollbar check box

11. Now comes the first moment of truth. Can the PROJECT_DATA data block retrieve records? Launch the application. When the form is displayed, place your insertion point into the **Projects** frame. Execute a query. If you have entered the SELECT statement correctly, records display in the data block. If you receive an error, you did not enter the SELECT statement correctly from Case Project 3. Recheck the statement.
12. Open the Object Navigator and format the PROJECT_DATA data block to resemble Figure 4-48.
13. Add the WORK_ORDERS data block to the PROJECTS tab page. Select this block and launch the Layout Wizard. Make the following selections and settings:
    - **Canvas**: MAIN
    - **Tab Page**: PROJECTS (be sure to set this correctly)
    - **Selection**: Select the following available items: WORK_ORDER_ID, WO_DESCRIPTION, WO_LOCATION, APPROVED_BY, and ASSIGNED_TO
    - **Width**: Change the width of WO_DESCRIPTION and WO_LOCATION to **90**
    - **Style**: TABULAR
    - **Frame Title**: WORK ORDERS
    - **Records Displayed**: 4
    - **Scroll bar**: Check the Display Scrollbar check box

Format the WORK_ORDERS data block per Figure 4-48. This figure illustrates the PROJECTS tab page after the default settings and minor formatting has been added.

14. The next set of tasks create the default WORK_ORDERS tab page. Select the **WO_SEARCH_CRITERIA** control block and launch the Layout Wizard. Make the following selections and settings:
    - **Canvas**: MAIN
    - **Tab Page**: NEW TAB PAGE (be sure to perform this correctly)
    - **Selection**: Select all of the available items
    - **Width**: Change the width of the WO_LOCATION and WO_DESCRIPTION items to **90**
    - **Style**: TABULAR
    - **Frame Title**: WORK ORDER SEARCH VARIABLES
    - **Records Displayed**: 1

15. Select the tab page created in Step 14 in the Object Navigator and change the name to **WORK_ORDERS**.
16. Select the **WORK_ORDERS** tab page and press the **F4** key. This opens the object's Property Palette. Locate the Label property. Change the value to **WORK ORDERS**. This changes the name on the tab.
17. Format the WO_SEARCH_CRITERIA data block to resemble Figure 4-49.

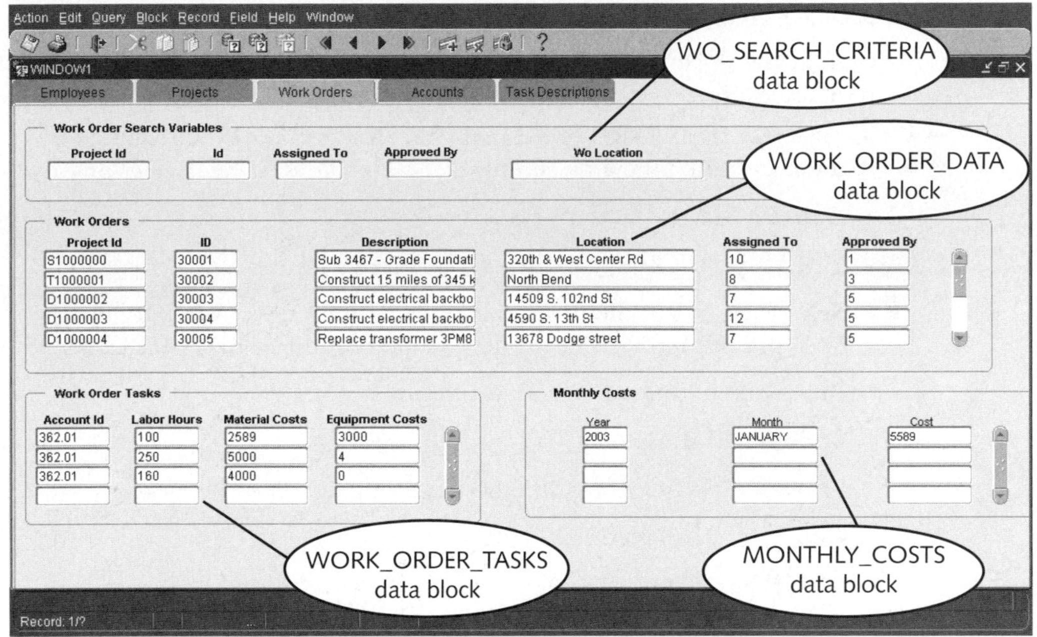

Figure 4-49 WORK_ORDERS tab page displaying budget data

18. Add the WORK_ORDER_DATA data block to the WORK_ORDERS tab page. Select the **WORK_ORDER_DATA** data block and launch the Layout Wizard. Make the following selections and settings:
    - **Canvas**: MAIN
    - **Tab Page**: WORK_ORDERS (be sure to perform this correctly)
    - **Adding Items**: Add the following available items to the tab page: WORK_ORDER_ID, WO_DESCRIPTION, WO_LOCATION, ASSIGNED_TO, APPROVED_BY, and PROJECT_ID
    - **Width**: Change the width of WORK_ORDER_ID, WO_DESCRIPTION, and WO_LOCATION to **90**
    - **Style**: TABULAR
    - **Frame Title**: WORK ORDERS

- **Records Displayed**: 5
- **Scroll bar**: Check the Display Scrollbar check box

19. Now comes the second moment of truth. Can the WORK_ORDER_DATA data block successfully return records? Launch the application. Click the various tabs at the top of the form until the WORK_ORDERS_DATA data block displays. This tab page should be furthest to the right. Place your insertion point in the data block and execute a query. The application should return records. If you receive a database error, check the SELECT statement you entered in Case Project 3.
20. Format the WORK_ORDER_DATA data block to resemble Figure 4-49.
21. Add the WORK_ORDER_TASKS data block to the WORK_ORDERS tab page. Select the **WORK_ORDER_TASKS** data block and launch the Layout Wizard. Use the following settings:
    - **Canvas**: MAIN
    - **Tab Page**: WORK_ORDERS (be sure to perform this correctly)
    - **Selection**: Select the following available items: ACCOUNT_ID, LABOR_HOURS, MATERIAL_COSTS, and EQUIPMENT_COSTS
    - **Prompts**: Change the prompt titles to suit yourself
    - **Style**: TABULAR
    - **Frame Title**: WORK ORDER TASKS
    - **Records Displayed**: 4
    - **Scroll bar**: Check the Display Scrollbar check box
22. Format the WORK_ORDER_TASKS data block to resemble Figure 4-49.
23. Add the MONTHLY_COSTS data block to the WORK_ORDER tab page. Select the **MONTHLY_COSTS** data block and launch the Layout Wizard. Use the following settings:
    - **Canvas**: MAIN
    - **Tab Page**: WORK_ORDERS (be sure to perform this correctly)
    - **Selection**: Select the following available items: YEAR, MONTH, and COST
    - **Prompts**: Change the prompt titles to suit yourself
    - **Style**: TABULAR
    - **Frame Title**: MONTHLY COSTS
    - **Records Displayed**: 4
    - **Scroll bar**: Check the Display Scrollbar check box
24. Format the MONTHLY_COSTS data block to resemble Figure 4-49.

25. Execute the form and determine whether the WORK_ORDER_DATA, WORK_ORDER_TASKS, and MONTHLY_COSTS data blocks return data. Perform the query on the WORK_ORDER_DATA data block. If the block doesn't return data, you must debug the SQL. You probably forgot to link the data blocks using the Master-Detail Data Block Wizard page. If your form is working, it should look similar to Figure 4-49.
26. Add the ACCOUNTS data block to the form on a new tab page. Select the **ACCOUNTS** data block and launch the Layout Wizard. Use the following selections and settings:
    - **Canvas**: MAIN
    - **Tab Page**: NEW TAB PAGE (be sure to set this correctly)
    - **Selection**: Select all of the available items
    - **Prompts**: Change the prompt titles to suit yourself
    - **Style**: TABULAR
    - **Frame Title**: ACCOUNTS
    - **Records Displayed**: 15
    - **Scroll bar**: Check the Display Scrollbar check box.
27. Select the tab page created in Step 26 in the Object Navigator and change the name to **ACCOUNTS**.
28. Select the **ACCOUNTS** tab page and press the **F4** key. This opens the object's Property Palette. Locate the Label property. To change the name on the tab, change the value to **ACCOUNTS**.
29. Add the TASK_DESCRIPTIONS data block to the form on a new tab page. Select the **TASK_DESCRIPTIONS** data block and launch the Layout Wizard. Use the following selections and settings:
    - **Canvas**: MAIN
    - **Tab Page**: NEW TAB PAGE
    - **Selection**: Select all of the available items
    - **Prompts**: Change the prompt titles to suit yourself
    - **Style**: TABULAR
    - **Frame Title**: TASK DESCRIPTIONS
    - **Records Displayed**: 15
    - **Scroll bar**: Check the Display Scrollbar check box
30. Select the tab page created in Step 29 in the Object Navigator and change the name to **TASK_DESCRIPTIONS**

31. Select the **TASK_DESCRIPTIONS** tab page and press the **F4** key. This opens the object's Property Palette. Locate the LABEL property. To change the name of the tab, change the value to **TASK DESCRIPTIONS**.
32. Add the WO_INSTRUCTIONS data block to the form as a stacked canvas. Select the **WO_INSTRUCTIONS** data block and launch the Layout Wizard. Make the following selections and settings:
    - **Canvas**: NEW CANVAS
    - **Type**: STACKED (be sure to set this correctly)
    - **Selection**: Select all of the available items
    - **Prompts**: Change the prompt titles to suit yourself
    - **Width**: Set the width of the WORK_ORDER_DESCRIPTION, WORK_ORDER_LOCATION, and WORK_ORDER_INSTRUCTIONS to **90**
    - **Style**: FORM
    - **Frame Title**: WORK ORDER INFORMATION
    - **Records Displayed**: 1
33. Select the tab page created in Step 32 in the Object Navigator and change the name to **WO_INSTRUCTIONS**.
34. Color the PROJECT_ADD, WO_INSTRUCTIONS, and MAIN canvases using a soft fill color. For the figures in this book, a light green was used for the MAIN canvas and a light yellow for the PROJECT_ADD and WO_INSTRUCTION canvases.

At this point, you have created the basic Budgeting form components and you (and your user) can actually operate the prototype. Most of the formatting is by default. You could now begin using some of the skills you learned in this chapter, but this would be wasted effort. In the Case Project sections to come, you will be adding descriptive items, such as employee names, to the data blocks. The user will be much happier seeing a name rather than a payroll number.

You will also be adding check boxes, radio groups, buttons, and other objects. As you add these components to the form, you will be practicing the skills that you learned in this chapter.

CHAPTER

5

Controlling Form Behavior and Format Using Properties, Property Classes, and the Property Palette

In this chapter you will:

- Learn the purpose of properties and property types
- Operate the Property Palette
- Create and use property classes
- Create and use visual attributes
- Control form navigation using properties
- Learn about important block properties
- Create reusable components using object groups and libraries
- Create and use SmartClasses
- Change properties during runtime

As the roadmap in Figure 5-1 depicts, this chapter focuses primarily on using the Property Palette to modify properties that control form behavior. The Property Palette is the third major Forms Builder IDE tool and is used to set scores of object properties. Properties are values that control a specific form format or behavior. A property can be the X coordinate of a canvas, the font size of a frame title, or the range of values that can be entered into an item, or it can be used to control whether a master data block can delete records if child records exist. You have been introduced to properties and the Property Palette in other chapters, but there hasn't been a discussion of how to operate the tool or how to format and control the behavior of the form using properties. Before working with properties, you needed to learn the skills for setting up the form.

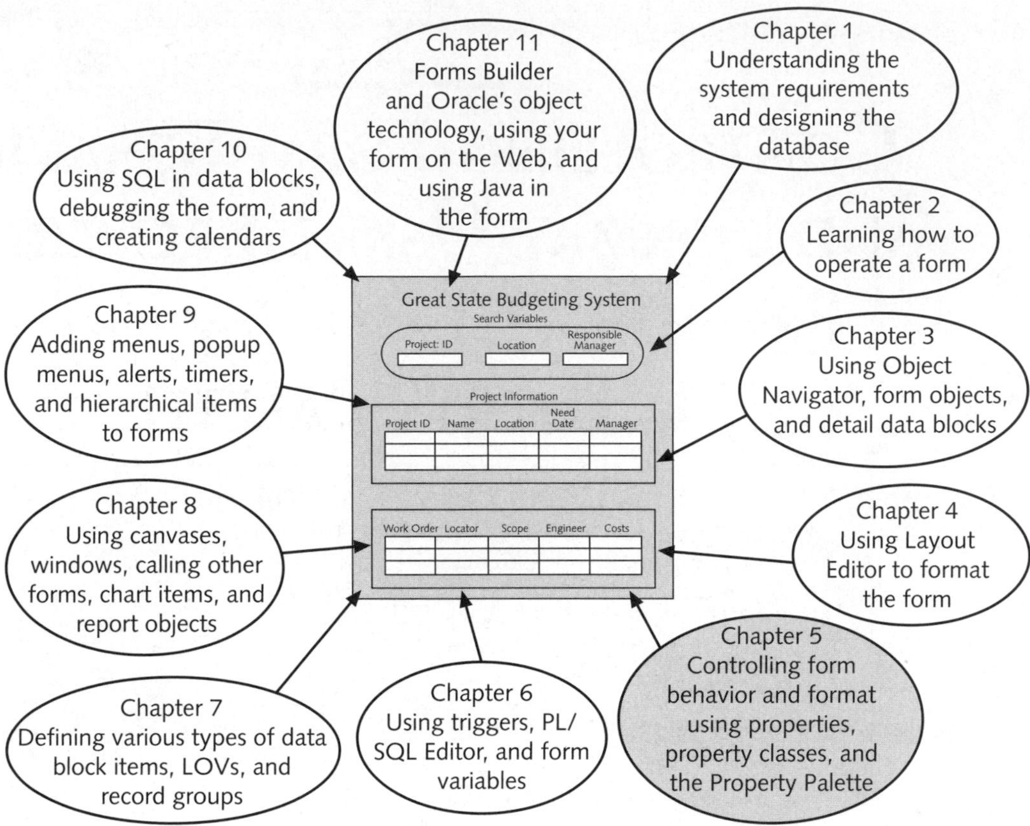

Figure 5-1 Roadmap

This chapter takes you to the next level. You learn how to set numerous form properties simultaneously and to visually compare the properties of two different items. You are introduced to property classifications and also learn how to use visual attributes and property classes to ensure that like objects have the same property values. This chapter also discusses some commonly used data block properties. And you are introduced to object libraries that allow you to reuse form components. Finally, this chapter introduces you to several Forms Builder built-in subprograms. Built-in subprograms are Oracle-developed procedures. Several of these subprograms are used to change form properties at runtime. You can set colors, order your data differently, or hide items with these built-in subprograms.

PROPERTIES AND PROPERTY TYPES

A property is a form module setting that controls a form attribute such as an item's data type, the order in which records are displayed, the color of the canvas, or an item prompt. Generic programs are composed of settings that control some feature of the application. If you were writing a program years ago in COBOL or FORTRAN or an application in HTML today, you would write statements that place characters at a specific point in the layout or that construct a specific format. Each displayed character or place to receive data has to be individually spelled out. To illustrate, Listing 5-1 contains a portion of the HTML code used on my Web site. Notice that I wrote a number of commands such as WIDTH, ALIGN, and COLOR. Each of the commands is the same as a property setting in Forms Builder. The difference is that Forms Builder is a fourth-generation tool that allows you to avoid writing these types of commands. Forms Builder's graphic user interface does a great deal of work for you. You use Forms Builder to be productive, just as you use Microsoft FrontPage or Macromedia Dreamweaver to be productive in creating HTML scripts. It's possible to write your HTML scripts in a product such as Microsoft Word, but it is preferable to use a fourth-generation tool. All of the fourth-generation tools actually create compiled programs, just as for COBOL, FORTRAN, and HTML. These programs all have numerous settings, and, in the case of Forms Builder, the settings are defined as property values.

5

Listing 5-1 HTML code

```
<tr>
    <td width="100%"><h1 align="center"><font color="#008080">
           <big>Realistic Software Training</big></font></h1>
    <p align="center"><strong><big><big>A Totally Unique Oracle
             Trainer/Developer/Consultant</big></big></strong></p>
    </td>
  </tr>
```

One of the hardest things for a new Forms Builder developer is to identify the needed property and to locate the form object in which it is set. Appendix B can help you, because all properties are grouped by type in the Property Palette. Properties that pertain to height, width, X position, or Y position are grouped under Physical properties. Using Appendix B, you can locate the Physical properties and identify the potential form objects that have that property. Appendix B not only lists all properties by type of property, it also lists the objects that have that property. This is useful because the same property can be associated to several objects. Because lower-level object property settings supersede higher-level object settings, it is important to identify all objects that have the same property. For example, if a data block has a setting of 10 for the Number Of Records Displayed property and a frame has a setting of 5, the frame value of 5 will be used.

OPERATING THE PROPERTY PALETTE

The Property Palette is the only Forms Builder tool that can modify any form property. This ability distinguishes it from other tools that can modify only selected properties, such as the Layout Editor and wizards. You can display the Property Palette through a number of methods:

- Double-clicking any object(s) in the Object Navigator
- Double-clicking any object(s) in the Layout Editor
- Pressing the F4 key
- Selecting Tools/Property Palette from the menu
- Right-clicking the mouse button to open a popup menu and selecting the Property Palette menu option

Forms Builder synchronizes the properties in the Property Palette with the currently selected object(s). When the Property Palette is displayed, it lists the appropriate properties and their values. If the Property Palette is launched and an object is not selected, the Property Palette contains no properties.

To practice using the Property Palette, follow these steps:

1. Create a new form. Add a data block to the module. The data block should be based on the EMP table. The style should be Form and one record should be displayed.
2. Display the Object Navigator by pressing the **F3** key.
3. Select the **EMP** data block and launch the Property Palette by pressing the **F4** key.
4. Scroll through the Property Palette and notice the different property types and sets of properties under each property type.
5. Save the form for later practice.

Entering Property Values

It is relatively easy to enter property values. The Property Palette has a number of tools that enable you to select or easily enter a value. These tools are shown in Figures 5-2 through 5-5.

- **Drop-down List**: Displays a list of values for your selection (see Figure 5-2).
- **Text Item**: Allows you to type in a value (see Figure 5-2).

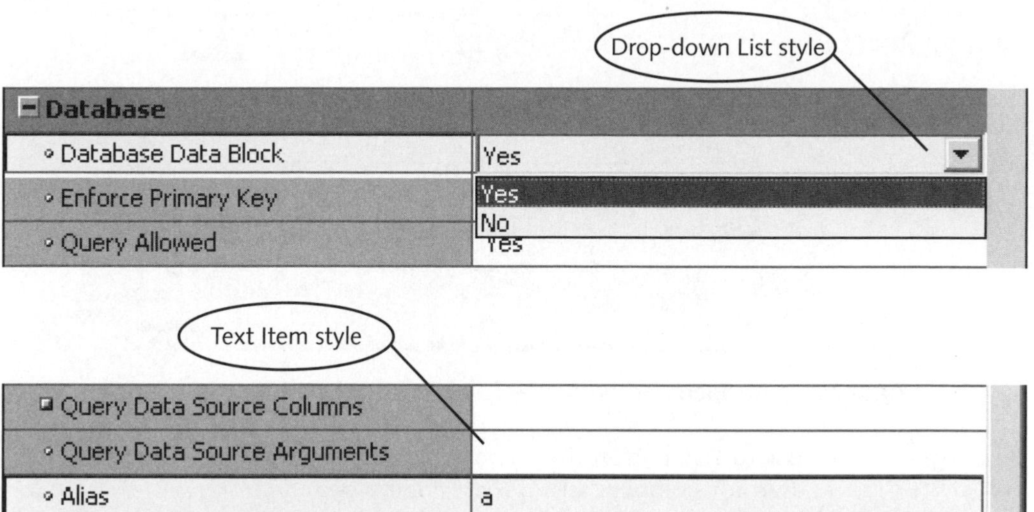

Figure 5-2 Drop-down list and Text Item styles

- **Editor**: A text item that contains an Editor button. The editor is a handy device for entering complex values such as a SELECT statement Where clause (see Figure 5-3).

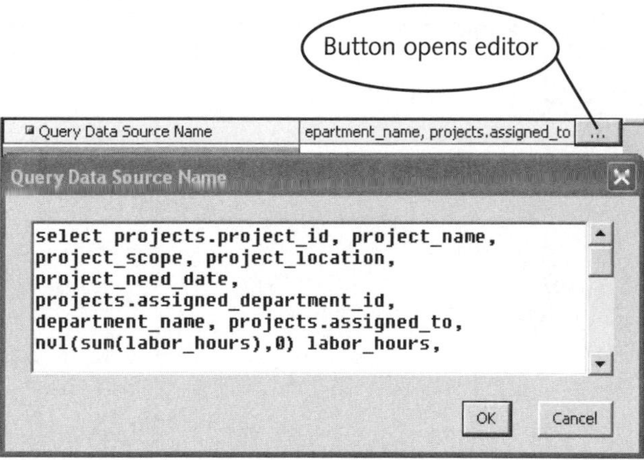

Figure 5-3 Property entry tools—Editor style

- **Color Palette**: A text item that employs a color palette used to view and select a color (see Figure 5-4).

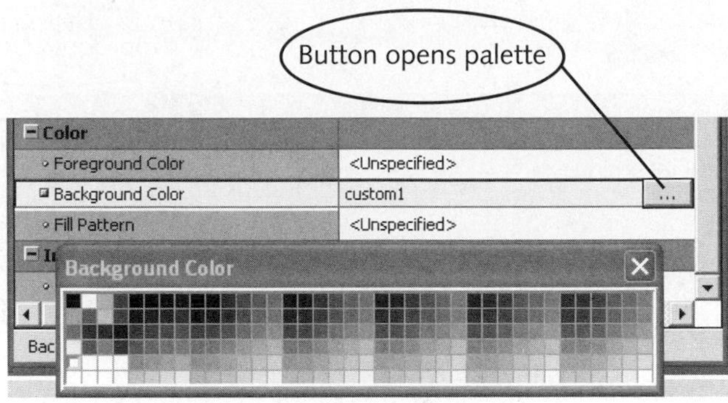

Figure 5-4 Property entry tools—Color Palette style

- **Button**: A button that appears in the property. The button opens a dialog box used for complex settings (see Figure 5-5).

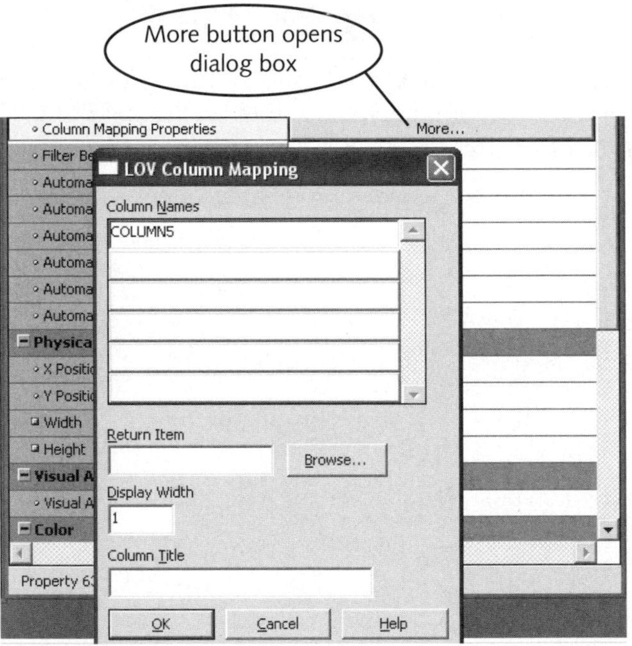

Figure 5-5 Property entry tools—Button style

As soon as you place the insertion point into a property, Forms Builder displays a description of the property in the status bar at the bottom of the Property Palette. This description can help you understand the use of the property.

As practice, perform the following steps to set the canvas color and the sort order of the EMP data block.

1. Open the practice form in the Object Navigator and locate the EMP property.
2. Locate the Canvas object and open a Property Palette for the item by pressing the **F4** key.
3. Locate the Background Color property. Click inside the property text item to display a button to the right of the text item. Click this button to open the Background Color palette.
4. Locate the EMP data block in the Object Navigator. Open the Property Palette by double-clicking the **EMP** data block icon.
5. Locate the ORDER BY Clause property. Click inside the property text item to display a button in the text item. Click the button to open the ORDER BY Clause editor. Enter **EMPNO** and click **OK**.
6. Launch the form and determine if the canvas color has changed and if the records are sorted by employee number (EMPNO).
7. Save the form for later practice.

Setting Properties for Multiple Objects

As you practice developing forms, you learn that it can be time consuming to set properties, especially if you have to set the properties individually. For example, because Oracle is case sensitive, many developers prefer to set the Case Restriction property of all items to UPPER. Forms Builder does not have a wizard for setting this property, and therefore the developer must set the property in the item's Property Palette by selecting each item (to open the Property Palette) and setting the property.

Fortunately, Forms Builder allows the developer to set multiple item properties simultaneously using the Property Palette. If you select multiple objects (by holding down the Shift or Control keys while selecting the objects) and launch the Property Palette, Forms Builder displays a multiple-selection Property Palette. If you set a property in this palette, Forms Builder sets the corresponding property on all selected objects, thereby saving you a considerable amount of time.

You do not have to select the same types of objects when performing a multiple selection. You can select any combination in the Object Navigator or the Layout Editor. When Forms Builder displays the multiple-selection Property Palette, these two different sets of properties can be listed:

- **INTERSECTION view**: Displays the common properties for the selected objects (Figure 5-6a). This view is indicated when the Intersection/Union tool squares display a whitened area.

- **UNION view**: Displays all properties for the selected objects (Figure 5-6b) even if some of the selected objects do not have this property. This view is indicated when the Intersection/Union tool square icons are darkened.

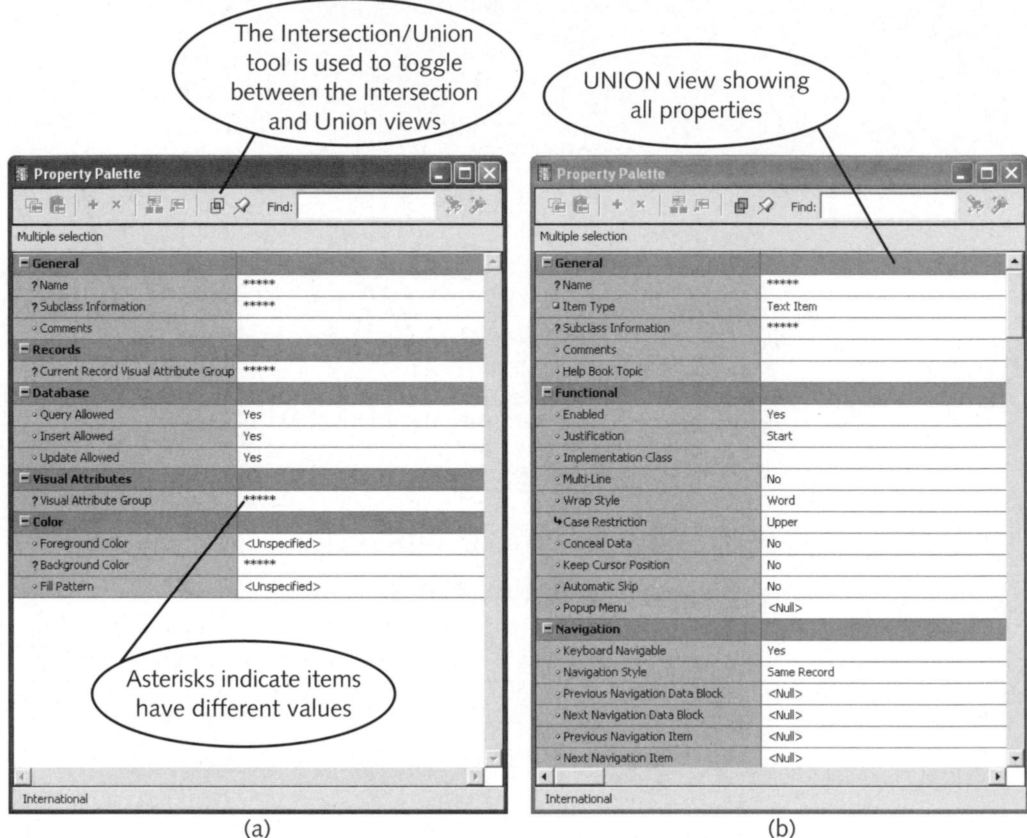

Figure 5-6 Multiple-selection Property Palettes in the INTERSECTION and UNION view modes

The UNION view is the better of the two views, because it allows the developer to see all properties. If a selected object does not have the updated property, the update does not affect the object. Updates only affect the objects that have the property.

To change the Property Palette view, click the Intersection/Union tool.

Figures 5-6a and 5-6b illustrate both views of the multiple-selection Property Palettes. A data block and all of its child data items were selected in the Object Navigator. These objects have few common properties; thus there is a significant difference in the property lists. Another important feature of the list is the properties that are preceded by a question mark (?) and whose values are populated with asterisks (*****). This indicates that several of the items have different values. For example, the Name property in Figure 5-6a and the

Column Name property in Figure 5-6b are populated with asterisks. This is because each selected object must have a unique name, and data items should be associated to different database columns.

The asterisk values can be modified. In the cases of the Name and Column Name properties, it doesn't make sense to change the values. However, if you selected all of the data items on your form and the Height property contained asterisks, this would suggest that the items have different values. It would be perfectly proper to modify the Height property setting, thereby insuring that all data items have the same height. If a property in the Property Palette has a readable value, all selected common objects have this value.

As practice, open a multiple-selection Property Palette and change the views by following these steps:

1. Open the Object Navigator and display the practice form.
2. Select the following objects: the canvas, each of the EMP data block items, and the **EMP** data block.
3. Press the **F4** key to open the multiple-selection Property Palette.
4. Use the Intersection/Union tool to change views. Notice the items that have asterisks.
5. With the palette in UNION mode, locate the Case Restriction property. Change the value to **UPPER**.
6. Launch the form and determine whether values are uppercase.
7. Save the form for later practice.

Comparing and Copying Properties from Multiple Property Palettes

At times, it is necessary to compare the properties of two or more objects. You can open a multiple-selection Property Palette, but that won't show you what the different property values are. The Pin/Unpin tool at the top of the Property Palette allows you to view multiple occurrences of the Property Palette by using the yellow pin icon that represents this tool. The tool can be toggled on and off. You can identify the mode as follows:

- **Unpin mode**: When the Property Palette is in this mode, the tool displays a side view of the pin showing the pinpoint (see Figure 5-7). This mode causes the contents of the Property Palette to change every time a new object is selected.
- **Pin mode**: When the Property Palette is in this mode, the tool displays the pin head as if the pin were pushed into an object (see Figure 5-7). This mode prevents Forms Builder from changing the property list every time a new object is selected. Forms Builder also launches a new Property Palette each time you launch a palette for a new object.

Figure 5-7 illustrates two Property Palettes, one in Unpin mode and the other in Pin mode.

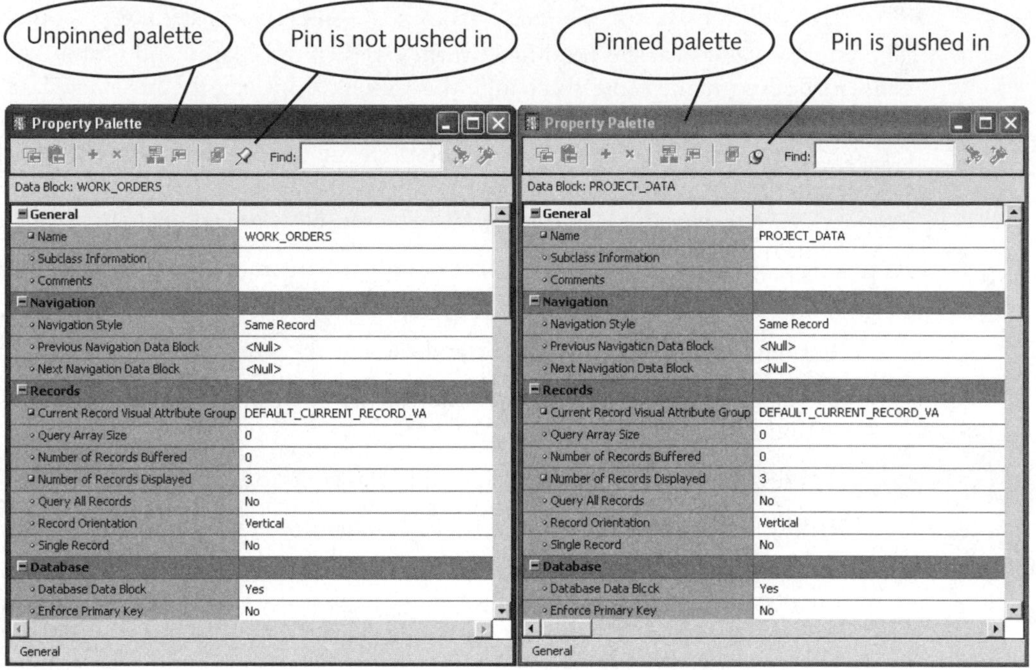

Figure 5-7 Pinned and unpinned Property Palette annotations

To pin a Property Palette and display a second palette, perform the following steps:

1. Launch the Property Palette for a selected object.
2. Pin the palette by clicking the Pin/Unpin tool. A yellow pinhead should appear.
3. Select another object and launch the Property Palette.

After viewing the palettes, you may decide to modify properties in either the Pin or Unpin Palette. You can update any property, or you may copy one or more properties from one palette to the other. The Property Palette Copy Properties and Paste Properties tools allow you to perform this task. These tools are in the top-left corner of the toolbar (see Figure 5-8) in the Property Palette. The following list describes techniques for copying one property:

1. Place the insertion point into the box of the property description or value to be copied.
2. Click the **Copy Properties** tool of the originating palette.

3. Select the target Property Palette or any property within the target Property Palette. This shifts the input focus to that Palette.
4. Click the **Paste Properties** tool of the receiving palette. The copied properties are placed into the corresponding property.

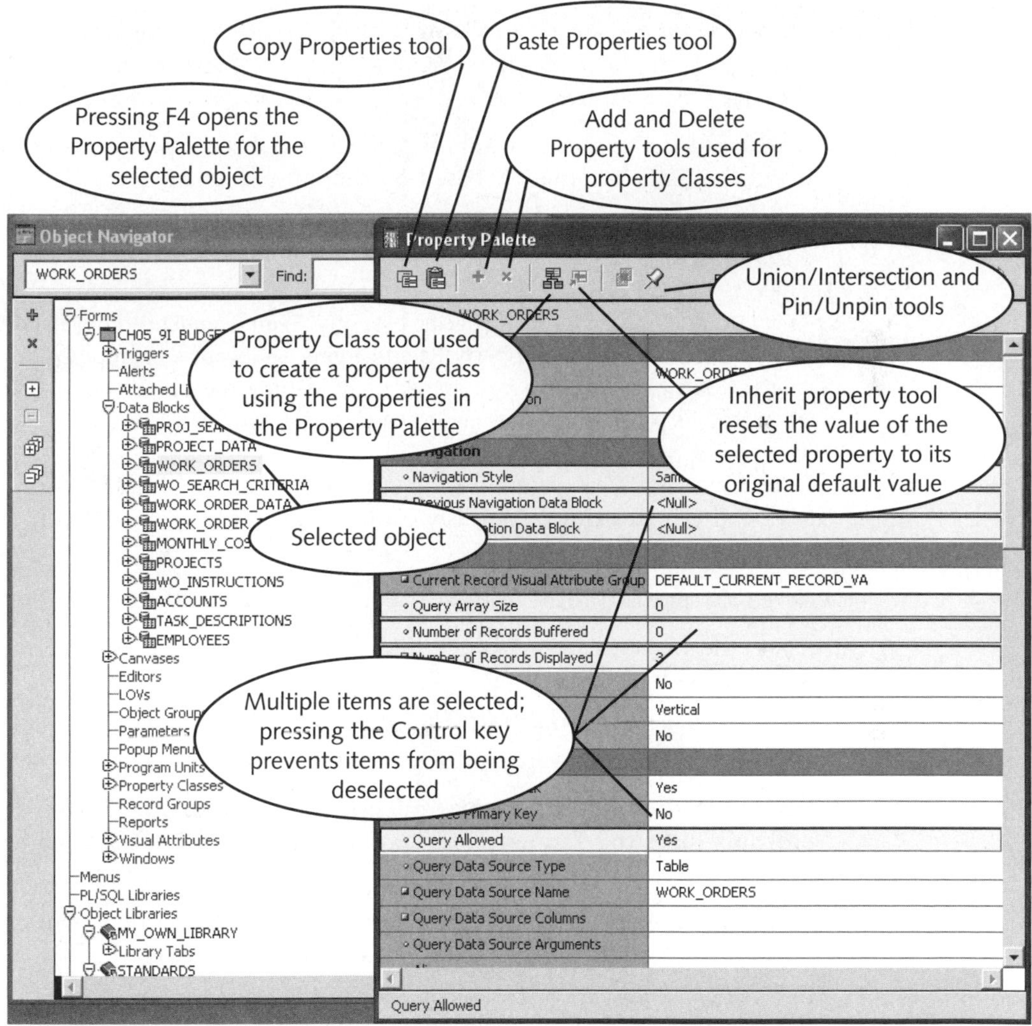

Figure 5-8 Copy Properties tool, Paste Properties tool, and multiple property selections

It is also possible to copy multiple properties between the items. To select multiple properties without deselecting a property, hold down the Shift or Control keys while selecting properties. The Shift key allows you to select multiple properties located between two selected properties. The Control keys allow you to select (or deselect) individual properties anywhere in the palette. When you use multiple properties, they look different from other Forms Builder multiple selections. The bevel of the selected property changes to inset rather than coloring the background, as can be seen in Figure 5-8.

Searching for Properties

The Property Palette has several tools for locating a specific property. These tools are the same as the Find tools located in the Object Navigator and are described as follows:

- A text box for entering search criteria. The insertion point moves to the first occurrence of the property based on the entered characters.
- Two search tools that perform forward and backward searches based on the entered search value.

It is often difficult to locate a specific property. Even experienced developers scroll up and down the Property Palette trying to locate the property. The search tools may not help you immediately identify the proper object, but they may help you avoid scrolling in search of the property.

As practice, follow these steps to open Property Palettes for the HIREDATE and MGR items, view both palettes simultaneously, and copy the HIREDATE Width property to MGR:

1. Open the practice form in the Object Navigator.
2. Open the Layout Editor. Notice that the HIREDATE and MRG items have different widths.
3. Double-click the **HIREDATE** item to open a Property Palette. Click the **Pin** tool. Move the Property Palette to the right side of the IDE window.
4. Double-click the **MGR** item to open its Property Palette. Forms Builder will probably place this Property Palette over the pinned HIREDATE palette. Move the MGR palette to the left to display both palettes.
5. Enter **WI** into the HIREDATE Property Palette search text item. Notice that the Width property appears at the bottom of the palette.
6. Place your insertion point into the Width property. Click the **Copy Properties** tool.
7. Locate the MGR item Width property. Place your insertion point into the property's text item. Click the **Paste Properties** tool to copy the new value into the item.

8. Press the **F2** key to open the Layout Editor. Notice that the MGR and HIREDATE items have the same width.

9. Save the form for later practice.

Creating and Using Property Classes

Forms Builder has a form object called a **property class** that is used to ensure that objects have the same property settings. Property classes are a set of properties that can be assigned to one or more objects. The property class properties override existing object properties. The action of assigning a property class to an object is called **inheritance**. A property class can be assigned to any form object, but a particularly good use of a property class is setting item properties.

To create a property class, follow these steps:

1. Open the Object Navigator and select the **Property Classes** object.

2. Create a new property class object by clicking the **Create** tool.

3. Open a Property Palette for the new property class.

4. Add properties to the property class using the Properties dialog box. Open this dialog box by clicking the Add Property tool located at the top of the Property Palette (see Figure 5-9).

5. To identify the property, scroll through the list or place a search value in the FIND text item and click **Enter**.

6. Highlight the object and click **OK**. The property is moved to the Property Palette.

Figure 5-9 illustrates the Property Palette for a typical property class. The figure also depicts the Properties dialog box that is used to choose properties, as well as the corresponding Object Navigator property class object.

To delete a property from the property class, perform the following steps:

1. Open the Property Palette for the property class.

2. Select the property.

3. Click the **Delete Property** tool (see Figure 5-9) to delete the property.

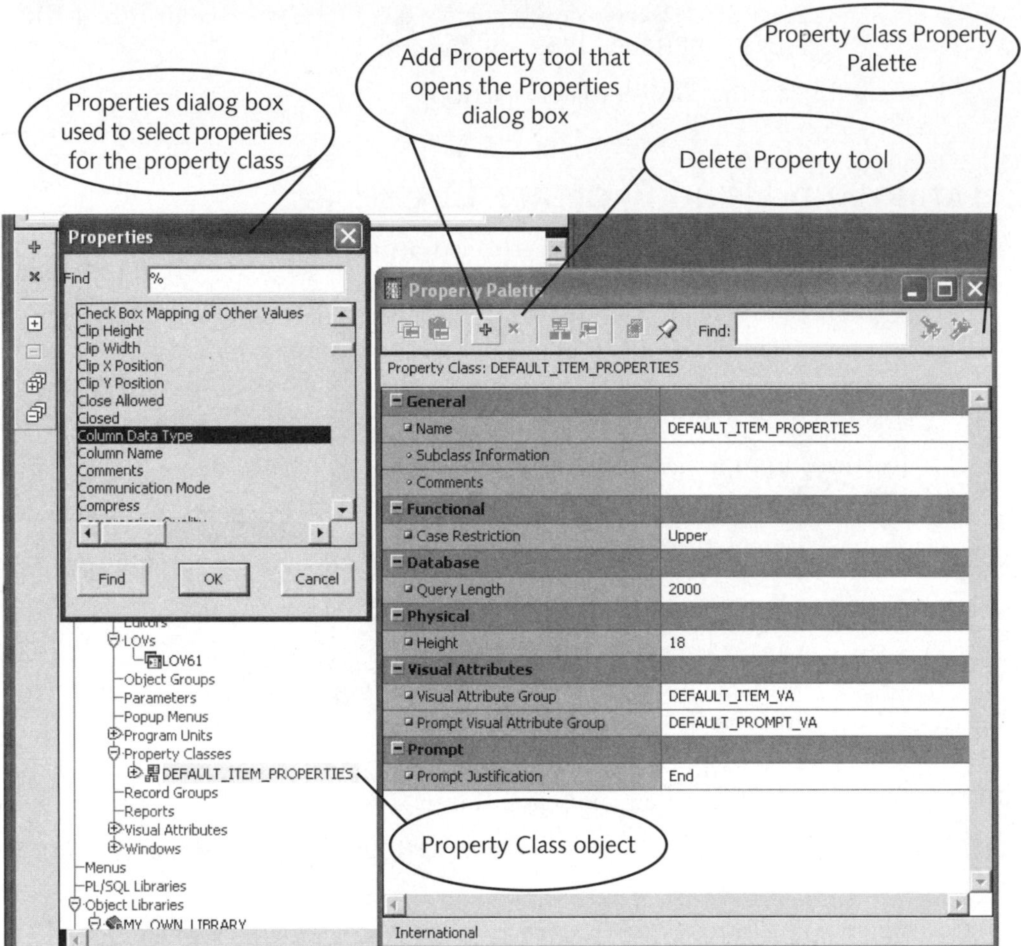

Figure 5-9 Property class properties and the Properties dialog box

After a property class has been created, it can be assigned to an object. Perform the following steps to assign a property class to an object:

1. Open the Property Palette for the target object.
2. Select the Subclass Information property. A button appears on the right side of the text item (see Figure 5-10).
3. Click the **Subclass Information property editor** button. The Subclass Information dialog box opens.
4. Select the **Property Class** radio button (see Figure 5-10).

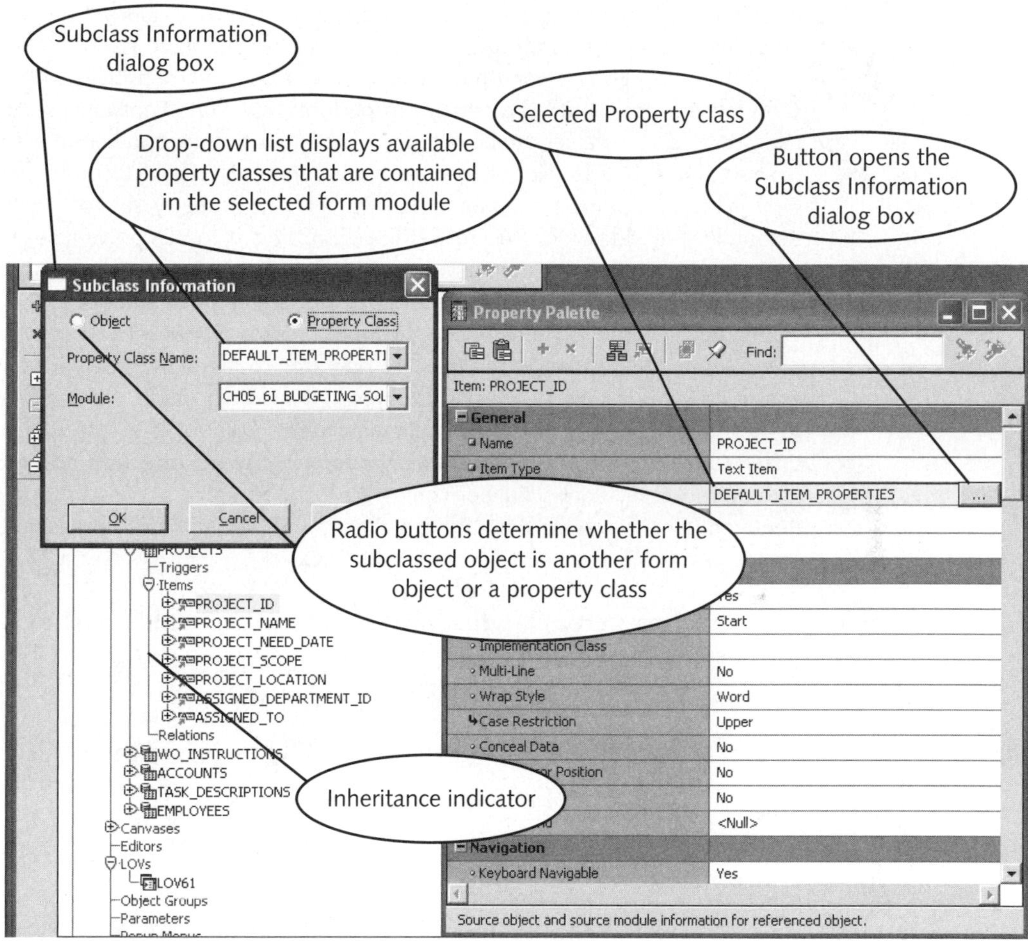

Figure 5-10 Subclass Information dialog box and the object and property annotations

5. Select the property class from the drop-down list and click **OK**. The class is now assigned to the object, thereby overriding the object's corresponding properties.

Properties that receive their values from a property class or an object that is assigned a property class are annotated in the Object Navigator and Property Palettes. Object Navigator objects are annotated with a small red arrow at the bottom-left corner of the object icon. Property Palette properties are annotated with a black downward arrow to the left of the property. These annotations are shown in Figure 5-10 along with the Subclass Information dialog box.

It is common to format all text items with the same property values. Common properties are the font, font size, and font weight. Setting the Case Restriction property to UPPER is a good practice due to Oracle's case sensitivity. If you allow mixed case, it may be difficult to perform SQL statement against the tables. Mixed-case values can be difficult to use in arguments. Another property to set is Required. Data block items that correspond to NOT-NULL constrained Oracle table columns (i.e., primary keys) have this property set to YES by default by the Data Block Wizard. Setting this property to YES prevents users from navigating from the item until a value is entered. This often causes users problems when they want to navigate to a part of the form and not enter a value into the Required item. When the input focus is moved into a Required item, Forms Builder does not allow the operator to leave the item without entering a value. Forms are initially displayed in the Normal mode. It is common for the operator to want to immediately change the mode to the ENTER QUERY mode to retrieve a record into the form. If the input focus drops into a Required item, Forms Builder forces the user to enter a value into the Required item before the operator can change the modes. This is a nuisance, so it is best to set the Required property to NO.

As practice, create a property class that changes the background color to WHITE by following these steps. The property class can then be assigned to the data block items:

1. Open the practice form in the Object Navigator.
2. Locate the Property Classes object in the Object Navigator.
3. Click the **Create** tool to create a new property class.
4. Double-click the new property class icon to open a Property Palette for the property class.
5. Click the **Add Property** tool to open the Properties dialog box.
6. Locate and select the **Background Color** property. Click **OK** to add the property to the property class.
7. Set the background color to WHITE.
8. Open the Object Navigator and select the **EMPNO** item. Press the **F4** key to open the Property Palette.
9. Locate and select the **Subclass Information** property. When the text item changes to a More button, click the button.
10. Click the **Property Class** radio button. Open the Property Class Name drop-down list and select the newly created property class. Click **OK**.
11. Locate the Background Color property in the EMPNO Property Palette. Notice the property class designation.

12. Locate the EMPNO item in the Object Navigator. Notice the property class designation on the item.
13. Perform steps 8 through 10 for the remaining data block items.
14. Open the Layout Editor and notice that the text items now have a white background.
15. Save the form for later practice.

CREATING AND USING VISUAL ATTRIBUTES

Visual attributes are similar to property classes, except that they only contain format properties, such as font name, font size, or background color. The purpose of a visual attribute is to eliminate the number of properties that require setting. Placing the format property settings into a visual attribute and assigning the visual attribute to objects reduces the labor by several factors. You may even assign a visual attribute to a property class. When the property class is assigned to the object, the visual attribute setting is used.

The following list describes the three different types of visual attributes. The available properties change with the type selected:

- **Common**: Properties that pertain to the object as a whole. Data blocks, data items, canvases, windows, alerts, and LOVs use this type of visual attribute.
- **Title**: Properties that pertain to an object's title properties. Frames use this type of visual attribute.
- **Prompt**: Properties that pertain to data block item prompt properties.

Figure 5-11 depicts a Visual Attribute Property Palette. The settings are representative of a commonly used visual attribute that is assigned to a form's data block items. The Color settings control the background and foreground colors, whereas the Font properties control the text settings.

To create a visual attribute, follow these steps:

1. Open the Object Navigator and select the **Visual Attributes** object.
2. Click the **Create** tool.
3. Select the new **Visual Attributes** object and launch the Property Palette by pressing the **F4** key.
4. Modify the properties.

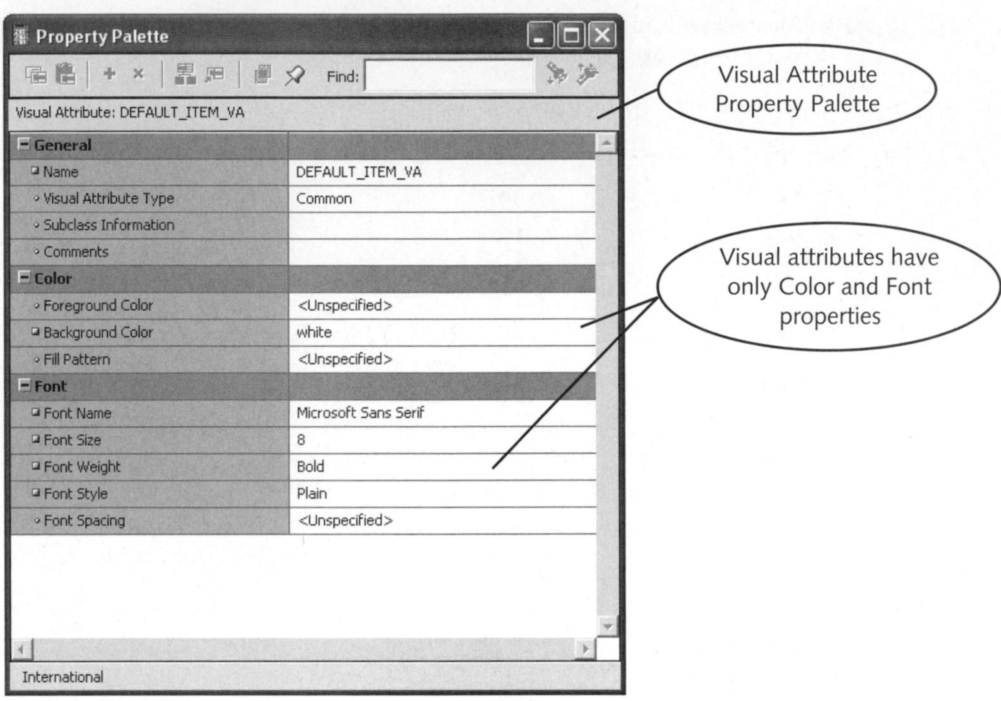

Figure 5-11 Visual Attribute Property Palette

To assign a visual attribute to an object, perform these steps:

1. Open the target object's Property Palette.
2. Locate the Visual Attributes section of the Property Palette.
3. Click the **Visual Attribute Group**, **Prompt Visual Attribute Group**, or the **Frame Title Visual Attribute Group property** drop-down list to open a list of available visual attributes. The drop-down lists display visual attributes that can be used in the property. The Visual Attribute Group list displays common types of visual attributes, and the Prompt Visual Attribute Group and Frame Title Visual Attribute Group property lists display prompt and title types of visual attributes.
4. Select the desired visual attribute. The inherited symbol appears next to the target object's overridden properties.

Visual attributes are often used with two other form objects: the data block's and data block item's Current Record Visual Attribute Group properties. The property causes the substitution of the visual attribute for the object's regular settings whenever a record is made the current record. Using the visual attribute in the data block property applies the visual attribute settings on each item in the current record. When the visual attribute is used in the data block item property, the settings apply to only one item in the record.

This technique is handy for multiple-record tabular style layouts, especially master-detail layouts. Master-detail layouts generally contain a multiple-row data block. When the input focus is moved to a record in the multiple-row data block, an operator can always identify the current record by locating the blinking insertion point. When the user moves the insertion point out of the multiple-row data block, the insertion point blinks in the new data block. However, one of the records in the original data block is still the current record. It is a good practice to make the user aware of all current records. Changing a format characteristic, such as the font color of the current record using the Current Visual Attribute Group property, is an effective device. Many developers simply change the current record's foreground color to red by using the property.

As practice, follow these steps to create a current visual attribute that changes the current item's font color to red:

1. Open the practice form in the Object Navigator.
2. Locate and select the **Visual Attributes** object. Click the **Create** tool.
3. Select the newly created visual attribute and press the **F4** key to open its Property Palette.
4. Locate the Foreground Color property and change it to **RED**.
5. Locate and select the frame object. Press the **F4** key to display its Property Palette.
6. Locate the Layout Style property and change it to **TABULAR**.
7. Locate the Number of Records Displayed property and change the value to **5**.
8. Locate and select the **EMP** data block in the Object Navigator. Double-click its icon to open a Property Palette.
9. Locate and select the **Current Record Visual Attribute Group** property. A drop-down list symbol displays in the text item. Open the drop-down list and select the newly created visual attribute.
10. Launch the form and execute a query. Scroll through the records noticing that the current record has red text.
11. Save the form for later practice.

CONTROLLING FORM NAVIGATION USING PROPERTIES

The Forms Builder properties that control form navigation are located in the form module, the data block, and the data block item objects. Before you place a form into production, you must review navigation, and these properties are an important determinant of form navigation.

Default form navigation is based on the position of the data blocks and their respective items in the Object Navigator. When a form is launched, the form **input focus** lands on the first listed data block item in the first listed data block (see Figure 5-12). Every time the user presses the Tab key, the form input focus moves to the next listed data block item, until the last item is reached. Pressing the Tab key again moves the input focus back to the first data block item of the same record. This is called **Same Record navigation** and is repeated until the user places the insertion point into another block where that data block's style of navigation begins.

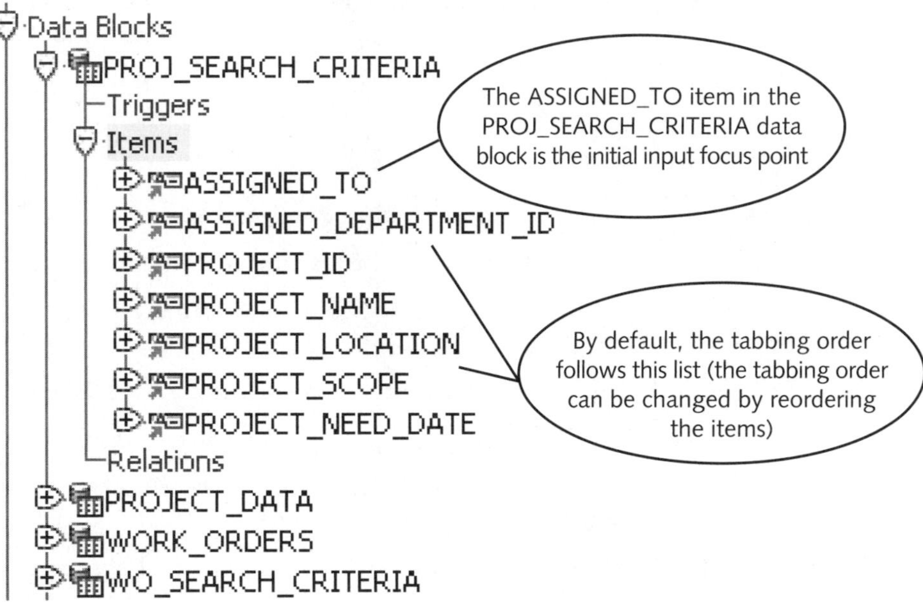

Figure 5-12 Object Navigator showing the default navigation

Data block objects have the following Navigation Style properties that change how block navigation occurs:

- **Same Record**: When tabbing from the last item in a record, the insertion point is returned to the first item in the current record.
- **Change Record**: When tabbing from the last item in a record, the insertion point is moved to the first item in the following record.
- **Change Data Block**: When tabbing from the last item in a record, the insertion point is moved to the first item in the following data block.

Data block objects have two other properties that are used when the Change Data Block style is selected. These properties are:

- **Previous Navigation Data Block**: Identifies the previous navigation data block.
- **Next Navigation Data Block**: Determines the next navigation data block.

These properties override the default order that the Object Navigator determines for the item. Default navigation can also be modified using data block item properties. The first set of properties prevents the operator from tabbing into a data item as presented in the list that follows:

- **Keyboard Navigable**: Prevents the user from moving into the item using the Tab key. The only way to shift the input focus into the item is with the mouse.
- **Mouse Navigable**: Prevents the user from using the mouse to shift the input focus into the item. This property is only available for list items, radio group items, push button items, hierarchical trees, and check box items.
- **Query Allowed**: Prevents the user from moving the input focus into the item by any means when the data block is in the Query mode. It is a good idea to prevent users from tabbing into items that are not used to enter selection criteria. This can save the user from tabbing through unnecessary items.
- **Item Type**: Setting the item type to DISPLAY ITEM prevents any navigation into the item. Display items cannot receive the input focus.

Data block items have two additional properties that are used to override the Object Navigator default item list: Previous Navigation Item and Next Navigation Item. They determine the previous and following tab item. A drop-down list can be used to set these properties. Only an item in the same data block can be used as a value.

Some navigation properties are located in the form module object, and their scope covers the entire form. The Mouse Navigation Limit property that is used to limit the use of the mouse contains the following four settings:

- **FORM**: Limits the use of the mouse to any item in the form. This is the default.
- **DATA BLOCK**: Limits the use of the mouse to any item in the current data block.
- **RECORD**: Limits the use of the mouse to any item in the current record.
- **ITEM**: Limits the use of the mouse to the current item.

If you choose not to use the FORM setting, forms with multiple blocks become a problem, and you need a mechanism to move the input focus. The following mechanisms can be used:

- Create push button items that move the input focus between data blocks.
- Use the Function keys to move the input focus. The Block Menu function key displays a menu of the data blocks. The user can select the desired block. Keys also exist to navigate to other records and items.
- Set up the data item properties to allow tabbing to different items, records, and data blocks.

When a form is launched, Form Runtime tries to move the input focus into the first data block that has navigable items. By default, this is the first listed data block in the

Object Navigator. If this block does not contain navigable items, Form Runtime moves to a subsequent data block until a navigable item is found. If none are found, Form Runtime terminates the application. If you would like Form Runtime to begin its search in a data block other than the top listed data block, the First Navigation Data Block property is available. This form module property is used to override the default initial data block.

As practice, perform the following steps to change several navigation properties and determine their effect on the form:

1. Launch the practice form and execute a query. Tab through the items and notice the tabbing order.
2. Close the form and open the Object Navigator. Locate and expand the EMP data block object. Change the order of the items. Launch the form and tab through the items. Notice that the tab order reflects the changes you made in Step 1. Close the form.
3. Locate and select the **EMP** data block object. Press the **F4** key to open its Property Palette.
4. Locate the Navigation Style property. Change the value to **CHANGE RECORD**. Launch the form, execute a query, and tab through the data items. Notice that the insertion point changes records after tabbing through the items. Close the form.
5. Locate and expand the EMP data block object, displaying the data block items. Select the **HIREDATE**, **MGR**, and **ENAME** items. Press the **F4** key to open a multiple-selection Property Palette. Locate the Keyboard Navigable property. Set the value to **NO**. Launch the form, execute a query, and tab through the data items. Notice that the insertion point does not move into the HIREDATE, MGR, and ENAME items. Close the form.
6. Select the form module object in the Object Navigator and press the **F4** key to open the Property Palette. Locate the Mouse Navigation Limit property. Change the value to **RECORD**. Launch the form and execute a query. Attempt to use the mouse to move the insertion point to a different record. Notice that this can no longer be done. Close the form.
7. Change the Mouse Navigation Limit property to FORM, which is the default value. Save the form for later practice.

IMPORTANT DATA BLOCK PROPERTIES

The data block object contains a variety of properties of which you should be aware. Some of these properties determine whether queries can be performed, whether inserts can be made, what the source of the data is, whether a scroll bar will be displayed, or whether the default WHERE clause is used by the data source. The data block object contains properties that significantly improve your form design. It is recommended that you review these data block properties every time you create a form. The following are important data block properties that have not yet been discussed:

- **Number of Records Displayed**: Determines how many records the data block displays.
- **Where Clause**: Contains default selection criteria that is appended to the SELECT statement generated by the data block, thereby filtering the retrieved records. The Where keyword is optional when using this property, and all normal Oracle syntax is allowable in the value.
- **ORDER BY Clause**: Contains an ORDER BY clause that is appended to the SELECT statement generated by the data block.
- **Database Block**: Determines whether the block displays data from the Oracle database.
- **Insert Allowed**: Determines whether records can be added to the database from the data block.
- **Update Allowed**: Determines whether records can be updated in the data block.
- **Delete Allowed**: Determines whether records can be deleted from the data block.
- **Query Allowed**: Determines whether a query can be performed from the data block. This property prevents the data block from entering the Query mode.

The Where Clause property is commonly used when navigating from one form to another. For example, you have developed a form that displays a list of departments. You want to select one department and navigate to another form that displays the employees for the department. To display only the employees for the specific department, you must pass the department value to the called form. This value is normally placed in the Default Where property using a special built-in subprogram discussed later in this chapter.

The data block almost always uses the Order By property, which determines how the displayed records are sorted. Database records are stored in a random fashion, and unless an ORDER BY clause is placed into this property, the displayed records will be in the same random order. Your users will be much happier if you use the property and sort the records.

The Query Allowed property determines whether the data block can perform a query. In some cases, you want to create a form used only to add new records. The Case Project PROJECT_ADD form is an example of such a form. This property helps you achieve this effect by preventing the form from retrieving records to the form. On the other hand, setting the Insert Allowed property prevents the user from adding records to the database. When this property is used, the data block will not allow the operator to type a value into the blank data block row used to insert records. Setting the Delete Allowed property prevents the user from deleting records. Setting the Update Allowed property prevents the updating of a record. These are handy properties when you have developed a form that is to be used only for viewing records. Systems commonly have forms set so that data can only be viewed.

The data block has other properties, but the previously discussed properties are the most commonly used and will be worth your time to evaluate each time you create a data block.

Creating Reusable Components Using Object Groups and Libraries

An **object library** is a Forms Builder file object that is composed of form components. The object library components can consist of any form object such as a canvas, window, visual attribute, or trigger and can be used in other forms. This reusability is a powerful form tool and helps you standardize your forms. As a first step in building a form, you can bring object library components into your form. This standardizes the form with other forms that have used the object library. Another benefit of an object library is that it saves you time in form development, because you do not have to re-create the canvases, property classes, triggers, and other commonly used form components.

When you become experienced using Forms Builder, you will know what form property settings and form objects work best. This will allow you to develop your own design style, and you will want the underlying mechanics of your forms to be similar. You will use the same fonts, toolbars, canvas sizes, and components in your forms. You will find that 30 percent of your forms will be exactly the same. After you have identified your preferred design style and the common components, object libraries allow you to place the components into the library file for later use. You can then move these objects into a new form, saving yourself considerable development time. Depending on your needs, it is possible to have a large number of object libraries, but at the minimum you should have an object library with the following items:

- Visual attribute used for regular items
- Visual attribute used for prompts
- Visual attribute used in the current record's visual attribute properties
- Canvas object with predefined height and width properties set
- Window object with predefined height and width properties set
- Toolbar canvas with the standard tools used in your forms
- Standard push button items used in your forms

- Generic alert. **Alerts** are modal dialog boxes displayed when it is necessary to warn the user. Alerts will be discussed in a later chapter.
- Default **popup menu**. A popup menu is a menu that is opened by clicking the Right Mouse button. Popups perform standard functions, such as querying, creating records, and deleting records.
- Any triggers that are part of your design

An **object group** is a grouping of form components. It is a form object that can reside as part of the form or as an object in an object library. The benefit of the object group is the grouping. If you have a series of objects, such as those described in the preceding bulleted list, it is efficient to place the objects into a group. When an object group is added to the form from an object group (or from another form using the Object Navigator Copy/Paste methods), all of the object group's components objects are placed in the form at one time. This is preferable in many instances to the moving of individual items into the form.

Creating an Object Group

Object groups are form objects and are created in the Object Navigator. To create an object group, perform the following steps:

1. Open a form module in the Object Navigator.
2. Locate the Object Groups node within the form module.
3. To create a new object group object, select the **Object Groups** object and click the **Create** tool.
4. Drag any form component into this object. The objects can only be dragged from the current form.

Objects can be removed from the object group by selecting the object and clicking the **Delete** tool or pressing the **Delete** key.

Objects groups can be copied between forms by dragging the group from one form to another. After you drop the group into a new form's object group node, Forms Builder copies each of the group's items into the proper form node. Figure 5-13 depicts a form after the DEFAULT_FORM_OBJECTS object group was placed in the form. Notice that the group's objects appear in the various form nodes. Forms Builder automatically copied these objects from the group. If you delete the object groups, the copied objects remain in the form under their respective object nodes.

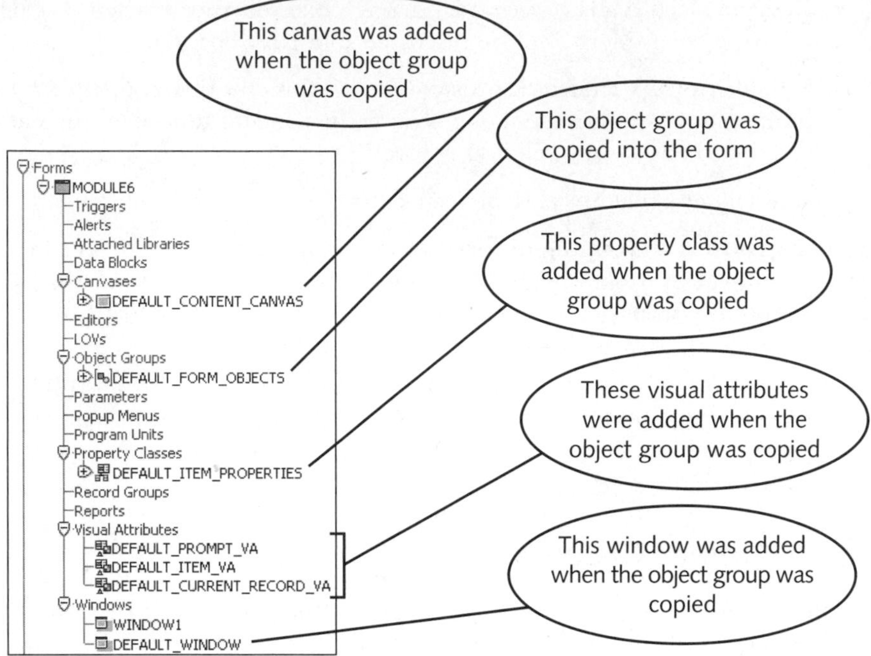

Figure 5-13 Object group placed into a form

A link exists between a form object and its group equivalent. You cannot change the name of the group object in the Object Navigator. To change the name, you must open the group object's Property Palette and change the Name property. Because the object and group are linked, changing the Name property also changes the name of the object's related form object. In fact, if you change any group object property, the corresponding form object's property is also changed, and likewise changing a form object's property affects the group object's property.

As practice, perform the following steps to create an object group using components from your practice form:

1. Open the practice form in the Object Navigator.
2. Locate and select the **Object Groups** object. Create an object group by clicking the **Create** tool.
3. Locate the property class you created in a previous practice session. Click and drag the property class into the object group. The property class displays as an Object Group Children object in the Object Navigator.
4. Locate the visual attribute you created in a previous practice session. Click and drag the visual attribute into the object group.

5. Save the form for later practice.
6. Leave the practice form open in the Object Navigator. Locate the Forms node in the Object Navigator and click the **Create** tool to create a new form module.
7. Locate and select the practice form object group. Drag the object group into the new form module. Place the object group in the Object Groups node. An alert displays. You should press the Copy button rather than the Subclass button.
8. Notice that the object group was placed into the new form. In addition, the object group's property class and visual attribute were copied into the Property Classes and Visual Attributes object nodes.

These steps demonstrated how an object group can be used to populate a number of form objects.

Creating an Object Library

An object library is a Forms Builder file object with a file extension of .olb. The object library is a useful device that holds form objects: canvases, data blocks, object groups, visual attributes, data block items, triggers, or anything else you may want to reuse. The object library file, when brought into the Object Navigator, opens each time you start a session making it readily available for adding and extracting components. You should think of it as a tool chest that helps you develop your systems more effectively and efficiently.

The STANDARDS OFGSTND1 Object Libraries

The object library components are displayed in the Object Library dialog box (see Figure 5-14). Objects are stored in a series of user-defined library tabs. A **library tab** is similar to a form tab page. Library tabs are simply tools to further segregate your components. Figure 5-14 illustrates the OFGSTND1 and the STANDARDS (STNDRD20.OLB) object libraries that are part of the default Forms Builder installation.

The STANDARDS object library comes with Form Builder 6*i*.

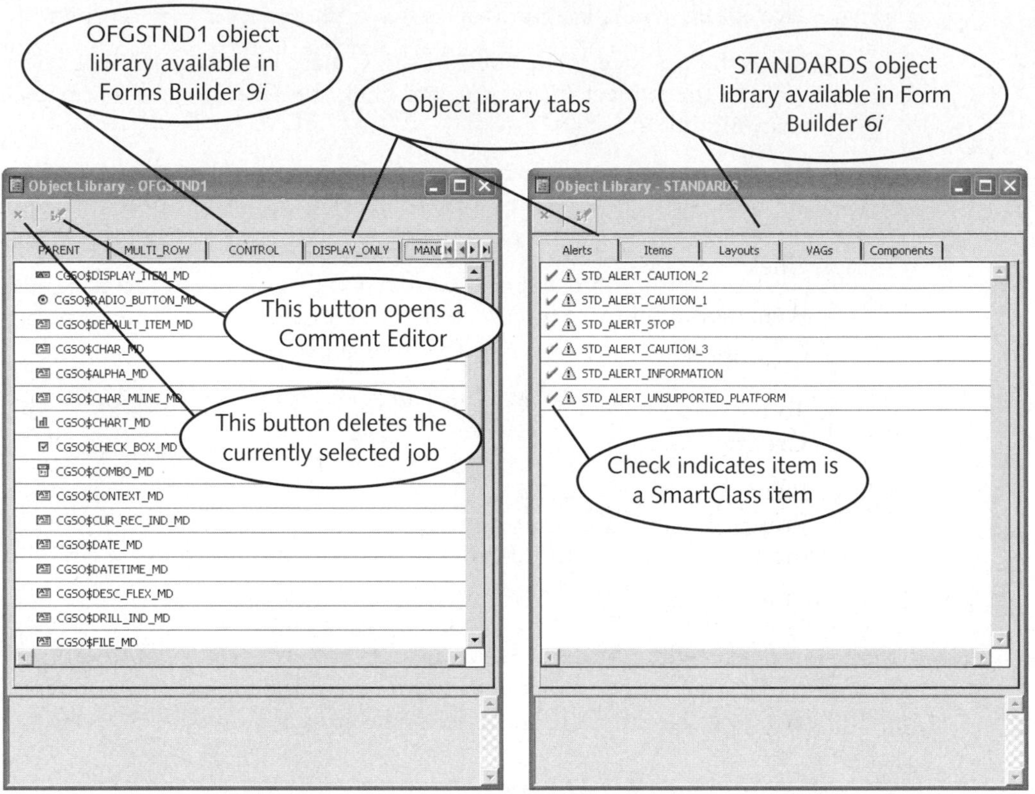

Figure 5-14 OFGSTND1 and STANDARDS object library dialog boxes

The OFGSTND1 object library comes with Forms Builder 9*i*. Oracle has provided these components to help you standardize your applications. You should look over these components to determine their usefulness, but you are not required to use them. The following list outlines the various STANDARDS library tabs:

- **Alerts**: Six different types of alerts that are modal dialog boxes used to notify the user of an event, such as an error.
- **Items**: Fourteen types of items. The items range from buttons with icons to text items formatted for a particular type of date.
- **Layouts**: Six layout styles ranging from horizontal toolbars to tabular frames.
- **VAGs**: Seven visual attribute groups used to format ToolTip, the current record, and text items.
- **Components**: A variety of PL/SQL scripts and tools that enable you to create wizards, use hierarchical items, and display calendars.

The PL/SQL components are of special interest. They contain some scripts that allow you to develop wizards for your forms similar to the Data Block Wizard. The tab also contains a Calendar object used to display an actual calendar that is used to select a date. These topics require knowledge of triggers and are discussed in a later chapter.

Creating, Populating, and Using an Object Library

To create an object library and a library tab, you would perform the following:

1. Open the Object Navigator and select the **Object Libraries** node.
2. Click the **Create** tool.
3. Rename the library in the Object Navigator.
4. Save the library using the File/Save menu option.
5. To create a library tab, select the **Library Tabs** child node and click the **Create** tool.
6. Rename the new library tab and the library tab's Label property using the Property Palette. You can only open a library tab Property Palette by pressing the F4 key or selecting the Tools/Property Palette menu selection.

You should note that the name of the library page and the name displayed on the tab differ, as illustrated in Figure 5-15. In this example, the library tab name was changed in the Object Navigator. You can see that it changed the name on the VISUAL_ATTRIBUTES tab but left the Label property as LIB_TAB1. The Label property controls what is displayed on the library tab and is only changeable in the object's Property Palette.

The following are techniques for populating and using the object library:

- **Populating the object library**: Select a form object and drag it into the appropriate tab.
- **Placing an object on the form**: Select an Object Library object and drag it into the appropriate node within the form module.
- **Deleting objects from the object library**: Select the Object Library object and click the **Delete** tool or press the **Delete** key.

As practice, follow these steps to create an object library using components from the practice form. You then move these components into a new form module:

1. Open the practice form in the Object Navigator.
2. Select the **Object Libraries** node and click the **Create** tool to create a new object library.
3. Select the newly created object library and name it **PRACTICE**.
4. Select the **Library Tabs** child node and click the **Create** tool. This creates a new a library tab.

5. Select the tab and press the **F4** key to open a Property Palette for the library tab. Change the tab Name property to **PROPERTY_CLASSES**. Change the tab Label property to **PROPERTY_CLASSES**. Close the Property Palette.
6. Repeat steps 4 and 5. Change the Name and Label properties of this object tab to **VISUAL_ATTRIBUTES**.
7. Repeat steps 4 and 5. Change the Name and Label properties of this object tab to **OBJECT_GROUPS**.
8. Double-click the icon to the left of the PRACTICE object library to open the Object Library dialog box.
9. Click the **VISUAL_ATTRIBUTES** library tab in the Object Library dialog box. This brings the tab to the front.

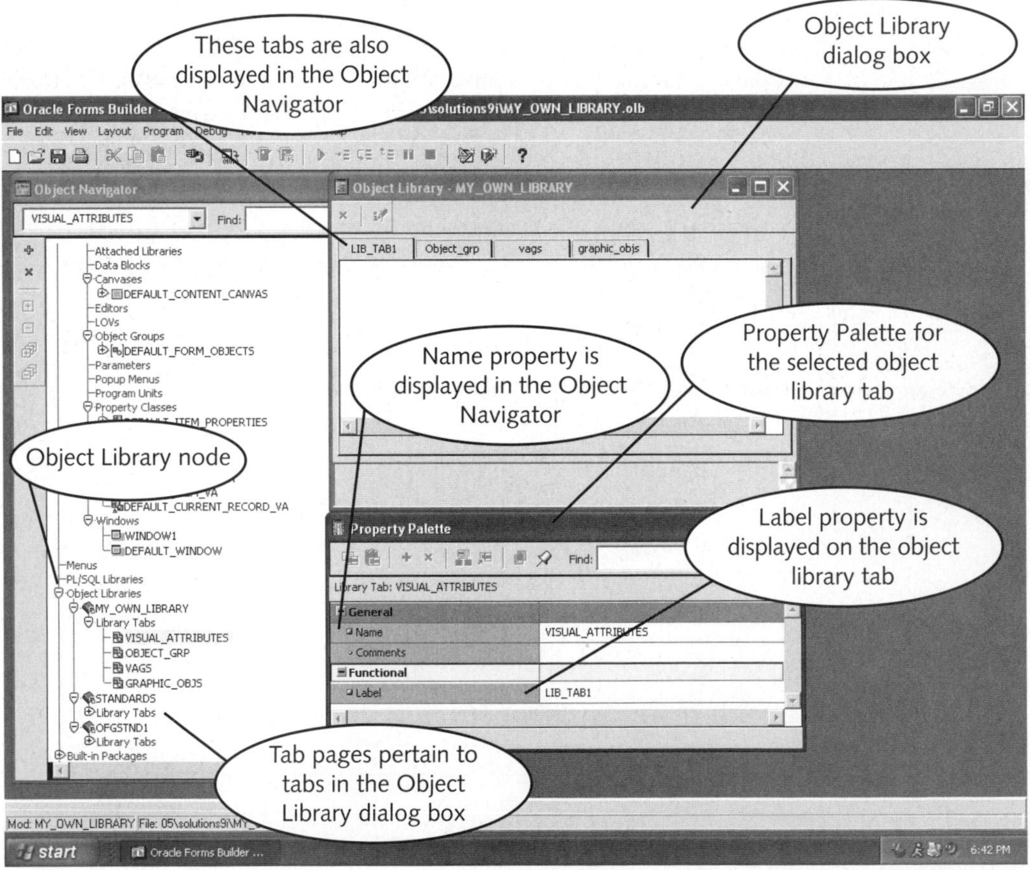

Figure 5-15 Object Navigator Library Tabs node, Object Library tab, and library tab's Property Palette displaying Name and Label properties

10. Locate the visual attribute in the practice module. Drag the visual attribute into the VISUAL_ATTRIBUTES library tab.
11. Click the **PROPERTY_CLASSES** library tab in the Object Library dialog box. Locate the property class in the practice module. Drag the property class into the PROPERTY_CLASSES library tab.
12. Click the **OBJECT_GROUPS** library tab in the Object Library dialog box. Locate the object group in the practice module. Drag the object group into the OBJECT_GROUPS library tab.
13. Select the **PRACTICE** object library. Click the **File/Save** menu option. This opens the Save As dialog box that you can use to save the object library.
14. Create a new form module in the Object Navigator.
15. Drag and copy the property class, visual attribute, and object library from the PRACTICE object library into the module.

These steps demonstrate the ability to save form components in an external file and reuse them in another file.

CREATING AND USING SMARTCLASSES

Forms Builder has an enabled Right Mouse button. Pressing this button opens a popup menu (see Figure 5-16) that allows you to select various common tools or displays, such as the Property Palette or one of the wizards. Popup menus help the user avoid having to move the insertion point to a specific tool. The popup menu opens adjacent to the insertion point. If the desired tool is on the display, mouse movement is greatly diminished. (A later chapter shows you how to create popup menus for your forms.)

One of the selections on the popup menu shown in Figure 5-16 is called **SmartClasses**. This option is used to add library objects to your form. The menu option displays object library components that you have identified as members of a SmartClass. Whenever a form object, such as a canvas, is selected anywhere in Forms Builder, all comparable object library components from any object library currently attached to the Object Navigator display. The objects displayed by this option change depending on the currently selected object. For example, only object library data block items are displayed when a form data block item is currently selected. When a window is selected, Object Library window objects are displayed. If the object libraries do not contain a comparable object, the SmartClasses option is disabled. SmartClass items can be added to the form by selecting the item from the popup menu.

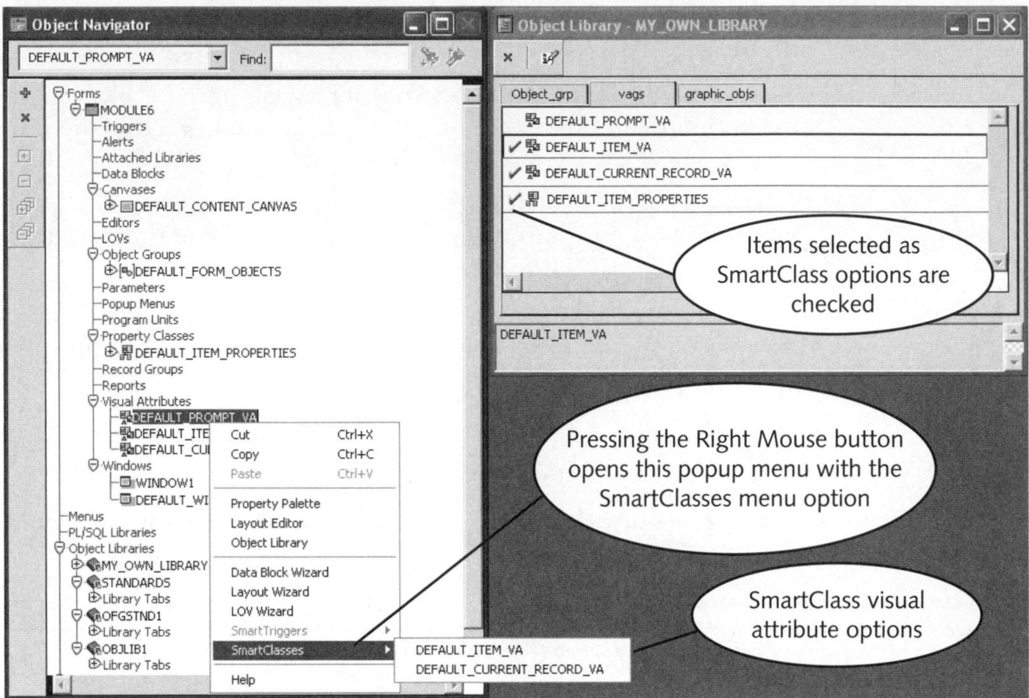

Figure 5-16 Oracle 9*i* Forms Builder popup menu, SmartClasses option panel, and object library displaying SmartClass objects

The SmartClasses option is only enabled when an object library is loaded into the Object Navigator and the currently selected form object is the same type as an object in an attached object library.

Figure 5-16 illustrates the Forms Builder popup menu, the SmartClasses options, the SmartClasses opened palette, and the object library containing the objects. Notice that the object library components that appear in the SmartClass Object Palette are checked. This indicates that they have been designated as members of a SmartClass.

Notice that in Figure 5-16 a description of the selected object library item is displayed in the bottom panel of the Object Library dialog box. Descriptions and SmartClass designations are added using the Edit menu, as shown in Figure 5-17.

This menu does not appear on the Edit menu in Form Builder 6*i*. The main menu options change and an Object menu appears.

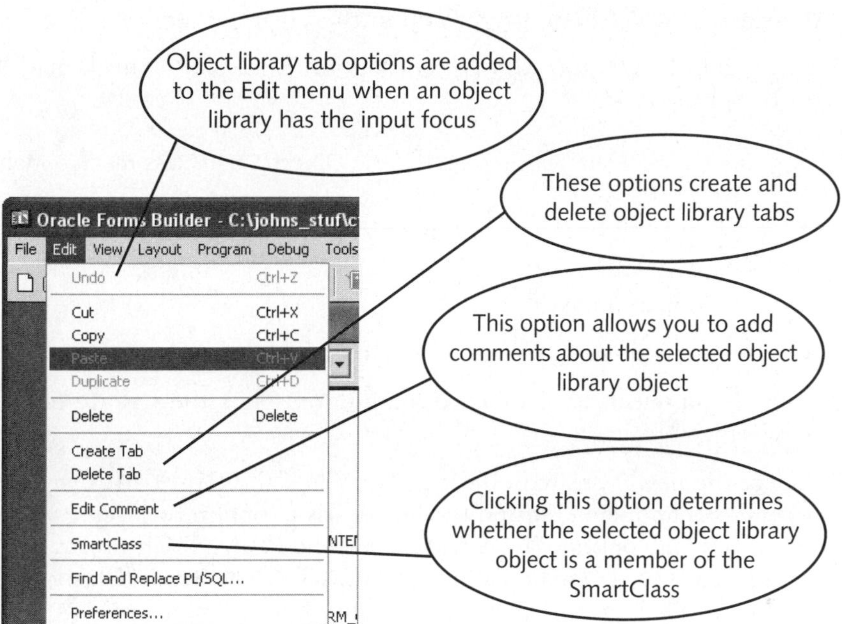

Figure 5-17 Oracle 9*i* Edit menu that is enabled when the Object Library dialog box has the input focus

The options appear on the menu when the Object Library dialog has the input focus or is selected. This menu contains options for maintaining the object library. The following are the menu options:

- **Create Tab**: Adds a library tab to the currently selected object library.
- **Delete Tab**: Deletes the currently selected object library tab along with any item on the tab.
- **Edit Comment**: Opens a Comments dialog box used to maintain the currently selected object's description that appears at the bottom of the Object Library dialog box.
- **SmartClass**: Designates the currently selected object as a member of the SmartClass. If this option is checked, the currently selected object is a member of the SmartClass. Clicking this option changes the designation.

As practice, perform the following steps to designate several of the PRACTICE object library components as SmartClass components, and add them to a form using the SmartClass menu option:

1. Locate the PRACTICE object library you created in the previous practice in the Object Navigator. Object libraries generally remain attached to Forms Builder, even if you close the session. If the PRACTICE object library is not visible, you may have to load it using the File/Open menu option. The object library has a file extension of **.olb**.

2. Locate and select the object group in the object library.
3. Select the **Edit/SmartClass** menu option to display a check mark to the left of the property class.

If you are using Form Builder 6*i*, select the **Object/SmartClass** menu option.

4. Save the object library.
5. Create a new form module.
6. Locate and select the **Object Group** node. Click the **Create** tool to create a new object group.
7. Select the newly created object group. Click the **Right Mouse button** to open a popup menu. Expand the SmartClasses option by placing your insertion point over the option. This SmartClass is the PRACTICE object library object group that was designated a SmartClass. Click the **SmartClass**. Notice that the form object group now has the inheritance designation.

These steps demonstrate how to create and use a SmartClass.

Changing Properties at Runtime

A great deal of your development time will be spent setting form properties using the various Forms Builder tools. The properties you set are those the form will use when the form is executed. However, as you become a skilled form developer, you will want to change these properties while the form is operating for any of the following reasons:

- Change how the data is sorted by modifying the Order By property
- Make it possible to enter the item by modifying the Update Allowed property
- Change the background color of an item to red if it is outside a variance range by changing the item's visual attribute
- Disable or enable an item by modifying the Enabled property

The list of possibilities is endless, but you can be assured that your users will want runtime changes to properties.

Properties are changed through a built-in subprogram placed inside a trigger. These are devices that will be discussed in greater depth in the next chapter. However, this chapter is about properties, and you should be introduced to several of these property-changing built-in subprograms. The two most commonly used are the Set_block_property and the Set_item_property built-in subprograms.

The Set_Block_Property Built-In Subprogram

Built-in subprograms are either **procedures** or **functions** that are executed by a trigger in a PL/SQL code block that is executed. The Set_block_property built-in is a procedure and is placed inside the trigger as a statement of its own. Many of Oracle's built-ins are **overloaded**, which means multiple built-ins have the same name. Each built-in's parameters differentiate it from any others with the same name. This is understandable because the properties have different needs. For example, changing the scroll bar location requires X and Y coordinates. The Set_block_property built-in, used to change this property, must have two value parameters, one each for the new X and Y coordinates. In the same vein, the Set_block_property used to change the Order By property only requires a single value parameter. Overloading occurs when several procedures have the same name but have different parameter lists. Many of the built-in programs used to reset form properties have this feature.

The Set_block_property is typical of a property-changing built-in. It has the following syntax template:

```
SET_BLOCK_PROPERTY(block_name, property, value1,
                        value2);
```

The first parameter identifies the block. The value can either be a variable populated with the name (i.e., `emp`) or the actual block name enclosed by single quotation marks. The second parameter is the target property. This value may or may not be the same name as the data block property. In addition, not all data block properties can be modified. It is best to look at the Forms Builder Help facility to identify the specific property name values. This parameter is not enclosed with single quotation marks, because it is a variable name. The value parameters can contain a number, text, or variable depending on the property to be modified. Text values require single quotation marks, whereas variables and numbers do not. In some cases, the parameter consists of a Boolean variable such as PROPERTY_VALUE that should not be enclosed by single quotation marks.

The following are three example statements using the EMP practice table. They represent three commonly performed runtime property changes. The first statement changes the ORDER BY Clause property, the second changes the Insert Allowed property, and the third changes the Where Clause property. Note that the property parameter uses DEFAULT_WHERE rather than the name used in the Property Palette.

```
        SET_BLOCK_PROPERTY('emp', order_by, 'fk_department,
last_name desc');
SET_BLOCK_PROPERTY('emp', insert_allowed, property_false);
SET_BLOCK_PROPERTY('emp', default_where,
              'last_name = :global.lname');
```

You may have noticed the `:global.lname` characters in the last example. This is a **global variable**, which is defined as a variable that exists throughout the user's session across all Oracle Forms applications. The global variable is created when it is initialized. A variable of some kind, either a global variable or a form parameter object, is needed because the condition has a character argument. If a character argument such as PALINSKI is placed in the parameter value, a compilation error occurs. The single quotation marks surrounding the argument will mix up the compiler; thus, a variable is needed. Oracle then appends the entire character expression to the SELECT statement. When it encounters the variable name, it references the variable and uses its value to filter the result set.

The Set_Item_Property and the Set_Item_Instance_Property Built-In Subprograms

Two built-in subprograms can be used to change a data block item property. These are Set_item_property and Set_item_instance_property. The difference between the two built-ins is that the former modifies the property for every occurrence of the item, and the latter only modifies the property for a specific item. For example, Set_item_instance_property can be used to identify exceptions by changing the background color of an item whose value is out of a specific range. This built-in changes only selected items, while Set_item_property changes every item. Thus, Set_item_property is not an effective tool for identifying exceptions, whereas the Set_item_instance_property built-in is.

These two built-ins have the same features as discussed in the "The Set_block_property Built-In Subprogram" section. They are overloaded procedures that modify a variety of properties. The following are two examples. The first example disables the EMPNO data item in the EMP data block. The result is that the value is dimmed and the user cannot manipulate the value. The second example changes the background of a specific record to red.

```
SET_ITEM_PROPERTY('emp.empno', enabled, property_false);
SET_ITEM_INSTANCE_PROPERTY('emp.sal', current_record,
visual_attribute,'exception_visual_attribute');
```

The second example requires additional explanation. The Set_item_instance_property built-in cannot change an item's background color. It can only change the visual attribute for the item. Because the visual attribute has a background color property, assigning a visual attribute with a background setting to the data block item has the same effect. The other feature you should be aware of is the second parameter. It is used to identify the specific record instance. The example used the variable CURRENT_RECORD that sets the current record background. This is a number parameter, and other record instances could be modified.

WHERE YOU ARE AND WHERE YOU'RE GOING

You have now seen the three most important Forms Builder tools: the Object Navigator, the Layout Editor, and the Property Palette. You have learned that a major part of developing a form is locating an object and setting a property. If you were prototyping an application for users, you would be ready for them to initially review the form. The forms would operate with the basic Form Runtime behaviors, plus whatever modifications you added as a result of setting properties. You have not yet added any custom programming to the form.

After viewing this early prototype, your users will request specific behaviors, probably based on logic. This will require you to develop PL/SQL code blocks that are executed at a specific time. These code blocks contain the IF-THEN-ELSE constructs that allow you to add specialized behavior to your form. This is the topic covered in Chapter 6.

Chapter Summary

- A property is a setting that controls some of the features of an application.
- Applications are composed of numerous settings, and Oracle forms also have many settings.
- Properties are grouped by type in the Property Palette.
- One of the best ways to locate a property is to determine its type of functionality and the form objects that have this type of property.
- The Property Palette uses text items, drop-down lists, editors, color palettes, and dialog boxes to help you enter values.
- A multiple-selection Property Palette can be used to set the properties for many objects simultaneously.
- Multiple-selection Property Palettes have two different views: INTERSECTION lists common properties, and UNION lists all selected object properties.
- The Property Palette Pin/Unpin tool can be used to view two property palettes at the same time.
- A property class is a form component that has a number of properties. It can be assigned to a form object to override the object's default properties.
- Property classes are assigned to the object using the object's Subclass Information property.
- A visual attribute is a form object that has a number of format properties. It is assigned to different data blocks and data block item properties.
- Data blocks and data block items have a Current Record Visual Attribute property that is used to modify the record format when the record is currently selected.
- Default form navigation is determined by the listing of data blocks and data block items in the Object Navigator.
- The data block and data block items have properties that can override the default form navigation.

- Properties exist in the data block that can prevent the mouse from moving outside a block, record, or item.
- The data block has properties that can be used to filter and sort returned records. It also has properties that can prevent the block from performing Data Manipulation Language (DML) operations.
- An object group is a form object that groups various form objects. It can be used to duplicate the grouped objects in another form.
- An object library is a Forms Builder module that is used to save form objects for reuse.
- Forms Builder has an enabled Right Mouse button that opens a popup menu that is used to launch Forms Builder tools.
- SmartClass is an option on the Forms Builder popup menu. It launches a palette of object library components that can be added to the form.
- The STANDARDS and OFGSTND1 object libraries were developed by Oracle and have a variety of form components.
- Properties can be changed at runtime using built-in subprograms that are procedures or functions developed by Oracle.

REVIEW QUESTIONS

1. Match the following terms that have appeared in this chapter with their descriptions:

a. ******	________________	Built-in subprogram used to modify a data block's property while the form is running.
b. Property class	________________	Oracle-developed procedure or function that performs a special task such as setting a property.
c. Global variable	________________	Built-in subprogram used to set a single occurrence of a data item's property.
d. Object library	________________	A menu palette that appears adjacent to the insertion point when the Right Mouse button is clicked.
e. F4 key	________________	A form object that has formatting properties. When it is assigned to a data block item, it overrides a number of the item's default properties.
f. Set Block property	________________	Causes the input focus to move to the first navigable item in the record when tabbing from the last item in the record.

g. Same Record property	______________	Data block item property that prohibits the block from performing a query.
h. Built-in subprogram	______________	Popup menu option that displays object library components that can be copied into the form.
i. Pin / Unpin tool	______________	A variable that exists throughout the user session. Its scope is not limited to the PL/SQL procedure or the application.
j. Visual attribute	______________	Object library file extension.
k. Keyboard Navigable property	______________	Built-in subprogram used to set a data block's properties while the form is operating.
l. Popup menu	______________	Data item property that determines whether the user can use the Tab key to enter the item.
m. SmartClass	______________	Indicates that some of the selected objects have different values.
n. Object group	______________	Displays the Property Palette.
o. Intersection tool	______________	Property Palette tool that causes the Property Palette for a specific item(s) to remain open when another item is selected.
p. Set_item_ instance_property	______________	A Forms Builder file object that contains form components for use by other forms.
q. .olb	______________	Causes only the common properties to be displayed in a multiple-selection Property Palette.
r. Query Allowed property	______________	A form object consisting of a set of form objects. Adding a form object to a form causes a number of form objects to be created that correspond to the group's objects.
s. Set_item_property	______________	Form object that has a number of properties. The object can be assigned to other objects, overriding their default properties.

2. What are properties and why are they important to you as a developer?

5

3. You have selected all of a data block's items. How can you deselect one of the items without deselecting all of the items?
4. Identify two ways of controlling the tab order of a data block's items.
5. You want to make the following changes to your form:
   a. Change a data block's number of displayed records from 15 to 10.
   b. Add a title to a window object.
   c. Change the weight of a prompt.
   d. Enable the insertion point to move to the next data block when tabbing from the last data item in the record.
   e. Sort the displayed records by the employees' HIREDATE values.
   f. Prevent the user from deleting any record from the data block.
   g. Determine whether any item is Subclassed.
   h. Make sure the form only places uppercase values into the Oracle database.

   Identify each of the Subclassed item's property types and the name of the target property.
6. You have just opened a form for maintenance and notice that the form has a property class object. How can you determine which form objects are using the property class?
7. A user just called you on the phone about a three-deep master-detail data block form (grandparent, parent, and child). The user cannot determine which record is selected in the middle or parent block. What can you do to help the user?
8. You have selected all of the items in a data block and opened a multiple-selection Property Palette. You are having difficulty locating the Height property. Besides turning in a TAR (trouble report) to Oracle, what can you do?
9. You have just placed a new form into production and received a phone call from an annoyed user. When the user first places the form in the QUERY mode, the insertion point is placed in the EMPNO data block item. The user wants to place a value in the ENAME item, but cannot move the insertion point from the EMPNO data block item. What is the likely cause of the problem? Name three things you can quickly do to solve this problem? What is the best solution?
10. You have just completed a rather complex, prototype form that is the first form in the system. You have asked the business expert to review the form. After the review, the business expert requests a different font, font size, and font weight for the prompts and the data items. Identify three ways to change the format properties of all data items. What is the best solution? Why?
11. You are working on a form that has several data blocks. The data blocks are on different canvases. When you launch the form, the wrong data block (and canvas) is displayed. You think the problem is caused by the input focus initially moving into the wrong data block when the form is launched. Name two ways of fixing this problem.

12. You have just been named the manager of a development project to build a system with 20 to 30 different forms built by five different programmers. What can you do to maintain consistency between the forms in the system?

    One of your developers has just completed an object library for use on your project. You are reviewing the object library (see Figure 5-18) for use within your development group. What comments do you have for the developer?

13. How can you use the Set_block_property built-in as a security device?

14. Which data block properties cannot be modified using the Set_block_property built-in?

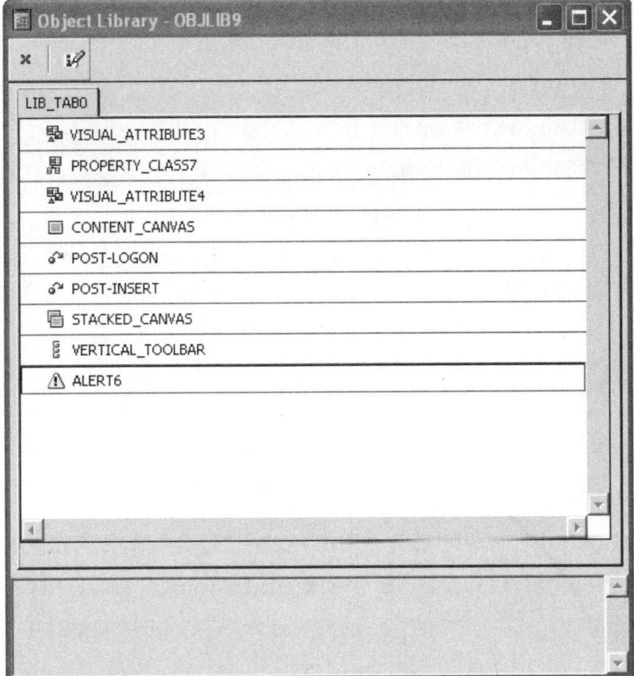

Figure 5-18 Object Library dialog box

Exam Review Questions

1. You developed a form that has a number of related items. You want to keep these items together. What Forms Builder tool would you use?
    a. Property class
    b. Object group
    c. Subclass information
    d. SmartClass

2. A form you developed has a program unit, object group, and a property class. You want to save these for use in other forms. What can you do?
   a. Place them on the Form Server.
   b. Subclass them using the original form.
   c. Create a SmartClass.
   d. Place them in an object library.
   e. Place them in a Forms library.
3. You have created a master-detail form. The master block displays one record. When you tab through the master record, the insertion point returns to the first item in the row. Which Navigation Style property setting should you use to place the insertion point into the detail block record after tabbing through the master record?
   a. Change the block setting in the detail block.
   b. Change the block setting in the master block.
   c. Change the record setting in the detail block.
   d. Change the record setting in the master block.
4. Each property in the Property Palette is preceded by an icon. Which icon indicates that the property value was inherited?
   a. Circle
   b. Arrow
   c. Arrow with a cross
   d. Square
5. Which data block properties control form navigation?
   a. Navigation Style, Previous Navigation Block, and Next Navigation Block
   b. Navigation Style, Previous Navigation Block, and Mouse Navigation Limit
   c. Mouse Navigation Limit, First Navigation Data Block, and Enabled
   d. Navigation Style, Keyboard Navigable, and Mouse Navigation Limit

HANDS-ON ASSIGNMENTS

1. In this assignment, you compare the property palettes of two different data block items.
   a. Create a new form.
   b. Add a data block based on the DEPT table. The layout style should be Form with only one record displayed.
   c. Open the Property Palette for the DNAME data block item.
   d. Pin the Property Palette opened in Step c using the Pin/Unpin tool.
   e. Open a Property Palette for the LOC data block item.

f. Compare the properties in the Property Palettes.

g. Using the Object Navigator, color the canvas using a color of your choice. This required you to locate the canvas object, open its Property Palette, and set the Background Color property. Did you have trouble opening the Property Palette because you forgot to Unpin the Property Palette?

h. Select the newly created canvas object in the Object Navigator. Change the name to **DEFAULT_CONTENT_CANVAS**.

i. Set the Height property to **390** and the Width to **600**.

j. Select the newly created window object in the Object Navigator. Change the name to **DEFAULT_WINDOW**.

k. Save the form as **ch05ex01.fmb**.

2. In this assignment, you set several data block properties that affect the record sorting and the data item fonts. Use form module **ch05ex01.fmb** in this assignment:

a. Add a detail data block to the form. The data block should use the EMP table as a data source. It should also be a Tabular style layout that displays 10 records.

b. Open the Property Palette for the DEPT data block. Add the following to the Order By clause: **DEPTNO**.

c. Open the Property Palette for the EMP data block. Add the following to the Order By clause: **HIREDATE DESC, ENAME**.

d. Execute the form and determine whether it is sorting the displayed records correctly.

e. Select all of the form data block items using the Object Navigator.

f. Open a Multiple-selection Property Palette for the selected items.

g. Make the following changes:

Font Name: MS SANS SERIF

Font Weight: BOLD

Font Size: 10

h. Execute the form and determine whether it is operating correctly and the formatting changes have taken effect.

i. Create a visual attribute named DEFAULT_ITEM_VA with the following settings:

Font Name: ARIAL

Font Size: 12

Font Style: ITALIC

Background Color: WHITE

j. Select all the form data block items using the Object Navigator.

k. Open a Multiple-selection Property Palette for the selected items.

l. Assign the visual attribute to the Visual Attribute Group property in the Property Palette.

m. Execute the form and view the changes.

n. Repeat Step j. Locate the Font Size property in the Property Palette. Notice the inheritance symbol.

o. Reset the Visual Attribute Group property to **DEFAULT**.

p. Save the form as **ch05ex02.fmb**.

3. In this assignment, you are asked to set a variety of form properties using a property class. Use form module **ch05ex02.fmb**.

a. Change the DEFAULT_ITEM_VA visual attribute properties as follows:

Font Name: MS SANS SERIF

Font Style: PLAIN

Font Weight: BOLD

Font Size: 8

b. Create a new visual attribute object named DEFAULT_PROMPT_VA. Add the following settings using its Property Palette:

Visual Attribute Type: PROMPT

Prompt Font Name: MS SANS SERIF

Prompt Font Size: 8

Prompt Font Weight: BOLD

Prompt Font Style: PLAIN

c. Create a property class named **DEFAULT_ITEM_PROPERTIES**.

d. Add the following properties and values to the property class. You must first add the properties using the Add Properties button and then set the values as follows:

Prompt Visual Attribute Group: DEFAULT_PROMPT_VA

Visual Attribute Group: DEFAULT_ITEM_VA

Case Restriction: UPPER

Query_Length: 100

Prompt Justification: END

Height: 18

e. Open the Object Navigator and select all data block items.

f. Open a multiple-selection Property Palette for the items.

g. Locate the Subclass Information property and open the Subclass Information dialog box.

h. Select the **Property Class** radio button.

i. Select the **DEFAULT_ITEM_PROPERTIES** value from the Property Class Name Drop-down List.

j. Click **OK**.

k. Execute the form and identify the format changes caused by the property class.

l. Open a Property Palette for the EMPNO data block item. Identify the properties that have inherited values.

m. Save the form as **ch05ex03.fmb**.

4. In this assignment, you create an object group using the form module **ch05ex03.fmb**. This object group is then copied into and used in a new form.

   a. Create a new visual attribute object called **DEFAULT_CURRENT_RECORD_VA**.

   b. Open the **DEFAULT_CURRENT_RECORD_VA** object and set the Foreground property to **RED**.

   c. Create an object group called **DEFAULT_FORM_OBJECTS**.

   d. Move the following objects into the DEFAULT_FORM_OBJECTS group created in Step c:

      DEFAULT_CONTENT_CANVAS (Delete the canvas' child frames before copying the canvas into the object group. Otherwise the frames will be added to a module using this object.)

      DEFAULT_WINDOW

      DEFAULT_PROMPT_VA

      DEFAULT_ITEM_VA

      DEFAULT_CURRENT_RECORD_VA

      DEFAULT_ITEM_PROPERTIES

   e. Save the form as **ch05ex04a.fmb**.

   f. Create a new form module.

   g. Drag and copy the DEFAULT_FORM_OBJECTS object group into the Object Group node of the new form module.

   h. Identify all of the objects that were added to the form module as a result of Step g.

   i. Add a data block based on the DEPT table to the form. The style should be Form, and it should only have one record. Be sure to specify DEFAULT_CONTENT_CANVAS as the canvas.

   j. Add a detail data block to the form based on the EMP table. The style should be TABULAR, and it should have ten records. Be sure to specify DEFAULT_CONTENT_CANVAS as the canvas.

k. Open the Property Palette for the EMP block. Assign the DEFAULT_CURRENT_RECORD_VA visual attribute to the Current Record Visual Attribute property. This ensures that the current record in the EMP block will have red text.

l. Open a Multiple-selection Property Palette for the data items.

m. Locate the Subclass Information property and open the Subclass Information dialog box.

n. Click the **Property Class** radio button.

o. Select the **DEFAULT_ITEM_PROPERTIES** value from the Property Class Name Drop-down List.

p. Click **OK**.

q. Save the new form as **ch05ex04.fmb**.

r. Execute the form. If you encounter a message stating that an item may be placed outside the canvas, you may have to open the Layout Editor and locate the item on the canvas. Forms Builder can occasionally place an item outside the canvas by default. How is this form different from the **ch05ex04a.fmb** form created in Steps 4a through 4e?

5. In this assignment, you create an object library that you can begin to use in your forms. Use form module **ch05ex04.fmb** in this assignment.

   a. Select the **Object Libraries** node in the Object Navigator.

   b. Using the Create tool, create an object library named **MY_OWN_LIBRARY**.

   c. Open the Object Library dialog box by double-clicking the **MY_OWN_LIBRARY** icon. Create three tabs in the object library using the Object Navigator Create tool or the Object menu. The tabs should be named:

   OBJECT_GRP

   VAGS

   GRAPHIC_OBJS

   d. Move the following components individually from the **ch05ex04.fmb** module into the MY_OWN_LIBRARY object library:

   DEFAULT_FORM_OBJECTS: OBJ_GRP

   DEFAULT_CONTENT_CANVAS: GRAPHIC_OBJS

   DEFAULT_WINDOW: GRAPHIC_OBJS

   DEFAULT_PROMPT_VA:VAGS

   DEFAULT_ITEM_VA:VAGS

   DEFAULT_CURRENT_RECORD_VA:VAGS

   DEFAULT_ITEM_PROPERTIES:VAGS

   e. Save the object library naming it **MY_OWN_LIBRARY**. You now have some basic components that you can use in this course. The objects can be added as part of the object group or individually.

   f. Re-create the master-detail form in Hands-on Assignment 4 using the object library components.

6. The purpose of this assignment is to demonstrate the effect of the Query Allowed, Insert Allowed, Update Allowed, and Delete Allowed data block properties. Use form module **ch05ex04.fmb**.
   a. Open the DEPT data block Property Palette and locate the Query Allowed property. Set the property to **NO**.
   b. Launch the form and attempt to execute a query. Were you successful?
   c. Reset the Query Allowed property to **YES**.
   d. Open the EMP data block Property Palette.
   e. Locate the Insert Allowed property, and set it to **NO**.
   f. Locate the Update Allowed property, and set it to **NO**.
   g. Locate the Delete Allowed property, and set it to **NO**.
   h. Launch the form and display records. Attempt to add, update, or delete any of the employee records. Were you successful?

CASE PROJECT: GREAT STATE ELECTRIC BUDGETING SYSTEM

In this section of the Case Project, you use the Property Palette, property classes, and the object library that you created in Hands-on Assignment 5 to format the Budgeting form data items. You are asked to format all the form data blocks and data items using visual attributes and property classes. The system has some lengthy data items that you are asked to format, so that they appear on two lines. You are also asked to format all the MAIN canvases tab pages. Finally, you set the Order By properties for all data blocks that appear on the MAIN tab canvas.

Your Work

1. Open the budgeting form in the Object Navigator. Open in the Object Navigator the object library called MY_OWN_LIBRARY that you created in Hands-On Assignment 5. Drag the **DEFAULT_PROMPT_VA**, **DEFAULT_ITEM_VA**, and **DEFAULT_CURRENT_RECORD_VA** objects into the Budgeting form's Visual Attribute node.
2. Drag the object library's **DEFAULT_ITEM_PROPERTIES** object into the Budgeting form's Property Class node.
3. Assign the **DEFAULT_CURRENT_RECORD_VA** visual attribute to the Current Record Visual Attribute Group property for all the multiple-record data blocks. These blocks are: PROJECT_DATA, WORK_ORDERS, WORK_ORDER_DATA, WORK_ORDER_TASKS, MONTHLY_COSTS, ACCOUNTS, TASK_DESCRIPTIONS, and EMPLOYEES. It will save you time if you use a Multiple-selection Property Palette.
4. Open the Object Navigator and select all of the form's data block items. You may want to select the Data Blocks node and click the **Expand All** tool.

5. Open a Multiple-selection Property Palette for the selected items.
6. Set the Subclass Information property to **DEFAULT_ITEM_PROPERTIES**.
7. Set the Required property to **NO**. You can deselect the items and collapse the data blocks using the Collapse All tool.
8. Several items in the form are lengthy. The Query Length property of these items was set to 100 as a result of the DEFAULT_ITEM_PROPERTIES property class. Open the form's **DEFAULT_ITEM_PROPERTIES** property class and set the Query Length property to **2000**.
9. Run the form and review the data item properties. If you do not like the font size or font properties, modify the visual groups and property classes to suit yourself. This changes all the items in the form.
10. After viewing the EMPLOYEES tab page, it has been determined that it is not wide enough to display each record on a single line. The decision has been made to display four records, each record on two lines. Perform the following steps:
    a. Change the EMPLOYEES Frame Layout Style property to **FORM**.
    b. Set the Distance Between Records property to **10**.
    c. Place a format mask on the SSN data item. The format mask should display the dashes in the value. Use the following value: 999"-"99"-"9999. The nines are the standard numeric placeholder. Any character enclosed by double quotation marks is always inserted into the text item. Set the Maximum Length property of the SSN item to **11**.
    d. Set the tab order so that the user tabs across each row correctly. Change the Navigation style so that the operator moves to the following record at the end of a record. This is done by setting the **EMPLOYEES** Data Block Navigation Style property to **CHANGE RECORD**.
    e. Format the EMPLOYEES tab page so that it is similar to the page shown in Figure 5-19.

It can be difficult to format multiple-record Form style layouts similar to Figure 5-19 by clicking and selecting data items. It may be easier to temporarily set the Number Of Records Displayed property to 1 for the formatting and then change it to 4 when you are finished working. You can also use the technique of selecting items(s) in the Object Navigator. Selecting an item in this tool causes the same item to be selected in the Layout Editor.

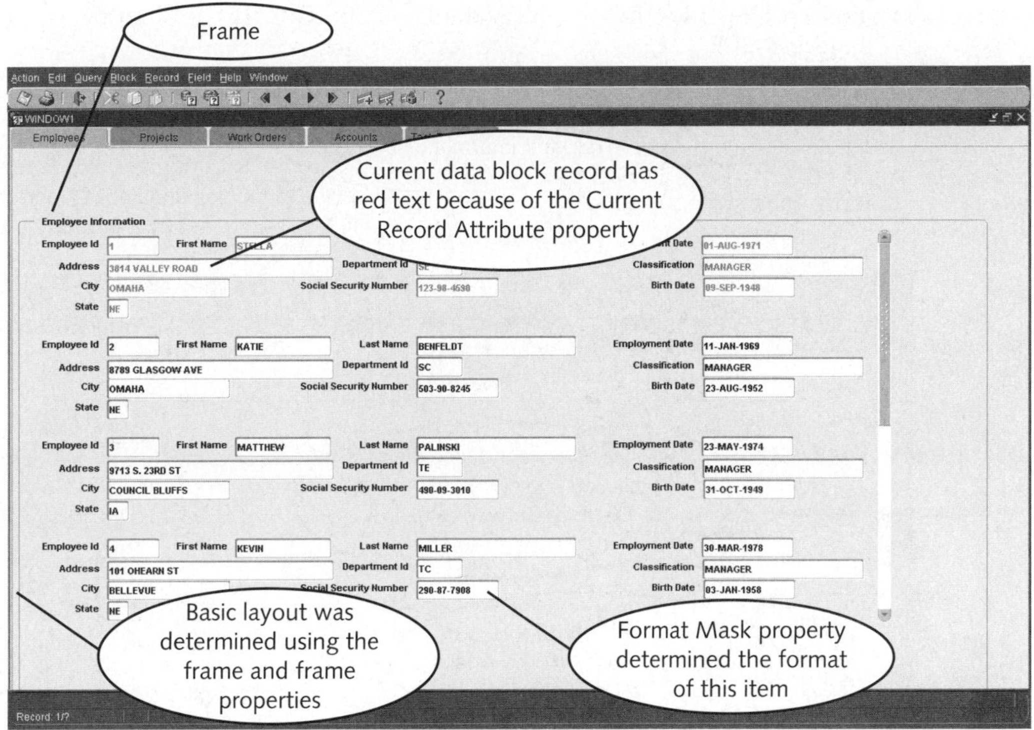

Figure 5-19 EMPLOYEES tab page

The formatting in Step 10e was done using frame properties. Frames can be hard to use. We will not use frames on the remainder of the canvases. You will be asked to delete the frames and perform your formatting. You should compare the formatting work you did in Step 10e to what you accomplish in the following steps:

a. Open the Object Navigator and delete all three frames on the PROJECTS tab page. (This can also be done in the Layout Editor.)
b. Format the **PROJ_SEARCH_CRITERIA** data block on the PROJECTS tab page (shown in Figure 5-20).
c. Place the data items in the following order: ASSIGNED_TO, ASSIGNED_DEPARTMENT_ID, PROJECT_ID, PROJECT_NAME, PROJECT_LOCATION, and PROJECT_NEED_DATE. The search variable you expect to be used most often is placed on the left.
d. Set the tab order to be the same as the data items listed in Step c.
e. Change the prompt locations according to Figure 5-20 or as you like.
f. Place a rounded rectangle around the data items.
g. Add the following boilerplate text above the frame: **Project Search Variables**.
h. Center the entire layout.

11. Format the PROJECT_DATA items on the PROJECTS tab page (shown in Figure 5-20).

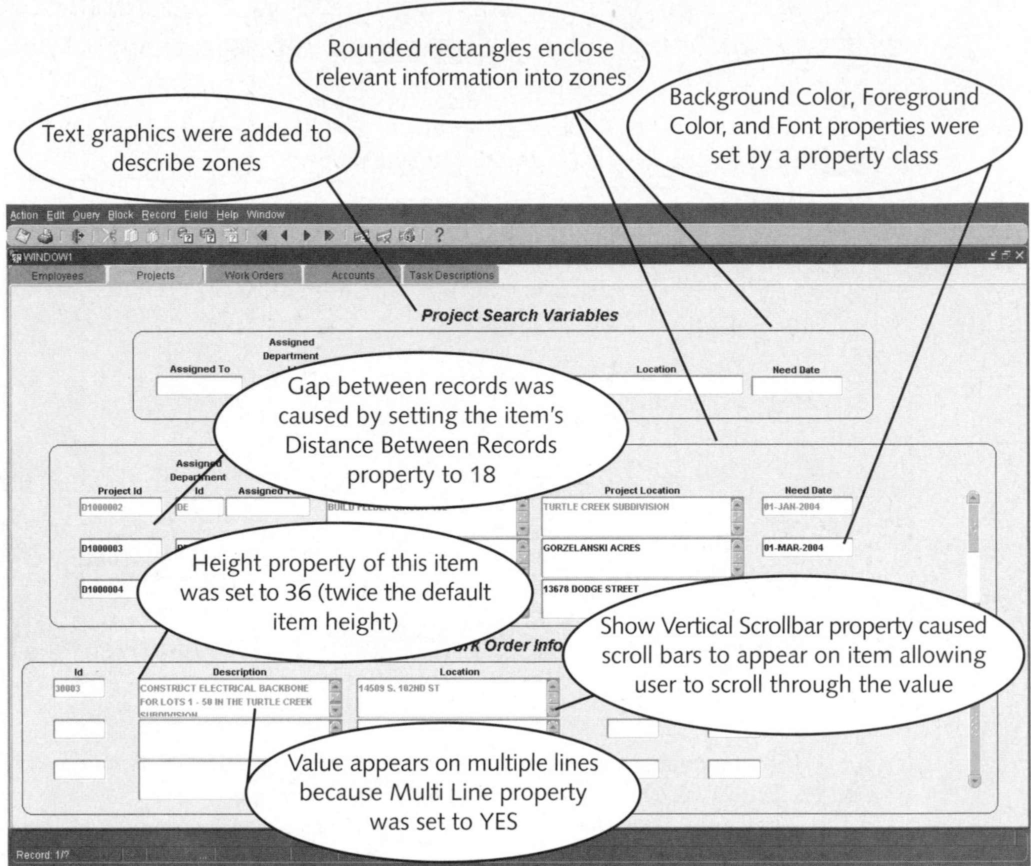

Figure 5-20 PROJECTS tab page after formatting and setting properties

12. Place the data items in the following order: **PROJECT_ID**, **ASSIGNED_DEPARTMENT_ID ASSIGNED_TO**, **PROJECT_NAME**, **PROJECT_LOCATION**, and **PROJECT_NEED_DATE**.
13. Set the tab order to match the data item layout. The PROJECT_NAME and PROJECT_LOCATION data items are lengthy. These items should be shown on two lines. The remainder of the data items will be displayed on one line. The steps that follow achieve this layout:
    a. Select the **PROJECT_NAME** and **PROJECT_LOCATION** data items and open a multiple-selection Property Palette.
    b. Set the Height property to **36**.
    c. Set the Width property to **180**.
    d. Set the Multi Line property to **YES**. This causes the text to wrap.
    e. Set to Wrap Style to **WORD**.

f. Set the Show Vertical Scrollbar property to **YES**. This places a scrollbar next to each of the items. The scrollbar can be used to view any hidden text.

g. Select the **ASSIGNED_TO**, **ASSIGNED_DEPARTMENT_ID**, **PROJECT_ID**, and **PROJECT_NEED_DATE** items. Set their Distance Between Records properties to **18**.

h. Draw a rounded rectangle around the data items.

i. Add the following boilerplate text above the rounded rectangle: **Project Information**.

j. Resize the scroll bar.

k. There is a gap in the items on the right side. This gap will be used for summary columns in a future installment.

l. Center the layout in the form.

14. Format the WORK_ORDERS data block items on the PROJECTS tab page (shown in Figure 5-20) by performing the following steps:

    a. Place the WORK_ORDERS data block items in the following order: WORK_ORDER_ID, WO_DESCRIPTION, WO_LOCATION, APPROVED_BY, and ASSIGNED_TO. The WO_DESCRIPTION and WO_LOCATION data items are lengthy. These items should be shown on two lines. The remainder of the data items will be displayed on one line. Use the following steps to achieve this layout.

    b. Select the **WO_DESCRIPTION** and **WO_LOCATION** data items.

    c. Set the Height property to **36**.

    d. Set the Width property to **180**. Set the Multi-Line property to **YES**. This causes the text to wrap.

    e. Set the Wrap Style property to **WORD**.

    f. Set the Show Vertical Scroll bar property to **YES**. This places a scroll bar next to each of the items. The scroll bar can be used to view any hidden text.

    g. Select the **WORK_ORDER_ID**, **APPROVED_BY**, and **ASSIGNED_TO** items. Set their Distance Between Records property to **18**.

    h. Draw a rounded rectangle around the data items.

    i. Add the following boilerplate text above the rounded rectangle: **Work Order Information**.

    j. Resize the scroll bar.

    k. There is a gap in the items on the right side, which will be used for summary columns in a future case project.

    l. Center the layout in the form.

15. Launch the form and execute a query on the PROJECTS tab page. Be sure that your insertion point is in the PROJECT INFORMATION area.

16. Format the WO_SEARCH_CRITERIA data block on the WORK_ORDERS tab page (shown in Figure 5-21) by performing the following steps:
    a. Delete all the child Frame objects for the WORK_ORDERS tab page.
    b. Place the WO_SEARCH_CRITERIA data items in the following order: PROJECT_ID, WORK_ORDER_ID, ASSIGNED_TO, APPROVED_BY, WO_LOCATION, and WO_DESCRIPTION. Place the search variable that you expect to be used most frequently on the left to reduce the number of tabbing actions the user must perform.
    c. Set the tab order to match that of the data items listed in Step b.
    d. Change the prompts according to Figure 5-21 or as you wish.
    e. Place a rounded rectangle around the data items.
    f. Add the following boilerplate text above the frame: **WORK ORDER SEARCH VARIABLES**.
    g. Center the entire layout.

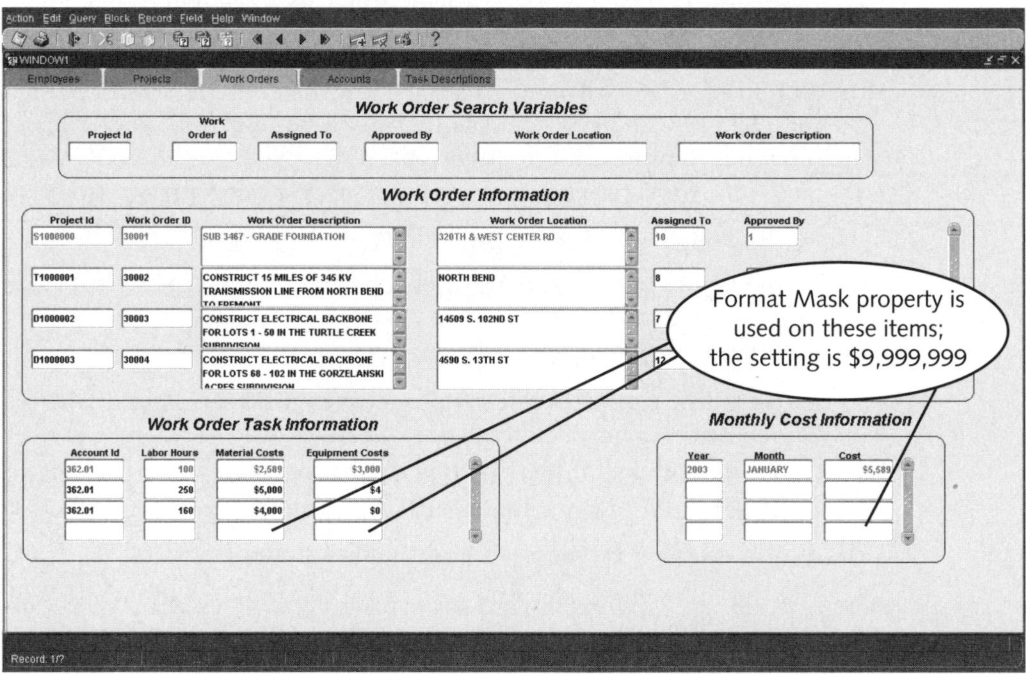

Figure 5-21 WORK_ORDERS tab page after formatting

17. Format the WORK_ORDER_DATA data block (shown in Figure 5-21) by performing the following steps:
    a. Place the WORK_ORDER_DATA data block items in the following order: PROJECT_ID, WORK_ORDER_ID, WO_DESCRIPTION, WO_LOCATION, ASSIGNED_TO, and APPROVED_BY.

b. Set the tab order to match Step a.

c. Select the WO_DESCRIPTION and WO_LOCATION items.

d. Set the Height property to **36**.

e. Set the Width property to **180**.

f. Set the Multi-Line property to **YES**. This causes the text to wrap.

g. Set the Wrap Style to **WORD**.

h. Set the Show Vertical Scroll bar property to **YES**. This places a scroll bar next to each of the items. The scroll bar can be used to view any hidden text.

i. Select the **PROJECT_ID**, **WORK_ORDER_ID**, **ASSIGNED_TO**, and **APPROVED_BY** items. Set the Distance Between Records property to **18**.

j. Draw a rounded rectangle around the data items.

k. Add the following boilerplate text above the rounded rectangle: **Work Order Information**.

l. Resize the scroll bar.

m. There is a gap in the items on the right side, which will be used for summary columns in a future Case Project.

n. Center the layout in the form.

18. Format the WORK_ORDER_TASKS items on the WORK_ORDERS tab page (shown in Figure 5-21) by performing the following steps:

    a. Place the data items in the following order: ACCOUNT_ID, LABOR_HOURS, MATERIAL_COSTS, and EQUIPMENT_COSTS.

    b. Set the tab order to match the data item layout.

    c. Draw a rounded rectangle around the data items.

    d. Add the following boilerplate text above the rounded rectangle: **Work Order Task Information**.

    e. Resize the scroll bar.

    f. Add the following format mask to the LABOR_HOURS item: **99,999**.

    g. Add the following format mask to the MATERIAL_COSTS and EQUIPMENT_COSTS data items: **$9,999,999**.

    h. Right-justify the LABOR_HOURS, MATERIAL_COSTS, and EQUIPMENT_COSTS data items. There are gaps in the items, which will be used for task description and account description items in a future Case Project.

19. Format the MONTHLY_COSTS items on the WORK_ORDERS tab page (shown in Figure 5-21) by performing the following steps:

    a. Place the data items in the following order: YEAR, MONTH, COST.

    b. Set the tab order to match the data item layout.

    c. Draw a rounded rectangle around the data items.

d. Add the following boilerplate text above the rounded rectangle: **Monthly Cost Information**.

e. Resize the scroll bar.

f. Add the following mask to the COST item: **$9,999,999**.

g. Right-justify the COST data items.

20. Open and execute the form. Be sure to put the insertion point into the Word Order Information layout area before executing the query.

If you cannot see the entire form within the browser applet window, the **formsweb.cfg** file located on your machine has a height and width setting that can be used to increase the size of the applet window. You may also adjust the resolution of your display.

21. Format the ACCOUNTS data items on the ACCOUNTS tab page by performing the following steps:

    a. Delete the ACCOUNTS tab page frame.

    b. Format the tab page so that it resembles Figure 5-22.

22. Format the TASK_DESCRIPTIONS data items on the TASK_DESCRIPTIONS tab page by performing the following steps:

    a. Delete the frame under the TASK_DESCRIPTIONS tab page.

    b. Format the tab page so that it resembles Figure 5-23.

23. Set the Order By clause for each of the data blocks. The following are the data blocks and the Order By clause settings:

    PROJECT_DATA: PROJECT_ID

    WORK_ORDERS: WORK_ORDER_ID

    WORK_ORDER_DATA: WORK_ORDER_ID

    WORK_ORDER_TASKS: WORK_ORDER_TASK_ID

    MONTHLY_COSTS: YEAR, MONTH

    ACCOUNTS: ACCOUNT_ID

    TASK_DESCRIPTIONS: TASK_ID

    EMPLOYEES: EMPLOYEE_ID

24. Launch the form and test whether each data block is ordering the records. If you entered incorrect values in this step, you will not be able to retrieve records and will have to correct the values.

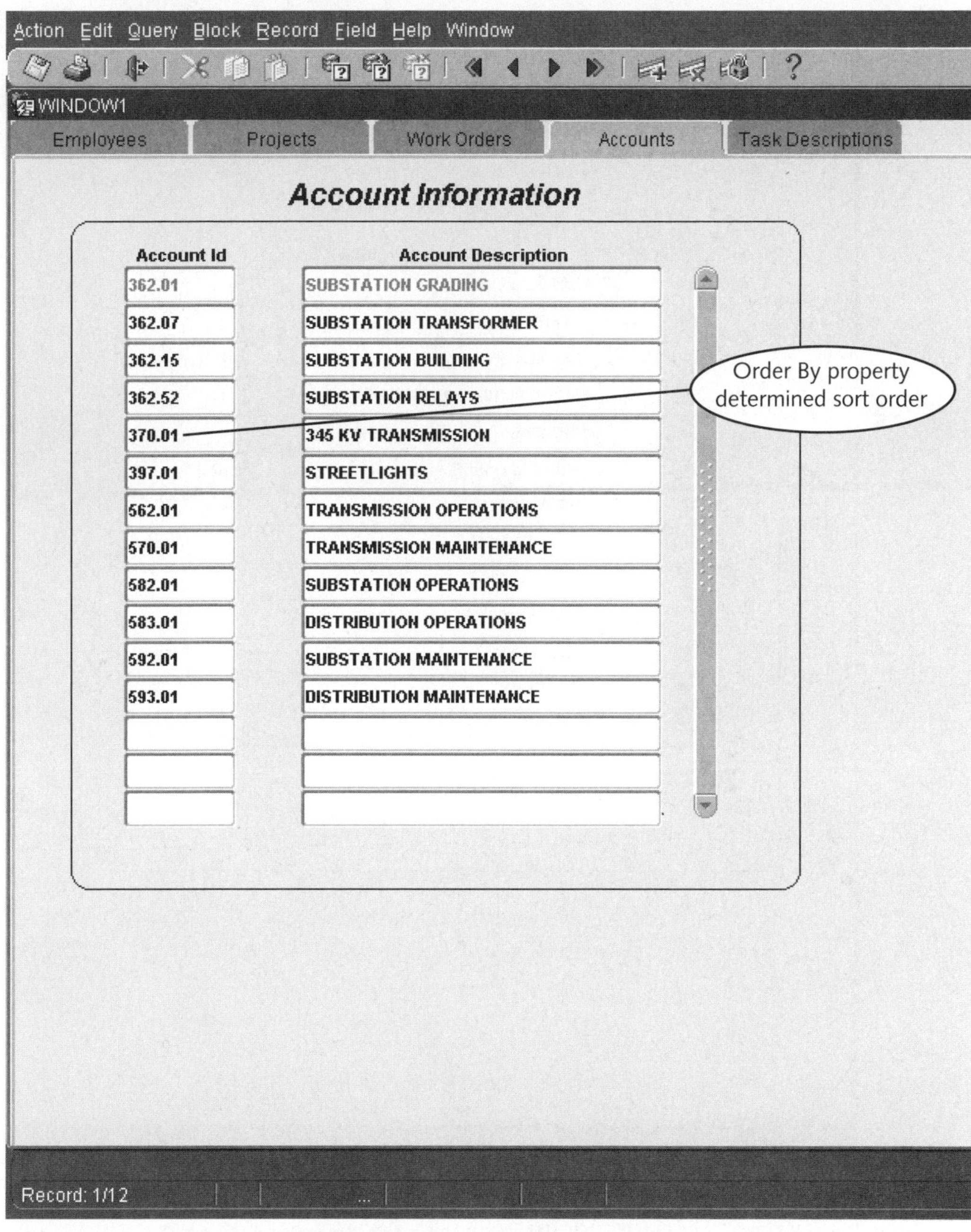

Figure 5-22 ACCOUNTS tab page after formatting

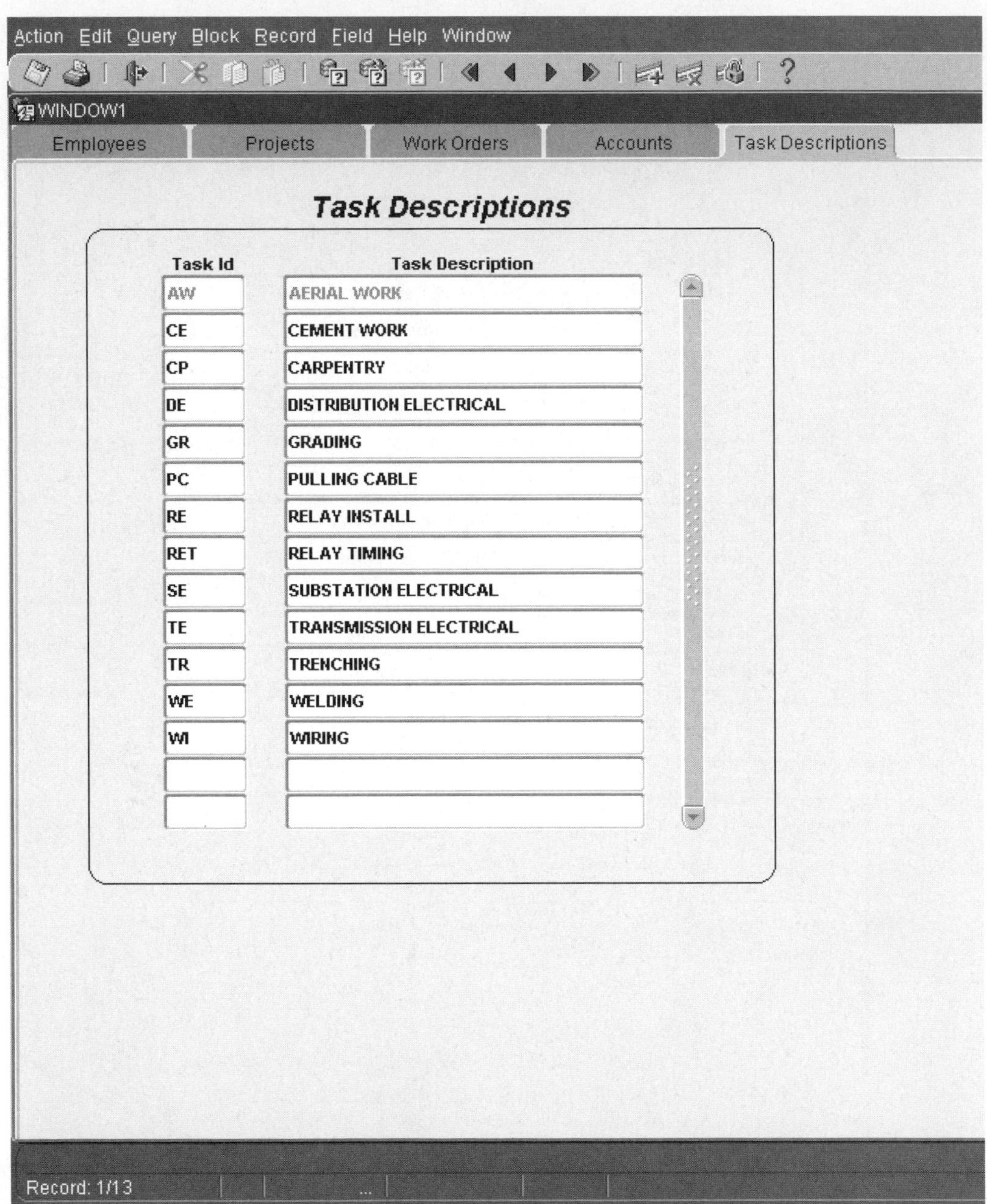

Figure 5-23 TASK_DESCRIPTIONS tab page after formatting

CHAPTER

6

USING TRIGGERS, THE PL/SQL EDITOR, SYNTAX PALETTE, AND FORM VARIABLES

In this chapter you will:

- ♦ Learn how to use triggers to add your own programming logic to a form
- ♦ Understand the various types of triggers
- ♦ Create and use SmartTriggers
- ♦ Use the PL/SQL Editor
- ♦ Use built-in subprograms when appropriate
- ♦ Use miscellaneous PL/SQL constructs and built-in tools
- ♦ Trap form errors
- ♦ Create your own stored procedures
- ♦ Use form parameters, global variables, and system variables
- ♦ Modify the action of function keys

As the roadmap in Figure 6-1 depicts, this chapter covers the tools, variables, and Oracle functions that allow you to use PL/SQL to fine-tune the behavior of your forms, so you need a basic understanding of PL/SQL. In the previous chapter, you used properties to control a form's behavior. This chapter continues with a discussion of how to control a form by employing PL/SQL scripts using triggers. By the end of this chapter you will be able to:

- Define form edit routines to ensure that entered data is correct.
- Perform an action such as displaying another form or running a report when a button is pressed.
- Initialize variables when the form is opened.
- Redefine or disable the behavior of the function keys.

- Execute secondary SELECT statements that fetch descriptive values when a record is fetched into the data block.
- Perform your own data manipulation language (DML) operations when a form event occurs.

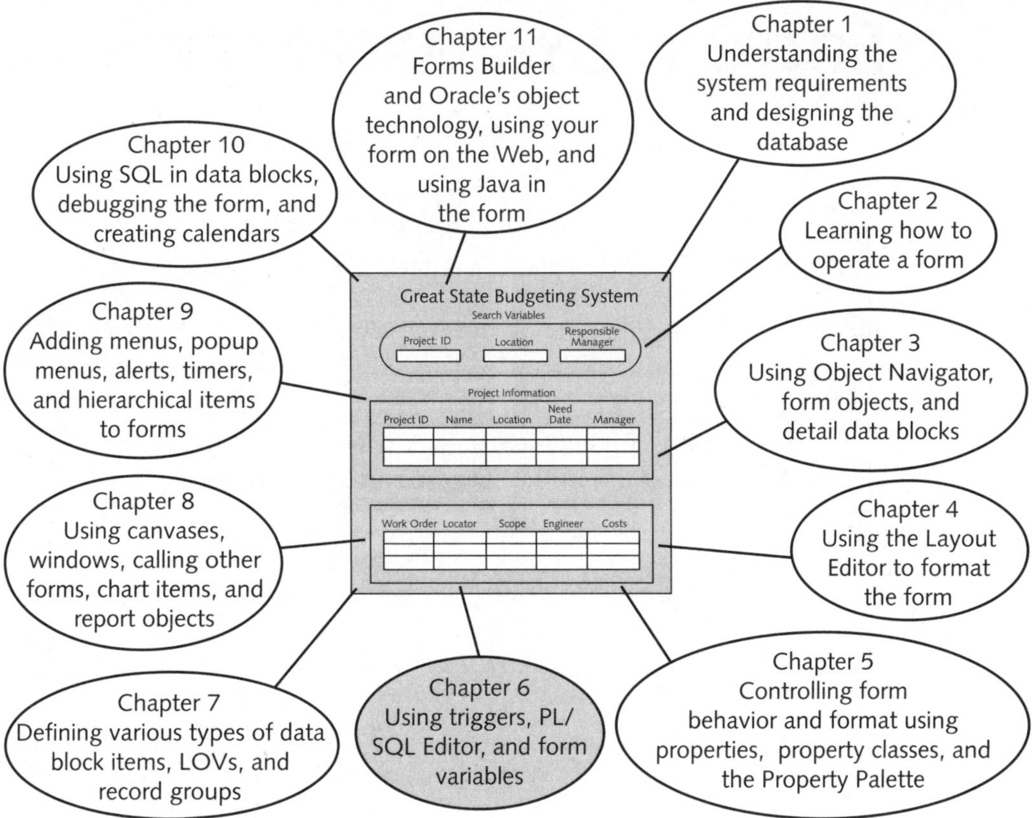

Figure 6-1 Roadmap

The forms that you have created to this point perform many functions but will probably never be put into production. Your users will want you to add security into a form, place the current date into a text item when the user tabs into it, or press a button (or a toolbar tool) to execute a query. They will want the application to perform as much of their work as possible. The topics in this chapter show you how to make your forms work for users. A form is powerful without the use of triggers and PL/SQL, but your forms enter an entirely new level when you learn to customize their behavior with PL/SQL.

The Forms Builder 9*i* PL/SQL Editor depicted in this chapter and throughout the book differs in format slightly from the 6*i* PL/SQL Editor. Because these differences are limited to format, they should not pose any difficulties for the 6*i* user.

TRIGGERS AND TRIGGER TYPES

Oracle forms are event driven, which means that programs or PL/SQL statements are executed when an event takes place on the form. Sample events include the clicking of a button, the retrieval of a record, and the execution of an INSERT statement. Each of these actions is called a **triggering event** or **trigger** for short. Every conceivable form event is associated with a named trigger, and a typical form uses many of these triggers to execute PL/SQL statements. For example, the Budgeting Case Project (shown in Figure 6-2) uses a variety of triggers to enhance or redefine functionality including the following:

- **Key-Others trigger**: Disables the function keys. This trigger is often used when a form designer wants all functions disabled except those launched by clicking a button.
- **When-Button-Pressed trigger**: Calls the ADD_PROJECT stacked canvas, calls the WO_INSTRUCTIONS stacked canvas, closes the ADD_PROJECT and WO_INSTRUCTIONS canvases, commits changes to the form, closes the form, launches an LOV (list of values), and executes a query on the PROJECT_DATA data block.
- **When-Radio-Changed trigger**: Dynamically changes the PROJECT_DATA Order By property.
- **Post-Query trigger**: Summarizes project and work order costs and identifies the first and last names of the ASSIGNED_TO and APPROVED_BY items.
- **Pre-Insert and Pre-Update triggers**: Execute a form procedure that checks that the WORK_ORDER_ID and WO_DESCRIPTION items have values. If the items do not have values, the trigger rings and terminates the DML transaction.
- **On-Populate-Details and On-Check-Delete-Master triggers**: Created by Forms Builder to coordinate the records in the PROJECT_DATA and WORK_ORDERS data blocks.

These triggers are fairly typical of those in every form. It is important for you to know that a form generally requires substantial PL/SQL programming in the form of procedures, stored procedures, and triggers. In addition, you should remember that all PL/SQL is executed as the result of a trigger firing.

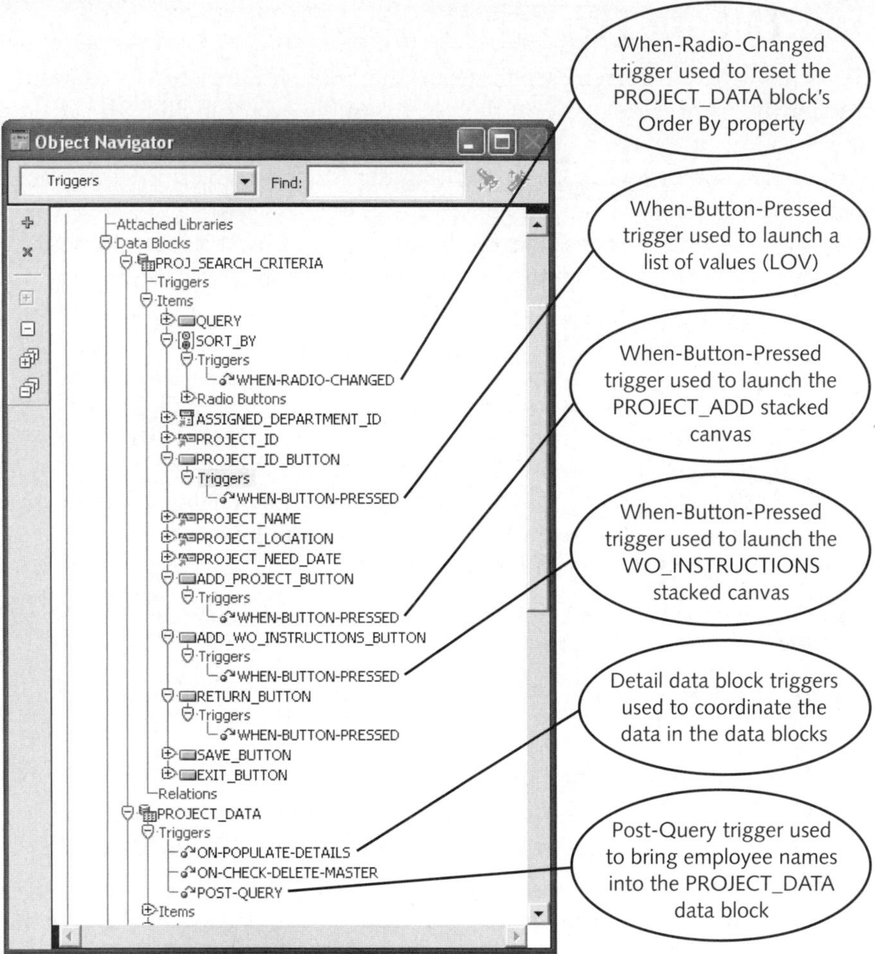

Figure 6-2 Various triggers used by the Budgeting Case Project application

A trigger is a form object that associates an event with one or more PL/SQL statements. The PL/SQL statements can be:

- Custom-built, stored, and form procedures
- Oracle-developed, built-in subprograms, such as Set_item_property
- SELECT statements
- DML statements, such as INSERT, UPDATE, and DELETE
- DDL statements, such as CREATE TABLE
- Any PL/SQL construct, such as the basic code block, IF-THEN-ELSE constructs, looping structures, exception handlers, and cursors

A trigger is fired when it is executed. One of the most difficult tasks in Forms Builder is to determine the proper trigger to use. This difficulty arises because of the need to identify the event that causes the trigger to fire. There are many possible events that occur in normal form transactions. If you choose the incorrect event, your trigger may not fire or may fire at the wrong moment.

The first step in adding PL/SQL statements to your form is to identify the type of action that causes the particular PL/SQL statements to execute. For example, you may want to test inputted values against a series of edits when the operator attempts to tab from an item, or to calculate derived values for each record fetched into a data block, or to initialize values when the form is launched. Each of these example tasks are performed when a different event occurs. Your task is to identify the correct event.

To limit the search for a trigger, you can first identify the event type. This limits your search, because Oracle has categorized the triggers by event type. When determining the proper trigger, examine the eight trigger type categories to see where your needed trigger fits. The trigger types are listed in Table 6-1.

Table 6-1 Trigger types

Trigger type	Description
Block-processing	Fires as a result of a block record management event. Examples: the When-Create-Record trigger is fired when an attempt is made to create a record; the When-Clear-Record trigger fires when the block is cleared of records.
Interface event	Fires as a result of a user action, such as clicking a button or activating a window.
Master-detail	Fires as a result of an event that requires coordination between related blocks. Creating a relation object automatically results in the creation of a trigger.
Message-handling	Fires as a result of an error or informational message. The names of these types of triggers often begin with the prefix On.
Navigational	Fires as a result of a navigational event, such as placing the cursor into a text item or moving the input focus into a data block. This type of trigger can be fired before or after the event. The keywords, Pre and Post, designate when the trigger will be fired as a result of the event, and the names of these types of triggers begin with the prefixes Pre or Post.
Query-time	Fires before or after a query is executed.
Transactional	Fires as a result of a DML action, such as the insertion, deletion, or commit of a record. These triggers can be fired before, after, or as a replacement for the DML action. The names of these triggers often begin with the prefix On.
Validation	Fires as a result of a validation action occurring on the record or item. The names of these triggers often begin with the prefix When.

Understanding the Difference Between Key, On, Post, Pre, and When Triggers

Triggers can be further classified by the prefix of their names, such as Key, On, Post, Pre, or When. Table 6-2 defines the trigger prefixes and shows examples of trigger use.

Table 6-2 Trigger name prefixes and descriptions

Trigger prefix	Description	Usage example	Examples
Key	These types of triggers supercede the normal function key functionality. For example a Key-Entqry (Enter query) trigger is fired when the function keys that place a data block into the Enter Query mode are pressed. They are used to replace or enhance the normal functionality of the Control function key.	A Key-Entqry (Enter query) trigger can be defined so that the input focus moves to a particular data block, such as a master data block, before the Enter-Query command is executed.	Key-Entqry (Enter query), Key-Exeqry (Execute query), Key-Commit (Commit form change), Key-Exit (Exit the form)
On	These types of triggers supercede the launching transaction. For example, the statements in an On-Insert trigger replace the INSERT statement issued by the data block. Typical transactions that are superceded by an On trigger are DML operations or form operations, such as clearing and repopulating a detail data block after changing records in the master data block.	On-Insert triggers can be used to uppercase new values before placing them into a table or to add records to tables not associated to the data block, such as a summary table.	On-Insert, On-Delete, On-Error, On-Message, On-Rollback, On-Check-Delete-Master
Post	These types of triggers fire as a result of a database transaction or form event. They contain supplemental statements that are executed after the action occurs. Unlike the On triggers, they do not replace normal form operations. For example, a Post-Query trigger fires after a record is fetched to the data block.	A Post-Query trigger is commonly used to bring descriptive information into a data block. For example, the EMP table has a column named DEPTNO, which is the employee's department number. A Post-Query trigger can be used to return the department name for the employee.	Post-Insert, Post-Update, Post-Query, Post-Logon, Post-Record

Table 6-2 Trigger name prefixes and descriptions (continued)

Trigger prefix	Description	Usage example	Examples
Pre	These types of triggers fire as a result of a database transaction or form event. They contain supplemental statements that are executed before the action occurs. Unlike the On triggers, they do not replace normal form operations. For example, a Pre-Insert trigger fires before the form executes an INSERT statement.	Pre-Insert, Pre-Update, and Pre-Delete triggers are often defined as security mechanisms. A security factor is evaluated by these triggers when the specified DML operation occurs. If the security check fails, the trigger terminates the intended DML transaction.	Pre-Insert, Pre-Update, Pre-Query, Pre-Logon, Pre-Record
When	These types of triggers fire as a result of a form action. For example, a When-New-Form-Instance trigger is fired when the form is initially launched.	A When-Button-Pressed trigger is used with form buttons. When the button is clicked, the trigger's statements are executed. Buttons and When-Button-Pressed triggers are used on toolbars to open new modules or stacked canvases, or to execute a query.	When-Button-Pressed, When-Checkbox-Changed, When-Mouse-Click, When-New-Form-Instance

See Appendix B for a complete listing of Triggers.

Triggers fire in a predetermined order. To make matters even more complex, different triggers can fire sequentially based on the same actions. For example, Figure 6-3 displays the Object Navigator with three triggers displayed under the EMPNO data block item. These are the Pre-Text-Item, When-Validate-Item, and Post-Text-Item triggers, which are fired when events occur in the EMPNO data block item. The triggers are fired in a sequential order, and a single event fires the latter two. The Pre-Text-Item trigger fires first. As its name implies, it fires before the insertion point enters the EMPNO text item.

The next two triggers both fire when the user moves the insertion point to another data item. The When-Validate-Item trigger fires first and the Post-Text-Item second. The difference between the two triggers is that the Post-Text-Item fires every time the input focus leaves the text item. The When-Validate-Item does not.

When a user moves from a data item that has been modified, the form first validates the new values against the item's validation properties. This validation consists of testing the modified value against the item's properties (i.e., Required, Primary Key, and Lowest Allowed Value). It also fires any associated When-Validate-Item trigger, which enhances the validation. If this validation is successful, the form begins moving the insertion point causing the Post-Text-Item trigger to fire.

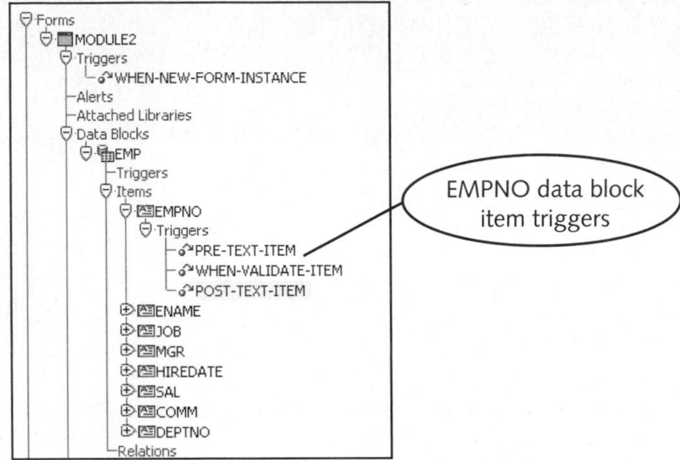

Figure 6-3 EMPNO data block item triggers

If both triggers fire when an operator tabs from the item, does it matter if you use the When-Validate-Item or the Post-Text-Item trigger? Yes, it does. The When-Validate-Item trigger only fires when a value has been modified. After the value is validated, the trigger will not execute if you once again move the insertion point from the data item. The Post-Text-Item trigger fires every time the insertion point is moved.

The point of this discussion is that there are subtle differences between many triggers. If you choose a trigger that fires conditionally, such as the When-Validate-Item trigger rather than the Post-Text-Item trigger, your form may not operate as you want. Conversely, if you choose the Post-Text-Item trigger rather than the When-Validate-Item trigger, your form may perform needless work. Thus, to be an effective form developer, it is important to understand the sequence and the exact conditions that fire a trigger.

It is often difficult to determine the order in which triggers are fired or whether a trigger is performing the necessary work. For example, if a trigger contains an IF-THEN-ELSE construct, you will not be sure if you have used the wrong trigger and it didn't fire or if the IF-THEN construct condition is incorrect.

The Message built-in subprogram can help you overcome this problem. The built-in displays text in the form's status line when it is executed. Place the built-in within the target trigger and execute the form. You can observe whether the trigger has been fired by observing the messages in the status area. The following is a template of the Message built-in:

```
Message ('your message test');
```

Trigger Scope

Triggers can be assigned to the form, a data block, or data item. In some cases, a trigger can only be assigned to a specific type of object. For example, a When-New-Form-Instance trigger is fired when the form is initially launched. It can be assigned only to the form module. It cannot be assigned to a data block or a data block item. Some triggers can be assigned to a form, a data block, or a data block item. The Post-Change trigger, which is fired after a change is made to a data block item, can be assigned to any of a data block's items, data blocks, or forms.

The level of the assignment influences the scope of the trigger. Triggers associated to a data block item are only fired when an event occurs in the data block item. Likewise, the same trigger associated to a data block only fires as a result of an action that affects the data block. The trigger assigned to the data block has a greater scope than the trigger assigned to the data block item. The trigger assigned to the form has the greatest scope of all. Figure 6-4 depicts three Post-Change triggers. One is assigned to the form, one to a data block, and one to an item.

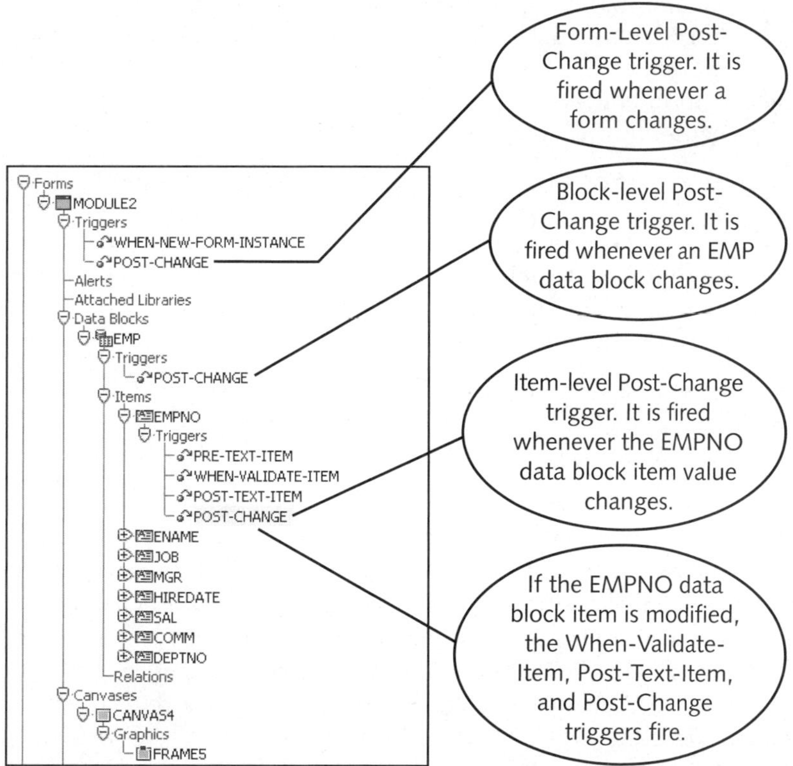

Figure 6-4 Object Navigator displaying Post-Change triggers assigned to the form, data block, and data block item

As a form developer, you determine the desired scope of each trigger that is added to the form, so that the trigger is fired at the proper time. For example, if you place some edits in a Post-Change trigger and the edits pertain to a specific item, the trigger should be associated to the item. If the trigger is assigned to a data block, it fires every time something changes in the form. This increased scope causes the trigger to fire more than was intended producing unexpected results, the least harmful of which is that the computer performs more work than necessary.

Trigger Restrictions

Besides its scope of control, each individual trigger may have characteristics or restrictions, as follows:

- **Legal commands**: Legal commands are commands that can be fired in a trigger. Triggers can fire SQL and DML statements and **restricted** and **unrestricted** built-ins, such as Set_item_property or Execute_query. Some triggers are restricted to the types of commands they can execute. Restricted built-ins affect navigation in a form. They may only be called from triggers that are fired while no navigation is occurring. For example, you may not place a Commit_form built-in used to commit form changes in a Post-Text-Item trigger, because the trigger is fired as the result of moving from an item. On the other hand, the Commit_form built-in can be used in a When-Button-Pressed trigger, because this trigger is not fired as a result of navigation.
- **Enter Query mode**: Certain triggers, such as the On-Insert and Pre-Insert, cannot be fired when a data block is in the Enter Query mode. This makes sense, because the data block only contains search values. In addition, some built-in subprograms, such as Commit_form, cannot be executed by a trigger that is fired in the Enter Query mode. This too makes sense, because the data block does not have records to save.
- **On failure**: Triggers perform different actions if triggers fail. Some triggers do nothing if they fail. Other triggers, such as the When-Validate-Item trigger, terminates the navigation and returns the input focus to the original point.

If you are using restricted built-ins in the wrong type of trigger, Forms Builder compiles and executes the form. However, Forms Builder issues an error message and terminates the trigger when it is fired. Both Appendix B and the Forms Builder Help Facility supply useful information about triggers, including when triggers fire, what restrictions apply to each one, and what happens when triggers fail to fire. The Help Facility generally gives you an explanation of the trigger's properties and even examples of code that might be used in the trigger. Figure 6-5 shows the Help screen for the When-Validate-Item trigger.

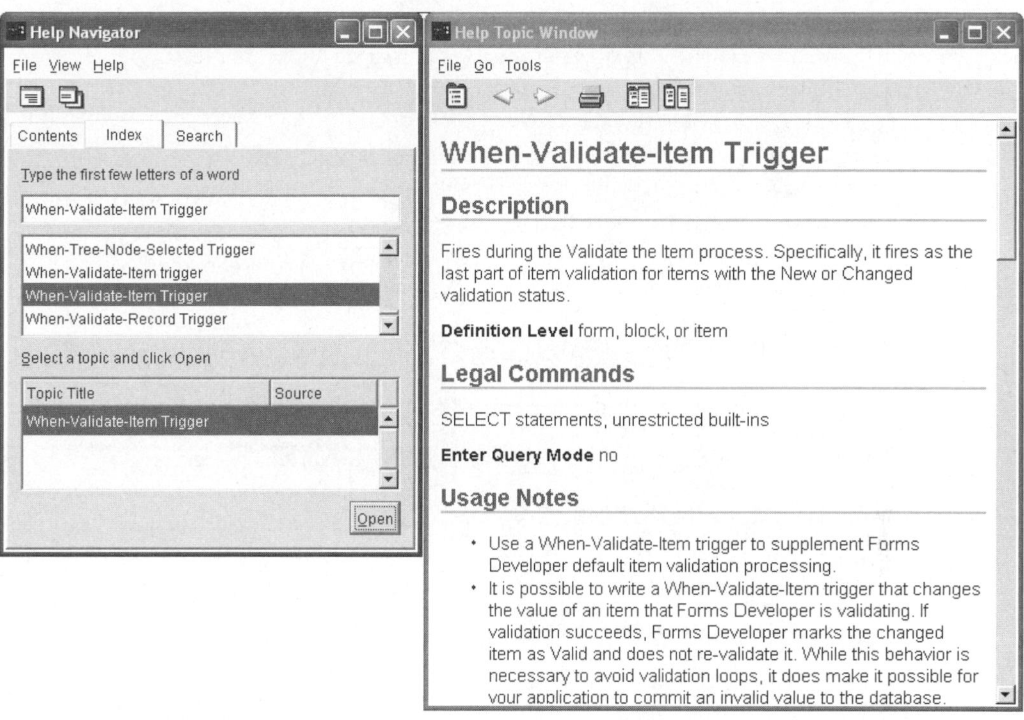

Figure 6-5 When-Validate-Item Trigger Help screen

Creating Triggers and Using Smart Triggers

Triggers are form child objects and are created in the Object Navigator. To create a trigger, perform the following steps:

1. Determine the scope needed for the trigger (i.e., form, data block, or item).
2. Select the object (form, data block, or item) that corresponds to this scope.
3. Locate the Triggers node under the selected object. This can be located by expanding the object.
4. Click the **Create** tool to open the Triggers dialog box (see Figure 6-6).
5. Select the desired trigger and click **OK**. A PL/SQL Editor opens for the trigger script entry (see Figure 6-6).
6. Enter the PL/SQL statements into the PL/SQL Editor. Forms Builder does not create a trigger unless it has at least one statement.
7. To compile the PL/SQL statements, click the **Compile PL/SQL Code** tool. This checks the script syntax.
8. Click **OK**.

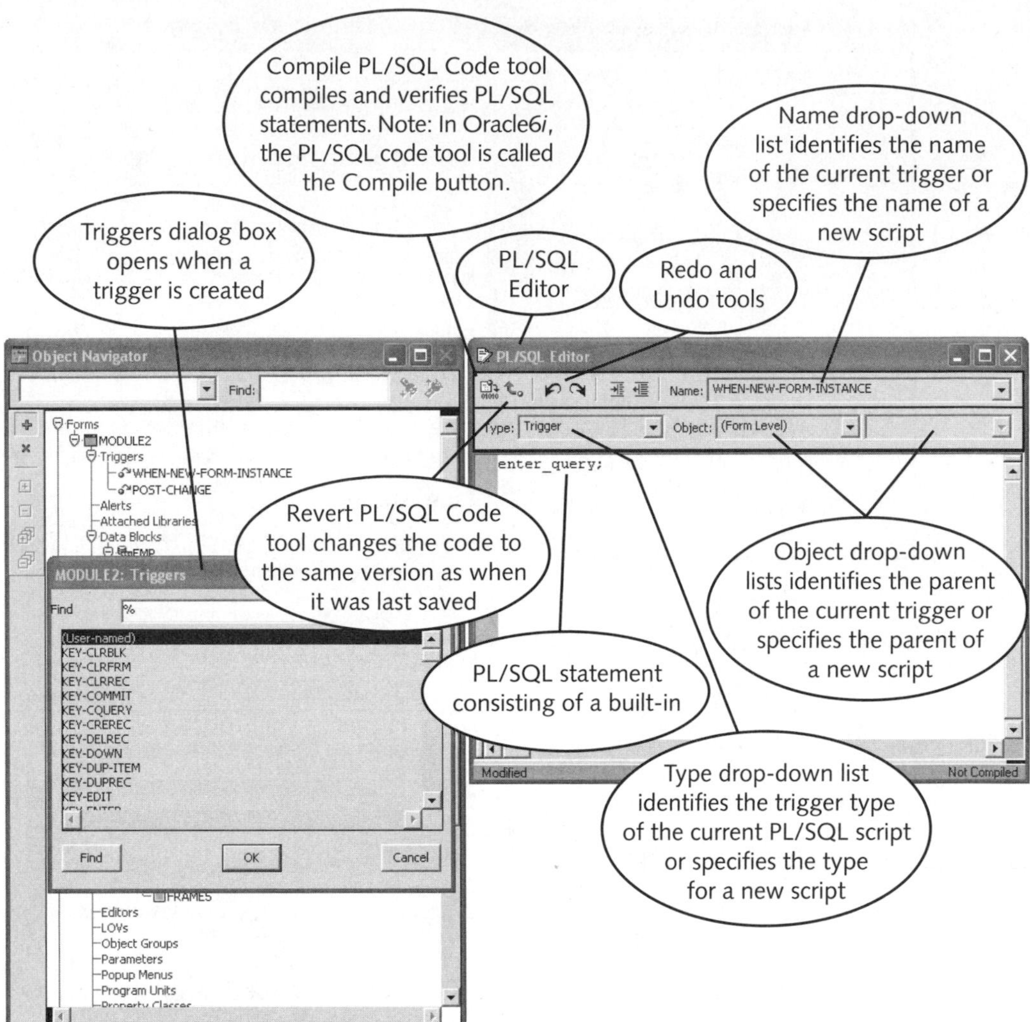

Figure 6-6 Triggers dialog box, the PL/SQL Editor displaying a statement, and the Compile PL/SQL Code tool

Now that you've seen the steps needed to create a trigger, it is useful to practice adding a trigger to a form yourself.

1. Open the Object Navigator and create a new form module.
2. Start the Data Block wizard and create a data block based on the DEPT table.
3. Use the Layout Wizard to create a layout for the data block. The style should be Form and one record should be displayed.
4. Open the Object Navigator to locate and expand the LOC data block item. Select the **Triggers** node under the LOC data block item.

5. Click the **Create** tool to open the Triggers dialog box.
6. Select the **Pre-Text-Item** trigger from the list. Click **OK** to open the PL/SQL Editor for the trigger. Add the following code:
   ```
   Bell;
   Message ('This is the PRE-TEXT-ITEM trigger');
   ```
7. Click the **Compile PL/SQL Code** tool to ensure that the trigger is correct.
8. Repeat steps 4 through 7. In this iteration, create a When-Validate-Item trigger using this script:
   ```
   Bell;
   Message ('This is the WHEN-VALIDATE-ITEM trigger');
   ```
9. Repeat steps 4 through 7. In this iteration, create a Post-Text-Item trigger using this script:
   ```
   Bell;
   Message ('This is the POST-TEXT-ITEM trigger');
   ```
10. Launch the form and execute a query.
11. Tab through the form several times while watching the status line for messages. When you tab into the LOC item, the Pre-Text-Item message displays. When you tab from the LOC item, the Post-Text-Item displays.
12. Tab into the LOC text item and modify the value.
13. The When-Validate-Item message should appear before the Post-Text-Item message when you tab out of the item. Note that when the form issues two or more messages at a time, the first message is displayed on the status line. The second and subsequent messages are displayed in a modal dialog box, because Forms Builder wants to ensure that the operator sees them.
14. Tab through the text items again and determine whether all three triggers are fired with each tabbing loop. The When-Validate-Item message does not appear again unless you modify the LOC value.
15. Save the form for later practice.

The previous practice demonstrated two things: that triggers fire at different times, and the differences between the functioning of the When-Validate-Item and Post-Text-Item triggers.

The Triggers dialog box (Figure 6-6) that was mentioned in Step 5 lists all triggers that can be used for the target object. Only triggers that are valid for the particular object are shown. Those that are ineligible due to their scope or other factors are not shown. You can generally locate the trigger by scrolling through the list. However, because there are numerable triggers, the dialog box has search capabilities that help you reduce the list to one or more specific triggers, thereby reducing your searching time. To perform a search, follow these steps:

1. At the top of the Triggers dialog box pictured in Figure 6-7 is a Find text box with a wild-card (%) symbol in the box. Enter a value into this box before, after, or before and after the % symbol.
2. Click the **Find** button. The list box contents are filtered to match the entered value.

Figure 6-7 shows a sample Triggers dialog box using the Search text item.

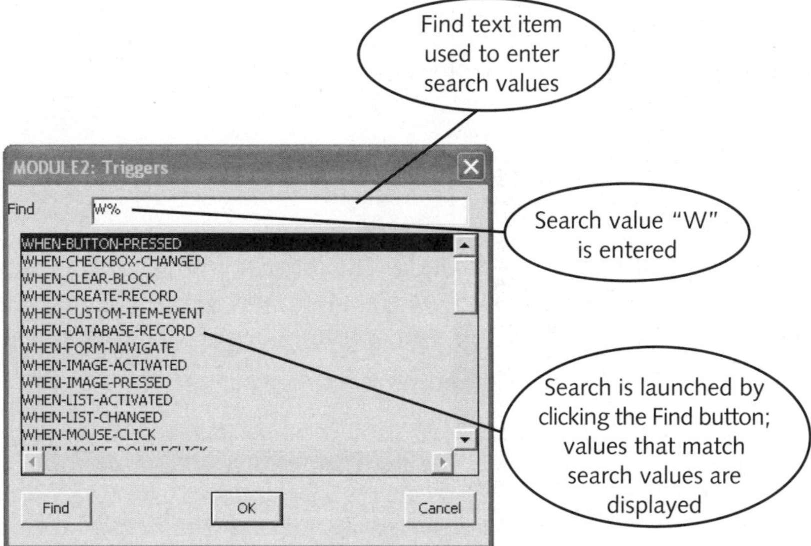

Figure 6-7 Triggers dialog box displaying triggers that begin with "W"

SmartTriggers is a handy feature of Forms Builder and a possible replacement for the Triggers dialog box. SmartTriggers are similar to the SmartClasses discussed in Chapter 5. Oracle has identified the most commonly used triggers for each form object. The most common triggers appear on the SmartTriggers Palette for the currently selected object. The triggers change depending on the selected item. For example, when the form module is selected, the palette displays the When-New-Form-Instance, Pre-Form, and Post-Form triggers. When a data block is selected, the When-New-Block-Instance, When-New-Record-Instance, Pre-Block, Post-Block, and When-Validate-Record triggers display. As you can see, this is a completely different list. Figure 6-8 illustrates the SmartTriggers menu palette for a data block.

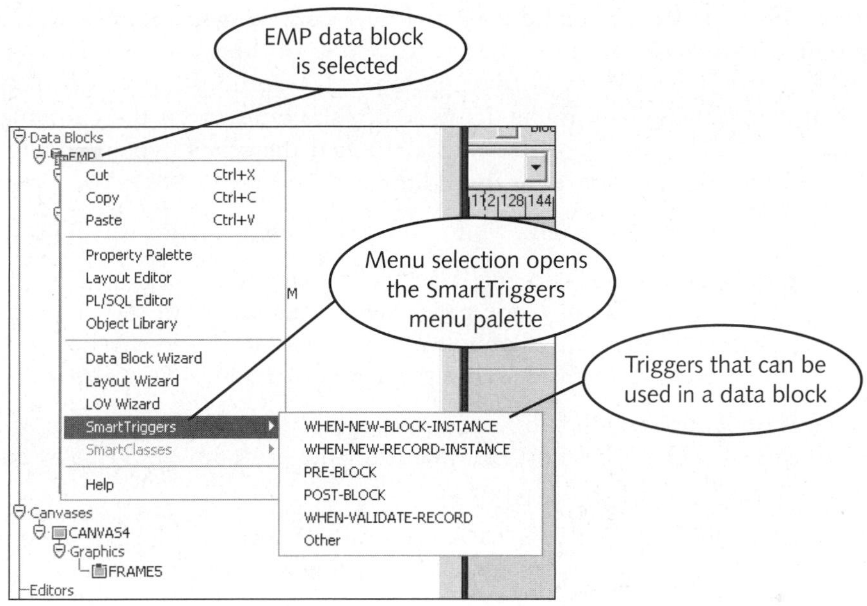

Figure 6-8 Data block SmartTriggers menu palette

To open the SmartTriggers Palette, click the Right Mouse button or select the Program/SmartTriggers menu selection.

For practice using smart triggers, follow the steps below:

1. Using the form you created in the previous practice, open the Object Navigator and select the first **Triggers** node (the form-level Triggers node).
2. Click the **Right Mouse button** to open the popup menu.
3. Locate and click the **SmartTriggers** options to open a submenu. Notice the various triggers that are displayed. Do not select a trigger.
4. Repeat steps 2 and 3 using the DEPT data block Triggers node. Notice that some of the triggers have changed.
5. Repeat steps 2 and 3 using the LOC data block Triggers node. Notice that the displayed trigger list has changed again.

Using the PL/SQL Editor

The PL/SQL Editor is a Forms Builder tool that creates and maintains PL/SQL code blocks. It is also sometimes called the Program Unit Editor. The PL/SQL Editor can be used to enter a trigger's statements, create and maintain functions and stored procedures that exist in the form or in the database, and create PL/SQL objects.

Figure 6-9 shows the PL/SQL Editor containing a single incorrect PL/SQL statement. The assigned variable Sysdte is an incorrect spelling of the Oracle variable Sysdate that returns the current date. This error was introduced to demonstrate the syntax-checking abilities of the PL/SQL Editor. The figure depicts the Editor after the Compile PL/SQL Code tool was clicked and Forms Builder checked the script syntax encountering an error. The following are features of the Editor:

- **Source Code pane**: The white pane that is used to enter PL/SQL statements.
- **Error Code pane**: The gray-black pane that is displayed beneath the Source Code pane. The Error Code pane does not appear until the program unit is compiled. Clicking the Compile PL/SQL Code tool in the Editor or compiling the entire form identifies the errors that appear in this pane.
- **Error location**: Clicking a message in the Error Code pane causes the input focus to shift to the most likely spot for the error in the script or code block displayed in the Source Code pane.
- **Sizing handle**: The line that separates the Source and Error Code panes can be used to resize either pane. Click the line and drag to resize.
- **Compile PL/SQL Code tool**: The tool that compiles the contents of the Source Code pane. This causes any errors to appear in the Error Code pane.
- **Revert PL/SQL Code tool**: The tool that returns the Source Code pane statements to the condition they were in at the last module save point.
- **Undo tool**: The tool that removes modifications one at a time until the save point is reached.
- **Redo tool**: The tool that returns removed modifications.
- **Indent tool**: The tool that indents the current statement line.
- **Outdent tool**: The tool that removes the indent of the current statement line.
- **Name drop-down list**: The list that displays PL/SQL objects that have the same characteristics as the identified object and type values.
- **Type drop-down list**: The list that identifies the type of PL/SQL displayed in the Editor. The options are Program Unit, Trigger, or Menu Item Code. Changing this value causes a different type of PL/SQL object to appear in the Source Code pane.
- **Object drop-down list**: The list that displays PL/SQL objects of the type identified in the drop-down list.

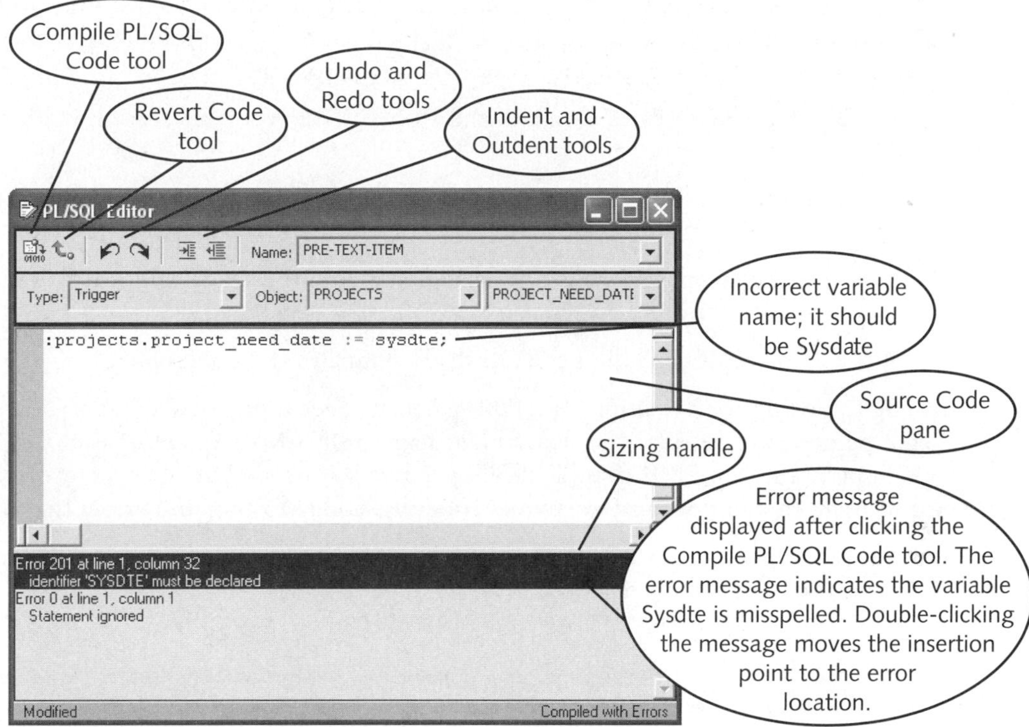

Figure 6-9 PL/SQL Editor displaying an error

The following features of the PL/SQL Editor facilitate code entry:

- Automatic indenting.
- Distinctive colors for keywords, comments, and string values.
- Selection of multiple columns of text, as well as lines of source code. You can select multiple columns by pressing the Alt key while dragging the cursor up or down.
- Unlimited undo/redo. Edits can be entered until the last Save.
- Selected text can be copied or moved by dragging and dropping. To move the text, simply drag the highlighted text. Be sure to select the text and release the mouse button before trying to drag it.

The PL/SQL that you place into the PL/SQL Editor can be a simple value assignment statement, as shown in Figure 6-9. You can also use the PL/SQL constructs, as well as your own procedures, functions, and packages. In addition, you can use built-ins such as the Set_item_property that Oracle provides.

Figure 6-9 contains a single statement that is not enclosed by a PL/SQL code block. You do not have to place the trigger scripts in a PL/SQL code block, unless you need to declare trigger variables or cursors, or need to perform exception handling. In those cases you must enclose the script in the PL/SQL code block. The following is a simple summary of the PL/SQL anonymous code block sections and keywords:

- **Declare**: Defines variables and PL/SQL objects. This section begins with the Declare keyword.
- **Executable**: Contains the statements that will be executed. This section starts with the Begin keyword.
- **Exception**: Contains error handlers that are used to trap errors. This section begins with the Exception keyword.
- **End**: Contains the keyword that terminates the code block.

The following is an example of a Post-Query trigger using a code block. The purpose of the trigger is to retrieve the department name (DNAME) value for each employee that is displayed in the EMP data block. A code block is needed because a cursor was defined and used. In addition, an Exception clause was added to trap any errors that may occur.

```
Declare
  Cursor a is select dname from dept
            Where dept.deptno = :emp.deptno;
Begin
  Open a;           -- Opens the cursor or executes the SELECT statement
  Fetch a into :emp.department_name;    -- Places the retrieved value
                                into the form item
  close a;           -- Closes the cursor
exception
  when others then
         Message ('A database error has occurred');
End;
```

Variables that are declared within the PL/SQL form object have the scope limitation of the code block. This is consistent with PL/SQL. However, it is often necessary and possible to reference form data block items and parameters from within the trigger, as done in the previous listing. The FETCH statement populated a data block item called EMP.DEPARTMENT_NAME. Notice that it was necessary to qualify the DEPARTMENT_NAME item with the name of the data block. In addition, the variable reference was preceded with a colon (**:**). Examine the following variable reference template. All referenced variables not created by the trigger must follow this template:

```
:block_name.data_item_name
```

BUILT-IN SUBPROGRAMS AND TYPES OF BUILT-INS

Oracle has developed numerous built-in subprograms (see Appendix E) for use in forms. A **built-in subprogram** is an Oracle-developed procedure or function that performs a specific action. In Chapter 5, you were introduced to the Set_item_property built-in that is used to change an item property. In a previous section of this chapter, you saw that the Message built-in displays a message in the form's status area. Oracle has developed scores of built-ins that you can use to supplement basic form actions: the Enter_query built-in places the current data block into the Enter Query mode, the Next_record built-in moves the cursor to the next record in the data block, and the Open_form built-in launches another form from an existing form.

There are over 100 built-in subprograms, and as you may have noticed from the previous examples, they are are named for the function they perform. Aptly named, Next_item moves the input focus to the next data block item. The Execute_query built-in causes the data block to be placed into the Query mode, which in effect causes the data block to issue a SELECT statement and return a result set to the data block. As you develop your form and add functionality, you can probably find a built-in with the functionality you need as its name. You can quickly find the desired built-in by searching either Appendix E or the Forms Builder Help Facility. You will be introduced to additional built-ins in the following chapters as various Oracle topics are introduced, such as calling new forms or populating LOVs.

Built-in Properties

You should be aware of several built-in subprogram restrictions, including the following:

- **Enter Query mode**: This property is similar to the trigger restriction discussed earlier in the chapter. It determines whether the built-in can be executed when the form is in the Enter Query mode. The Next_block built-in is an example of a built-in that cannot be fired in this mode, because it performs navigation out of the block. However, the Next_item built-in can be fired in the Enter Query mode, because the insertion point remains in the data block.
- **Built-in type**: Built-ins can be either restricted or unrestricted. **Restricted built-in subprograms** affect navigation in the form. They can only be called from triggers while no internal navigation is occurring. For example, the Commit_form built-in that saves form changes cannot be executed from a Pre-Text-Item trigger. However, it can be executed from a When-Button-Pressed trigger. An **unrestricted built-in subprogram** can be executed in any trigger. The Find_canvas built-in that returns the ID of the current canvas is an example of an unrestricted built-in.

- **Parameters**: Some built-ins require parameters. Built-ins are equivalent to stored procedures and functions. Stored procedures and functions sometimes need data supplied by the calling program to function. This outside data is supplied to the built-in through a parameter list. The Show_alert built-in, for example, requires a parameter that identifies the alert name. The Next_Block built-in is an example of a built-in that does not require a parameter, because it uses the data block's Next Block property value to determine the next navigable block.

Whenever you add a built-in to a trigger, you should take into account each of the previously listed features. For example, if you want to save records using the Commit_form built-in, which is a restricted trigger, you must identify a trigger that allows the use of restricted triggers, such as When-Button-Pressed. A trigger such as Next-Item cannot be used because it cannot execute restricted built-ins. If you want to avoid your forms submitting error messages because of invalid built-ins, you must identify whether the built-in is restricted or whether the built-in can be executed when the data block is in the Enter Query mode. Finally, you should identify the parameters of the built-ins and ensure that the parameters are properly valued when the built-in is executed. The Syntax Palette, discussed in the next section, helps to identify built-ins and parameters.

MISCELLANEOUS PL/SQL CONSTRUCTS AND BUILT-IN TOOLS

As you begin to develop complex forms, you may encounter several difficulties. First, you may find that you have many triggers and PL/SQL constructs. In some cases, you may want to change a reference because the referenced item's name changed or to correct an error in the form logic. It might be difficult to identify which trigger you need to modify, possibly because it is a child object. It is sometimes necessary to expand, open, and review every trigger in the Object Navigator to find the reference, which can be a time-consuming task. A second problem that can occur is writing the proper PL/SQL construct. PL/SQL has many different constructs, and it is sometimes necessary to research through a PL/SQL manual to find the correct syntax. This can also be a time-consuming task. A third lengthy task is identifying the name of a built-in and the necessary parameters. Fortunately, Forms Builder has two tools that shortcut the task of locating a PL/SQL reference. It also has a tool that can be used to identify and place a PL/SQL construct into your trigger, saving you a great deal of investigation. These tools, the Syntax Palette, the Find and Replace PL/SQL menu option, and the Show PL/SQL Only menu option, are discussed in the following sections.

Using the Syntax Palette to Write PL/SQL Code

The Syntax Palette is an excellent aid for writing your PL/SQL code blocks. The Syntax Palette is depicted in Figure 6-10 along with the PL/SQL Editor displaying a PL/SQL construct and built-in templates. The PL/SQL construct and built-in were placed in the Editor by the Syntax Palette. The Syntax Palette consists of two tabs: the PL/SQL tab that displays various PL/SQL constructs and the Built-ins tab that displays various built-ins. These tabs can be used to paste basic code blocks and built-in subprogram templates into an open PL/SQL Editor. You can use the Syntax Palette to write a significant portion of your PL/SQL code.

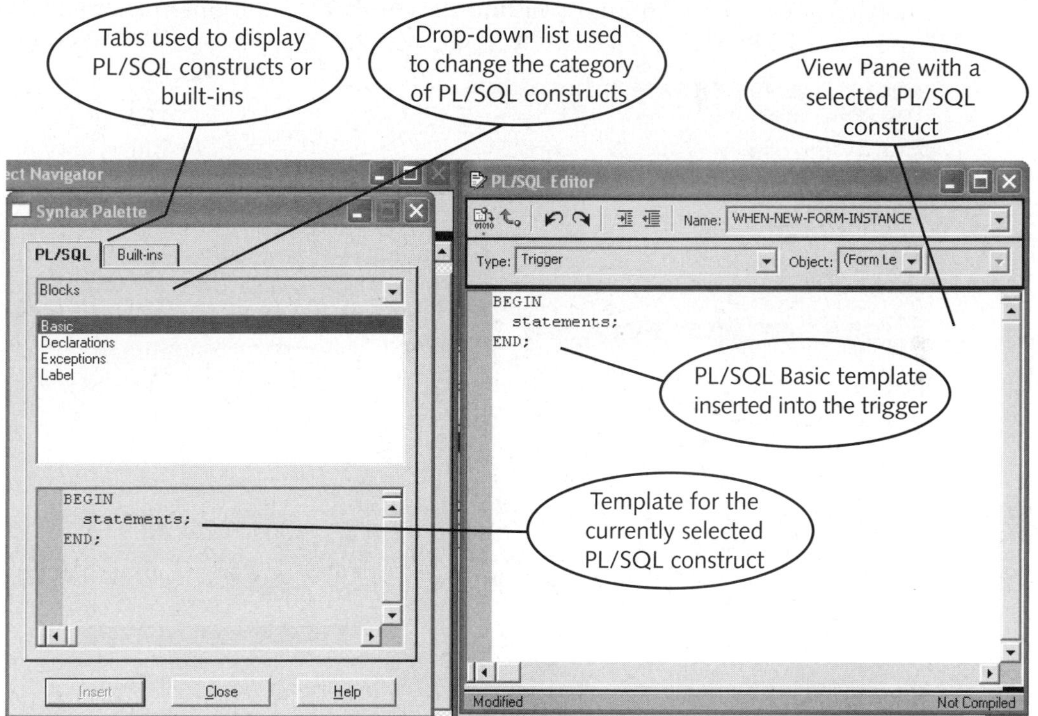

Figure 6-10 Syntax Palette displaying the PL/SQL tab and PL/SQL editor that has been populated with a PL/SQL template

The PL/SQL tab allows you to paste a PL/SQL construct into the open PL/SQL Editor at the location of the insertion point. The PL/SQL tab has the following features:

- A drop-down list that displays the various PL/SQL constructs available for insertion into the PL/SQL Editor
- A View window that depicts the PL/SQL construct template for the currently selected pick list construct

The Built-ins tab is similarly constructed. However, it has three components, as follows:

- A drop-down list that displays the various built-in types
- A list box that displays the built-ins for the selected built-in type
- A View pane that shows the selected built-in along with its various parameters

As you scroll through the list of built-ins on the Built-ins tab (see Figure 6-11), notice that the list displays various built-ins multiple times. The built-in names are repeated because Oracle has overloaded many of the built-ins. **Overloading** means that different procedures can have the same name but must be differentiated by their parameters. This is the case of the built-ins displayed in the list box. To find the correct built-in, you must click each built-in until you find the one with the proper parameters.

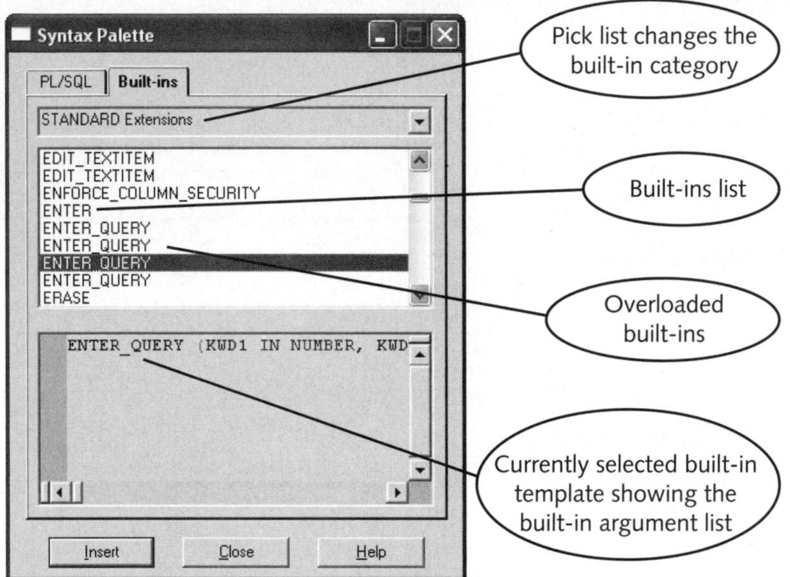

Figure 6-11 Syntax Palette Built-ins tab showing overloaded built-ins

To add a template PL/SQL construct or built-in to a PL/SQL script, perform the following steps:

1. Identify the trigger and open a PL/SQL Editor for the object. The Syntax Palette may be opened without the PL/SQL Editor being opened. However, the Insert button on the Syntax Palette button will not be enabled.
2. Use the drop-down lists and list box to locate the PL/SQL construct or built-in.
3. Select the PL/SQL construct or the built-in on the Syntax Palette view pane. Click the Insert button on the Syntax Palette. The selected construct or built-in is added to the editor.

To open the Syntax Palette, select the Tools/Syntax Palette menu selection.

Now try your hand with the Syntax Palette. The following practice session steps you through creating a trigger that places the form in the Enter Query mode when the form is first opened by the Syntax Palette:

1. Using the practice form, open the Object Navigator and locate the form-level Triggers node.

2. Select the **Triggers** node and click the **Create** tool to open the Triggers dialog box. Create a When-New-Form-Instance trigger.
3. Select the **Tools/Syntax Palette** menu option to open the Syntax Palette.
4. Use the Syntax Palette to locate and add the basic PL/SQL code block construct to the trigger. This construct looks similar to the following example. Click the **Insert** button to move the template to your trigger.

```
BEGIN
    statements;
END;
```

5. Move the cursor inside the PL/SQL Editor. Remove the STATEMENTS line.
6. Using the Syntax Palette, change to the Built-ins tab. Locate the Enter_query built-in. Four built-ins are listed; choose the one without the parameter list. Place the built-in where the STATEMENTS line resided.
7. Execute the form. Notice that the form is placed in the Enter Query mode when it is first launched. The When-New-Form-Instance trigger you created was fired when the form was first opened. It executed the code block containing the Enter_query built-in.
8. Save the form for later practice.

Locating PL/SQL Elements

Occasionally, it is important to locate all occurrences of a variable or other PL/SQL object. Perhaps a table or item name has changed, or you are searching for a line of programming that does not work. This often happens after adding substantial PL/SQL code to the form. Trying to locate these references one at a time can be tedious, especially if the code blocks are long.

The Edit/Find and Replace PL/SQL menu option helps you identify the occurrences of a variable. The option opens the Find and Replace in Program Units dialog box, as shown in Figure 6-12. Some of the features of the dialog box are as follows:

- **Find What text box**: Used to enter the search value. In Figure 6-12, this is the value CLEAR. This value was entered to locate built-ins that start with the letters "CLEAR".
- **Expression button**: Opens a palette of searchable expressions such as the `\w` characters that denote white space.
- **Replace With text box**: Used to enter a replacement value.
- **Look Where list box**: Lists the Object Navigator objects. Forms Builder searches only the selected objects for the target value.
- **Results list box**: Lists all program units that have the target values. Clicking any item in the list opens a PL/SQL Editor for the item.

- **Find All button**: Begins the search of the selected items.
- **Replace All button**: Replaces occurrences of the target value within the selected objects.
- **Replace button**: Replaces the currently selected occurrence of the target value.
- **Edit button**: Moves the insertion point to the occurrence of the target value. You can then manually change the value.

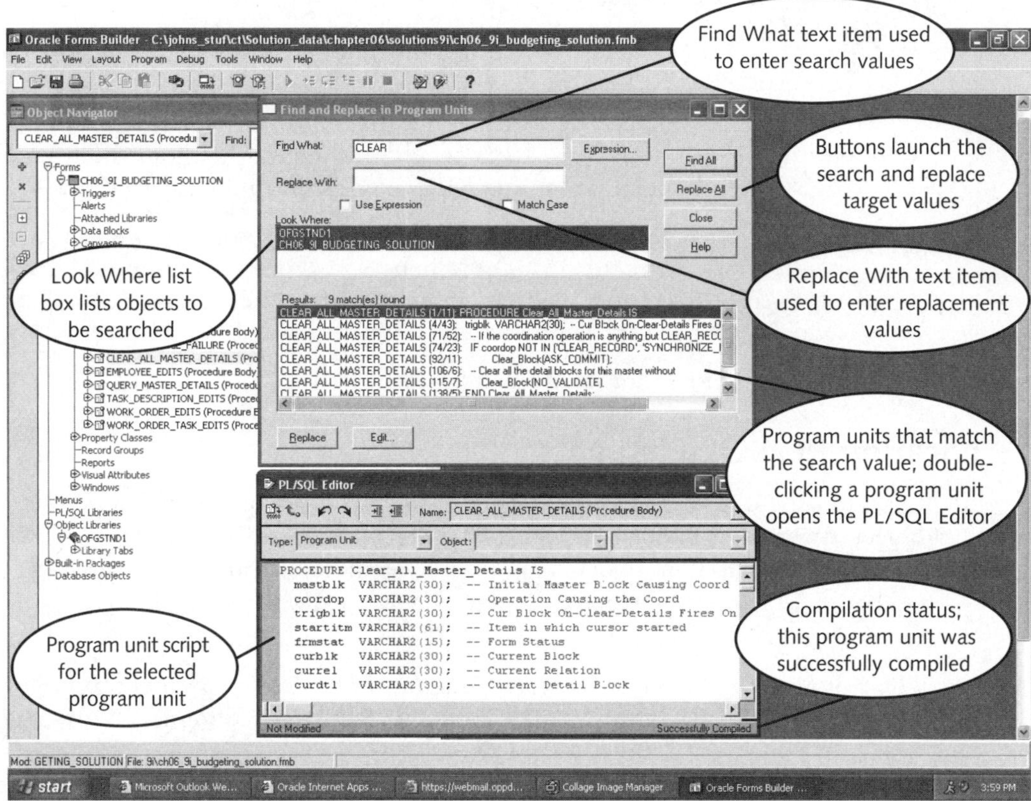

Figure 6-12 Find and Replace in Program Units dialog box and the PL/SQL Editor for the selected object

For a short practice session using the Program Units dialog box, perform the following steps:

1. Using the practice form, select the **Edit/Find and Replace PL/SQL** menu option to open the Find and Replace in Program Units dialog box.
2. Enter **IS A** in the Find What text box.
3. Click **Find All**. Notice that the triggers you created in the first practice session appear.

4. Enter **IS THE** in the Replace With text box. Click **Replace All**. This replaces the original characters.
5. Locate the Post-Text-Item trigger under the LOC data item. Open a PL/SQL Editor for the trigger. Notice that the characters in the Message built-in changed in all of the form's triggers.
6. Save the form for later practice.

Show PL/SQL Only Menu Option

The last PL/SQL location tool to be discussed in this chapter is the Show PL/SQL Only menu selection. Depending on complexity, form modules can have many triggers and form objects. You will often find it necessary to locate a trigger, such as when a form is not behaving in the appropriate manner or you are not sure that you have added a trigger. As we have seen, it is possible to use the Expand All tool to display all of the form objects and triggers. You can then scroll through the list and attempt to find the appropriate PL/SQL object. This can be a difficult chore for lengthy forms.

A preferable method is to change the Object Navigator view by using the Show PL/SQL Only menu selection. This view, illustrated in Figure 6-13, displays only form objects that have PL/SQL. Notice the difference in the number of form objects displayed between the Regular view and the Show PL/SQL Only view.

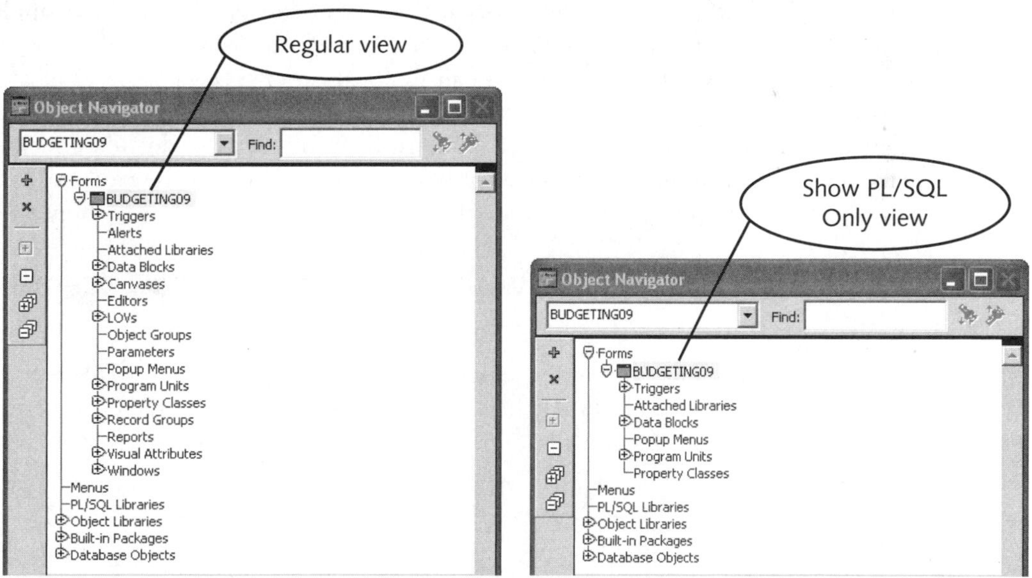

Figure 6-13 Two Object Navigator views: Regular and Show PL/SQL Only

Now try your hand at it by performing the following steps.

1. Open the practice form in the Object Navigator.
2. Select the **Form** module object and click the **Expand All** tool to display all the form's components.
3. Select the **View/Show PL/SQL Only** menu option. This removes many of the form objects from view.
4. Return the Object Navigator to its original state by deselecting the View/Show PL/SQL Only menu option.

TRAPPING ERRORS AND CAUSING EXCEPTIONS

As a developer, you will be trapping or handling exceptions that may occur in your PL/SQL code blocks. Form exceptions often occur when the database returns a database exception to the form. Common database exceptions sent to the form include executing a trigger SELECT statement that causes no records to be returned, violating a database constraint such as the NOT NULL constraint, or attempting to update a record that is locked by another user. Exceptions can also occur due to errors in your PL/SQL scripts. If you do not handle the exception, Forms Builder terminates the trigger and issues the operator an error message, which the operator usually finds incomprehensible.

By not placing exception handlers in their triggers, novice developers allow applications to issue unintelligible messages and scripts to terminate abnormally. This is a poor practice, and it is best to place exception handlers in all PL/SQL scripts. Developers want to have control over their programs. They do not want their scripts to be terminated without performing the work that was intended. They also do not want a default Oracle exception leaving the operator puzzled about what has happened. Trapping the exceptions allows you to keep the information in your form clear so that the operator knows how to proceed.

Handling Form Exceptions with the When Others Exception Handler

To handle exceptions, developers enclose their PL/SQL trigger statements in a code block. The PL/SQL code block has an Exception clause that handles exceptions and errors. This clause allows you to define an exception handler for each type of exception. You can use the Oracle-named exceptions, such as No_data_found, or you can create your own. Any good PL/SQL book fully describes how to use the Exception clause to handle exceptions.

As a developer, it is a good idea to place your trigger scripts in a code block and include the When Others catch-all exception. This exception traps any exception encountered by the code block. It allows the code block to be terminated with the developer in control, because the developer designed statements to be executed after an exception is encountered. These statements can consist of the Commit_form built-in that saves changes or the Message built-in that allows the developer to send a custom message to the operator. A When Others handler should be used in any form code block that issues SQL commands.

To illustrate, Figure 6-14 depicts a Post-Query trigger that is commonly used in forms to return descriptive information to the data block record after it is fetched. Post-Query triggers fire for each row fetched from the database. Figure 6-14 illustrates a Post-Query trigger that returns the full department name from the DEPT database table for each record fetched from the EMP table. The purpose of the trigger is to display the full department name rather than the department code value that is contained in the EMP table. If the SELECT statement does not find a match for the DEPTNO value, an exception handler in the Exception clause returns UNKNOWN.

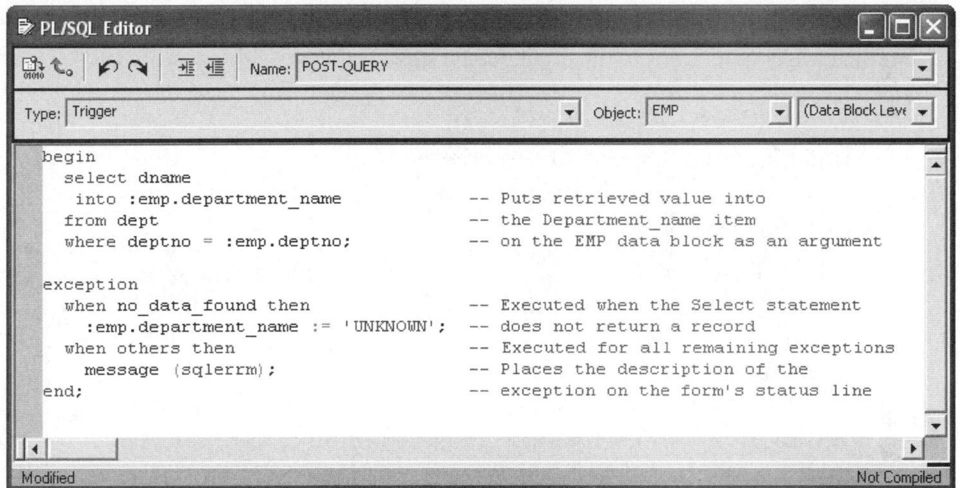

Figure 6-14 Post-Query trigger containing When No_data_found and When Others exception handlers

The Post-Query trigger code block contains the following two exception handlers:

- **When No_data_found**: This exception is used if the SELECT statement does not return a value. It places the value UNKNOWN into the EMP data block DEPARTMENT_NAME data item when this exception occurs.
- **When Others**: This is the catch-all exception handler. It is placed last in the Exception clause because it traps any exception not trapped by a preceding exception handler. In this example, the When No_data_found exception is a predecessor exception. An example of one of the different database exceptions that may be trapped by the When Others exception is the Too_many_rows exception, which is caused by the retrieval of more than one record by the SELECT statement. The Sqlerrm message variable is used

in the exception handler. The variable contains the actual message returned by the Oracle database. The Message built-in displays this Sqlerrm value on the status line, giving the operator a more accurate message than the generic Forms Builder error message issued when an exception handler is not included in the code block. All code blocks that contain SQL or DML statements should have this handler.

Comments can be placed into a PL/SQL code block using two different symbols:

1. --: Comments any line text to the right
2. /* */: Comments all text between the start and finish symbols, even if the text is on multiple lines.

Terminating the Trigger with the RAISE FORM_TRIGGER_FAILURE Statement

In some cases, you want to stop trigger processing because of an edit failure or another reason. Forms Builder allows you to stop trigger processing using the Form_trigger_failure built-in, which is launched using the PL/SQL RAISE command. RAISE is a PL/SQL command that causes a specified exception to occur. The Form_trigger_failure built-in terminates the trigger, stops all form processes, and rolls back any transactions to the start of the trigger statements.

Figure 6-15 illustrates the use of the Form_trigger_failure built-in. It is used in a When-Validate-Record trigger that is fired when the operator attempts to commit the record or navigate out of the data block. This is the trigger you would use to ensure that an item's value is correct. The Figure 6-15 edit ensures that the operator enters a COMM (commission) value for all salesmen. If the operator does not, an exception is raised causing a bell to sound, a message to be displayed, and navigation stopped until the value is corrected.

Here's a chance to practice using the When-Validate-Record block-level trigger:

1. Open the Object Navigator and create a new form module.
2. Start the Data Block Wizard and create a data block based on the EMP table. The form style should be Form and one record should be displayed.
3. Locate and expand the EMP data block and its Triggers node.
4. Select the EMP data block's **Triggers** node and click the **Create** tool to open the Triggers dialog box.
5. Select the **When-Validate-Record** trigger and click **OK**. A PL/SQL Editor window opens for the new trigger. Use the Figure 6-15 PL/SQL script for the trigger.

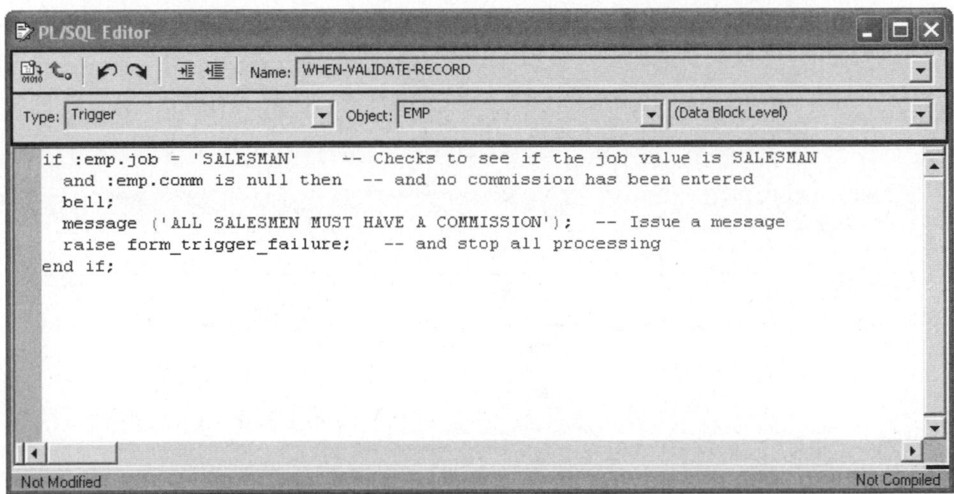
PL/SQL Editor
Name: WHEN-VALIDATE-RECORD
Type: Trigger
Object: EMP
(Data Block Level)
if :emp.job = 'SALESMAN' -- Checks to see if the job value is SALESMAN
and :emp.comm is null then -- and no commission has been entered
bell;
message ('ALL SALESMEN MUST HAVE A COMMISSION'); -- Issue a message
raise form_trigger_failure; -- and stop all processing
end if;
Not Modified
Not Compiled

Figure 6-15 When-Validate-Record trigger ensuring all salesmen have a commission value entered

6. Execute the form displaying an employee record. Change the employees' JOB value to SALESMAN and delete any value in the COMM data item. When the record is saved, the changes will cause the edit to fail and the RAISE Form_trigger_failure command to be executed terminating the commit process.
7. Save the form changes and determine whether the trigger works.
8. Save the form for later practice.

Raising Your Own Exceptions Using Exception Handlers

As an alternative to the Form_trigger_failure built-in discussed in the previous section, you can also use the PL/SQL code block Exception section to handle specific events. This style consists of using the RAISE command to move the processing to a custom handler in the code block Exception section. This style of exception handling alerts the user of a condition, but does not stop all processing as does the Form_trigger_failure built-in. Custom handlers allow the operator to control events after a variance occurs. The Form_trigger_failure built-in terminates the processing without offering the developer a chance to perform tasks, such as saving records. Raising a custom error and using the Exception section to execute statements allows the developer to perform desired actions. To illustrate this distinction, the When-Validate-Record trigger using the Form_trigger_failure built-in shown in Figure 6-15 was modified and is shown in Figure 6-16. The following changes were made:

- A custom exception called Null_commission_value was added.
- An exception handler called Null_commission_value was added.

- The Bell and Message built-ins were moved to the Exception section as statements for the Null_commision_value exception handler.
- The Form_trigger_failure built-in exception was replaced with the Null_commission_value custom exception.

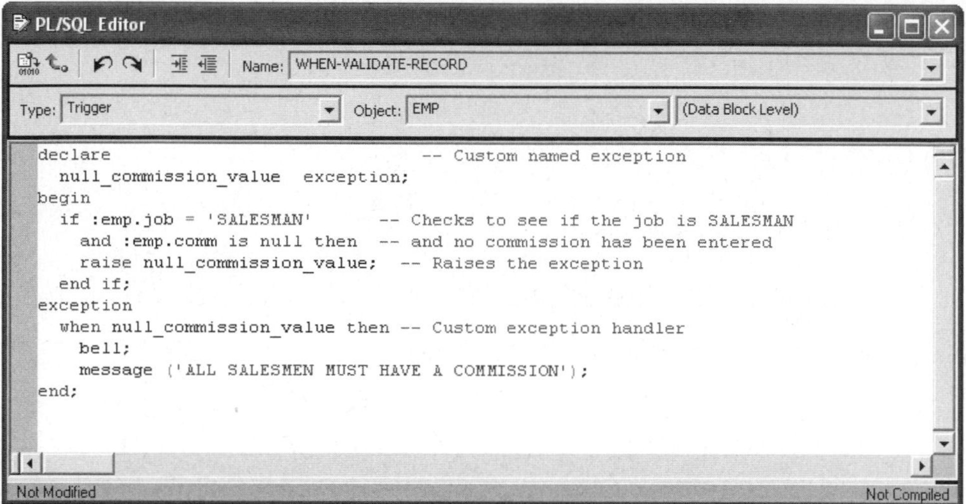
PL/SQL Editor
Name: WHEN-VALIDATE-RECORD
Type: Trigger
Object: EMP
(Data Block Level)
declare -- Custom named exception
null_commission_value exception;
begin
if :emp.job = 'SALESMAN' -- Checks to see if the job is SALESMAN
and :emp.comm is null then -- and no commission has been entered
raise null_commission_value; -- Raises the exception
end if;
exception
when null_commission_value then -- Custom exception handler
bell;
message ('ALL SALESMEN MUST HAVE A COMMISSION');
end;
Not Modified
Not Compiled

Figure 6-16 PL/SQL editor containing a code block using custom exception handlers

The result of these changes is a trigger that notifies the operator that the COMM value is missing but does not roll back the trigger execution. All work accomplished before the RAISE command is maintained, and the action that launched the trigger continues to completion. If you would like to use the scheme and still roll back the transaction, add the RAISE Form_trigger_failure statement to the exception handler.

For practice in modifying triggers, perform the following steps:

1. Open the practice form in the Object Navigator and locate the EMP data block's When-Validate-Record trigger.
2. Double-click the trigger to open a PL/SQL Editor for the trigger. Modify the When-Validate-Item trigger using the script in Figure 6-16.
3. Test the new trigger and determine how it works. You should see the exception messages, but the trigger should complete successfully and not prevent the record from being saved.
4. Save the form for later practice.

CREATING YOUR OWN STORED PROCEDURES OR PROGRAM UNITS

Forms Builder allows you to develop your own functions, procedures, and packages for a form. The items are exactly the same as the PL/SQL objects that you create within the database, with one difference: these PL/SQL objects are used only within the form and not through accessing the database. Form program units are handy when you use the same PL/SQL code in several places within a form. It is not a good practice to have multiple instances of the same code, because it wastes time entering the code multiple times and is difficult to ensure that modifications are made and tested in each of the code locations. So, if your form has multiple instances of the same code, you should develop a program unit and call the unit from your triggers.

The following are steps you would use to create and compile a form program unit:

1. Locate and highlight the Program Units form object in the Object Navigator.
2. Click the Create tool to open the New Program Unit dialog box (Figure 6-17).

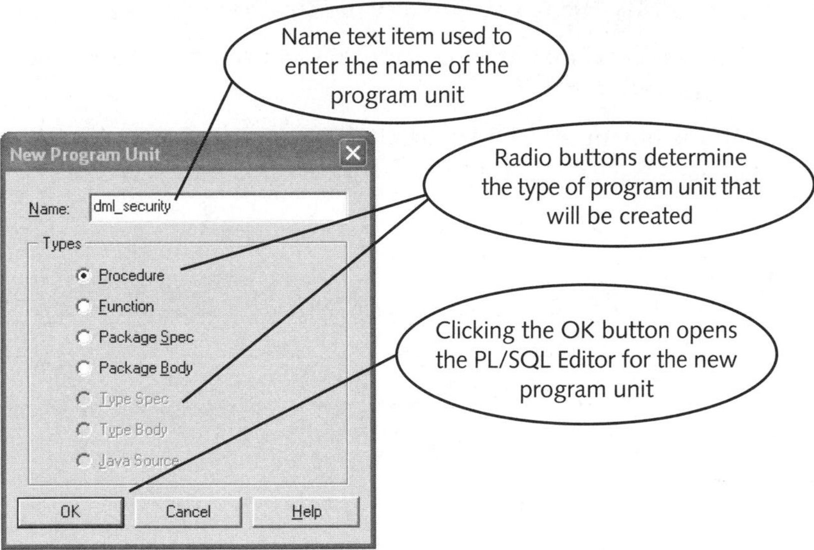

Figure 6-17 New Program Unit dialog box

3. Enter the program unit name and click the appropriate radio button.
4. Click OK to open the PL/SQL Editor for the program unit.
5. Enter the PL/SQL code block into the PL/SQL Editor.
6. Compile the code block.
7. Enter the new program unit into the appropriate trigger.
8. Test the application.

To illustrate the use of a single program unit in multiple triggers within a form, the next practice session steps you through the development of a program unit used to control which users can update a record. Assume that you are to develop a security scheme that allows a user to only create, update, and delete employee records from the user's department. If the user does not have the same department number (DEPTNO) value as on the modified record, the DML transaction is terminated. There are three DML operations (INSERT, UPDATE, and DELETE) that must be controlled with the same security code block. The security programming is the same for each of the transactions but must be used in Pre-Insert, Pre-Update, and Pre-Delete triggers to control the different events. The triggers are to fire before the DML transaction. If the operator does not have valid security, the trigger terminates the transaction.

Using your practice form, create a program unit that can be used in Pre-Insert, Pre-Update, and Pre-Delete triggers to control who is allowed to make a DML transaction on the EMP data block. Practice these functions by performing the following steps:

1. Open the practice form in the Object Navigator.
2. Delete the EMP data block **When-Validate-Record** trigger.
3. Locate and select the **Program Units** node. Click **Create** to open the New Program Unit dialog box.
4. Name the program unit **DML_SECURITY**, click the **Procedure** radio button, and click **OK** to open the PL/SQL Editor.
5. Enter the script shown in Figure 6-18.

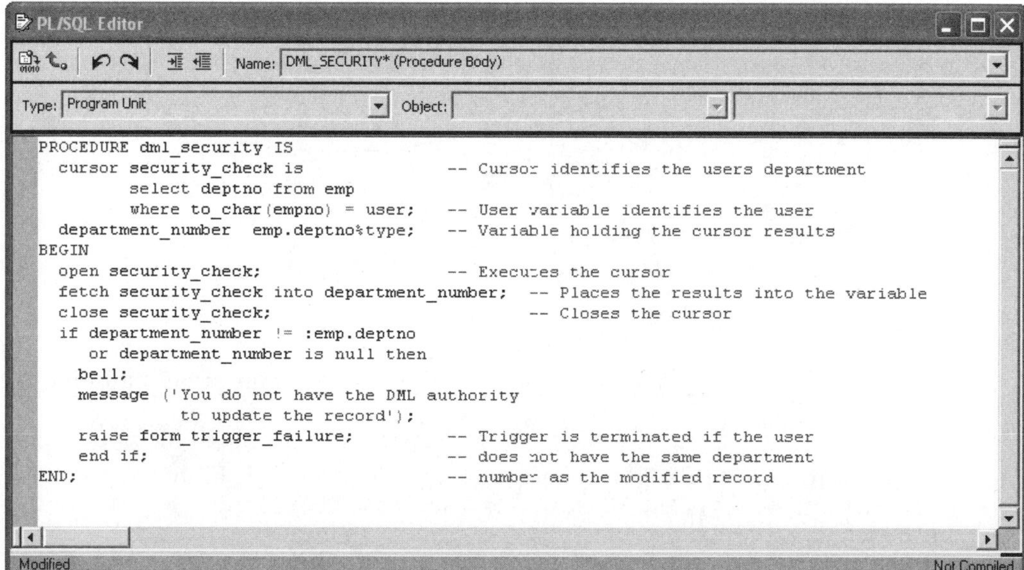

Figure 6-18 DML_SECURITY program unit

The figure depicts a PL/SQL Editor for the DML_SECURITY program unit. The program unit contains a cursor that is used to retrieve the department number (DEPTNO) for the user. The variable USER is a Forms Builder variable that contains the name or identification of the user. When a user logs on to Oracle, Forms Builder puts the user account into this variable. The USER variable can be referenced at any time in the Oracle session to identify the user.

If the user had logged on using the default Oracle ID, SCOTT, the value of the USER variable will be SCOTT. If you choose not to use the USER variable, you can substitute any other user-identification scheme. Many Web applications require the user to enter an ID and password into a page before entry into the system. The values can be placed in global variables (discussed in the next section) and passed from form to form as needed.

When the DML_SECURITY program unit is executed, the OPEN Security_check cursor command executes the referenced cursor and launches its SELECT statement. The value returned by the cursor (SELECT statement) is fetched into the DEPARTMENT_NUMBER variable. This variable is compared to the operator's department number. If the values do not match, the program unit sounds a bell, issues a message, and stops the transaction.

6. Compile the **DML_SECURITY** program unit. If it compiles correctly, close the PL/SQL Editor.
7. Locate and select the form-level **Triggers** node. Press the **Create** tool to open the Triggers dialog box. Select the **Pre-Insert** trigger and click **OK** to open the PL/SQL Editor.
8. Enter the **DML_SECURITY** program unit into the PL/SQL Editor as shown in Figure 6-19. The DML_SECURITY program unit is a procedure, and its name can be used as a statement.

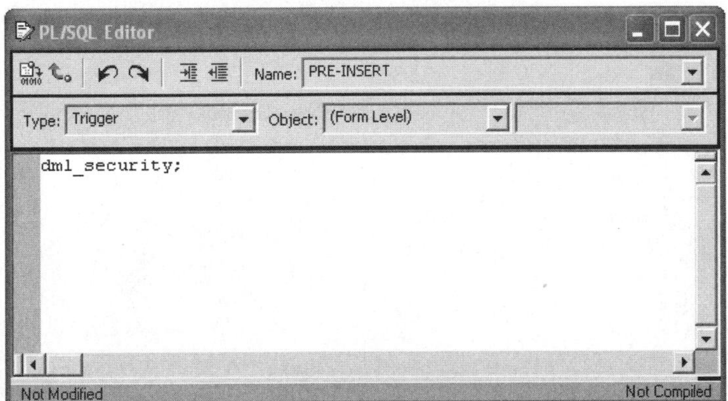

Figure 6-19 Pre-Insert trigger that calls the DML_SECURITY program unit

9. Compile the trigger and close the PL/SQL Editor.

10. Create Pre-Update and Pre-Delete triggers using steps 7 through 9.
11. After creating the triggers, launch the form. The value of the USER variable is your Oracle ID. It is highly unlikely that this value matches any of the employee number (EMPNO) values in the EMP. Thus, you should not be able to insert, update, or delete records. Attempt to insert, update, and delete records in the form, and determine whether the program unit prevents DML operations for unauthorized operators. Figure 6-20 illustrates the practice form after the Commit button was clicked. Notice the error message displayed on the status line.

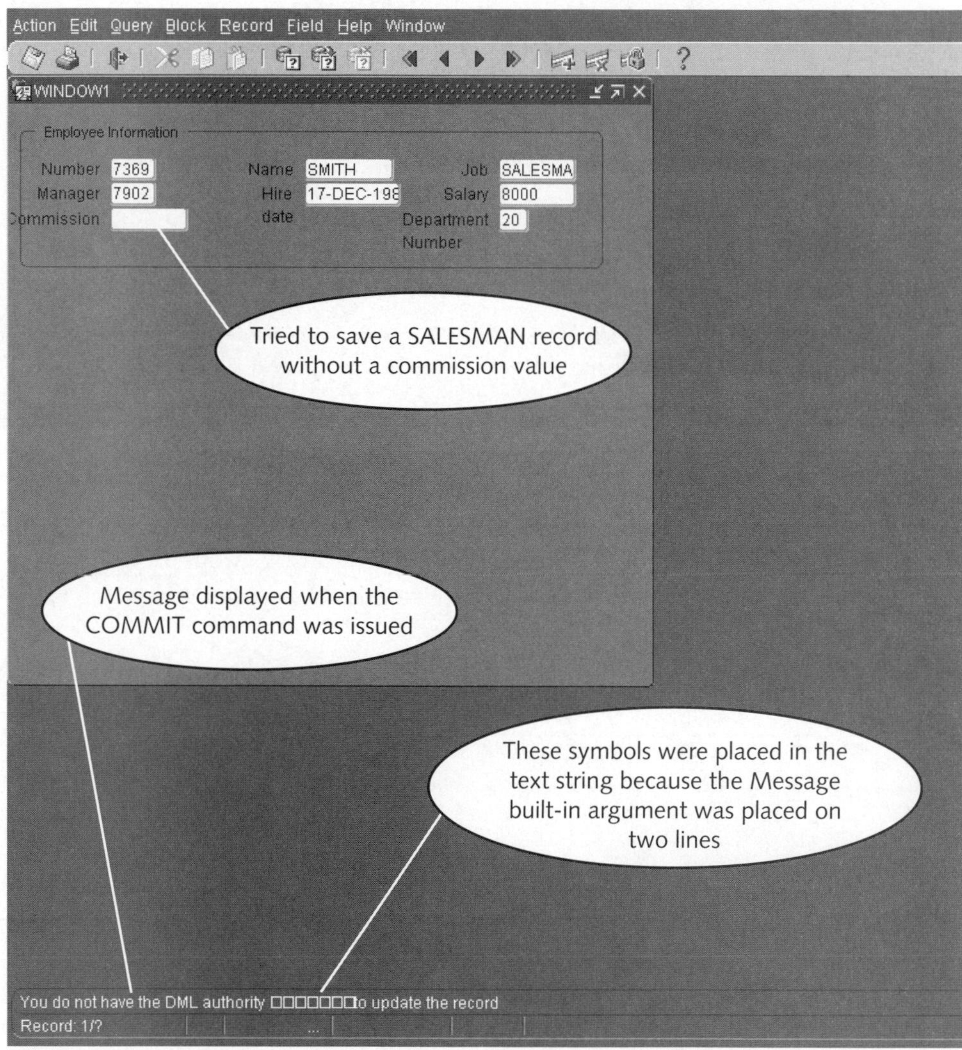

Figure 6-20 Practice form displaying a security error message after a COMMIT command was issued

12. Close the form and delete the **Pre-Insert**, **Pre-Update**, and **Pre-Delete** triggers.
13. Save the form for later practice.

Using Form Parameters, Global Variables, and System Variables

Applications require variables and information about the system. They need to pass information or values between different code blocks and even between different applications. This section covers three types of variables:

- Form parameters that have a form module scope
- Global variables that have a runtime session scope
- System variables that provide information or control features about the system

6

Using Form Parameters

Form parameters are variables that exist within the form. Parameters can be used in triggers, as property values, or anywhere else a variable is needed. Their primary importance is passing information into the form when the form is launched. For example, suppose your system has a form that displays a list of departments and you want to give users a button that calls another form that displays the employees for a selected department. To limit the employee records, you must pass the selected department number (DEPTNO) to the called Employee form. The Employee form then uses the department number as an argument in the data block's Where Clause property. A parameter is one of the tools that enable you to achieve this task.

To create a parameter, you would select the Parameters object node and click the Create tool.

A parameter is a form object and has the following properties that can be set in the Property Palette:

- **Name**: Parameter name
- **Parameter Data Type**: Determines the type of value stored in the parameter
- **Parameter Length**: Parameter length
- **Parameter Initial Value**: Default parameter value

Figure 6-21 illustrates the triggers and parameters that are needed to pass the DEPTNO value to a called form, so that the Where Clause property can be set causing the data block to retrieve only the employees for a specific department. Three Forms Builder tools are depicted. The first is the PL/SQL Editor that illustrates a When-Button-Pressed trigger. This trigger contains a New_form built-in subprogram that launches the Employee form. The built-in has four parameters:

- The name and location of the Employee form.

- Roll back mode setting. The default, TO_SAVEPOINT, rolls back uncommitted changes to the last Save point.
- Query mode setting. Determines whether the called form can be used for DML operations or only to query data.
- Parameter list. The name of the parameter list that contains the variables that will be passed to the called application.

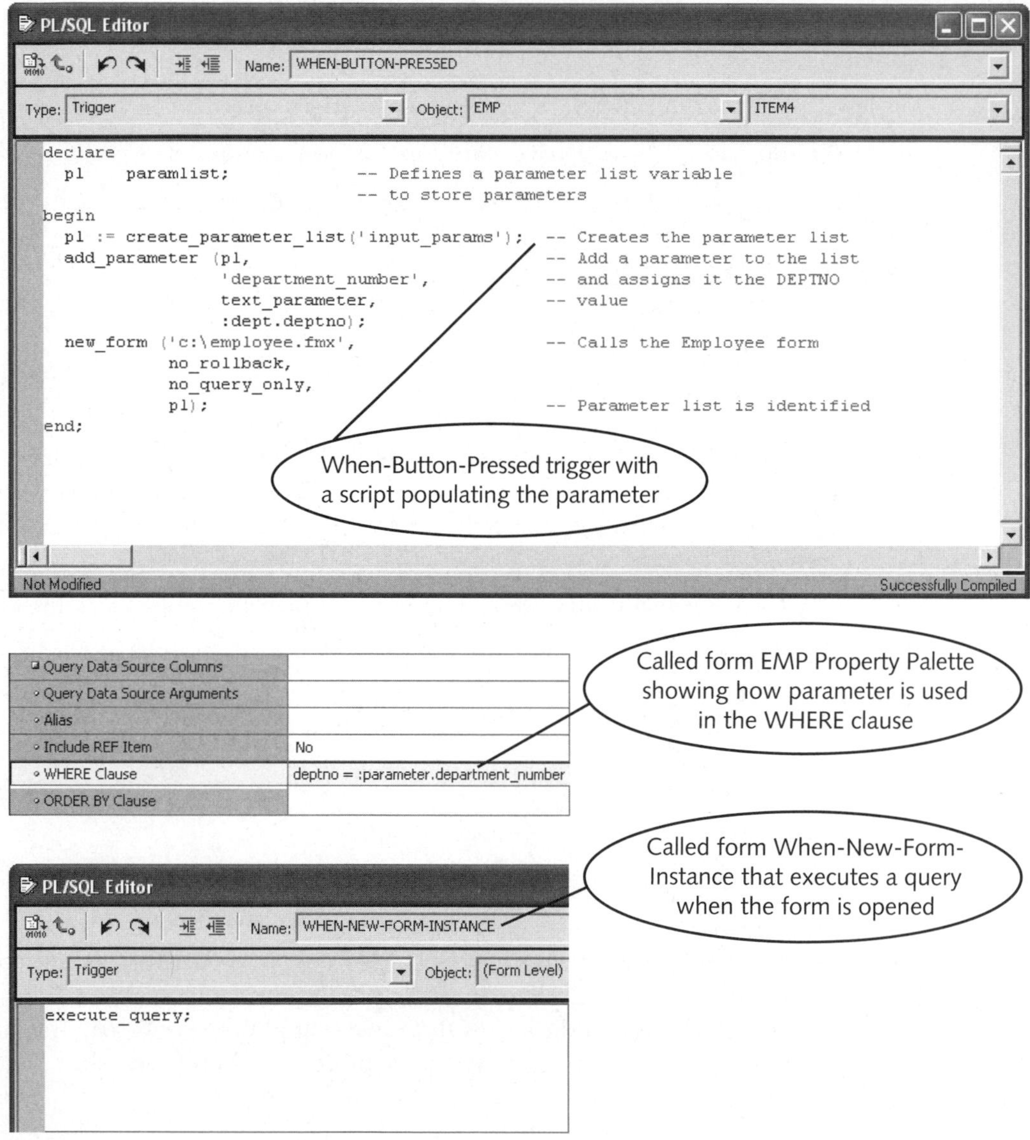

Figure 6-21 When-Button-Pressed trigger, Property Palette, and the When-New-Form-Instance trigger

The most complicated part of the script is the parameter list. To pass parameters, a list must be defined and the parameter added to the list. This was done with the Create_parameter_list and the Add_parameter built-ins. The DEPTNO value was added to the list with the later command.

The second tool shown in Figure 6-21 is a Property Palette for the Employee form. It shows the Where Clause property that references the parameter. Notice that the parameter is qualified by ":parameter". This qualification is necessary whenever the parameter is used. Placing this parameter into the property ensures that only the proper employees will be displayed.

The third tool is a PL/SQL Editor for the When-New-Form-Instance trigger that executes the query when the form is displayed. It contains the Execute_query built-in that brings the data back to the data block.

Using Global Variables

Global variables are variables that exist throughout the form session. When a form is executed, Forms Builder establishes a global area of memory. The global memory area stores variables that can hold values that can be used by all forms executed in the session. The variables are called global variables, and they are used to store user IDs and passwords, or to pass values between forms. Global variables have the following characteristics:

- Unlike parameters, they do not have to be defined as objects in the form.
- It is not necessary to create a parameter list to pass global variables (as shown in the previous section).
- Because global variables reside in memory, it is possible to assign their values by simply referencing them (i.e., :global.variable := 90).
- Global variables can be defined anywhere in the form session.
- Global variables are created when they are assigned a value. A data type and length is not necessary because Forms Builder sets these attributes based on the assigned value. The following is an example of creating a global variable:

```
global.department_number := :dept.deptno;
```

In the above template, the global variable DEPARTMENT is assigned the value of the DEPTNO data item in the DEPT data block. Global variables are always qualified by the Global keyword. A NULL value may also be assigned to the variable. Variables remain in memory until the Forms Builder session is terminated or the Erase built-in is executed. The following is an example of using this built-in:

```
Erase('global.department_number');
```

To illustrate the difference between using parameters and global variables, the example used in the last section for calling a form and passing a variable was modified using global variables. Figure 6-22 displays the modified scripts. Notice the difference between the When-Button-Pressed triggers in the two figures:

- A parameter list variable was not created.
- A parameter list was not created.
- Built-ins to populate the list are not needed.

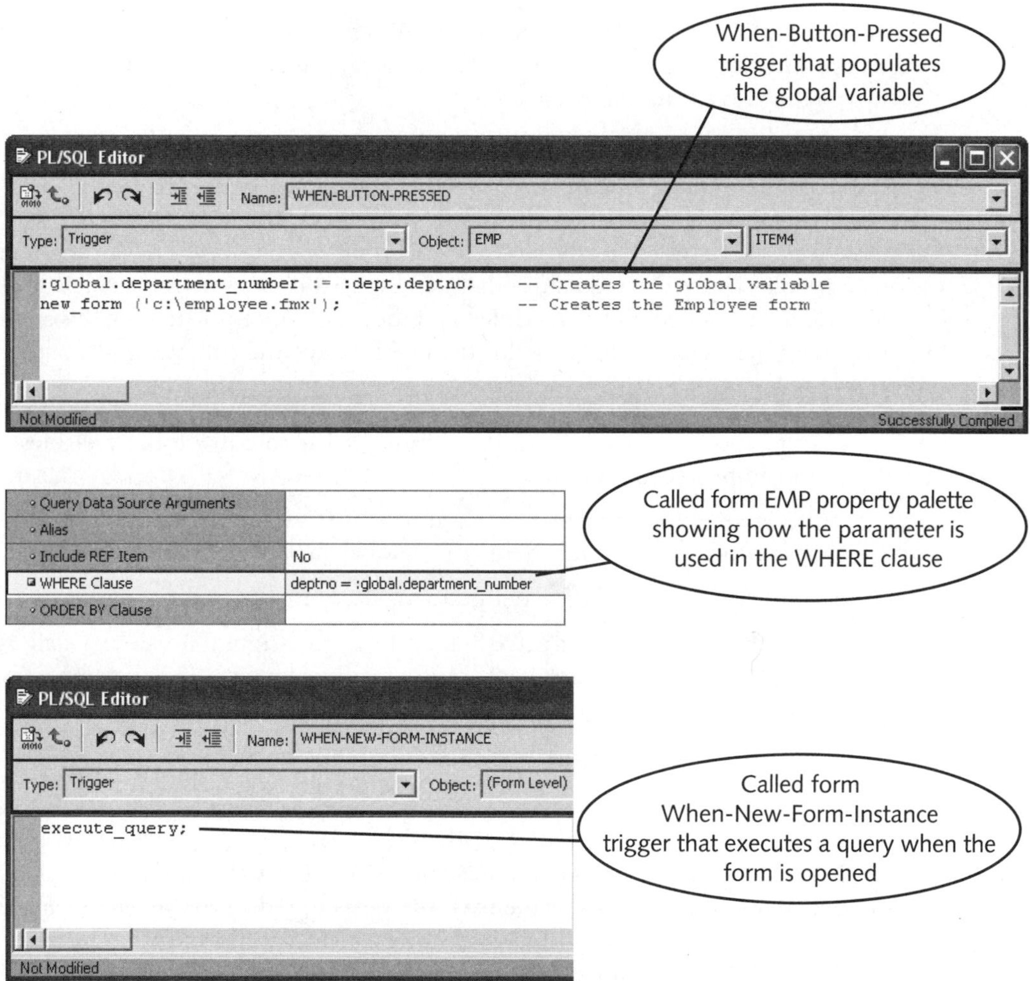

Figure 6-22 When-Button-Pressed trigger, Property Palette, and the When-New-Form-Instance trigger

The net difference is that fewer statements are needed to pass data between screens. You should also notice that the global variable was placed into the Where Clause property in place of the form parameter. The two techniques have exactly the same results.

Using System Variables

A **system variable** either tracks or controls form states. The following are several examples of form states:

- The currently selected record is the last record in the data block.
- The current data block is in the Enter Query mode or has changed values.
- The state of the current record. **States** indicate that the record is new and can be inserted into the data, the record has been updated, or the record is to be used to enter search values.

System variables and their values are important to you, and you will find that it is often necessary to determine the form state. The variables help you control the form behavior. For example, a form operator can by default, navigate into a new blank record after scrolling through a data block's records. As a developer, you may want to create a trigger (see Figure 6-23) that disables the ability of the operator to scroll into this blank record after the last record in the result set is reached. The Last_record and Block_status system variables can be used to control this behavior. As illustrated in Figure 6-23, the variables can be used in a Pre-Record trigger, which is fired before navigation into a record.

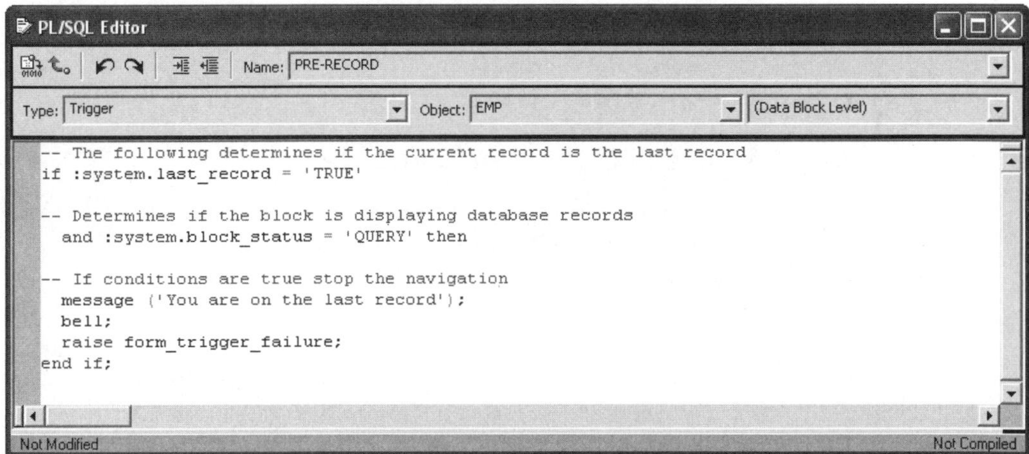

Figure 6-23 Pre-Record trigger and system variables to prevent navigation past the last data block record

The Last_record system variable is used in the trigger to determine whether the current record is the last data block record. If it is, the trigger sounds a bell, issues a message, and executes the RAISE Form_trigger_failure statement to terminate the navigation preventing the operator from opening the blank record at the end of the data block's result set.

The Block_status system variable is another useful variable that is placed in the example Pre-Record trigger. It is used in the IF-THEN construct to prevent the trigger's statement from executing when the form is in the Enter Query mode. In this mode, the data block is blank, and the current record is the last record. It is only desirable for the trigger statements to be executed when the data block contains records.

System variables must be qualified by the :System keyword. Appendix C details the system variables. The following is a short practice on creating a Pre-Record trigger:

1. Open the practice form in the Object Navigator.
2. Locate and expand the EMP data block exposing its Triggers node.
3. Select the **Triggers** node and click the **Create** tool to open the Triggers dialog box.
4. Select the **Pre-Record** trigger and click **OK**.
5. Add the Figure 6-23 script to the trigger. Click the **Compile PL/SQL Code** tool to check for errors. Close the PL/SQL Editor when finished.
6. Launch the form and execute the query. Scroll through the records and determine whether you will be able to scroll to the blank record at the end of the result set.
7. Save the form for later practice.

The MESSAGE_LEVEL System Variable

An Oracle form issues a wide variety of messages ranging from informational messages, such as that issued when a record is saved, to messages issued as a result of a severe database error. It can sometimes be inconvenient to have these messages displayed. For example, it is common to issue DML statements from the form as a result of clicking a button. The DML updates a database table that is not related to the form's data block. If you issue a COMMIT statement from the button trigger, Forms Builder issues a "No Changes to Save" warning message, even though the button script may have updated a table. The message was issued because the block did not have a modified status. It is inconvenient and confusing to the user to see this message.

Forms Builder allows you to suppress many of the messages including the "No Changes to Save" message. All form messages have a ranking of 0 (the default), 5, 10, 15, 20, and 25. The more severe the message, the greater the value. The Message_level system variable allows you to suppress messages based on the level value. For example, setting the message level to 25 suppresses the "No Changes to Save" warning, along with quite a few other messages. Whenever you issue DML statements that are not related to a data block, it is a good practice to use the MESSAGE_LEVEL system variable. Before the COMMIT statement, the MESSAGE_LEVEL variable is set higher. The COMMIT command is issued, and the MESSAGE_LEVEL is then returned to the normal level. The following depicts these statements:

```
:system.message_level := 25;
commit;
:system.message_level := 0;
```


MODIFYING FUNCTION KEY FUNCTIONALITY

Every Oracle form, whether used on the Web or in the client-server environment, has function keys defined. The function keys can be used to display errors, place the form into the Enter Query mode, duplicate a record, or to perform a host of other useful tasks. Each of the function keys is associated with a particular trigger. For example, the Key-Entqry trigger is fired when the Enter Query function key is pressed.

The function keys generally work well; however, it is sometimes necessary to override the default behavior. Here is an example: by default, pressing the Accept function key (the name of the key on the Function key menu) fires the Key-Commit trigger (the type of trigger that corresponds to the Accept key) and issues a Commit_form built-in that saves changes in the form. Perhaps you would like to ensure that the user has the authority to modify and save the form records before the issuance of the Commit_form built-in by the Accept function key. This requires you to modify the behavior of the Accept key.

It is possible to modify function key behavior by placing a Key trigger into the form. All control and function key triggers begin with the word Key. The Key-trigger overrides and defines the associated function key behavior. Figure 6-24 depicts a PL/SQL Editor containing a Key-Commit trigger that redefines the Accept function key. Looking at the script, notice that it contains the DML_SECURITY procedure. This is the same security script first seen in Figure 6-18. If the user who presses the key does not have security, the DML_SECURITY procedure executed by the Key-Commit trigger terminates the trigger by raising the Form_trigger_failure exception. This prevents the Commit_form built-in from firing. On the other hand, if the user has the proper security, the trigger executes the Commit_form built-in that saves the modified data. It is necessary to add this built-in to the script, because the default key behavior is discarded when the trigger is redefined. If it were not added to the trigger script, nothing would happen if the user passed the security check.

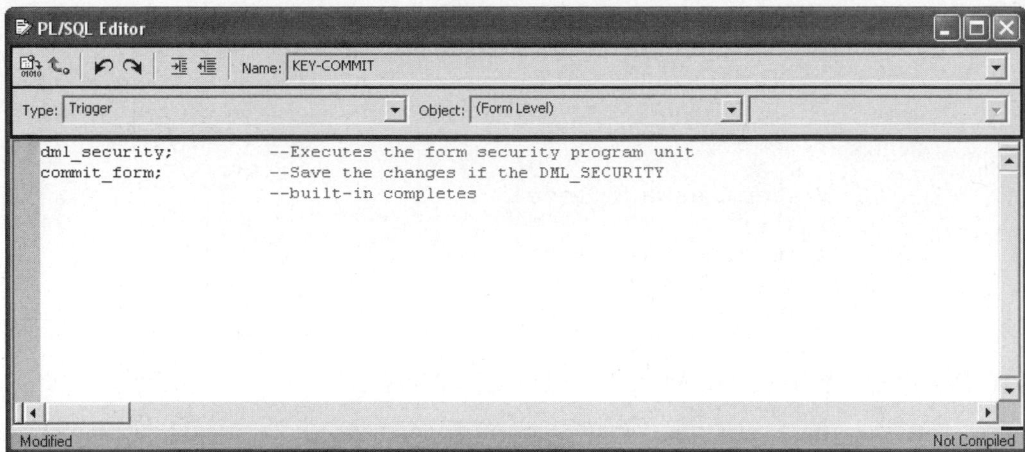

Figure 6-24 Key-Commit trigger that checks for user security

Key-trigger scope is the same as other triggers. Key-triggers can be defined at the form, data block, or item level. Form-level triggers are launched by an action anywhere within the form. Data block- and item-level triggers have a smaller range.

Disabling All Function Keys Using the Key-Others Trigger

All function keys can be disabled using the Key-Others trigger. In some cases, you may choose to disable this functionality and force the user to rely on the form buttons and toolbar tools. Disabling function keys can demystify form behavior for the user—sometimes fewer options are better than more options.

Figure 6-25 illustrates a Key-Others trigger. Because it is a trigger, it must have at least one statement. In this case, the statement was the word 'null;" which means nothing. Other statements can also be used, such as a message that says the function keys have been disabled.

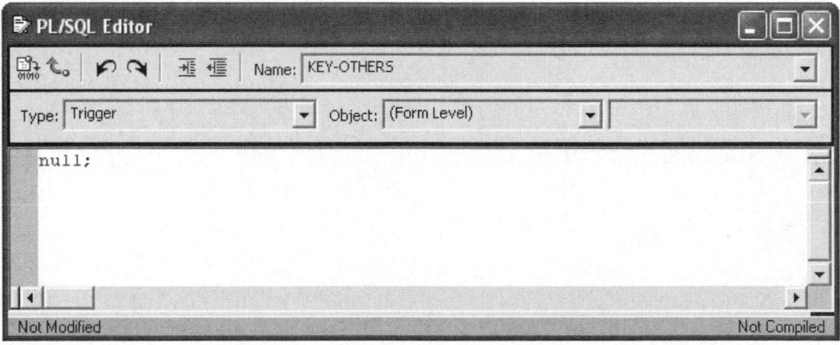

Figure 6-25 Key-Others trigger containing a NULL statement

You must be extremely careful when using the Key-Others trigger. It disables all default functionality in the form, so that the operator cannot tab between data items, execute a query, or even exit the form. If you decide to use this feature, your form must have buttons or toolbar tools that execute the desired procedures. You can also re-enable the function keys you need for the form by redefining the particular function key. For example, if you want to use the Exit key or the Exit toolbar tool, you can define a Key-Exit trigger with the Exit_form built-in, as illustrated in Figure 6-26.

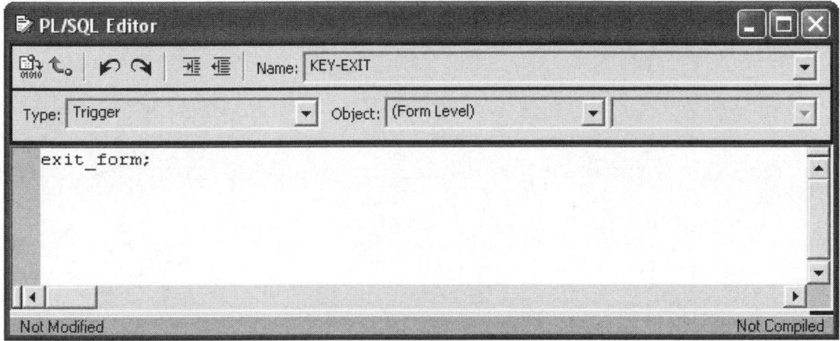

Figure 6-26 Key-Exit trigger that re-enables the Exit control key

Simulating a Function Key with the Do-key Built-in

Most forms are built so that the operator can perform a procedure using several tools. It is common to allow an operator to execute a query using a menu option, a toolbar tool, a button, a function key, or even a popup menu selection. When you decide that one of the function keys needs special instructions, you must be sure to place the same instructions into all of the form tools (i.e., toolbar tool, button, and function key) that perform the same function.

For example, a previous section discussed the need to place a security script into the Accept key. If you don't put the equivalent code into the form's toolbar tool, menu, form button, or popup menu, the operator may be able to save records without the proper privileges. It can be time consuming to locate and modify the different form tools that perform the same functions. In addition, it is easy for a developer to fail to identify one of the tools. A better approach is to modify the form procedure functionality by redefining the function key and simulating its execution with the Do_key built-in. The Do_key built-in simulates the pressing of a target function key. Each time this built-in is executed, it is exactly the same as using the function key. To complete our example, let's say that a Save button was placed in a form that required security to save records. In this case, the following When-Button-Pressed trigger statement, shown in Figure 6-27, simulates the pressing of the Accept key. It performs the simulation by executing the Key-Commit trigger that redefined the Accept key's behavior. You might note that the Do_key built-in has one parameter—the built-in that replicates the target function key's functionality.

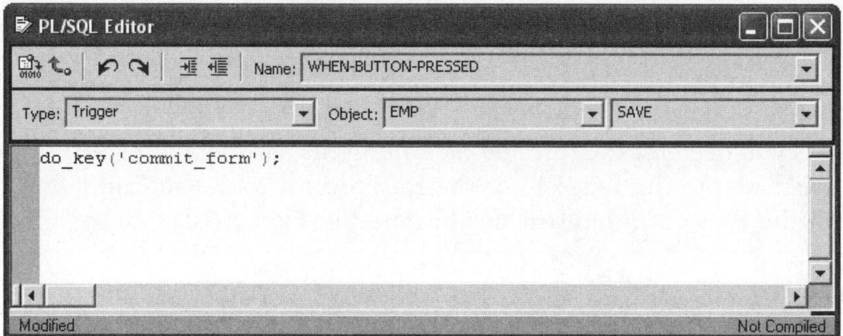

Figure 6-27 When-Button-Pressed trigger that executes the Key-Commit trigger

For practice creating a form level Key-Others trigger, perform the following steps:

1. Open the practice form in the Object Navigator.
2. Locate the form-level Triggers node. Using Figure 6-25 as an example, create a Key-Others trigger.
3. Execute the form and attempt to perform a query or exit the form. You should not be able perform either action.
4. Close the form. You may have to use the Windows Task Manager because none of the function keys or tools work.
5. Using Figure 6-26 as an example, create a form-level Key-exit trigger.
6. Execute the form and attempt to perform a query or exit the form. You should not be able to perform the query, but you should be able to exit from the form.
7. Close the form.

Where You Are and Where You're Going

This chapter added several useful development tools to your arsenal.

Your forms can now deviate from the default form behavior, because you now see how custom PL/SQL statements can be added to the form. This chapter covered common events that can fire or execute the code. You have also seen a number of essential built-in programs that you can use in your forms to perform special functions. This chapter also discussed how to create and pass variables between forms and triggers within the form. You have also seen how to customize the behavior of the function keys.

The forms that we have seen thus far displayed the data in text items. In the next chapter, you learn how to change these items into radio buttons, check boxes, and a number of other item types. This chapter started you on your way to supercharging your forms. The next chapter guides you further on the path by showing you tools that help eliminate a great deal of data entry.

CHAPTER SUMMARY

- Oracle forms are event driven. The programming statements are executed when an event takes place in the form.
- A trigger is fired when a specific event occurs.
- A trigger is a child object of a form object, such as the form, data block, or data item. The parent object determines the trigger scope.
- Triggers can be categorized by their prefixes. The prefix types are Key, On, Post, Pre, and When.
- Triggers fire in a specific order. It is important to determine the sequence of trigger firings.
- Triggers fired as a result of navigation may not execute SQL statements.
- Some triggers cannot be fired in the Enter Query mode.
- The SmartTriggers option on the Object Navigator popup menu is useful for identifying possible triggers.
- The PL/SQL Editor is the Forms Builder tool for entering PL/SQL statements.
- Compiling the PL/SQL code determines whether the code has syntax errors.
- Oracle has developed a variety of built-in subprograms that perform functions, such as moving the cursor or executing a query. Some of the built-ins are procedures that can be statements of their own, and some are functions that are used as assignment arguments.
- Many triggers are restricted, meaning the built-in cannot be called while navigation is occurring.
- The Syntax Palette is a tool that can be used to add PL/SQL constructs and built-ins to the program unit.
- The Exception section of the PL/SQL script is used to trap errors and exceptions.
- The RAISE Form_trigger_failure statement stops trigger processing and rolls back the form state to the start of the trigger.
- The When Others exception can trap any exception or error.
- Parameters can be added to the form to accept values from a calling application.
- Global variables have a session scope and are automatically passed between forms. The ERASE command can be used to remove them from memory.
- System variables are used to test or control a specific form state.
- The Message_level system variable is used to suppress messages.
- The Key-Others trigger suppresses all other Key triggers unless they are specifically defined.

REVIEW QUESTIONS

1. Match the following terms that have appeared in this chapter with their descriptions:

    a. /*   */ ______ An Oracle-built procedure or function that performs a form task.

    b. Key-Others ______ A set of characters that are used to comment one or more lines of PL/SQL code.

    c. Program unit ______ A class of triggers that are fired when an event occurs.

    d. Parameter list ______ A class of triggers that are fired before an event occurs.

    e. Trigger scope ______ A trigger that disables all default function keys.

    f. When-Others ______ Identifies the range in which a trigger can be fired.

    g. On triggers ______ A form variable that can be tested to determine if a specific condition exists.

    h. Global variable ______ A variable that can be passed from the form runtime executable to the starting form.

    i. Do_key ______ A dialog box that is displayed after clicking the Create tool when a trigger node is selected.

    j. Syntax Palette ______ A trigger that replaces a procedure.

    k. Fired ______ The catch-all exception handler that should be placed in all PL/SQL code blocks.

    l. When trigger ______ A tool palette that can be used to add PL/SQL code templates and built-ins to the PL/SQL Editor.

    m. Parameter ______ A list of variables that can be passed to an object such as a form.

    n. Post trigger ______ A built-in subprogram that simulates the pressing of a function key.

o. Triggers dialog box	________	A form PL/SQL object created by the developer.
p. Built-in subprograms	________	A variable that can exist throughout a Forms Builder session and can be referenced by multiple forms.
q. System variable	________	Oracle's name for executing a trigger.
r. Form_trigger_failure	________	A class of triggers that are executed after an event occurs.
s. Pre trigger	________	A built-in subprogram that terminates trigger processing and returns the form to the state it was in before the firing of the trigger.

2. Describe the difference between a form event and a trigger.
3. Why is it a good practice to add exception handlers to your program units?
4. What type of trigger would you use to ensure that a valid value was entered into the form? What trigger or triggers could you use? At what form level would you place the trigger?
5. A user requested that you place the current date into a text item whenever the user places the mouse into the item. This will eliminate the need for the user to add the value. What type of trigger should you use? If the field is the HIREDATE item in the EMP data block, what would the statement look like?
6. What type of trigger would you use to replace the default DELETE statement issued by a data block? What trigger or triggers could you use? At what form level would you place the trigger?
7. Order the following trigger types in the logical firing sequence: On, Post, When, Pre, and Key.
8. You have just compiled a newly created PL/SQL code block in the PL/SQL Editor. Many syntax errors were listed in the Error Message pane. What is the quickest way to locate the potential problem in the code block?
9. What is the difference between a restricted and unrestricted built-in? Can you use the Execute_query built-in within a Post-Text-Item trigger? Can you execute the Create_record built-in in a Pre-Text-Item trigger?
10. What happens if a trigger receives an error message from the Oracle database? Can this situation be avoided? How?
11. If you have the same PL/SQL script that is used in numerous places in the form, what kind of problems can occur? What can you do to avoid these problems?
12. Discuss the pros and cons of using global variables and form parameters.

13. You have a trigger that performs an action if a record is changed in the data block. How can you determine whether a value was changed?
14. You have a form that computes a value in a text item before the record is saved. You redefined the Accept function key to perform this function before saving the changes. Several weeks after the form was put into production, a user called and said that the calculation does not occur when the Save button is clicked. Can you think of a potential defect that is causing the problem?
15. You developed a master-detail form. After deploying the form, you noticed that occasionally users placed their insertion points in the detail block when they pressed the Enter Query tool or the Enter Query function key. This placed the detail block into the Enter Query mode rather than the master block and caused the users problems, because they had to cancel the query, move the insertion point to the master block, and place the master block into the Enter Query mode. What can you do to eliminate this problem?
16. You are debugging a program unit. You suspect that a particular set of statements is causing your problem. You would like to disable these lines from executing, but you don't want to remove them from the code block. What should you do?
17. You have just created your first form. Your supervisor mentioned that you should use the Key-Others trigger to disable the unused function keys. You placed the Key-Others trigger into your form, and now you can't operate it. What should you do?

Exam Review Questions

1. The location of a trigger in a form's hierarchy determines its scope. At which level should you define a trigger to ensure that it fires based on an event across the data block?
   a. Record
   b. Form
   c. Item
   d. Data block
2. Which trigger type would you use to assign values for search criteria?
   a. Pre
   b. On
   c. Post
   d. When
   e. Key

3. When you call a specific form, you want the values to be initialized. What type of trigger would you use to perform this task?
   a. Pre
   b. On
   c. Post
   d. When
   e. Key
4. You are creating a When-New-Form-Instance trigger. What constructs will be implicitly included?
   a. Begin and End
   b. Begin, Executable, and End
   c. Begin, Declaration, and End
   d. Declaration, Begin, and End
   e. Declaration, Exception, and End
5. What are SmartTriggers?
   a. SmartClass triggers
   b. Object library triggers
   c. Common form triggers
   d. Common triggers appropriate for a specific object

Hands-on Assignments

1. In this assignment, you create a new form using the EMP table as a data source. You add a trigger that populates the EMP data block when the form is opened and also add a When-Validate-Item trigger that ensures that the DEPTNO value is a valid department number.
   a. Open the Object Navigator and create a new form module.
   b. Create a data block based on the EMP table. The data block should display 10 records in a Tabular layout.
   c. Locate and create the form-level **Triggers** node. Click the **Create** tool to open the Triggers dialog box. Select the **When-New-Form-Instance** trigger and click **OK** to launch a PL/SQL Editor for the trigger.
   d. Add the following built-in to the trigger:

      ```
      Execute_query;
      ```
   e. Click the **Compile PL/SQL Code** tool to ensure that you entered the statement correctly.
   f. Launch the form and confirm that the form executes a query and populates the EMP data block when the form is opened.

g. Close the form.

h. Locate and expand the **DEPTNO** data block item exposing its Triggers node.

i. Select the DEPTNO data block item **Triggers** node. Click the **Create** tool to open the Triggers dialog box. Select the **When-Validate-Item** trigger, and click **OK** to open the PL/SQL Editor. Add the following script to the trigger:

```
Declare
   Cursor a is select deptno from dept
               Where deptno = :emp.deptno;
   A_var      a%rowtype;
begin
   open a;
   fetch a into a_var;
   if a%notfound then
     bell;
     message ('You have entered an incorrect department value');
     raise form_trigger_failure;
   end if;
end;
```

j. Click the **Compile PL/SQL Code** tool to ensure that the script is correct.

k. Launch the form. Change the department number of any record to **11** (an incorrect value) and tab out of the data item. An error message should be displayed, and you will be prevented from moving out of the DEPTNO text item until the value is correct.

l. Close the form.

m. Save the form as **ch06ex01.fmb**.

2. You have decided that you prefer if possible to have your form validations in one executable rather than in various triggers. To make this change, you decided to delete the When-Validate-Item trigger you created for the DEPTNO data item in Hands-on Assignment 6-1. You decided to use form-level Pre-Insert and Pre-Update triggers instead. To avoid having duplicate edit codes, you want to create a form program unit and use the program unit in each of the triggers. Use the form you created in Hands-on Assignment 6-1 (**ch06ex01.fmb**).

   a. Open form **ch06ex01.fmb** in the Object Navigator.

   b. Locate and select the **DEPTNO When-Validate-Item** trigger.

   c. Double-click the icon to the left of the trigger, which opens its PL/SQL Editor.

   d. Copy the trigger script and close the PL/SQL Editor.

   e. Delete the trigger.

   f. Locate and select the **Program Units** node in the Object Navigator. Click the **Create** tool to open the New Program Unit dialog box. Click the **Procedure** radio button and name the program unit **APPLICATION_EDITS**. Click **OK** to open the PL/SQL Editor.

g. Paste the copied trigger script into the new program unit. Be sure to copy it between the Begin and End keywords. Click the **Compile PL/SQL Code** tool to ensure that the script is correct.

h. Open the Object Navigator and locate the form-level Triggers node. Select the **Triggers** node and click the **Create** tool to open the Triggers dialog box. Select the **Pre_Insert** trigger and click **OK** to open the PL/SQL Editor.

i. Add the following statement to the trigger:

```
Application_edits;
```

j. Click the **Compile PL/SQL Code** tool to ensure that the trigger is correct. Close the PL/SQL Editor.

k. Create a form-level Pre-Update trigger by repeating steps i through k.

l. Launch the program and test the triggers and program units by trying to add an employee for department 31 and updating the DEPTNO value of an existing employee to 31.

m. Close the form and save as **ch06ex02.fmb**.

3. The purpose of this assignment is to show you how to trap a database error and modify the normal database error message. When database error messages shown to the user are cryptic, you should add a more meaningful message. A form-level On-Error trigger will be used to trap the error. Whenever an error occurs, Forms Builder generates an error value and places it into a variable named ERROR_CODE. The trigger traps the code returned by Oracle for violating a Primary Key constraint.

   In this assignment, you insert an employee record into the database containing the payroll number of an existing employee. This causes a constraint error, because the EMPNO column contains a Primary Key constraint. Use the form you created in Hands-on Assignment 6-2 (**ch06ex02.fmb**) for this exercise.

   a. Open form **ch06ex02.fmb** in the Object Navigator.

   b. Run the form and add a new employee. The EMPNO value is **7934** and DEPTNO value is **10**.

   c. Save the record. This should generate the default error message indicating that the record cannot be created.

   d. Close the form.

   e. Locate and expand the EMP data block exposing the data block Triggers node.

   f. Select the **Triggers** node and click the **Create** tool to open the Triggers dialog box. Create a block-level On-Error trigger. Add the following script:

```
if error_code = 40508 then  -- 40508 Is and Oracle error code
     bell;
 message ('You have already added this employee to the database');
else
 message (ERROR_TEXT);
end if;
```

g. Run the form and add a new employee. The EMPNO value is **7934** and DEPTNO value is **10**.

h. Save the record. Notice the new message.

i. Save the form as **ch06ex03.fmb**.

4. It is good configuration management to name the forms in a system and have the name available for the operator. Many developers place the name of the form on the screen. Forms Builder has a seldom-used function key called Key Menu. By default, this function key displays a list of data blocks for your selection and navigation. This key can be re-programmed to display information about the form rather than the menu, eliminating the need to put information directly on the screen. In this assignment, you redefine this key to display the name of the application, the date it was last modified, and the name of the developer. Use the form you created in Hands-on Assignment 6-3 (**ch06ex03.fmb**).

   a. Open form **ch06ex03.fmb** in the Object Navigator.

   b. Locate and select the form-level Triggers node. Click the **Create** tool to open the Triggers dialog box. Select the **Key-Menu** trigger and click **OK** to open the PL/SQL Editor.

   c. Add the following code to the trigger:

```
Message ('Module CH06EX04  last modified on today's date by your name');
```

   d. Click the **Compile PL/SQL Code** tool to ensure that the trigger is correct.

   e. Launch the form and press the **Key Menu** function key. This is the Control + B key combinations on the Web and the F5 key in client-server mode. The configuration message should appear.

   f. Save the form as **ch06ex04.fmb**.

5. This assignment consists of placing a number of miscellaneous triggers into the **ch06ex04.fmb** form module.

   a. Open form **ch06ex04.fmb** in the Object Navigator.

   b. Locate the HIREDATE data block item. Expand the item, and expose and select its **Triggers** node. Click the **Create** tool to open the Triggers dialog box.

   c. Select the **Pre-Text-Item** trigger and click **OK** to open the PL/SQL Editor.

   d. This trigger places the current date into the item if it does not have a value when the user navigates into the item. Use the following script:

```
if :emp.hiredate is null then
  :hiredate := sysdate;
end if;
```

   e. Click the **Compile PL/SQL Code** tool to ensure that the code is correct.

   f. Run the form. Place your cursor into a row. Tab to the **HIREDATE** item and delete its value. Tab through the record returning to the HIREDATE item. Notice that the current date is placed into the blank item when you tab into it.

g. Close the form.

h. Locate the Visual Attributes node in the Object Navigator. Click the **Create** tool. Select the newly created visual attribute and press **F4** to open a Property Palette. Set the following properties:

Name:	ERROR
Background Color:	RED

i. Open the **APPLICATION_EDITS** program unit. Add the following built-in to the script. The built-in should precede the RAISE Form_trigger_failure statement. It will cause any invalid DEPTNO (department number) value to change to red text when the operator attempts to save a record.


```
Set_Item_Instance_Property ('emp.deptno', current_record,
                            visual_attribute, 'error');
```

j. Click the **Compile PL/SQL Code** tool to ensure that the code is correct.

k. Run the form and test the trigger by changing a DEPTNO value to **11** and saving the changes. The background of the modified record should turn red.

l. Save the form as **ch06ex05.fmb**.

6. In this assignment, you disable the function keys using the Key-Others trigger and enable several others.

a. Open form **ch06ex05.fmb** in the Object Navigator.

b. Locate and select the form-level **Triggers** node. Click the **Create** tool to open the Triggers dialog box. Select the **Key-Others** trigger and click **OK** to open the PL/SQL Editor.

c. Add the following script to the trigger:

```
message ('Your form is currently in the '||:system.mode ||' mode');
```

d. Click the **Compile PL/SQL Code** tool ensuring the script is correct.

e. Repeat steps b through d creating a form-level Key-Exit trigger using the following script:

```
Exit_form;
```

f. Repeat steps b through d creating a form-level Key-Entqry trigger using the following script:

```
Enter_query;
```

g. Repeat steps b through d creating a form-level Key-Exeqry trigger using the following script:

```
Execute_query;
```

h. Repeat steps b through d creating a form-level Key-Commit trigger using the following script:

```
Commit_form;
```

i. Launch the form. Press the **Delete Record** function key and notice that the message returns the current data block status. Operate the form and make sure that you can place the form into the Enter Query mode, execute a query, save the records, and exit the form.

j. Save the form as **ch06ex06.fmb**.

7. Using the form you created in Hands-on Assignment 6-6, place the following items into your MY_OWN_LIBRARY object library that you created in Hands-on Assignment 5-5:

   a. When-New-Form-Instance trigger

   b. Key-Menu trigger

   c. On-Error trigger

You will be able to move these triggers into forms that you create.

CASE PROJECT: GREAT STATE ELECTRIC BUDGETING SYSTEM

In this section of the Case Project, you enter a variety of triggers into the forms and create triggers that perform the following functions:

- Generate the next employee number
- Generate the next work order number
- Place the current date into the EMPLOYMENT_DATE data item
- Prevent records from being modified in the WORK_ORDERS, WORK_ORDER_TASKS, EMPLOYEES, ACCOUNTS, and TASK_DESCRIPTIONS data blocks unless all of the proper fields have a value

Your Work

When a record is first created, the employment date is generally the current date. Populate the EMPLOYEES data block, EMPLOYMENT_DATE, with the current date. This trigger fires when the user tabs into the EMPLOYMENT_DATE item. If the item contains a null value, the trigger populates the item with the current date and thus eliminates the need for the operator to enter it.

1. Open the Budgeting form in the Object Navigator.
2. Select the **Triggers** node under the EMPLOYEES.EMPLOYMENT_DATE data item. Click the **Create** tool to open the Triggers dialog box.
3. Select the **Pre-Text-Item** trigger and click **OK** to open the PL/SQL Editor.

4. Enter the following script into the Editor:

```
If :employees.employment_date is null then
        :employees.employment_date := sysdate;
end if;
```

5. Run the form and determine whether the trigger is operating correctly.

You want to prevent the user from creating or modifying an employee record unless the EMPLOYEE_ID, DEPARTMENT_ID, EMPLOYMENT_DATE, and CLASSIFICATION fields have values. If these fields do not have values, the transaction should stop and the user should be notified. This script will be used in the block-level Pre-Insert and Pre-Update triggers. Because the script is the same for both triggers, create a program unit for the edits and use the program unit in the triggers by performing the following steps:

6

1. Open the Object Navigator, select the **PROGRAM UNITS** node, and click the **Create** tool to open the New Program Unit dialog box.
2. Click the **Procedure** radio button and name the procedure **EMPLOYEE_EDITS**. Click **OK** to open the PL/SQL Editor.
3. Enter the following script into the program unit:

```
PROCEDURE employee_edits IS
BEGIN
  if :employees.employee_id is null
        or :employees.department_id is null
        or :employees.classification is null
        or :employees.employment_date is null then
        bell;
        message ('You must enter an employee id, department id,
              current position, and employment date values');
        raise form_trigger_failure;
 end if;
END;
```

4. Click the **Compile PL/SQL Code** tool to ensure that the trigger is correct.
5. Create Pre-Insert and Pre-Update triggers under the EMPLOYEES data block that call the EMPLOYEE_EDITS program unit. The script for each of these triggers is:

```
Employee_edits;
```

6. Run the form and test whether the Pre-Insert and Pre-Update triggers operate correctly.
7. The WORK_ORDERS data block needs similar Pre-Insert and Pre-Update triggers. The triggers prevent a user from modifying the database if the WORK_ORDER_ID and WO_DESCRIPTION data items are NULL. Create a program unit named **WORK_ORDER_EDITS** that is similar to EMPLOYEE_EDITS and create Pre-Insert and Pre-Update triggers that use this program unit. Launch the form and test the triggers.

8. The WORK_ORDER_TASKS data block needs similar Pre-Insert and Pre-Update triggers. The triggers prevent a user from modifying the database if the TASK_DESCRIPTION_ID and ACCOUNT_ID data items are NULL. Create a program unit named **WORK_ORDER_TASK_EDITS** that is similar to EMPLOYEE_EDITS and create Pre-Insert and Pre-Update triggers that use this program unit. Launch the form and test the triggers.
9. The ACCOUNTS data block needs similar Pre-Insert and Pre-Update triggers. The triggers prevent a user from modifying the database if the ACCOUNT_ID and ACCOUNT_DESCRIPTION data items are NULL. Create a program unit named **ACCOUNT_EDITS** that is similar to EMPLOYEE_EDITS and add Pre-Insert and Pre-Update triggers that use this program unit. Launch the form and test the triggers.
10. The TASK_DESCRIPTIONS data block needs similar Pre-Insert and Pre-Update triggers. The triggers prevent a user from modifying the database if the TASK_ID and TASK_DESCRIPTION data items are NULL. Create a program unit named **TASK_DESCRIPTION_EDITS** that is similar to EMPLOYEE_EDITS and add Pre-Insert and Pre-Update triggers that use this program unit. Launch the form and test the triggers.

Your users want the form to generate new employee IDs. You have been asked to create a trigger that generates the next available employee ID. The ID will be generated when the operator double-clicks in the EMPLOYEE_ID data item and the current record is in the Insert mode. To accomplish this, perform the following steps:

1. Open the Object Navigator. Locate and expand the EMPLOYEES data block EMPLOYEE_ID item exposing its Triggers node.
2. Select the **Triggers** node and click the **Create** tool to open the Triggers dialog box.
3. Select the **When-Mouse-Doubleclick** trigger and click **OK** to open the PL/SQL Editor.
4. Enter the following script:

```
begin
        if :system.record_status = 'NEW'
                  and :employees.employee_id is null then
           select nvl(max(employee_id),0) + 1
            into :employees.employee_id
           from employees;
       end if;
exception
          when others then
            bell;
            message ('An error occurred and the number was not generated');
end;
```

5. Launch the form and test the trigger.

Work order numbers are generated in the WORK_ORDERS data block on the PROJECTS tab page. You are to write a trigger that generates the next sequential work order number when the operator double-clicks in the WORK_ORDER_ID data item. This trigger should only operate when the current record is in the Insert mode. To accomplish this, perform the following steps:

1. Open the Object Navigator and create a **When-Mouse-Doubleclick** trigger for the WORK_ORDERS.WORK_ORDER_ID data item.
2. Use the following script:

```
begin
        if :system.record_status = 'NEW'
                  and :work_orders.work_order_id is null then
           select nvl(max(work_order_id), 0) + 1
            into :work_orders.work_order_id
           from work_orders;
        end if;
exception
         when others then
           bell;
           message ('An error occurred and the number was not generated');
end;
```

You have decided that function keys will not be used in this form. Instead, the user will click buttons to perform all functions (buttons are created in the next chapter's Case Project). Disable the control keys by creating a form-level Key-Others trigger. The trigger should only have a single statement: NULL. Create a form-level Key-Exit trigger that allows you to shut down the form. The script is: exit_form;

CHAPTER

7

DEFINING DATA BLOCK ITEM TYPES, LOVS, AND RECORD GROUPS

In this chapter you will:

- Learn about the block item types
- Use text and display items at the proper time
- Create and use a check box
- Create and use a radio group
- Create and use a poplist, Tlist, or a combo box
- Add an image to your form
- Create and use a button
- Create and use a calculated item
- Create and use a list of values (LOV) in your form
- Learn about static and programmatically created record groups

The roadmap pictured in Figure 7-1 shows that this chapter introduces you to tools that enhance the user interface. Previous chapters covered text items that are used to display and modify data. This chapter shows you how to change the text item so that you can enter multiple lines of text in one item. You also see that a text item can be changed to a number of other formats that potentially ease the entry of data. Examples of other formats include check boxes that allow the user to enter data by checking a box, radio groups that allow the user to click a radio button, and drop-down lists for selecting values. This chapter also introduces you to **LOVs** (lists of values), which are dialog boxes of values that can be called to validate or populate a data block item. By the end of this chapter, you will you have worked with all the major tools that are required for creating an efficient form.

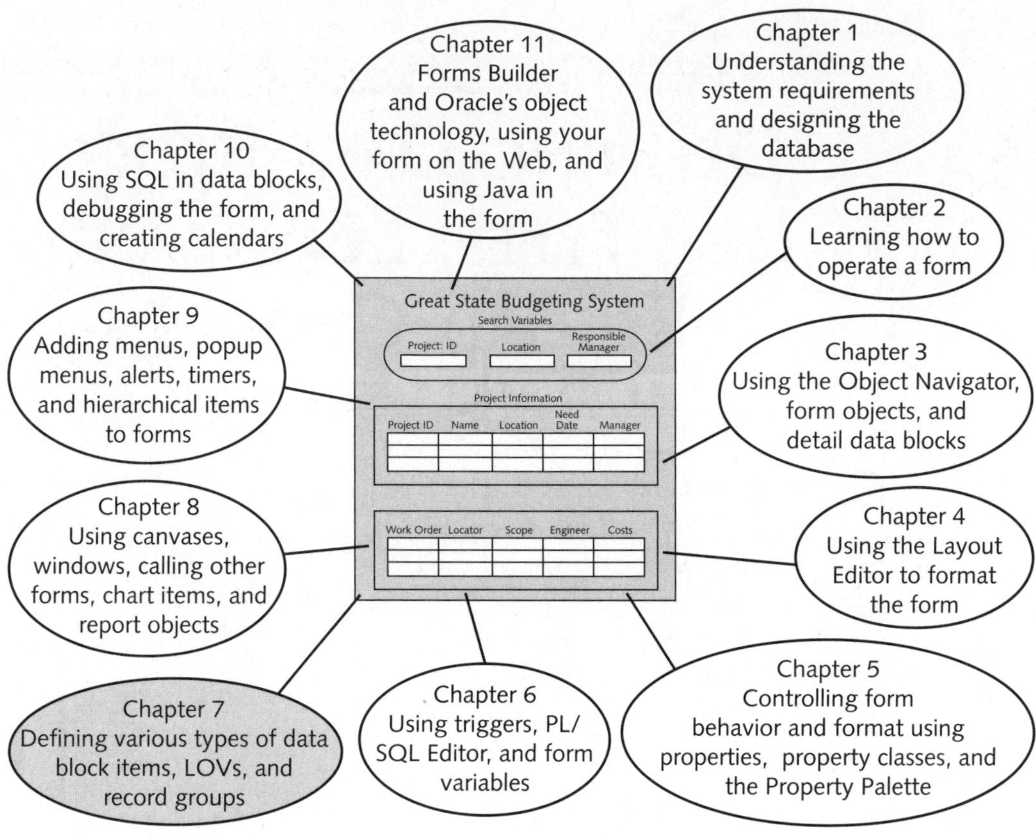

Figure 7-1 Roadmap

Block Item Types

The forms that you design contain data blocks that interact with the database. To this point, every form that you have seen contained text items. The text item is the most common type of data block item in Forms Builder. It is used to display a database value or to receive a different value from the user. There are actually 15 different types of data items. These items range from text items to radio groups and buttons. Some of the item types are used in conjunction with a data block. Others, such as a **hierarchical tree item** that displays an object list, can only be used in a control block. You use the Item Type property to change an item to any type. When you do so, Forms Builder changes the item's properties to conform to the chosen type. Table 7-1 lists and describes item types.

Table 7-1 Item types

Item type	Description
ActiveX control	An item that uses a custom control, such as a spin dial (obsolete in 9*i*).
Bean Area	An item that uses a JavaBean as a control for the item.
Chart Item	An Oracle Graphics Builder chart.
Check Box	An item that appears as checked or unchecked. This item is used when only two mutually exclusive values can be entered.
Display Item	An item that can only display a value. This item cannot be modified.
Hierarchical Tree	An item that displays lists of related values allowing the user to expand and collapse branches. The Object Navigator is an example of this item.
Image	An item that displays an image, such as a **bmp** or **jpeg** file.
List Item	An item that displays a static or dynamic set of values. This item can be a Poplist, Combo Box, or a Tlist.
OLE container	An item that displays an OLE object (obsolete in 9*i*).
Push Button	A button item. This item can appear as a button on the form or as a tool on a toolbar.
Radio Group	A set of mutually exclusive radio buttons. Each button represents a different item value.
Sound	An item that allows the user to load, play, edit, and save a sound file (obsolete in 9*i*).
Text Item	An item that is used to display and modify a value.
User Area	An area that stores and displays a user-defined item.
VBX Control	Used with Microsoft Windows 3.1 only (obsolete in 9*i*).

7

Creating an Item and Specifying Its Type

Of the several ways to create an item, the most common is to use the Layout Wizard Data Block page (see Figure 7-2). After you identify the items that will appear in the layout, it is possible to determine the item type on the Data Block page. Selecting any of the objects enables the Item Type Drop-down list to be used to set the item. The default item type is Text Item.

A second way of creating an item is to select the Item tool on the Layout Editor toolbar. See Figure 7-3, which illustrates the toolbar and a newly created image item. The toolbar has a tool for most of the available item types. To use these tools, you would perform the following steps:

1. Activate the tool by clicking it.
2. Place the insertion point on the canvas at the location where the item is to appear.

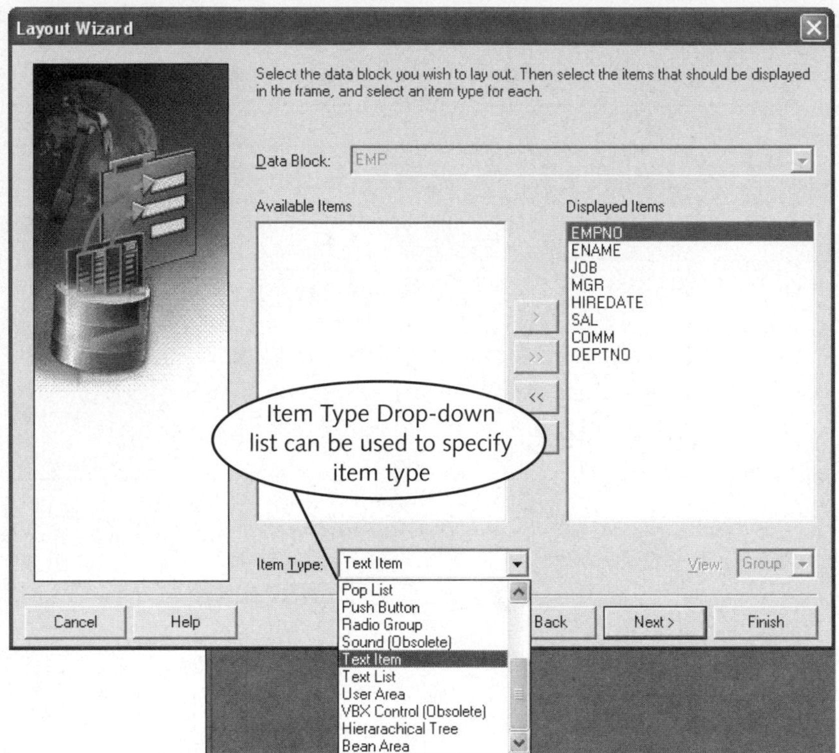

Figure 7-2 Layout Wizard Data Block page displaying available item types

3. Click and hold the Left Mouse button.
4. Size the item by dragging the insertion point.
5. Release the Left Mouse button when the size is correct.

The third method is to create the item object in the Object Navigator. An item is created by selecting the data block Items node and clicking the Create tool. The item type can then be set by opening the item's Property Palette and setting the Item Type property (see Figure 7-4). This property can be used to change the type of any form block item.

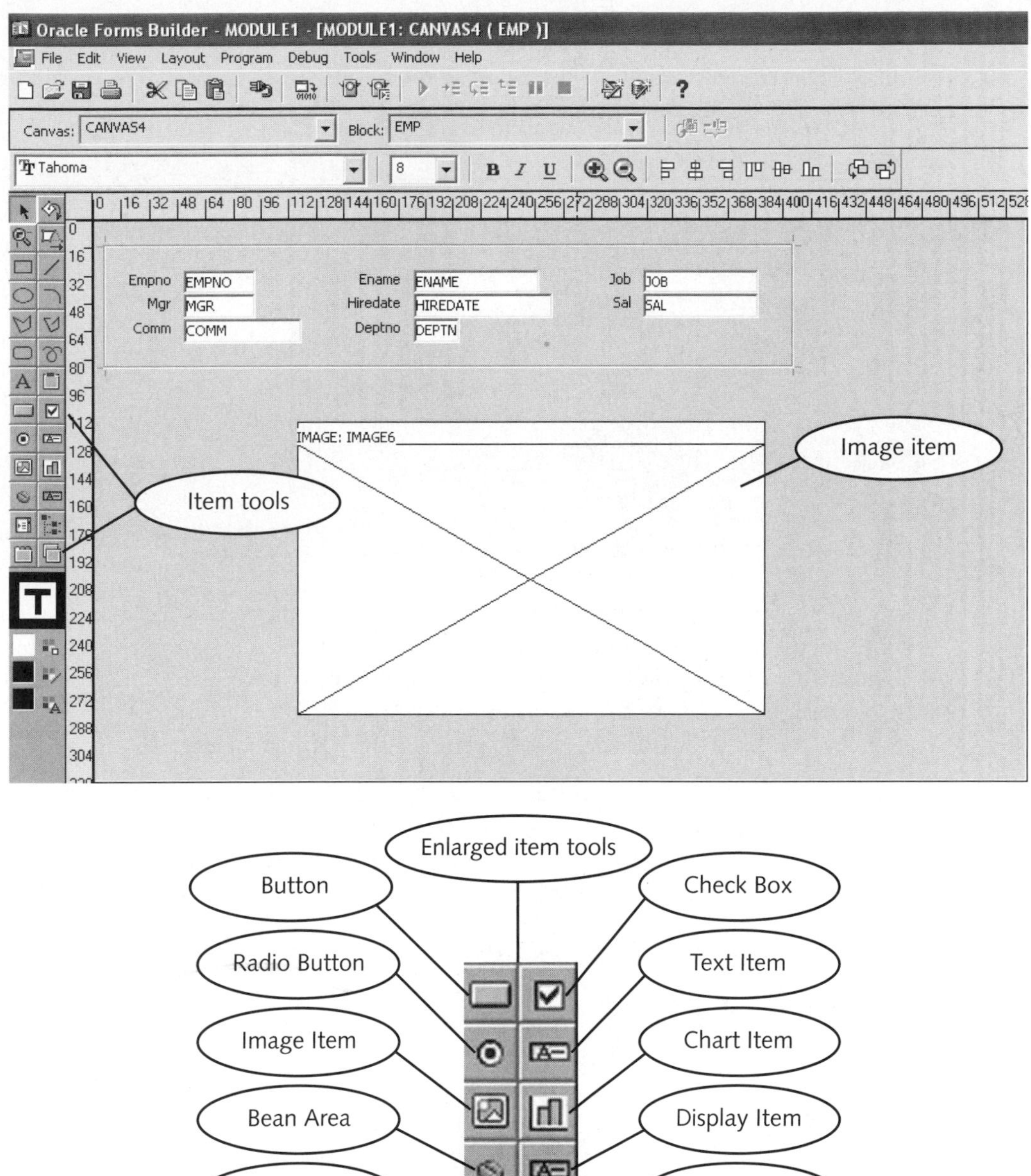

Figure 7-3 Layout Editor item tools and newly created image item

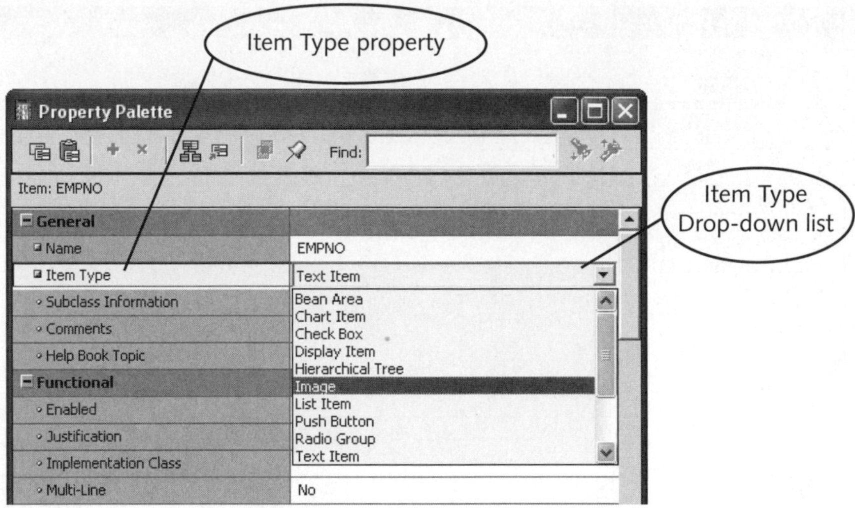

Figure 7-4 Property Palette and the Item Type Drop-down list

The last method of creating an item is to copy and paste it. This is an especially good technique when adding text items. The new items have the same properties and triggers as those from which they are copied. The only drawback of this method is that Forms Builder might not paste the new item into the proper data block. It is always necessary to check the locations of the pasted items in the Object Navigator.

Each item type has its own unique Object Navigator icon (shown in Figure 7-5). In general, the icons make the items easy to differentiate. However, display and text item icons look somewhat similar. They both consist of a box with the character "A". The difference is that the display item icon is slightly darkened.

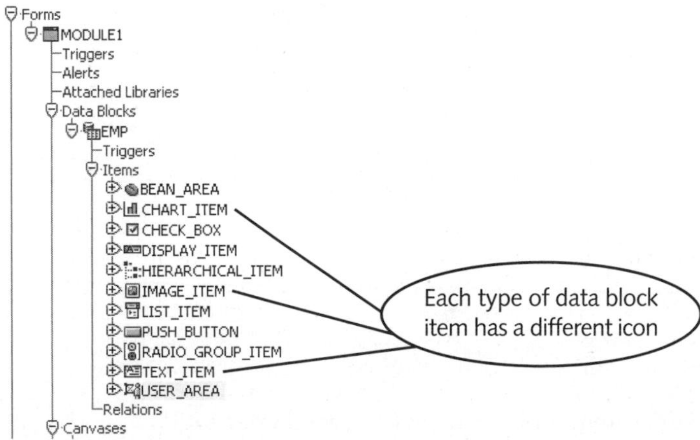

Figure 7-5 Object Navigator and item type icons

Item Behavior Properties

Text and display items have a number of properties that are useful to you as a developer. These properties can be used to perform the following functions: display a single record, even though the item is in a multiple-record data block; prevent the entry of a value; perform a range check on a value; and perform a case-insensitive query. These properties are available for many but not all item types. Commonly used item properties are: Automatic Skip, Case Insensitive Query, Case Restriction, Column Name, Database Item, Format Mask, Highest Allowed Setting, Initial Value, Insert Allowed, Lowest Allowed Value, Number of Records Displayed, Primary Key, Query Allowed, Query Length, Query Only, Required, and Update Allowed. The names of the properties are fairly descriptive. You can read descriptions of these properties in Appendix B.

Hints and Tooltips

Forms Builder has two features that allow you to display informational messages to the user: hints and Tooltips (see Figure 7-6 for examples of both). A **hint** is a message that appears on the status line of a form whenever the operator navigates into a specific item. The message can be used to describe the input format of the value or to display other pertinent information about the item. A hint is actually an item property that can be set for each item. Hints also have a complementary property called Display Hint Automatically. If this property is set to YES, the hint message is displayed whenever the operator navigates to the item. If it is set to NO, the operator must press the appropriate function key to display the message.

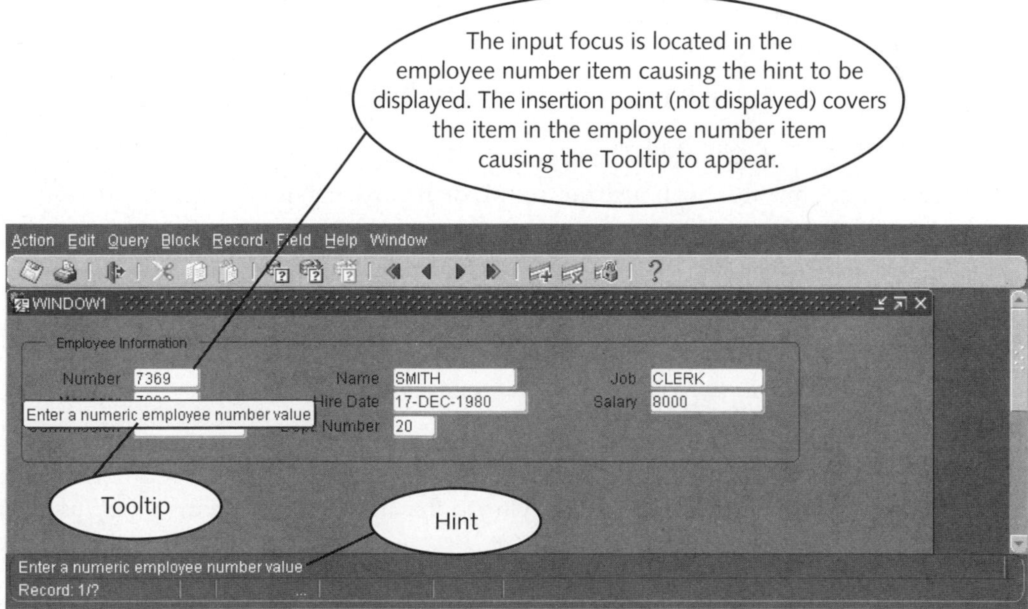

Figure 7-6 Example of a hint and Tooltip

Hints are an old Forms Builder feature designed for character-based systems used on mainframes. A more recent innovation is the **Tooltip**. This is a message that is displayed whenever the insertion point is placed over an item. Toolbars often have Tooltips to explain the functions of each of their tools. Forms Builder enables you to add a Tooltip to any form item. Set the Tooltip message by modifying the item's Tooltip property. Forms Builder also has a complementary property called Tooltip Visual Attribute. This property is used to format the Tooltip.

Of the two features, the Tooltip is more likely to grab the user's attention, because it appears where the user is currently looking. Hints are displayed on the status line, which the user may not even notice. The primary benefit of the hint is its length. The status line can accommodate a longer message.

To practice setting item properties, perform the following steps to create a new form module and data block based on the EMP table. The data block should be a Form style and display one record:

1. Open the Object Navigator and create a new form module. Using the Data Block and Layout wizards, add a new data block based on the EMP table. The layout will be form with one record displayed.
2. Expand the EMP data block and select the **EMPNO** item.
3. Open the selected item's Property Palette by double-clicking the **EMPNO** item icon or pressing the **F4** key.
4. Set the corresponding values for the following properties:

   Hint: **ENTER A NUMERIC EMPLOYEE NUMBER VALUE**

   Display Automatic Hint: **YES**

   Tooltip: **ENTER A NUMERIC EMPLOYEE VALUE**

   Required: **NO**
5. Save the form as **practice01.fmb** for later use.
6. Launch the form. Make sure the input focus is in the **EMPNO** item. Notice the hint displayed on the left side of the status line.
7. Place your cursor over the **EMPNO** item. Notice the Tooltip that appears.

USING TEXT AND DISPLAY ITEMS

Text and display items are the two most common form items, and both are used to display character and numeric data. They differ in that a text item can be used to modify a value, whereas a display item cannot. Because display items are read-only, users cannot tab or place the insertion point into the item. This makes them a good choice for descriptive values that are added to a data block to describe another value. For example, the DEPTNO column (department number) in the EMP table is a code. It is useful to display the DNAME value from the DEPT table, along with the DEPTNO value. However, because DNAME is a descriptive value that does not relate to the block's data source, it cannot be updated. For this reason, display items are excellent tools to use with these values. Display items are also good tools for items that should not be updated, such as primary key value. Table 7-2 shows differences between a display and text item.

Table 7-2 Text item and display item differences

Item feature	Display item	Text item
Must be read-only	Yes	No
Can control case with a property	No	Yes
Can display data on multiple lines within the item	No	Yes

Text Items and the Multi-Line Property

Text items have a Multi-Line property that allows the value to be displayed on multiple lines. In the Case Project, several items have lengths of 100 or more. In fact, the WO_INSTRUCTIONS column in the WORK_ORDERS table from the Case Project has a length of 2000. It is impractical and, in the case of WO_INSTRUCTIONS, impossible to display the entire value on one line. For these types of values, it is best to enable the operator to place the insertion point into the item and display additional text as the cursor is moved to the end of the item.

The Multi-Line property allows you to avoid this problem and display more of the value. It allows you to increase the height of the object rather than the width, in order to see the value. The property also allows you to have more diverse information in your data block. It is common to have a large column in a table used to record comments or other textual information. Setting the column length to 2000 and the data type to VARCHAR2 gives the operator a location for entering a lengthy value without taking up disk space when the field is not used.

Text items also have two useful properties that are related to the Multi-Line property as follows:

- **Wrap Style**: Determines when the text is moved to a new line. The default is WORD, which moves any partially complete word onto a new line. The CHARACTER setting breaks a word, leaving orphan characters whenever the item width is met. The NONE setting does not wrap the value.
- **Show Vertical Scroll Bar**: Causes a scroll bar to be displayed on the right side of the item. This tool allows the operator to scroll through the text.

Figure 7-7 illustrates a multi-line text item that contains Lincoln's Gettysburg Address. It contains a scroll bar and uses the Word wrap style.

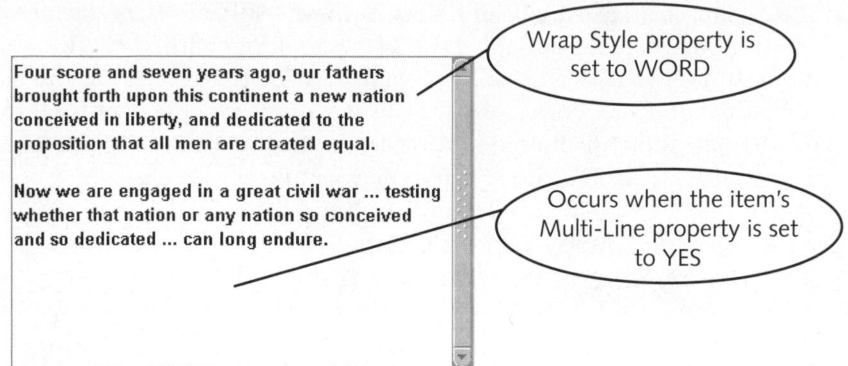

Figure 7-7 Multi-line item

Concealing Data

Text items have a useful feature that can be used for the entry of passwords or other security values. Many systems require their operators to enter a user name and password before entry into the system to authenticate the operator. It is common practice to conceal or hide the password so that onlookers cannot see the value. An especially effective tool changes any typed character into a meaningless symbol, such as an asterisk (*). This enables the user to know that a character was typed but keeps an onlooker from knowing what character was entered.

The Conceal Data property does just that. It displays an asterisk in place of any character that is entered. Figure 7-8 illustrates this property. The ENAME item's Conceal Data property was set to YES. A value was entered, and asterisks appear in the text item.

In this exercise, you practice and evaluate the concepts learned in this section.

1. Open the form you saved in the last practice session **(practice01.fmb)** in the Object Navigator.
2. Open the Layout Editor and select the **ENAME** (employee name) item.
3. Double-click the **ENAME** item to open a Property Palette for the item.
4. Change the Conceal Data property to **YES**.
5. Double-click the **MGR** (manager) data item. Change the Item Type property value from TEXT ITEM to **DISPLAY ITEM**.
6. Run the form and execute a query. Notice that the ENAME value contains asterisks. Enter a value into the **ENAME** item. Notice that the value is concealed.
7. Try to enter a value into the **MGR** item. Notice that you cannot tab or place your insertion point into the item. Close the form.

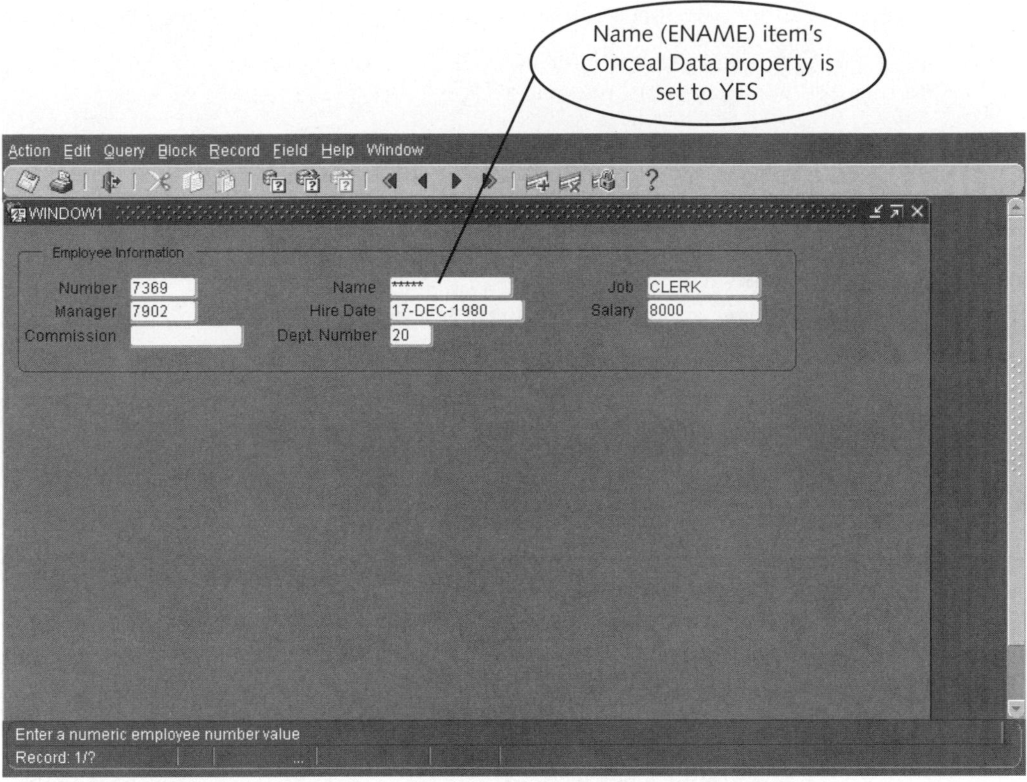

Figure 7-8 Using the Conceal Data property to hide the ENAME item value

8. Open the Layout Editor. Click the **Text Item** tool. Place a new text item on the canvas. Grab the ends of the text item and size it approximately 100 × 200 points.
9. Open a Property Palette for this item. Set the following properties to the corresponding values:
   - Multi-Line: **YES**
   - Wrap Style: **WORD**
   - Show Vertical Scroll Bar: **YES**
   - Database Item: **NO**
   - Maximum Length: **2000**
10. Launch the form, perform a query, and add the Gettysburg Address or several paragraphs from this book into the item, until you understand how the item is used. Be sure to try indenting with the Tab key. Notice that it does not indent but moves the input out of the text item to another item.
11. Close the form and change the Wrap Style property to **CHARACTER**.

12. Launch the form and add text. Compare how the item operates now.
13. Save the form for later use.

CREATING AND USING A CHECK BOX

A **check box** is a graphic item that is used when the item can only have one of two values. An entity attribute, such as gender, is a good example. Check boxes are also used in questionnaires when an answer is YES or NO. The benefit of the check box is that users do not have to type in a value; they simply check or uncheck the check box by clicking it.

Check boxes are created using any of the methods mentioned earlier in this chapter. The properties that you set for check boxes are listed here:

- **Label**: Check boxes are essentially text items that have a check box and descriptive text inside the item. Check boxes do not have prompts. The meaning of the check box is identified by the text within the item. The Label property is used to document the descriptive text that is displayed within the item.
- **Value when Checked**: Identifies the item value when the box is checked.
- **Value when Unchecked**: Identifies the item value when the box is unchecked.
- **Check Box Mapping of Other Values**: Determines whether the box is checked or unchecked and if the item has a value different from those designated in the previous two properties.

The Check Box Mapping of Other Values property is important to consider. Should you decide to set this property value to CHECKED, whenever the item contains a NULL, the box is checked. This can be misleading, because the operator could believe that the item has a value other than NULL. Thus, you may want to leave this property value as UNCHECKED.

Because a check box item is really a text box, it has its own fill color. You cannot set the Fill property to NO FILL, because the check box resides in the item. If the fill is removed, the check box is also removed. If you want the label to appear to reside on the canvas rather than inside the item, you must set the fill color of the check box item to the same color as the underlying canvas. Figure 7-9 illustrates two check boxes. The top description uses the same color fill as the canvas; the bottom description uses the default white fill.

The When-Check-Box trigger is used in conjunction with a check box. It is fired after an action occurs on the check box. It can be used to issue DML commands or to perform other work, such as populating another item.

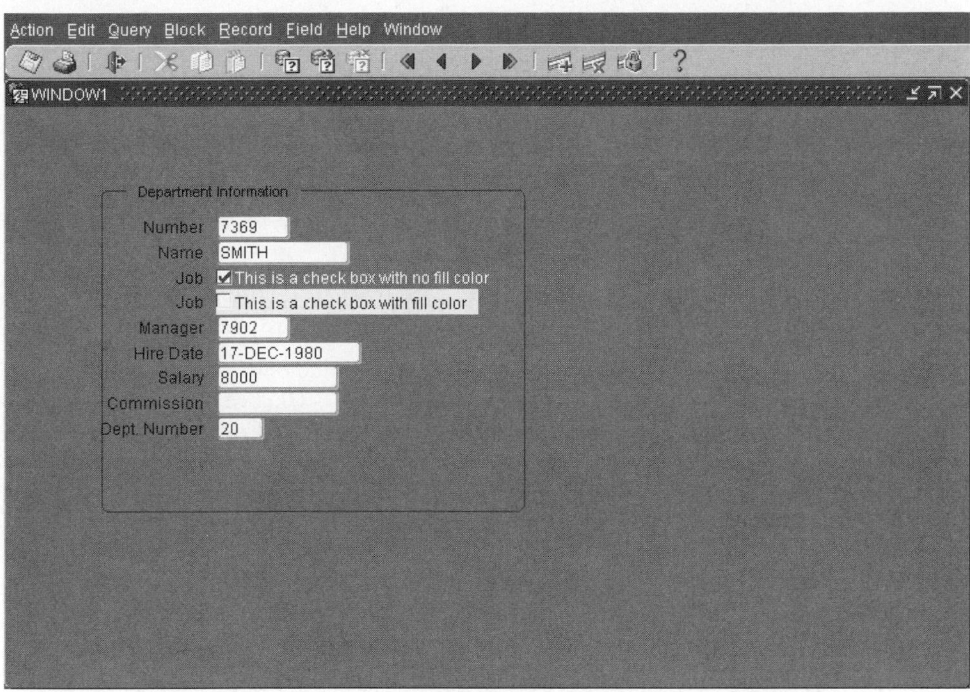

Figure 7-9 Example check boxes with and without the canvas color fill

In this exercise, you practice the concepts learned in this section.

1. Open the practice form **practice01.fmb** in the Object Navigator.
2. Locate and double-click the **JOB** item to open a Property Palette for the item and make the following changes:
   a. Change the Item Type property to **Check box**.
   b. Set the Value When Checked property to **MANAGER**.
   c. Set the Label property to **CHECK WHEN EMPLOYEE IS A MANAGER**.
   d. Set the Check Box Mapping of Other Values property to **UNCHECKED**.
   e. Open the Layout Editor. You will probably not see the entire check box label. Select the **JOB** item and move it to an open location. Resize the item so that its Label value can be seen.
   f. Launch the form. Execute a query and scroll through the records. Notice that all MANAGERS display a check mark.
   g. Save the form for later use.

Creating and Using Radio Groups

A **radio group item** is used when the item has more than two values. The group consists of a series of mutually exclusive buttons. These buttons are called **radio buttons**, and they represent distinct item values. They are placed inside a group, because only one of the buttons can be selected at a time, just as only one button can be selected on a car radio. The button that is currently selected supplies the value to the item. Radio groups allow the user to avoid having to type in a value.

When an item is designated as a radio group, Forms Builder adds a Radio Button child node under the item (see Figure 7-10). You must then add a radio button object for each possible value. To illustrate, the JOB item has five distinct values: PRESIDENT, MANAGER, SALESMAN, ANALYST, and CLERK. In Figure 7-10, five objects were created for the five distinct values. Forms Builder then creates five radio button objects, each with a radio button and a descriptive label.

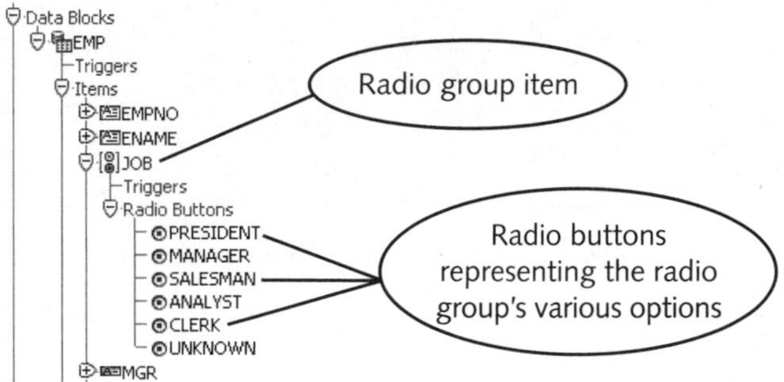

Figure 7-10 Object Navigator displaying the JOB radio group and radio buttons

Radio buttons do not have prompts; they have labels similar to check boxes. Radio groups and buttons have properties similar to check boxes, but the properties are located on both the radio group and radio buttons. The properties are:

- **Label**: The text that describes the radio button. It is located in the radio button area to the right of the button. This property is located on the radio button object.
- **Value**: The value represented by the radio button. This property is located on the radio button object.
- **Mapping of Other Values**: This property determines which button should be selected if an undefined value is encountered. This property is located on the radio group object.

To create a radio group and buttons, you would perform the following steps:

1. Create an item using one of the methods described earlier in this chapter.
2. Open the item's Property Palette and set the Item Type property to RADIO GROUP.

3. Set the Mapping of Other Values property.
4. Open the Object Navigator and locate the radio group.
5. Create a radio button object under the radio group for each distinct item value.
6. Double-click a radio button to open its Property Palette. Set the Label and Value properties.
7. Repeat Step 6 for each radio button.
8. Open the Layout Editor. The radio buttons are located in the top-left corner of the canvas at position 0,0. The buttons overlie each other.
9. Click the radio button and drag it to the desired location on the canvas.
10. Resize the radio button and set the fill color.
11. Repeat steps 9 and 10 for each radio button.

Figure 7-11 depicts a form with a set of radio buttons for the JOB data item in the EMP table. The Unknown button is currently selected, because the form is not displaying any values. The UNKNOWN value was set as the default value in the Mapping of Other Values property.

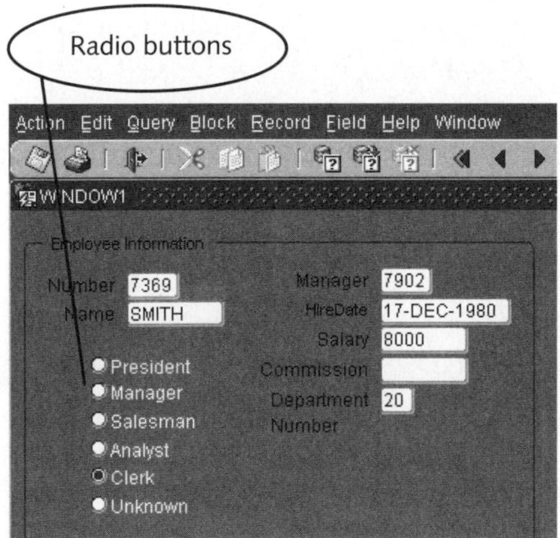

Figure 7-11 JOB radio buttons

In the following exercise, you practice the concepts learned in this section:

1. Open the practice form **practice01.fmb** in the Object Navigator.
2. Open a Property Palette for the JOB data item.
   a. Set the Item Type property to **RADIO GROUP.** Notice that the properties change because the JOB item formerly was a check box.

b. Change the Item Type back to **CHECK BOX**. Notice that the radio group properties return along with the original values. Return the Item Type to **RADIO GROUP**.

c. Set the Mapping of Other Values property to **UNKNOWN**.

d. In the Object Navigator, expand the **JOB** item.

e. Select the **Radio Buttons** node. Click the **Create** tool six times creating six child radio buttons for the JOB radio group item. They should be named: **PRESIDENT**, **MANAGER**, **SALESMAN**, **ANALYST**, **CLERK**, and **UNKNOWN**.

f. Set the radio button properties. Each item's Label and Radio Button Value properties should be the same value as its name (i.e., the PRESIDENT item has a label of President and a radio button value of PRESIDENT).

g. Open the Layout Editor. The radio buttons are located in the top-left corner of the canvas at position 0,0. They overlie each other.

h. Select the top **radio button**. Resize the item so that the label is displayed and move the radio buttons to a visible location. Set the fill color if necessary.

i. Repeat Step h for each of the radio buttons.

j. Operate the form and launch a query. Scroll through the records and watch the radio group values change.

k. Modify one of the employee records setting the JOB value to **UNKNOWN**. Save the record. Use SQL*PLUS to see what value was placed in the database.

l. Save the form for later use.

Creating and Using a Poplist, TList, or a Combo Box

The next Forms Builder item type is a **list item**. This type allows the operator to choose a value from a list of values. There are three styles of list items (see Figure 7-12) that are determined by the List Style property. The styles are:

- **Combo Box**: Allows the operator to enter one or more characters into the item. When the list is displayed by clicking the open list arrow on the right side of the item, Forms Builder locates the first occurrence of the characters in the value list and populates the item with this value. If this item is not the proper value, the operator can choose a different value. This style works best when the values list is long or it would be inconvenient for the operator to type values into the item.
- **Poplist**: Is similar to the combo box style except that the operator cannot type a value. The operator must open the list and select a value.

- **Tlist**: Consists of a text item and two tools located on the right portion of the text item. The top tool is the Up tool and increases the value in the text item when it is pressed. The bottom tool is the Down tool and decreases the value when it is pressed. When this style is used, the user never sees a list of values. The user must use the Up and Down tools to locate the desired value.

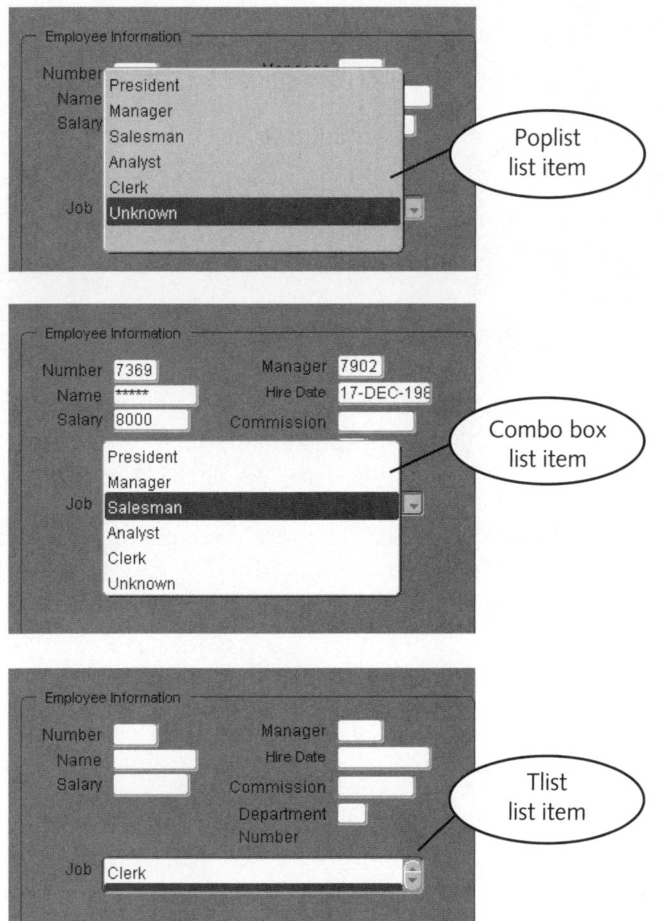

Figure 7-12 List item styles

List item objects have the following three properties of interest:

- **List Style**: This property determines the list style. Styles include POPLIST, TLIST, and COMBO BOX.
- **Mapping of Other Values**: This property determines which list value to use if the item contains a value not on the list.
- **Element in List**: Opens the List Elements dialog box used to enter the static list values (see Figure 7-13).

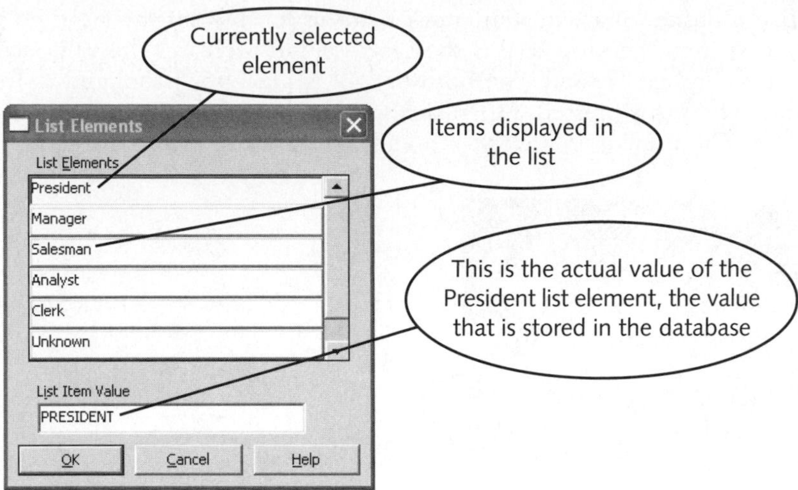

Figure 7-13 List Elements dialog box

Static values are added to the item using the List Elements dialog box (see Figure 7-13), which contains two sections. The top section is used to record the value description displayed in the list and in the form. In Figure 7-13, this is the mixed-case version of the JOB values. Mixed case was used because it is more readable than uppercase. At the bottom of the dialog box is a List Item Value text item. This item contains the actual item value for the selected display value. This is the value that is stored in the database. List items are useful in masking codes, because the operator does not have to see codes or non-descriptive values.

Values are entered into the List Elements dialog box by:

1. Placing the insertion point into the first open List Elements row and entering a value description.
2. Moving the insertion point into the List Item Value text item and entering the item's actual value.

Lists are not ordered. They display the values in the order that they are listed in the List Elements dialog box. It is often necessary to put the values into a specific order or to modify an existing list. The following directions describe how to insert a new row or delete an existing row for the dialog box:

- **Inserting a new row**: A new row can be inserted immediately after the selected row by pressing the Control and Shift keys and clicking the right arrow button.
- **Deleting an existing row**: The currently selected row can be deleted by pressing the the Control and Shift keys and clicking the Left Arrow button.

To create a list item, you would perform the following steps:

1. Create a block item using any of the techniques discussed earlier in the chapter.
2. Open the Property Palette for the list item.
3. Set the Item Type property to LIST ITEM.
4. Set the List Style property to the desired style.
5. Set the Mapping of Other Values property.
6. Click the Elements in List property. Click the **More** button to open the List Elements dialog box.
7. Add the value descriptions and values.
8. Close the dialog box and test by executing the form and using the list item.

List items have a When-List-Changed trigger that is fired each time a list value is changed.

Adding List Values Dynamically

It is possible to replace or add a value list to an item. This can be useful when the value list can change. For example, our practice database has a table named DEPT. It contains the names and IDs of the various departments. The department number column is a foreign key to the employee records in the EMP table. Developers like to use list items for these kinds of database columns, especially if the number of values is limited. The list would displace the descriptive names, and the non-descriptive foreign key value is saved in the database. However, if a new department is added to the database, you will have to modify the application. In this case, it is preferable to have the list added to the item dynamically at runtime. You can then avoid modifying the application.

The Populate_group and the Populate_list built-ins are the appropriate tools for adding a set of values to the list item. The Populate_group built-in is a function that executes a SELECT statement and populates a record group. A **record group** is a form object that holds a set of records or static values. The benefit of a record group is that the record set it holds can be passed to a calling object, such as a list. Creation of a record group is discussed later in this section. For now, it is important to know only that the record group is a form object that can receive and hold a set of records returned by a SELECT statement. The following is a template for the built-in:

```
Numeric_variable := populate_group('record_group_name');
```

The Populate_list built-in is a procedure that is used to populate the list item. The built-in has two parameters. The first is the ID or name of the list item (i.e., EMP.JOB). The second is the ID or name of a record group. The Populate_list built-in passes the item. A template for this built-in is as follows:

```
Populate_list('list_item_name', 'record_group_name');
```

Figure 7-14 illustrates a trigger that queries the DEPTNO table and adds the values to the DEPTNO list item. The built-ins were placed in a form-level When-New-Form-instance trigger that is fired when the form is first opened. The Populate_group function was executed first. It populates a record group called DEPARTMENT. The Populate_list procedure is then executed populating the DEPTNO list item in the EMP block.

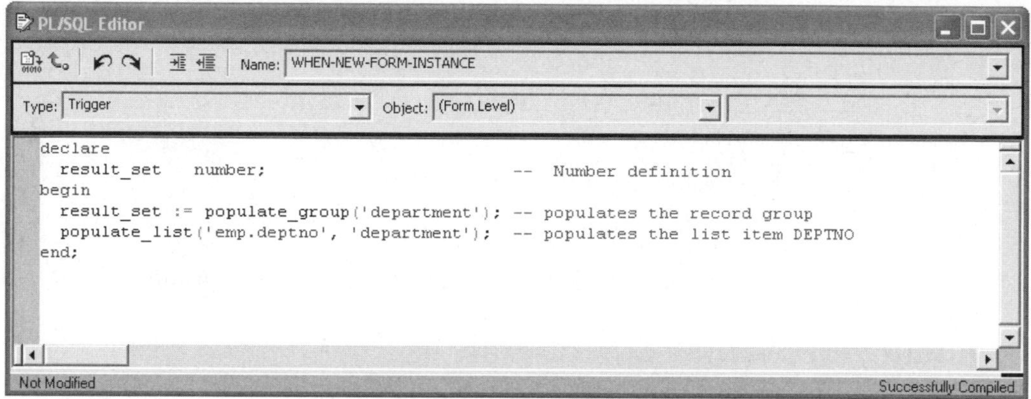

Figure 7-14 When-New-Form-Instance trigger that populates a record group and a list item

It is important to remember the following concepts about adding list values at runtime:

- The record group SELECT statement should contain two expressions. The first expression supplies the list label values. The second expression supplies the actual value. The following SELECT statement can be used to populate the DEPTNO list item:

```
SELECT dname, deptno from dept;
```

The DNAME values will be displayed in the list item, and the DEPTNO values will be the item's actual value.

- The list item must have a default static list, even though it is populated dynamically. The form does not compile if it is omitted.

Single elements can also be added and removed from the list by using two built-ins: Add_list_element and Delete_list_element. The Add_list_element built-in has the following four parameters:

- **List ID or Name**: The name or Oracle ID of the list item.
- **List Index Value**: A number that determines the location of the inserted element. All list elements have values with the first element number 1.
- **Label Value**: The value that is displayed on the inserted element row.
- **Item Value**: The element's actual value.

The following is a syntax template for the Add_list_element built-in:

```
Add_list_element('list_name', index_value', 'label', 'value');
```

The Delete_list_element has two parameters, the LIST_ID and the index value.

In the following exercise, you practice the concepts learned in this section:

1. Open the practice form **practice01.fmb** in the Object Navigator. Double-click the **JOB** data item to open its Property Palette.
2. Set the following properties:
   - Item Type: **LIST ITEM**
   - List Style: **POPLIST**
   - Mapping of Other values: **UNKNOWN**
3. Click the **Elements in List** property and open the List Elements dialog box by clicking the **More** button.
4. Add the following elements and corresponding list item values. Overtype the default element and value.
   - President: **PRESIDENT**
   - Manager: **MANAGER**
   - Salesman: **SALESMAN**
   - Analyst: **ANALYST**
   - Clerk: **CLERK**
   - Unknown: (no value should be added)
5. Run the form and execute a query.
6. Move your insertion point to the JOB item and open the list for the item. Select a different job value for the item. Notice that the JOB item is populated with your selected value. Close the form.
7. Change the JOB data item List Style to **TLIST**. Run the form and operate the list.
8. Change the List Style to **COMBO BOX**. Run the form and operate the list.
9. Enter **CL** into the JOB combo box. Open the list. Notice that CLERK is selected in the list.
10. Save the practice form for later use.

7

Adding an Image to the Form

Adding images to a form can make it more useful and pleasing to view. For example, you may want to display an employee's image in a form or possibly an equipment schematic that has been scanned into a file. An item can be made to hold images by changing the Item Type property to IMAGE. Image items can hold and display the following types of image files: **bmp**, **cals**, **gif**, **jfif**, **pict**, **ras**, **tiff**, and **tpic**.

Image items have the following unique properties:

- **Image Format**: Identifies the type of image file that the item will display.
- **Image Depth**: Determines the image depth setting applied to an image being read from or written to a file in the file system. Valid values are: ORIGINAL, MONOCHROME, LUT (Lookup Table), and RGB (Red, Green, Blue).
- **Compress Quality**: Determines whether an image object should be compressed, and if so, to what degree.
- **Display Quality**: Determines the quality of the display. The poorer the quality, the better the performance.
- **Show Palette**: Causes an Image-Manipulation Palette to be displayed adjacent to the image. The Palette has tools to zoom, pan, or rotate the image.
- **Sizing Style**: Used when the image size does not match the size of the image item. Settings are: CROP, which displays only the portion of the full image that fits in the display rectangle, and ADJUST, which scales the image to fit within the display rectangle.

Populating the Image Item

Images cannot be associated to the image item during application design; they must be placed into the image item during runtime. There are two techniques for populating the item: 1) executing the Read_image_file built-in; 2) cutting an image into the clipboard and pasting it into the image item. The Read_image_file built-in can be fired from a form-level When-New-Form-Instance trigger or from an item-level When-Button-Pressed trigger. The latter trigger is effective, if the operator wants see an image only at particular times. The following script can be used to populate the image item in either of the two triggers:

```
Read_image_file ('c:\photo_file.bmp', 'BMP', 'photo.picture');
Read_image_file ('c:\photo_file.bmp', 'BMP', 'photo.picture1');
```

Figure 7-15 depicts two images in a Web form that are displayed using the script shown above in a When-Button-Pressed trigger. Two images are displayed to show you the differences that result from their properties. The properties are listed in Table 7-3. The CROP setting used in the left picture did not reduce the image as the ADJUST setting did. You should also notice that the right picture does not have a palette, even though the property was set. The palette is not displayed in Web forms. It is only used when the form is used in a client-server environment.

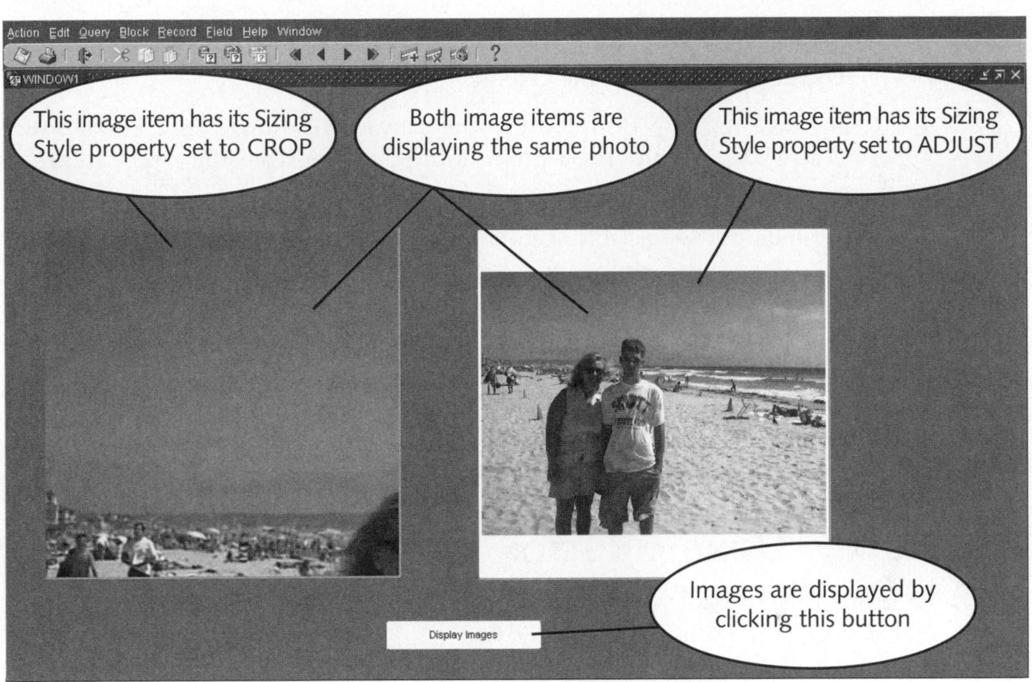

Figure 7-15 Two image items populated with the Read_image_file built-in

Table 7-3 Image property setting used for Figure 7-15

Property	Left picture setting	Right picture setting
Show Palette	NO	YES
Sizing Style	CROP	ADJUST

You should not confuse image items with imported images that are used in a form. Forms Builder allows you to import an image into the form using the File/Import/Image (6*i*) menu selections. These options only appear when the Layout Editor is the current IDE window. This tool opens the Import Image dialog box. The dialog box is used to identify and import an image into the form. The image can then be used like any other graphic object, such as a rectangle, arc, or line. The image item, on the other hand, is an item just like any other item. It is only used to hold an image that is brought into the form.

In the following exercise, you practice the concepts learned in this section by creating a new form module:

1. Open the Object Navigator and create a canvas.
2. Create a control block. This is a data block not associated to a table.

3. Open the Layout Editor.
4. Click and activate the **Image Item** tool.
5. Move the insertion point to the canvas. Hold down the **Left Mouse** button and drag the insertion point until you have sized the image item to approximately 3" square.
6. Open the Object Navigator and create a form-level When-New-Form-Instance trigger. Use a script similar to the previous Read_image_file example that populates the image item.
7. Launch the form and determine whether the image is displayed.
8. Change properties on the image item and determine their effect.
9. This form can be discarded since it is not used in other practice sessions.

CREATING AND USING A BUTTON

Buttons are extremely useful graphical tools for forms. Because a form is an event-driven application, the When-Button-Pressed trigger associated to a button can launch an event. In the previous section, you saw that a button was used to execute the Read_image_file built-in that populated the image item. Buttons are commonly used to perform the same actions as function keys or to launch other forms or applications such as a report. An operator, especially an infrequent operator, often forgets the proper function key. However, the operator does not have trouble locating and clicking a button. Thus, buttons are useful tools for enabling the operator to perform needed tasks.

Buttons are sometimes placed on the normal canvas at strategic locations. They are also used on toolbars. Each of these toolbar tools is actually an **iconic button**. In essence, these are buttons that display an image rather than text. A button is an item that is listed under a data block, but it does not have any properties that associate it to the database, such as Database Item, Query Only, and Update Allowed. However, a button does have several properties that are useful for you:

- **Label**: Text that is displayed on the button
- **Iconic**: Determines whether the button is iconic
- **Icon Filename**: Name of the file that supplies the image for the button

To create a button, you would perform the following steps:

1. Click the Button tool on the Layout Editor toolbar.
2. Locate where you want to place the button. Click and hold the Left Mouse button while dragging and sizing the button.
3. Double-click the button and open its Property Palette.

4. Set the Label, Iconic, and Icon Filename properties.
5. Open the Object Navigator and locate the button object. Create a When-Button-Pressed trigger.

You will often place a button in a form in order to place the form into the Enter Query mode or to launch a query. When the button is added to a master-detail form, it must be associated to a data block. This block might be the master block, the detail block, or even a control block. If the Enter_query built-in is executed by the button's When-Button-Pressed trigger, the built-in will place its associated data block into the Enter Query mode. It's useless to put a detail block or a control block into the Enter Query mode, because a control block cannot execute a query and the detail block always uses master block search values. Thus, when using a button to place a block into Enter Query mode or to execute a query, be sure to use the Go_block built-in to move the input focus to the proper block before executing the query.

In the following exercise, you practice the concepts learned in this section:

1. Using the practice form **practice01.fmb** based on the EMP data block, create four buttons that perform the following functions:
   - Places the EMP data block into the Enter Query mode
   - Places the data block in the Query mode and executes a SELECT statement
   - Saves changes to the form
   - Exits or closes the form

   a. Open the practice form **practice01.fmb** in the Object Navigator.

   b. Open the Layout Editor and click the **Button** tool.

   c. Locate a spot on the canvas and place and size the button.

   d. Select the newly created button and click the **Copy** tool or press the **Control + C** keys.

   e. Paste the button on the canvas using the **Paste** tool or the **Control + V** keys. The pasted button may overlie the original button.

   f. Select the button and drag the new button to the desired location. The original button will remain in its original location

   g. Repeat steps e through f.

   h. Use the Format tools to properly size and arrange the buttons. Double-click the first button to open its Property Palette. Set the Name property to **ENTER** and the Label property to **ENTER QUERY**.

i. Click the second button to display its properties in the Property Palette. Set the Name property to **EXECUTE** and the Label property to **EXECUTE QUERY**.

j. Click the third button to display its properties in the Property Palette. Set the Name property to **SAVE** and the Label property to **SAVE**.

k. Click the fourth button to display its properties in the Property Palette. Set the Name property to **EXIT** and the Label property to **EXIT**.

l. Open the Object Navigator and create a When-Button-Pressed trigger under the ENTER button data block item. Place the following script into the trigger:

```
Enter_query;
```

m. Create a When-Button-Pressed trigger under the EXECUTE button data block item. Place the following script into the trigger:

```
Execute_query;
```

n. Create a When-Button-Pressed trigger under the SAVE button data block item. Place the following script into the trigger:

```
Commit_form;
```

o. Create a When-Button-Pressed trigger under the EXIT button data block item. Place the following script into the trigger:

```
Exit_form;
```

p. Launch the form and use the buttons to place the form into the Enter Query mode, execute a query, save changes, and exit the form.

Creating and Using a Calculated Item

Forms Builder contains a handy feature that enables you to turn an item into a **calculated item**. The calculation can be based on a summarization or a formula. Rather than creating a calculation in a Post-Query trigger and then populating a display item, the formula can be placed directly into the item and calculated when the data block is populated. Calculated items can be used to compute ages of employees based on the current date and a birth date. Another example of a calculated item is the total of a department's employee wages based on the records in a detail data block. Figure 7-16 illustrates a form that contains a calculated item that summarizes the detail block's salary values.

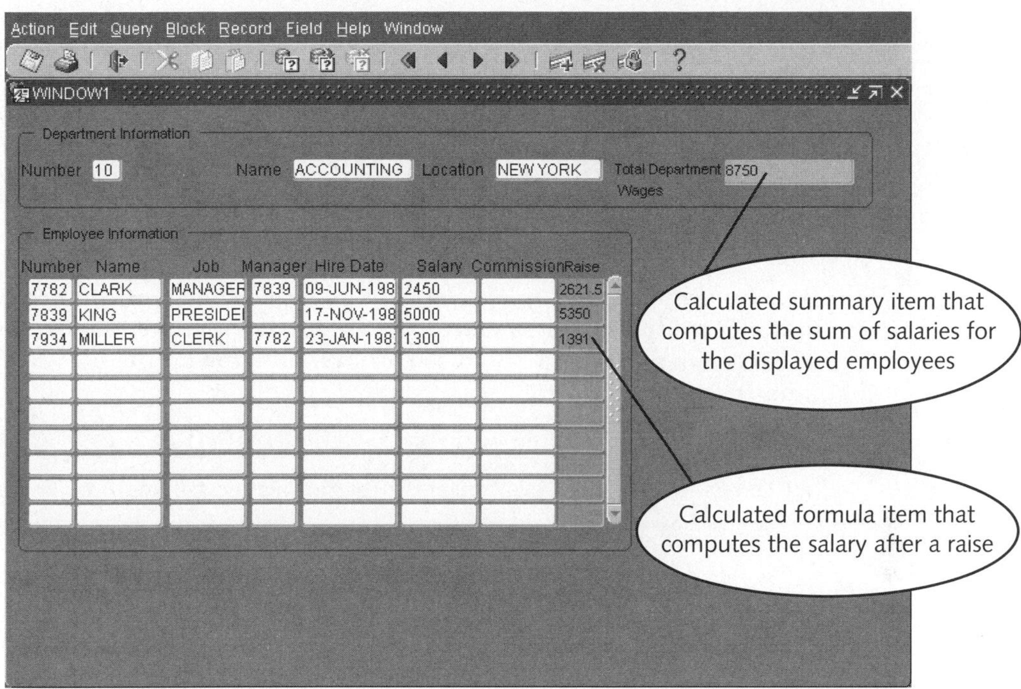

Figure 7-16 Calculated item displaying a department's total employee salaries

Table 7-4 lists a number of properties on both the item and the data block that must be set when placing a calculated item in the form.

Table 7-4 Calculated item properties

Property name	Property location	Description
Calculation Mode	Item	Determines whether the item conducts an aggregation or a calculation based on a formula. Values are NONE, SUMMARY, or FORMULA.
Formula	Item	Launches a Formula dialog box that calculates a value. This property is used only when the Calculation Mode property is set to FORMULA.
Summary Function	Item	Determines the type of aggregation to be performed. Settings are NONE, AVG, COUNT, MAX, MIN, STDDEV, SUM, and VARIANCE.
Summarized Block	Item	Identifies the data block on which the aggregation is to be performed.
Summarized Item	Item	Identifies the data block item that is to be summarized.
Precompute Summaries	Data Block	Causes the data block's records to be summarized. The values are summarized for the calculated item before they are displayed.

To add a Summary calculated item to a form, you would perform the following steps:

1. Open the Layout Editor and activate the Text Item or Display Item tool.
2. Place the item on the canvas.
3. Open the Object Navigator and make sure the calculated item is on the same block that is to be summarized.
4. Open the item's Property Palette.
5. Because this item is in a detail block, it is likely to be repeated because the data block displays multiple records. Change the calculated item's Number of Items Displayed property to **1**. This overrides the data block's Number of Items Displayed property.
6. Set the Calculation Mode property to SUMMARY.
7. Set the Summary Function property to the desired calculation type.
8. Set the Summarized Block property to the name of the summarized block.
9. Set the Summarized Item property to the name of the summarized data block item.
10. Open the Property Palette for the summarized data block. Set the Precompute Summaries property to YES.

There are fewer steps to create a formula column. These steps are:

1. Open the Layout Editor and activate the Text Item or Display Item tool.
2. Place the item on the canvas.
3. Open the Object Navigator and make sure the calculated item is in the same block that supplies the values for the formula.
4. Open the item's Property Palette.
5. Set the Calculation Mode to FORMULA.
6. Click the Formula property and the More button to open the Formula dialog box.
7. Enter the formula.

There are several things to remember about calculated items:

- A calculated item cannot summarize another calculated item.
- Calculated items can only reside in the summarized block or in a block that has only one record, such as a control block.

In this exercise, you practice the concepts learned in this section. You are creating a new practice master-detail form similar to that shown in Figure 7-16. The DEPT table should be the data source of the master block. The EMP table should be the data source of the detail block. You will add a formula column to the EMP block that computes salaries after a 7% raise. To accomplish these functions, perform the following steps:

1. Create a new form module in the Object Navigator.
2. Create a data block based on the DEPT table using the Data Block and Layout Wizards. The block style should be Form, and one record should be displayed.
3. Create a detail data block based on the EMP table using the Data Block Wizard and Layout Wizard. The block style should be Tabular, and ten records should be displayed.
4. Open the Layout Editor and activate the **Display Item** tool.
5. Place the text item on the canvas. It should be located close to the EMP values.
6. Open the Object Navigator and make sure the text item is associated to the EMP block by moving the item to the EMP block.
7. Open a Property Palette for the item.
8. Set the following properties:
   - Name: **RAISE**
   - Data Type: **NUMBER**
   - Calculation Mode: **FORMULA**
   - Prompt: **RAISE**
   - Prompt Attachment Edge: **TOP**
9. Click the **Formula** property to activate it and display the Editor button. Click the button to open the Formula dialog box. Use the following script:

   ```
   :emp.sal * 1.07
   ```
10. Run the form and determine if the calculation is correct.

Now you add a calculated item to the form that summarizes the department's salaries.

1. Open the Layout Editor and activate the **Display Item** tool.
2. Place the display item on the canvas. It should be located close to the DEPT values.
3. Open the Object Navigator and make sure the item is in the EMP block.
4. Open a Property Palette for the item.
5. Set the following properties:
   - Name: **TOTAL_WAGES**
   - Prompt: **TOTAL DEPARTMENT WAGES**

7

- Data Type: **NUMBER**
- Calculation Mode: **SUMMARY**
- Summary Function: **SUM**
- Summarized Block: **EMP**
- Summarized Item: **RAISE**
- Number of Items Displayed: **1**

6. Open a Property Palette for the EMP data block.
7. Set the EMP data block Query All Records property to **YES**.
8. Launch the form and test by executing a query.
9. Save the form for later practice.

ADDING AND USING A LIST OF VALUES (LOV) IN YOUR FORM

Forms Builder has a special object called a LOV that is used to populate and validate a text item value. A **LOV** is a dialog box that is associated with specific form items. The operator can open the LOV and select the value from the displayed list. A LOV can be used in the Enter Query mode to identify selection criteria and in the Normal mode to populate or validate a value. A LOV uses a record group as its source of values. The record group generally uses a SELECT statement as its data source. Thus, the LOV can generate a dynamic set of values. Like list items, LOVs identify values. However, a LOV has the ability to display hundreds and thousands of values. The list item is not effective for displaying more than a dozen values. The LOV allows the operator to scroll through the values or to limit the displayed values based on an entered value.

Figure 7-17 depicts a LOV that displays employee names and IDs. The depicted LOV illustrates several LOV features:

- **Find text item**: Limits the records displayed by the LOV. Entry of a value into the item and clicking the Find button causes Forms Builder to eliminate any values that do not match the criteria. Forms Builder places the wild card symbol (%) into the item by default. It is best to enter several characters and use the wild card symbol. It's often easier to locate values by using fewer search characters. Fewer search characters allow similarly spelled values to display.
- **Value list box**: Displays the values that match the search criteria. When the Find text item contains only %, all of the record group records are returned. Highlighted values are placed into the form items.
- **Find button**: Refreshes the value list using the Find text item value to limit values.

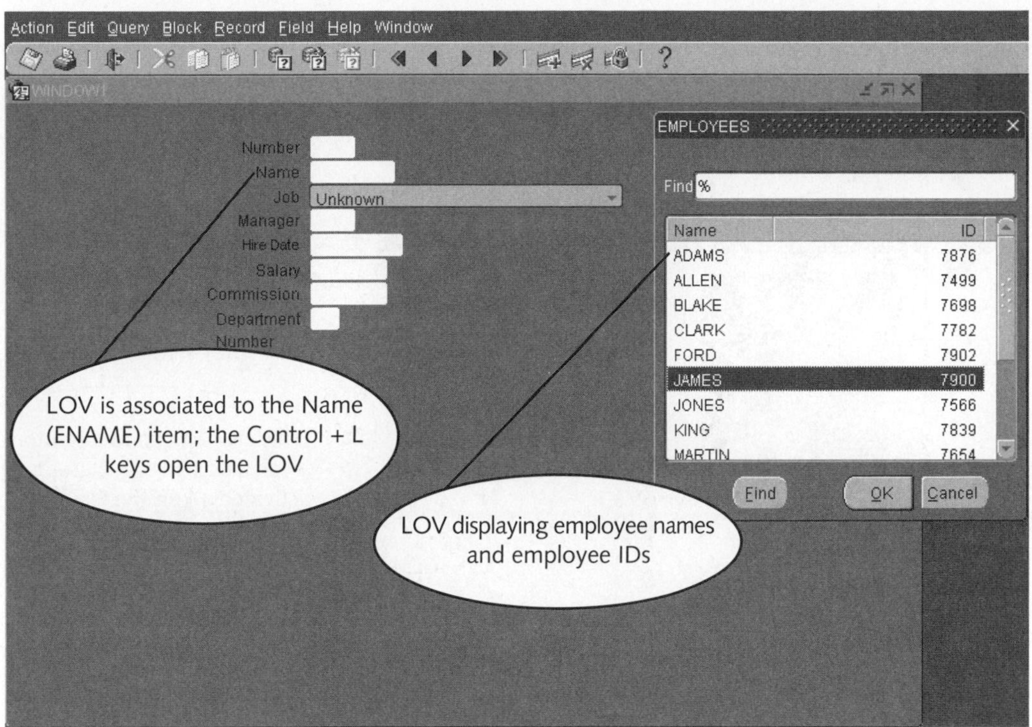

Figure 7-17 LOV displaying employee values

A number of steps are required to create a LOV and its record group. It is possible to create a LOV manually, as was done in older versions of Forms Builder. However, the easiest method is to use the Oracle LOV Wizard, which Oracle has added to the IDE. You would use the following steps to create a LOV:

1. Open the Object Navigator and select the LOVs object.
2. Click the Create tool. This procedure opens a dialog box with two radio buttons asking whether you want to use the wizard or not. Choose the radio button that signifies your intent to use the wizard. As an alternate, you may select the LOV Wizard on the Tools menu.
3. The first wizard page is the Source page (Figure 7-18), which is used to specify whether the LOV will use as a data source a new record group or an existing record group. Selecting the Existing Record Group button enables the drop-down list used to identify a record group.

7

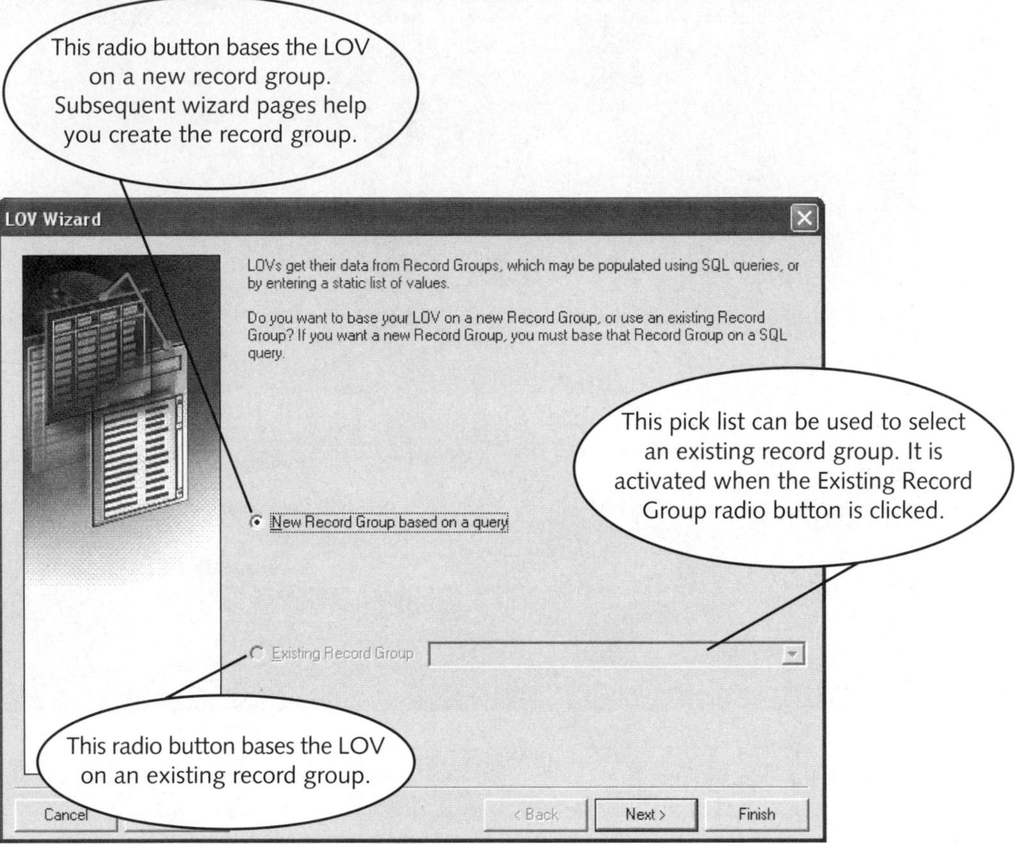

Figure 7-18 LOV Wizard Source page

4. If you selected the New Record Group option on the Source page, the SQL Query page appears as the next wizard page. The SQL Query page (Figure 7-19) is used to add the SELECT statement that will be used in the record group. The page has options for connecting to the database, checking the syntax of the SELECT statement, and launching Query Builder. Query Builder, which is used to create the SELECT statement, is not covered in this text. Forms Builder does not allow you to move from this page unless the SELECT statement is valid.

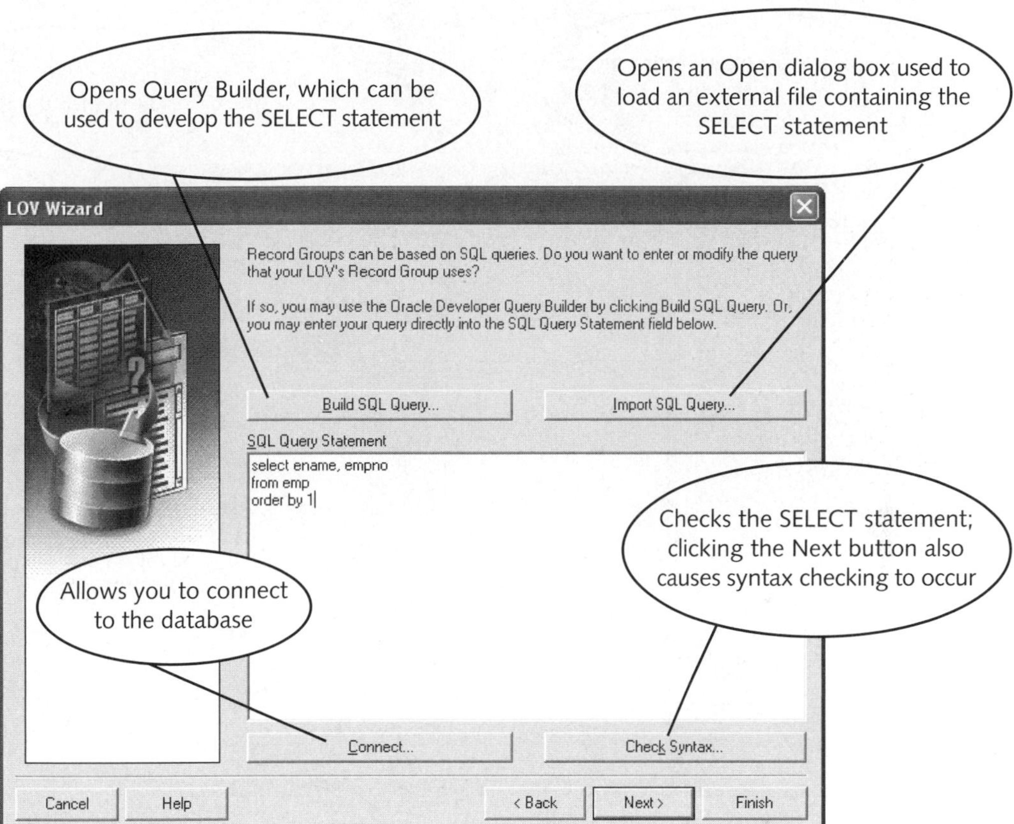

Figure 7-19 LOV Wizard SQL Query page

5. The Column Selection page is next and is used to identify the columns that appear in the LOV. The order shown in the right pane is the order in which they are displayed in the LOV. If you intend to filter the LOV records based on one of the LOV columns, be sure to select that item first. The LOV Wizard Column Selection page is displayed in Figure 7-20.

7

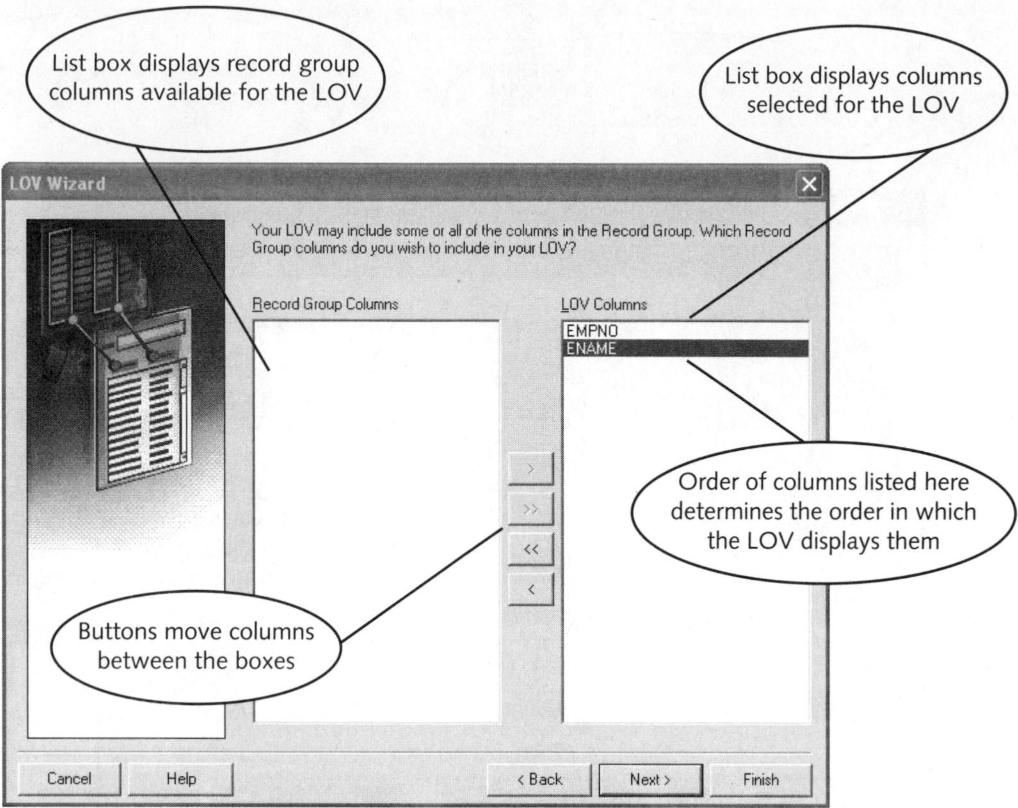

Figure 7-20 LOV Wizard Column Selection page

6. The next page is Column Display (Figure 7-21), which is used to enter a custom column heading. The list box on the right contains four columns: Column (non-changeable), Title, Width, and Return Value. You may modify any of the latter three column properties. Return Value identifies the form item that will receive the selected value. Sometimes columns are placed in the LOV for descriptive purposes only. It is not necessary to populate the return value for these types of columns. Setting the column width to 0 hides the column values, which will not appear in the LOV but can still be used to return a value to a form item. This page has two other features:
   - A radio button named Automatically size columns that overrides the list box width settings. It is a good idea to check this box.
   - A Look up return item button that opens a list box that displays form items that are available to receive a value from the LOV.

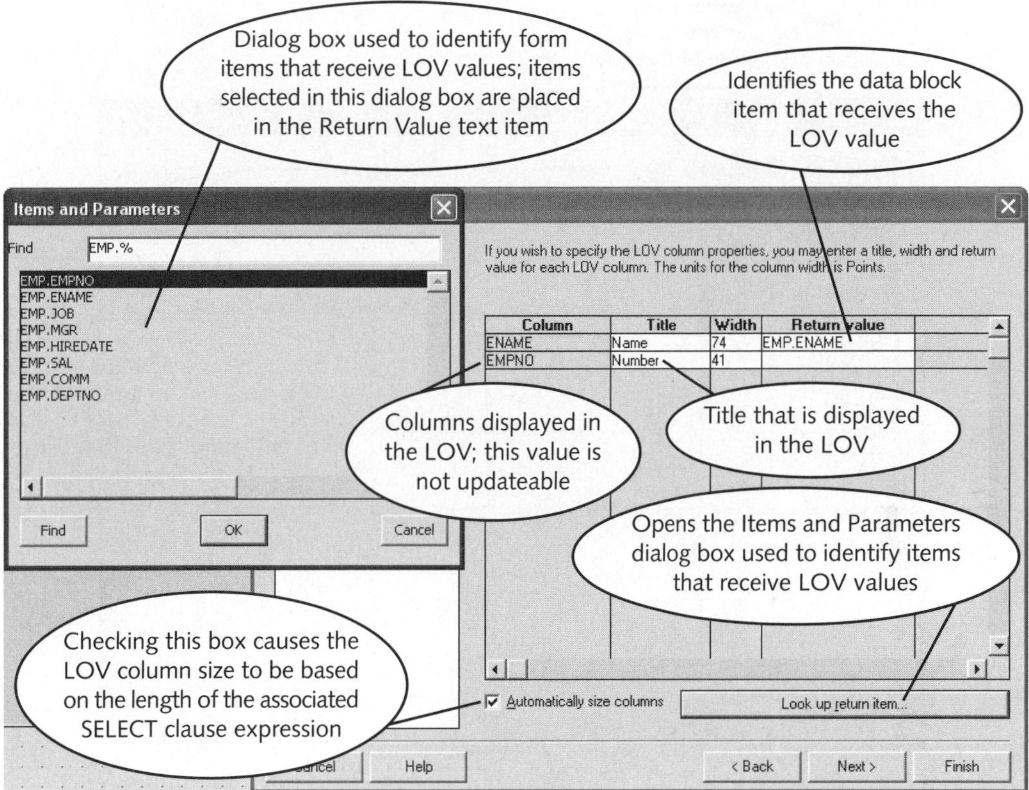

Figure 7-21 LOV Wizard Column Display page

The next LOV Wizard page is the Display page (see Figure 7-22), which determines the displayed position of the LOV, as well as its overall size and title. This page has the following features and settings:

- **Title text item**: Records the LOV's title
- **Width text item**: Sets the width of the LOV in points
- **Height text item**: Sets the height of the LOV in points
- **Radio buttons**: Determine the position of the LOV when it is displayed. The automatic positioning option puts the LOV in the exact center of the form. The manual option enables the left and top text items that allow you to set a different location.

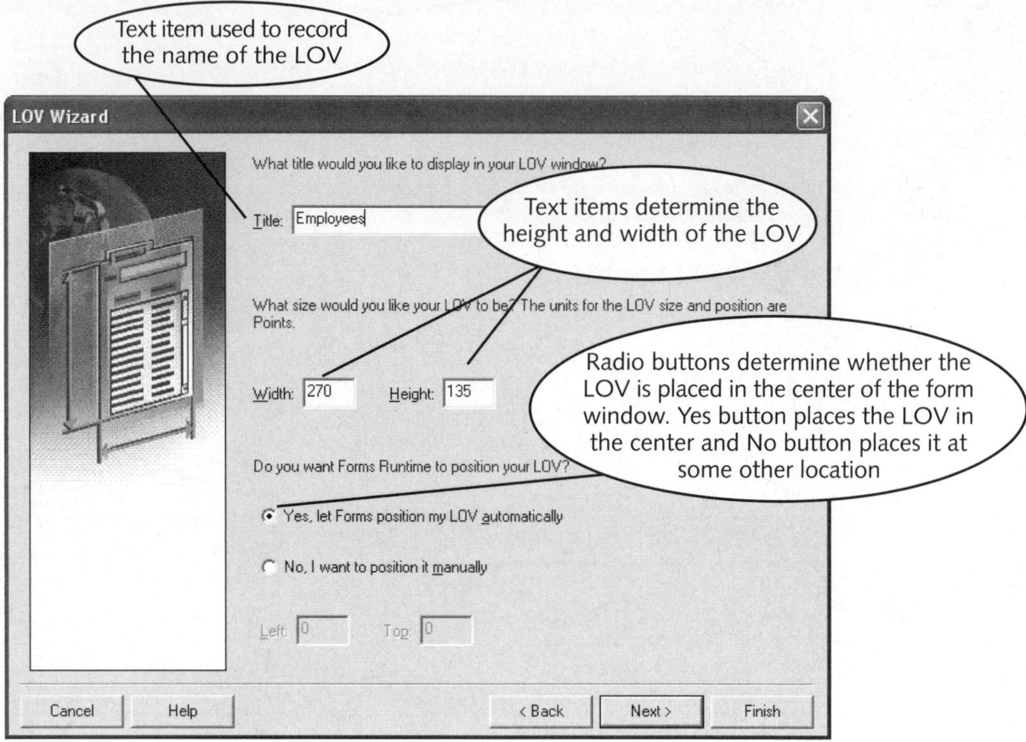

Figure 7-22 LOV Wizard Display page

7. The Advanced Options page, shown in Figure 7-23, is next. Settings on this page can affect the performance of the LOV. The settings are:
   - **Retrieve rows at a time**: Determines the number of records fetched to the screen at one time. The larger the value, the better the performance, but the longer it takes to display the initial values. The smaller the value, the quicker the initial records are displayed, but the longer it takes to scroll through the records.
   - **Refresh record group data before displaying LOV**: Causes the LOV's record group to be repopulated each time the LOV is opened.
   - **Let the user filter records before displaying them**: Disables the automatic population of the record group. This option allows you to enter search criteria into the LOV before the matching records are returned and is useful when the LOV can return a large number of records.

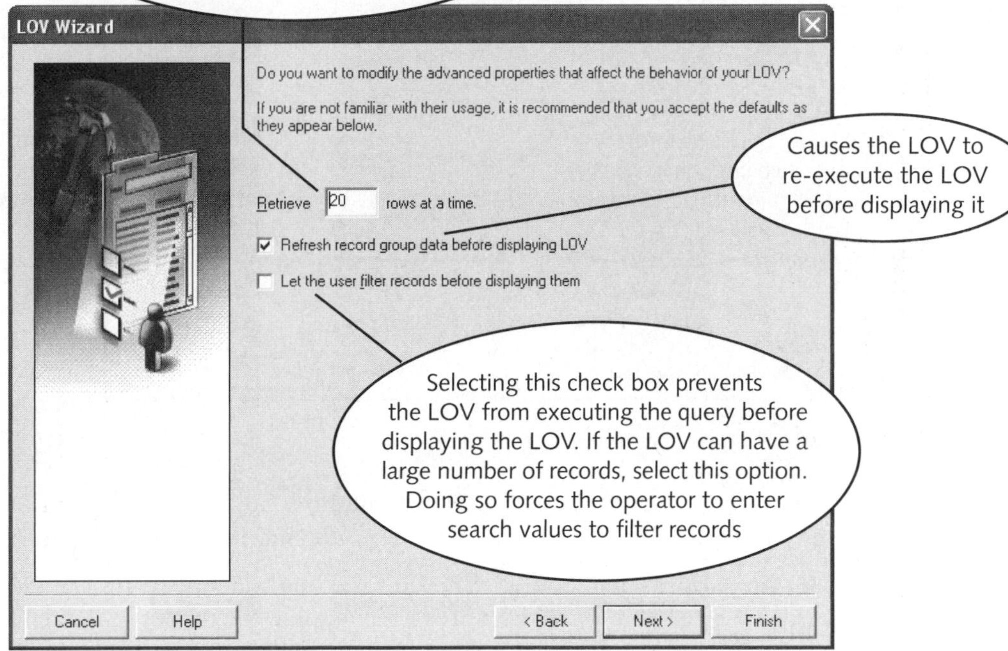
This setting limits the number of records displayed. A lower setting can decrease the response time of the initial display of the LOV. However, it increases the time needed to scroll through the LOV values. A higher value has the opposite effect
LOV Wizard
Do you want to modify the advanced properties that affect the behavior of your LOV?
If you are not familiar with their usage, it is recommended that you accept the defaults as they appear below.
Causes the LOV to re-execute the LOV before displaying it
Retrieve 20 rows at a time.
Refresh record group data before displaying LOV
Let the user filter records before displaying them
Selecting this check box prevents the LOV from executing the query before displaying the LOV. If the LOV can have a large number of records, select this option. Doing so forces the operator to enter search values to filter records
Cancel
Help
< Back
Next >
Finish

Figure 7-23 LOV Wizard Advanced Options page

8. The last LOV Wizard setting page (Figure 7-24) is the Items page, which is used to associate a LOV to a form item. By default, a LOV opens when the operator moves the insertion point into an item associated with a LOV and presses the appropriate function key. The LOV can also be opened:
   - Automatically when the operator moves into the item
   - As the result of pressing the proper function keys
   - After the operator enters an incorrect value and attempts to tab from the item

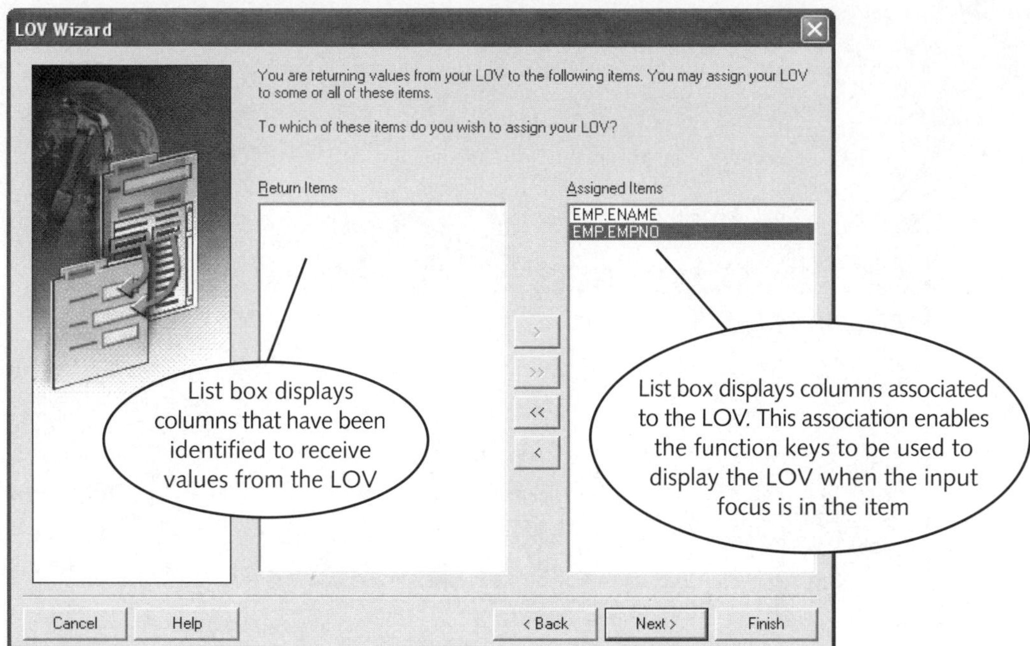

Figure 7-24 LOV Wizard Items page

A LOV cannot be opened using any of these methods, unless it is assigned to the item. The Items page shown in Figure 7-24 has the following features and settings:

- **Return Items list box**: Lists the return items identified on the Column Display page. These are the only items eligible for the assignment. If LOV columns are not associated to a return item, this list box is blank.
- **Assigned Items list box**: Lists the return items assigned to the LOV.

Forms Builder creates two objects when you complete the LOV Wizard. These are the LOV and record group. Forms Builder also gives the objects default names, such as LOV1, LOV2, or LOV3. Fortunately, the LOV and the record group have the same name, so that you can determine the related LOVs and record groups. However, your forms will probably contain a number of LOVs, and it will be difficult for you to identify the LOVs unless you give them your own descriptive names. Thus, after you create a LOV, you should modify both the LOV and record group names in the Object Navigator.

In the following exercise, you practice the concepts learned in this section. Using the practice form **practice01.fmb** that was based on the EMP table, you create a LOV that populates the EMPNO and ENAME items.

1. Open the form in the Object Navigator.
2. Start the LOV Wizard by selecting the **LOV Wizard** menu selection on the Tools menu.
3. On the LOV Wizard Source page, click the **New Record Group Based On A Query** radio button. Click **Next**.
4. Enter the following SELECT statement into the SQL Query page:

   ```
   Select ename, empno from emp order by ename
   ```

5. Click **Next**.
6. On the Column Selection page, move the **ENAME** and **EMPNO** items to the LOV Columns list box. Click **Next**.
7. On the Column Display page, add the following settings:
   - Change the ENAME title to **NAME**.
   - Set the ENAME Return Value setting to **EMP.ENAME** using the Look up return item button.
   - Change the EMPNO title to **ID**.
   - Set the EMPNO Return Value setting to **EMP.EMPNO** using the Look up return item button.
   - Check the **Automatically Size Columns** check box.
8. Click **Next**.
9. On the LOV display page, set the following values:
   - Add the following to the Title text item: **EMPLOYEES**.
   - Set the Width to **210**.
   - Set the Height to **230**.
   - Select **Yes, let Forms position my LOV automatically**.
10. Click **Next** to open the Advanced Options page. Keep the default settings.
11. Click **Next** to open the Items page. Move both the **EMP.EMPNO** and **EMP.ENAME** values to the Assigned Items list box.
12. Click **Finish**.
13. Open the Object Navigator, rename the newly created LOV, and record group object to **EMPLOYEE_NAMES**.
14. Open a Property Palette for the ENAME item. Change the Conceal Data property to **NO**.

15. Open the form and execute a query. Place your insertion point into the EMPNO item. To open the LOV, press the **F9** key (client-server) or the **Control + L** keys (Web).
16. Select a record and click **OK**. Notice that the EMPNO and ENAME columns are populated.
17. Enter the letter **M** in the Find text item. Click the **Find** button to filter the list.
18. Save the form for a later practice session.

Changing the LOV After It Was Created

After you have created the LOV, it is sometimes necessary to modify it. The user may decide the values should be ordered in a different manner or may want to add columns to the LOV record. It is easiest to make these changes by selecting the LOV in the Object Navigator and starting the LOV Wizard. The LOV Wizard dialog box (Figure 7-25) opens with tabs on the top of each of the pages. Locate the proper page and modify the appropriate property.

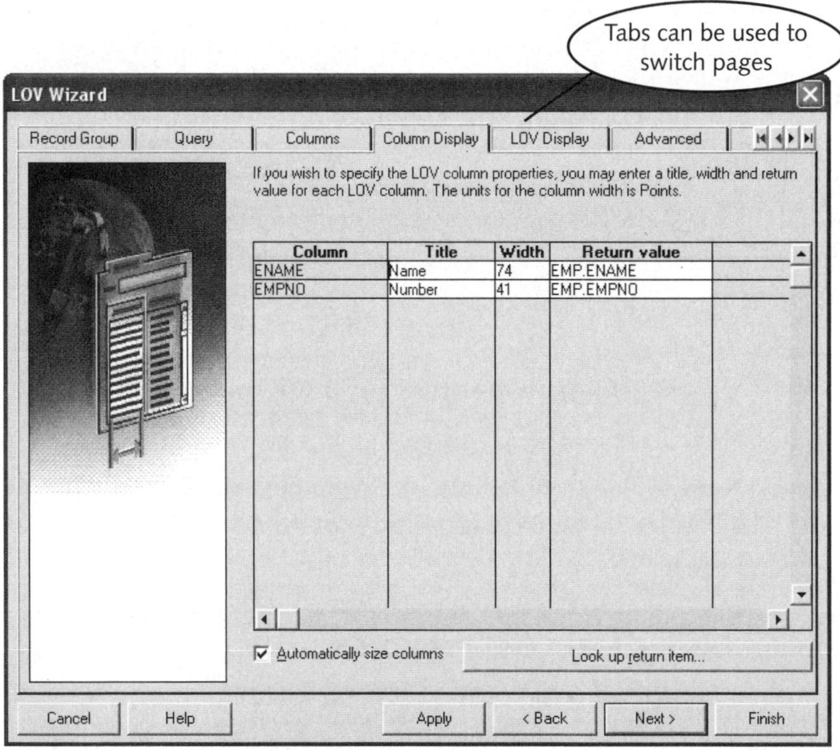

Figure 7-25 LOV Wizard dialog box

You can also modify the LOV by resetting properties in the Property Palette. In fact, the following LOV behaviors can be set only through properties:

- The LOV contents can be used to validate an entered value. The property used to set this validation is called Validate From List.
- LOVs can have different foreground and background colors and fonts. These properties are located in the LOV Property Palette.
- You can set the insertion point to automatically move to the next form item after a value is selected from the LOV. The Automatic Skip property determines this behavior.
- The Automatic Select property causes the LOV value to be placed into the form item when the LOV list only contains a single row.

The important LOV properties are spread across the form item, the LOV, and the record group. Table 7-5 helps you locate the important properties by listing the following: the item on which they are located, whether they can be set in the LOV Wizard, and a short description.

Table 7-5 Properties affecting the LOV

Form object	Property name	Can be set in the wizard	Description
Item	List of Values	Yes	Identifies the LOV to be used by the item.
Item	List X Position	Yes	Identifies the LOV's top-left corner X coordinate relative to the screen.
Item	List Y Position	Yes	Identifies the LOV's upper-left corner Y coordinate relative to the screen.
Item	Validate From List	No	Causes Forms Builder to validate any entered value using the LOV.
LOV	Title	Yes	LOV title.
LOV	Record Group	Yes	Identifies the record group to be used by the LOV.
LOV	Column Mapping Properties	Yes	Opens a LOV Column Mapping dialog box (Figure 7-26) that associates a record group value to a form item, sets the width of the LOV value, and sets the LOV value title. This dialog box works like the List Elements dialog box shown in Figure 7-13.
LOV	Filter Before Display	Yes	Delays the execution of the record group until the operator has a chance to enter selection values. This property should be used if the record group could return many values.
LOV	Automatic Display	No	Displays the LOV automatically each time the operator navigates into the item associated to the LOV.

Table 7-5 Properties affecting the LOV (continued)

Form object	Property name	Can be set in the wizard	Description
LOV	Automatic Select	No	Re-executes the record group's SELECT statement each time the LOV is called.
LOV	Automatic Skip	No	Causes the insertion point to move to the next form item after an item was selected from the LOV.
LOV	Automatic Position	Yes	Places the LOV in the center of the form. This property overrides the properties set in the item.
LOV	Automatic Column Width	Yes	Automatically sizes the width of the LOV columns.
Record group	Record Group Type	Yes and No	Determines whether the record group values will be based on a SELECT statement or will be a static list. The LOV Wizard can only specify that the record group will be based on a query. You must modify this property on the Property Palette if the record group is to be based on a static set of values.
Record group	Record Group Query	Yes	Record group's SELECT statement.
Record group	Record Group Fetch Size	Yes	Determines how many records will be fetched to the LOV at a time.
Record group	Column Specifications	Yes	Determines the column name, data types, and lengths used in the record group. These values are normally set based on data dictionary values when the record group is created.

LOVs and Validation

A LOV is often used to add foreign key values to a data block. Foreign keys are values that are used to relate different table instances. For example, you may want to associate an employee with a department and a work order to a project or to a specific line in an invoice. Regardless of the association, you want a correct value entered. If you don't get the proper value, the integrity of the database is lost because it contains records that have no parents. Thus, it is a good idea to validate all values against a parent table whenever possible, and in the case of foreign key items it is always possible.

The LOV property, Validate From List, allows you to validate values against the list prepared by the LOV. If this property is set to YES, the LOV is called when the operator attempts to move from the form item. If the entered value does not exist in the LOV value list, Forms Builder prevents navigation from the item and displays the LOV. The operator cannot navigate from the item until a proper value has been entered.

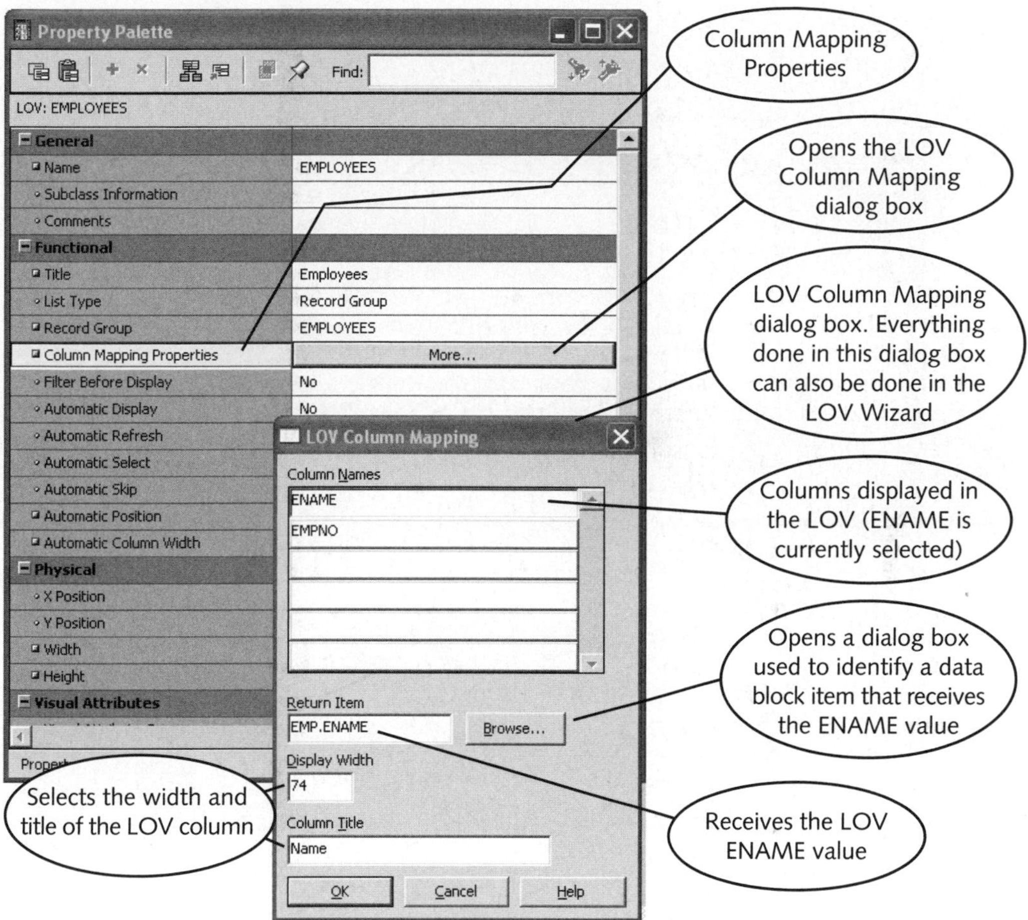

Figure 7-26 LOV Column Mapping dialog box

This feature is illustrated in Figure 7-27. A LOV was associated to the EMPNO item. The operator attempted to enter a value of 35 into the item, which is an invalid value. When the operator attempted to navigate from the item, the LOV was launched.

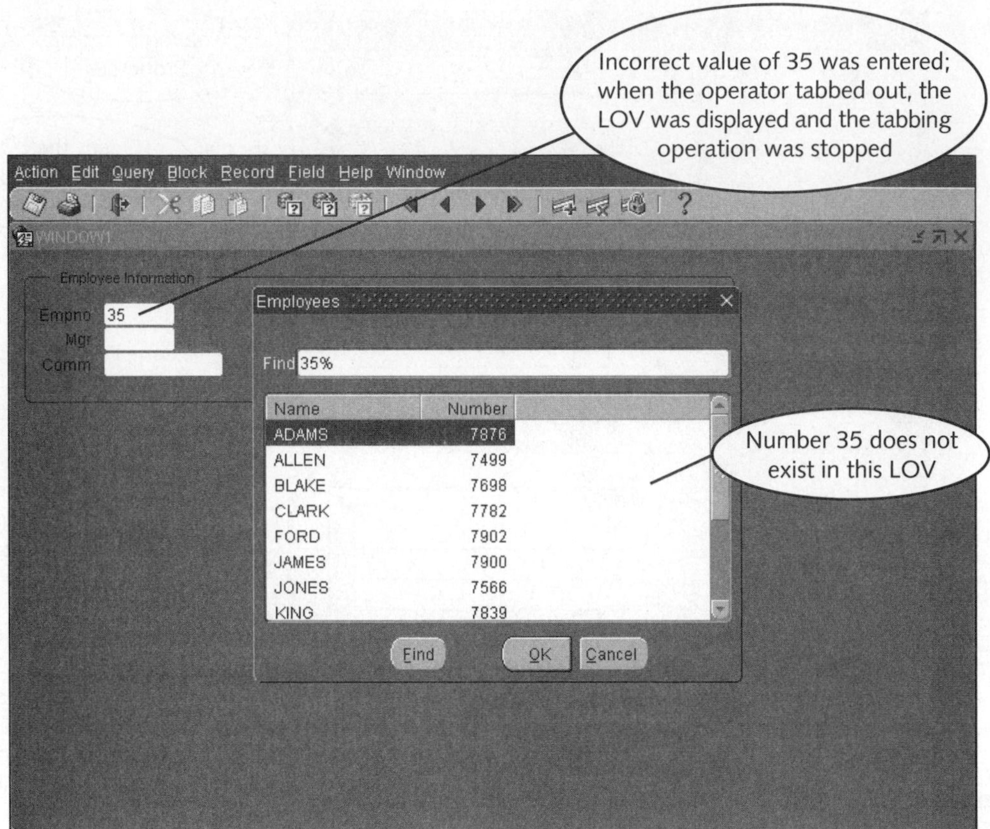

Figure 7-27 LOV displayed after an incorrect value was added into the EMPNO item

Displaying the LOV with a Button

When the insertion point is in an item associated to a LOV, by default LOVs are opened by pressing the F9 key (client-server) or the Control + L keys (Web). There are several problems associated with the default method:

- Users have difficulty identifying a form item that is associated to a LOV. To determine whether an item has an associated LOV, the user must look at the status line (see Figure 7-28). Each time the user navigates into an item that has a LOV, Forms Builder displays a message on the status line. However, users generally do not notice this message at the bottom of the screen.
- Users are not likely to remember which function key to press to open the LOV, and they seldom open the Help Facility to find the proper key.

- If the user happens to realize that an item has a LOV and remembers the function key, the user must move the insertion point to the item and then press the appropriate function key. This requires two actions by the user. If possible, you should minimize user actions.

For these reasons, it is best to place a button next to form items that have associated LOVs and structure the form so that the user clicks the button to open the LOV. The button is in plain view of the user and helps the user recognize that the item has a LOV. In addition, the user need not remember the proper function key to press or perform multiple actions. Figure 7-28 illustrates just such a button that is adjacent to the ENAME item and contains the pipe symbol (| |). It is a good idea to put a symbol on the button. Based on the symbol, users quickly understand the functionality. If you want to use other symbols, such as a Down arrow, change the button into an iconic button and associate it to a graphic file.

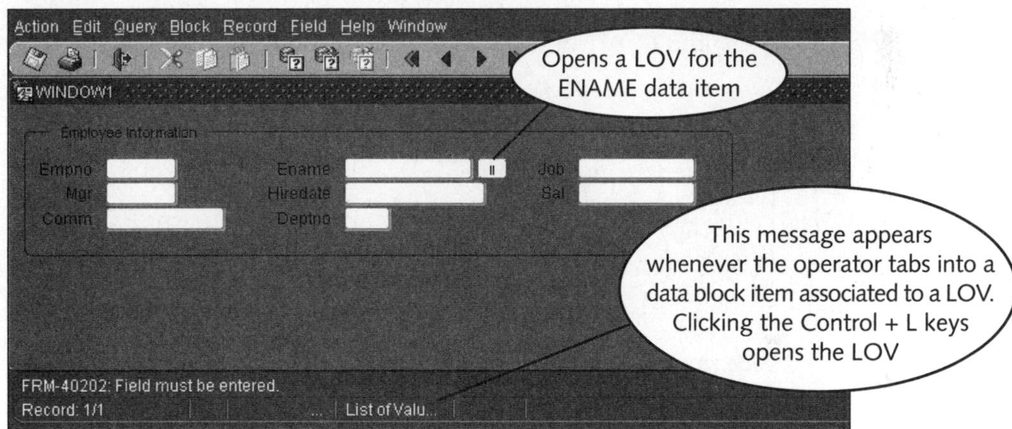

Figure 7-28 Form indicating the EMPNO column has an associated LOV and containing a button that opens a LOV

LOVs can be programmatically opened using the Show_lov built-in. This built-in is a function that is used as part of an expression. It opens the LOV and returns a Boolean value to a variable. A template script using the built-in is included in the following steps.

To create a button that opens a LOV, you would perform the following steps:

1. Open the Layout Editor and activate the Button tool.
2. Place and hold the Left Mouse button while sizing the button adjacent to the form item that uses the LOV.
3. Double-click the button item to open its Property Palette. Name the button appropriately and add the pipe symbol (| |) to the Label property.

4. Open the Object Navigator and locate the button. Expand the button object displaying the Triggers node. Select the node.
5. Click the Create tool to open the Triggers dialog box. Select the When-Button-Pressed trigger. This opens the PL/SQL Editor for the trigger.
6. Enter the script that opens the LOV using the following code template:

```
DECLARE
 lov_displayed     boolean;
begin
 lov_displayed := show_lov('name_of_the_lov');
end;
```

7. Compile the trigger to ensure that it is syntactically correct.
8. Launch the form and test the button.

In this exercise, you see the effect of the Validate From List property and you create a button that opens the LOV you created in the previous practice session.

1. Using the **practice01.fmb** form, determine the effect of the Validate From List property by performing the following steps:
   a. Open the Layout Editor and select the **EMPNO** item.
   b. Double-click the **EMPNO** item to open its Property Palette.
   c. Change the Validate From List property to **YES**.
   d. Open the form and execute a query.
   e. Place your insertion point into the EMPNO item.
   f. Enter **36** into the item and tab from the item. The LOV should display because 36 is an invalid item.
   g. Select a valid value from the LOV and tab from the item. You should now be able to tab from the item without displaying the LOV.
2. This is the second part of the practice. In this section, you create a button that opens the EMPLOYEE_NAMES LOV.
   a. Open the Layout Editor and activate the **Button** tool.
   b. Place and size this button adjacent to the EMPNO form item.
   c. Double-click the new button to open its Property Palette.
   d. Set the following properties:
      - Name: **EMPNO_BUTTON**
      - Label: | |
   e. Open the Object Navigator and select the **EMPNO_BUTTON Triggers** node.

f. Using the SmartTriggers popup menu option (Right Mouse button), create a When-Button-Pressed trigger.

g. Use the following script in the trigger. Be sure to compile the script before leaving the PL/SQL Editor.

```
Declare
  Lov_displayed       boolean;
Begin
  Lov_displayed := show_lov('employee_names');
End;
```

h. Launch the form and test the button. You should be able to display the LOV by clicking the button.

i. Save the form for later use.

STATIC AND PROGRAMMATICALLY CREATED RECORD GROUPS

As stated earlier, record groups are holders of values that can be passed to a form object, such as a LOV. In the previous section, you saw that the record group contains a SELECT statement. This is the most common type of data source for the record group. However, record groups can also contain static values, just as a list item can. The static list can also be used in a LOV, but the record group must be created before the LOV. In order to associate a static record group to the LOV, you choose the Existing Record Group radio button on the LOV Wizard Source page (see Figure 7-18). This activates the LOV Drop-down list, allowing you to select the static record group.

In several cases, a LOV static list may be preferable to a list item:

- A list item is limited to one value or element per row, but the LOV has no limits on the number of columns per row.
- The list item is displayed in the form item and cannot effectively display more than seven or eight values because of the form size. The LOV can be displayed anywhere in the form and can display many more values, because it has scroll bars and the filter option that can limit the number of records.

If your form item has a fixed set of values and the number is greater than seven, you should consider using a static record group in a LOV, rather than a list item. Figure 7-29 illustrates a LOV that displays a static list of JOB values. Compare this to the list items depicted in Figure 7-12.

To create a static record group, you would perform the following steps:

1. Open the Object Navigator and select the Record Groups node.

   Click the Create tool to open the New Record Group dialog box depicted in Figure 7-30.

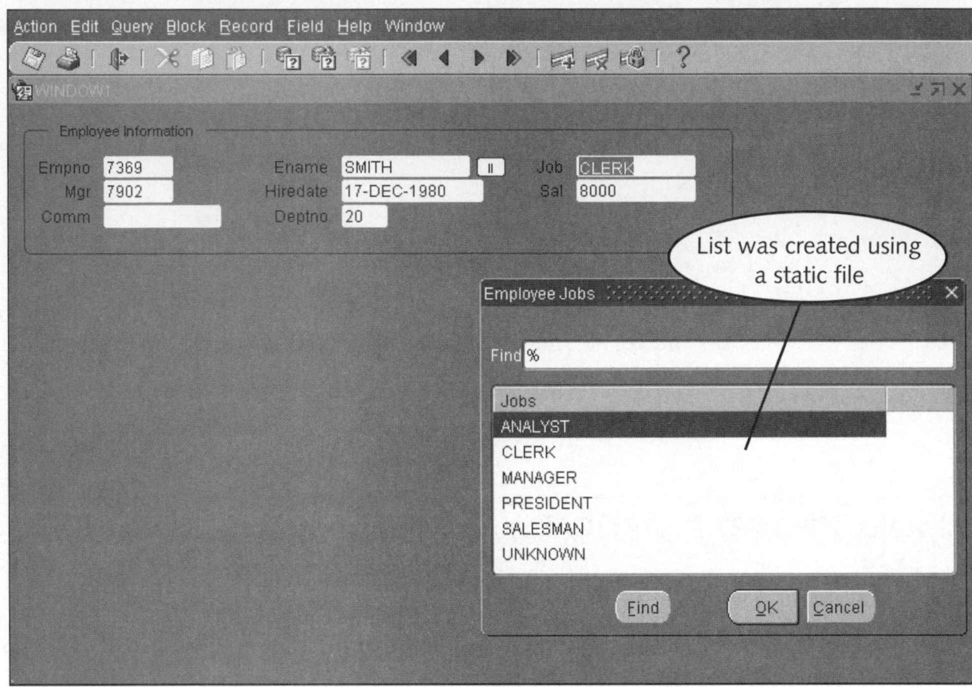

Figure 7-29 LOV displaying a static record group of JOB values

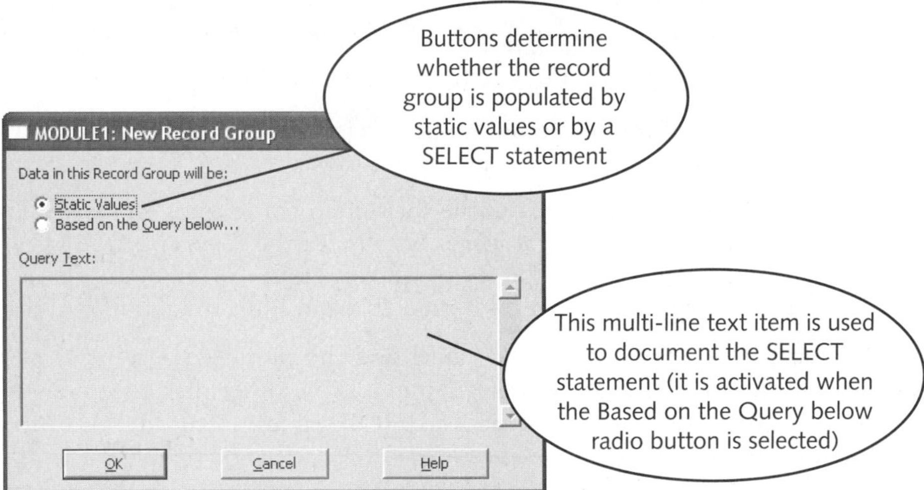

Figure 7-30 New Record Group dialog box

2. Select the Static Values radio button and click OK to open the Column Specification dialog box depicted in Figure 7-31.

The Column Specification dialog box is used to enter columns and values. The Column Names list contains an entry for each column in the record group. The Data Type and Length text items are used to document the value's characteristics. The Column Values list is used to enter the values that appear in the column. The record group can have multiple columns. The values in each column are associated to each other by their indexes. For example, if three columns were specified, the values on the first row of each column would be displayed on the same row.

3. Populate the Column Specification dialog box.
4. Click OK. The record group is now ready to use.

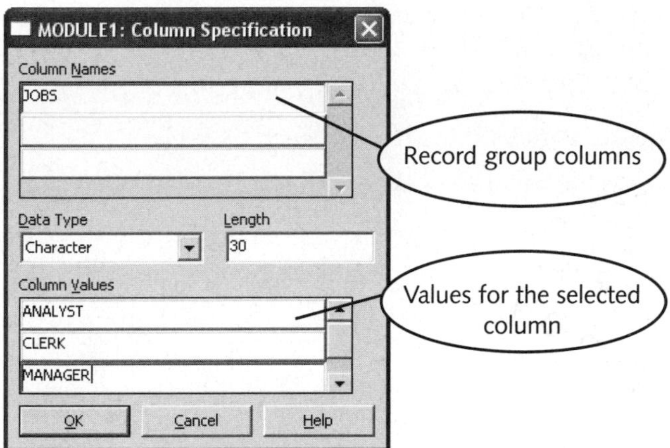

Figure 7-31 Column Specification dialog box

Elements can be added and deleted from the Column Specification dialog box lists using the Control + Shift + > and Control + Shift + < keys.

In this exercise, you practice the concepts learned in this section. Using the **practice01.fmb** practice form, add a LOV to the JOB item that displays a static record group by following these steps:

1. Open the Object Navigator. Locate and double-click the **JOB** data block item to open its Property Palette. Change the Item Type property to **TEXT ITEM**.
2. Open the Object Navigator and select the **Record Groups** node, and click the **Create** tool to open the New Record Group dialog box.
3. Click the **Static Values** radio button.
4. Click **OK** to open the Column Specification dialog box.
5. Add the following column name: **EMPLOYEE_JOBS**.

6. Add the following EMPLOYEE_JOBS column values: **ANALYST**, **CLERK**, **MANGER**, **PRESIDENT**, and **SALESMAN**.
7. Click **OK**.
8. Open the Object Navigator and change the name of the record group to **JOB_STATIC_LIST**.
9. Select the **Tools/LOV Wizard** menu selection to start the LOV Wizard.
10. On the LOV Wizard Source page, click the **Existing Record Group** radio button and select the **JOB_STATIC_LIST** record group created in Step 8. Click **Next**.
11. On the LOV Column selection page, move the EMPLOYEE_JOBS value to the LOV Columns list. Click **Next**.
12. On the LOV Column Display page, perform the following tasks:
    - Check the **Automatically Size Columns** check box.
    - Set the Return Value to **EMP.JOB**.
    - Click **Next**.
13. On the LOV Display page, perform the following tasks:
    - Add **EMPLOYEE POSITIONS** to the Title text item.
    - Change the Height to **200**.
    - Click **Next**.
14. Do not make any changes on the LOV Advanced Options page. Click **Next**.
15. On the LOV Items page, move the **EMP.JOB** value to the Assigned Items list. Click the **Finish** button.
16. Locate the new LOV in the Object Navigator. Change the name to **EMPLOYEE_JOBS**.
17. Launch the form. Navigate into the JOB item. Press the appropriate function key that launches the LOV. Notice that the LOV is displaying the static list that you created in Step 5.
18. Save the form.

Changing the Record Group Query Programmatically

It is possible to change the record group SELECT statement programmatically using the Populate_group_with_query built-in. This feature can be useful when you want to filter records using the SELECT statement Where clause. For example, assume that you want the LOV used in the practice form to display all of the employees, if the DEPTNO item is blank. However, if the DEPTNO item has a value, you want the LOV to display only employees for that department. This technique can have two advantages. If the LOV is used in the Enter Query mode and the operator selected an employee who did have a

DEPTNO value that matched the entered DEPTNO value, no records would be returned because of the value mismatch. A second benefit to changing the SELECT statement Where clause is that fewer records are displayed by the LOV.

The Populate_group_with_query built-in is a function that must be called as an assignment to a numeric variable. It is an overloaded function. The more commonly used version requires the name of the record group and the new SELECT statement as parameters. The following is a template of the command:

```
Populate_group_with_query('record group', 'select statement');
```

In this exercise, you practice the concepts learned in this section. Using the **practice01.fmb** form that you have saved, modify the When-Button-Pressed trigger with the Populate_group_with_query built-in. If the form's DEPTNO value is blank, the trigger ensures that the original SELECT statement that displays all of the employees is used. If the DEPTNO values are not blank, a SELECT statement that limits the LOV employees to those that have the same DEPTNO value should be used. To accomplish these tasks, perform the following steps:

1. Open the **practice01.fmb** form and select the EMPNO_BUTTON button item's **When-Button-Pressed** trigger. Double-click the trigger to open its PL/SQL Editor.
2. Modify the trigger script as follows. Be sure to compile the script before closing the PL/SQL Editor.

```
declare
       lov_displayed        boolean;
       num_var              number;
begin
       if :emp.deptno is not null then
         num_var := populate_group_with_query ('employee_names',
                             'select ename, empno
                              from emp
                              where deptno = :emp.deptno');
       else
         num_var := populate_group_with_query ('employee_names',
                             'select ename, empno
                              from emp');
       end if;
       lov_displayed := show_lov('employee_names');
end;
```

3. Launch the form and test the trigger.
4. Execute a query on the form. Scroll through the list of employees. Each time a DEPTNO value changes, click the **LOV** button. Notice a different set of employees for each DEPTNO value.

5. Place the form into the Enter Query mode and launch the LOV. Notice that it now displays all employees.
6. Close the form.

Where You Are and Where You're Going

In this chapter, you used various item types to increase a form's operating efficiency and to control data integrity. The use of LOVs, list items, radio groups, and check boxes reduce the keystrokes performed by the form operators and ensure that the proper values are entered into the data block items. In the next chapter, you begin to see how various canvases interact to make a complete system, you learn how to call additional canvases from a form, and you also learn to make toolbars using iconic buttons and to create and format tab pages.

Chapter Summary

- Text items are the most common type of data block item. In fact, they are the default item type.
- There are 15 different types of text items. The Item Type property allows you to change an item from one type to another.
- The Layout Editor has tools for creating most of the different types of items. Click the tool to activate it and the place the item on the canvas.
- When creating an item anywhere other than in the Object Navigator, be sure to check in which data block the item was placed. Forms Builder may have placed it in the wrong block.
- Items have a variety of properties that control their behaviors. Properties can be used to disable the item during the Enter Query, Insert, or Normal modes.
- All items have a Hint property that causes the form to display a descriptive message on the status line when a user navigates to the item.
- All items have a Tooltip property that causes the form to display a descriptive message over the item.
- A display item is similar to a text item except that it is read-only.
- A Multi-Line property exists on text items. This property allows the value to be displayed on multiple lines. This property is useful for lengthy items.
- Text items also have a Wrap Style property and a Show Vertical Scroll Bar property that can be used in conjunction with the Multi-Line property.
- The Conceal Data property causes the entered value to be concealed by displaying asterisks in the item rather than the entered value.

- A check box item is used when the item can contain one of two values.
- Radio group items and radio buttons are used when items contain two or more mutually exclusive values.
- A list item allows the operator to choose the value from a list of values.
- A combo box is a list item type that allows the operator to enter a partial value that is used as search criteria when the list is opened.
- A poplist is a list item type that displays a list of values.
- A Tlist is a list item type that has Up and Down tools that change the value.
- List item values can be added dynamically using the Populate_group and Populate_list built-ins. The latter populates a record group that is transferred to the list item by the Populate_list built-in.
- An image item displays an image provided to the form from an external source. The Read_image_file built-in is used to place the image into the item.
- Buttons are items that can cause an event. A button can be displayed on the form or on a toolbar. The Toolbar tool is an iconic button displaying an image.
- Calculated items can be used to summarize a set of values or to compute a value based on a formula.
- A LOV is a dialog box that displays a list of values. The LOV values can be added to the item or used to validate an entered value.
- Record groups are used to populate a LOV. The record group can be based on a SELECT statement of a static value list.
- LOVs are launched by default using a function key. It is better to launch the LOV from a button adjacent to the item using the Show_lov built-in.

Review Questions

1. Match the following terms that have appeared in this chapter with their descriptions:

a. Show_lov	________________	A sizing Style property value that cuts a portion of an image to fit the image item space.
b. Hint	________________	An item property that allows the value to be displayed on more than one line.
c. Text item	________________	A dialog box associated with an item that displays a list of values for selection or validation.
d. CROP	________________	An item used to represent a series of mutually exclusive values.

e. Tlist	________	A property that prevents the form operator from entering an invalid value.
f. Populate_group_ with_query	________	An item property that causes a message to be displayed when the cursor is placed over an item.
g. Multi-Line	________	A read-only item type.
h. Radio button	________	An item that is used when the item only has two values.
i. LOV	________	An item that allows the user to enter several characters into the item before searching for the value.
j. Tooltip	________	A button that displays an image rather than text.
k. Radio group	________	The most common type of data block item used to add, update, and display values.
l. Calculated item	________	A form object that stores a set of records and can be passed to a list item or LOV.
m. Validate From List	________	A built-in that programmatically displays a LOV.
n. Check box	________	A radio group and check box item property that determines the value to be used when the item encounters an undefined value.
o. Display item	________	A built-in that changes a record group's SELECT statement.
p. Combo Box	________	A property used to change an item from one type to another.
q. Precompute Summaries	________	An item that summarizes a data block item's values.
r. Mapping of Other Values	________	An item property that forces an operator to enter a value before navigation can occur.
s. Required	________	A built-in that places a record group into a list item.
t. Iconic button	________	A list item type that causes Up and Down buttons to appear on the item.

u. Populate_list	______________	Property that causes a scroll bar to appear adjacent to an item. The scroll bar is used to view parts of the value that may be hidden.
v. Item type	______________	Data block property that must be set to YES in order to provide a summarized value to a calculated item.
w. Show Vertical Scroll Bar	______________	A graphic item that represents a distinct value in a set of values.
x. Record group	______________	A message that is displayed on the form status line when the user tabs into an item.

2. Identify a situation in which a display item is preferable to a text item.
3. Identify a situation in which a poplist is preferable to a combo box.
4. Identify one reason for the use of a static record group versus a record group based on a SELECT statement.
5. A user just called you and said that he is having trouble retrieving a record from the database. You suspect that the problem is a case restriction mismatch between the database and the form. What can you do to correct the problem?
6. You have placed a button in a multiple-record tabular data block. The button appears once for each data block row that is displayed on the form. What can you change so that the button appears just once?
7. You just received a call from a user who says a particular LOV is displayed in the center of the form. The user said that the LOV is covering the item it is associated with and wants the LOV moved to a different part of the form. What can you do to help the user?
8. You have an employee form that has the date the employee was hired and the date the employee was born. Your users would also like to see the employee's age and the number of years with the company. What can you do to provide this information?
9. You have just created a poplist that is used to enter department codes. You have decided to display the full department name in the list rather than the code that will actually be placed in the item. When you open the list during runtime, you can only see the first several characters of the department name. Why did this happen and what can you do?
10. You have a user who keeps forgetting how to format a date. What can you do to help the user remember the format?
11. Can an item be populated by two different LOVs? If so, how can you program this?
12. Can the same LOV be used for two different instances of the same item in a form (i.e., an instance on a control block and an instance on a data block)?

13. You have a form that uses a LOV to identify customers and customer accounts. There are approximately 5,000 customers. When you operate the LOV, it takes several minutes to display the value list. What can you do to make this procedure faster?
14. You just got off the phone with one of your users. The user has been operating a master-detail form that you created. The user dislikes scrolling through the detail block records to see how many have been retrieved and instead wants something in the form that identifies the number of records returned by the detail block. What can you do to help the user?
15. You are implementing an equipment database. One of the pieces of information the user must enter is the manufacturer code. There are approximately 25 different manufacturers and the list grows occasionally. What can you do to help the operator efficiently add the proper manufacturer code?
16. What kinds of entity attributes are candidates for having their Query Allowed properties set to NO?
17. You have just entered seven elements into a list item. You noticed that two of the values are out of order. What can you do to correct this?
18. You are developing a form that displays invoices for a particular customer. Ten different divisions and 50 departments within the divisions will use the form. A sequential account number identifies the customer. When customers call, they seldom remember their account numbers. You created a LOV to be used to identify the customers and their account numbers. Each division has different customers, but a customer may call any division or department. Because the customer will be on the phone, you want the operator to scroll through the fewest number of customer names as possible. What can you do to minimize the number of customers in the LOV yet retain it as an all-purpose tool?
19. A user wants to see a tabular multiple-record data block sorted in three possible ways. The user would like to be able to designate the sort order at runtime and have an indication of how the records are sorted. Can you think of a way to do this?

Exam Review Questions

1. Which Forms Builder object eliminates repeated queries against external tables and holds records that can be used in Forms Builder applications?

    a. Combo box

    b. List item

    c. Radio group

    d. Record group

2. Which LOV property allows you to populate an item automatically when the LOV returns a single record?
   a. Automatic Select
   b. Automatic Display
   c. Automatic Refresh
   d. Filter Before Display
3. You have a data block item whose value can only be one of three different types. Which input item type would work best for you
   a. LOV
   b. Check box
   c. Radio group
   d. Record group
4. Which check box characteristic occurs when the Check Box Mapping of Other Values property is enabled?
   a. The check box can have more than two values.
   b. The check box can be ignored in the Enter Query mode.
   c. The check box can display checked or unchecked.
   d. The check box will use the Mouse Navigate property.
5. Which of the following Forms Builder objects is the most similar to a database table?
   a. Parameter
   b. Group object
   c. Record group
   d. List of values

Hands-on Assignments

1. In this assignment, you add a display item to a form to hold descriptive department information. You are also asked to disable several of the form items during the Enter Query mode.
   a. Create a new form module named **ch07ex01.fmb**. Add a data block to the form using the EMP table as a data source. The layout should be Form with one record in the form.
   b. Open the Object Navigator and change the EMPNO item Required property to **NO**.
   c. Use the Display Item tool to add a display item to the form to hold the EMP data block (see Figure 7-32). This item displays the DNAME value (department name) that corresponds to the value in the employee's DEPTNO item.

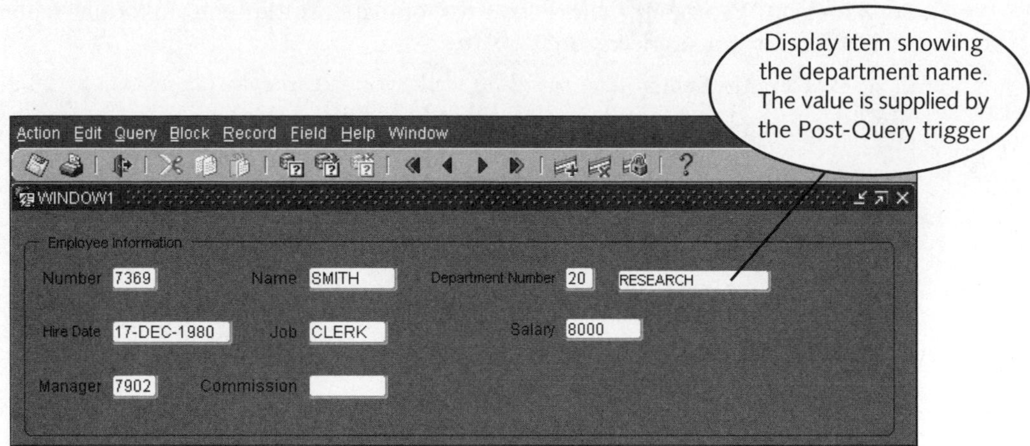

Figure 7-32 Hands-on Assignment 7-1 form

d. Double-click the new display item to open its Property Palette. Enter the following property settings:

- Name: **DEPARTMENT_NAME**
- Database Item: NO

e. Open the Object Navigator and create a block-level Post-Query trigger under the EMP block.

f. Add the following script to the trigger:

```
Begin
   SELECT dname
       Into :emp.department_name
    From dept
    Where deptno = :emp.deptno;
  Exception
When others then :emp.department_name := 'ERROR';
        End;
```

g. Open the Object Navigator. Select the **JOB**, **MGR**, **HIREDATE**, **SAL**, **COMM**, and **DEPTNO** items.

h. Open a multiple selection Property Palette for the selected items. Change the Query Allowed property to **NO**.

i. Launch the form and place it into the Enter Query mode. Attempt to enter values into all of the items except EMPNO (employee number) and ENAME (employee name). You should not be able to enter values into these items in this mode.

j. Execute the query. Attempt to modify the form items. You should be able to do so.

k. Notice that the department names are now being displayed.

l. Save the form as **ch07ex01.fmb**.

2. In this assignment, you modify the form you created in Hands-on Assignment 7-1, **ch07ex01.fmb**. You create a LOV that displays the various departments for selection into the DEPTNO and DEPARTMENT_NAME items. Because the DEPARTMENT_NAME value is displayed, there is no need to display the DEPTNO value. It will be made invisible to save canvas real estate. Finally, you will be asked to create a button that opens the Department LOV.

a. Open module **ch07ex01.fmb** in the Object Navigator.

b. Locate the DEPTNO data block item and open its Property Palette. Set the following properties to the corresponding values:

- Visible: **NO**
- Canvas: **Null**

c. Locate the DEPARTMENT_NAME data block item and open its Property Palette. Set the following properties to the corresponding values:

- Prompt: **DEPARTMENT**
- Prompt Attachment Edge: **START**

d. Start the LOV Wizard.

e. Select the **New Record Group** radio button on the Source page. Click **Next**.

f. Add the following SELECT statement to the SQL Query page:

```
Select dname, deptno from dept order by 1
```

Click **Next**.

g. On the Column Selection page, move both the **DNAME** and **DEPTNO** items to the LOV Columns list. Click **Next**.

h. On the Column Display page, set the following values:

- DNAME Title: **NAME**
- DNAME Return Value: **EMP.DEPARTMENT_NAME**
- DEPTNO Title: **Delete the value**
- DEPTNO Width: **0**
- DEPTNO Return Value: **EMP.DEPTNO**
- Automatically Size Columns: **YES**

i. The DEPTNO values were set to disable the LOV from displaying the item. However, the DEPTNO value will still be selected into the DEPTNO form item for database integrity. Click **Next**.

j. On the next page, set the LOV title to **VALID DEPARTMENTS**. Set the Height value to **200**.

k. Because the LOV is opened using a button, and the only way the operator can place a value into the DEPTNO field is with a selection from the LOV, it is not necessary to associate the LOV with an item. Create the LOV by clicking the **Finish** button.

l. Open the Object Navigator. Change the new LOV and record group object names to **DEPARTMENTS**.

m. Open the Layout Editor. Activate the **Button** tool. Place the button to the right of the Department text item (see Figure 7-33).

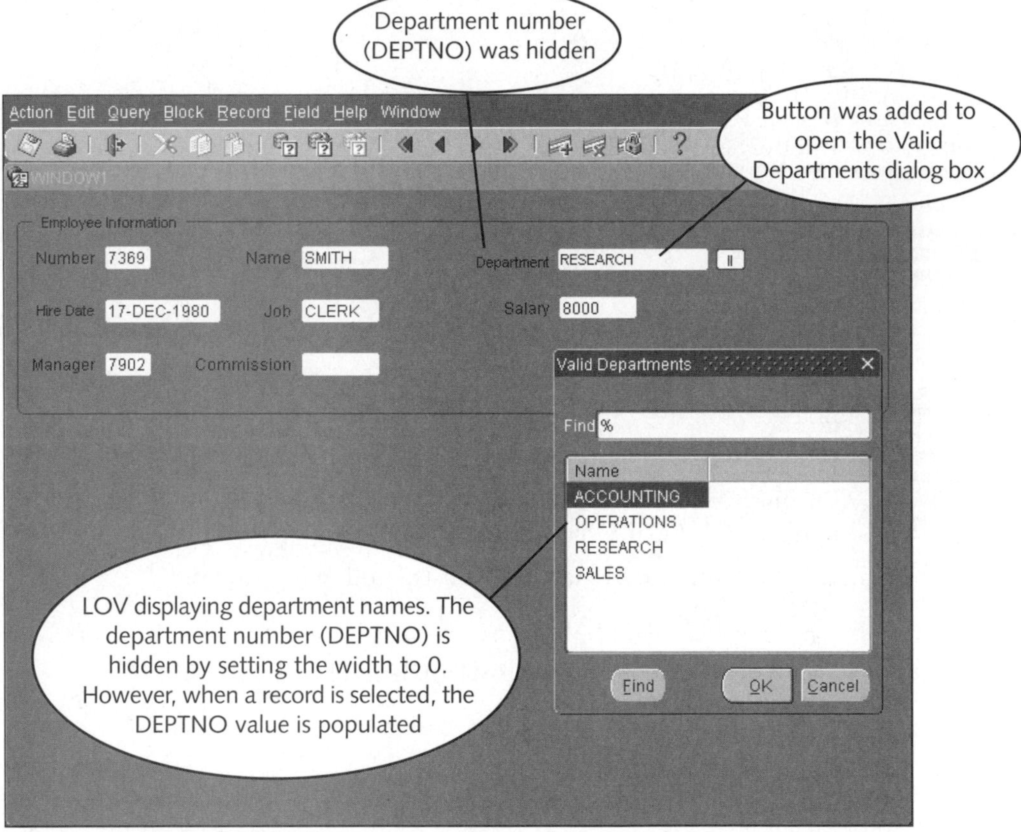

Figure 7-33 Hands-on Assignment 7-2 form

n. Double-click the button to open its Property Palette. Set the following properties:

- Name: **DEPARTMENTS_BUTTON**
- Label: | |

o. Open the Object Navigator. Create a When-Button-Pressed trigger for the DEPARTMENTS_BUTTON item. Use the following script:

```
Declare
       Lov_displayed        boolean;
Begin
       Lov_displayed := show_lov('departments');
End;
```

p. Run the form and test the LOV. Change some values and make sure that the department name also changes.

q. Save the form as **ch07ex02.fmb**.

3. In this assignment, you disable the function keys and add buttons to the form. The buttons are used to perform basic form functions.

a. Open form **ch07ex02.fmb** in the Object Navigator.

b. Expand the Object Navigator **Triggers** node and add a form-level Key-Others trigger. Add the following command to the trigger:

```
message('Function key has been disabled, please use a button');
```

c. Open the Layout Editor. Activate the **Button** tool and place a button item in the form.

d. Double-click the new button and set the following properties:

- Name: **ENTER_QUERY**
- Label: **ENTER QUERY**
- Width: **68**
- Height: **18**

e. Open the Layout Editor. Select the **ENTER_QUERY** button. Copy the item using the Control + C keys. Paste the item using the Control + V keys.

f. Repeat Step d. The Name and Label properties should be set to **QUERY**.

g. Create another button by repeating steps e and f. On this iteration, the button properties should be set to **SAVE**.

h. Create a fourth button by repeating steps e and f. On this iteration, the button properties should be set to **EXIT**.

i. Open the Object Navigator and create a When-Button-Pressed trigger under the ENTER_QUERY button item. Add the following command to the trigger:

```
enter_query;.
```

j. Open the Object Navigator and create a When-Button-Pressed trigger under the QUERY button item. Add the following command to the trigger:

```
execute_query;
```

k. Open the Object Navigator and create a When-Button-Pressed trigger under the SAVE button item. Add the following command to the trigger:

```
commit_form;
```

l. Open the Object Navigator and create a When-Button-Pressed trigger under the EXIT button item. Add the following command to the trigger:

```
exit_form;
```

m. Launch the form and attempt the following:

- Place the form into the Enter Query mode.
- Execute a query.
- Save a modification.
- Close the form.

n. Figure 7-34 illustrates the completed form. Save this form as **ch07ex03.fmb**.

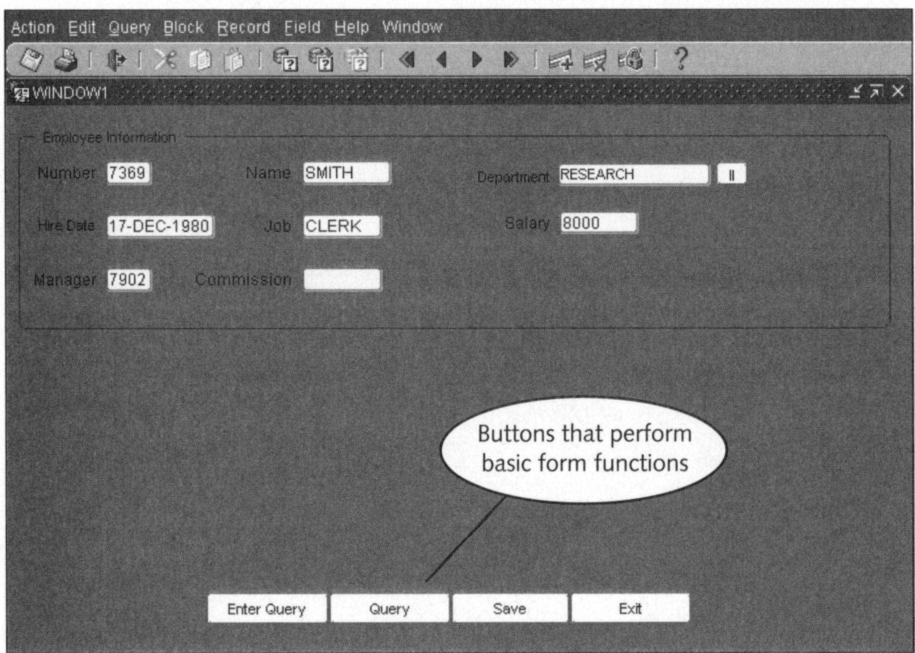

Figure 7-34 Hands-on Assignment 7-3 form

4. In this assignment, you add some Tooltip messages to the buttons created in previous assignments.

   a. Open the form **ch07ex03.fmb**.

   b. Open the Object Navigator.

c. Double-click the **ENTER_QUERY** button item displaying its Property Palette. Set the Tooltip property to place the data in **ENTER QUERY MODE**.

d. Double-click the **QUERY** button item displaying its Property Palette. Set the Tooltip property to **EXECUTES A QUERY**.

e. Double-click the **SAVE** button item displaying its Property Palette. Set the Tooltip property to **Saves the records**.

f. Double-click the **EXIT** button item displaying its Property Palette. Set the Tooltip property to **Exits the form**.

g. Launch the form. Place your cursor over each of the buttons and notice the message.

h. Close the form and create a visual attribute. Open a Property Palette for the visual attribute. Set the following properties:

- Name: **TOOL_TIP_VA**
- Background Color: **WHITE**

i. Assign the visual attribute to each of the form's buttons. The visual attribute should be added to the Tooltip Visual Attribute property.

j. Launch the form. Experiment with different colors to determine the best one to use on the Web.

k. Move the TOOL_TIP_VA to your object library.

l. Save the form as **ch07ex04.fmb**.

5. In this assignment, you create a Directory style form. A Directory style form changes the default form behavior style. A control block is placed in the form for the entry of the selection values. These values are transferred to the database block using Copy From properties located on specific data block items. This style of application always displays the selection values, and this is something a database block does not do. This feature is greatly appreciated by the form operators. This type of application requires the function keys and buttons to be programmed to ensure that the form executes the query on the correct data block. For example, if the user enters a value into a control block item and executes a query using the Execute Query function key, no records are returned because the input focus remains in the control block. The Go_block built-in must be added to ensure that the query always occurs on the correct block.

a. Open the Object Navigator and create a new form module.

b. Using the Data Block Wizard and Layout Wizard, create and format a data block based on the EMP table. The block should have a Tabular style and display 10 records.

c. Open the Layout Editor and move the data block down so that 1 or 2 inches of space appear above the EMP data block.

d. Double-click the **EMPNO** item to open a Property Palette. Set the Required property to **NO**.

e. Open the Object Navigator and add a control block to the form. Name the block **SEARCH**.

f. Move the **SEARCH** data block above the EMP data block in the Object Navigator.

g. Select and copy the **EMPNO** and **ENAME** items in the EMP data block.

h. Paste the **EMPNO** and **ENAME** items into the SEARCH control block.

i. Open the Property Palette for the EMPNO and ENAME items in the SEARCH control block. Set the following properties:

- Database Item: **NO**
- X Position: **0**
- Y Position: **0**

j. Open the Layout Editor. The EMPNO and ENAME items are located at the top-left corner of the canvas. They were placed there so that they do not overlie the items from which they were copied. Move them to a convenient location.

k. Double-click the original **EMPNO** item in the EMP data block. Set the Copy Value From Item property to **SEARCH.EMPNO**.

l. Double-click the original **ENAME** item in the EMP data block. Set the Copy Value From Item property to **SEARCH.ENAME**.

m. Create a form-level Key-Exeqry trigger. Add the following script to the trigger:

```
Go_block('emp');
Execute_query;
```

n. Launch the form. Enter **CLARK** into the ENAME search column. Press the **Execute Query** function key. Notice that the form retrieved a matching record and retained the original search values.

o. Save the form as **ch07ex05.fmb**.

6. In this assignment, you copy various form components that you have created in these assignments into your MY_OWN_LIBRARY object library.

a. Open form **ch07ex04.fmb**.

b. Double-click the **MY_OWN_LIBRARY** object library. Click the **GRAPHIC OBJS** tab.

c. Drag the following form objects into the GRAPHICS OBJS tab: **DEPARTMENTS_BUTTON** button, **ENTER_QUERY** button, **QUERY** button, **SAVE** button, and the **EXIT** button.

CASE PROJECT: GREAT STATE ELECTRIC BUDGETING SYSTEM

In this portion of the Case Project, you continue to modify your forms, making them more descriptive and easier to use. You add display items that contain the task and account descriptions, employee names, and computed costs for a task, work order, and project. You also create numerous LOVs, list items, and a radio group that allows the form operator to change sort order on the fly. At the end of this portion of the Case Project, the PROJECTS and WORK_ORDERS tab pages will be close to final form.

Your Work

The first task is to add a QUERY button to the PROJECTS tab canvas. This canvas is a Directory style application. The QUERY button ensures that the query always begins on the correct data block. In addition, you modify selected Copy From properties to populate the block with search values from the PROJ_SEARCH_CRITERIA control block. This is done to keep the PROJECT_DATA data block in sync with the values entered in the PROJECT_SEARCH_CRITERIA control block. To accomplish these tasks, follow these steps:

1. Open your object library and display the buttons you added in Hands-on Assignment 7-6.
2. Open the Object Navigator with your budgeting application displayed.
3. Copy the **QUERY** button from the object library to the PROJ_SEARCH_CRITERIA control block.
4. Open the button's Property Palette.
5. Set the following properties:
   - Visible: **YES**
   - Canvas: **MAIN**
   - Tab Page: **PROJECTS**
6. Open the Layout Wizard and position the **QUERY** button on the PROJECTS tab page in the top-left corner of the form.
7. Open the Object Navigator, locate the QUERY button, and open the PL/SQL Editor for its When-Button-Pressed trigger. Add the following as the first line of the script; do not delete the existing built-in:

   ```
   go_block ('project_data');
   ```
8. Compile the trigger and close the PL/SQL Editor.
9. Open a Property Palette for the ASSIGNED_DEPARTMENT_ID item in the PROJECT_DATA data block. Set the Copy Value From Item property to **PROJ_SEARCH_CRITERIA.ASSIGNED_DEPARTMENT_ID**.
10. Open a Property Palette for the PROJECT_ID item in the PROJECT_DATA data block. Set the Copy Value From Item property to **PROJ_SEARCH_CRITERIA.PROJECT_ID**.
11. Open a Property Palette for the PROJECT_NAME item in the PROJECT_DATA data block. Set the Copy Value From Item property to **PROJ_SEARCH_CRITERIA.PROJECT_NAME**.

12. Open a Property Palette for the PROJECT_LOCATION item in the PROJECT_DATA data block. Set the Copy Value From Item property to **PROJ_SEARCH_CRITERIA.PROJECT_LOCATION**.
13. Open a Property Palette for the PROJECT_NEED_DATE item in the PROJECT_DATA data block. Set the Copy Value From Item property to **PROJ_SEARCH_CRITERIA.PROJECT_NEED_DATE**.
14. Launch your form and perform the following queries:
    a. Press the **QUERY** button with no values entered into the SEARCH VARIABLES area. All project records should be displayed.
    b. Enter **SE** into the DEPARTMENT ID item. Press the **QUERY** button. One project should be displayed.
    c. Remove the **SE** value from the DEPARTMENT ID item. Enter **%3467%** into the project NAME item. Click the **QUERY** button. Two projects that contain the value in their names appear.
15. Perform other queries using combinations of all the search fields.

The next task is to add a similar QUERY button to the WORK_ORDERS tab page. To add the button, perform the following steps:

1. Open your object library and display the buttons you added in Hands-on Assignment 7-6.
2. Open the Object Navigator and expand the **WO_SEARCH_CRITERIA** data block.
3. Copy the **QUERY** button from the object library to the WO_SEARCH_CRITERIA control block.
4. Open the button's Property Palette.
5. Set the following properties:
    - Visible: **YES**
    - Canvas: **MAIN**
    - Tab Page: **WORK_ORDERS**
6. Open the Layout Wizard and position the **QUERY** button on the WORK_ORDERS tab page in the top-left corner.
7. Open the Object Navigator, locate the QUERY button, and open the PL/SQL Editor for its When-Button-Pressed trigger. Add the following as the first line of the script (do not delete the existing built-in):

```
go_block ('work_order_data');
```

8. Compile the script and close the editor.
9. Open a Property Palette for the WORK_ORDER_ID item in the WORK_ORDER_DATA data block. Set the Copy Value From Item property to **WO_SEARCH_CRITERIA.WORK_ORDER_ID**.

10. Open a Property Palette for the PROJECT_ID item in the WORK_ORDER_DATA data block. Set the Copy Value From Item property to **WO_SEARCH_CRITERIA.PROJECT_ID**.
11. Open a Property Palette for the ASSIGNED_TO item in the WORK_ORDER_DATA data block. Set the Copy Value From Item property to **WO_SEARCH_CRITERIA.ASSIGNED_TO**.
12. Open a Property Palette for the APPROVED_BY item in the WORK_ORDER_DATA data block. Set the Copy Value From Item property to **WO_SEARCH_CRITERIA.APPROVED_BY**
13. Open a Property Palette for the WO_LOCATION item in the WORK_ORDER_DATA data block. Set the Copy Value From Item property to **WO_SEARCH_CRITERIA.WO_LOCATION**.
14. Open a Property Palette for the WO_DESCRIPTION item in the WORK_ORDER_DATA data block. Set the Copy Value From Item property to **WO_SEARCH_CRITERIA.WO_DESCRIPTION**.
15. Launch your form and perform the queries to test the buttons and the properties.
16. Add a similar QUERY button to the EMPLOYEES, ACCOUNTS, and TASK_DESCRIPTIONS tab pages using the same steps used on the PROJECTS and WORK_ORDERS tab pages. Note that you will have to set the Number of Items Displayed properties to 1.

7

The next task is to change the ASSIGNED_DEPARTMENT_ID item in the PROJECT_SEARCH_CRITERIA control block to a list item. This item is located on the PROJECTS tab page. Great State has only six departments so a list item can be used effectively.

1. Open the Layout Editor and locate the ASSIGNED_DEPARTMENT_ID item. Double-click the item to open a Property Palette. Change the following properties:
   - Item Type: **LIST ITEM**
   - List Style: **POPLIST**
2. Click the **Elements in List** property (and the **More** button) to open the List Elements entry tool. Add the following list elements and list element values:
   - Distribution Construction: **DC**
   - Distribution Engineering: **DE**
   - Substation Construction: **SC**
   - Substation Engineering: **SE**
   - Transmission Construction: **TC**
   - Transmission Engineering: **TE**
3. You should also add one blank element and a corresponding blank value. This is needed so that the item can contain a blank value. To create a blank row, place your insertion point into a blank element row and delete its corresponding value.

4. Resize the width of the ASSIGNED_DEPARTMENT_ID item so that the new values can be displayed.
5. Launch the form and test the list item

In the next part of this project, you provide better information about the tasks. Currently, the Work Order Task Information area on the WORK_ORDERS tab page does not contain a task description or an account description. The TASK_DESCRIPTION_ID is a foreign key to the TASK_DESCRIPTIONS table. The TASK_DESCRIPTION_ID item must be in the block, but the value is not displayed because it does not have any real meaning to the user. The task description has the meaning.

In this task, you create a display item populated by a Post-Query trigger so that the task description is displayed. This same Post-Query trigger populates an account description display item you will also add to the form. To accomplish these tasks, perform the following steps:

1. Open the Layout Editor and display the **WORK_ORDERS** tab page.
2. Activate the **Display Item** tool and place the item in the WORK_ORDER_TASKS area to the left of the ACCOUNT_ID text item.
3. Double-click the new display item opening its Property Palette. Set the following properties:
    - Name: **TASK_DESCRIPTION**
    - Maximum Length: **25**
    - Height: **18**
    - Database Item: **NO**
    - Prompt: **TASK DESCRIPTION**
    - Prompt Attachment Edge: **TOP**
4. Open the Layout Editor and redisplay the **WORK_ORDERS** tab page.
5. Activate the **Display Item** tool and place the item in the WORK_ORDER_TASKS area to the right of the ACCOUNT_ID text item.
6. Double-click the new display item opening its Property Palette. Set the following properties:
    - Name: **ACCOUNT_DESCRIPTION**
    - Maximum Length: **25**
    - Height: **18**
    - Database Item: **NO**
    - Prompt: **ACCOUNT DESCRIPTION**
    - Prompt Attachment Edge: **TOP**

7. Open the Object Navigator and make sure that the newly created ACCOUNT_DESCRIPTION and TASK_DESCRIPTION items are associated to the WORK_ORDER_TASKS data block.
8. Create a Post-Query trigger in the WORK_ORDER_TASKS data block by using the following script:

```
begin
  select task_description
  into :work_order_tasks.task_description
  from task_descriptions
  where task_id like (:work_order_tasks.task_description_id||'%');
exception
  when others then :work_order_tasks.task_description := 'UNKNOWN';
end;
begin
  select account_description
    into :work_order_tasks.account_description
  from accounts
 where account_id = :work_order_tasks.account_id;
exception
 when others then :work_order_tasks.account_id := 'UNKNOWN';
end;
```

9. Launch the form and test the Post_Query trigger. Figure 7-35 illustrates the Work Order Task Information area after the display items have been added.

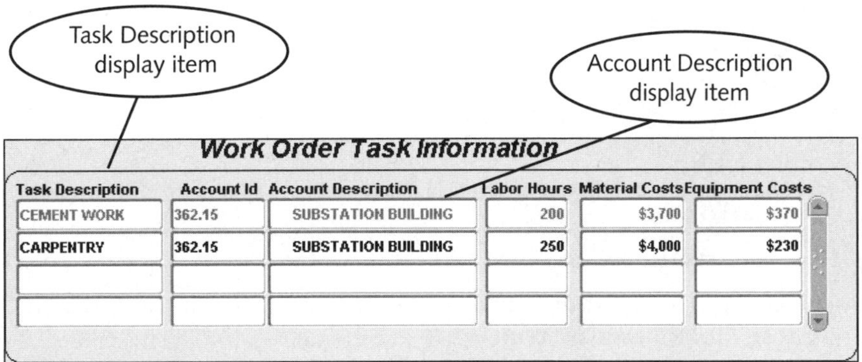

Figure 7-35 Work Order Task Information form area after display items have been added

The next task is to add a LOV for the Work Order Task Information area that is used to populate the TASK_DESCRIPTION_ID and TASK_DESCRIPTION Information. A button will be used to open the LOV. To accomplish these tasks, perform the following steps:

1. Start the LOV Wizard.

7

2. Use the following settings:
   - Select the **New Record Group** radio button
   - Add the following SELECT statement:

```
select task_description, task_id
 from task_descriptions
 order by 1
```

3. Move both columns into the LOV Columns list.
4. Check the **Automatically size columns** check box.
5. Set the TASK_ID Width to **0**.
6. Set the TASK_ID return value to: **WORK_ORDER_TASKS.TASK_DESCRIPTION_ID**.
7. Set the TASK_DESCRIPTION return value to **WORK_ORDER_TASKS.TASK_DESCRIPTION**.
8. Set the Title to **WORK ORDER TASKS**.
9. Set the Height to **250**.
10. Open the Object Navigator and change the name of the new record group and LOV to **TASKS**.
11. Create the button that launches the LOV. Drag the DEPARTMENTS_BUTTON from the object library to the WORK_ORDER_TASKS data block in the Object Navigator.
12. Open a Property Palette for the DEPARTMENTS_BUTTONS. Set the following properties:
    - Name: **TASK_BUTTON**
    - Visible: **YES**
    - Canvas: **MAIN**
    - Tab Page: **WORK_ORDERS**
13. Open the Layout Editor and place the button adjacent to the TASK_DESCRIPTIONS display item.
14. Open the Object Navigator and locate the When-Button-Pressed trigger for the newly added TASK_BUTTON. Open a PL/SQL editor for the item. Modify the script according to the following:

```
declare
       lov_displayed     boolean;
begin
       lov_displayed := show_lov('tasks');
end;
```

15. Compile the script and close the editor.
16. Launch the form and test the button and the LOV.

The next task is to add another LOV in the Work Order Task Information area. This LOV will be used to populate the ACCOUNT_ID item and has another wrinkle in that it will validate values entered into the ACCOUNT_ID item. You have chosen to allow the form operator to enter values into the item rather than solely selecting them from the LOV, because many of the form operators are familiar with the accounts and would like to enter the value freehand rather than selecting it from a list. To accomplish these tasks, perform the following steps:

1. Start the LOV Wizard.
2. Select the **New Record Group** radio button.
3. Use the following SELECT statement:

```
select account_id, account_description,
from accounts
order by 1
```

4. Move both columns into the LOV Columns list.
5. Check the **Automatically Size Columns** check box.
6. Set the ACCOUNT_ID return value to **WORK_ORDER_ TASKS.ACCOUNT_ID**.
7. Set the TASK_DESCRIPTION return value to **WORK_ORDER_ TASKS.ACCOUNT_DESCRIPTION**.
8. Set the Title property to **ACCOUNTS**.
9. Set the Height property to **250**.
10. Move the ACCOUNT_ID item to the Assigned Items list.
11. Open the Object Navigator and change the name of the new record group and LOV to **ACCOUNTS**.
12. Create the button that launches the LOV. Drag the **DEPARTMENTS_BUTTON** from the object library to the WORK_ORDER_TASKS data block in the Object Navigator.
13. Open a Property Palette for the DEPARTMENT_BUTTON. Set the following properties:
    - Name: **ACCOUNT_BUTTON**
    - Visible: **YES**
    - Canvas: **MAIN**
    - Height: **18**
    - Tab Page: **WORK _ORDERS**
14. Open the Layout Editor and place the button after the ACCOUNT_ID text item.

7

15. Open the Object Navigator and locate the When-Button-Pressed trigger for the newly added ACCOUNT_BUTTON. Open a PL/SQL editor for the item. Modify the script according to the following:

```
declare
        lov_displayed     boolean;
begin
        lov_displayed := show_lov('accounts');
end;
```

16. Compile the trigger and close the editor.
17. Open a Property Palette for the ACCOUNT_ID item in the WORK_ORDER_TASKS data block. Set the Validate From List property to **YES**.
18. Launch the form and test the button and the LOV. Be sure to enter an incorrect value into the ACCOUNT_ID item to determine whether validation is working.

The next task is to add a calculated formula item to the WORK_ORDER_TASKS data block and the WORK_ORDERS tab page (see Fig 7-36). This item will compute the total cost of each task by adding the material costs, equipment costs, and the labor hours multiplied by a $50 hourly rate. To accomplish these tasks, perform the following steps:

1. Open the Layout Editor and place a new display item in the WORK_ORDER_TASKS area.
2. Double-click the display item opening its Property Palette. Set the following properties:
    - Name: **TASK_COSTS**
    - Data Type: **NUMBER**
    - Format Mask: **$999,999**
    - Calculation Mode: **FORMULA**
    - Formula: :**work_order_tasks.material_costs + :work_order_tasks.equipment_costs**

      + (:work_order_tasks.labor_hours * 50)
    - Database Item: **NO**
    - Visible: **YES**
    - Canvas: **MAIN**
    - Data Block: **WORK_ORDER_TASKS**
    - Tab Page: **WORK_ORDERS**
    - Prompt: **TASK COSTS**
    - Prompt Attachment Edge: **TOP**
    - Height: **18**

3. Open the Object Navigator and make sure the TASK_COSTS data block item is associated to the WORK_ORDER_TASKS data block.
4. Launch the form and test whether the formula column is computing costs correctly.

You would like to see a total work order cost for each work order on the WORK_ORDERS tab page. This item will consist of a display item on the WORK_ORDER_DATA block. A Post-Query trigger will be used to compute the value. This trigger will be placed on the WORK_ORDER_DATA data block. To accomplish these tasks, perform the following steps:

1. Open the Layout editor and place a display item in the Work Order Information area on the WORK_ORDERS page (see Figure 7-36).
2. Double-click the display item and set the following properties:
   - Name: **WORK_ORDER_COSTS**
   - Format Mask: **$999,999**
   - Data Type: **NUMBER**
   - Database Item: **NO**
   - Visible: **YES**
   - Canvas: **MAIN**
   - Prompt: **WORK ORDER COSTS**
   - Prompt Attachment Edge: **TOP**
   - Height: **18**
   - Distance Between Records: **18**
   - Tab Page: **WORK_ORDERS**
3. Open the Object Navigator and make sure the WORK_ORDER_COSTS data block item is associated to the WORK_ORDER_DATA data block.
4. Create a Post-Query trigger under the WORK_ORDER_DATA data block. Place the following script into the trigger:

```
begin
       select sum(material_costs +
                  equipment_costs +
                  (labor_hours * 50))
       into :work_order_data.work_order_costs
       from work_order_tasks
       where wo_work_order_id = :work_order_data.work_order_id
       group by wo_work_order_id;
exception
 when others then :work_order_data.work_order_costs := 0;
end;
```

5. Compile the trigger and close the editor.
6. Launch the form and test the trigger.

7

You have made great progress in this installment. You can complete most of the remaining form objects without detailed step-by-step instructions. For the remainder of this portion of the Case Project, most of the tasks are repeats of steps you performed in the previous chapter, so the project manager is confident that you can complete the remainder of this portion of the Case Project. You will only be given detailed instructions for new tasks.

1. You have reviewed the WORK_ORDERS tab page and do not like the fact that it is displaying the employee IDs rather than names. You are to:
   - Hide the APPROVED_BY and ASSIGNED_TO data items and display the employees' names in this data block (see Figure 7-36). This is similar to what was done for the TASK_DESCRIPTION_ID and TASK_DESCRIPTION items.
   - Modify the WORK_ORDER_DATA block Post-Query trigger to populate the assigned and approved by employee names you added in the previous step.
   - Create LOVs for each of the APPROVED_BY and ASSIGNED_TO items.
   - Place buttons adjacent to the APPROVED_BY and ASSIGNED_TO items to open the LOVs.

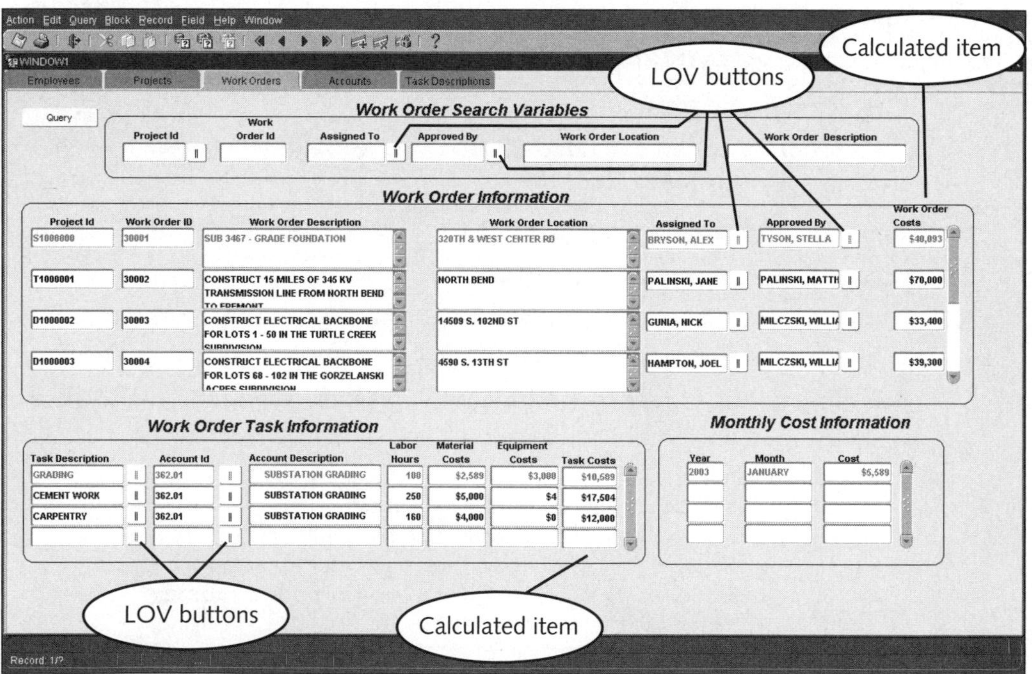

Figure 7-36 WORK_ORDERS tab page

2. You have taken one last look at the WORK_ORDERS tab page. You like the fact that LOVs are opened by a button for the PROJECT ID, ID, ASSIGNED_TO, and APPROVED_BY search variables in the WO_SEARCH_CRITERIA data block. Please be sure to include the first 30 characters of the project name in the PROJECT_ID LOV. When you are finished, the tab page should look similar to Figure 7-36. You may find it quicker to copy and paste the WORK_ORDER_DATA LOVs and buttons into the WO_SEARCH_CRITERIA data block.
3. You have reviewed the PROJECTS tab page. In general, you like the form but would like some additional summary information and LOVs. Add the following to this tab page:
   a. A display item similar to task 8 on the Work Order Information area of the form. Hint: you can copy and modify the WORK_ORDER_COSTS item and Post-Query trigger from the WORK_ORDER_DATA data block to save time. Beware though; there will be modifications to the trigger.
   b. Hide and replace the **ASSIGN_TO** and **APPROVED_BY** items in the WORK_ORDERS data block with their employee names. This is similar to what was done in the WORK_ORDER_DATA data block.
   c. Add a display item called **PROJECT_COSTS** to the PROJECT_DATA data block on the PROJECTS tab page that summarizes the total project costs. Create a Post-Query trigger using the following script:

```
begin
       select sum(material_costs+equipment_costs+(labor_hours*50))
                into :project_data.project_costs
       from projects, work_orders, work_order_tasks
       where projects.project_id = work_orders.project_id(+)
        and work_orders.work_order_id =
work_order_tasks.wo_work_order_id(+)
        and projects.project_id = :project_data.project_id
       group by projects.project_id;
exception
       when others then :project_data.project_costs := 0;
end;
```

   d. Create a LOV on the Project Search Variables area to populate the PROJECT_ID item. Hint: You may try copying the LOV used on the WORK_ORDERS tab page and modifying the Column Mapping Properties.
5. The last work is to add two radio buttons to the PROJECTS tab page. In most cases, the users would like to see the projects displayed by project ID. However, there are times when the form operator will want to see the projects by need date. This type of sort will be important when the engineering managers are assigning projects, because projects with the more recent need date must be worked on first.

7

In this task, you are to make the project ID the default sort order of the PROJECT_DATA data block. You then add two radio buttons that will allow the operator to change the sort order on the fly. To accomplish these tasks, perform the following steps:

a. Open the Object Navigator and create a radio group item in the PROJECT_SEARCH_CRITERIA control block. Name this item **SORT_BY**.

b. Create two radio buttons under the SORT_BY radio group. Name them **NEED_DATE** and **PROJECT_ID**. Open a Property Palette for the SORT_BY radio group. Set the following properties:
   - Mapping of Other Values: **P**
   - Canvas: **MAIN**
   - Tab Page: **PROJECTS**

c. Open a Property Palette for the NEED_DATE radio button. Set the following properties:
   - Label: **NEED DATE**
   - Radio Button Value: **N**
   - Visible: **YES**

d. Open a Property Palette for the PROJECT_ID radio button. Set the following properties:
   - Label: **PROJECT ID**
   - Radio Button Value: **P**
   - Visible: **YES**

e. Open the Layout Editor and place the radio buttons beneath the QUERY button.

f. Create a When-Radio-Changed trigger under the SORT_BY radio group item. Use the following script:

```
if :proj_search_criteria.sort_by = 'N' then
  set_block_property ('project_data', order_by, 'project_need_date desc');
else
  set_block_property ('project_data', order_by, 'project_id');
end if;
```

g. Open a Property Palette for the PROJECT_DATA data block. Set the Order By Clause property to **PROJECT_ID**.

h. Launch and test the form. Figure 7-37 depicts the completed form.

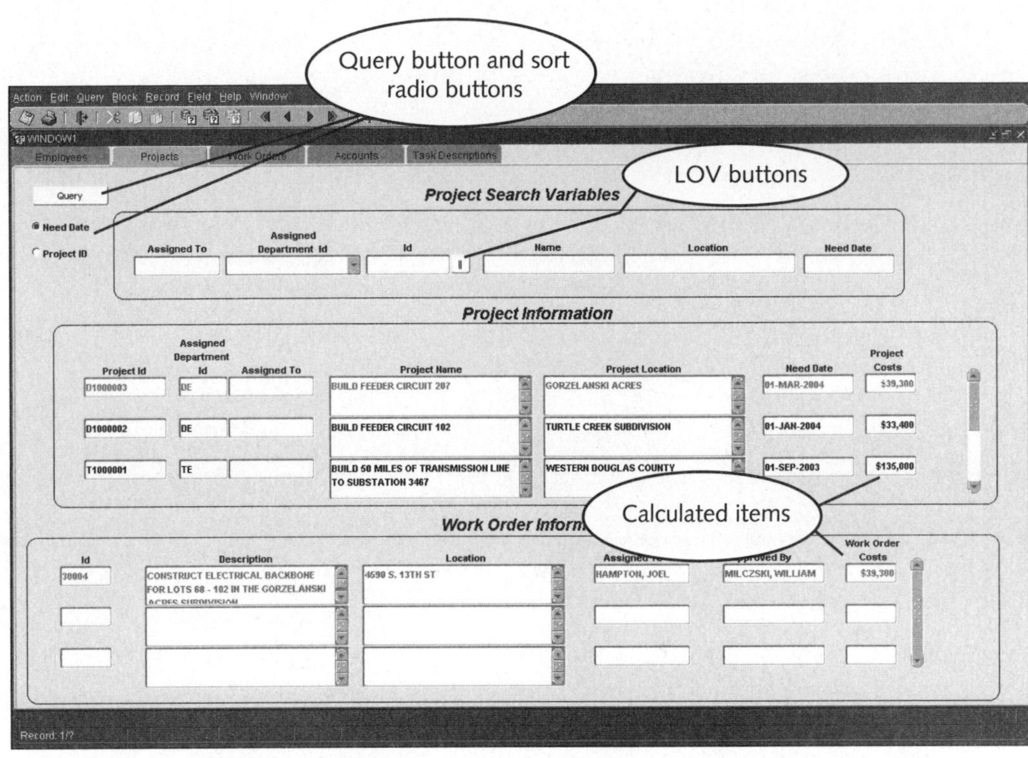

Figure 7-37 PROJECTS tab page displaying projects by need date

7

CHAPTER

8

CANVASES, WINDOWS, CALLING OTHER FORMS, CHART ITEMS, AND REPORTS

In this chapter you will:

- Learn about the behavior of canvases and window types
- Create and use stacked canvases
- Create and format tab canvases
- Call other forms
- Create toolbar canvases
- Create and use chart items
- Call a Web document from a form
- Create and use Reports objects

This chapter focuses on using and calling canvases, charts, and reports from your form. Looking at the roadmap, Figure 8-1, you see that this chapter shows you how to create and call dialog boxes from your form. The chapter discusses how to format the tab canvases and tab pages that you have been using in the Budgeting Case Project. You also learn how to associate a stacked canvas with its own window to create a dialog box for your forms. The chapter also teaches you to create your own form wizard, which is similar to the wizards used in Forms Builder. The last part of the chapter shows you how to create and deploy charts and reports in your forms.

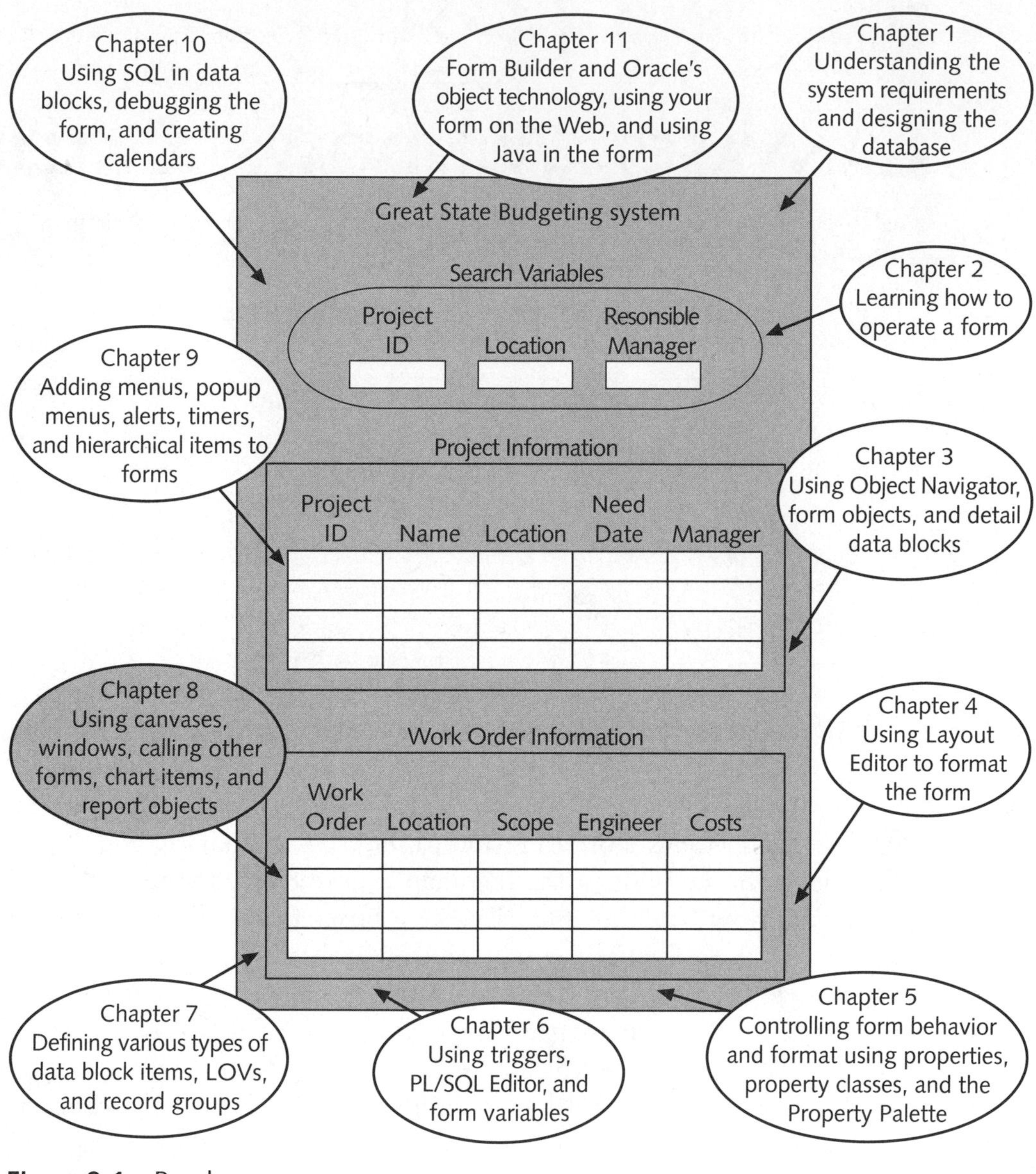

Figure 8-1 Roadmap

Canvas and Window Types and Behaviors

You should know from earlier discussions that a canvas is a form graphic object that is viewed by the operator. Anything that is viewed must be placed on a canvas. Canvases are displayed inside a window, which can be larger or smaller than the canvas. If the canvas is larger than the window, the window has scroll bars that allow the operator to view all parts of the canvas. Canvases can also overlay other canvases, just as a graphic component can overlay other graphic components. The overlaying or **stacked canvas** can be in the same window as the base canvas or it can be in its own window that appears above or within the base window. Dialog boxes are stacked canvases that are associated with their own windows. The varieties of canvas and window types that can be set through their properties give you a number of options as a developer.

The first step is to understand the different types of canvases, which are detailed in the following list:

- **Content**: A main form canvas. All forms must have at least one content canvas.
- **Stacked**: A secondary canvas. This canvas can overlay or cover a portion of a content canvas. Stacked canvases are most commonly used as popup menus and often require the creation of an additional form window. Once the stacked canvas is created, the window and canvas are associated with each other. The window can be dragged around the runtime window covering a portion of the underlying content canvas.
- **Tab**: A content canvas that consists of a series of tab pages. The current tab page overlays adjacent tab pages. You navigate between the pages by clicking the page's tab, which is always visible.
- **Horizontal toolbar**: A canvas that is attached to a window or on the form. It displays above the window's primary canvas if it is attached to the window and displays above the window if it is attached to the form. The canvas generally contains a series of buttons (or tools) that perform various functions.
- **Vertical toolbar**: The vertical toolbar is the same as the horizontal toolbar, except it appears on the left side of the canvas.

Canvas and Window Properties

The properties of canvases and windows are used to associate each to the other, change the type of canvas, or to control how the window operates. The following are canvas properties:

- Canvas Type
- Raise On Entry
- Viewport X Position On Canvas
- Viewport Y Position On Canvas
- Window

The following are window properties:

- Hide On Exit
- Close Allowed
- Horizontal Toolbar Canvas

- Icon Filename
- Inherit Menu
- Maximize Allowed
- Minimize Allowed
- Minimized Title
- Modal
- Move Allowed
- Primary Canvas
- Resize Allowed
- Show Horizontal Scrollbar
- Show Vertical Scrollbar
- Window Style

The canvas and window property names describe their purpose. You can view detailed descriptions of the properties in Appendix B.

Understanding Window Styles

The Window Style property determines whether the window is displayed in the document or dialog mode as depicted in Figure 8-2. This figure shows the same form in two different modes. To produce Figure 8-2, two different runtime applications were launched. The top application that is partially cut off by the runtime window is displayed in a document window. The lower application that is displayed above the runtime window is a dialog window. The difference between the two is that the dialog style raises the window above the runtime window and allows the operator to move the dialog anywhere within the computer screen. The document style keeps the window within the runtime frame. When the window is moved toward the edge, the runtime frame covers the window.

The Window style property works differently when the window is displayed on the Web than in the client/server environment. Although the DIALOG property setting raises the window above the runtime (client/server) or applet area (Web), the range of movement is different. Dialog style windows displayed on the Web can only be moved within the Web browser window. Dialog windows in the client/server environment may be moved anywhere within the Windows desktop.

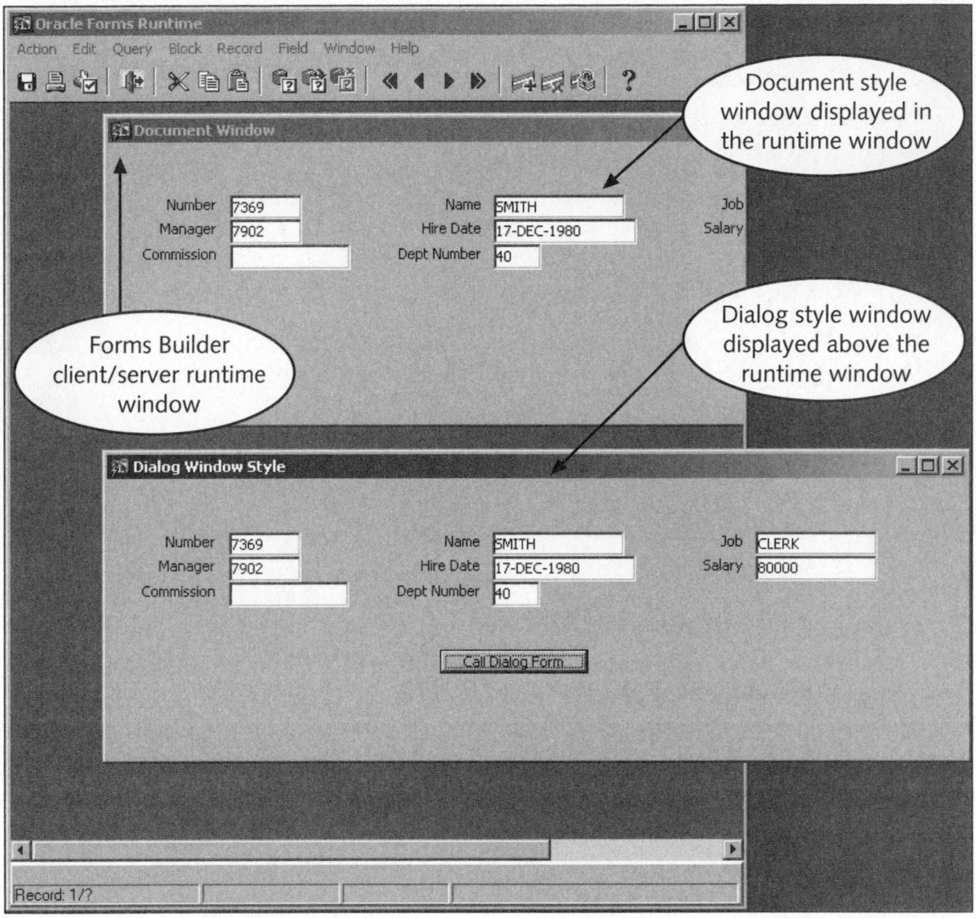

Figure 8-2 Dialog and document windows displayed in client/server runtime engine window

This practice session allows you to see the effect of the various properties on a form. You change various properties and run the form in the client/server (6*i* only) and Web runtime environments (6*i* and 9*i*):

1. Create a new form that uses the EMP table as a data source. The data block should contain one record and the style should be Form.
2. Open the Object Navigator, locate the canvas object, and open a Property Palette for the canvas. Change the default name to EMP_CANVAS. Locate the form window object. Set the Window Style property to **DOCUMENT**.
3. Save the form as **practice0801.fmb**. If you are using Form Builder 6*i*, run the form in the client/server environment. You will repeat the following steps again running the form in the Web environment. If you are using Forms Builder 9*i*, execute the form in the Web environment, because 9*i* does not support the client/server environment.

4. Move the window to the left so that the runtime frame covers half the window.
5. Close the form and set the Window Style property to **DIALOG**.
6. Repeat Step 4. Notice the difference caused by changing the Window Style property.
7. Move the window to the center of the runtime frame and resize the window.
8. Minimize the window.
9. Maximize the window.
10. Close the application and open the Object Navigator. Locate the window object and open a Property Palette. Set the following properties:

    Title: **EXAMPLE WINDOW TITLE**

    Move Allowed: **NO**

    Resize Allowed: **NO**

    Maximize Allowed: **NO**

    Minimize Allowed: **NO**
11. Launch the form and repeat steps 7 and 8. Notice the effects of the property changes.
12. Close the application and reset the Move Allowed, Resize Allowed, Maximize Allowed, and Minimize Allowed properties to the original values. Change the Window Style property to **DOCUMENT**.
13. Close the form. If you are using Forms Builder 9*i* or Form Builder 6*i* on the Web, proceed to Step 14. If you are using Form Builder 6*i* in the client/server environment, launch the form in the Web environment and repeat Steps 4 through 12. Determine if there are any differences between the client/server and Web environments.
14. Save form **practice0801.fmb** for later use.

USING STACKED CANVASES

A stacked canvas is a canvas that overlays a content canvas. A content canvas is the base window canvas. Each application normally has at least one content canvas. A stacked canvas can be used to cover a portion of the content canvas or as the canvas of a dialog box that is displayed within another window. Chapter 4 discussed how to display a content canvas in the Layout Editor and how to display the stacked canvas over a content canvas in the editor. This section discusses how to use and call a stacked canvas.

Displaying a Canvas

Stacked canvases and, in fact, all canvases are displayed by navigating into an item on the canvas. Canvases without a data block item cannot be displayed. Thus, to display a stacked canvas you must navigate to an item on the canvas. Forms Builder then places the canvas within the designated window at the position specified by the following properties of the canvases: Viewport X Position On Canvas and Viewport Y Position On Canvas. If these properties are set to 0,0, the top-left corner of the canvas is displayed in the top-left corner of the window. If the canvas is to be used as a dialog box that is called from another canvas, the 0,0 settings should probably be used.

Figure 8-3a, 8-3b, and 8-3c illustrate three application views. Figure 8-3a is a view that displays the content canvas. The window actually has two canvases: one that is displayed and a stacked canvas that is hidden. Both canvases have Viewport X Position On Canvas and Viewport Y Position On Canvas properties of 0,0. This means that they are displayed in the same place. The content canvas is displayed because the input focus resides in the block on that canvas.

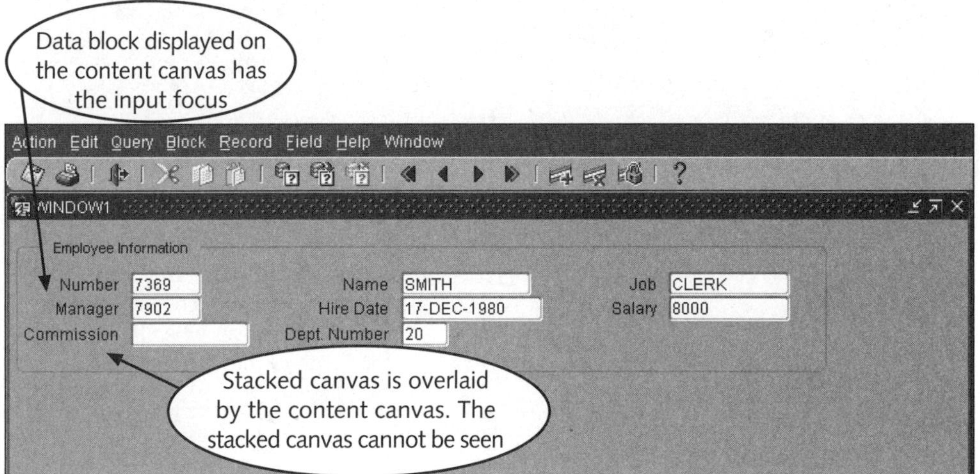

Figure 8-3a The content canvas containing the EMP data block overlays a stacked canvas containing the DEPT data block

The second application (Figure 8-3b) displays the stacked canvas over the EMP items on the content canvas. The stacked canvas was displayed when the user tabbed into the canvas. Forms Builder automatically places the canvas that has the input focus on top.

The third application (Figure 8-3c) displays both canvases. The stacked canvas is displayed because its Viewport Y Position On Canvas property was set to 200. It is displayed on top of the content canvas, because the content canvas did not have any items or graphic objects in the space occupied by the stacked canvas.

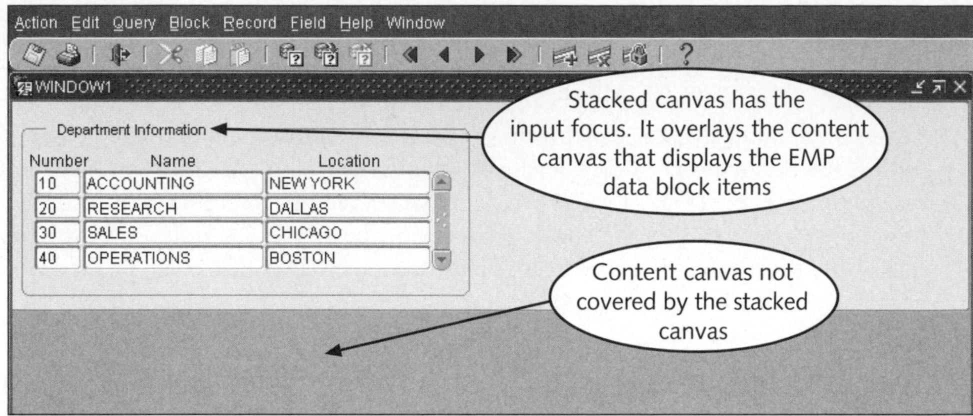

Figure 8-3b The stacked canvas containing the DEPT data block overlays a portion of the content canvas

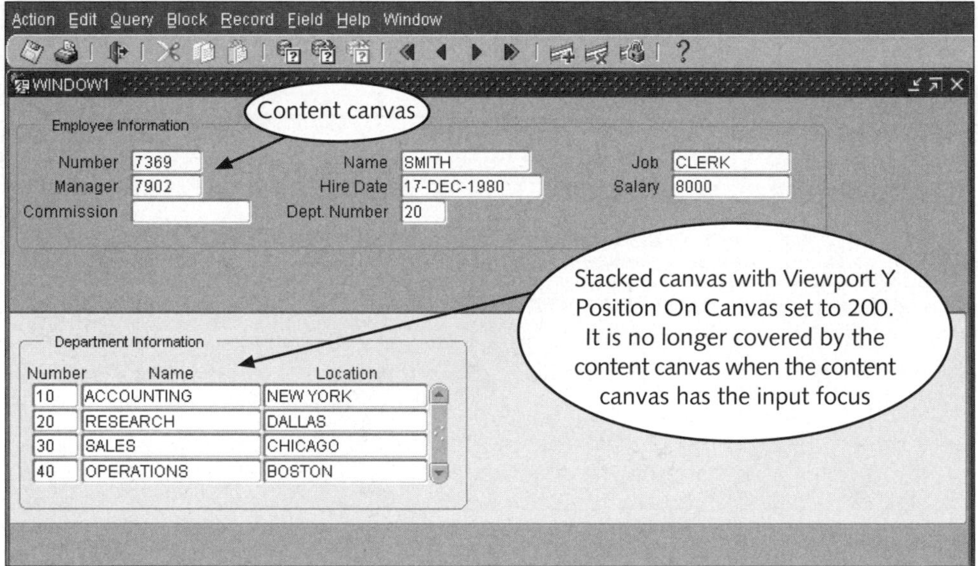

Figure 8-3c The stacked canvas positioned below the EMP data block

Stacked canvases are generally used as the basis of a dialog box that is displayed over the content canvas. They can also be used to overlay parts of another canvas as you saw in Figure 8-3b and Figure 8-3c. To create a dialog box using a stacked canvas you would perform the following steps to associate the stacked canvas to its own window:

1. Create a stacked canvas and place some items on the canvas. This can be done using the Layout Wizard or the Layout Editor.
2. Use the Layout Editor to format the stacked canvas.

3. Create a window object. Set the window object's Primary Canvas property to the name of the stacked canvas. This ensures that the stacked canvas is used if the window is opened.
4. Set the other window properties to suit your application's needs.
5. Open the Object Navigator for the stacked canvas and change the object's Window property to the name of the window created in Step 3. This ensures that the canvas uses the window if the canvas is displayed by navigation.
6. Set the Viewport X Position On Canvas and Viewport Y Position On Canvas properties to 0,0.

Figure 8-4 illustrates a stacked canvas placed in a window. The dialog box window displays the same stacked canvas depicted in Figures 8-3b and 8-3c. When the canvas is placed in its own window, it can be moved, resized, minimized, or made modal to substantially enhance your application.

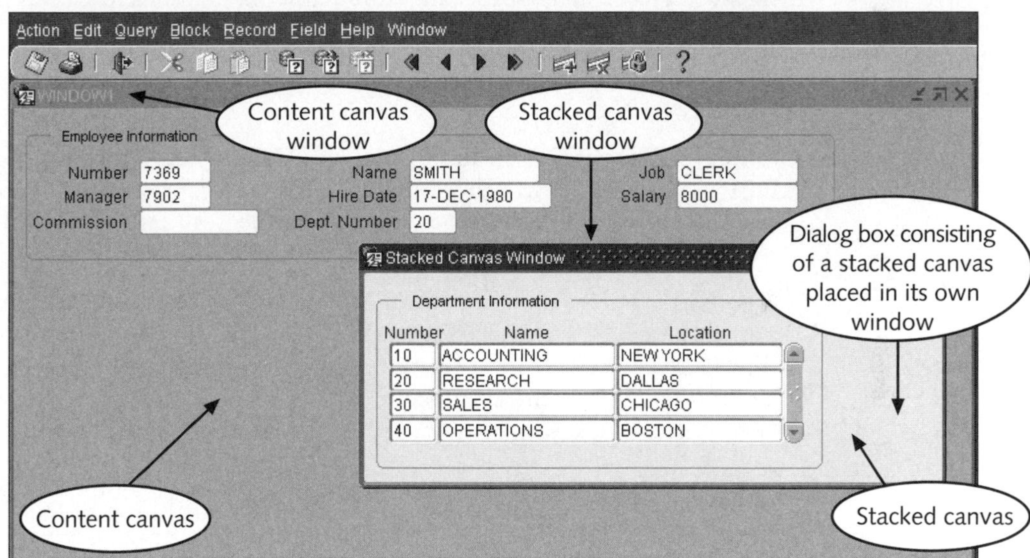

Figure 8-4 Dialog box displaying a stacked canvas

It is common to use called dialog boxes to see or create auxiliary information. All forms have limited space. One of your challenges as a designer is to place the items in this space, although it is common to have insufficient space. Dialog boxes allow you to place items and display them only when the user actually needs them. For example, the Case Project has a WO_INSTRUCTIONS item that can have a length of 2,000 characters. Because this type of item can take a great deal of form space, it can best be made into a dialog box that is displayed whenever the operator needs to see the instructions.

Two practice sessions on calling stacked canvases and creating dialog boxes are outlined as follows:

1. In the first practice session, you create a stacked canvas that is displayed over a content canvas. You then navigate into the stacked canvas causing it to display. To accomplish these tasks, perform the following steps:
   a. Using the **practice0801.fmb** form from the previous practice, *make sure* the EMPNO Required property is set to **NO**. Start the Data Block Wizard.
   b. Using the Data Block Wizard, create a data block based on the DEPT table. No relationship is needed.
   c. Start the Layout Wizard. Make sure that you place the DEPT data block on a new canvas using a setting of **NEW CANVAS** and a Type setting of **STACKED**. Only one DEPT data block record should be displayed in the FORM style.
   d. In the Object Navigator, change the name of the stacked canvas object to **DEPT_CANVAS**.
   e. Locate the DEPTNO item in the DEPT data block. Set the Required property to **NO**.
   f. Open the Layout Editor and format the **DEPT** data block on the DEPT_CANVAS. Size the **DEPT_CANVAS** to be smaller than the form's content canvas, so that you can see the content canvas while displaying the DEPT_CANVAS stacked canvas.
   g. Open a Property Palette for the EMP data block. Set the Navigation Style property to **CHANGE DATA BLOCK**. This causes the input focus to shift to the DEPT block after the operator tabs though the EMP data block items. When the shift occurs, the stacked canvas displaying the DEPT data block will be displayed.
   h. Repeat Step g for the DEPT data block. This causes the input focus to shift to the EMP data block after the operator tabs through the data block items. This in turn causes the stacked canvas to be hidden.
   i. Launch the form. Tab through the EMP and DEPT items displaying the DEPT and EMP canvases.
   j. Close the form. Change the DEPT_CANVAS canvas Viewport Y Position On Canvas property to **200**.
   k. Launch the form. Both canvases should now be displayed, because the stacked canvas does not cover the data items in the EMP data block.

2. In this practice session, you place the stacked canvas into a window creating a dialog box. Perform the following steps:
   a. Using the same practice form, create a window object.
   b. Open the new window object's Property Palette. Set the following:
      Name: **STACKED_CANVAS**
      Title: **STACKED CANVAS WINDOW**
      Height: Same as the stacked canvas Height property, approximately 150.
      Width: Same as the stacked canvas Width property, approximately 350.
      Primary Canvas: **DEPT_CANVAS**
   c. Open the Property Palette of the DEPT_CANVAS canvas. Set the following properties:
      Window: **STACKED_CANVAS**
      Viewport Y Position On Canvas: **0**
   d. Save and launch the form. Tab through the EMP data block until the STACKED_CANVAS window is displayed. Notice that it is in its own window and can be moved and resized.
   e. Click the content canvas. Notice that the stacked canvas is placed behind the content canvas.
   f. Retain the form for later practice.

Launching Windows and Canvases

Canvases are displayed as a result of two events: the input focus moves to an item on the canvas or the window associated to the canvas is opened. In the previous practice session, the Navigation Style property of the data blocks was changed to CHANGE DATA BLOCK. After the operator tabbed through a record, the input focus changed to the next block displaying the canvas. A data block's items can also be placed on different canvases. As the operator tabs between items, the canvases associated to the items are automatically displayed.

Forms Builder has two built-in subprograms that perform these same basic functions. The Go_item built-in moves the input focus to a designated item. The Go_block built-in moves the input focus to the first navigable item in the designated block. These two commands are good techniques for opening new canvases. It can be extremely confusing for an operator to have canvases appear and disappear in a form as a result of tabbing, so it is better to have a button or toolbar that displays the canvas. In this way, operators are always aware that they are displaying new canvases, because they must click the button.

It is also a good idea to have a button on the stacked canvas that moves the focus back to the base content canvas. This causes the content canvas to overlay the stacked canvas. These buttons use the Go_item or Go_block built-in to change the input focus.

To reinforce and practice the techniques described in this section, use the **practice0801.fmb** form from the previous practice session to add a button that calls the other canvas to each of the canvases. To do so, perform the following steps:

a. Open the **practice0801.fmb** form in the Object Navigator.

b. Open the Layout Editor, and place a button on the EMP_CANVAS canvas that displays the EMP data block. Be sure to associate the button to the EMP canvas.

c. Open a Property Palette for the new button. Set the following properties:

   Name: **DEPARTMENT_BUTTON**

   Label: **DEPARTMENTS**

d. To create a When-Button-Pressed trigger for the DEPARTMENTS_BUTTON button, use the following statement:

```
Go_block ('dept');
```

e. Open the Layout Editor and add a button to the DEPT_CANVAS canvas that displays the DEPT block. Be sure to associate the button with the DEPT data block.

f. Open the Property Palette for the new button. Set the following properties:

   Name: **EMPLOYEE_BUTTON**

   Label: **EMPLOYEES**

g. Create a When-Button-Pressed trigger for the EMPLOYEE_BUTTON button. Use the following statement, which moves the input focus to the EMP data block:

```
Go_block ('emp');
```

h. Save and launch the form to test the buttons. The buttons cause the dialog box to appear and disappear. Figure 8-5 illustrates the two canvases and buttons.

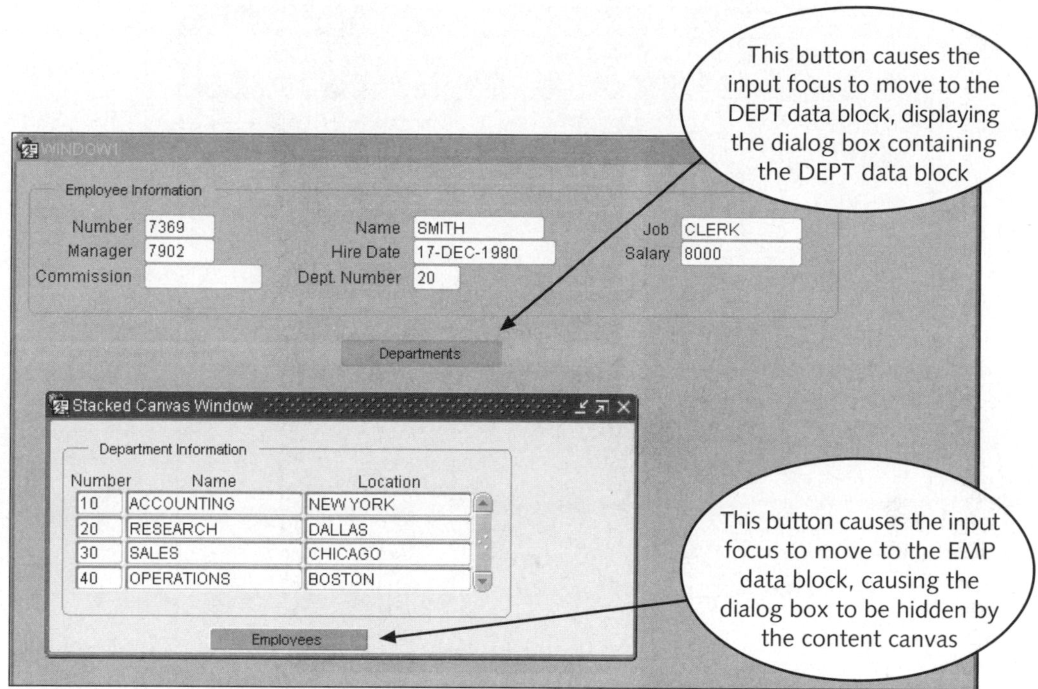

Figure 8-5 EMP_CANVAS and DEPT_CANVAS and buttons that display the canvases

8

Creating and Formatting Tab Canvases

A **tab canvas** is a canvas that consists of a series of pages. The Budgeting Case Project form (see Figure 7-36) is an example of a tab canvas with multiple pages. The pages are very similar to a stacked canvas. The page currently being viewed overlays the other pages. The tabs can be placed on any of the four canvas edges, so that each page has a tab on one of the edges that is always visible. The operator can display different pages by selecting the tab. Figure 8-6 illustrates a tab canvas with two tabs on the left side of the canvas.

A tab canvas is useful, especially since most systems consist of a series of forms that offer different views of the database, and operators often move around through the various forms. For instance, an operator using a budgeting system may want to add a new project to the database, review the costs of an existing work order, identify the work order tasks that must be performed, or add an employee to the database. All of these tasks are functionally different and require different forms. Tab pages offer a mechanism that enables the operator to quickly locate and navigate to the various forms. The proper form can be easily located, because the tabs are always visible to the operator. Navigation is quick because Forms Builder does not have to open a new application for each called form—all of the tab pages are already open.

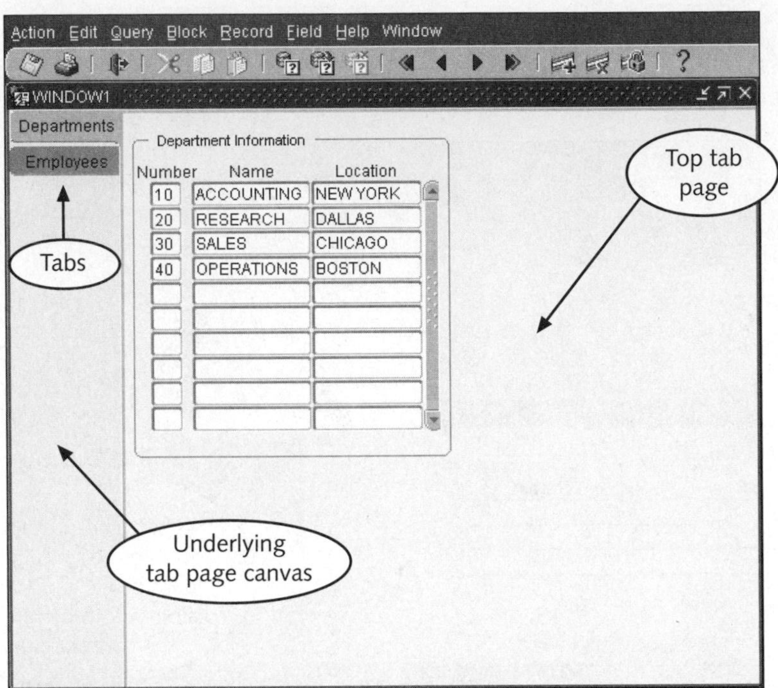

Figure 8-6 Tab canvas and two tab pages

Tab canvases are also useful tools for the Web. If each form is a different application, you must continually download applications over the Web, thus slowing performance. This is especially wasteful if you need to open the same application repeatedly. If you place the forms into one application using tab pages, the operator encounters an initial delay downloading a larger application, but the navigation to different forms within the system is much quicker.

You create a tab canvas in the same manner in which you create other canvases. You can use any one of the following three techniques:

1. Using the Layout Wizard Canvas page, select **TAB** as the type style option and set the Tab Page option to **NEW TAB PAGE** (see Figure 8-7).
2. Using the Object Navigator, select the Canvases node and click the Create tool. Open the Property Palette for the new canvas. Change the Canvas Type property of the canvas to **TAB CANVAS** on the Create A Tab Page.
3. Using the Layout Editor, select the **Tab Canvas** tool and draw a canvas in the work area.

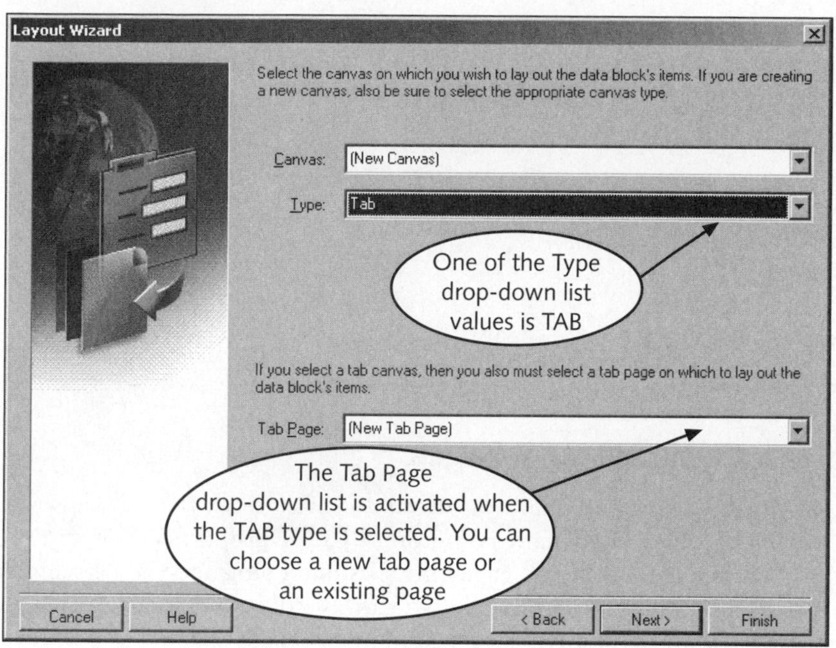

Figure 8-7 Layout Wizard Canvas page displaying the options needed to create a new tab canvas and tab page

Tab pages are graphic objects that exist underneath the tab canvas object in the Object Navigator, as shown in Figure 8-8. This figure displays a tab canvas called CANVAS4 and two child tab pages called PAGE5 and PAGE9. After creating the tab canvas, tab pages could be created in the following two ways:

- Using the Layout Wizard, select the NEW TAB PAGE option.
- Using the Object Navigator, select the Tab Pages node and click the Create tool.

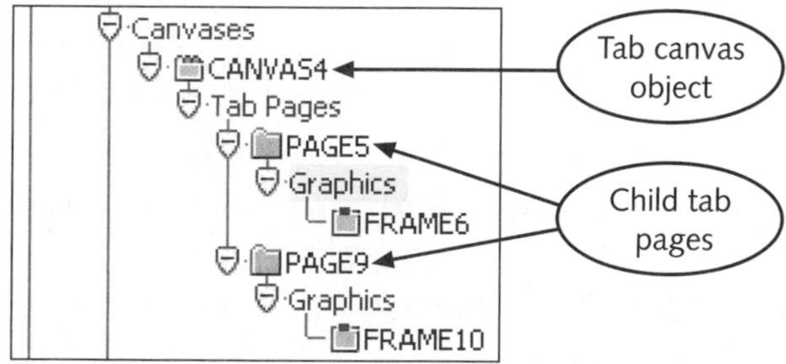

Figure 8-8 Object Navigator view of a tab canvas object and two child tab page objects

Because the tab canvas and tab pages are related, tab canvas properties influence the tab page. For example, all of the tab pages have the same height and width, because these

8

properties are set on the canvas. However, the tab page has properties that supercede the canvas properties. The following are canvas and tab page properties (a complete description of the properties can be found in Appendix B):

- Bevel (canvas)
- Corner Style (canvas)
- Width Style (canvas)
- Active Style (canvas)
- Tab Attachment Edge (canvas)
- Label (page)

Coloring Tab Canvases and Pages

Tab pages can be colored to stand out from a canvas. Both the tab canvas and the tab page have Background Color and Foreground Color properties. You can see from the shading in Figure 8-9 that the tab page body has one color, and the tabs and area around the tab pages are a different color. The tab canvas' color and format properties control the tabs and the area around the tab pages. The tab page properties control the format within the page body, override the parent tab canvas properties, and default to the canvas property if tab page properties are not set.

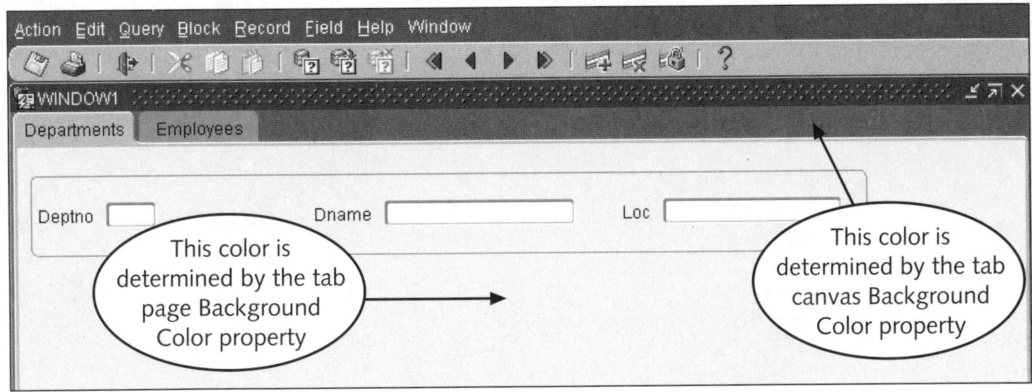

Figure 8-9 Example of using different colors for the tab canvas and tab page

For practice with creating and formatting tab pages, perform the following the steps:

1. Create a new form with a tab canvas. The canvas has two pages: one for the DEPT table and one for the EMP table.

   a. Open the Object Navigator and create a new form.

   b. Create a data block for the DEPT table using the Data Block Wizard.

c. Place the DEPT data block on a new tab canvas using the Layout Wizard. Be sure to select the **TAB** type and **NEW TAB PAGE** settings on the Layout Wizard Canvas page. The style should be Tabular with 10 records displayed.

d. Locate this tab page in the Object Navigator and name the page **DEPARTMENTS**.

e. Locate and open a Property Palette for the DEPTNO data block item in the DEPT data block. Set the Required property to **NO**.

f. Create a second data block for the EMP table using the Data Block Wizard. There is no relationship between this block and the DEPT data block.

g. Using the Layout Wizard, place the EMP data block on the tab canvas. Be sure to select the **existing tab canvas** and the **NEW TAB PAGE** settings on the Layout Wizard Canvas page. The style should be Tabular with 10 records displayed.

h. Locate the new tab page in the Object Navigator and name the page **EMPLOYEES**.

i. Locate and open a Property Palette for the EMPNO data block item in the EMP data block. Set the Required property to **NO**.

j. Open the Property Palette for the tab canvas. Set the Tab Attachment Edge property to **LEFT**.

k. Open the Layout Editor and format and size the tab pages so that all items are displayed.

l. Save the form as **practice0802.fmb**. If you are using Form Builder 6*i*, launch the form in both the Web and client/server environments, and try to notice the difference. Forms Builder 9*i* developers will not be able to see the differences.

2. In this practice session, you format the tab canvas and tab pages by performing the following steps:

a. Open the Property Palette for the **practice0802.fmb** form tab canvas. Select a background color and foreground color value for the canvas.

b. Open the Property Palette for the DEPARTMENTS tab page. Set the following properties:

Label: **DEPARTMENTS**

Background Color: A color different than the tab canvas

c. Open the Property Palette for the EMPLOYEES tab page. Set the following properties:

Label: **EMPLOYEES**

Background Color: A color different than the tab canvas and the DEPARTMENT tab page

d. Save and launch the form using both the client/server and Web runtime engines (note that Forms Builder 9*i* developers cannot use the client/server engine). Close the form.

e. Modify the following properties of the tab canvas: Bevel, Corner Style, Width Style, Active Style, and Tab Attachment Edge. Use the various settings for these properties. Then run the form and notice the effect of these property settings. If you are a Form Builder 6*i* developer, run the form in both the client/server and Web environments.

f. Save the form for later practice.

CALLING OTHER FORMS

The previous section described how tab pages are effective tools for displaying various system screens. If you choose not to place all your forms into one application, you must call the other applications. Forms Builder has three built-in subprograms for locating and executing a form from an existing form. These built-ins are described in Table 8-1.

Table 8-1 Built-in subprograms that call other applications

Name of built-in subprogram	Description
Call_form	Launches another form application and leaves the calling application open. The operator must return to the calling application.
New_form	Launches another form application and replaces the calling application. The operator cannot return to the calling application.
Open_form	Launches another form application and leaves the calling application open. This command allows multiple database connections to occur.

The functions of each of the following subprograms vary slightly. The Call_form and Open_form built-ins leave the calling form open. These executables overlay the calling form with the called form. The original form remains under the called application. When the operator closes the called application, the original application is redisplayed with the same data it had when it called the form. These built-ins are useful tools when the operator is opening applications for auxiliary information and wants to return to the original application. These built-ins are not the best options when the operator continues to open other applications including those similar to the calling form. Because the calling forms remain open, the operator can eventually run out of memory and crash his machine. Even without a crash, the operator has to close numerous forms before exiting the system.

The New_form built-in closes the calling application each time it is executed. The memory and closing problems are eliminated using this built-in; it does not, however, allow the operator to return to the original form. When designing such a form, you should contact the system engineer to determine the purpose of the called form. The system engineer should be familiar with how the system operates and may be able to identify the situations in which the operator wants to close the calling application as well as those in which the operator probably wants to return to the calling form.

There are slight differences between the Call_form and Open_form built-ins. The Call_form built-in does not save any modifications in the calling form when it calls another application, and this can cause problems. For example, assume you have updated a record without committing the change, and you then call a second application using the Call_form application and modify the called form. When you issue a COMMIT command, Forms Builder issues the following error message, which is pictured in Figure 8-10: "FRM-40403: A calling form has unapplied changes. Save not allowed." The operator cannot save the changes in the called form until the changes are made in the calling form. This means that the operator must close the called form, save the changes in the calling form, open the called form, and redo the modifications. Obviously, such a situation should be avoided whenever possible.

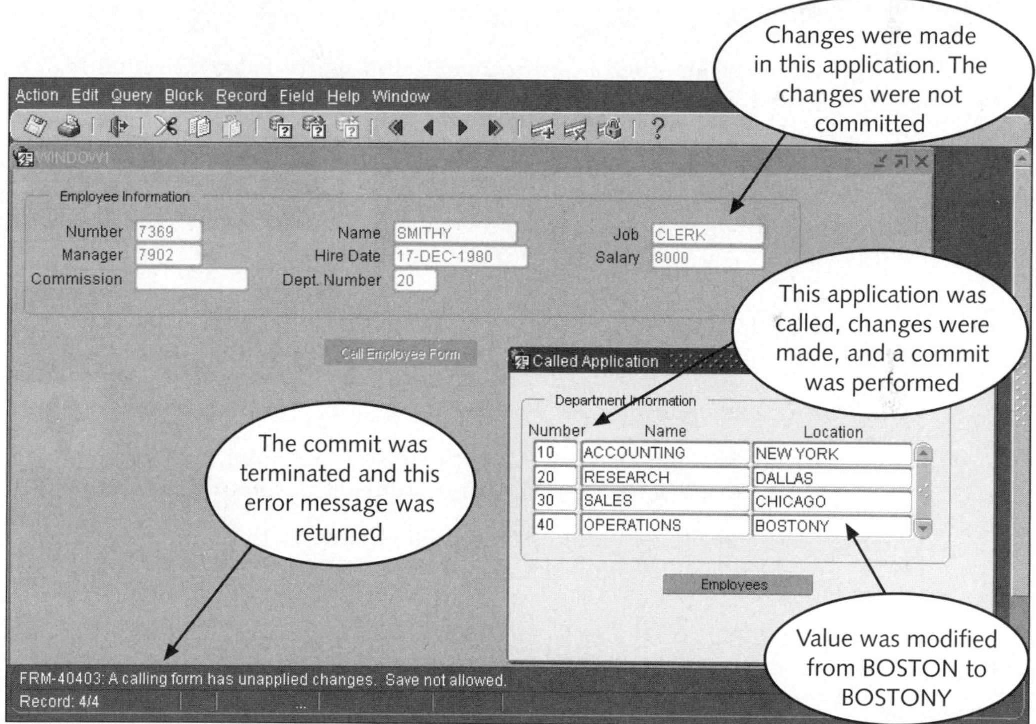

Figure 8-10 FRM-40403 error message caused by making changes in a called form with pending changes in the calling form

The Open_form built-in allows the operator to avoid the error. This built-in commits the changes for both forms. Call_form, however, has several features not allowed with Open_form. Call_form can disable the called application's DML (insert, update, and delete) functionality. The built-in has a parameter value named QUERY_ONLY that disables the called form's ability to issue INSERT, UPDATE, or DELETE statements. It can also hide or not hide the calling form. The NO_HIDE option causes any portion of the calling form to be displayed that is not overlaid by the called form. Thus, if the called form is smaller than the calling form, portions of the calling form are displayed (see Figure 8-10). The HIDE option totally removes the calling form from view regardless of size.

Calling an Application Using a Button

An excellent way to call another application is through a button, which can be placed on a canvas or on a toolbar canvas. The user can click the button and see the called application. To create a button that calls another application, you would perform the following steps:

1. Open the Layout Editor and display the button's canvas.
2. Activate the Button tool on the toolbar.
3. Place and size the button on the canvas.
4. Double-click the button to open its Property Palette. Set the Name and Label properties.
5. Open the Object Navigator and select the new button's Triggers node.
6. Create a When-Button-Pressed trigger for the button by using one of the following template scripts:

```
Open_form ('name and location of the form');
Call_form('name and location of the form', hide);
Call_form('name and location of the form', no_hide);
New_form('name and location of the form');
```

Two practice exercises on calling other applications are outlined as follows.

1. In the first practice session, perform the following steps to call form module **practice0801.fmx** using form module **practice0802.fmb**:
   a. Open form module **practice0802.fmb** in the Object Navigator. Open the Layout Editor and display the **DEPARTMENTS** tab.
   b. Add a button to the tab page. Make sure the button is associated to the DEPT data block. If you look at the Layout Editor, you will see ten buttons. The multiple buttons were created by placing the button item on the DEPT data block. DEPT is a multiple-item data block. The appearance of multiple buttons will be corrected in the next step.
   c. Open the button's Property Palette and set the following properties:

      Name: **EMPLOYEE_FORM**

      Label: **Open Employee Form**

      Number of Items Displayed: **1**

d. Create a When-Button-Pressed trigger for the button by using the following script (be sure to precede "practice0801" with the module file path):

```
Call_form ('practice0801', no_hide);
```

e. Save and launch the form. Click the **EMPLOYEE_FORM** button. The called form, **practice0801**, should display. To return to the calling form, click the **window** of the called form and drag it away. Be sure to compile the **practice0801** form before performing this step. You can only call the compiled version of the form.

2. In this second practice session, you see the differences between the Open_form and Call_form built-ins. Perform the following steps:

   a. Launch the form created in the last step of the preceding practice session.

   b. Select the DEPARTMENTS tab and execute a query on this tab page form. Modify one of the records.

   c. Click the **button** that calls the Employee form.

   d. Execute a query on this form. Modify one of the records and attempt to save the changes. You should receive a "FRM-40403" error.

   e. Close the browser without saving the data.

   f. Change the When-Button-Pressed trigger script to the following (add the file path to the module name):

   ```
   Open_form ('practice0801');
   ```

   g. Repeat steps b through d. Notice that you should now be able to save the changes.

   h. Close the called form. Notice that the original application is still displayed with the same records.

   i. Close the browser.

   j. Change the When-Button-Pressed trigger script to the following (add the file path to the module name):

   ```
   New_form ('practice0801');
   ```

   k. Save and launch the form.

   l. Click the **EMPLOYEE_FORM** button and call the Employee form.

   m. Close the application. This should terminate the session rather than returning you to the calling application, since the Employee form was called using the New_form built-in.

Creating and Using a Toolbar Canvas

Horizontal and **vertical toolbar canvases** are the last remaining types of canvases to be discussed in this chapter. They are similar to stacked canvases in that they can overlay a portion of the canvas that is displayed within a window. They are displayed horizontally at the top of the canvas or vertically on the left side of the canvas. The tools that reside on the toolbar canvas are iconic buttons, each button with a When-Button-Pressed trigger. The toolbar tools can perform basic form activities, such as placing a form into the Query mode, executing a query, or saving changes. These tools are also handy for placing the buttons that launch other applications. Placing these buttons on a toolbar that is displayed with each window can add consistency to your system.

The toolbar canvas can be assigned to a window or to an application. When the toolbar is assigned to the window, the toolbar appears within the window frame (see Figure 8-11). The toolbar appears within the window's viewport, which is the part of the window that displays the canvas. The canvas is displayed below or to the right of the toolbar, depending on whether it is a vertical or horizontal toolbar (see Figure 8-11).

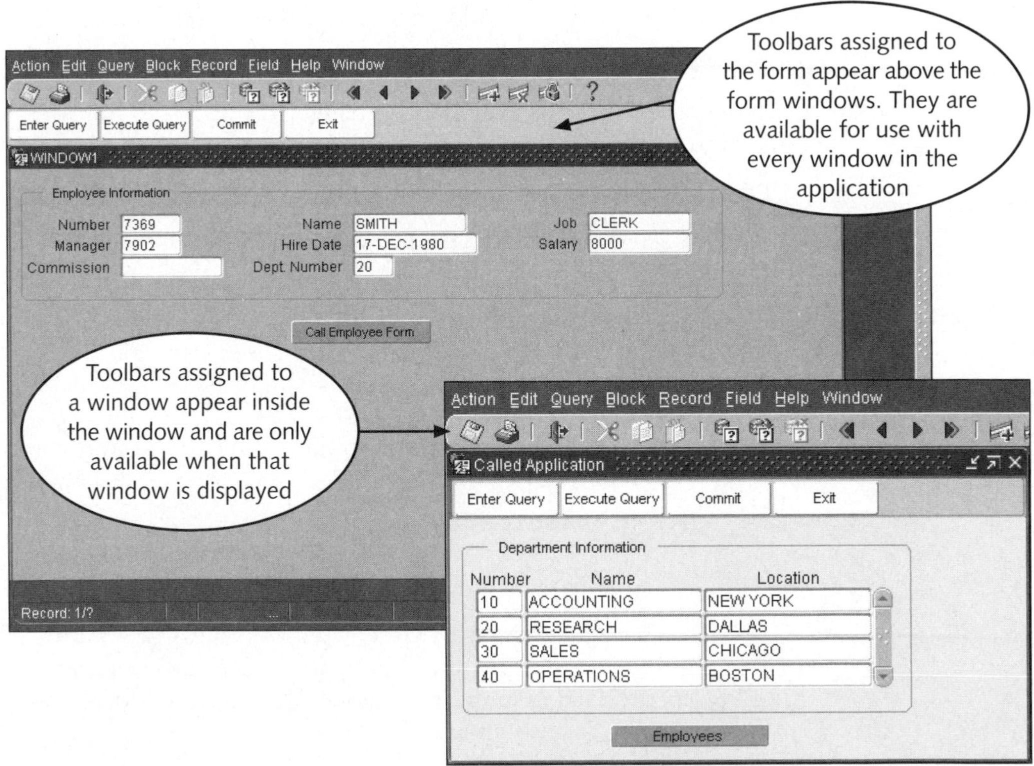

Figure 8-11 Horizontal toolbars assigned to the application and to the window

To create a toolbar, you would perform the following steps:

1. Open the Object Navigator and create a canvas object.
2. Open the Property Palette of the canvas and set the following properties:
   Canvas Type: **Horizontal Toolbar** or **Vertical Toolbar**
   Height or Width: **20** (or a value of your preference)
3. Open the Layout Editor and place the buttons on the canvas. Buttons must not be larger than the canvas.
4. Associate each button with a When-Button-Pressed trigger that contains the appropriate built-in.
5. Associate the toolbar canvas to either the window or the application. Toolbars are associated to the application using the Form Vertical Toolbar Canvas property or the Form Horizontal Toolbar Canvas property. An application can have both horizontal and vertical toolbars simultaneously. Toolbars are associated to the window using the Form Vertical Toolbar Canvas property or the Form Horizontal Toolbar Canvas property.

For more practice creating toolbars, two exercises are outlined as follows.

1. In the first practice session, you create a horizontal toolbar that has buttons or tools that place the form into the Enter Query mode, execute a query, and call another application. Perform the following using the **practice0802.fmb** form module:
   a. Open the **practice0802.fmb** module in the Object Navigator and create a canvas object.
   b. Open a Property Palette for the canvas and set the following properties:

      Name: **TOOLBAR_CANVAS**

      Canvas Type: **HORIZONTAL TOOLBAR**

      Height: **20**
   c. Open the Layout Editor and display the TOOLBAR_CANVAS. Create three buttons by following these steps:
      - Activate the **Button** tool.
      - Place a button on the TOOLBAR_CANVAS canvas.
      - Double-click the **button** opening its Property Palette. Set the following properties:

        Name: **ENTER_QUERY**

        Label: **ENTER QUERY**

        Number of Items Displayed: **1**

        Tooltip: **PLACES THE FORM IN THE ENTER QUERY MODE**

d. Close the Property Palette. Select and copy the **ENTER_QUERY** button.

e. Paste the copied button onto the TOOLBAR_CANVAS canvas. The pasted button will overlay the copied button. Drag the **button** to the right of the ENTER_QUERY button.

f. Double-click the **pasted button** opening its Property Palette. Set the following properties:

   Name: **EXECUTE_QUERY**

   Label: **EXECUTE QUERY**

   Tooltip: **RETRIEVES RECORDS TO THE FORM**

g. Repeat steps d and e.

h. Double-click the **pasted button** to open its Property Palette. Set the following properties:

   Name: **CALL_EMPLOYEE_FORM**

   Label: **EMPLOYEE FORM**

   Tooltip: **OPENS THE EMPLOYEE FORM**

Figure 8-12 illustrates the toolbar at this point.

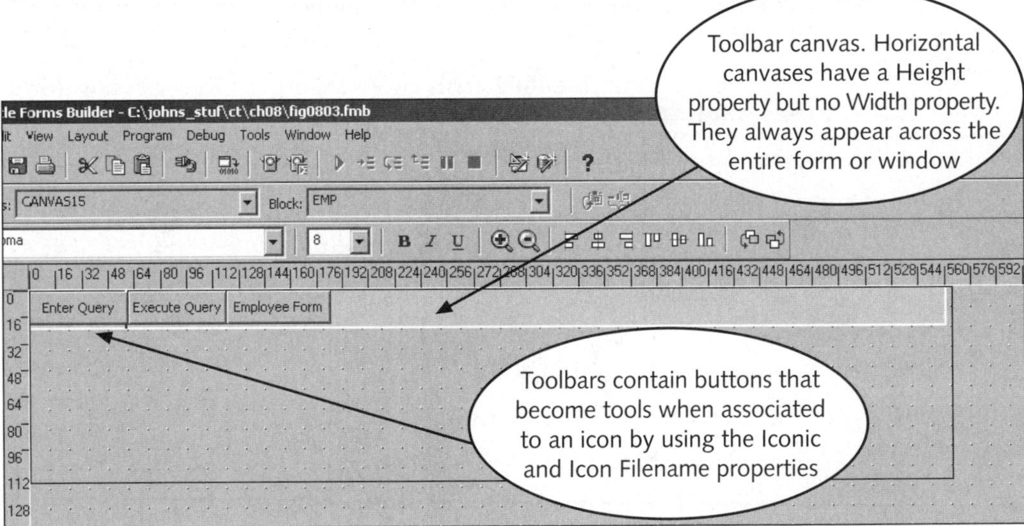

Figure 8-12 Horizontal Toolbar

i. Open the Object Navigator and locate the ENTER_QUERY button. Create a When-Button-Pressed trigger using the following script:

```
Go_block ('dept');
Enter_query;
```

j. Locate the EXECUTE_QUERY button. Create a When-Button-Pressed trigger using the following script:

```
Go_block ('dept');
Execute_query;
```

k. Locate the CALL_EMPLOYEE_FORM button. Create a When-Button-Pressed trigger using the following script (add the file path to the form name):

```
Open_form ('practice0801');
```

l. Locate the form module icon in the Object Navigator. Open a Property Palette for the item. Set the Form Horizontal Toolbar Canvas property to **TOOLBAR_CANVAS**.

m. Save the form and then launch it to test the toolbar and buttons.

Because the buttons do not display an icon, you must locate an icon file and attach it to the button using the Iconic and Icon Filename properties.

2. In this second practice session, you assign the TOOLBAR_CANVAS canvas to the window rather than to the applications:

   a. Open the **practice0802.fmb** form module in the Object Navigator.

   b. Open a Property Palette for the form module. Set the Form Horizontal Toolbar Canvas property to **NULL**.

   c. Open a Property Palette for the form's window. Set the Horizontal Toolbar Canvas property to **TOOLBAR_CANVAS**.

   d. Save and launch the form and notice the difference in the location of the toolbar.

   e. Close the form.

CREATING AND USING CHARTS IN FORMS

Form Builder 6*i* allows you to create a chart item within the IDE. Both 6*i* and 9*i* allow you to display a chart in a form using a chart item. The 9*i* chart items do not work very well because of the move to the Web. The 6*i* charts, however, work very well.

A chart item displays data block values graphically rather than in a tabular data block. A chart item can display the values as a line graph, bar graph, or a pie chart and in other manners. Charts displayed in a chart item are created by Oracle's Graphics Builder tool. Graphics Builder is a tool that has been part of Oracle's Developer suite for many years. It is used to create a chart file that has an extension of **.ogd**. This file can then be used in a form or a report. When the file is launched, a SELECT statement is executed and the results are returned to the form or report. The following sections discuss how to create and display a chart in your form.

Using the Chart Wizard to Create a Chart

Form Builder 6*i* has a Chart Wizard that can be called to create a chart (9*i* does not have a Chart Wizard). The 6*i* wizard is located on the Tools menu along with the other wizards. However, this tool is generally disabled, which means it cannot be launched. To enable the Chart Wizard option, three things must be done:

1. A data block must be created. The charted values are based on the result set returned to the data block.
2. A canvas must be created.
3. A chart item must be placed on the canvas and selected. If you use the Layout Editor Chart Item tool to add and place the item on the canvas, Form Builder displays the New Chart Object dialog box (see Figure 8-13) prompting you to use the Chart Wizard or to build the chart manually. The latter option will not open the Chart Wizard.

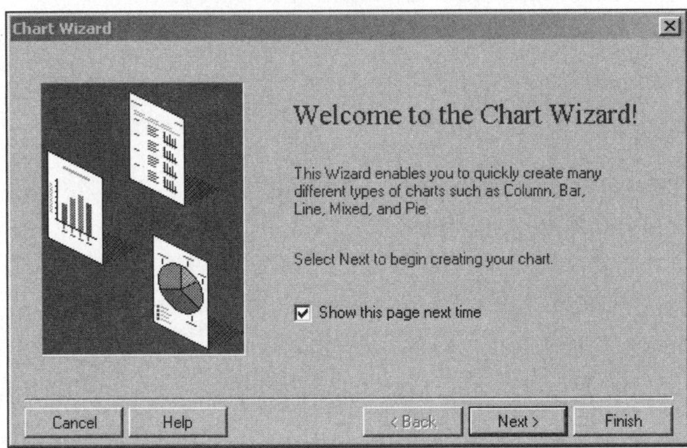

Figure 8-13 Chart Wizard dialog box

The first page of the Chart Wizard is the Welcome page. It has no real purpose and can be disabled by unchecking the Show This Page Next Time check box. The first page of consequence is the Type page (see Figure 8-14), which is used to identify the type of chart. This page has three components:

- **Title text item**: Text item used to enter the title of the chart.
- **Chart Type list box**: This list box displays the types of charts that are available. The image to the left of the box depicts the selected chart type.
- **Chart Subtype list box**: This list box displays the various subtypes of charts. The values in this list change with the selected chart type.

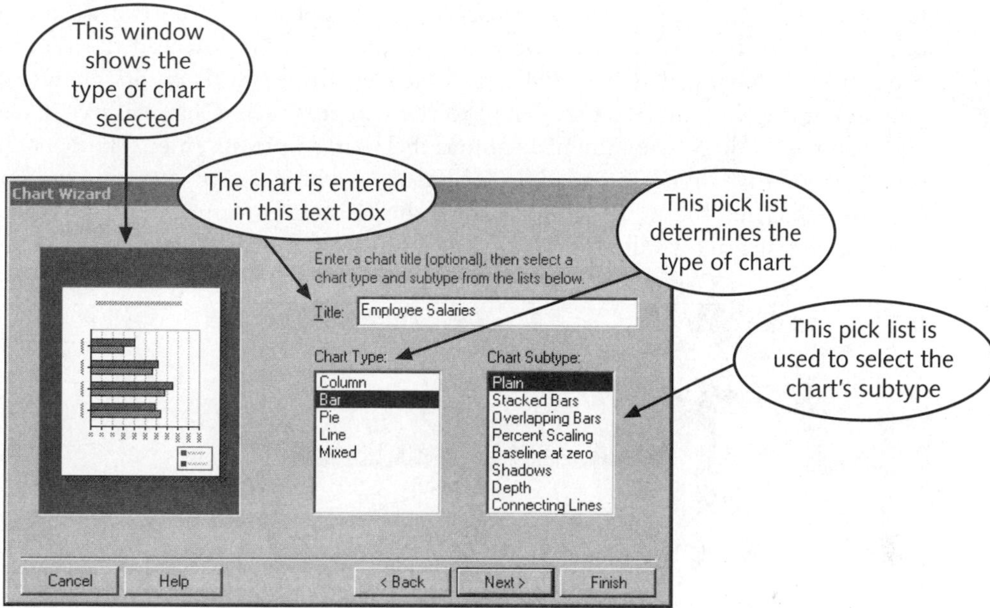

Figure 8-14 Chart Wizard Type page

The Block page (see Figure 8-15) is the second wizard page. This page contains a list box that displays the names of all of the form's data blocks that contain items. The chart values are based on the values returned by this data block.

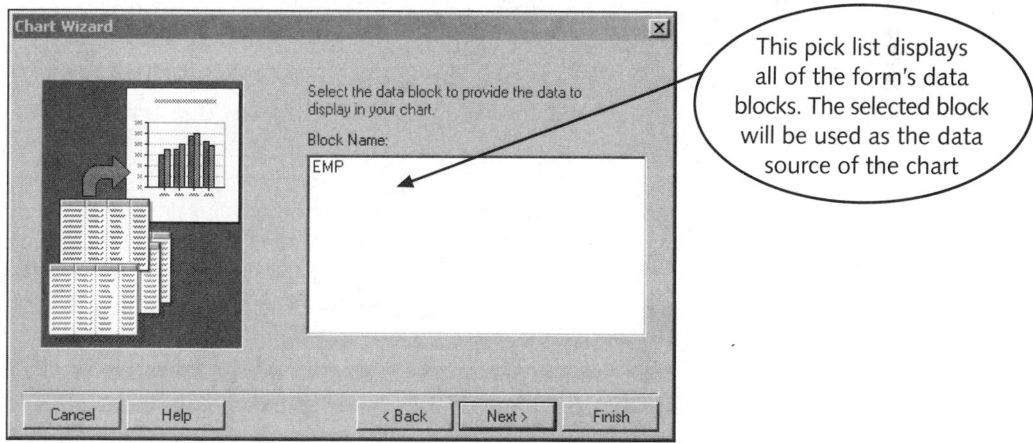

Figure 8-15 Chart Wizard Block page

The third page is used to identify the data block items that describe the measured values. This is called the Category page and is shown in Figure 8-16. The NAME (ename) item was selected as the Category Axis. The value appears as NAME instead of ENAME, because the ENAME Name property was changed to NAME and the Column Name property was changed to ENAME, so that the proper SQL could be written. These changes also gave a more precise label to the category axis. Charts always have numeric and character values. The numeric value is the charted measurement. The character value describes or gives meaning to the charted measurement. For example, when charting employee salaries, the value of the salary is the numeric measurement, and the employee name is the character value that gives the measurement meaning.

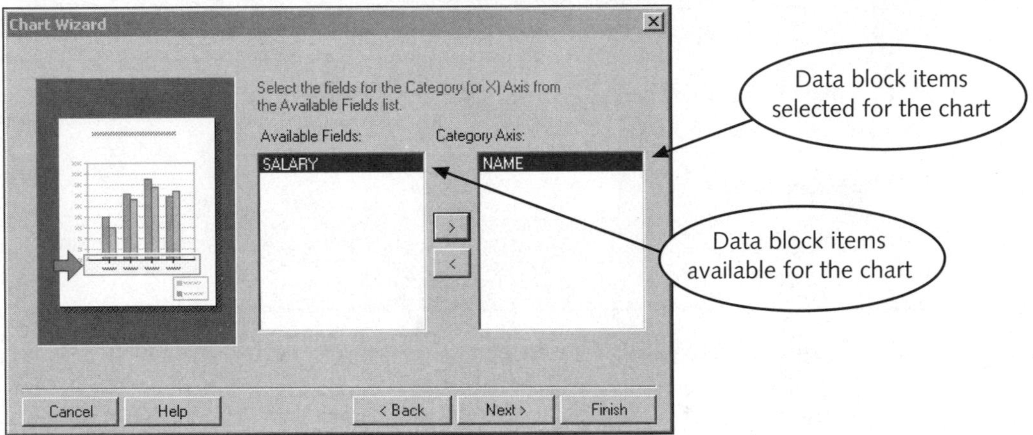

Figure 8-16 Chart Wizard Category page

This page displays all the items of the selected data block. You must select one or more items. You should pick the character value on this page, because the page is used to identify the descriptive variable. Using the employee salary example, the NAME data item should be selected. Items are selected by moving them from the Available Fields list box to the Category Axis list box.

Even though the wizard page mentions the X axis, the values may not appear along that axis. The placement of the values depends on the type of chart. Vertical and horizontal bar graphs display the values along different axes. The key to remember is that this page refers to the descriptive variable.

The fourth page is the Values page (depicted in Figure 8-17), which is used to select the value items. The same rules outlined in the previous paragraph for the Category page apply to this page.

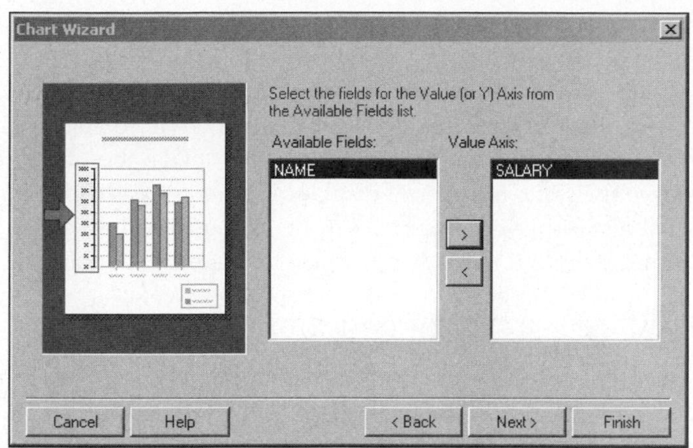

Figure 8-17 Chart Wizard Values page

8

The last wizard page is the File Name page, illustrated in Figure 8-18, and it completes the chart creation steps. This page has a File Name text item. This is the name of the Oracle Graphics file that is used by the form's chart item.

Form Builder 6*i* puts a default name into this item and saves the file in its default directory unless the name and file directory is changed. You may change the file name or use the Save As button to open a Save As dialog box to identify a different directory for the file.

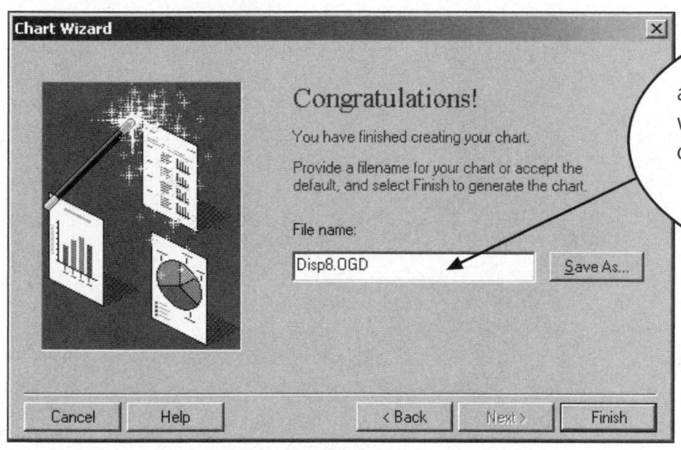

Figure 8-18 Chart Wizard File Name page

Clicking the Finish button on the Chart Wizard File Name page creates the graphics file, sets the properties for the chart item, closes the wizard, and displays a template chart on a canvas. Figure 8-19 depicts the example chart item. Form chart items are generally related to a data block whose values are displayed in a Tabular style format with multiple records, as shown in the Figure 8-19 example. When you first place the chart item in this block, the chart items have the same number of displayed instances as the other data block items. The Number of Items Displayed property can be changed to 1 in order to correct this problem. At this point, the chart is ready and the form can be launched.

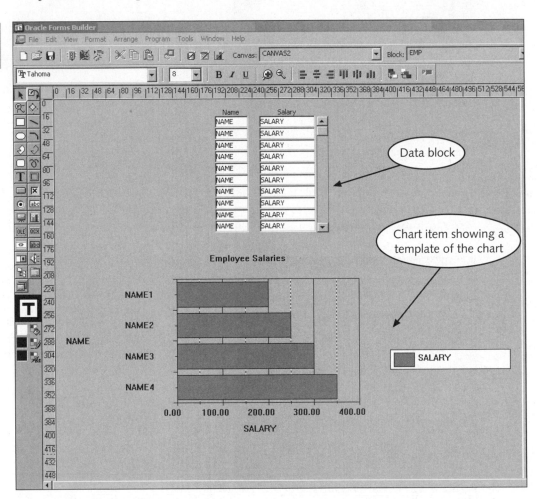

Figure 8-19 Chart item on a canvas in Form Builder 6*i*

Figures 8-20 and 8-21 depict the finished charts in both the client/server runtime environment and the Web environment. Figure 8-20 illustrates the Employee Salaries chart using the client/server runtime engine with the X and Y axis labels displayed. However, the labels are missing in the Web environment. You can see that some Forms Builder tools are not totally available for Web applications at this point, and the client/server environment is more robust, as demonstrated in this example. However, Oracle is working diligently to make the Web runtime engine just as robust as the client/server.

Chart item is populated when the data block is populated. The Update On Query property controls this task

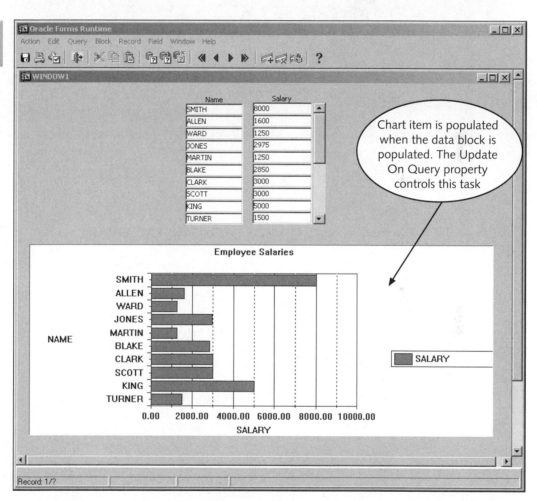

Figure 8-20 Form Builder 6*i* Employee Salaries chart displayed in client/server form

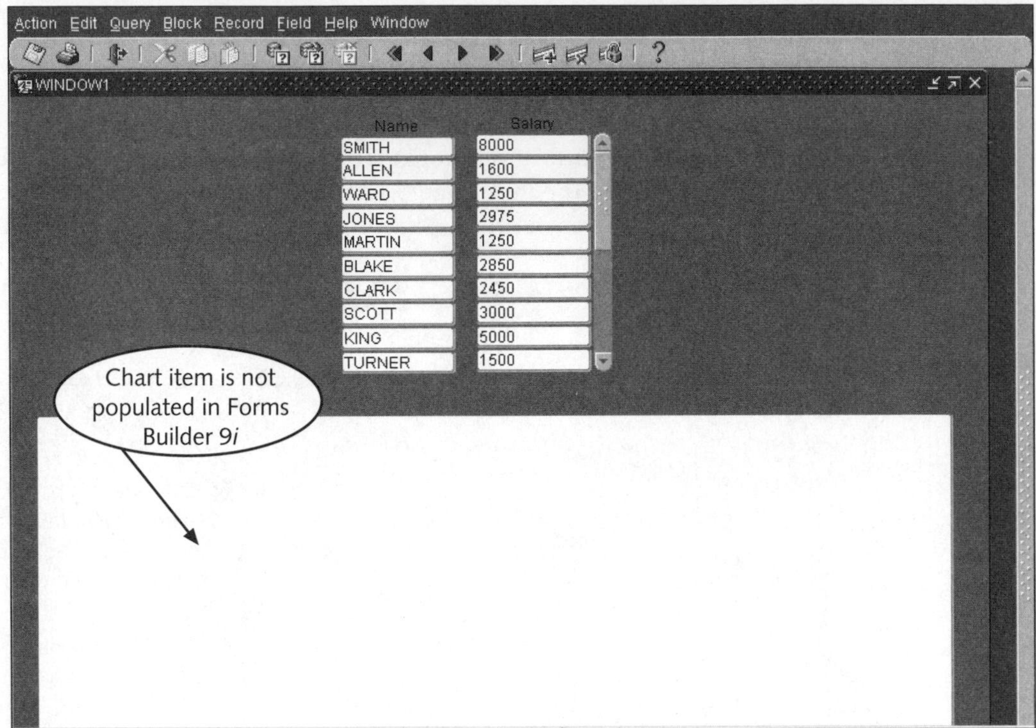

Figure 8-21 Forms Builder 9*i* Employee Salaries chart displayed in Web browser form

One final point concerns formatting of the chart. You may select the chart item and launch the Chart Wizard repeatedly. You can change the settings that are available in the wizard, but the wizard is limited in its formatting options. To enhance the chart, you must use Oracle's Graphics Builder, a tool that has many useful functions but is unfortunately outside the scope of this book.

Populating the Chart and Chart Item Properties

A chart item is initially populated when the data block on which it is based is populated. Thus, when you execute the first query against the data block, the chart is also populated with the results of the query. You should note that the chart item does not contain by default all records that could potentially appear in the data block. It only contains records that have been returned to the data block. If you enter selection criteria into the data block and limit the retrieved records, the chart item shows only the limited set returned to the block. This is an interesting feature and allows users to customize their charts. For example, a division manager can use a chart item to see all employee salaries, while a department manager can use the search values to limit the values to employees in his department. Thus, many different levels in a company can use the same chart item.

By default, the chart updates its values each time a query occurs on the data block or each time a commit occurs on the data block. However, it is possible to use the Update On Query and Update On Commit properties to suppress this update. The default for these properties is YES, so changing the property to NO suppresses the update.

Two other important properties are Execution Mode and Communication Mode. The Execution Mode property has two settings: BATCH (the default) and RUNTIME. The RUNTIME setting launches Oracle Graphics Runtime and displays the graph within Oracle Graphics. The operator can then use Graphics to save the graph. The graph is also displayed within the form. The BATCH setting simply displays the graph within the form chart item. The operator cannot save the graph.

The Communication Mode property determines where control resides. The SYNCHRONOUS setting (the default) determines that control returns to the form only after the chart item has been populated. The ASYNCHRONOUS setting causes the control to return to the form immediately after the update process has been started. A chart item has several other properties, which can be viewed in Appendix E.

For practice create an employee salary chart similar to the previous example on the tab page form, perform the following steps:

1. Open form module **practice0802.fmb** in the Object Navigator. Note that this practice session is intended for Form Builder 6*i* in the client/server environment.
2. Create a new tab page object named **SALARIES**. Open its Property Palette and set the Label property to **SALARY CHART**.
3. Open the Object Navigator and display the **SALARIES** tab page.
4. Open the Layout Editor and increase the size of the tab canvas so that it covers the work area.
5. Activate the **Chart Item** tool. Place a chart item on the SALARIES tab page. This should open the New Chart Object dialog box. Select the **Chart Wizard** option by clicking the OK button.
6. If the Chart Wizard Welcome page appears, click the **Next** button to display the Chart Wizard Type page. On this page, select the **BAR** chart type and the **Stacked BARs** chart subtype. Enter **EMPLOYEE SALARIES** into the Title text item. Click **Next**.
7. On the Block page, select the **EMP** block. Click **Next**.
8. On the Category page, move **ENAME** to the Category Axis list box. Click **Next**.
9. On the Values page, move **SAL** to the Value Axis list box. Click **Next**.
10. On the File Name page, click the **Finish** button. This creates the chart item and its file.

11. Open a Property Palette for the new chart item. Set the Number of Items Displayed property to **1**. You may also have to set the X Position property to place it on the tab page.
12. Run the form using both the Client/Server and Web runtime engines. Execute a query on the EMP block to populate the chart.
13. Close the form.
14. Open the Layout Editor and display the **SALARIES** tab page.
15. Select the **chart item** and click the **Chart Wizard** tool. This opens a Chart Wizard.
16. Click the **Type** tab. Select a different type and subtype setting to create a different chart. Click the **Finish** button.

If you click **Cancel**, the chart item is deleted.

17. Execute the form and populate the chart item.

CALLING A WEB DOCUMENT FROM THE FORM

An Oracle Web form has the ability to call and display a Web document. This can be an **.html**, **.pdf**, or other document. The document can even be a page from someone's Web site, such as *www.oracle-trainer.com*, a report created by Oracle Reports Builder, a Java Server Page.

The Show_document built-in calls a Web document. It is one of the procedures included in Forms Builder's Web package. The following is a template of the built-in:

```
Web.show_document ('url', 'target')
```

The URL argument is the name of a Web document location. For example, "*HTTP://www.oracle-trainer.com*" is the argument that would be used to display the Web page for the *www.oracle-trainer.com* Web site. The second variable, TARGET, determines how the document is to be displayed. There are four possible values as follows:

- **_self**: Loads the document into the same window as the source document
- **_parent**: Loads the document into the parent window containing the hypertext reference
- **_top**: Loads the document into the window containing the hypertext link, replacing any frames currently displayed in the window
- **_blank**: Causes the document to load into a new, unnamed top-level window

To illustrate the display of a Web document and as practice, add a button to the **practice0802.fmb** practice form to display a Web page. (Note that this practice is intended for Forms Builder 9*i* only.) Perform the following steps:

1. Open the **practice0802.fmb** form module in the Object Navigator.
2. Open the Layout Editor and add a button to one of the TOOLBAR_CANVAS horizontal canvases. Double-click the **button** opening its Property Palette. Set the following properties:

   Name: **DISPLAY_PAGE**

   Label: **DISPLAY PAGE**

   Number of Items Displayed: **1**
3. Open the Object Navigator and select the **TRIGGERS** node under the DISPLAY_PAGE button item. Click the **Create** tool and create a When-Button-Pressed trigger using the following script:

   ```
   Web.show_document('http://www.oracle-trainer.com', '_blank');
   ```
4. Save and launch the form. Click the **DISPLAY_PAGE** button. A Web page should be displayed in its own Web browser window.
5. Close the form and the Web browser window. Open the trigger and experiment with the _self, _parent, and _top arguments.

8

CREATING AND USING REPORTS OBJECTS

In a previous section, you saw that a chart item in a data block calls a Graphics Builder file, passes the results of a data block query to the file, and displays the formatted results in a chart item. Forms Builder also has the ability to call an Oracle Reports Builder module from a form. This is similar to calling a Graphics file, but different in that the form does not have an item such as a chart item to display the report on the form.

Oracle reports called from a form are displayed differently depending on whether they are called from Form Builder 6*i* or Forms Builder 9*i*, and whether the report is displayed in the client/server or Web environment. Form Builder 6*i* has the ability to print the file or display it online in the Reports Builder Previewer but only if the form is executed in a client/server environment. If the form is deployed on the Web, the report is displayed within the Web browser. Forms Builder 9*i* does not have the ability to launch the Previewer and can only print the report or display the report in the Web browser.

It is common to launch a report from a form, and Forms Builder allows you to launch any Reports Builder module whether it is related to the data in the form or not. However, sometimes users want the report to display the same records displayed in a data block. Forms Builder can also pass information to the Reports Builder module that allows the report to duplicate the records displayed in the data block. Passing the current data block query to a report module allows the user to print the data block result set. This section shows you how to create a Forms Builder Reports object that is associated to a Reports Builder module and is used to launch the Report Builder module.

The Reports object is a form object used to store information needed to call and produce the Reports Builder report. It is similar to and, in fact, replaces a parameter list that is passed to Reports Builder when the report is created. The Reports object has a number of properties: Filename, Execution Mode, Communication Mode, Data Source Data Block, Query Name, Report Destination Type, Report Destination Name, Report Destination Format, Report Server, and Other Reports Parameters. Appendix B contains detailed descriptions of these properties.

Creating a Reports Object

A **Reports object** is a form object that is called and stores values that are passed to Reports Builder. Reports objects can be associated to a data block or can be completely independent of a data block. The Reports object is associated to a data block when the Data Source Data Block property contains the name of a form data block. When this property is populated, the data block's Where clause argument values are passed to the Reports Builder module, thus ensuring that the report contains the same values as the data block. If you do not associate the Reports object to a data block, the Where clause argument values are not passed to the report and the report contents are based solely on the SELECT statement in the report.

If you choose to associate a report to a data block, when you create the reports object, Forms Builder automatically launches Reports Builder. Forms Builder passes the data block items and the SELECT statement used by the data block to Reports Builder. Reports Builder then creates a SELECT statement based upon the data block's SELECT statement, and you can use the Reports Builder Reports Wizard to complete the report. The Forms Builder Reports object will have all of the information in its properties to identify the report and pass it the proper Where clause arguments.

Reports objects are form-level objects and are located in the Object Navigator. To create a Reports object based on a data block, you would select the Reports node in the Object Navigator and then click the Create tool. This would launch the New Report dialog box depicted in Figure 8-22. The dialog box has the following features:

- **Radio buttons**: The dialog box contains two radio buttons. If the Create New Report File radio button is selected, clicking the OK button creates a new blank Reports Builder module and loads the new module into Reports Builder. The developer can then complete the report using the Reports Builder IDE. The Use Existing Report File radio button is used to associate an existing report to the Reports object. Reports Builder is not launched if this radio button is selected.

- **Filename text item**: This text box is used to document the name of the Reports Builder module to be associated to the Reports object. Only one of the text items is activated at a time.
- **Browse buttons**: The top Browse button is used to open a Save As dialog box that allows you to locate a directory to store the new Reports Builder module. The bottom Browse button opens an Open dialog box that is used to identify an existing Reports Builder module.
- **Base Report on Block check box**: This check box determines whether the report is based on a data block's SELECT statement. If it is checked, Forms Builder passes the data block's SELECT statement to Reports Builder. Reports Builder then sets up parameters for each of the statement's expressions and creates a query using the statement.
- **Select button**: Launches a list of form data blocks that are associated to the reports object.

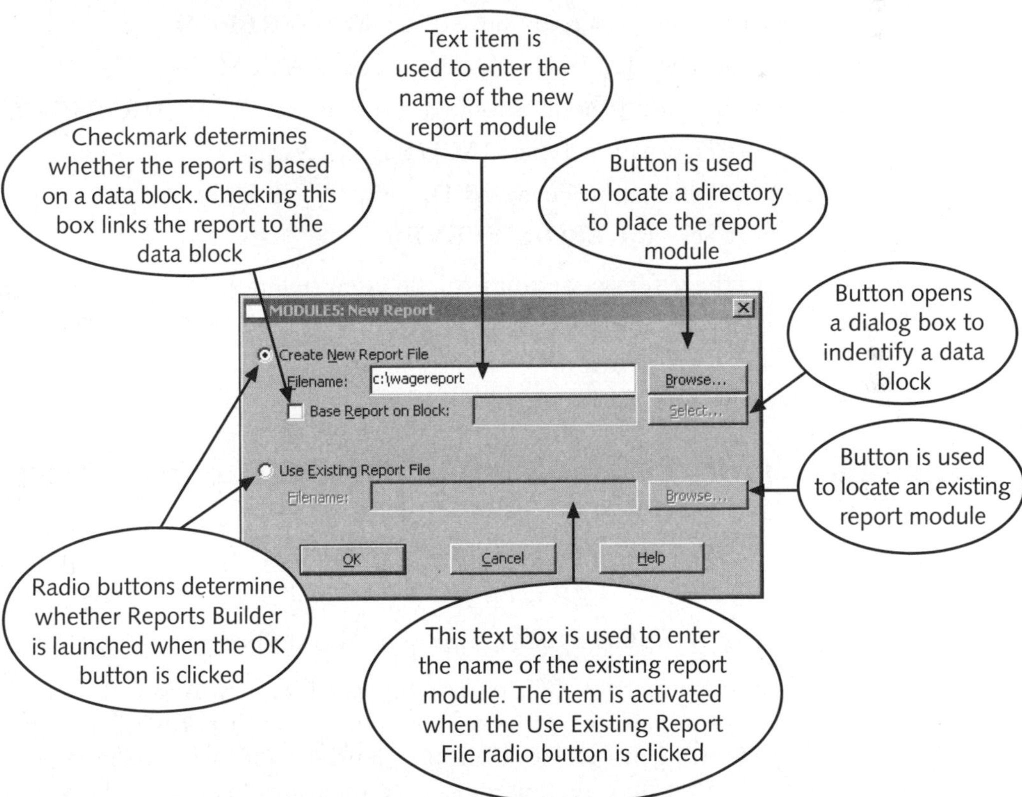

If the developer selects the Create New Report File option, clicking the OK button launches Reports Builder. It is beyond the scope of this book to cover Reports Builder and the Reports Wizard used to construct the report. However, you are given a sample

Reports Builder report module named **wagereport.rdf** to use in creating a Reports object in the following practice. (Note that this practice is intended for Forms Builder 9*i*.) Perform the following steps:

1. Open the **practice0802.fmb** module in the Object Navigator.
2. Locate the Reports node and click the **Create** tool to open the New Report dialog box. Perform the following tasks:
   a. Select the **Use Existing Report File** radio button.
   b. Enter the following in the Filename text item (modify the value with the actual file path on your system):

      C:\wagereport
3. Click **OK**. Open a Property Palette for the new Reports object. Set the following properties:

   Name: **WAGEREPORT**

   Filename (should already be set): **C:\WAGEREPORT**

   Execution Mode (should already be set): **BATCH**

   Communication Mode (should already be set): **SYNCHRONOUS**

   Report Destination Type: **CACHE**

   Report Destination Format: **PDF**

   Report Server: **REPORTSERVER**

The purpose of the latter two settings will be discussed in the "Report Destination Types and Forms" section later in this chapter. Also note that the Report Server setting is only needed for Web reports using Forms Builder 9*i*.

4. Save the form for later practice.

Calling a Reports Builder Module Using a Reports Object

Before you can call a report module from Forms Builder, a reports service must be started on the client using a DOS command. The following command installs a service named TESTREPORTS:

```
Rwserver —install testreports testreports
```

If the command is successful, a dialog box opens asking if you want to set up a permanent service. You may not have the authority to set up a permanent service on your computer, and setting up services on all clients is outside the scope of this book. However, you can set up a temporary service on your client. This allows you to call a Web report from a form. To set up a temporary service on your computer, execute the following command from a DOS prompt (the name of the service is arbitrary):

```
Rwserver server reportserver
```

After this command is executed, an Oracle9*i*AS Reports Services dialog box opens. This dialog box and the Command Prompt window are depicted in Figure 8-23. You should close the Command Prompt window and minimize the Oracle9*i*AS Reports Services dialog box. You can shut down the service by clicking the Shutdown button.

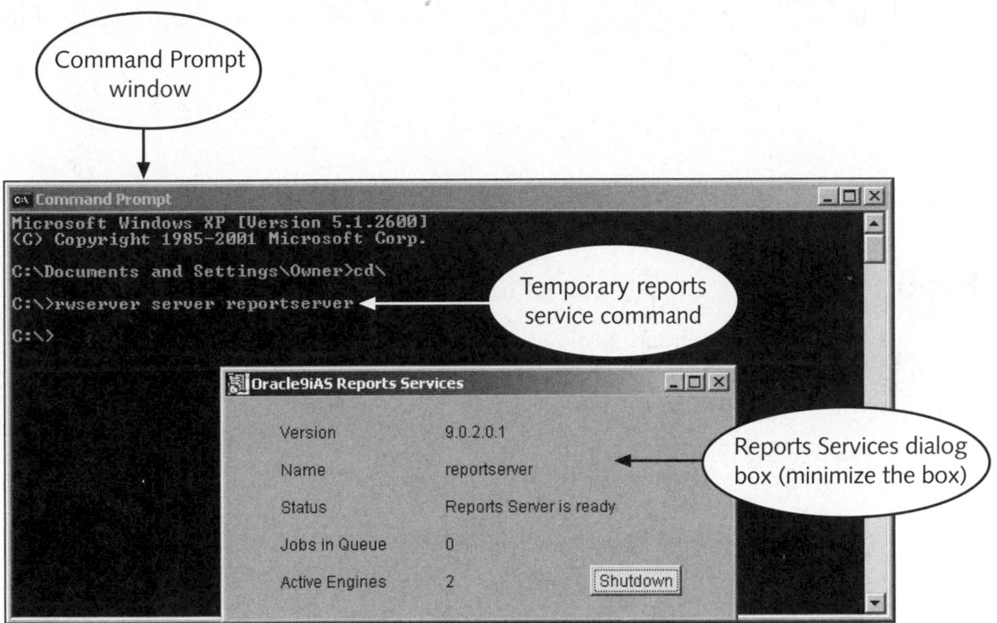

Figure 8-23 Setting up a temporary reports service using the Command Prompt window and the Oracle9*i*AS Reports Services dialog box

Forms Builder 9*i* can only execute a Reports Builder module using the Run_report_object built-in subprogram. Form Builder 6*i* can use this executable as well as the Run_product and Host built-ins discussed in a later section. The Run_report_object built-in is a function that returns a character string. The built-in is overloaded; however, it is normally executed using one parameter—the name of the Reports object. Because it is overloaded, you can also add a parameter list. This built-in performs the following tasks:

- Reads the Reports object properties
- Launches the Reports Builder runtime engine
- Passes Form Runtime (6*i*) or Forms Server (9*i*) the Oracle ID, password, and host string needed to access the Oracle database
- Passes the report file name to Reports Builder

- Passes parameters to Reports Builder
- Displays the report (Form Builder 6*i* only;) Forms Builder 9*i* reports can only be displayed using the Web.Show_document built-in

The Run_report_object built-in can be launched from any trigger, but the most logical choice is a When-Button-Pressed trigger associated to a button. The following is a template for this trigger:

```
Declare
     Return_string varchar2(100);
Begin
     Return_string := run_report_object('report_object_name');
End;
```

Report Destination Types and Formats

The output of a Reports Builder report can be sent to a variety of locations. The locations are values of the Reports object property named Report Destination Type. The following are the Report Destination Type property values:

- **PREVIEW**: The Oracle Reports Builder Previewer (this is not an option for Forms Builder 9*i*)
- **FILE**: Electronic version stored in a file on a hard disk
- **PRINTER**: Printed on paper
- **CACHE**: Electronic version in memory
- **SCREEN**: Displayed on the screen

The reports can be output in several different formats, and these formats can be used as values for the Reports object Report Destination Format property. The values are: PDF, HTML, HTML CSS, HTML CSSIE, RTF, and DELIMITED. The PDF setting is an especially good option; it causes Reports Builder to create a PDF version of the report. This version looks exactly like the version you created in Reports Builder. If you choose the other options, Reports Builder changes the format to conform. In addition, when you print the report using PDF, it looks exactly like the report you designed, whereas printing in HTML does not. The only negative about PDF is that a PDF view product, such as Adobe Acrobat, is needed, but this product is available on most workstations.

For this reason, the Report Destination Format property was set to PDF in the previous practice. When you view the WAGEREPORT report, it will look exactly as designed in Reports Builder. In addition, the Report Destination Type property was set to CACHE. This placed the report in memory rather than on the hard disk, so that the report was not written to the hard drive. If the operator wants to save the report, it can be saved when it is displayed in a Web browser.

Executing and Viewing a Reports Builder Report Illustration

In this section, you complete the practice form you started in the previous practice session, allowing you to display a PDF version of the WAGEREPORT report in a Web browser. Before starting this practice session, you need to understand the When-Button-Pressed trigger that launches and displays the report.

To dynamically create and display a report in a Web browser from a form, you need to run two built-ins:

- **Run_report_object**: Creates the actual report output
- **Web.Show_document**: Displays the report in the Web browser

It is possible to place the two built-ins in the trigger in consecutive statements. However, the Web.Show_document built-in might execute before the report is completed. Ideally, this built-in should execute only when the report has been completed. Thus, a delay device is needed to prevent the built-in from executing prematurely. Figure 8-24 depicts just such a device, the When-Button-Pressed trigger. This trigger has the following features:

- **Find_report_object function call**: Determines the internal Oracle name of the WAGEREPORT object.
- **Run_report_object function call**: Produces the PDF version of the report output that will reside in cache.
- **Report_object_status function call**: Determines the current status of the report.
- **WHILE loop**: Checks the report status. It uses a built-in called Report_object_status to determine the report status. As long as the status is "RUNNING", "OPENING REPORT", or "ENQUEUED", the loop is executed. When the report is complete the loop is terminated.
- **Web.Show_document procedure call**: Locates the PDF report and displays it in a new Web browser window. The procedure contains a lengthy argument containing several concatenated variables of which you should be aware. The COMPUTER_NAME variable is the name of your client. This is the name the client received when the operating system was installed. You can determine this name by viewing the Web browser Address drop-down list when it is displaying an Oracle form. Another variable is V_REP_SERVER, which is the internal Oracle name of the reports service.

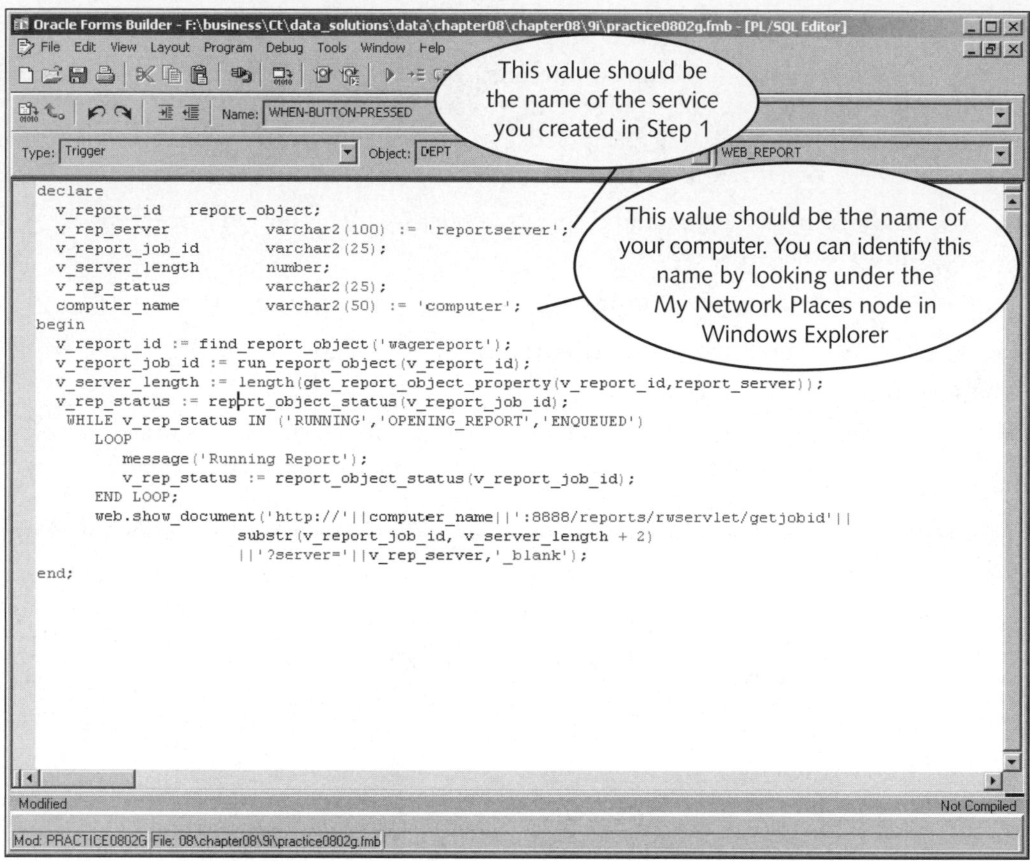

Figure 8-24 When-Button-Pressed trigger used to produce and display the WAGEREPORT report

As practice, complete the modification to the **practice0802.fmb** module that will enable it to create and display the WAGEREPORT report. Perform the following steps:

1. Start a reports service by following these steps:
   a. Open a Command Prompt window by selecting the **Start/All Programs/Accessories/Command Prompt** menu options.
   b. Navigate to the root directory by entering: **CD**
   c. Enter the following command on the command line of the window:

      Rwserver server reportserver

Remember that this step is only necessary once per session, not every time you create a report.

2. Open the **practice0802.fmb** form module in the Object Navigator.

3. Open the Layout Editor and display the **EMPLOYEES** tab page. Add a button to the TOOLBAR_CANVAS horizontal canvas. Double-click the **button** to open its Property Palette. Set the following properties:
   Name: **WEB_REPORT**
   Label: **RUN WAGEREPORT**
   Number of Items Displayed: **1**
4. Open the Object Navigator, and locate and expand the WEB_REPORT button object displaying its Triggers node. Click the **Create** tool to produce a When-Button-Pressed trigger. Enter the script from Figure 8-24 making sure that you enter the name of your computer along with the name of the service you established in Step 1. A copy of the script has been supplied with the data files.
5. Compile the trigger. Save and launch the form. When you click the **RUN WAGEREPORT** button, a report similar to the one displayed in Figure 8-25 should be displayed.

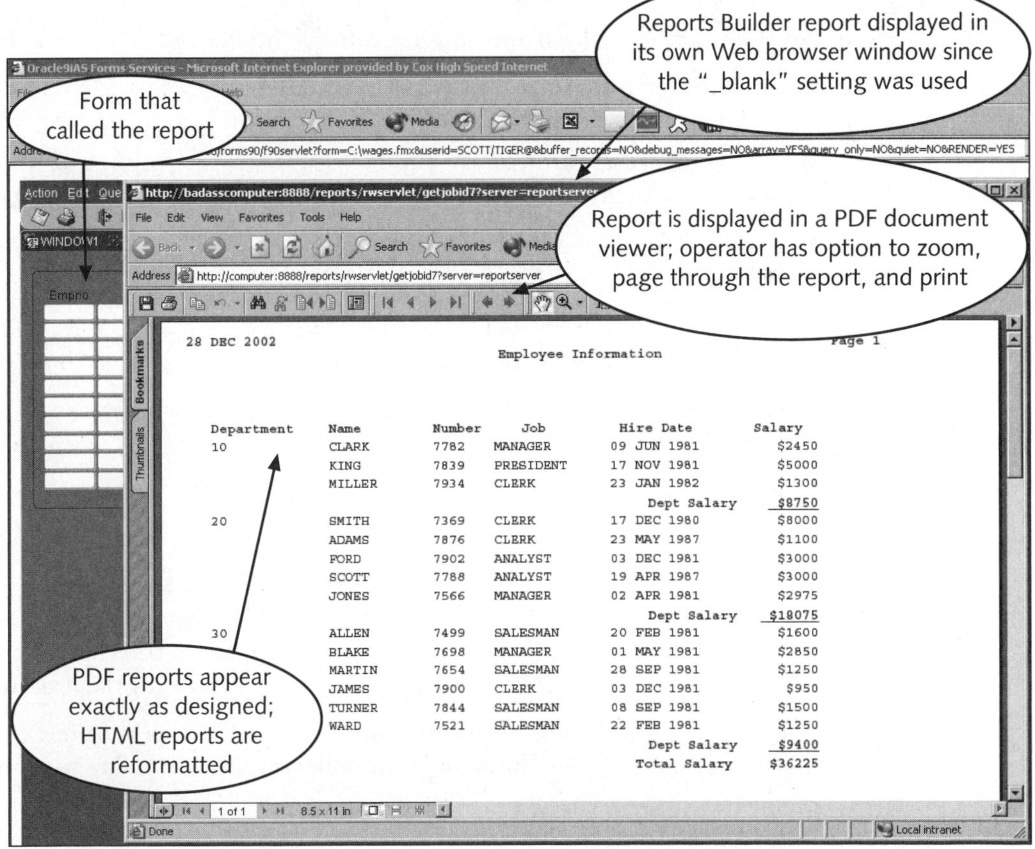

Figure 8-25 WAGEREPORT PDF output displayed in a Web browser window

Using the Run_product and Host Built-ins in Form Builder *6i* to Launch a Report

In Form Builder (6*i* and before), reports were executed using either the Run_product or Host built-in, which are somewhat similar. The main difference is that the Host built-in requires the Oracle ID to be embedded as a parameter within the built-in. This can be a problem in that Oracle IDs are supposed to be protected and secret. Placing the Oracle ID in the built-in opens the possibility of someone accessing the source code **.fmb** file and obtaining the Oracle ID. The Run_product built-in is similar in nature to the Run_report_object built-in, because it passes the Oracle ID used by the current operator to initiate the session.

The Run_product built-in is a procedure. It has a number of parameters that are listed as follows:

- **Product**: A constant that identifies the product runtime engine to be launched. Options are GRAPHICS (for Graphics Builder), REPORTS (for Reports Builder), and BOOK for Oracle Book.
- **Module**: Displays the name and location of the file that is to be executed.
- **Communication Mode**: Determines whether the object is to be run synchronously or asynchronously.
- **Execution Mode**: Determines whether the object is run in batch or runtime mode.
- **Location**: Identifies whether the file is located in the file system or in the database. Values are FILESYSTEM and DB.
- **Parameter List**: Identifies the parameter list passed to the object. This is the same type of list as was discussed in the Parameter section of Chapter 6.
- **Display**: Specifies the name of the Forms Builder chart item that displays the chart.

The following is the template for the built-in:

```
Run_product(reports, 'file name and location', synchronous, runtime,
            Filesystem, parameter_list_name, null);
```

In the previous template, the last parameter is DISPLAY. This parameter value is not used for a report. Thus, a NULL value was placed in the parameter. If you do not plan to pass a parameter list to the report module, place the keyword NULL in that parameter.

The Host built-in can also be used to both launch one of Oracle's runtime engines and to execute any operating system command. The following is a template for the built-in:

```
Host ('system command');
```

To launch Reports Builder runtime using the Host built-in, the system command string must contain the name of the runtime executable and any other parameter that you want to pass to the runtime executable. These parameters can consist of the file name, Oracle ID, or a parameter list. The following is a simple example of a command:

```
Host('C:\ORANT\BIN\RWRUN60.EXE
     USERID=SCOTT/TIGER REPORT=test.RDF ');
```

Of the three built-ins—Run_report_object, Run_product, and Host—the Run_report_object built-in is the easiest to use. The Run_product built-in requires you to build a parameter object and set all of the built-in parameters correctly. Because this can be difficult, Oracle created a Reports object that has properties, which is easier to use.

Where You Are and Where You're Going

At this point, you know how to create a form and how to open other form windows and applications. You also know how to call reports and chart items from your forms. In the next chapter, you learn to use a menu to tie your applications together. You also see how to create a popup menu that is launched by the Right Mouse button. Finally, you learn to add alerts that display informational messages to your form.

Chapter Summary

- There are two different window styles: document and dialog.
- A document style window exists within the runtime engine window. A dialog style window is raised above the runtime window and allows the operator to move it anywhere within the computer screen.
- The Viewport X Position On Canvas and Viewport Y Position On Canvas properties determine where the stacked canvas is located within the window.
- Windows and canvases are displayed by navigating into an item on the canvas.
- Windows are always associated to a canvas. Canvases are always associated to a window through properties.
- The Go_item and Go_block built-in subprograms can be used to programmatically move the input focus to an item and display a canvas or window.
- Buttons are useful form tools for launching a window or canvas.
- A tab canvas is a canvas that consists of a series of pages that are tabbed at the top to allow the user to display an associated page by clicking a tab.
- Tab pages and tab canvases can be colored differently. Tab pages originally default to the tab canvas colors. The canvas Background Color property determines the tab page colors.

- Horizontal and vertical toolbar canvases can be attached to a window or to the application.
- Toolbar canvases attached to the application appear within the application's frame.
- Toolbar canvases attached to the window appear within the window.
- Toolbar tools are iconified buttons that have a When-Button-Pressed trigger.
- Chart items are used to display Oracle Graphics objects.
- Chart items display the contents of a form data block in a graphical rather than a tabular format.
- Chart items are automatically updated when a query or commit is performed on a data block. This can be suppressed using chart item properties.
- A form can have a Reports object that links a data block to a specific report.
- The Run_report_object built-in is used to execute a report associated to a Reports object.
- Reports Builder modules can also be executed from a form using the Run_product and Host built_ins.

REVIEW QUESTIONS

1. Match the following terms that have appeared in this chapter with their descriptions:

a. Run_product	________	Determines the style of the tab on a tab page.
b. Call_form	________	A built-in procedure that displays a Web document.
c. Go_block	________	A window style that allows the window to float above the runtime engine window.
d. Stacked canvas	________	A built-in that launches a new application, leaving the existing applications open. Modifications that exist in the calling and called forms are saved
e. **.ogd**	________	A property that identifies the canvas to display when a window is opened.
f. Run_report_ object	________	Property that causes a single chart item to appear when the chart item resides on a multi-record data block.
g. Tab page	________	A set of PL/SQL objects that resides in an external file but can be used by a form.

h. Content canvas	______________	Properties that determine the location in which a stacked canvas appears within a window.
i. Dialog window	______________	A built-in that can be used to launch Reports Builder runtime. This built-in does not require the Oracle ID to be placed in the parameter list.
j. Viewport properties	______________	A graphics Builder file extension.
k. Open_form	______________	A built-in that moves the input focus to the first item in the designated block.
l. **Show.web_ document**	______________	A type of canvas that can overlay another or is used within a wizard.
m. Update On Commit property	______________	A base canvas over which other canvases can be placed.
n. Host	______________	A built-in that moves the input focus to a specified data block item.
o. Number of Items Displayed property	______________	Determines on which edge the tab will appear on a tab canvas.
p. Document window	______________	A built-in that launches a new application leaving the remaining application open. This built-in requires that modifications that occur in the calling form be saved before changes can be saved in the called form.
q. Primary Canvas property	______________	A built-in that issues a command to the operating system. It can be used to launch Reports Builder runtime.
r. Tab Attachment Edge property	______________	A built-in that launches a Reports object.
s. New_form	______________	A property that controls whether a chart item is updated when a COMMIT statement is issued.
t. Attached library	______________	A type of canvas that consists of a series of overlapping pages that are displayed by clicking a tab.

8

u. CORNER_STYLE property ____________ A style of window that resides inside the Forms Builder runtime window.

v. Go_item ____________ A built-in that calls another application and replaces the calling application.

2. Explain the differences between each of the canvas types. Identify at least one situation for which a particular canvas type is the best solution.
3. Identify a situation in which a modal window is needed. Identify a situation in which a dialog window is needed. Identify a situation in which a document window is needed.
4. You have a window that displays both vertical and horizontal scroll bars. What can you do to eliminate the scroll bars?
5. Name four ways of displaying a stacked canvas.
6. A user called you on the phone. The user is operating a form that has a data block in which the items are displayed on two canvases. One of the canvases is a content canvas. The second canvas is a stacked canvas inside a dialog window. You had planned to have the user open the dialog by using a button. The user noticed that this window automatically opens when tabbing past the last item on the content canvas. The user wants you to suppress this and have the window open only when the button is clicked. What can you do to achieve this effect?
7. Why are tab canvases and pages excellent Web tools? What are their disadvantages?
8. A user called you on the phone and said that he is having trouble identifying the current tab page. Is there something you can do to help?
9. You've just used the Layout Wizard to place a new data block on a canvas. You wanted to place this block on a new tab page on an existing tab canvas. You forgot to change the settings in the wizard, and the data block was placed on the content canvas. Is it possible to correct this without deleting the data block?
10. A different user called you on the phone about a form you developed. The form has a button that calls a stacked canvas in a dialog window. This stacked window is used to enter comments about the piece of equipment displayed in the calling form. If the user has modified a value in the equipment form and then modifies a value in the Comments dialog box, Forms Builder does not allow the user to save the changes. You told the user to save the changes in the equipment form before calling the Comments form. The user doesn't like this option. What other options do you have?
11. Name at least five form functions for which you would create tools on every application toolbar.
12. Explain the differences between assigning a toolbar to a window and the form application.

13. Why would you want to employ a wizard in your system? Can you name some real-world situations in which using a wizard would be useful?
14. When creating a chart with the Chart Wizard, what type of items would you select on the Category page? What type of items would you select on the Values page?
15. You are using the Object Navigator and just created a new chart item. You have opened the Tools menu and notice the Chart Wizard option is disabled. What's the problem?
16. Can you offer an example of when it's disadvantageous to update a chart item automatically whenever a query or commit command is issued?
17. Explain how the Run_report_object, Run_product, and Host built-ins operate differently to execute a report.
18. What is the difference between creating a chart in the Batch mode and the Runtime mode?
19. In Forms Builder, when you initially create an object, the wizards are displayed as a series of pages with Next and Back buttons. When you use the wizards to modify the previously created objects, the pages are displayed as a series of tabs on a tab canvas. Is it possible accomplish the same thing with the wizard pages that you create in a form? If so, how is it accomplished?

Exam Review Questions

1. How are data blocks and windows related?
   a. A block is assigned to a window; therefore, it is displayed in the window.
   b. A block can be assigned to a canvas. Because the canvas can be assigned to many windows, a block can be displayed in multiple windows.
   c. A block can be assigned to a single canvas, and the canvas can only be assigned to a single window. Therefore, a block can only be displayed in a single window.
   d. A block can be assigned to a canvas. Therefore, a block can be displayed in multiple windows.
2. You created a form and intend to use it as a modal dialog window. Which built-in should you use?
   a. Go_form
   b. New_form
   c. Open_form
   d. Call_form

3. Which statement is true?
   a. A canvas cannot contain non-display items.
   b. A window can have only one canvas but multiple blocks.
   c. A data block can contain many items, and the items cannot be displayed in multiple windows.
   d. Items can be displayed on only one canvas at a time.
4. Which two built-ins can be used to run a report from forms?
   a. Open_form
   b. Call_form
   c. Run_product
   d. Run_report_object
   e. Set_report_object_property
5. Using the Chart Wizard, you are adding a chart to your form. Which data source supplies data for the values and category axes?
   a. Selected query
   b. Graphics query
   c. Form data block
   d. Query Name property
   e. Data Source property

HANDS-ON ASSIGNMENTS

1. In this assignment, you create a form that has a data block based on the EMP table. The main purpose of this form is to maintain the EMP records. This form should have a When-Validate-Item trigger that validates the DEPTNO item. If the entered value does not exist in the DEPT table, the trigger displays an error message. Operators can then click a button that opens a dialog box that allows them to enter a new DEPT record and subsequently pass the edit. To accomplish these tasks, perform the following steps:
   a. Create a new form module. Create a data block based on the EMP table and place it on a content canvas. One record should be displayed and the layout style is Form.
   b. Open a Property Palette for the EMPNO item on the EMP datablock. Change the item's Required property to **NO**.
   c. Create a data block based on the DEPT table. This data block should be placed on a new stacked canvas. One record should be displayed and the layout style is Form. Do not relate this data block to the EMP data block.

d. In the Layout Editor, resize the newly created DEPT stacked canvas. The Height should be approximately 80 and the Width approximately 496.

e. Open the Object Navigator. Change the name of the content canvas to **EMPLOYEES** and the name of the stacked canvas to **DEPARTMENT**.

f. Open a Property Palette for the existing form window. Set the following properties:

   Name: **MAIN**

   Title: **EMPLOYEE UPDATE FORM**

   Primary Canvas: **EMPLOYEES**

g. Create a new Window object. Set the following properties:

   Name: **DEPARTMENT**

   Title: **ADD NEW DEPARTMENT**

   Primary Canvas: **DEPARTMENT**

   X Position: **20**

   Y Position: **50**

   Width: **496**

   Height: **80**

h. Open a Property Palette for the DEPARTMENT canvas. Set the Window property to **DEPARTMENT**.

i. Using the Object Navigator, locate the DEPTNO item in the EMP data block.

j. Create a When-Validate-Item trigger for the DEPTNO item. The script will alert the operators when they enter an invalid DEPTNO value. Use the following script:

```
Declare
       Dept_var  dept%rowtype;
Begin
       Select *
       Into dept_var
       From dept
       Where deptno = :emp.deptno;
Exception
       When others then
            Bell;
            Message ('You have entered an invalid department number');
End;
```

k. Open the Layout Editor and add a button next to the DEPTNO item on the EMPLOYEES canvas. Position it as shown in Figure 8-26, which shows the button after it has been labeled.

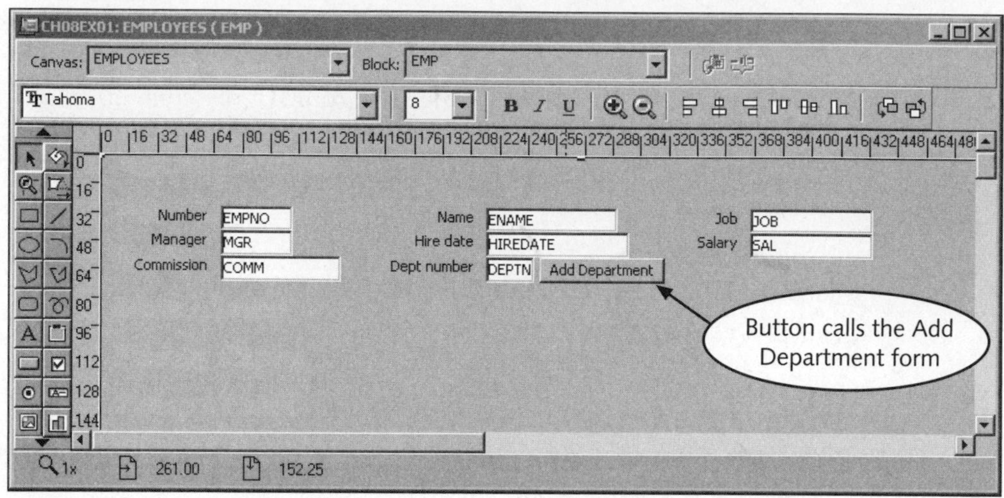

Figure 8-26 The EMPLOYEES canvas after addition of the button

l. Open a Property Palette for the button. Set the following properties:

   Name: **ADD_DEPT**

   Label: **ADD DEPARTMENT**

m. Create a When-Button-Pressed trigger for the ADD_DEPT button. Use the following script:

```
Go_block ('dept');
```

n. Open a Property Palette for the DEPT data block. This step ensures that this data block is used only to add new departments. Set the following properties:

   Update Allowed: **NO**

   Delete Allowed: **NO**

   Query Allowed: **NO**

o. Run the form. Query a record on the Employee Update Form window.

p. Change the Dept. Number text item value to **78** and tab out of the item. This should cause the bell to sound and the message to be displayed.

q. Change the **Dept. Number** text item to its original value.

r. Click the **Add Department** button, launching the Add New Department dialog box, which is shown in Figure 8-27.

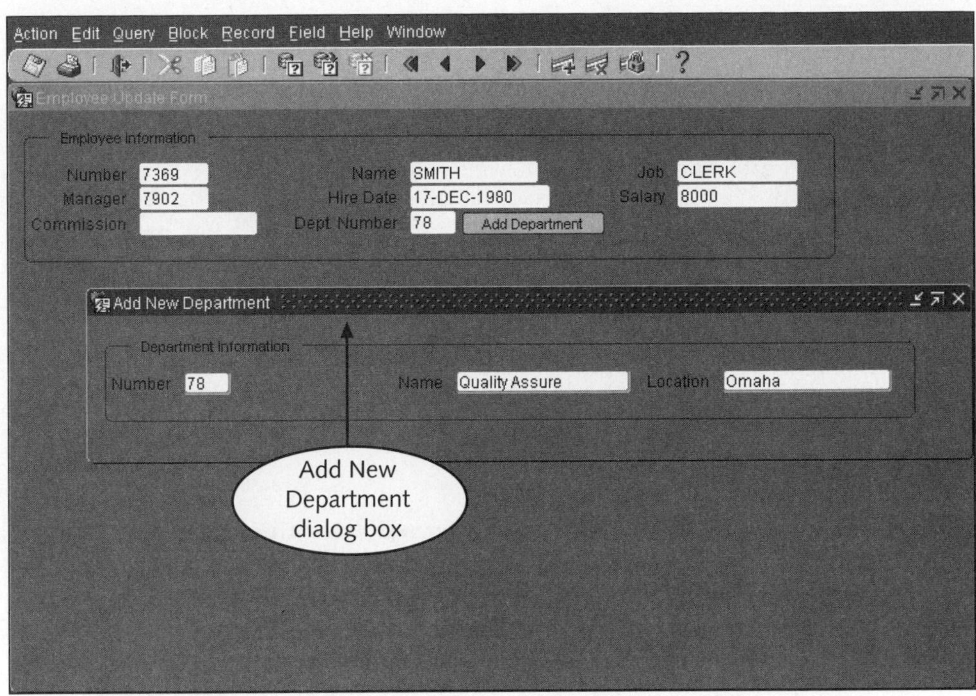

Figure 8-27 The Add New Department dialog box

s. Using the Add New Department dialog box, fill in the following values:

   Number: **78**

   Name: **QUALITY ASSURE**

   Location: **Omaha**

t. Now try to change the Department Number to **78**. To place the Add New Department behind the Employee Update form, click the underlying canvas with your insertion point.

u. For extra practice, put a button in the Add New Department window that navigates to the MAIN canvas.

v. Save the form as **ch08ex01.fmb**.

2. In this assignment, you create a series of tab pages that access various Oracle Data Dictionary views. To accomplish this task, perform the following steps:

   a. Create a new form module in the Object Navigator.

   b. Create a data block using the USER_OBJECTS table. This table is owned by SYS.ID. When browsing for the table on the Data Block Wizard Table page, check the Other Users and Views check box. Use the following settings:

   Columns to Select: **OBJECT_NAME**, **OBJECT_TYPE**

   Canvas Type: **TAB**

Tab Page: **NEW TAB PAGE**

Layout Style: **TABULAR**

Records Displayed: **15**

Display Scrollbar: **CHECKED**

c. Open a Property Palette for the new tab canvas. Set the following properties:

Name: **DATABASE**

Width Style: **VARIABLE**

Active Style: **BOLD**

d. Open a Property Palette for the new tab page. Set the following properties:

Name: **OBJECTS**

Label: **DATABASE OBJECTS**

e. Using the Data Block Wizard and Layout Wizard, create a new data block based on the USER_TAB_COLS view, which is owned by SYS.ID. This is a detail data block using USER_OBJECTS as the master block. The data block is linked by the OBJECT_NAME and TABLE_NAME columns. The tab page displays the columns for the selected table on the OBJECTS page. Use the following settings:

Columns to Select: **TABLE_NAME, COLUMN_NAME, DATA_TYPE, DATA_LENGTH,** and **NULLABLE**

Join Condition: **USER_TAB_COLS.TABLE_NAME = USER_OBJECTS.OBJECT_NAME**

Canvas Type: **TAB**

Canvas Name: **DATABASE**

Tab Page: **NEW TAB PAGE**

Layout Style: **TABULAR**

Records Displayed: **15**

Scrollbar Displayed: **CHECKED**

f. Open a Property Palette for the new tab page. Set the following properties:

Name: **COLUMNS**
Label: **COLUMNS**

g. Save the form as **ch08ex02.fmb.**

h. Run the form. Perform a query on the OBJECTS tab page. Open the COLUMNS tab and view the various columns.

3. In this assignment, you create a horizontal toolbar for the Employee form created in the first assignment. This toolbar contains tools to toggle between the EMPLOYEES and DEPARTMENT canvases. It also has buttons to place the

form into the Enter Query mode, execute a query, commit the changes, and exit the form. Using form module **ch08ex01.fmb**, perform the following steps:

a. Open the Object Navigator and create a new canvas.

b. Open a Property Palette for the canvas and set the following properties:

   Name: **TOOLBAR**

   Canvas Type: **HORIZONTAL_TOOLBAR**

   Height: **20**

   Window: **MAIN**

c. Open the Object Navigator and create four items in the EMP data block.

d. Open the first item and set the following properties:

   Name: **ENTER_QUERY**

   Item Type: **PUSH BUTTON**

   Label: **ENTER QUERY**

   Canvas: **TOOLBAR**

   Height: **20**

e. Open the second item and set the following properties:

   Name: **EXECUTE_QUERY**

   Item Type: **PUSH BUTTON**

   Label: **EXECUTE QUERY**

   Canvas: **TOOLBAR**

   Height: **20**

f. Open the third item and set the following properties:

   Name: **SAVE**

   Item Type: **PUSH BUTTON**

   Label: **SAVE**

   Canvas: **TOOLBAR**

   Height: **20**

g. Open the fourth item and set the following properties:

   Name: **EXIT**

   Item Type: **PUSH BUTTON**

   Label: **EXIT**

   Canvas: **TOOLBAR**

   Height: **20**

h. To create a When-Button-Pressed trigger for the ENTER_QUERY button, use the following script:

```
go_block ('emp');
Enter_query;
```

i. To create a When-Button-Pressed trigger for the EXECUTE_QUERY button, use the following script:

```
go_block ('emp');
Execute_query;
```

j. To create a When-Button-Pressed trigger for the SAVE button, use the following script:

```
Commit_form;
Go_block ('dept');
Clear_block;
Go_block ('emp');
```

k. To create a When-Button-Pressed trigger for the EXIT button, use the following script:

```
Exit_form;
```

l. Open a Property Palette for the ADD_DEPT button and set the following properties:

Canvas: **TOOLBAR**

X Position: **0** (places this button with the other buttons)

Y Position: **0**

Height: **20**

m. Select the ADD_DEPT button in the Object Navigator. Use the Copy tool to copy the item and then paste the item into the DEPT data block using the Paste tool. This button is used to return the input focus to the EMPLOYEES data block.

n. Open a Property Palette for the new button. Set the following properties:

Name: **EMPLOYEE_FORM**

Label: **RETURN TO EMPLOYEE FORM**

Height: **20**

o. Open the Layout Editor and display the TOOLBAR canvas. All the buttons should be located in the top-left corner. Select and drag the **buttons** so that they appear similar to those shown in Figure 8-28.

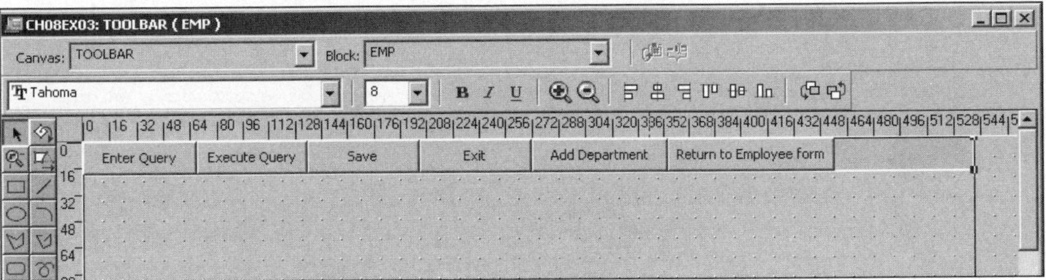

Figure 8-28 Horizontal toolbar canvas

p. Open the Object Navigator and locate the DEPTNO item on the DEPT data block. Set its Required property to **NO**.

q. Open the Property Palette for the form object. Set the Form Horizontal Toolbar Canvas property to **TOOLBAR**.

r. Execute the form and test all the buttons.

s. Save the form as **ch08ex03.fmb.**

4. In this assignment, you create a new tabular form that lists the records in the EMP table. You add a button to this form that opens the **ch08ex03.fmb** application. The twist in this assignment is that the called form displays the selected employee in the new form. You have to pass the EMPNO value to the called form, so that it can retrieve the proper employee and display the value in the **ch08ex03.fmb** form.

   a. Create a new form module based on the EMP table. Use the following settings:

      Layout Style: **TABULAR**

      Number of Records Displayed: **10**

   b. Create a visual attribute named **CURRENT_RECORD**. Set the Foreground Color property to **RED**. This attribute is used to identify the currently selected record.

   c. Open a Property Palette for the EMPNO item. Set the Required property to **NO**.

   d. Open a Property Palette for the EMP data block. Set the Current Record Visual Attribute Group property to **CURRENT_RECORD**.

   e. Open the Layout Editor and place a button on the canvas.

   f. Open a Property Palette for the button. Set the following properties:

      Name: **CALL_EMP_FORM**

      Label: **EMPLOYEE FORM**

      Number of Items Displayed: **1**

g. Create a When-Button-Pressed trigger for the CALL_EMP_FORM button. Use the following script:

```
global.empno := :emp.empno; -- assigns the value of empno to a global variable
:open_form('c:\ct\chapter08\ch08ex03a'); -- use the actual location of your files
```

One of the easiest ways of passing the foreign key value to a called form is to assign the foreign key to a global variable. The variable is then in memory and can be accessed from any form. In this example, a trigger populates the global variable. A When-New-Form-Instance trigger evaluates the global variable. If it contains a value, the data block's Where Clause property is modified using the global variable as an argument.

When using this technique, two things must be done. The global variable should be defined with a NULL value when the user initiates a session. This is generally accomplished by using a When-New-Form-Instance trigger in the startup form. This prevents a form from inadvertently referencing the global variable before it is defined, which causes the form to issue an error message. Creating the global variable as the first step in a session eliminates this error.

The global variable should always contain a NULL value, except when it is used to pass a value. This prevents the Where clause from reusing the value inadvertently. Always assign the global variable a NULL in these two circumstances: when the global variable is defined, and immediately after it is used and the value is no longer needed. You should notice that in the following When-New-Form-Instance trigger, the global variable is initialized immediately after a query is performed on the target data block.

h. Open the **ch08ex03.fmb** module.

i. Create a form-level When-New-Form-Instance trigger using the following script:

```
If :global.empno is not null then
    Set_block_property('emp', default_where, 'empno = :global.empno');
End if;
Execute_query;
:global.empno := null;
set_block_property('emp', default_where, ' ');
```

j. Save the form as **ch08ex03a.fmb.** Compile the **ch08ex03a.fmb** module. Note that it is important that the **ch08ex03a.fmb** module be compiled. Forms Builder will not be able to locate the file unless this is done.

k. Save the original, newly created form as **ch08ex04.fmb**. Run the form and query the data block displaying all of the EMP records.

l. Select a record and click the **CALL_EMP_FORM** button. The second form should appear displaying the appropriate employee record.

m. Close the form. The original form should now be displayed.

n. Select a second record and see if the called form displays the correct record. You should be able to see the original form by dragging the **EMPLOYEE UPDATE FORM**.

o. Close the form.

p. Save the form as **ch08ex04.fmx.**

5. In this assignment, you see the difference between the Open_form built-in and the New_form built-in.

a. Open module **ch08ex04.fmx.**

b. Locate the CALL_EMP_FORM button and modify the When-Button-Pressed trigger. Change the Open_form built-in to **New_form**.

c. Save the form as **ch08ex05.fmb.**

d. Execute the form. Query the data block to display all the EMP records.

e. Select a record and click the **CALL_EMP_FORM** button. The second form should appear, displaying the appropriate employee record.

f. Close the form. The original form should be gone and the session is terminated.

Case Project: Great State Electric Budgeting System

In this portion of the Case Project, you place the PROJECTS and WO_ INSTRUCTIONS canvases into their own windows. The PROJECTS canvas is an insert-only form that is launched with a button located on a horizontal toolbar located in the application. The WO_INSTRUCTIONS canvas is an update-only application. The work order instruction column is too large for the WORK_ORDERS tab page, because the layout is tabular and the column can have a large amount of data. Placing this item on its own custom form will allow the engineer to use multi-line text items to enter and maintain the instructions. The form will be called from a button located on the horizontal toolbar. In this installment, you also add tools to the toolbar for committing the records and exiting the system. To accomplish these tasks, perform the following steps:

1. Open the Budgeting application.
2. In the Object Navigator, create two new Window objects.
3. Open a Property Palette for the first Window object and set the following properties:

   Name: **ADD_PROJECT**

   Title: **ADD NEW PROJECTS**

   Primary Canvas: **PROJECT_ADD**

   Window Style: **DOCUMENT**

   X Position: **60**

Y Position: **100**

Height: **324**

Width: **540**

4. Open a Property Palette for the PROJECT_ADD canvas. Set the Window property to **ADD_PROJECT**. This associates the canvas with the window.
5. Open a Property Palette for the second window object. Set the following properties:

   Name: **ADD_INSTRUCTIONS**

   Title: **MAINTAIN WORK ORDER INSTRUCTIONS**

   Primary Canvas: **WO_INSTRUCTIONS**

   Window Style: **DOCUMENT**

   X Position: **60**

   Y Position: **100**

   Width : **540**

   Height: **324**
6. Open a Property Palette for the WO_INSTRUCTIONS canvas. Set the Window property to **ADD_INSTRUCTIONS**.
7. Open a Property Palette for the last remaining window. This was the original window. Set the following properties:

   Name: **MAIN_WINDOW**

   Title: **ENGINEERING BUDGETING SYSTEM**

   Primary Canvas: **MAIN**

   Width: **900**

   Height: **600**
8. In the Object Navigator, create a new canvas. Open a Property Palette and set the following properties:

   Name: **TOOLBAR**

   Canvas Type: **HORIZONTAL TOOLBAR**

   Height: **20**
9. Open the Layout Editor and display the TOOLBAR canvas. Set the background color to suit your preferences.
10. Open the Object Navigator and create a new control block named **BUTTONS**. Make sure this data block is the last data block in the Object Navigator.
11. Add five data block items to the BUTTONS canvas. Name the buttons **ADD_PROJECT_BUTTON**, **WO_INSTRUCTIONS_BUTTON**, **CLOSE_DIALOG_BUTTON**, **SAVE_BUTTON**, and **EXIT_BUTTON**.

12. Open the Property Palette and set the Label property for each button item to conform with its name and how it appears in Figure 8-29.
13. Open multiple selection Property Palettes for the buttons. Set the following properties:

    Item Type: **PUSH BUTTON**

    Height: **20**

    Canvas: **TOOLBAR**

    X Position: **0**

    Y Position: **0**
14. Open the Layout Editor and format the TOOLBAR canvas according to Figure 8-29.

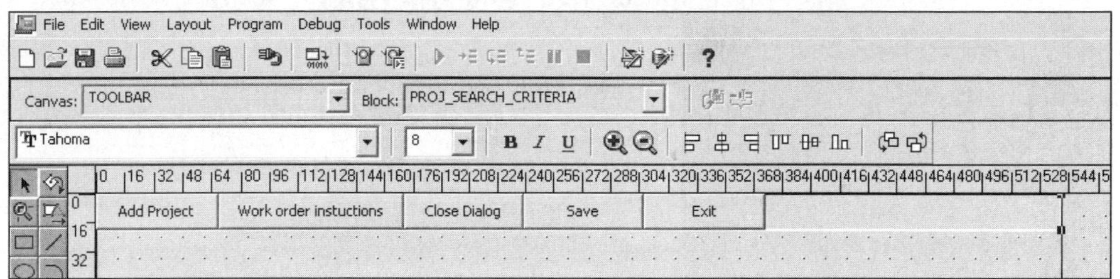

Figure 8-29 Budgeting system toolbar and buttons

15. Open a Property Palette for the Query buttons. They are located in the PROJ_SEARCH_CRITERIA, WO_SEARCH_CRITERIA, ACCOUNTS, TASK_DESCRIPTIONS, and EMPLOYEES data blocks. Set the NEXT NAVIGATION ITEM property to itself. This prohibits the operator from tabbing from the button.
16. Create a When-Button-Pressed trigger for the ADD_PROJECT_BUTTON item. Use the following script:

    ```
    Go_block('projects');
    ```
17. This step prohibits the PROJECT_ADD data block from performing any DML operations other than adding projects. Open a Property Palette for the PROJECTS data block. Set the following properties:

    Query Allowed: **NO**

    Update Allowed: **NO**

    Delete Allowed: **NO**
18. Create a When-Button-Pressed trigger for the WO_INSTRUCTIONS_ BUTTON item. This trigger opens the WO_INSTRUCTIONS window and executes a query. The window should always display the work order data for the

currently selected row in the WORK_ORDER_DATA block. This trigger and the next step ensure that this happens. Use the following script:

```
If :work_order_data.work_order_id is null then
   Bell;
   Message ('You have not selected a work order on the Work Orders tab');
else
   Go_block('wo_instructions');
   Execute_query;
END IF;
```

19. Open a Property Palette for the WO_INSTRUCTIONS data block WORK_ORDER_ID item. Set the following properties:

    Item Type: **DISPLAY ITEM** (ensures the primary key cannot be updated)

    Copy Value From Item: **WORK_ORDER_DATA.WORK_ORDER_ID**

20. In the Object Navigator, open a multi-item Property Palette for the following WO_INSTRUCTIONS data block items: WO_DESCRIPTION, WO_LOCATION, WO_INSTRUCTIONS. Change the following properties to make the items multiple selection:

    Multi-Line: **YES**

    Wrap Style: **WORD**

21. This step ensures that the WO_INSTRUCTIONS data block is used only to update work order information, because the WORK_ORDERS data block is the data block used to add records. Open a Property Palette for the WO_INSTRUCTIONS data block. Set the following properties:

    Insert Allowed: **NO**

    Delete Allowed: **NO**

22. Open the Layout Editor and display the WO_INSTRUCTIONS canvas. Format it to resemble Figure 8-30.

23. Create a When-Button-Pressed trigger for the CLOSE_DIALOG_BUTTON item. This trigger causes the ADD_PROJECT and the ADD_WO_INSTRUCTIONS windows to disappear if they are overlaying the main tab canvas by using the following script:

    ```
    Hide_window('add_project');
    Hide_window('wo_instructions' );
    ```

24. Create a When-Button-Pressed trigger for the SAVE_BUTTON item by using the following script:

    ```
    Commit_form;
    ```

25. Create a When-Button-Pressed trigger for the EXIT_BUTTON by using the following script:

    ```
    Exit_form;
    ```

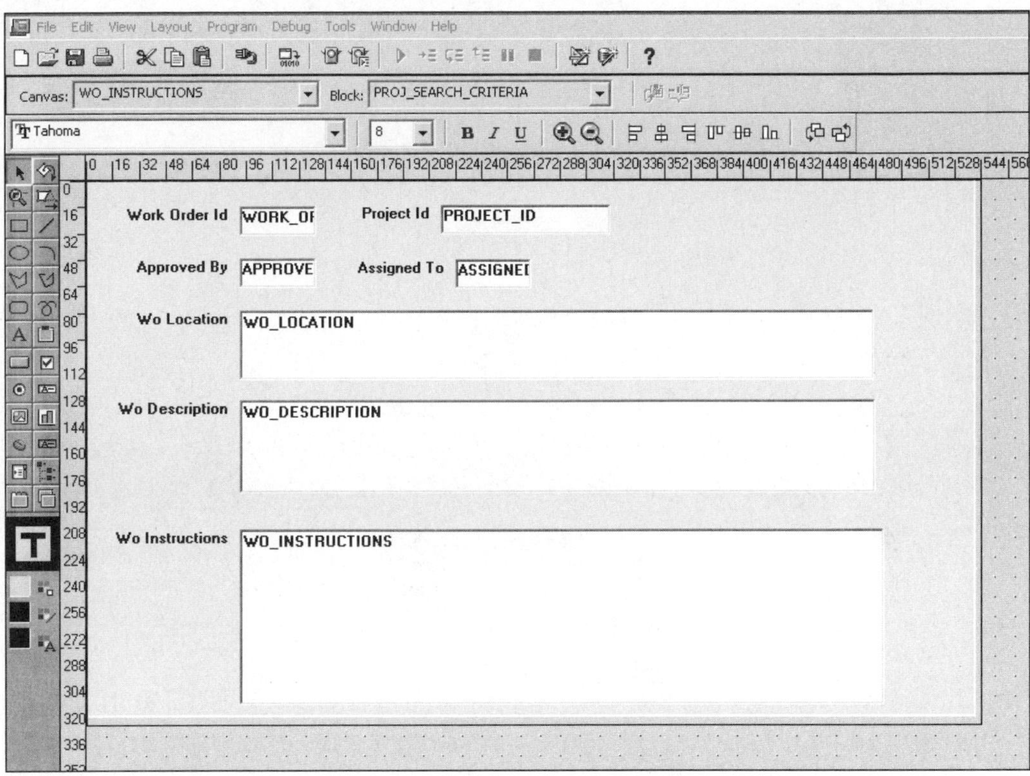

Figure 8-30 WO_INSTRUCTIONS canvas after formatting

26. In this step, you link the TOOLBAR canvas to the application, and the canvas will be visible when you execute the application. Open a Property Palette for the form object. Set the Form Horizontal Toolbar Canvas property to **TOOLBAR**.
27. Test your form by doing the following:
    a. Launch the form. Does your button bar appear?
    b. Execute a query on the WORK_ORDERS tab page. Select a **row**. Click the **WO_INSTRUCTIONS** button. The WO_INSTRUCTIONS window should appear.
    c. Click the **CLOSE_DIALOG_BUTTON** button. The display of the WO_INSTRUCTIONS window should end.
    d. Click the **ADD PROJECTS** button. The corresponding form should appear.
    e. Select another work order and click the **WO_INSTRUCTIONS** button. The window should open with the selected work order information.
    f. Click the **CLOSE_DIALOG_BUTTON** button. The display of both windows should end.
    g. Click the **EXIT** button. The session should terminate.
28. Save your form for the Case Project in the next chapter.

CHAPTER

9

ADDING MENUS, POPUP MENUS, ALERTS, TIMERS, AND HIERARCHICAL TREE ITEMS TO FORMS

In this chapter you will:

- Use menus to consolidate applications into systems
- Create and use popup menus
- Use alerts to grab an operator's attention
- Create timers in your forms
- Add and use hierarchical tree items
- Create database objects through your form
- Trap and handle error messages
- Learn about mouse events

Looking at the roadmap in Figure 9-1, you can see that this chapter continues to build on the skills that you have been developing throughout this book. In the previous chapters, you have learned to build a variety of different types of forms and to call other forms and windows using buttons and toolbars. In this chapter, you learn to consolidate your applications into a system using a drop-down menu. Systems that you build are likely to have far more applications than you have space to display on a toolbar. The standard Forms Builder drop-down menus help your operators easily identify the system choices when there are too many to be displayed simultaneously on a toolbar.

This chapter also covers two useful tools: popup menus and alerts. A **popup menu** is a menu that is opened by right-clicking the mouse button. An **alert** is a modal dialog box that informs the operator of an event. This chapter also discusses hierarchical tree items. These items can be used to display data in a hierarchy of parent and child nodes. Trees allow your users to drill down to a lower level of detail. Finally, this chapter covers a number of miscellaneous topics, such as creating timers, trapping error messages, and creating your DDL and SQL statements within a form.

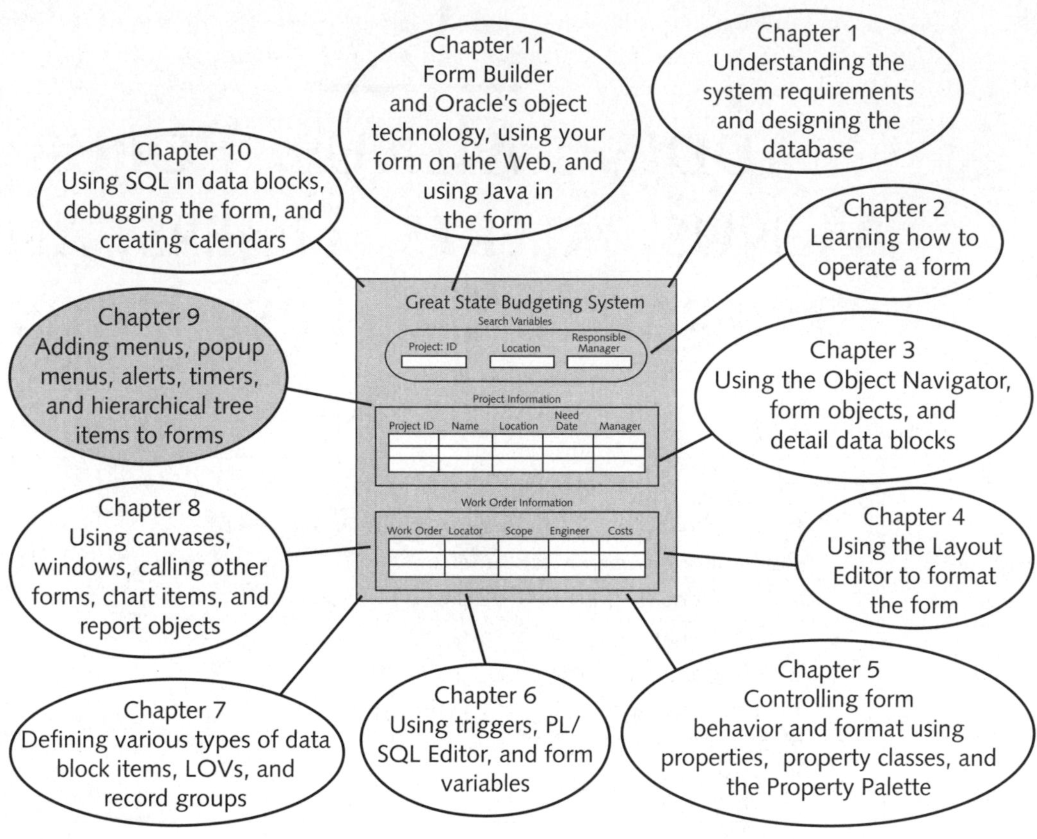

Figure 9-1 Roadmap

Using Menus to Consolidate Applications into Systems

Most systems contain a large number of applications, which operators access and use to perform tasks. For example, the Great State Budgeting System has forms for the following functions: creating projects; maintaining employee records, accounts, and task descriptions; identifying work orders; and estimating costs. Operators must be able to easily call each of these forms to perform a specific function. In Chapter 8, you saw that tab pages can be used for this purpose, but unfortunately there is a limitation to tab pages. After the width of the screen is filled, the operator cannot see the remaining applications, and most systems have far too many applications to label each with a tab. You can use menus to solve this problem and to organize your system's many applications for easy access.

The menu that you have been using in Forms Builder's IDE (see Figure 9-2) is an example of a drop-down menu that groups numerous applications into a series of menu palettes. At the top of the menu are palette or submenu headings that classify the various sets of options. Clicking the palette heading opens the palette with the various options. Several of the options shown in Figure 9-2, such as SmartTriggers, have right-facing arrows, which indicate that a submenu is available. Placing the cursor over this option opens the submenu, displaying more options. The expansion and collapse of submenus allow you to compress more options into a limited space. Some of the menu options have hot keys or keyboard shortcuts. For example, the Ctrl+C key combination listed next to the Copy menu option copies the selected object to the Clipboard. You can also define hot keys for your menu options. In the next several sections, you learn to create a menu as complex as the Forms Builder IDE menu.

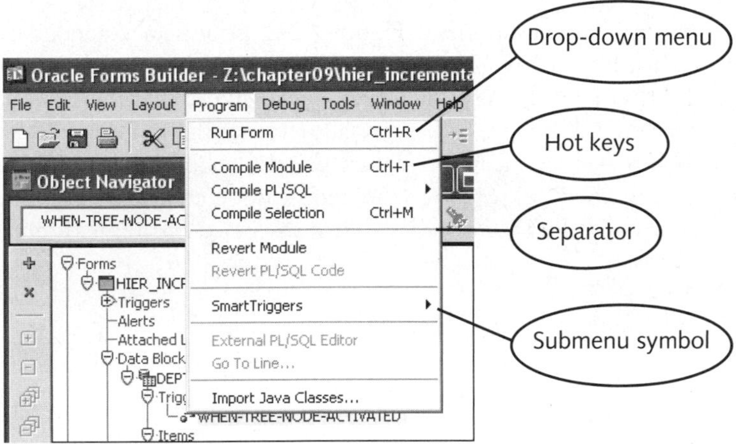

Figure 9-2 Forms Builder IDE drop-down menu

9

Menu Modules

A menu is a module that cannot be executed on its own. The module can only be executed when it is called from a form. A different menu module can be attached to each form in a system, or a module can be assigned to the first application opened and then passed to each subsequent application. In Forms Builder, you may have noticed that the menus change depending on the currently active screen. When the Object Navigator is selected, the menu and options differ from those displayed when the Property Palette is selected. This same feature can be deployed in your system forms. Assigning a specific menu to each form allows you to achieve this same effect. On the other hand, if you assign only a menu to the startup application, the menu is automatically transferred to each called application, provided the called application does not have its own menu. This transfer ability allows the developer to build one menu and use it on many forms.

A menu is its own module. Forms Builder has two types of menu modules: the source code binary file that has a file extension of **.mmb** and a compiled version with an extension of **.mmx**. The **.mmb** file is used inside of the Forms Builder IDE and is built using the Menu Editor. The compiled **.mmx** is the version assigned to the form and executed at runtime. The executable menu module is created by compiling the **.mmb** file.

To compile a menu module (or the form module), you would perform these steps:

1. Select the module.
2. Click the Compile Module tool on the toolbar.

Throughout this book, you have been building and executing applications. The changes that you made were evident when the form was displayed, and you did not have to compile the form to see the changes. The reason is that the Forms Builder IDE has a general preference, called Build Before Running, which compiles the form module before it is executed. However, this preference compiles only the executed module, not attached files, such as the menu module. To see the changes in a menu, you must compile the file before running the form.

A menu module has a number of components. Figure 9-3 illustrates an expanded menu module in the Object Navigator. You have seen most of the components of the menu in other sections of this book. The menu can use the Parameters, Object Groups, Visual Attributes, and other components shown in Figure 9-3, just as a form uses them. The menu component is the object that contains the menu option design palette, selections, and PL/SQL that is executed by the menu. The menu object and subobjects can be created with the Create tool in the Object Navigator or in the Menu Editor that is discussed in the next section.

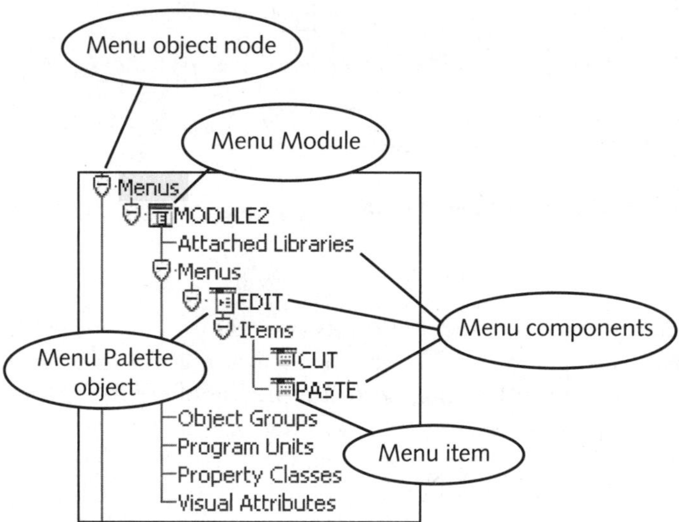

Figure 9-3 Object Navigator and an expanded menu module object

Menu Editor

The Menu Editor of Forms Builder (Figure 9-4) graphically depicts the menu. It is far easier to use the editor than to create the menu in the Object Navigator. To open the Menu Editor, you would use one of these methods:

- Double-click a menu module object in the Object Navigator.
- Select any item within the menu module and select the Tools/Menu Editor menu option.

The Menu Editor in Figure 9-4 displays a menu (Form_MENU), a drop-down menu below this menu (APPLICATIONS_MENU), and a submenu for (REPORTS_MENU).

If you look at the Object Navigator depicted next to the Menu Editor, you can see the three menu objects. Notice that the Form_MENU menu object has a child menu item called APPLICATIONS. Figure 9-4 displays a Property Palette for this item. Notice that the Submenu Name property has a value of APPLICATIONS_MENU. This means that the menu option will display a menu named APPLICATIONS_MENU, which is the second menu on the Object Navigator. The APPLICATIONS_MENU will be a drop-down menu because the options were created with the Create Down tool. The last menu item is the REPORTS menu option. This option calls a submenu called REPORTS_MENU, which has a single option. This option is displayed to the right because the Create Right tool was used. You know that the Form_MENU menu and its subordinate menus are being displayed because its name appears in the Display Menu drop-down list at the top of the Menu Editor. The select menu as indicated by this drop-down list always displays at the top-left of the editor.

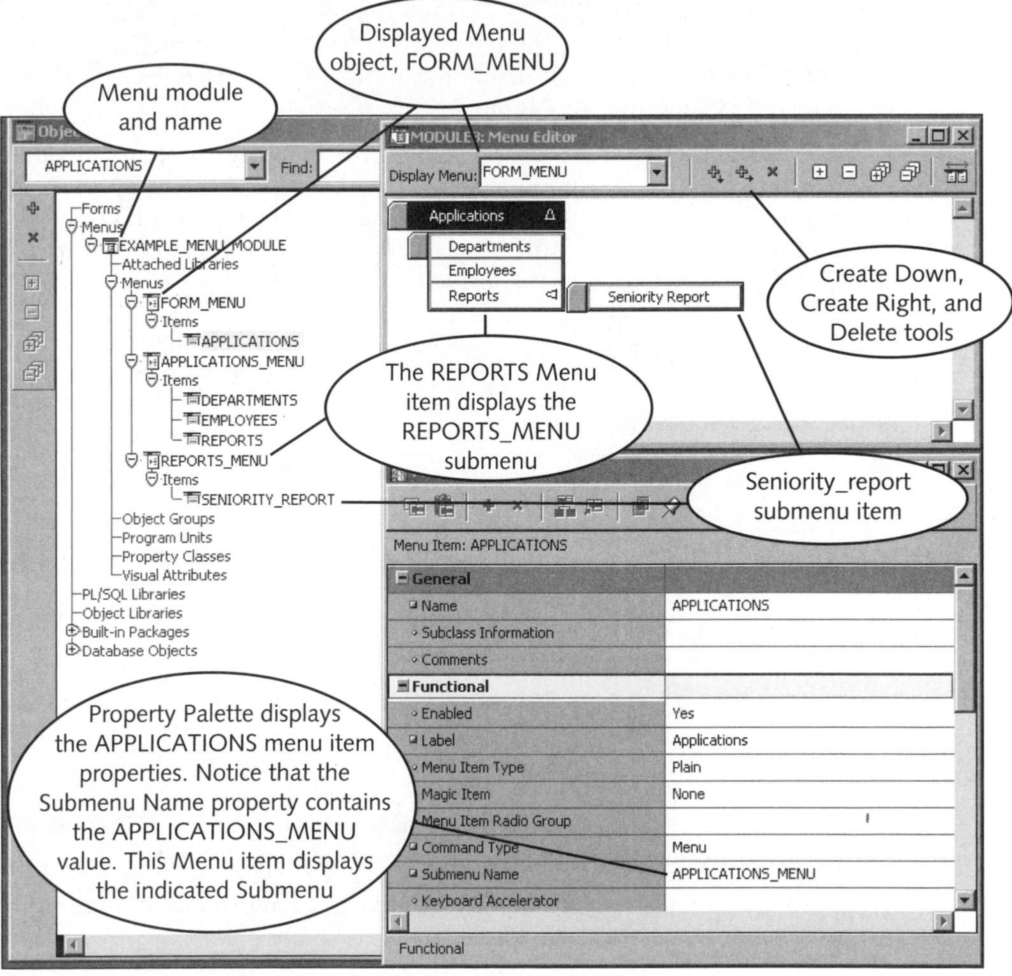

Figure 9-4 Menu Editor and a drop-down menu

9

Each of the menus has several items that are options on the menu you create. The items are used to call a form, execute a procedure, or call another menu. In the case of the Reports item, it calls the REPORTS_MENU menu. The purpose of this discussion was to show you the relationship between the graphic menu display and the Object Navigator, and you should now be able to set up a basic menu in the Menu Editor.

The Menu Editor has a number of tools for cutting, copying, and pasting items. It also has several tools for expanding and collapsing menus. In addition, the following four tools are extremely useful for creating your menus:

- **Create Down tool**: Creates a new item directly below the currently selected item. This tool has a downward-pointing arrow.
- **Create Right tool**: Creates a new submenu and item to the right of the selected item. This tool also associates the original item to the submenu. This tool has a right-pointing arrow.
- **Delete tool**: Deletes the currently selected item. If the item is associated to a submenu, it does not delete the submenu; it only deletes the menu item. A red X identifies this tool.
- **Switch Orientation tool**: Changes the orientation of the menu. A vertical drop-down menu can be changed to a horizontal menu by clicking this button. Figure 9-5 illustrates the same menu as depicted in Figure 9-4 after the Switch Orientation tool was clicked. This tool is located furthest to the left and is identified by a two-headed red arrow.

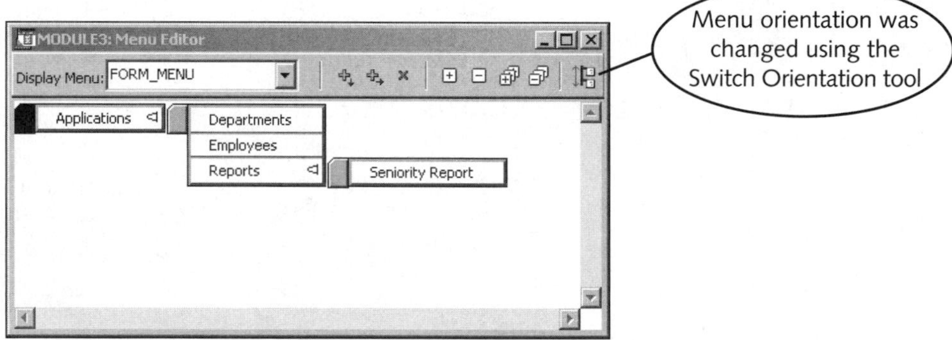

Figure 9-5 Menu depicted in Figure 9-4 after the orientation was changed to vertical

Creating a Menu

Now that you understand the menu functions, you can create a menu module and a menu. To do so, you would use the following procedure:

1. To create a new menu module, select the Menus module node in the Object Navigator and click the Create tool.
2. To create a menu object within the new menu module (file), select the Menus object node, which is a child of the Menus module, and click the Create tool.

3. Open the Menu Editor by double-clicking the new menu object or selecting the Tools/Menu Editor menu selection.
4. The Menu Editor initially displays a single new item.
5. Place your insertion point into the item. You can then change the label that is displayed on the item by typing over the value. This also changes the name of the item in the Object Navigator.
6. Use the Create Down or Create Right tool to add another item or submenu.
7. Repeat Steps 5 and 6 until all items and submenus are completed.
8. Add PL/SQL statements to all items (not shown yet).
9. Close the Menu Editor.
10. Save and compile the module.

Any menu option that is not associated to a submenu must have a PL/SQL script associated to it. This is discussed in the next section.

Adding Statements to Menu Items

For the menu option to function, a command must be associated to the menu item. Five types of commands can be associated to menu items, although you will probably use only the first three:

- **Null**: Specifies that the item does not perform an action. This is required for separator items.
- **Menu**: Calls another menu.
- **PL/SQL**: Invokes a PL/SQL script or built-in subprogram, such as Open_form. This is the default menu item type.
- **Plus**: Opens an SQL*Plus session.
- **Macro**: Executes an SQL*Menu macro. You should avoid this option.

The menu item's Command Type property determines the type of item. You probably don't have to set the property, because Forms Builder sets the type to PL/SQL by default or to MENU whenever a submenu is added. Set the property by opening the item's Property Palette and changing the property value.

Commands are entered in two ways: by opening the item's PL/SQL Editor (for PL/SQL items) or by using the Command Text Editor (for other types). The editors are opened in two ways:

- Double-clicking the menu item icon in the Object Navigator (see Figure 9-6).
- Opening the item's Property Palette and clicking the Menu Item Code property's More button (see Figure 9-6).

The menu item can open any PL/SQL code block. If sophisticated processing must be done, it can be opened using a menu option. However, it is typical to use menu items to open forms and perform routine functions such as cutting, pasting, or executing a query. You will probably be entering standard Open_form and Execute_query type built-ins as the item scripts.

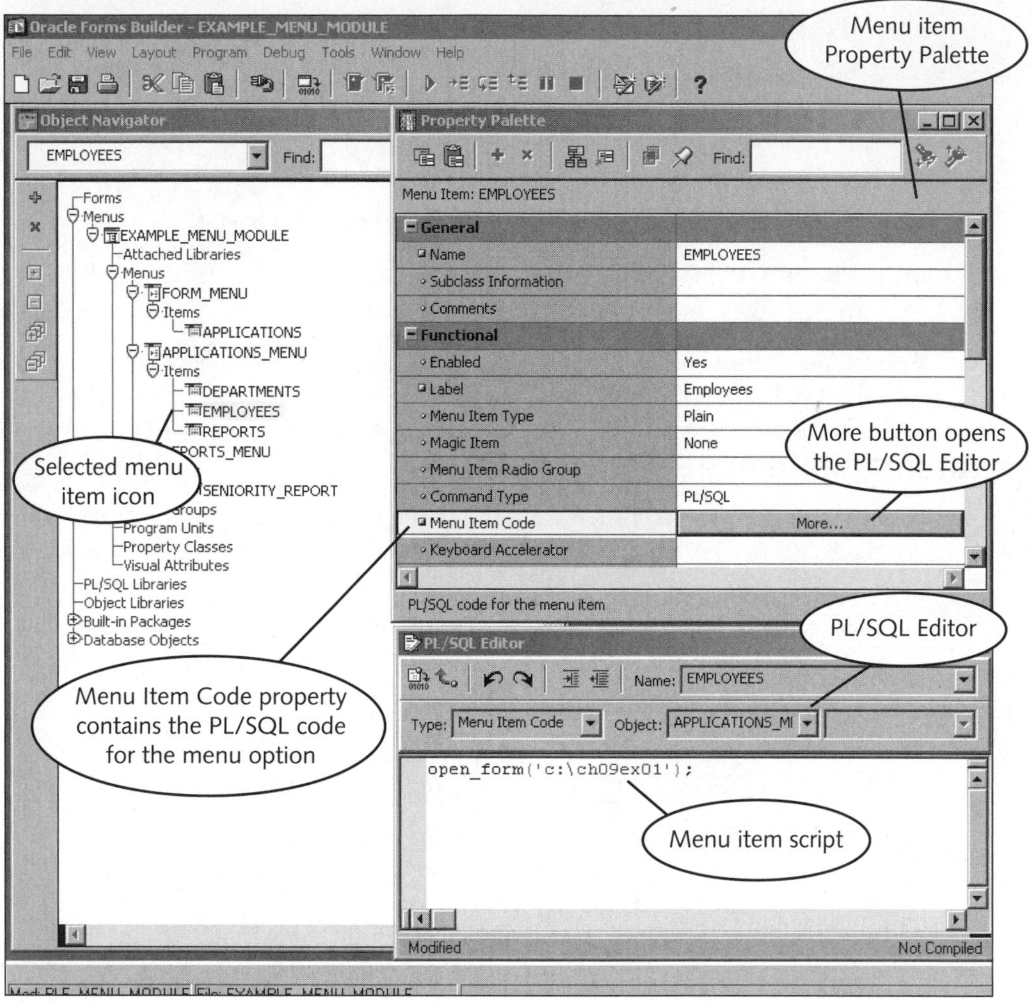

Figure 9-6 Menu item icon and More button used to open the item's PL/SQL Editor

Associating a Menu to a Form

A menu is associated to a form through form properties. These properties are:

- **Menu Source**: Identification of the storage location of the menu file. Choices are DATABASE and FILE. The default is FILE.
- **Menu Module**: Name of the menu module. The full file path of this item must be set if the FILE option is used and the module does not reside in the default Forms Builder directory.

To associate a menu to a form, you add the name of the menu module to the Menu Module property.

In the practice session that follows, you follow steps to create a simple menu that calls forms you created in the Chapter 8 exercises and calls built-ins that perform simple form actions:

1. Open the Object Navigator and create a new menu module (file) by selecting the Menus module mode and clicking the **Create** tool.
2. Save the menu module as **practice0901.mmb.**
3. Select the **Menus** node within the **practice0901.mmb** module. Do not be confused with the Menus module node, which is at the file node level. The menus node is the second menu module node, and it follows the Attached Libraries node. Click the **Create** tool on the Menus object node to produce a new default menu. Name this menu **FORM_MENU**.
4. Open the Menu Editor by double-clicking the **FORM_MENU** menu object item. You will create a menu similar to the one depicted in Figure 9-7 using the Create Down and Create Right tools.

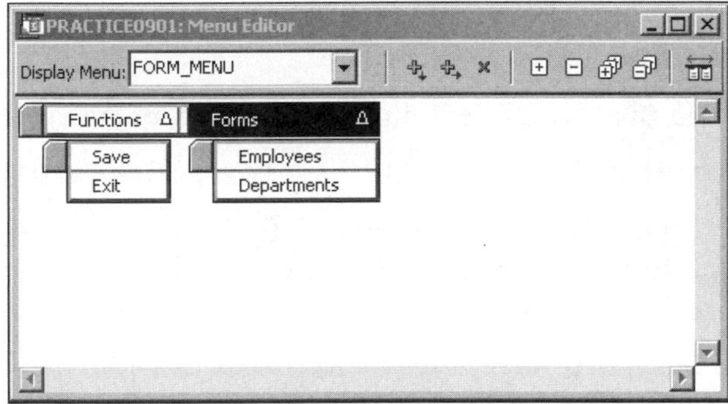

Figure 9-7 Practice menu

5. When you open the Menu Editor, you should see one option called <NEW_ITEM>. Overtype this value with the value **FUNCTIONS**. This can be done by clicking the item twice very slowly. Press **Enter** to cause Forms Builder to accept the change.
6. Click the **Create Down** tool to add a new option below the current one. Overtype the default option name with **SAVE**. Press **Enter** to cause Forms Builder to accept the change.
7. Click the **Create Down** tool to add an option below the SAVE option. Overtype the default option name with **EXIT**. Click **Enter** to cause Forms Builder to accept the change.

8. Select the **FUNCTIONS** option and click the **Create Right** tool. Overtype the default name with **FORMS**. Click **Enter** to cause Forms Builder to accept the change.
9. Click the **Create Down** tool. Overtype the default option name with **EMPLOYEES**. Click **Enter** to cause Forms Builder to accept the change.
10. Click the **Create Down** tool. Overtype the default option name with **DEPARTMENTS**. Click **Enter** to cause Forms Builder to accept the change.
11. Close the Menu Editor and return to the Object Navigator. Notice that the menu items have the names you typed into the Menu Editor.
12. Add the PL/SQL scripts to the menu items by opening the PL/SQL Editor for each item. Open the PL/SQL Editor by double-clicking the **menu item** and supply the scripts for the following menu items:

    SAVE: **COMMIT_FORM;**
    EXIT: **EXIT_FORM;**
    EMPLOYEES: **new_form('c:\practice0901');** be sure to use the correct file path
    DEPARTMENTS: **new_form('c:\practice0902');** be sure to use the correct file path
13. Save the module file as **practice0901.mmb**.
14. Compile the file using the Compile Module tool at the top of Forms Builder.
15. Open the **practice0801.fmb** module and save it as **practice0901.fmb**.
16. Open the Property Palette for the **practice0901.fmb** form module. Set the Menu Module property to **c:\practice0901.mmx**. Be sure to use the correct file path. Save and compile the **practice0901.fmb** form module.
17. Open the **practice0802.fmb** form and save it as **practice0902.fmb.** Remove the **DEFAULT&SMARTBAR** setting in the form Menu Module property. Save and compile this form.
18. Open form **practice0901.fmb**. Select all the various options. Notice that the menu remains when new applications are called.

Menu Security

Oracle has incorporated security that is based on a role into its menus. A **role** is an Oracle database security object that is granted database privileges. These privileges can be **object privileges**, such as the ability to select, update, or modify tables, or they can be **system privileges**, such as Create Table. Roles are then granted to specific user accounts. You can control who operates the menu by associating roles to the menu. Forms Builder identifies the roles assigned to the current user and permits the user to employ the menu options, if the role matches those associated to the menu.

To add security to your menus, you would perform the following steps:

1. Open a Property Palette for the menu module.
2. Set the Use Security property to YES.
3. Select the Module Roles property and activate the More button. Click the button to open the Menu Module Roles dialog box.
4. Enter the role names into the dialog box.

Figure 9-8 illustrates a menu module Property Palette and the Menu Module Roles dialog box.

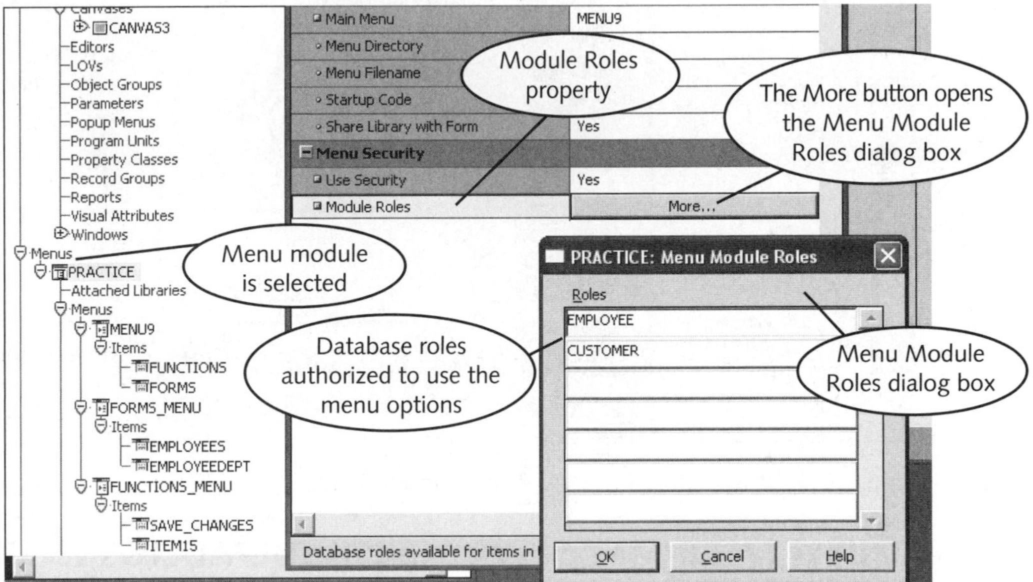

Figure 9-8 Menu module Property Palette and the Menu Module Roles dialog box

The next steps are performed on the individual menu items. You must determine which role(s) are needed to use the option. Each menu item has an Item Roles property that opens a Menu Item Roles dialog box (see Figure 9-9) that is used to identify the roles that can use the option. A second property, Display without Privilege, determines whether or not the menu option is even visible to the operator. A value of NO hides the option for any user not assigned the proper role.

5. Open a **Property Palette** for the menu item requiring security.
6. Set the **Item Roles** and **Display without Privilege** properties for the menu item.
7. Repeat steps 1 and 2 for each menu item requiring security.
8. Save and compile the file.

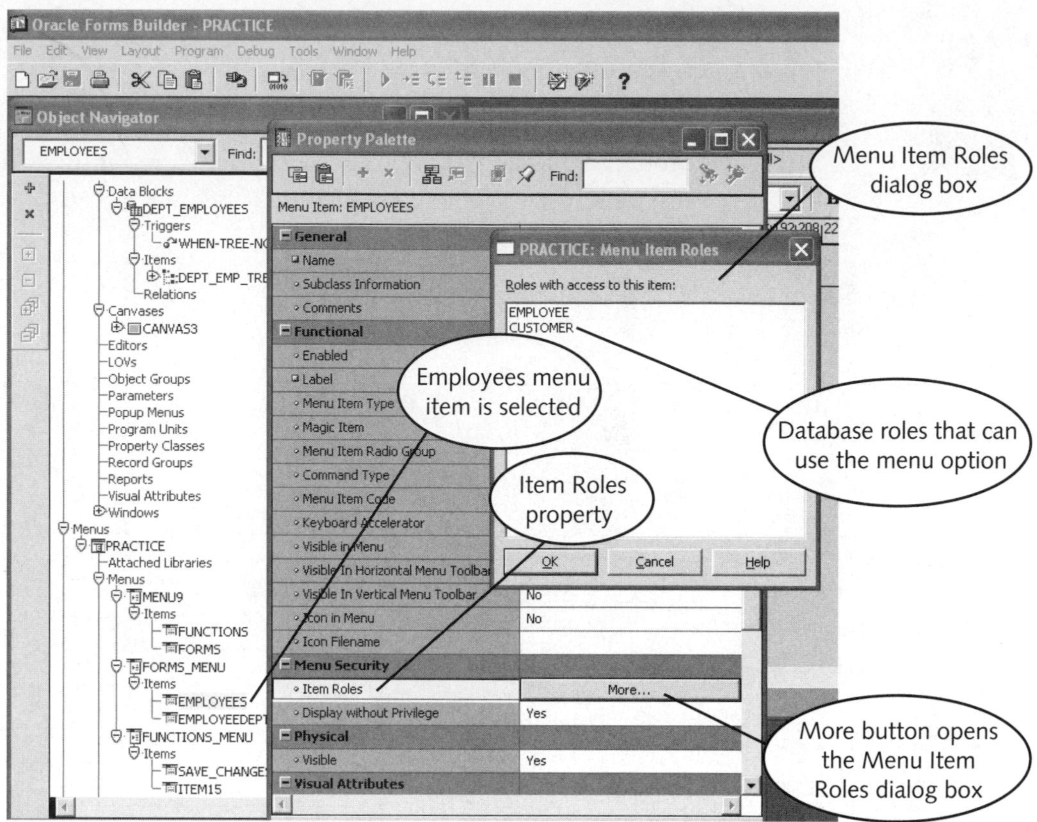

Figure 9-9 Menu item Property Palette and the Menu Item Roles dialog box

Menu Item Types, Magic Items, and the DEFAULT&SMARTBAR

When you set up a menu, you can choose among a variety of different types. The default type is Plain, which consists of text displayed on the menu option. You can also design a menu using the Radio and Check item types that allows the operator to place a check in a check box or click a radio button next to the menu item. These types of menu items are used when it is necessary to determine whether the item has been selected. For example, a check in a Check item indicates that the item was selected. It is possible to add a separator to the menu, which consists of an item that displays a horizontal line designating the segregation of options. Finally, a menu item can be set up to perform standard tasks, such as cutting and pasting. The Menu Item Type property is used to add the features to the menu.

Figure 9-10 illustrates several types of menu items. The Functions menu palette is open. The first two items, Cut and Paste, are Magic item types (defined in the next paragraph) and perform standard cut and paste operations. Below these items is a horizontal bar that acts as a separator to distinguish the operating functions, which are displayed above the separator, from the form functions, which are displayed below the separator. The Save Changes menu item has a check to its left. This item is a check menu item and the check indicates that the option has been chosen. The Exit menu item is an example of the plain type.

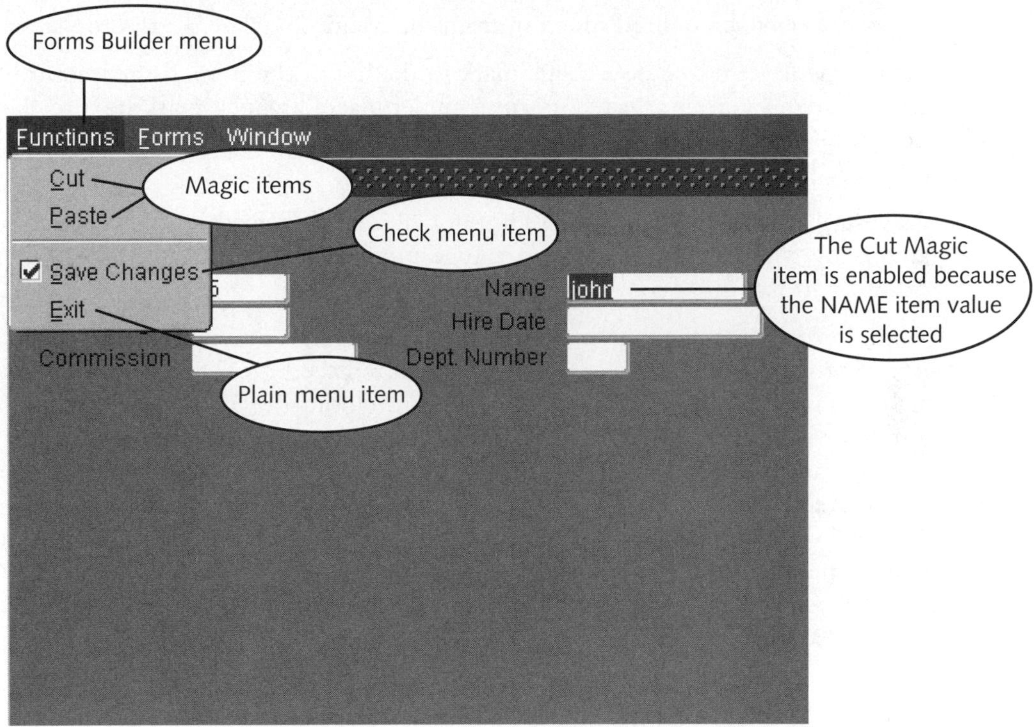

Figure 9-10 Magic, Check, and Plain menu items

A **Magic menu item** is one that is associated to a standard operating system function. When an item is designated as this type, Forms Builder identifies the hot key (e.g., Control + C for copy) for the function and places it to the right of the option on the menu. The hot key can change depending on the operating system (i.e., Windows or UNIX). Forms Builder determines the proper hot key for the particular operating system and associates it to the item. It also places the hot key symbols next to the item on the menu. You can see an example of this by opening the Forms Builder File menu. Notice the Ctrl + O designation next to the Open option. This indicates that the Control + O keys can be used to open a file.

Forms Builder also determines whether the item should be disabled. In Figure 9-10, you know that the Cut Magic menu item is enabled because the text has been selected in the form. The Paste Magic menu item is not enabled because nothing has been copied to the Clipboard. These functions work exactly as they do in all other Windows applications. You can designate 11 different types of functions: None, Cut, Copy, Paste, Clear, Undo, Help, About, Quit, Window, and Page Setup.

To designate a menu item as a Magic item, you would perform the following steps:

1. Select the menu item and open a Property Palette for the item.
2. Set the Menu Item Type property to **MAGIC**.
3. Select the desired function from the Magic Item property drop-down list.

Check menu items toggle a check mark to the left of the item. If the item is unchecked and the menu item is selected, Forms Builder places a check mark next to the item the next time it is displayed. It works in the opposite way if the item is checked when it is selected.

As described earlier, separators are horizontal lines displayed on the option. Create separators by changing the Menu Item Type property to SEPARATOR. Separator items cannot perform an action.

While either viewing Figure 9-10 or performing the previous practice, you probably noticed that the menu you added to the form replaced the default toolbar that has been attached to the forms you have executed throughout this book. This toolbar is actually a menu called DEFAULT&SMARTBAR and is the default menu that Oracle places in all applications. It is also the default Menu Module property setting. When you assigned the menu to the application, you replaced this value with the name of your menu file. If you do not want the default toolbar menu as your own menu and do not want to have a menu for your application, you can remove the DEFAULT&SMARTBAR setting. This is handy if you add your own toolbar to your form.

DEFAULT&SMARTBAR is actually a fairly good menu, but because it is a default menu, it probably lacks some of the options that you want. DEFAULT&SMARTBAR is not a file that you can modify. However, Oracle has provided a menu file called **menudefs.mmb** that mimics DEFAULT&SMARTBAR. You may open this file in Forms Builder and modify it according to your needs.

You may have also noticed that the DEFAULT&SMARTBAR menu has tools on the bottom of the menu. This is not a horizontal toolbar canvas but is actually a feature of menus. Each menu item has an Icon Filename and a Visible In Horizontal Toolbar property. If you place an icon file name into this property and set the Visible In Horizontal Toolbar property to YES, Forms Builder displays the icon below the menu, much as icons are displayed by the DEFAULT&SMARTBAR menu. To create your own customized version of the DEFAULT&SMARTBAR, simply use the Menu Editor to add or remove items. You can modify the tools by adding icon file names to the Icon Filename. Icon files have a file extension of **.ico**.

Menu Module Properties

The previous chapter discussed a number of properties that affect a menu's features. There are, however, additional properties that are sometimes used. The menu module properties are Module Roles and Use Security. Each menu in the module has this property: Tear

Off Menu. Finally, the menu items have these properties: Command Text, Command Type, Display without Privilege, Enabled, Keyboard Accelerator, Icon Filename, Icon In Menu, Item Roles, Label, Magic Item, Menu Item Code, Menu Item Radio Group, Menu Item Type, Submenu, Visible In Horizontal Toolbar, Visible In Vertical Toolbar, and Visible in Menu. This chapter has described several of these properties and Appendix B describes the rest.

Creating and Using Popup Menus

The Forms Builder menu object that is a component of a form is the **Popup Menu** object. This menu pops up next to the insertion point when the Right Mouse button is clicked. This handy tool has been incorporated into most software applications in the past five years. Popup menus allow the operator to quickly execute a command without having to move the cursor to a toolbar, menu, or button. Having a command palette so readily available can dramatically reduce the time needed to perform tasks. Figure 9-11 illustrates a typical popup menu, which is displaying options for calling department and employee forms.

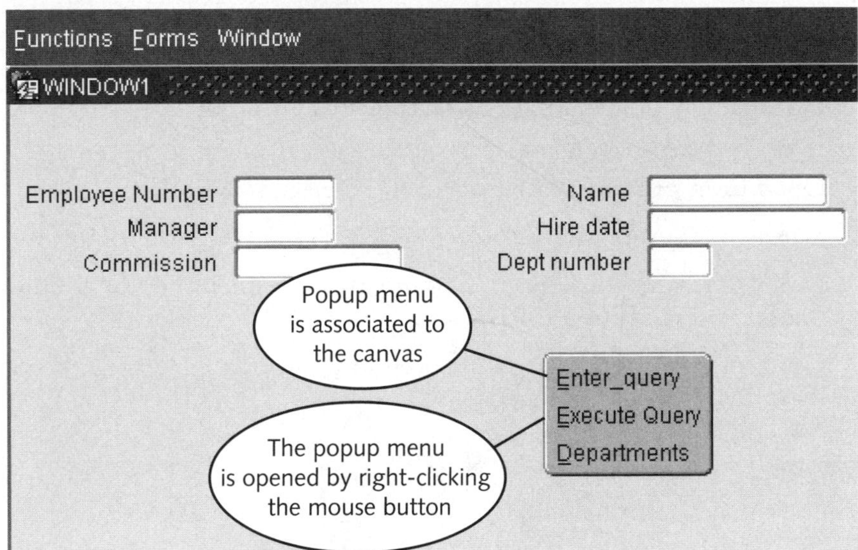

Figure 9-11 Popup menu containing a variety of item types

Common popup menu selections are often the normal form functions, such as executing a query or saving the changes. Other selections include navigation executables such as Go_block or executables that display a LOV. Actually, any menu option, toolbar tool, or form button can be an option on a popup menu. If the user can reduce mouse movement and prefers the popup menu, it's a good tool.

The one downfall of popup menus is the number of potential options that can be placed on them. A popup menu containing every option can be so long that it takes as long locating the option on the menu as it would to locate the tool on the form. Forms Builder compensates for this by allowing you to create numerous popup menus in a form module. It allows you to assign the popup menu to a canvas or item. This allows you to segregate options. For example, you could place each data block on different overlaying canvases and attach a different popup to each canvas. This allows you to create a custom popup menu for each data block.

To create a popup menu, you would perform the following steps:

1. Open a form module and select the Popup Menus node. Click the Create tool to create a popup menu object.
2. Select the Popup Menus object node. Click the **Create** tool. Name the new popup menu object **EMPNO_POPUP**.
3. Double-click the **new popup menu item** to open the Menu editor.
4. Open a Property Palette for each item and set the properties.
5. Add appropriate scripts to each of the menu items.
6. Assign the popup menu object to the appropriate canvas or data block item. Set the Popup Menu property. This property is located on canvas or data block items.

As practice, add a popup menu to the **practice0901.fmb** practice form by performing the following steps:

1. Open form **practice0901.fmb** in the Object Navigator.
2. Select the **Popup Menus** object node. Click the **Create** tool.
3. Double-click the **new popup menu item** to open the Menu Editor. Name the menu **EMPNO_POPUP**.
4. Using the same techniques employed in the last practice, create a menu similar to that depicted in Figure 9-12.

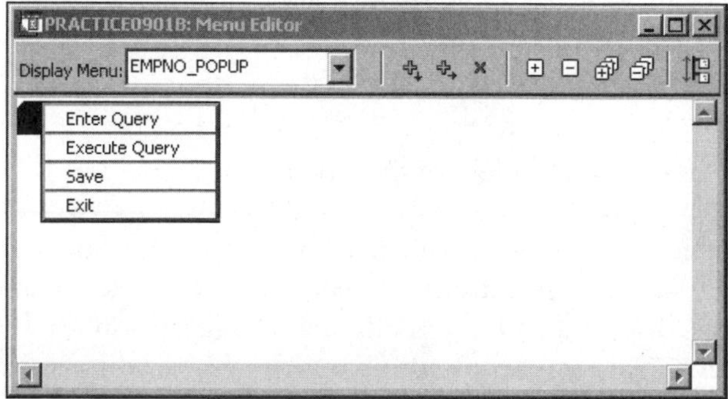

Figure 9-12 Practice popup menu

5. Open a PL/SQL Editor for each of the items for the EMPNO_POPUP popup menu object. The following are the names of the items to be added to the PL/SQL statement that will be executed by the item:
   - ENTER_QUERY: **ENTER_QUERY;**
   - EXECUTE_QUERY: **EXECUTE_QUERY;**
   - SAVE: **COMMIT_FORM;**
   - EXIT: **EXIT_FORM;**
6. Open the Property Palette for the EMP_CANVAS canvas object. Add the **EMPNO_POPUP** menu object to the EMP_CANVAS Popup Menu property.
7. Save and run the form. Test the popup menu by clicking the Right Mouse button when the insertion point is located in the EMP_CANVAS canvas.
8. Save the form for later practice.

USING ALERTS TO GRAB AN OPERATOR'S ATTENTION

At times you want to capture an operator's attention. For example, a security violation might have occurred, an operator is about to delete a record, or an operator is about to open a lengthy process. There are many events in a system about which you want to send a message to the operator and have the operator acknowledge its receipt. Alerts perform this function. When the alert opens, a modal dialog box opens displaying a message and one or more buttons. Because the operator cannot perform any action other than clicking one of the buttons in the alert, you can be assured the operator saw the message.

Figure 9-13 illustrates examples of alerts. An alert, which is always displayed in the exact center of the form where it is sure to capture an operator's attention, has several components:

- **Title**: A title that describes the purpose or nature of the alert.
- **Text**: Text that is displayed inside the alert.
- **Severity symbol**: A symbol representing the severity of the alert. The types are: Stop, Caution, and Note, as shown in Figure 9-13. The Stop alert is the most severe.
- **Buttons**: The alert can have one to three buttons, such as OK and Cancel, that represent options. Each alert must have at least one button.

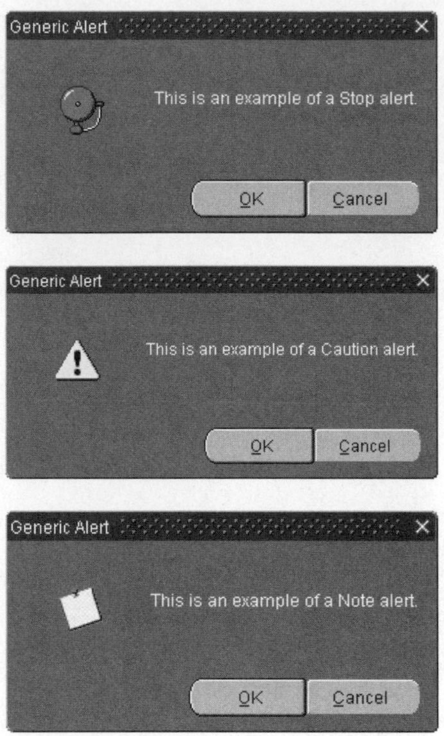

Figure 9-13 Stop, Caution, and Note alerts

To create an alert, you would perform the following steps:

1. Open the form module and select the Alerts object node. Click the Create tool.
2. Double-click the newly created alert to open its Property Palette.
3. Set the alert properties.

Alert Properties

Just as with any other form object, alerts have properties. The severity symbol is a property setting, as are the title, text, and buttons. The alert properties are Alert Style, Button 1 Label, Button 2 Label, Button 3 Label, Default Alert Button, Message, and Title. Appendix B contains descriptions of these properties.

Displaying the Alert

Alerts are displayed by the Show_alert built-in function. This function returns a numeric constant whose values are ALERT_BUTTON1, ALERT_BUTTON2, or ALERT_BUTTON3 and assigns the constant value to a variable. The following is a template of a typical statement:

```
Declare
 Alert_button          number;
Begin
 Alert_button := show_alert('alert_name');
End;
```

The built-in is a function and returns a value that represents the clicked button in order to allow you to use the value in an evaluation script. Different courses of action may be needed depending on the chosen button. For example, if the OK button is clicked, an action such as the execution of an INSERT statement may proceed. However, if a different button such as the Cancel button is clicked, the INSERT statement does not execute. The ability to use returned values in an IF-THEN-ELSE construct following the Show_alert built-in offers you a great deal of flexibility.

Generic Alert

Creating the many different alerts that a form can contain may be tedious. As the number of alerts increases, it can also become confusing. Although it is possible to create an alert for each situation, it is far more preferable to create one alert for the form and set the alert's properties programmatically to correspond to many different situations. This allows you to avoid continually creating new alert objects and setting the same property on every alert. Using the same alert repeatedly makes it easier to remember the name of the alert when preparing the launching PL/SQL statement. In fact, if you place a generic all-purpose alert in your object library, you do not even have to re-create it. Simply move it from the object library to your form module.

The Set_alert_property built-in procedures allow you to set the alert's Title and Message properties. The Set_alert_button_property built-in procedure allows you to set the Label property. This enables you to control the button's text as well as display properties. Setting the button Label property to a value causes it to be displayed even if its original value is blank. Setting the button Label property to NULL causes the property to default to its original value. If the original value was blank, the button disappears. The two built-ins allow you to control all of the major alert components except the style. If you want to use the different severity style alerts, you can create three different style alerts. The generic alerts can be created with steps similar to those used earlier. You need to populate only the properties that are not influenced by the built-ins because these cannot be changed programmatically. The following is a template of a script that sets the alert properties, opens the alert, and has an IF-THEN-ELSE construct.

```
Declare
  Alert_button          number;
Begin
  Set_alert_property ('alert_name', title, 'Error');
  Set_alert_property ('alert_name, alert_message_text',
                      'Alert message');
  Alert_button := show_alert('alert_name');
  If alert_button = 1 then
   Action1;
  Else
  Action2;
End if;
End;
```

As practice, add an alert to the **practice0901.fmb** form used in the previous practice session. The alert is executed from a When-Validate-Item trigger associated to the DEPTNO item in the EMP data block. If the operator enters a DEPTNO value that does not exist in the DEPT table, the alert is opened. To accomplish this task, perform the following steps:

1. Open the **practice0901.fmb** form in the Object Navigator.
2. Select the **Alerts** object node and click the **Create** tool.
3. Open a Property Palette for the new alert. Set the following properties:

   Name: **GENERIC_STOP**
   Alert Style: **STOP**
   Button 1 Label: **OK**
   Button 2 Label: **NO VALUE SHOULD BE SET FOR THIS PROPERTY**
   Button 3 Label: **NO VALUE SHOULD BE SET FOR THIS PROPERTY**
4. In the Object Navigator, expand the **EMP** data block and locate the DEPTNO item.
5. Create a When-Validate-Item trigger for the DEPTNO item. Use the Listing 9-1 script.

Listing 9-1 When-Validate-Item trigger script

```
declare
   alert_button    number;
   cursor a is select deptno from dept
          where deptno = :emp.deptno; --Determines whether
  a_var  a%rowtype;              -- the Deptno value exists
begin

 open a;
 fetch a into a_var;
```

```
    if a%notfound then     -- The DEPTNO value does not exist
      set_alert_property('generic_stop', title,
                  'Data Integrity error');
      set_alert_property('generic_stop', alert_message_text,
                 'Department number value does not exist');
      alert_button := show_alert('generic_stop');
      raise form_trigger_failure;
     end if;
     close a;
   end;
```

6. Save and open the form. Enter a value of **34** into the DEPTNO item in the EMP data block and tab from the item. This should cause the alert to display.
7. Save the form for later practice.

Creating Timers

In some cases, a developer may want an action to occur after a specific period of time. For example, you have a form that displays sensitive information, such as management salaries, and you are worried that a manager might leave the form open when away from the computer. So you would like the form to close after a period of time. A **timer** is the tool to use. It counts until a specified number of milliseconds is reached. When that time occurs, a timer-expired event occurs. Forms Builder has a When-Timer-Expired trigger that performs an action when the timer expired event happens. In the case of the sensitive form, a When-Timer-Expired trigger could be defined that issues an Exit_form built-in command when the trigger is fired.

Timers are created using the Create_timer built-in function, which is a trigger with three parameters:

- Name of the timer
- Number of millieseconds
- Keyword that determines whether the timer repeats after it expires (values are REPEAT and NO_REPEAT).

The following is a template of the function:

```
Timer := Create_timer('timer_name', 60000, no_repeat);
```

The function creates a timer named TIMER_NAME. It expires in one minute, or 60,000 milliseconds. One second equals 1,000 milliseconds; thus it takes a count of 60,000 to equal a minute. The third parameter in the preceding function determines whether the timer is repeated after it expires. In the case of the template, the timer is not repeated.

A form can have multiple timers, but only one When-Timer-Expired trigger. When the form has multiple timers, it is necessary to determine which timer expired. The Get_application_property built-in function is used to determine which timer expired.

This function returns or assigns the uppercase version of the timer name to a variable. This built-in can be placed inside the When-Timer-Expired trigger and used in an IF-THEN-ELSE construct to cause different actions to occur based on the timer that expires. The following is a template for a When-Trigger-Expired script that determines which timer is expired:

```
Declare
 Timer_that_expired            timer;
Begin
 Timer_that_expired := get_application_property(timer_name);
 If time_that_expired = 'first_time' then
    Action1;
 Else
    Action2;
 End if;
End;
```

There are two other built-ins that are used to delete and modify timers. These are the Delete_timer and Set_timer built-in procedures. The Set_timer built-in essentially replaces a current timer and has the same parameters as the Create_timer built-in. The Delete_timer built-in has only one parameter, which is the name of the timer. The following are templates for the built-ins:

```
Delete_timer('timer_name');
Set_timer('timer_name', milliseconds, repeat);
```

To practice creating timers, perform the following steps to create two timers in a form. The first timer closes the form 60 seconds after it is opened. The second timer tracks the number of seconds that have passed since the form was opened. To accomplish this task, perform the following steps:

1. Open the **practice0901.fmb** form used in the previous practice in the Object Navigator.
2. Locate and select the **Data Blocks** nodes in the Object Navigator. Click the **Create** tool and create a control block named **CT_BLK**. This is done by selecting the **Build a New Block Manually** radio button when the New Data Block dialog displays. The CT_BLK block is necessary for the text item that displays the timer count. If the text item is placed in a data block, the block is considered changed after the text item is modified. This causes Forms Builder to prompt the user to issue a COMMIT command when the form tries to close. Placing the item in a control block eliminates this, because the control block is not associated to a database table.
3. Open the Layout Editor and place a **text item** on the EMP_CANVAS canvas. Associate this text item to the CT_BLK control block.

4. Double-click the **new item** to open its Property Palette. Set the following properties:

   Name: **TIMER_COUNTER**
   Data Type: **NUMBER**
   Database Item: **NO**
   Initial Value: **0**
   Prompt: **TIMER_COUNT**
   Prompt Attachment Edge: **START**

   The initial value is set to 0, because a NULL value cannot be used in a calculation.

5. Create a form-level When-New-Form-Instance trigger with the Listing 9-2 script.

Listing 9-2 When-New-Form-Instance trigger

```
DECLARE
    timer_id Timer;
BEGIN
    timer_id := create_timer('minute_timer',
                             60000, no_repeat);
    timer_id := create_timer('second_timer',
                              1000, repeat);
END;
```

6. Create a form-level When-Timer-Expired trigger with the Listing 9-3 script.

Listing 9-3 When-Timer-Expired trigger

```
Declare
   Timer_that_expired            char(20);
Begin
   Timer_that_expired :=
                 get_application_property(timer_name);
   If timer_that_expired = 'SECOND_TIMER' then
      -- The following increments the timer
     :ct_blk.timer_counter := :ct_blk.timer_counter + 1;
      else
       exit_form; -- closes the form
      End if;
End;
```

7. Save and open the form and watch the counter until the form closes.

ADDING AND USING HIERARCHICAL TREE ITEMS

Hierarchical tree items are one of the most interesting items in Forms Builder. A **hierarchical tree item** is a ranked list of values or objects that you can sort through until you find the desired record. Figure 9-14 depicts a hierarchy of the practice database. The tree item is displaying the departments and the employees in the departments. The Forms Builder Object Navigator is another example of a hierarchical item. At the highest level are objects stored in the database. The hierarchical tree item allows you to expand an object and see child and grandchild objects. The ability to drill down to lower levels of detail is most useful, because most data is arranged in a hierarchy.

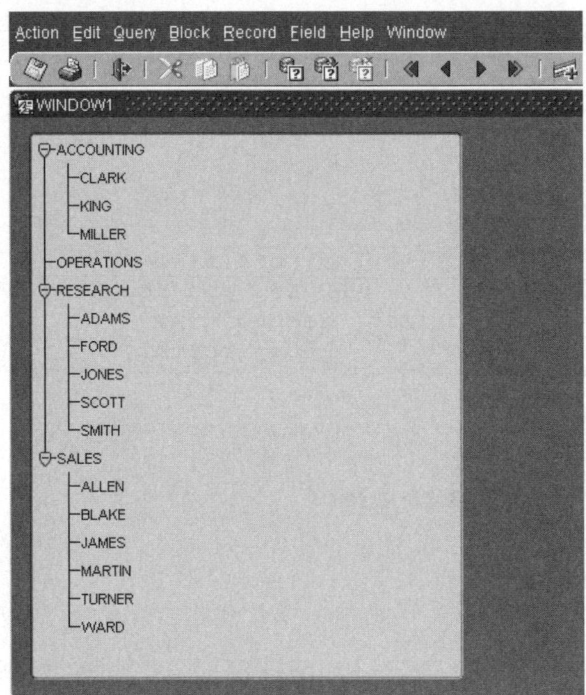

Figure 9-14 Hierarchical tree item of departments and employees

To illustrate the use of hierarchical tree items, consider the Case Project database, which is a hierarchy representative of many databases. As shown in Figure 9-15, at the highest level is a project. This is the first entity that must be created in the database. Each project can have zero to many work orders. A work order is a project's child entity, and also has its own child entity, tasks. Tasks also have children—the monthly costs. Wading through this four-level hierarchy of data is made easier for users by means of a hierarchical item.

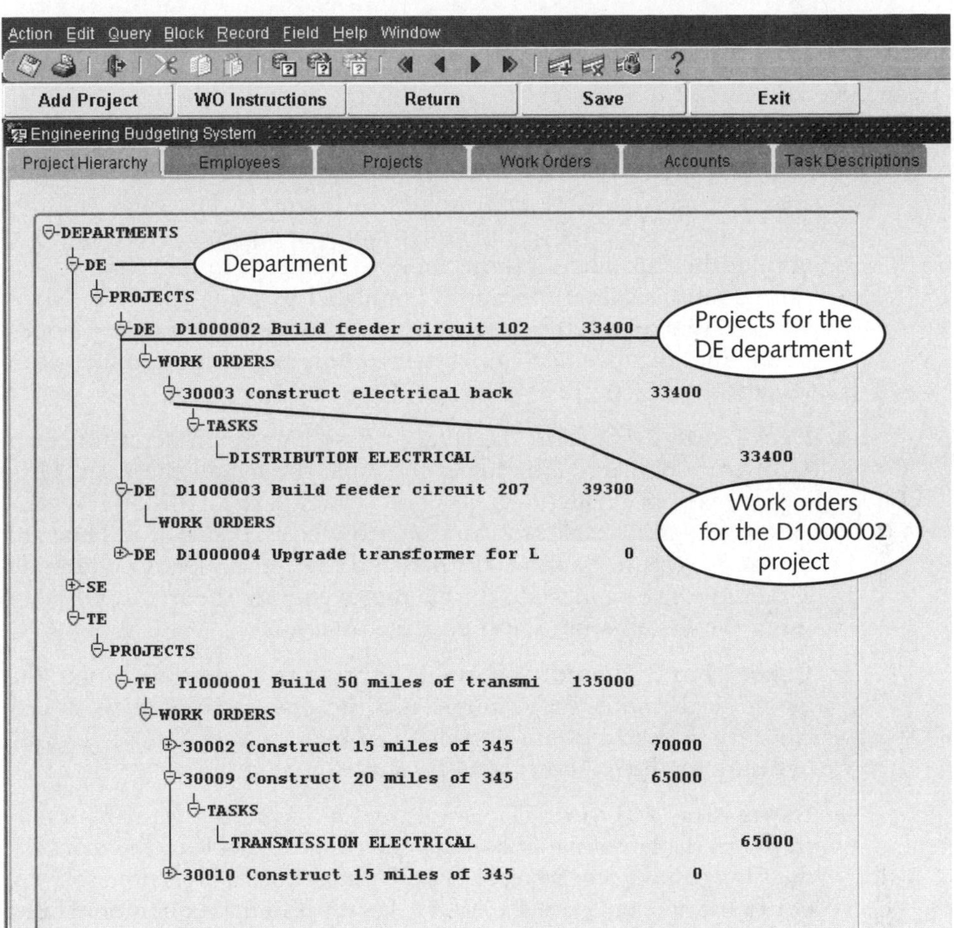

Figure 9-15 Example of data hierarchy

Understanding the Hierarchical Tree Item

A hierarchical tree item is like a text item, display item, or a radio group with a few differences. One difference is that the tree item must reside in a control block and must be the only item in the block. Unlike other items, a tree item has its own data source and the values displayed in the tree cannot be updated through the tree. Tree items can have a variety of properties, but the most important are the Data Query and the Record Group properties. One of these properties is associated to a SELECT statement that populates the hierarchical item. Regardless of the property used, the SELECT statement must have a special format.

The SELECT statement must contain five and only five expressions in the Select clause. If it contains more or less than five expressions, the tree item does not operate. The expressions from left to right are:

- **First Expression (State):** The state expression determines whether the record node is expanded or collapsed. Expanded means the children records are displayed. There are three values: 0, 1, and –1. The value 0 causes the child record to be displayed at the same level as the parent. The value 1 causes the node to be expanded, and the value –1 causes it to be collapsed. The value can be retrieved after the tree is populated by using the Ftree.Node_state package function. (Ftree is an Oracle-developed package that populates the tree item, expands nodes, and retrieves values. For more information, see the section titled "The Ftree Package" later in this chapter.)
- **Expression 2 (Level):** The level or rank expression determines how the records are displayed. The lower the rank, the higher the node. Using the hierarchy from Figure 9-15, projects would have a rank of 1, work orders a rank of 2, tasks a rank of 3, and monthly costs a rank of 4. This ranking causes projects to be displayed first and the remainder as child nodes needing expansion. The rank value can be retrieved after the tree is populated by using the Ftree.Node_depth package function.
- **Expression 3 (Value):** The value expression is the actual value that is displayed in the node. For example, it is the project number, work order number, or task description. This value can be retrieved after the tree is populated by using the Ftree.Node_label package function.
- **Expression 4 (Icon):** The icon expression identifies the symbol that is displayed to the left of the node value. This is comparable to the icons displayed in the Object Navigator to represent the different data block items. If you choose not to use an icon, place the NULL keyword in this expression. This value can be retrieved after the tree is populated by using the Ftree.Node_icon package built-in.
- **Expression 5 (Primary key):** The primary key expression identifies the primary key value(s) for the displayed value. This value is used to retrieve child node records, because the child records have this value as the primary key. This value can be retrieved after the tree is populated by using the Ftree.Node_value package built-in.

Sorting and Ranking the Values

The most difficult part of creating a tree item is to sort and rank values. The values are listed in the hierarchy in the exact manner that they are retrieved from the database using the SELECT statement. If you return your attention to Figure 9-14, you can see that the department's employees are listed below each department. The SELECT statement must produce two effects:

- Each record has the correct level.
- The children follow the proper parent.

Producing records at the correct level is easy. Because the records in each level essentially come from a record in a different table, the level can be hard-coded into the level expression. Department records can have a level value of 1, and employee records can have a level value of 2. Because the records come from two different tables and must appear on consecutive rows, the result sets are combined using the Union set operator. Listing 9-4 illustrates the SELECT statement and the returned result set.

Listing 9-4 Select statement that displays departments and employees

```
SQL> select 1 state, 1 lvl, dname val, null, deptno pk
     from dept
     union
     select 1 state, 2 lvl, ename val, null, empno pk
     from emp
     ;

    STATE       LVL VAL            N        PK
--------- --------- -------------- - ---------
        1         1 ACCOUNTING              10
        1         1 OPERATIONS              40
        1         1 RESEARCH                20
        1         1 SALES                   30
        1         2 ADAMS                 7876
        1         2 ALLEN                 7499
        1         2 BLAKE                 7698
        1         2 CLARK                 7782
        1         2 FORD                  7902
        1         2 JAMES                 7900
        1         2 JONES                 7566
        1         2 KING                  7839
        1         2 MARTIN                7654
        1         2 MILLER                7934
        1         2 SCOTT                 7788
        1         2 SMITHY                7369
        1         2 TURNER                7844
        1         2 WARD                  7521

18 rows selected.

SQL>
```

When looking at the Listing 9-4 result set, you should notice that the data does not match the results displayed in Figure 9-14. Herein lies the difficulty: how do you sort the result set so that the employees are listed under the proper department? You cannot sort based on any of the values in the result set. The answer is to compute a sort value for each row, but this too poses a problem. The SELECT statement must have five and only five expressions. A computed value would raise the number of expressions to six.

The answer is to create a database view that computes the sort value. The view can then be used as the data source for the tree item SELECT statement. The SELECT statement can order the rows based on the computed sort values, and it does not have to include the sort value in the Select clause. Listing 9-5 illustrates the view and SELECT statement that were used to populate the Figure 9-14 tree item.

Listing 9-5 View that computes a sort value and the result set

```
SQL> create or replace view dept_employee_hierarchy as
     select 1 state, 1 lvl, dname val, null icon, deptno pk,
            dname sort_value
     from dept
     union
     select 1 state, 2 lvl, ename val, null, empno pk,
            dname||ename sort_value
     from dept, emp
     where dept.deptno = emp.deptno;

View created.

SQL> select state, lvl, val, icon, pk, sort_value
     from dept_employee_hierarchy
     order by sort_value;

STATE LVL  VAL            I PK    SORT_VALUE
----- ---- -------------- - ----- ------------------
    1    1 ACCOUNTING          10 ACCOUNTING
    1    2 CLARK             7782 ACCOUNTINGCLARK
    1    2 KING              7839 ACCOUNTINGKING
    1    2 MILLER            7934 ACCOUNTINGMILLER
    1    1 OPERATIONS          40 OPERATIONS
    1    1 RESEARCH            20 RESEARCH
    1    2 ADAMS             7876 RESEARCHADAMS
    1    2 FORD              7902 RESEARCHFORD
    1    2 JONES             7566 RESEARCHJONES
    1    2 SCOTT             7788 RESEARCHSCOTT
    1    2 SMITH             7369 RESEARCHSMITHY
    1    1 SALES               30 SALES
    1    2 ALLEN             7499 SALESALLEN
    1    2 BLAKE             7698 SALESBLAKE
    1    2 JAMES             7900 SALESJAMES
    1    2 MARTIN            7654 SALESMARTIN
    1    2 TURNER            7844 SALESTURNER
    1    2 WARD              7521 SALESWARD
```

```
18 rows selected.

SQL>

End listing
```

Notice that the data in the result set is properly sorted. The employees are displayed under the proper department. The key to the sort value is concatenating the parent's sort value to its child. Notice that in the second row the sort value is "ACCOUNTINGCLARK". This is the concatenation of the DNAME and ENAME values. Because the child node is related to the parent node through primary and foreign keys, it is always possible to obtain the parent's sort value.

This technique even allows you to type or put labels on the various nodes. For example, the Object Navigator has names on each node or level type. When you expand the form object, you see children such as data blocks or canvases. You must click the type name to see the child nodes. To add names to your hierarchy, you simply place additional SELECT statements in the data source. Listing 9-6 illustrates a view that adds a DEPARTMENTS and an EMPLOYEES node to the result set. This result set has a DEPARTMENTS label node at the top of the hierarchy. If this node is expanded, the departments are displayed. Expanding a DEPARTMENTS node causes the EMPLOYEES label node to be displayed. The actual employees are displayed by clicking this node. Notice that Listing 9-6 supports this schema.

Listing 9-6 View containing label nodes

```
SQL> create or replace view dept_employee_hierarchy as
select 1 state, 1 lvl, dname val, null icon, deptno pk,
       dname sort_value
from dept
union
select 1 state, 3 lvl, ename val, null, empno pk,
       dname||ename sort_value
from dept, emp
where dept.deptno = emp.deptno
union
select 1 state, 0 lvl, 'DEPARTMENTS' val, null, 0, 'A'
from dual
union
select 1 state, 2 lvl, 'EMPLOYEES' val, null, 0,
       dname||'A'
from dept;
```

```
View created.

SQL>
SQL> select state, lvl, val, icon, pk, sort_value
  2  from dept_employee_hierarchy
  3  order by sort_value;

STATE LVL  VAL            I PK    SORT_VALUE
----- ---- -------------- - ----- ------------------
    1    0 DEPARTMENTS              0 A
    1    1 ACCOUNTING              10 ACCOUNTING
    1    2 EMPLOYEES                0 ACCOUNTINGA
    1    3 CLARK                 7782 ACCOUNTINGCLARK
    1    3 KING                  7839 ACCOUNTINGKING
    1    3 MILLER                7934 ACCOUNTINGMILLER
    1    1 OPERATIONS              40 OPERATIONS
    1    2 EMPLOYEES                0 OPERATIONSA
    1    1 RESEARCH                20 RESEARCH
    1    2 EMPLOYEES                0 RESEARCHA
    1    3 ADAMS                 7876 RESEARCHADAMS
    1    3 FORD                  7902 RESEARCHFORD
    1    3 JONES                 7566 RESEARCHJONES
    1    3 SCOTT                 7788 RESEARCHSCOTT
    1    3 SMITH                 7369 RESEARCHSMITHY
    1    1 SALES                   30 SALES
    1    2 EMPLOYEES                0 SALESA
    1    3 ALLEN                 7499 SALESALLEN
    1    3 BLAKE                 7698 SALESBLAKE
    1    3 JAMES                 7900 SALESJAMES
    1    3 MARTIN                7654 SALESMARTIN

STATE LVL  VAL            I PK    SORT_VALUE
----- ---- -------------- - ----- ------------------
    1    3 TURNER                 7844  SALESTURNER
    1    3 WARD                   7521  SALESWARD

23 rows selected.

SQL>
End listing
```

Recursive Data

The previous technique pertained to data entities that are related through binary relationships. Some data is related through unary relationships. Our practice database has such a relationship. Each record in the EMP table has a MGR column. This column represents the employee number of the employee's manager. Because the manager is an employee, the MGR value can be related to the EMPNO values. This is a unary relationship.

Rather than use UNION operators to combine several SELECT statements, you can use the Connect By clause to compute the values for the levels. Listing 9-7 illustrates just such a statement. It is using the Connect By clause to determine the managers and the manager's employees.

Listing 9-7 Using a Connect By clause to rank and sort values

```
SQL> column employee_name format a40
SQL> select level, empno, mgr,
  2      lpad(' ', level * 2)||ename employee_name
  3  from emp
  4  start with mgr is null
  5  connect by prior empno = mgr;

LEVEL EMPNO   MGR    EMPLOYEE_NAME
----- ------ ------ --------------
 1     7839           KING
 2     7566   7839      JONES
 3     7788   7566        SCOTT
 4     7876   7788          ADAMS
 3     7902   7566        FORD
 4     7369   7902          SMITHY
 2     7698   7839      BLAKE
 3     7499   7698        ALLEN
 3     7521   7698        WARD
 3     7654   7698        MARTIN
 3     7844   7698        TURNER
 3     7900   7698        JAMES
 2     7782   7839      CLARK
 3     7934   7782        MILLER

14 rows selected.

SQL>
```


Creating and Populating the Hierarchical Tree Item

Creating the hierarchical tree item is actually easy. After you have laid out the SQL, it is not much different than adding any other item to your form. Populating the tree item is equally simple. A built-in procedure named Populate_tree executes the SELECT statement and places the result set into the tree item. This procedure is part of the Ftree package that also contains variables that can be used to identify node values such as LEVEL, STATE, or PRIMARY KEY. The Populate_tree built-in has one parameter—the name of the hierarchical item. The following is a template of the procedure:

```
Ftree.populate_tree('block_name.tree_item_name');
```

The procedure must be placed inside a trigger. The When-New-Form-Instance trigger is a good place for this procedure, because it fires when the form is initially opened. Other choices are the When-Button-Pressed or When-New-Block-Instance triggers.

To add a hierarchical tree item to the form, you would follow these steps:

1. Open the Object Navigator and create a control block.
2. Open the Layout Editor and display the canvas on which the tree item is to be displayed.
3. Activate the Hierarchical Tree item tool by clicking it.
4. Place your cursor on the canvas. Click and hold the Left Mouse button. Drag the cursor to size the item. Release the mouse button when the size is correct.
5. Double-click the item to open its Property Palette.
6. Add a SELECT statement to the Data Query property.
7. Modify other properties as necessary.
8. Add a trigger to the form that opens the Ftree.Populate_tree procedure that populates the tree item.
9. Execute and test the hierarchical tree item.

As practice, create a hierarchical tree item that displays a DEPARTMENTS node label, the departments, an EMPLOYEES node label, and the employees for each department. To accomplish this task, perform the following steps:

1. Using the script in Listing 9-6, create the DEPT EMPLOYEE HIERARCHY view. This can be done in SQL*Plus.
2. Open a new form module in the Object Navigator.
3. Create a control block in this module. Name the control block **DEPT_EMPLOYEES**.
4. Create a canvas object. Set the following properties:

   Width: **600**
   Height: **500**
5. Set the window Height and Width properties to the same values as the canvas.
6. Open the Layout Editor and display the canvas.
7. Activate the **Hierarchical Tree** tool. Place your insertion point on the canvas and size the item by dragging the cursor while holding down the Left Mouse button. Set the Height property to 260 and the Width property to 325. Set other properties, such as Font Name and Background, as you wish.

8. Double-click the **item** to open its Property Palette. Add the following SELECT statement to the Data Query property:

```
select state, lvl, val, icon, pk
 from dept_employee_hierarchy
order by sort_value
```

9. Open the Object Navigator. Make sure the hierarchical tree item is in the DEPT_EMPLOYEES data block.
10. Change the name of the tree item to **DEPT_EMP_TREE_ITEM**.
11. Create a form-level When-New-Form-Instance trigger by using the following script:

```
Ftree.Populate_tree('dept_employees.dept_emp_tree_item');
```

12. Save this form as **practice0902.fmb** for use in the exercises at the end of the chapter.
13. Open the form and test it. Attempt to expand and collapse the various nodes.

Hierarchical Tree Item Properties

Hierarchical tree items have several properties that affect the operation of the tree item. These properties are Allow Empty Branches, Data Query, Multi-Selection, Record Group, Show Lines, and Show Symbols. You can see a complete description of these properties in Appendix B.

Hierarchical Tree Items and Performance

Hierarchical tree items are useful for drilling through massive amounts of data. However, they can cause performance problems due to the large number of record combinations or data paths. The number of records increases exponentially as the operator navigates through the tree. At the highest level, there are usually just a few records. Each child node level usually has more records than the parent node, because the nodes are related in one-to-many relationships. The more levels you have, the more combinations you have. For example, assume you have an application that displays orders for a large national company. At the top node you have four sales regions. Each sales region has an average of 13 states that comprise the region. Each state averages 12 sales offices. Each sales office has approximately 200 customers that generate roughly 10 orders per customer. If you develop a hierarchical tree item that holds all possible combinations of records, it would require the item to hold 1,248,000 records, as shown in the following calculation:

4 regions * 13 states * 12 offices * 200 customers * 10 orders = 1,248,000 records

It would take approximately ten minutes or more to load the records for this enormous amount of data into the hierarchical tree item. In addition, the operator's PC probably wouldn't have the memory needed to receive these records. This is a waste of computer resources and operator time, because the operator is probably interested in a small amount of data. As the following calculation shows, if you want to find a particular customer's order, you actually only need to wade through 239 records. To begin, you must see the four regions consisting of four records. After you select the region, you only need to see the 13 states that pertain to the region. You do not need to see the combinations of regions and states that are irrelevant. If the irrelevant records are dropped from the item, the calculation is no longer exponential and can be changed to additive as follows:

4 regions + 13 states + 12 offices + 200 customers + 10 orders = 239 records

Based on the this discussion, it should be clear that you do not want to bulk load all combinations of records into the tree item unless there are a limited number of branches. It is far better to issue incremental queries that populate the nodes as they are opened. This can be done using the When-Tree-Node-Activated trigger and the Ftree.Add_tree_data built-in. As the node is activated, the primary key of the parent record is passed to the trigger and used in the Where clause of the SELECT statement that populates the child node. This allows you to filter the records maintaining performance and memory.

Populating the Tree Item Incrementally

This section shows you how to incrementally populate a tree item by performing the following tasks:

- Analyzing the tree hierarchy and creating views
- Setting a trigger to populate the hierarchical item
- Populating the Data Query property with a SELECT statement
- Setting up the trigger that initially populates the hierarchical item
- Setting up the triggers that populate the hierarchical item incrementally

Analyzing the Tree Hierarchy and Creating Views

The first task in setting up the tree item to be populated incrementally is to set up the views. You can't have an all-encompassing view, such as the one depicted in Listing 9-6. It must be broken apart into several smaller SELECT statements that have a Where clause to filter records. To illustrate this technique, the following paragraphs describe how to incrementally populate the department and employees tree items discussed earlier in this chapter.

To determine the views and SELECT statements, it is necessary to understand how the tree item operates. The following describes the procedures that are performed:

- The DEPARTMENTS label node is initially displayed in an expanded state with the various departments available under the node in the collapsed state. A When-New-Form-Instance trigger populates the item with the DEPARTMENTS label and department values when the form is opened.

- When operators expand a particular department's node, the operator should see the EMPLOYEES label. Because there is only one label per department, there is no benefit to computing this label incrementally. It can be computed using the initial When-New-Form-Instance trigger.
- Expanding an EMPLOYEES label node causes the department's employees to appear. Because the number of employee records is exponentially larger than the department, this node is a good candidate for an incremental addition. The employee should be added to the hierarchical tree item incrementally using a When-Tree-Node-Activated trigger.

Based on the above analysis, two views and two triggers are needed. The first view adds the DEPARTMENTS label, the departments, and the EMPLOYEES label. The view is depicted in Listing 9-8. Compare this listing to Listing 9-6. Notice that the Select clause populating the employee nodes is missing.

Listing 9-8 View that initially populates the tree item


```
SQL> Create or replace view department_tree_view as
     select 1 state, 1 lvl, 'DEPARTMENTS' val,
            null icon, 0 pk, 'A' sort_value
     from dual
     union
     select -1, 2, dname, null, deptno, dname
     from dept
     union
     select -1, 3, 'EMPLOYEES', null, deptno, dname||'A'
     from dept;

View created.

SQL>
```

The second view, depicted in Listing 9-9, populates the department's employees when the EMPLOYEES label node is expanded. This view uses the first level even though it is on the fourth level. The view can have this value because the values are added as the first level under an existing node. This view does not need a sort field, because it is only adding employee names to the tree item. It does have a DEPTNO column named FILTER_VALUE. This value is used in a When-Node-Activate trigger that adds employee records to the tree to filter the employees, so that only employees for the parent department are displayed under the parent.

Listing 9-9 View that populates the employees

```
SQL> create or replace view employee_tree_view as
     select 1 state, 1 lvl, ename val, null icon, empno pk,
            deptno filter_value
     from emp;
```

```
View created.

SQL>
```

Populating the Data Query property with a SELECT Statement

After you have set up the views, the Data Query property must be populated with a SELECT statement that will use the first view. The When-New-Form-Instance trigger using the Ftree.Populate_tree built-in executes the SELECT statement to retrieve the record set from the DEPARTMENT_TREE_VIEW view. This record set adds the DEPARTMENTS label node, the department values, and the EMPLOYEES label node.

```
select state, lvl, val, icon, pk
from department_tree_view
order by sort_value
```

Setting up the Trigger that Initially Populates the Hierarchical Item

The Ftree.Populate_tree built-in is used in the When-New-Form-Instance trigger to initially populate the tree item. Figure 9-16 depicts the tree item after it is first populated. Notice that the DEPARTMENTS label node is expanded. This occurred as a result of placing a +1 state value in the DEPARTMENT_TREE_VIEW (see Listing 9-8). On the other hand, the individual department nodes are collapsed. This was caused by using the -1 state value in the DEPARTMENT_TREE_VIEW view.

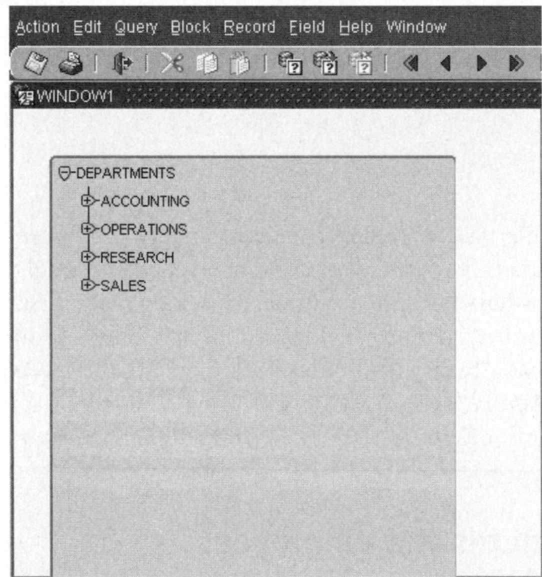

Figure 9-16 Tree item after it is initially populated with collapsed department value nodes

Setting up the Triggers that Populate the Hierarchical Item Incrementally

The previous tasks were very similar to the steps discussed earlier in the chapter that describe how to create and populate a hierarchical tree item at one time. Now comes the complex part—populating the hierarchical item incrementally. A When-Tree-Node-Activated trigger must be developed that has the following features:

- Ability to identify the type of node that was activated when several different types of nodes (DEPARTMENTS and EMPLOYEES) can be incrementally loaded. This feature determines which SELECT statement to use.
- Ability to populate the filter variable used in the SELECT statement with the primary key for the selected parent node (DEPTNO).
- Routine that ensures that the children for a parent node are only added *once*.
- Routine that ensures that the children nodes appear in as expanded rather than collapsed.

Listing 9-10 is a trigger that fulfills these objectives. As you look at the script, examine these features:

- It is important that the employees are not added twice to the item. The trigger must prevent the Ftree.Add_tree_data built-in from executing when the node has already been populated. By default, the EMPLOYEES label node contains the department's DEPTNO value in the fifth (primary key) expression. Step 3 in Listing 9-10 uses the Ftree.Get_tree_node property built-in to get this value and assign it to the global variable NODE_VALUE. Step 4 evaluates this value. If it is not equal to 0, the trigger enters the IF-THEN construct and executes the Ftree.Add_tree_data built-in that adds the child records. If the value is 0, this built-in is not executed. Step 8 immediately follows the built-in statement. It sets the primary key value of the EMPLOYEES label node to 0, preventing the repopulation of the children records.
- Step 7 contains an Ftree.Add_tree_data built-in. One of the parameters is a SELECT statement that retrieves values from the EMPLOYEE_TREE_VIEW view. It has a Where clause that uses the NODE_VALUE global variable as an argument. It is compared to the FILTER_VALUE column in the view. This argument ensures that only the employees for the activated department are retrieved.
- Step 5 retrieves the EMPLOYEES label node value. This value is EMPLOYEES. This is the indicator that determines which node type was activated and determines which SELECT statement should be used (if multiple node types could be incrementally populated). This value is used in Step 6.

Listing 9-10 Trigger script used to populate a tree item incrementally

```
DECLARE
      htree      item;                   --Holds the id of the hierarchy
      current_node    ftree.node;        --Holds the id
                                         --of the activated node
      executed_num number;               /*Holds the value indicating
                                           success or failure after a
                                           Record group is populated*/
      node_label  varchar2(10);          --Holds the label of
                                         --the activated node
BEGIN
/*Step 1: Populate a variable with the hierarchy id.*/
         htree := find_item('dept_employees.dept_emp_tree_item');
/*Step 2: Populate a variable with the id of the activated node*/
         current_node := :system.trigger_node;
/*Step 3: Populate a variable with the primary key value
          for the record displayed on the activated node.
          This should be the DEPTNO values if the node
          has never had child records added.
          Records with a value of 0 indicate the child
          records have added*/
         :global.node_val := ftree.get_tree_node_property(htree,
                                  current_node, ftree.node_value);
/*Step 4: Determines whether the current node has had
          child records added.  If node_val = ' ',
          then records have been added and the trigger
          will perform on more work.  If a different
          value exists, child records may be available
          for the node.  The tasks in the if-then
          structure should be executed*/
     if :global.node_val != 0 then
/*Step 5:  Place the label of the activated node record
           into a variable. This value is used to
           determine which Select statement to use
           for extracting records
           if there are more than 1 node that can be
           incrementally populated.  In this example,
           there is only one so this is placed here
           for example purposes*/
           node_label := Ftree.Get_Tree_Node_Property(htree,
                                 current_node, Ftree.node_label);
/*Step 6:  Populate the appropriate Record group and
           add the records to the hierarchy.  The
           first if-then construct is used if the
           activated node is an "EmployeeS" node.
           Other constructs can be added if there
           are other nodes that can be
           incrementally populated.*/
```

```
-- Beginning of the first if-then construct
        if node_label = 'EMPLOYEES' then
/*Step 7: Add the contents of the Record group
          as children to the activated node*/
         Ftree.Add_Tree_Data(htree, current_node,
              Ftree.parent_OFFSET, ftree.last_child,
              Ftree.query_text,
              'select state, lvl, val, icon, pk
               from employee_tree_view
               where filter_value = :global.node_val');
       end if;
/*Step 8: Changes the activated node value to 0.*/
         Ftree.Set_Tree_Node_Property(htree, current_node,
              Ftree.NODE_value, 0);
/*Step 9: Expands the activated node displaying
          the newly added child nodes*/
         Ftree.Set_Tree_Node_Property(htree, current_node,
              Ftree.NODE_state,
              ftree.expanded_node);
     end if;
end;
```


As practice, modify the tree item you created in the last practice so that it incrementally populates a department's employees when the operator double-clicks the EMPLOYEES node. To accomplish this task, perform the following steps:

1. Open an SQL*Plus session and create the **DEPARTMENT_TREE_VIEW** (Listing 9-8) and the **EMPLOYEE_TREE_VIEW** (Listing 9-9) views.
2. Open the Object Navigator for the **practice0902.fmb** form used in the last practice.
3. Locate the DEPT_EMP_TREE_ITEM tree item. Open the item's Property Palette and add the following SELECT statement to the Data Query property:

   ```
   select state, lvl, val, icon, pk
   from department_tree_view
   order by sort_value
   ```

4. Save and open the form. It should look like Figure 9-16. If you expand any of the nodes, you will not see any employee records. Close the form.
5. Open the Object Navigator. Create a When-Tree-Node-Activated trigger under the DEPT_EMP_TREE_ITEM item. Use the Listing 9-7 script that precedes this practice session.
6. Save and open the form. You can now see a department's employees by double-clicking the **EMPLOYEES** label node. The form that displays should be similar to Figure 9-17.

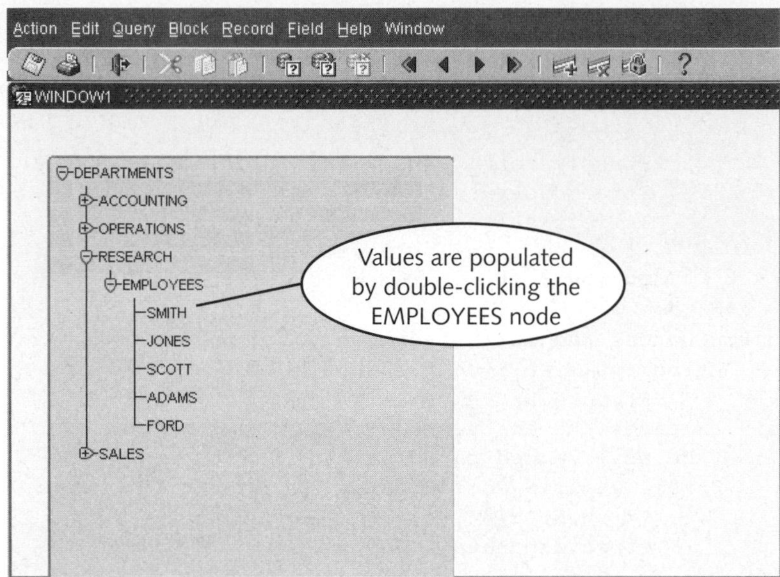

Figure 9-17 Hierarchical tree item that is incrementally populated by double-clicking the EMPLOYEES node

The Ftree Package

Throughout this chapter, you have seen numerous references to the Ftree package. As stated earlier, this is an Oracle-developed package that populates the tree items, expands nodes, and retrieves values. Table 9-1 describes the various package components.

Table 9-1 Ftree package built-ins

Name	Description
Add_tree_data	Adds a new set of data under the identified node
Add_tree_node	Adds a new node to the tree under the identified node
Delete_tree_node	Removes a node from the tree
Find_tree_node	Locates the next node that has a data value that matches the target value
Get_tree_node_parent	Determines the ID of the parent of the target node
Get_tree_node_property	Retrieves a property for a target node
Get_tree_property	Returns a specified tree property for a target node
Get_tree_selection	Returns the values for selected nodes
Populate_group_from_tree	Places the data within the tree into an existing record group
Populate_tree	Opens the query and places the results into the tree
Set_tree_node_property	Sets a property for a target node
Set_tree_property	Sets a specified tree property for a target node
Set_tree_selection	Selects or highlights the target node

CREATING DATABASE OBJECTS THROUGH YOUR FORM

Forms Builder has a built-in called Forms_ddl that allows you to create database objects at runtime. This built-in gives you flexibility, because you can use it to create tables that hold form data, messages, or created data, and you can also use it to open DML and other SQL statements that are actually written during runtime.

Another function that is often used in conjunction with Forms_ddl is Form_success. This function returns a Boolean value to indicate whether the last built-in was successful. This Boolean can be used in conjunction with the following built-ins: Go_block, Execute_query, and Forms_ddl. The Form_success built-in is similar to the Form_failure and Form_fatal built-ins. Those three built-in functions, Form_failure, Form_fatal, and Form_success, test for the three outcomes of a built-in.

To understand the use of the Forms_ddl and Form_success built-ins, examine the When-Button-Pressed trigger, which is presented in Listing 9-11. The purpose of this script is to create and populate a table that stores the total employee wages per department. The trick is that the date the table is created and populated is placed in the table name. This is a common technique for retaining enormous amounts of data. For example, a governmental agency retains the water flow rate of U.S. dams with readings kept for each second. Needless to say, much data is saved. To reduce the size of files and facilitate fast data retrieval, the date of the readings is embedded in the table name. The example in Listing 9-11 is a simplistic version of creating such a table from a form.

9

A variable named TODAYS_DATE was created to hold a character version of the current date. This variable is needed because the To_char function could not be embedded in the Forms_ddl built-in, because the compiler would not have understood the To_char function. The problem is the single quotation marks around the date format. When the compiler encounters these marks, it is programmed to assume that the parameter expression ended, and the compiler would not have understood the date picture parameter. A date picture is the format of the date. In this case it is MONDDYYYY. The trick is to use the To_char function to compute a value, assign the value to the variable, and then concatenate the variable value into the expression. You perform this function often in many programming languages.

The Forms_ddl built-in has one parameter—the DDL, DML, or SQL statement. The first Forms_ddl function call issues the expression contained in the parameter. It creates a table to hold the department wages. The Form_success function that returns a Boolean value is then used to test whether the CREATE TABLE statement was successful. If it was, the Forms_ddl function issues the DML INSERT statement to populate the newly created table. The Forms_ddl function was used again, because the current date must be embedded in the table name. The script then issues a COMMIT command that permanently saves the records.

Listing 9-11 Trigger script used to create and populate an Oracle table

```
declare
  todays_date          varchar2(9):=
                            to_char(sysdate, 'MONDDYYYY');
begin
      /* Following command creates the table */
      forms_ddl('create table
                  dept_wages_'||todays_date||
                  '(deptno number, dsal number)');
      if form_success then      -- Determines if
                                -- the create table command
                                -- was successful
        forms_ddl('insert into
                   dept_wages_'||todays_date||
                  '(deptno, dsal)
                   select deptno, sum(sal)
                   from emp
                   group by deptno');
-- The following suppresses messages
           :system.message_level := 25;
      commit;     -- saves the records
-- The following returns the
-- message level to its original state
      :system.message_level := 0;
-- The following tells the user everything is done
      message ('Table dept_wages_'||todays_date||
               ' created and populated');
   end if;
end;
```

As practice, create a new form that contains a button. The button opens the previous code script, creating and populating a table. To accomplish this task, perform the following steps:

1. Create a new form module in the Object Navigator.
2. Save this form as **practice0903.fmb.**
3. Open the Object Navigator and select the **Canvases** node. Click the **Create** tool to add a canvas to the table.
4. Select the **Data Blocks** node. Click the **Create** tool to add a control block to the form.
5. Open the Layout Editor and, using the toolbar tools, add a button item to the canvas.
6. Open the Object Navigator. Locate the newly created Push button. Create a When-Button-Pressed trigger, using the Listing 9-11 script.
7. Save and open the form. Click the **button** to execute the trigger and create and populate the table.

8. Close the form when you are finished.
9. Open an SQL*Plus session to verify that the table was created and populated. The table name begins with the prefix "DEPT_WAGES_" and ends with the current date.

TRAPPING AND HANDLING ERRORS

Various errors can crop up when you are operating a form, many as the result of incorrect programming. For example, you have defined a text item with a size larger than the corresponding table column. An error occurs when the operator uses the entire length to enter a new value and then tries to insert or update this larger value into the table. Other errors can occur because of database actions. For example, one user tries to update a record that has been locked by another user. These examples cause Oracle to return an error message to the form.

Regardless of the reason, hundreds of different types of errors can occur, and it is your responsibility to trap and handle them. If you do not handle the error, Oracle terminates the trigger and sometimes issues an undecipherable message. Here is another example: A Post-Query trigger was added to a block, and a SELECT statement was placed in the trigger. The Where clause was omitted causing the trigger to assign multiple values to a single data block item. This causes a Too_Many_Rows error. Figure 9-18 illustrates the error message returned by Forms Builder, which gives neither the developer nor the operator a clue as to the cause of the error. It simply states that the error was not handled.

9

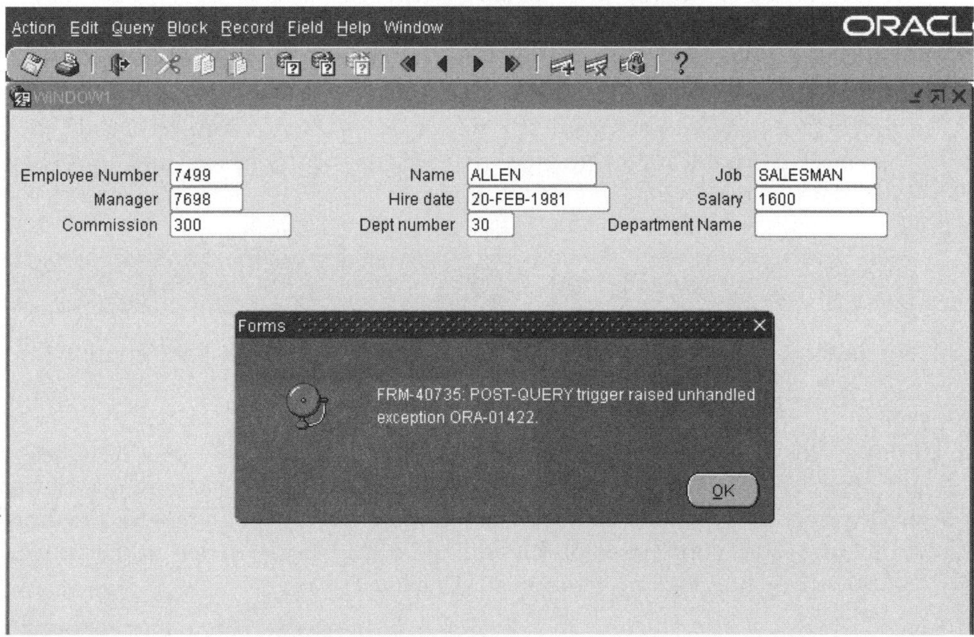

Figure 9-18 Unhandled form error message

One way to trap errors is to place an Exception clause and appropriate error handlers in your PL/SQL script. This technique allows your script to terminate successfully and gives you an opportunity to return a custom message to your operator. The following script is a modified version of the Post-Query trigger that caused the error depicted in Figure 9-18. An Exception clause is the modification. The clause contains an error handler that traps the Too_Many_Rows error. Too_Many_Rows is an error handler named by PL/SQL. Oracle has assigned a name to this error. This exception handler traps the error caused by omitting the Where clause in the SELECT statement. The error handler causes a message to be displayed to the user. The Message built-in is using a variable named Sqlerrm. **Sqlerrm** is a PL/SQL variable that returns the last error message that was received as the result of issuing an SQL statement. The SQLERRM variable was placed in the Message built-in so that an accurate message can be displayed to the operator. **Sqlcode** is a comparable variable. It returns the error code of the most recently issued SELECT statement.

```
begin
      select dname
       into :emp.dname
       from dept;
exception
      when too_many_rows then message (sqlerrm);
end;
```

Figure 9-19 illustrates a form using the modified Post-Query trigger script. Notice that the error message now reads "ORA-01422: exact fetch returns more than requested number of rows." While it is not the clearest message, it is far better than the unhandled form error depicted in Figure 9-18. The new message tells the operator or developer that more rows were returned than expected, which caused the error. The error handler also has the added advantage that it does not ring a bell and make the user close a modal dialog box to acknowledge the error for each record returned. The next practice session enables you to see the effects of handling and not handling the Too_Many_Rows error.

ORA-01422: exact fetch returns more than requested number of rows
Record: 1/?

Figure 9-19 Message displayed by the Too_many_rows error handler using the SQLERRM variable

Forms Builder has two additional built-ins that perform the same functions as Sqlerrm and Sqlcode: Dbms_error_text and Dbms_error_code. These built-ins return the latest error returned by the database. Error_text and Error_code are additional built-ins that return the latest runtime error. Error_code has a broader scope in that it returns Forms Builder error messages in addition to database errors.

The On-Error trigger can be used with the Error_text built-in to replace error messages with custom messages. For example, operators often make the mistake of placing a form into the Enter Query mode and entering record values as if in the Normal mode. When the user clicks the Commit key, a form error occurs, which is depicted in Figure 9-20.

FRM-41009: Function key not allowed. Press Ctrl+K for list of valid keys.

Figure 9-20 Form error message caused by trying to commit a record in the Enter Query mode

Because the Figure 9-20 error message is not intuitive, you should trap these types of errors and display your own custom messages. The On-Error trigger is fired whenever an error occurs. This trigger allows you to trap Forms Builder errors and substitute your own custom messages.

All error messages have a number. The error depicted in Figure 9-20 is FRM-41009. The FRM prefix indicates that it is a Forms Builder error, as does the leading 4. Database errors generally start with a 0. If a message can be associated to the FRM-41009 error within an On-Error trigger, it is possible to substitute a custom message. That is exactly what the following script does. An IF-THEN construct is placed inside the trigger, and the construct evaluates the type of error and substitutes the message with a custom message. The following is an example of a script that traps the FRM-41009 error.

```
if error_code = 41009 then  -- evaluates the error message
      message ('You have tried to save  -- message
           a record while the form
           is in the Enter-query mode.
           Please press the Exit button.');

   End if;
```

Figure 9-21 depicts the results of the trigger. It displays the custom message on the status line. If you want to trap other errors and substitute custom messages, simply add other conditions to the script.

As practice, add a Post-Query trigger that populates a DNAME column and trap the error. To accomplish this task, perform the following steps:

1. Open the Object Navigator and create a new form module named **practice0904.fmb**.
2. Create a data block based on the EMP data block. The data block should have a Tabular layout and display 10 records.
3. Locate the EMPNO data block item and set its Required property to **NO**.

4. Open the Layout Editor and add a text item to the form to receive the department name value returned by the Post-Query trigger. Set the following properties:

   Name: **DNAME**
   Database Item**: NO**
   Number of Items Displayed: **1**

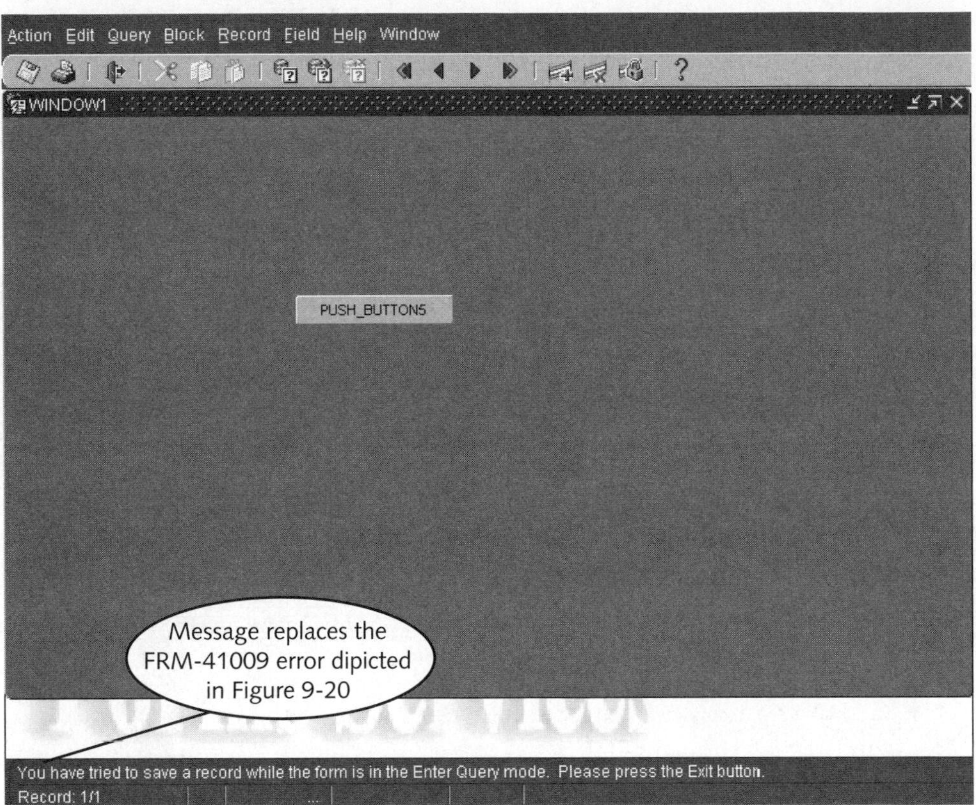

Figure 9-21 Form displaying a custom FRM-41009 error

5. Create a Post-Query trigger for the EMP data block. Use the following script, which causes a too_many_rows error:

```
Begin
   select dname
     into :emp.dname
    from dept;
end;
```

6. Save and open the form. Execute a query. Notice the error messages.

7. Close the form and modify the Post-Query trigger. Add the following Exception section to the script in Step 5:

```
exception
   when too_many_rows then message (sqlerrm);
```

8. Open the form and execute a query. Notice the difference that results from adding the exception handler.
9. Close the form and modify the trigger. Replace the Too_Many_Rows exception handler with the following exception handler:

```
When others then :emp.dname := 'UNKNOWN';
```

10. Open the form and execute a query. Notice that there is no longer a need to acknowledge messages.
11. Save the form.

Mouse Events and Mouse Effecting Properties

Forms Builder has a variety of triggers that pertain to mouse movements. You might not suspect that there are many events associated to the mouse, but there are actually seven as follows:

- **When-Mouse-Down**: Fires when the operator clicks a mouse button
- **When-Mouse-Up**: Fires when the operator releases a mouse button
- **When-Mouse-Click**: Fires after the operator clicks and releases a mouse button
- **When-Mouse-Doubleclick**: Fires after the operator clicks a mouse button twice
- **When-Mouse-Enter**: Fires when the mouse pointer enters a canvas or item
- **When-Mouse-Leave**: Fires when the mouse pointer leaves a canvas or item
- **When-Mouse-Move**: Fires when the mouse pointer moves within a canvas or item

Forms Builder also provides a number of system variables that can be used with the mouse triggers. These variables return values that identify the mouse button that was clicked, the "X" or "Y" position of the mouse insertion point, or the name of the cursor. The system variables are:

- **System.Mouse_button_pressed**: Identifies whether the Left, Middle, or Right Mouse button was clicked (the buttons are identified by the numbers 1, 2 and 3)
- **System.Mouse_button_modifiers**: Identifies the shift modifier (Shift or Control) key that was held down while clicking the mouse button

- **System.Mouse_canvas**: Returns the name of the canvas on which the insertion point is located
- **System.Mouse_item**: Returns the name of the item in which the insertion point is located
- **System.Mouse_record**: Returns the index number in which the record insertion point is located
- **System.Mouse_Offset**: Returns the offset between the first visible record and mouse record
- **System.Mouse_x_pos**: Returns the X position of the insertion point
- **System.Mouse_y_pos**: Returns the Y position of the insertion point

The following script illustrates the use of the triggers and the system variables. The trigger is a When-Mouse-Click trigger that contains two IF-THEN constructs. The first construct tests if the Right Mouse button was clicked. If the Right Mouse button is clicked, the EXECUTE_QUERY button is executed. Depending on your form design, this trigger can save mouse movement by enabling the operator to avoid having to click a button.

```
if :system.mouse_button_pressed = 1 then --
 left mouse button clicked
        enter_query;
end if;
if :system.mouse_button_pressed = 3 then --
 right mouse button clicked
        execute_query;
end if;
```

It should be noted that the second IF-THEN-ELSE statement will be executed only if you are using Form Builder 6*i* in the client/server environment. Forms Builder 9*i* does not fire the When-Mouse-Event triggers unless the left button is clicked. Clicking the right mouse button in Forms Builder 9*i* causes Forms Builder to look for and launch popup menus. Thus the script presented here can only be used for Form Builder 6*i*.

Forms Builder has a property that limits the movement of the cursor. This is the form property Mouse Navigation Limit. This property has three settings: FORM, BLOCK, and ITEM. The FORM setting allows the cursor to move to any spot in the form. The BLOCK setting limits movement to the current data block. To change blocks, the operator must click a block navigation control key. The ITEM setting confines the movement to the current item. This effectively eliminates the ability to move the cursor.

As practice, add the previously illustrated When-Mouse-Click trigger to the **practice0904.frm** form. Check to see if clicking the Left Mouse button places the form into the Enter Query mode and clicking the Right Mouse button executes a query.

Where You Are and Where You're Going

This chapter adds more tools to the repertoire you have developed. In previous chapters, you learned how to construct a form and call other forms. In this chapter, you learned how to combine these applications into a system using a menu. You have also learned about hierarchical tree items that can help you wade through data to reach the information you want. In the next chapter, you learn how to base a block on a SELECT statement rather than a table. This can greatly increase the form performance and search capabilities. You also learn how to override the default DML with your own statements. The chapter also discusses how to update a complex view using the Instead-Of trigger. Finally, the chapter discusses how to use stored procedures to perform your Form SQL functions.

Chapter Summary

- Most systems have a large number of interrelated forms and applications.
- Menus help operators easily identify the system's application choices.
- Menus are built using their own modules or files. The binary source code is contained in a file with an extension of **.mmb**. The compiled version of the menu is contained in a file with an extension of **.mmx**.
- The Menu Editor is used to construct menus.
- There are a variety of menu item types. The most common are Menu and PL/SQL. The Menu type calls another menu from a module. The PL/SQL type executes a PL/SQL statement or script. The script can contain built-ins, such as Enter_Query.
- Menu modules can be stored in the file system or in the database.
- Menus are associated to a form by populating the form-level property Menu Module File.
- Each form in a system can have its own menu or a menu can be passed between forms. If you do not specify a menu for an application, the currently opened menu module is passed.
- Security can be added to a menu using the Menu Roles property.
- A specific menu item can be secured using the item's Menu Item Roles property.
- A Magic menu item type is associated to a standard operating system function, such as cut, copy, or paste.
- DEFAULT&SMARTBAR is the default form menu. This menu is replaced when you assign a custom menu to a form.
- Menudefs.mmb is a menu module similar to DEFAULT&SMARTBAR that can be customized.

- Menus can have their own toolbars.
- A popup menu is a form component. Click the Right Mouse button to open the menu.
- Popup menus can be associated to a data block item or a canvas.
- Alerts are modal dialog boxes that are used to grab an operator's attention.
- There are three levels, or styles, of alerts: Stop, Caution, and Note. Each one displays a different symbol.
- Alerts are displayed using the Show_alert built-in function. Besides displaying the alert, this function identifies the alert button selected by the operator.
- It is preferable to have one alert for a form and change the alert's properties with the Set_alert_property built-in procedure.
- A timer is a form countdown tool.
- When a timer expires, it fires a When-Timer-Expires trigger.
- Timers track time in milliseconds.
- The Create_timer built-in function creates timers.
- A hierarchical tree item is an item similar to the Object Navigator that allows the operator to drill-down through various layers or branches of records.
- Hierarchical tree items must reside in a control block and must be the only item in the control block.
- SELECT statements populate the hierarchical tree items. They reside in the item's Data Query property or in the Record Group property.
- Tree item SELECT statements must have five and only five expressions. They are state, rank or level, displayed value or label, name of the icon, and primary key value.
- The Ftree package contains a variety of functions and procedures that influence a hierarchical tree item.
- It can be difficult to properly sort the rows that appear in a hierarchical item. It is best to create a view with a computed sort column and use the view in the hierarchical tree item.
- Recursive data is the easiest to sort in a hierarchical tree item.
- Databases with large numbers of records can encounter performance problems when using hierarchical items. When this happens you should use the When-Tree-Node-Activated trigger to populate the branches incrementally as they are activated.
- The Forms_ddl built-in allows you to create database objects while the form is running.

- The Forms_ddl built-in allows you to construct and execute a SELECT statement at runtime.
- The Form_success built-in returns a Boolean value to indicate whether the last built-in was successfully executed.
- A sign of professionalism is when the developer traps and handles errors that occur during runtime.
- Sqlerrm is a PL/SQL variable that returns the text returned by the database after the last SQL command is issued.
- Dbms_error_text is a built-in that performs the same function as Sqlerrm. It has an associated built-in called Dbms_error_code that returns the error code.
- Error_code and Error_text return codes and text associated to form and database errors.
- A variety of events and triggers are associated to clicking a mouse button.
- A variety of system variables return mouse conditions, such as the button clicked or the record the mouse was clicked on.

REVIEW QUESTIONS

1. Match the following terms that have appeared in this chapter with their descriptions:

a. Submenu	______________	A form device that is used to track time and perform a task at specific intervals.
b. Stop, Caution, Note	______________	A modal dialog box that is used for operator notification.
c. Timer	______________	A package of procedures and functions used to perform hierarchical tree item tasks.
d. State	______________	A graphical tool used to design a menu.
e. **.mmb**	______________	A menu item type that consists of a solid horizontal line.
f. Alert	______________	The default form menu module.
g. Menu	______________	Contains the text returned as a result of the most recent form action.
h. Forms_ddl	______________	A menu that is called from another menu in a menu module.
i. Ftree	______________	The hierarchical tree item property used to document the SELECT statement.

j. Sqlerrm	______________	The first expression in a hierarchical tree item. It determines whether the node is collapsed or expanded.
k. Hierarchical tree item	______________	A built-in that returns a Boolean value identifying whether the last built-in statement failed to execute.
l. Popup menu	______________	A built-in used to create database objects and custom DML and SQL commands.
m. Roles	______________	The second expression in a hierarchical tree item SELECT statement. It determines the rank or level at which the item appears in the hierarchy.
n. DEFAULT& SMARTBAR	______________	The binary menu module file extension.
o. Data Query property	______________	The three different styles of alerts.
p. Magic item	______________	A type of menu item that performs an operating system function.
q. Separator	______________	A Menu Editor tool that changes the menu orientation.
r. Level	______________	A form property used to associate the menu to the form.
s. Form_failure	______________	The PL/SQL variable that returns the message received from the database as a result of an SQL statement.
t. Switch Orientation	______________	An Oracle database privilege object that can be granted to a user. It is also used as a security device in a menu.
u. Error_text	______________	A form menu object that is opened when the Right Mouse button is clicked.
v. Menu Module property	______________	A form item that displays the results of a SELECT statement in a hierarchy. It allows an operator to drill down into detail.
w. Menu Editor	______________	A tool that contains a series of panels that display options. It is used to associate a series of related applications into a system.

2. What kind of commands can you execute from a menu?
3. What tool would you use to compute the levels for a hierarchical tree item when the data is recursive?

4. You have just constructed an Employee Information system. Management personnel use one of the forms to review salary information. You do not want this form available to nonmanagement personnel when the manager leaves the workstation. How can you secure the application?
5. You have just made some changes to a menu module file and saved the module. You then opened the form associated to the menu. You didn't see the modifications that you made. What is the problem?
6. You have a menu in a form that has a Reports menu item that displays a submenu of reports. You have decided that you want to promote the Reports item to the top layer of the menu. How can you do this without creating a new menu and options?
7. How can you use the menu palettes from a menu module in your form on a popup menu?
8. What kind of options would you place on a popup menu?
9. Why would you not want to load all of the records of a hierarchical tree when the item is first opened?
10. You have just created a hierarchical tree item that is based on a series of SELECT statements. Each level's records were grouped together rather than under the proper parent. What's wrong with this grouping?
11. Explain the difference between Sqlerrm, Dbms_error_text, and Error_text.
12. You developed a form that generates relay equipment numbers. Relays are purchased in bulks of 30 or more. When the technician receives the relays, he goes to your application and enters his payroll number (e.g., 3221 or 4598), the type of relay, and the number of relay numbers he needs. The system then generates the numbers and the records. The technician just called you to explain that he entered his payroll number, 6432, in the Amount of Relay Numbers text item. As a result, he generated 6,432 relay numbers when he only needs 28. He would like you to delete the additional records from the database. What can you do to prevent this from happening again?
13. How do you disable an alert object button so that it doesn't appear in the alert?
14. If you are testing a form and you encounter an error message you don't understand, what can you do to the form to give you clear information? What external sources can you use for more information?
15. The DBA called you on the phone to tell you that a user has called the help desk. The user was trying to update a record in a system you developed when he received an error message stating that another user was modifying the record. Upon investigation, you found a user who performs a number of record modifications every day. The user has not been very conscientious about committing the changes. Sometimes the user does not save the changes until she goes home for the day. In some cases, the records have been locked for up to eight hours. What tools from this chapter can you use to help the user to remember to commit changes after a reasonable period of time?

16. What are the three built-ins that return the results of executing a built-in?
17. How can you stop a timer?

Exam Review Questions

1. Which two form objects can be associated to a popup menu?
   a. Window
   b. Item
   c. Canvas
   d. Form module
   e. Frame
2. Which type of item can be used to perform a Windows paste operation?
   a. Separator
   b. Plain
   c. Magic
   d. Radio
   e. Check
3. You have just created a menu for your new Budgeting System. What two things must you do before running the menu with the Budgeting System application?
   a. Populate the form's Menu Module property with the menu file name
   b. Populate the form's window object's Menu Module property with the menu file name
   c. Compile the menu module
   d. Compile the form module
   e. Place the menu module in the same directory as the application
4. Which data type is returned by the Create_timer built-in?
   a. Number
   b. Timer
   c. Time
   d. Date
5. You created an alert containing Cancel and OK buttons. After the operator clicks a button, your application must determine which button was clicked. Which built-in can be used to determine this information?
   a. Display_alert
   b. Get_alert_property
   c. Get_alert_button_property
   d. Show_alert

HANDS-ON ASSIGNMENTS

1. In this assignment, you create a startup application that welcomes the operator to the practice system. You then create a menu that has functional commands such as placing the form into the Enter Query mode. It also has a menu palette that calls several of the forms you created in the practice sessions in the last chapter. The menu is slightly different than the practice menu in that it has magic items and a separator, and the options are laid out as submenus. Perform the following steps:
   a. Create a new form module and name it **ch09ex01.fmb**. Create a control block and name it **START_BLOCK**.
   b. Create a canvas and format it to resemble the canvas shown in Figure 9-22.
   c. Add a text item to the control block and to the canvas. This text item receives the input focus when the form is opened. Set the text item's Height property to **1** and the Width to **1** so that it is virtually invisible.

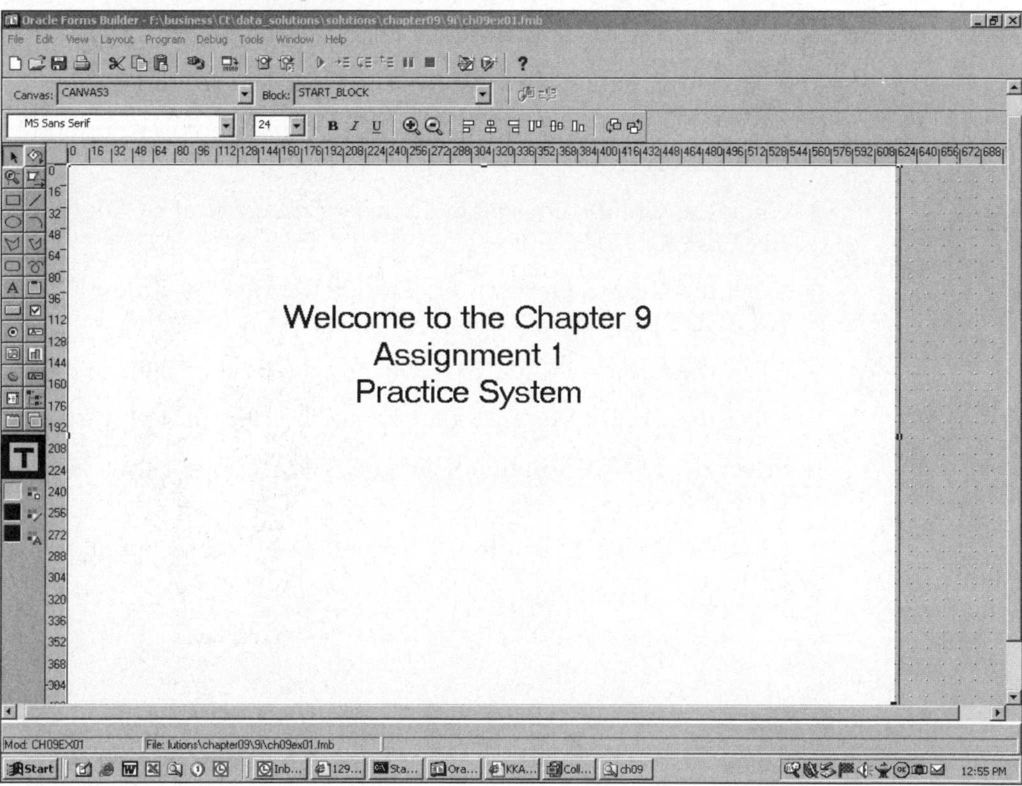

Figure 9-22 Assignment 1 system startup form

d. Open the Object Navigator and create and save a new menu module named **ch09ex01.mmb**. Open the Menu Editor and create a menu similar to that shown in Figure 9-23. Follow these steps:

- Select the **Menus** node and click the **Create** tool to create a menu palette object. Name this menu **EMPLOYEE_MENU**.
- Double-click the **menu object** to open the Menu Editor.
- An unnamed item displays in the Menu Editor. Overtype the <NEW_ITEM> value with the label **OPTIONS**. Press **Enter**.
- Click the **Create Down** tool. Change the label of this item to **FORM FUNCTIONS**.
- Click the **Create Down** tool. Change the label of this item to **FORMS**.
- Select the **FORM FUNCTIONS** option and click the **Create Right** tool. Change the label of this option to **CUT**.
- Click the **Create Down** tool. Change the label of this option to **COPY**.
- Click the **Create Down** tool. Change the label of this option to **PASTE**.
- Click the **Create Down** tool. Change the label of this option to **SEPARATOR**.
- Click the **Create Down** tool. Change the label of this option to **ENTER QUERY**.
- Click the **Create Down** tool. Change the label of this option to **EXECUTE QUERY**.
- Click the **Create Down** tool. Change the label of this option to **SAVE**.
- Click the **Create Down** tool. Change the label of this option to **EXIT**.
- Select the **FORMS** option. Click the **Create Right** tool. Name the option **CH08EX01**.
- Click the **Create Down** tool. Change the label of this option to **CH08EX02**.
- Close the Menu Editor.

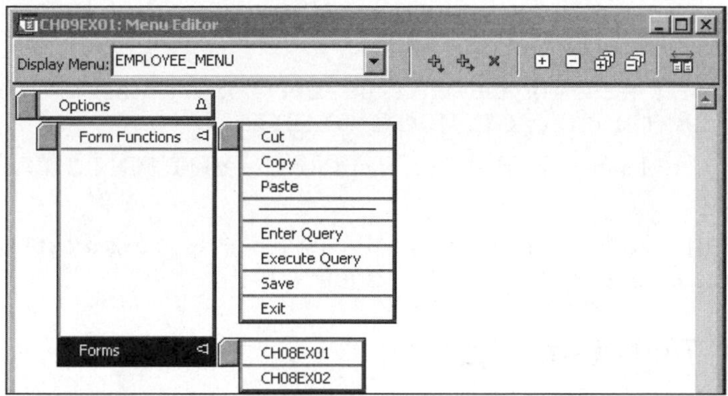

Figure 9-23 Assignment 1 menu

e. Open the Object Navigator and place the following commands into the identified menu items. The menu item names are in the left column:

   ENTER_QUERY: **ENTER_QUERY;**
   EXECUTE_QUERY: **EXECUTE_QUERY;**
   SAVE: **COMMIT_FORM;**
   EXIT: **EXIT_FORM;**
   CH08EX01: **open_form('c:\ch08ex01.fmx');** (be sure to add the correct file path)
   CH08EX02: **open_form('c:\ch08ex02.fmx');** (be sure to add the correct file path)

f. Open a Property Palette for the Cut, Copy, and Paste options. The Menu Item Type property should be set to **MAGIC**. Set the Magic Item property to match the item's name.

g. Open a Property Palette for the SEPARATOR item. Change the Menu Item Type property to **SEPARATOR**.

h. Save the menu module as **CH09EX01.mmb.** Compile the menu module.

i. Open the Object Navigator and locate the form module ch09ex01.fmb.

j. Open a Property Palette for the form. Place the name and file path of the **ch09ex01.mmb** menu module in the Menu Module property. Be sure to include the full file path.

k. Open the form and test all of the menu options.

2. In this assignment, you create a generic alert and open the same alert when two different errors occur. Entering a future hire date causes the first error. Failing to give the employee a salary causes the second error. The alert is opened before the record is inserted into the database. Perform the following steps:

   a. Create a new form module in the Object Navigator.

   b. Create a data block based on the EMP table. The layout should be the Form style displaying one record.

9

c. Locate, select, and open a Property Palette for the EMPNO item. Set the Required property to **NO**.

d. Open the Object Navigator and select the **Alerts** object. Click the **Create** tool. Name this alert object **GENERIC_ALERT**.

e. Open a Property Palette for the alert. Remove the **BUTTON 2 LABEL** property value.

f. Locate the HIREDATE item in the EMP data block. Create a **Post-Text-Item** trigger for the item. Use the script in Listing 9-12:

Listing 9-12 Post-Text-Item trigger

```
Declare
   Alert_button         number;
Begin
   If :emp.hiredate > sysdate then
        Set_alert_property('generic_alert',
                           alert_message_text,
                           'You have entered a
                            future hire date
                            for the employee');
      alert_button := show_alert('generic_alert');
            raise form_trigger_failure;
     end if;
end;
```

g. Create a form-level Pre-Insert trigger that prevents the operator from inserting a record into the database without a value in the SAL column. Use the script in Listing 9-13:

Listing 9-13 Form-level Pre-Insert trigger

```
Declare
   Alert_button         number;
Begin
   If :emp.sal is null then
        Set_alert_property('generic_alert',
                           alert_message_text,
                           'You must enter an
                            employee salary');
      alert_button := show_alert('generic_alert');
            raise form_trigger_failure;
     end if;
end;
```

h. Save the form as **ch09ex02.fmb.** Open the form and test the triggers. Add a future date into the HIRE DATE item and attempt to tab out of the item. Try to save the record without entering a value in the SAL column.

3. In this assignment, you modify the **ch09ex02.fmb** form you created in the previous exercise. You modify the Post-Text-Item trigger that monitors the HIREDATE value. You programmatically add a second button to the alert. Rather than making the operator enter a current hire date, the operator has the option of leaving the future date in the item. The alert is used to notify rather than prevent the entry of a future hire date.
   a. Open the **ch09ex02.fmb** form module in the Object Navigator.
   b. Locate the Post-Text-Item trigger under the HIREDATE item. Modify the PL/SQL script as follows (see Listing 9-14):

Listing 9-14 Post-Text-Item trigger modification

```
Declare
   Alert_button            number;
Begin
   If :emp.hiredate > sysdate then
        Set_alert_button_property('generic_alert',
                                   alert_button2,
                                   Label, 'Cancel');
        Set_alert_property('generic_alert',
                            alert_message_text,
                            'You have entered a
                             future hire date
                             for the employee');
         alert_button := show_alert('generic_alert');
         if alert_button = alert_button2 then
             raise form_trigger_failure;
         end if;
     end if;
end;
```

   c. Save the form as **ch09ex03.fmb**.
   d. Open the form and enter a future date into the HIREDATE item, and attempt to tab out of the item. Click **OK**. You should be able to move to the next item.
   e. Attempt the same operation as described in Step d, but this time click **Cancel**.

4. In this assignment, you modify form **ch09ex03.fmb** by adding a timer to the form that prompts the user to commit changes that are pending. The timer is created when Forms Builder attempts to lock a database record. This occurs when the operator modifies a value in the form. The timer opens the alert every minute until the timer is deleted after the records have been committed. This prevents the user from locking database records for unduly long periods of time.
   a. Open the **ch09ex03.fmb** module in the Object Navigator and save it as **ch09ex04.fmb**.

9

b. Create a form-level On-Lock trigger. This trigger is fired when a record is modified. Use the following script:

```
Declare
 Timer_id      timer;
Begin
 Lock_record;
 Timer_id := create_timer('lock_time', 60000, repeat);
End;
```

c. Create a form-level When-Timer-Expired trigger by using the following script:

```
Declare
 Alert_button          number;
Begin
Set_alert_property('generic_alert', alert_message_text,
                       'You have pending changes for longer
                        than 1 minute. Please save changes');
alert_button := show_alert('generic_alert');
end;
```

d. Create a form-level Post-Forms-Commit trigger that deletes the timer by using the following script:

```
Delete_timer('lock_time');
```

e. Save the form as **ch09ex04.fmb**.

f. Open the form and execute a query. Wait for one minute. Notice that the alert has not displayed.

g. Modify any value in the form. Wait for one minute. The alert should display.

h. Click **OK** in the alert to close it. Wait for a period of time. The alert should redisplay.

i. Commit the records. Wait for a period of time. The alert should not redisplay until you modify a record.

5. In this assignment, you create a hierarchical tree item that can be used to analyze department and employee salaries. At the top level are the departments and the sum of their employee salaries. The operator can drill down through any of these nodes to view individual employee salaries. Perform the following steps:

a. Open the Object Navigator and create a new form module.

b. Add a control block called **HIER_TREE** to the form.

c. Add a canvas to the form.

d. Open the Layout Editor and add a **Hierarchical Tree item** to the canvas. Name the tree item **DEPARTMENT_SALARIES**.

e. Log into SQL*Plus and create a view using the script in Listing 9-15. If you analyze the SELECT statement, you notice the following:

- The DEPARTMENTS label node, the DEPARTMENTS node, and the EMPLOYEES label node are expanded for the operator.
- The EMPLOYEES node is collapsed. Because the initial view is the summarized view, displaying the employees by default would clutter the display.
- The second SELECT statement contains an outer join. The outer join was needed to return the Operations department, which does not have any employees.
- The third and fourth SELECT statements do not have an outer join, so the EMPLOYEES label was not placed under the OPERATIONS department.

Listing 9-15 DEPARTMENT HIERARCHY view

```
Create or replace view
  department_hierarchy as
  select 1 state, 1 lvl, 'DEPARTMENTS' val,
    null icon, 0 pk, 'A' sort_value
  from dual
  union
  select 1, 2, rpad(dname,25, ' ')||
    to_char(sum(nvl(sal,0)),99999),
    null, dept.deptno, dname
  from dept, emp
  where dept.deptno = emp.deptno(+)
  group by dept.deptno, dname
  union
  select -1, 3, 'EMPLOYEES', null, 0,
    dname||'A'
  from dept,emp
  where dept.deptno = emp.deptno
union
  select -1, 4, rpad(ename,25, ' ')||
    to_char(nvl(sal,0),99999),
    null, empno, dname||ename
  from dept, emp
  where dept.deptno = emp.deptno;
```

f. Open a Property Palette for the DEPARTMENT_SALARIES item. Add the following SELECT statement to the Data Query property:

```
Select state, lvl, val, icon, pk
From department_hierarchy
Order by sort_value
```

9

g. Open the Object Navigator. Create a form-level When-New-Form-Instance trigger using the following script:

```
Ftree.populate_tree('hier_tree.department_salaries');
```

h. Save the form as **ch09ex05.fmb.** Open and test the form.

i. If the salary values are not aligned vertically in the hierarchical item, change the DEPARTMENT_SALARIES Font Name property to **COURIER**.

CASE PROJECT: GREAT STATE ELECTRIC BUDGETING SYSTEM

With the case in this chapter, you create a new tab page. Management will use the form to review projects, work orders, and their tasks. This tab page contains a hierarchical tree item. At the top of the tree are departments that are assigned a project. The cost of each project is displayed. The next level is the project's work orders followed by the project's tasks. Managers will use this screen to identify important projects and to quickly drill-down to the level of detail they need. Figure 9-24 depicts the completed form.

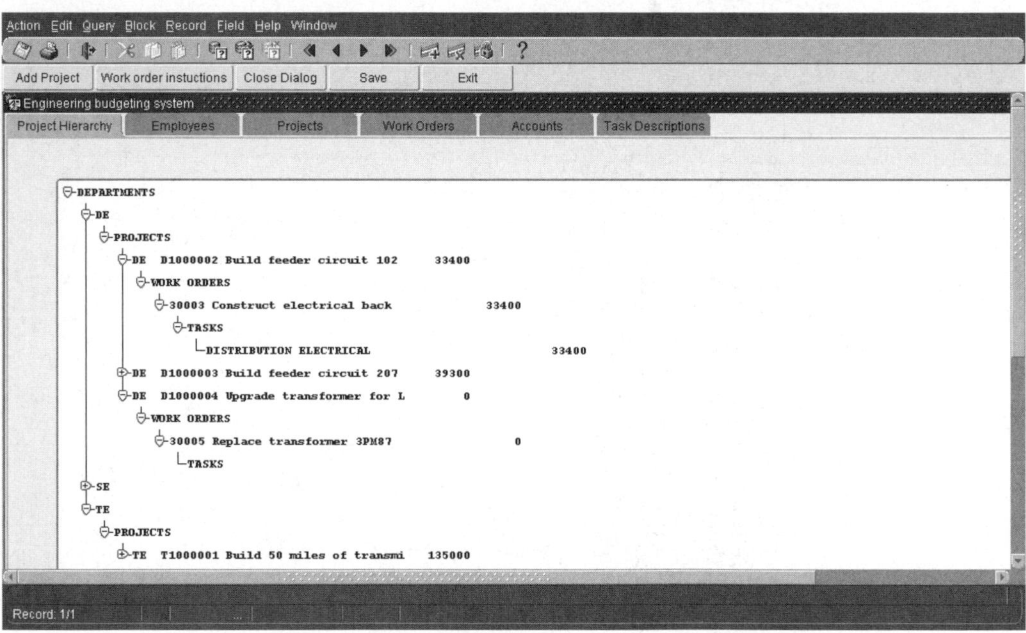

Figure 9-24 Budgeting system project hierarchy

To begin the process of creating a new tab page, perform the following steps:

1. Open the **Budgeting** application.

2. Open the **Object Navigator** and locate the MAIN canvas object. Create a new tab page under this canvas. Set the following properties:

   Name: **PROJECT_HIERARCHY**
   Label: **PROJECT HIERARCHY**

3. Open the **Object Navigator** and rearrange the tab pages so that the PROJECT_HIERARCHY tab page is listed first.

4. In the Object Navigator, create a control block named **PROJECT_HIERARCHY**. This data block should also be the first listed block.

5. Open the **Layout Editor**. Add a hierarchical tree item to the PROJECT_HIERARCHY tab page.

6. Open a Property Palette of the tree item. Set the following properties:

   Name: **PROJECT_HIERARCHY**
   Canvas: **MAIN**
   Tab Page: **PROJECT_HIERARCHY**
   Font Name: **COURIER**

7. Open a **SQL*Plus** session. Create a view using the Listing 9-16 script:

Listing 9-16 PROJECT_HIERARCHY view

```
create or replace view project_hierarchy as
select 1 state, 1 lvl, 'DEPARTMENTS' val,
       null icon, '0' pk, 'A' sort_value
from dual
union
select distinct -1, 2, assigned_department_id,
       null, assigned_department_id,
       'A'||assigned_department_id
from projects
union
select -1, 3, 'PROJECTS', null,
       assigned_department_id,
       'A'||assigned_department_id||'A'
from projects
union
select -1,4, pr.Assigned_department_id||
       ' '||pr.project_id||' '||
       rpad(substr(project_name,1,25),25)||' '||
       to_char(sum( (nvl(labor_hours,0)*50)
               +nvl(material_costs,0)
               +nvl(equipment_costs,0)),9999999),
       null, pr.project_id,
       'A'||pr.assigned_department_id||pr.project_id
from projects pr, work_orders wo,
     work_order_tasks wot
```

```
where pr.project_id = wo.project_id(+)
  and wo.work_order_id = wot.wo_work_order_id(+)
group by pr.assigned_department_id, pr.project_id, project_name
union
select 1, 5, 'WORK ORDERS', null,
       projects.project_id,
       'A'||projects.assigned_department_id||
       projects.project_id||'A'
from projects;
```

8. Leave SQL*Plus open, but return to Forms Builder.
9. Open a **Property Palette** for the PROJECT_HIERARCHY data block. Set the Data Query property of the PROJECT_HIERARCHY tree item by using the following script:

```
select state, lvl, val, icon, pk
from project_hierarchy
order by sort_value
```

10. Open the **Object Navigator** and create a When-New-Form-Instance trigger by using the following script:

```
Ftree.populate_tree('project_hierarchy.project_hierarchy');
```

11. Save the form. Launch the form and test the hierarchy that you just created.
12. Return to your SQL*Plus session. Create a view using the Listing 9-17 script:

Listing 9-17 Work_order_hierarchy view

```
create or replace view work_order_hierarchy as
select -1 state,1 lvl, work_order_id||' '||
      rpad(substr(wo_description,1,25),35,' ')||
           ' '||to_char(sum( (nvl(labor_hours,0)*50)+
                         nvl(material_costs,0)+
                         nvl(equipment_costs,0)),999999) val,
      null icon, wo.work_order_id pk,
      to_char(wo.work_order_id) sort_value,
      wo.project_id filter_value
from work_orders wo, work_order_tasks wot
where wo.work_order_id = wot.wo_work_order_id(+)
group by work_order_id, wo_description,
         wo.project_id
union
select -1, 2, 'TASKS', null, wo.work_order_id,
       to_char(wo.work_order_id)||'A', wo.project_id
from  work_orders wo, work_order_tasks wot
where wo.work_order_id = wot.wo_work_order_id(+)
union
select 1, 3,
       rpad(substr(task_description,1,25),45,' ')||
      ' '||to_char(sum( (nvl(labor_hours,0)*50)+
```

```
                              nvl(material_costs,0)+
                              nvl(equipment_costs,0)),999999) val,
        null icon, wo.work_order_id pk,
        to_char(wo.work_order_id)||'AB' sort_value,
        wo.project_id filter_value
 from work_orders wo, work_order_tasks wot,
      task_descriptions
 where wo.work_order_id = wot.wo_work_order_id(+)
   and task_description_id = task_id
 group by work_order_id,task_description,
         wo.project_id;
```

13. Return to Forms Builder and open the **Object Navigator**. Create a When-Tree-Node-Activated trigger under the PROJECT_HIERARCHY tree item. Use the Listing 9-18 script:

Listing 9-18 When-Tree-Node-Activated trigger

```
declare
   current_node                       ftree.node;
   executed_num                       number;
   node_label                               varchar2(12);
begin
   current_node := :system.trigger_node;
   :global.node_val := ftree.get_tree_node_property
                      ('Project_hierarchy.project_hierarchy',
                       current_node,
                       ftree.node_value);
   if :global.node_val != '0' then
      null;
      node_label := ftree.get_tree_node_property
                      ('Project_hierarchy.project_hierarchy',
                        current_node,
                        ftree.node_label);
      if node_label = 'WORK ORDERS' then
         ftree.add_tree_data
            ('project_hierarchy.project_hierarchy',
              current_node,
              ftree.parent_offset,
              ftree.last_child,
              ftree.query_text,
              'select state, lvl, val, icon, pk
              from work_order_hierarchy
              where filter_value = :global.node_val
              order by sort_value');
      end if;

      ftree.set_tree_node_property
          ('project_hierarchy.project_hierarchy',
```

9

```
                    current_node,
                              ftree.node_value, '0');

               ftree.set_tree_node_property
                    ('project_hierarchy.project_hierarchy',
                     current_node,
                     ftree.node_state,
                     ftree.expanded_node);
          end if;
      exception
          when others then message(sqlerrm);
      end;
```

14. Save and launch the form and test the hierarchy. You will be able to see a project work order by double-clicking on the WORK ORDERS node.

CHAPTER

10

USING SQL IN DATA BLOCKS, DEBUGGING, AND CREATING CALENDARS

In this chapter you will:

- Base your data blocks on custom SQL code to increase performance and enhance search capabilities
- Add your own DML statements to the data block
- Use Instead-Of triggers and database triggers
- Base a data block on PL/SQL stored procedures to perform SQL and DML operations
- Identify, create, and modify database objects using the Object Navigator
- Debug the form manually or with Forms Builder Debugger
- Add a calendar to a form

As the Figure 10-1 Roadmap shows, this chapter focuses primarily on replacing the default SQL statements that are generated by the data block with custom SQL statements. It is possible and often advantageous to replace the default SELECT, INSERT, UPDATE, and DELETE statements generated by the data block. This chapter discusses how and when it should be done.

In addition, this chapter shows you how to use PL/SQL stored procedures in your forms and also covers a number of other form topics, such as using database triggers, debugging forms, and creating a graphic calendar.

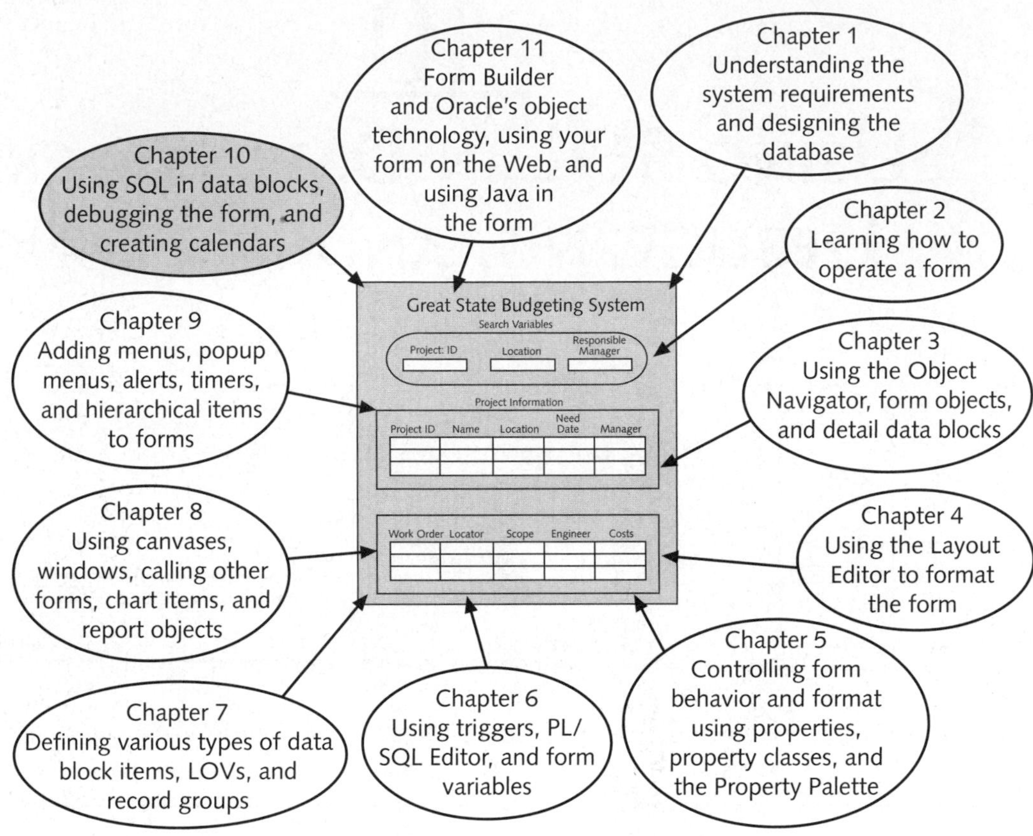

Figure 10-1 Roadmap

Basing a Data Block on Custom PL/SQL

The data blocks that you have created in the practice sessions throughout this book were based on a single table. When you created the data block, you identified the table by using the Data Block Wizard. Forms Builder created a data block based on the table and then selected table columns. This is how a developer often creates a data block, but there is one problem with basing your data block on a table: A single table often does not contain all the columns that you want to see on the data block row.

Because databases are normalized, a table does not have descriptive types of values. The descriptive values are placed in related tables of their own. As explained in Chapter 1, the second normal form of the Normalization process requires values that do not depend on the primary key to be placed in a table of their own. This is evident in Figure 10-2. The figure depicts a table relationship drawing of the practice database. The database has a DNAME (department name) column. This value is not placed in the EMP table along with DEPTNO (department number), because it does not depend on the primary key of that table (EMPNO). It depends on DEPTNO. Thus, it is placed in its own table. It is far better to record the DNAME value in a single record in the DEPT table than on every EMP table. The DNAME value can still be associated to an employee through the power of joining tables.

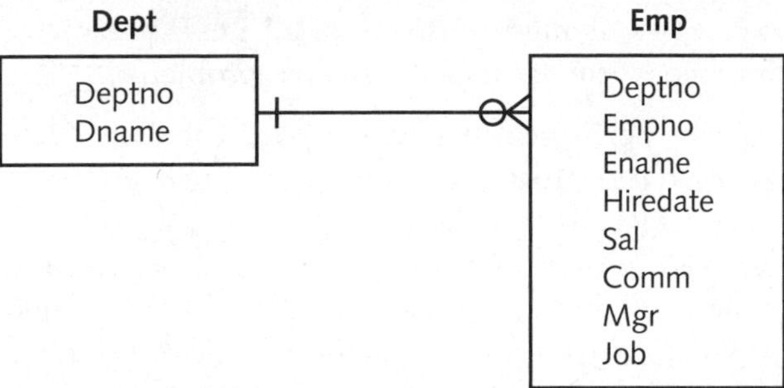

Figure 10-2 Table relationship drawing of the practice database

Databases can contain many descriptive types of tables, such as those described in the preceding paragraph, whose primary keys are foreign keys in other tables. Employee tables can contain foreign keys that relate to a department table. Projects and work orders can contain foreign keys that relate back to an employee table. These associations allow you to retrieve descriptive information to the entity. For example, they allow you to display the employee's department name rather than department number, or the employee's name rather than the employee ID. Good design, and especially conceptual clarity, dictates the placement of descriptions in your forms. Descriptive information helps the operator better understand the data—descriptions are easier to interpret than codes or numbers. For example, which is more descriptive: the employee number 3109 or the name John Palinski?

Data blocks can also contain summary information. For example, the book's Case Project application displays the summarized cost of the project with the project, and the summarized cost of the work with the work order. This is important information to the operator, but the information does not reside in the parent table. For all of these reasons, you should bring additional information into your block.

There are three ways to bring descriptive data into the form:

- Use a Post-Query trigger that executes a SELECT statement for each record returned to the data block. The SELECT statement retrieves the descriptive values based on the values of the data block's foreign keys.
- Use a complex view as the data source. The view SELECT statement joins the tables before any records are returned to the data block. The view then returns the descriptive values along with the base or parent record.
- Use a From Clause Query. FROM CLAUSE QUERY is a data block property value of the data block's Query Data Source Type property. It indicates that the Query Data Source Name property contains a SELECT statement. When the data block executes the query, it uses the Query Data Source Name property's SELECT statement as an in-line view to the SELECT statement created by the data block.

The Post-Query trigger is useful and commonly used, because the developer can use the Data Block Wizard to create the data block. The wizard ensures that the data block can properly issue the SELECT, INSERT, UPDATE, and DELETE statements. The other two techniques require the developer to create these statements. However, the Post-Query trigger has some deficiencies. It must perform a SELECT statement for every record selected. This additional work can cause performance problems.

Joining records can have definite performance benefits over the Post-Query trigger method, especially if Post-Query returns many records or a summarized value. Another disadvantage of the Post-Query trigger is that the descriptive values cannot be used as search arguments. Because they are related only to the block's data source, descriptive values cannot be used as arguments in the Where clause that is created by the data block. A third disadvantage is that the data block cannot update descriptive values returned by the Post-Query trigger. Forms Builder cannot use non-database columns in a DML statement issued by the data block.

The View and From Clause query methods have the advantage of using a join to combine records. This can increase the performance of your data retrieval by eliminating the secondary database queries performed by a Post-Query trigger. Another advantage is that the descriptive arguments can be used as search values, because the descriptive values are returned by the block's data source. The disadvantage of the view is that it resides in the database and might not get updated as needed. For example, many organizations require a DBA to create views, especially production views. As databases are moved from server to server, the DBA may forget to re-create the view, thus disabling the form. In addition, placing many views into the database clutters it; a database should contain as few objects as possible.

The From Clause query method has the advantage of containing the SELECT statement in the form. The disadvantage is that the Data Block Wizard cannot be used with this method. The SELECT statement is placed in the Query Data Source Name property. You must then manually create each data block item that is populated. To associate the data block item to a SELECT statement expression, give the data block item the same name as the expression, or place the expression name into the Column Name property of the data block items. You can use the Layout Editor to create the items and set the properties by opening the item's Property Palette from the editor.

A disadvantage to using views and the From Clause query method is that the data block cannot create or issue DML statements. By default, complex views cannot be updated by the database. Thus, without employing an Oracle database and Forms Builder triggers, data blocks based on views or using From Clause queries cannot issue DML statements. Fortunately, there are a number of tools that allow you to create custom DML statements for your data block. These tools are discussed in the next several sections.

To summarize, the Post-Query method of populating descriptive data block items is the easiest. However, using the From Clause query method offers better performance and additional search criteria. The latter is preferred when the data block displays considerable descriptive data or summarized values. Using a view as the data source is the least preferred method.

Basing a Data Block on a From Clause Query

When you decide to use a From Clause query as the data source of a block, you must set properties. The Data Block Wizard cannot be used, because it does not have a page for entering the SELECT statement. From Clause queries are created by setting the Query Data Source Type and Query Data Source Name properties. The former property determines the type of data source. The options are: TABLE, PROCEDURE, TRANSACTIONAL TRIGGER, and FROM CLAUSE QUERY. Figure 10-3 illustrates the Property Palette depicting the properties and the Query Data Source Name dialog box used to record the SELECT statement.

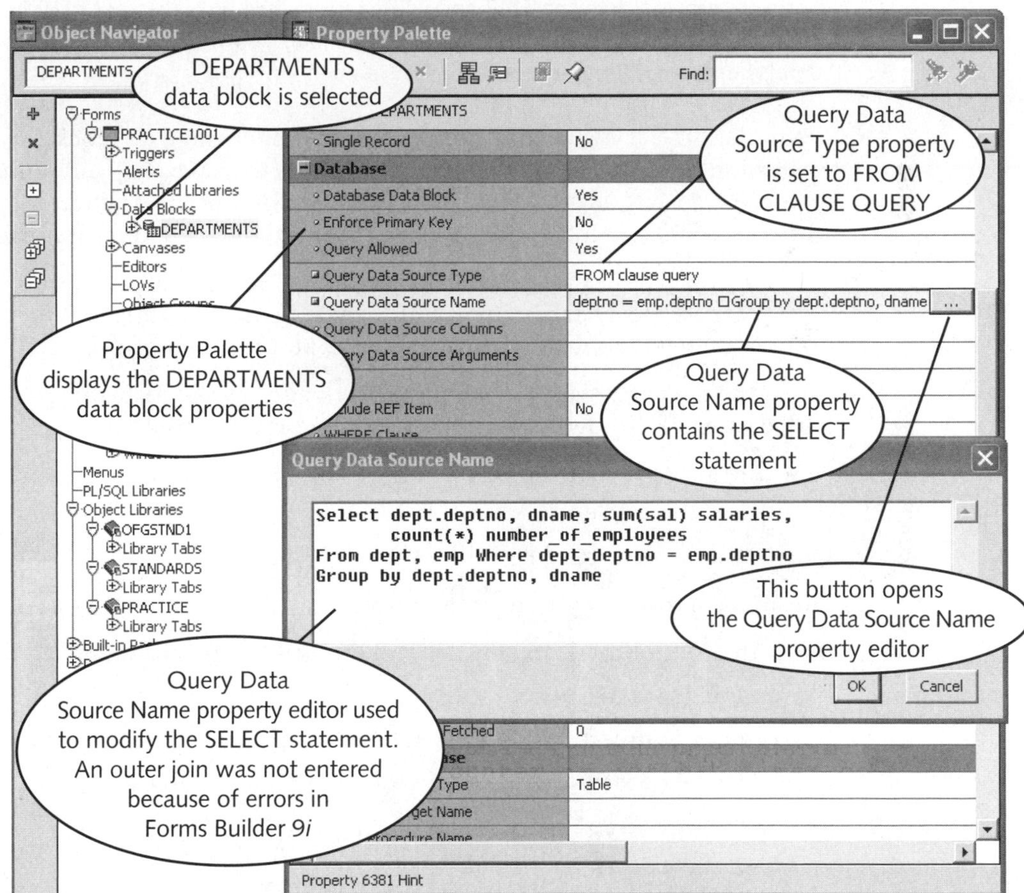

Figure 10-3 Data block Property Palette displays the Query Data Source Name property and the Query Data Source Name dialog box

To create a data block based on a From Clause query, you would perform the following steps:

1. Create a data block in the Object Navigator (do not use the wizard).

2. Open a Property Palette for the newly created block.
3. Set the Query Data Source Type property to FROM CLAUSE QUERY.
4. Click the Query Data Source Name property. A button appears on the right side of the item's text item. Click this button to open the Query Data Source Name dialog box.
5. Enter the SELECT statement into the dialog box.

There appears to be a bug in Forms Builder 9*i* that causes the SELECT statement to fail to return records when an outer join is used, an action you would normally perform with the EMP and DEPT tables. This bug does not exist in Form Builder 6*i*. If you need to use an outer join, you may prefer to use a database view rather than the From Clause query.

6. Open the Object Navigator. Create an item under the data block for each expression in the SELECT statement. It is best to make the name of the item match the corresponding expression name. If you choose a different name, you must set the item's Column Name property to the expression name.
7. Open a Property Palette for each of the items. Set the following properties: Name, Data Type, Database Item (YES), Maximum Length, and Query Length. Be sure to set the Primary Key property of one of the items to YES.
8. Open the Layout Wizard for the data block and set the formatting properties. The data block is now ready to be used to retrieve records.

As practice, create a data block based on a From Clause query. To do so, perform the following steps:

1. Create a new form module in the Object Navigator.
2. Create a control block in the new form.
3. Select the control block and open a Property Palette. Set the following properties:

   Name: **DEPARTMENTS**

   Query Data Source Type: **FROM CLAUSE QUERY**

   Query Data Source Name: Use the following select statement:

   ```
   Select dept.deptno, dname,
          sum(sal) salaries,
          count(*) number_of_employees
   From dept, emp
   Where dept.deptno = emp.deptno
   Group by dept.deptno, dname
   ```

4. Create four data block items under the DEPARTMENTS data block.

5. Open a Property Palette for the first item and set the following properties:

   Name: **DEPTNO**

   Data Type: **CHAR**

   Maximum Length: **30**

   Query Length: **50**

   Database Item: **YES**

   Primary Key: **YES**

6. Open a Property Palette for the second item and set the following properties:

   Name: **DNAME**

   Data Type: **CHAR**

   Maximum Length: **30**

   Query Length: **50**

   Database Item: **YES**

7. Open a Property Palette for the third item and set the following properties:

   Name: **SALARIES**

   Data Type: **NUMBER**

   Maximum Length: **30**

   Query Length: **50**

   Database Item: **YES**

8. Open a Property Palette for the fourth item and set the following properties:

   Name: **NUMBER_OF_EMPLOYEES**

   Data Type: **NUMBER**

   Maximum Length: **30**

   Query Length: **50**

   Database Item: **YES**

9. Open the Layout Wizard and format the DEPARTMENTS data block. The form style should be Tabular and ten records displayed.
10. Save the form as **practice1001.fmb.** Open the form and execute a query.
11. Attempt to update a value. You should not be able to do so.
12. Place the form into the Enter Query mode. Enter **#> 3** into the NUMBER_OF_EMPLOYEES item. Execute a query. The departments with more than three employees should be returned. This demonstrates a query against a calculated value.
13. Save the form for later practice.

ADDING YOUR OWN DML STATEMENTS

When a From Clause query or view are used as the block data source, the data block cannot construct DML statements. This was demonstrated in the previous practice. You must, therefore, find another mechanism to maintain the database. This mechanism can be one of the four On-type triggers in the list that follows; On-type triggers replace a specific form transaction:

- **On-Lock**: Fired when the data block attempts to lock a record in the table. This occurs whenever a value in the record is modified.
- **On-Insert**: Fired when the data block attempts to issue an INSERT statement.
- **On-Update**: Fired when the data block attempts to issue an UPDATE statement.
- **On-Delete**: Fired when the data block attempts to issue a DELETE statement.

An On-type trigger's PL/SQL code block replaces the DML statement that would normally be issued by the data block. When the data block is based on a view or From Clause query, the data block cannot lock a record in the database. Thus you cannot perform DML transactions. The On-Type triggers allow you to lock records and substitute a valid statement for the one issued by the data block. For example, the following SELECT statement was used in the last practice:

```
select dept.deptno, dname,
        sum(sal) total_salaries,
        count(*) number_of_employees
from dept, emp
where dept.deptno = emp.deptno
group by dept.deptno, dname
```

If the statement were placed in a view, the view could not be used to modify the database, because the statement is complex. Views that contain a Group By clause or aggregate functions cannot be used in DML statements. You might wonder why someone would want to update the view. An operator would never want to modify the Salaries expression, because it is a computed value. However, it is conceivable that the operator might want to modify the department name (DNAME) while viewing the data block item containing the aggregate values. Placing the following UPDATE statement in an On-Update trigger allows this to happen. The following is an example of an UPDATE statement that can be placed in an On-Update trigger:

```
Update dept set dname = :block_name.dname
Where dept.deptno = :block_name.deptno;
```

You can even use the On-Type triggers to modify multiple tables by placing two UPDATE statements into the trigger. You can also place calculations into the trigger or perform evaluations in the trigger. Triggers give you flexibility to manipulate items that appear in your form, such as updating values on a summary screen. This is something not normally done in a form.

Locking Database Records

Whenever a DML statement is issued against a table, the Oracle database locks the record so that another user cannot modify the record until a COMMIT statement is executed. Whenever a record in a form is modified, Forms Builder causes Oracle to lock the corresponding database record. A data block item property named Locking Mode controls when the form locking occurs. The default setting is AUTOMATIC, which means that Forms Builder communicates at once with the Oracle database and places a lock on the table. When an Oracle database is used as the data source, the AUTOMATIC setting acts the same way as the second setting, IMMEDIATE. If the AUTOMATIC setting is used for other databases, Forms Builder determines the locking mechanism used by the data source and attempts to behave as similarly to the IMMEDIATE method as possible. The third setting is DELAYED, and this setting causes Forms Builder to lock the record only when the change is posted to the database rather than while the user is editing the record. The actual change occurs when the form tries to commit the changes.

Whenever your form is based on a From Clause query or view and you modify a value, you must provide for record locking, or Forms Builder issues an error. By default, each time a value is modified on a data block row, Forms Builder attempts to place a database lock on the corresponding database record. The purpose of this is to prevent another user from modifying the record while changes are pending on the form. If Forms Builder cannot lock the database record, it issues an error message. As stated earlier, views cannot be updated and the records cannot be locked. A From Clause query also falls into this trap because it is an **in-line view**, and Forms Builder cannot lock the corresponding record. Thus, whenever a record based on a view or From Clause query is modified, Forms Builder cannot lock a record and issues an error message unless you provide a special mechanism to override the data block's default locking mechanism. Figure 10-4 illustrates the practice form that uses default locking after the department name (DNAME) column was modified. Forms Builder issued an FRM-40501 error.

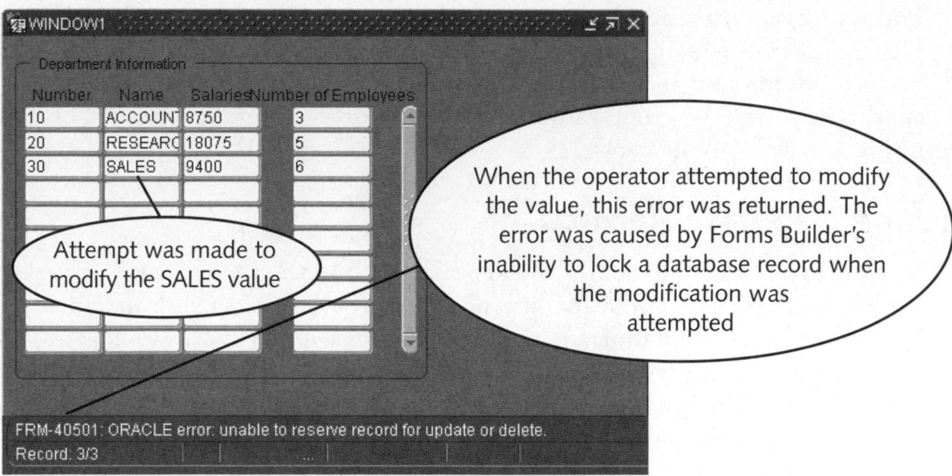

Figure 10-4 Forms Builder error caused by modifying a record based on a From Clause query

To prevent this error, you must add an On-Lock trigger to the data block, so that Forms Builder executes the trigger rather than the normal locking procedure. If you want the On-Lock trigger to simulate the DELAYED setting, place the following statement into the trigger. It allows the trigger to compile, but doesn't do any work such as attempting to lock a record when it is fired:

```
Null;
```

The trigger satisfies Forms Builder's need to lock the record without actually performing the lock. This is the same as using the DELAYED setting. If you want an immediate lock, you must issue a lock command, which is a SELECT statement with the For Update clause. Listing 10-1 shows the statement that can be used to lock the DEPT records that have been discussed in the previous sections:

Listing 10-1 On-Lock trigger

```
begin
select deptno
into :block_name.deptno
from dept
where deptno = :block_name.deptno
for update;
exception
     when others then
       message ('Error occurred
                    when locking record');
end;
```

This statement locks the record modified by the form operator. It is released when the record is committed. As practice for adding On-Lock and On-Update triggers to the practice form, perform the following steps:

1. Open the previous practice form, **practice1001.fmb**, and execute a query. Modify the **department name (DNAME) value.** This should cause the error depicted in Figure 10-4. Close the form.
2. Open the Object Navigator. Create an On-Lock trigger in the data block. Use the script contained in Listing 10-1 (be sure to use the correct block name).
3. Save the form as **practice1002.fmb** and perform Step 1 again. The error should no longer appear. Close the form.
4. Open the Object Navigator. Create an On-Update trigger using the following script:

   ```
   Update dept
   Set dname = :departments.dname
   Where deptno = :departments.deptno;
   ```

5. Save and open the form. Execute a query. Modify one of the DNAME values for one of the records. Commit the changes. You should now be able to modify records.
6. Close the form.

10

USING INSTEAD-OF AND DATABASE TRIGGERS

The Oracle database has two types of triggers: **database triggers** and **Instead-Of triggers**. Database triggers are fired before or after an INSERT, UPDATE, or DELETE statement. Database triggers are used in coordination with a DML transaction to execute a PL/SQL code block. They can also be used to perform edits before a transaction, generate values such as a unique record ID, generate an employee payroll number before an insert, or make sure all of the values saved in the database are uppercase. The benefit of a trigger is that the database manager makes sure that the PL/SQL code is executed. If someone modifies a table using an INSERT statement in SQL, the database trigger automatically executes the code. If a form operator issues an INSERT statement from a form, the database manager executes the code. No matter how the table is modified, the database trigger ensures that the PL/SQL code is executed.

The following script illustrates these concepts by creating a database trigger that generates a payroll number (EMPNO) for newly added EMP table records. EMPNO is a numeric value, and the script first determines the maximum existing value. This value is incremented by 1 and added to the EMPNO table column. The trigger allows the developer to avoid having to place the trigger code in the forms, which can be useful. If the same code is used in multiple forms, you can experience a code management problem when the code changes. Placing it in the database can solve this problem.

```
create or replace trigger payroll_number_gen
  before insert on emp
  for each row
declare
 cursor a is select max(empno) empno
   from emp;
 a_var   a%rowtype;
begin
 open a;
 fetch a into a_var;
 :new.empno := a_var.empno + 1;
 close a;
end;
/
```

After the trigger in the preceding code is created, whenever a form inserts a record into the EMP table, the database trigger fires, and the next employee number (EMPNO) value is generated and placed into the EMPNO column of the new record. If the operator queries the record, the new employee number (EMPNO) is displayed. Database triggers and stored procedures called from the form can make code management much easier.

A possible problem related to this method is when a database trigger fires and modifies a table value, the trigger value is not added to the form. The effect of this is that the record displayed in the form does not match the record in the database. As soon as you modify the record, Forms Builder attempts to lock the corresponding database record. Because the form record does not match the database record from the last time it was committed, this error message appears in the form (shown in Figure 10-5): "FRM-40654: Record has been updated by another user. Re-query to see change."

To avoid this error, you must clear the block and query the database again, so that the form record matches the database record. This can make your form operation somewhat cumbersome. Although it is a good idea to place your code into the database as a database trigger or a stored procedure, you must be careful about keeping the form record and database records synchronized.

The Instead-Of trigger is similar to a database trigger except that it is used in conjunction with a view to perform DML operations. The Instead-Of trigger references a view rather than a table and executes DML contained within the trigger's code block whenever a DML statement is executed against the view. Thus, if you are using a view as the data source of a block, you can avoid defining On-type triggers by creating an Instead-Of trigger in the database. Then, you can reference the view in numerous forms and applications without having to re-create the On-type triggers.

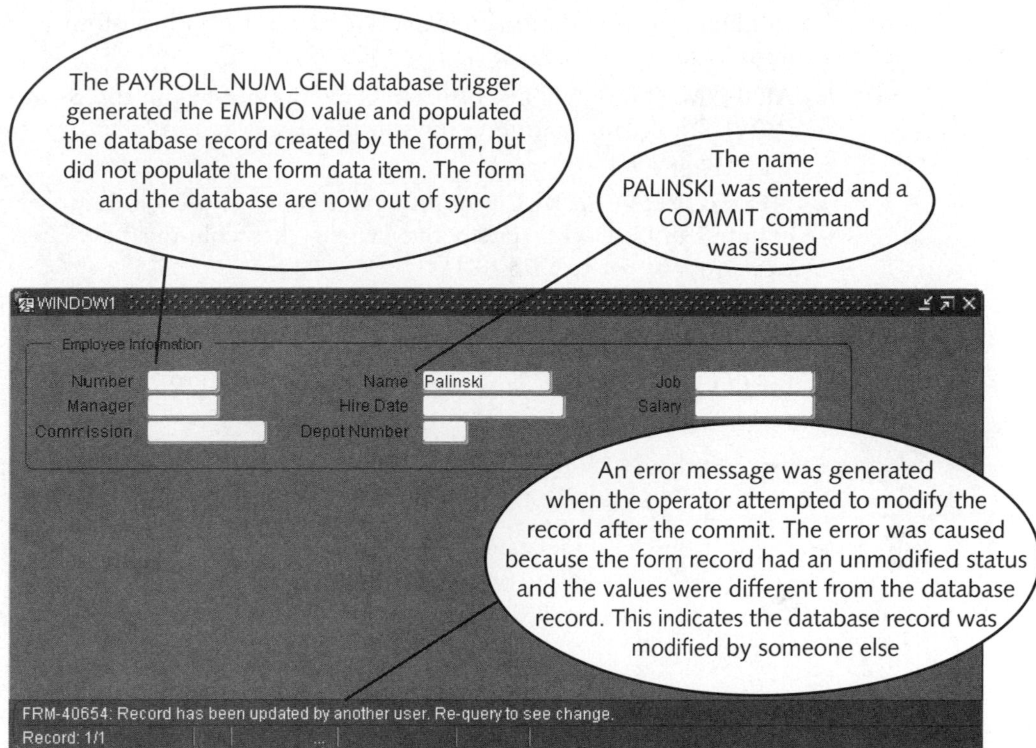

Figure 10-5 Error message returned after a form COMMIT command was issued causing an employee number (EMPNO) value to be generated, and the record was modified a second time

10

To base your data block on a view and use an Instead-Of trigger to perform DML, you would perform the following steps:

1. Create the view. You should consider placing each table's ROWID into the view. ROWID is an Oracle value that uniquely identifies the record. (See the following practice for an example of a view with ROWIDS.)
2. Create the Instead-Of trigger(s). Each DML operation probably needs a different trigger, because it is unlikely that the same code can be used for each type of operation.
3. Create the data block using the view as the table name.
4. Change the data block Key-Mode property to UPDATEABLE. This property determines how Forms Builder uniquely identifies a database row. If this step

is not done, you encounter an FRM-40602 error. You have four property options as follows:

- **AUTOMATIC** (default): Causes Forms Builder to use the record's ROWID to identify unique rows in the data source, if the data source supports ROWIDs.
- **NON-UPDATEABLE**: Causes Forms Builder to exclude primary key columns in UPDATE statements. Primary key columns have the Primary Key property set to YES.
- **UNIQUE**: Causes Forms Builder to use ROWID constructs to identify unique rows in an Oracle database.
- **UPDATEABLE**: Causes Forms Builder to issue UPDATE statements that include primary key values.

5. Make sure that at least one of the data block item's Primary Key properties is set to YES. Preferably, this is the ROWID or the actual primary key column.

As practice and to help you understand how to base a block on a view and an Instead-Of trigger, use the following steps to work through the creation of a complex view, an Instead-Of trigger that can update the view, and a form that updates tables using the Instead-Of trigger:

1. Log on to SQL*Plus. The following view joins the DEPT table and the EMP table, so that the department name (DNAME) is displayed with the employee record. An in-line view is used in the statement to compute the total cost of department wages. This value is used to compute the percentage of each employee's wages of the total. (Note: This practice requires an Oracle 9*i* database. The Oracle8*i* databases contain a bug that prevents the execution of this practice from Forms Builder.) Create the view in Listing 10-2.

Listing 10-2 EMPLOYEE VIEW view script

```
Create or replace view employee_view as
  Select dept.rowid dept_rowid,
         dept.deptno, dname,
         Emp.rowid emp_rowid,
         empno, ename, hiredate, sal,
         (sal/dept_sal) salary_percent
         from dept, emp,
          (select deptno,
            sum(nvl(sal,0)) dept_sal
           from emp
           group by deptno) dept_sal
           where dept.deptno = emp.deptno
             and  emp.deptno = dept_sal.deptno;
```

The NVL function was used along with the Sum aggregate function. When using in-line views with Forms Builder, you must be sure that the aggregate function returns a value or an error occurs.

2. Create **an** Instead-Of trigger (see Listing 10-3) that is used to update the EMP and DEPT tables using the view created in Step 1.

Listing 10-3 Instead-Of trigger view

```
Create or replace trigger employee_view_update
Instead of update on employee_view
For each row
Begin
   Update dept set dname = :new.dname
   Where rowid = :new.dept_rowid;
   Update emp set ename = :new.ename,
                  Hiredate = :new.hiredate,
                  Sal = :new.sal
   Where rowid = :new.emp_rowid;
End;
/
```


3. Open Forms Builder and create a new form module.
4. Create a data block using the Data Block Wizard. Use EMPLOYEE_VIEW as the data source. Select all of the view's **columns** for the data block.
5. Use the Layout Wizard to format the data block. Do not display the DEPT_ROWID and EMP_ROWID items. The form should be Tabular and display ten records.
6. Open a Property Palette for the EMPLOYEE_VIEW data block. Set the Key Mode property to **UPDATEABLE**.
7. Open a Property Palette for the DEPT_ROWID and EMP_ROWID items. Set the following properties:

   Primary Key: **YES**

   Maximum Length: **50**
8. Save the form as **practice1003.fmb.** Open the form and execute a query. The form should look similar to Figure 10-6.

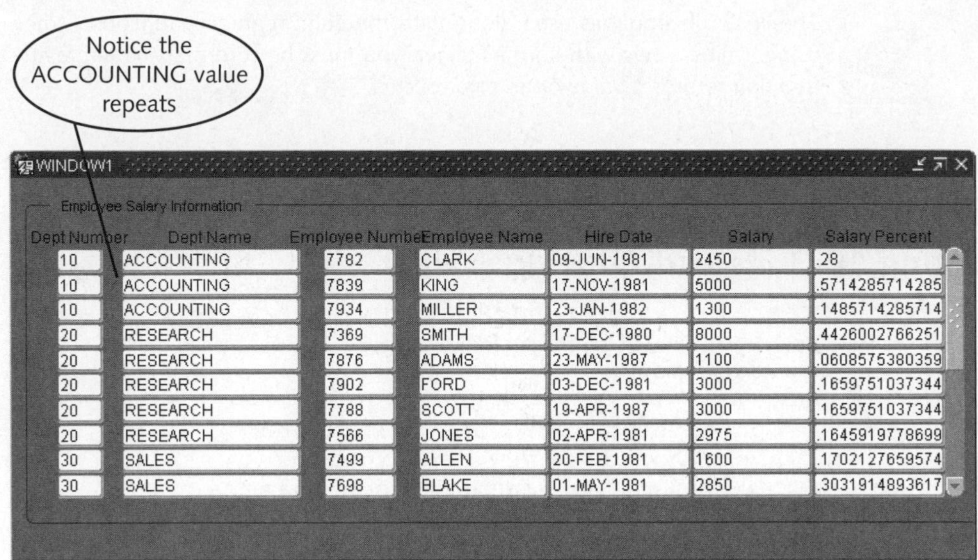

Figure 10-6 Form based on the EMPLOYEE_VIEW view before modification

9. Make the following changes to the first row:

   DNAME: **ACCT DEPT**

   ENAME: **CLARKSON**

10. Save the changes and execute the query. The results should appear similar to Figure 10-7. Notice that the DNAME value ACCOUNTING changed on three rows and the ENAME value changed on only one row. This is because of the complex join in the view. The DEPT record containing the ACCOUNTING value was joined to three EMP records.

Experts suggest that you should use the Instead-Of trigger view with caution. It may be difficult to debug forms after you have used the Instead-Of trigger view because a trigger modifies the values rather than the form. Even experienced developers may not be aware that a trigger exists and wonder why the form is reacting differently than it should.

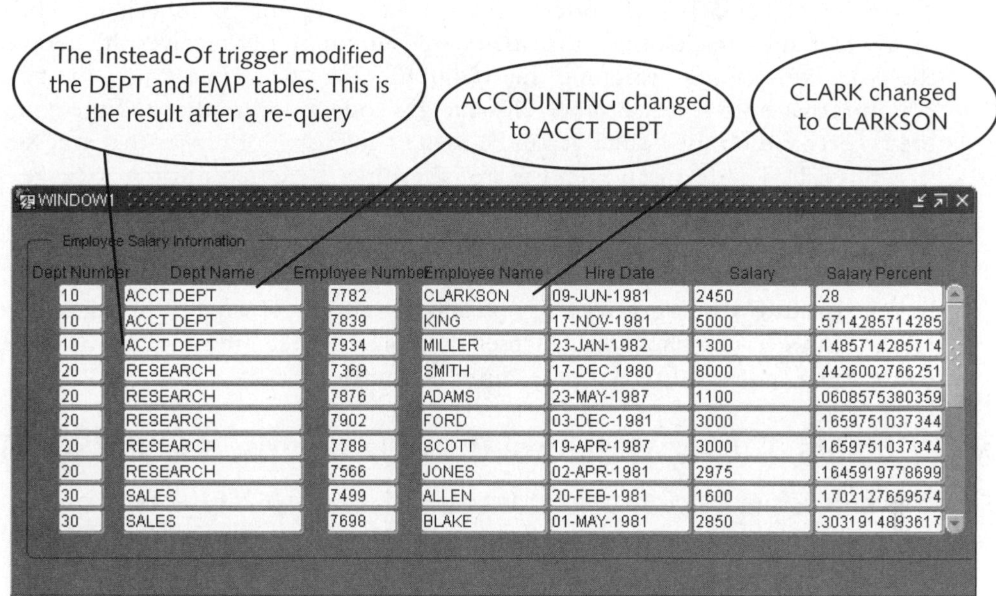

Figure 10-7 Form based on the EMPLOYEE_VIEW view after modification and re-query

10

Basing Your Block on PL/SQL Stored Procedures to Perform SQL and DML Operations

It is possible to base you data block on PL/SQL stored procedures. Basing the query functionality of a data block on PL/SQL stored procedures allows you to modify the result set before it is returned to the form. You can use IF-THEN-ELSE constructs to change values or even switch SQL statements. You can also use stored procedures to perform your DML operations, as well as add special edits, calculations, and formulas to the code block.

Using stored procedures in your forms also has an element of object-oriented design. If you develop a package of stored procedures, cursors, REF cursors, PL/SQL records, PL/SQL tables, functions, and variables that affect a specific set of data such as a table(s), you are using encapsulation. **Encapsulation** consists of enclosing or associating your data and its methods into an object. **Methods** are code scripts or programs that affect the object's data elements. They perform tasks such as querying the data, updating and deleting the data, or conducting edits. While scripts outside the package can still manipulate the data, placing all the PL/SQL objects that contain the business rules that pertain to the object into the package takes a big step towards object-oriented design and encapsulation.

A second object-oriented concept that packages support is inheritance. **Inheritance** means that any Oracle object that uses a type automatically receives the definitions with the type. For example, assigning the ADDRESS type to a table causes the table to have columns that hold street number, city, and zip code. Because the package contains all of the objects and business rules, it can be used in any form or report that accesses or modifies the data. The form and reports are inheriting the objects in the package. There are two important benefits of inheritance. The first is **reusability**, which means that each form and report uses the same code. This saves time and adds consistency across a system because the developer does not have to redevelop the same program. The second benefit is **code management**. If you modify an object in the package, the change is reflected in every application that uses the object. These are some powerful reasons for considering the use of stored procedures in your forms.

REF Cursors, Cursor Variables, PL/SQL records, and PL/SQL Tables

A **cursor** is an area of memory that holds a result set. A **REF cursor** is a reference to this area. To receive a query result set from a stored procedure, you must create a cursor variable. Looking at Figure 10-8, you can see that a **cursor variable** is a set of records returned by a SELECT statement that resides inside a stored procedure. A cursor variable is the object a REF cursor references. The cursor variable is composed of a series of PL/SQL records. A **PL/SQL record** is an object that consists of a series of attributes that match the expressions in a SELECT clause. A **PL/SQL table** is a series of indexed (by binary integer) PL/SQL records, which differ from cursor variables in that SELECT statements do not populate them. The stored procedures that perform DML operations use the PL/SQL records to transfer values.

The first step in setting up a data block to use a stored procedure is to create the PL/SQL objects. The first object to create is a PL/SQL record. The Type keyword initiates the definition, which also includes the name of the object, the type of object (record), and the record attributes. The following is a code template for the statement that defines a PL/SQL record:

```
Type record_name is record
     (attribute1 datatype,
      attribute2 datatype);
```

After the PL/SQL record has been defined, the PL/SQL table and cursor variables can be defined. These definitions also begin with the keyword Type, along with the type of object. Both definitions reference a PL/SQL record. The REF cursor definition uses the PL/SQL record as the return type. The PL/SQL table definition identifies the PL/SQL record as its basic component. The PL/SQL table definition has one more component—the Index By Binary_integer keywords. These keywords cause each record in the table to have an integer value beginning with the integer 0. The following are templates of the definitions:

```
Type cursor_variable_name is
     ref cursor return record_name;
Type table_name is
     table of record_name index
     by binary_integer;
```

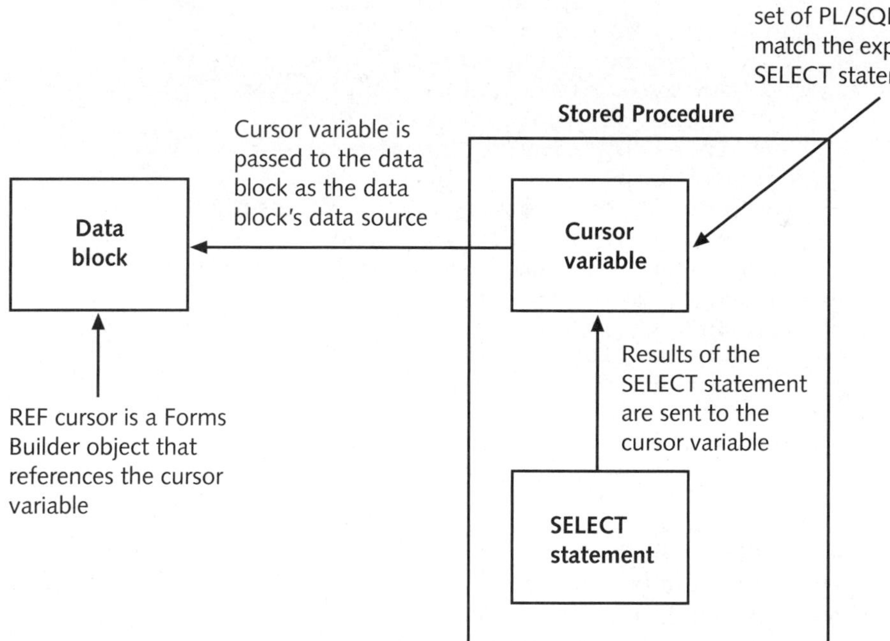

Figure 10-8 Relationships between a stored procedure, SELECT statement, cursor variable, and a data block

The PL/SQL object definitions are placed inside a package that encapsulates objects used in the form. To illustrate the use of the PL/SQL objects, the following sections describe how to use PL/SQL stored procedures to query and maintain the EMP table.

Before the form can be created, a package must be defined that contains the PL/SQL object types and the stored procedures. Listing 10-4 is a **package specification** for the objects used in the example. It has a definition for the PL/SQL record, the REF cursor, the PL/SQL, and for the procedures to query, lock, insert, update, and delete EMP records.

Listing 10-4 EMPLOYEE_OBJECTS package specification

```
create or replace PACKAGE
   employee_objects IS
   type employee_record is
        record (empno number(4),
                ename varchar2(10),
                job varchar2(9),
                mgr number(4),
                hiredate date,
                sal number(7,2),
                comm number(7,2),
                deptno number(2));
  type employee_ref_cursor is
        ref cursor return employee_record;
  type employee_plsql_table is
        table of employee_record
        index by binary_integer;
  procedure employee_query
    (dmlset in out employee_ref_cursor);
  procedure employee_record_lock
    (dmlset in out employee_plsql_table);
  procedure employee_record_insert
    (dmlset in out employee_plsql_table);
  procedure employee_record_update
    (dmlset in out employee_plsql_table);
  procedure employee_record_delete
    (dmlset in out employee_plsql_table);
END;
/
```

A package specification contains header information for public objects. Public objects are the objects that can be called by objects outside the package. This information consists of the type definitions, the names of the procedures and functions, and any parameters used by the stored procedures. The actual statements are contained in the **package body**. The EMPLOYEE_OBJECTS package body is detailed in Listing 10-5.

Listing 10-5 EMPLOYEE_OBJECTS package body

```
Create or replace PACKAGE body
   employee_objects IS
      procedure employee_query
      (dmlset in out employee_ref_cursor)
  is
  begin
     open dmlset for
       select empno, ename, job,
              mgr, hiredate,
              sal, comm, deptno
       from emp;
```

```
end;
procedure employee_record_lock
   (dmlset in out employee_plsql_table)
is
  empno_holder  number;
begin
   select empno
     into empno_holder
   from emp
   where empno = dmlset(1).empno
  for update;
end;
procedure employee_record_insert
   (dmlset in out employee_plsql_table)
is
  -- This cursor is used to
  -- generate an employee number (EMPNO)
  cursor a is
    select max(empno) empno from emp;
  a_var   a%rowtype;
begin
   -- This is an example of an edit
if dmlset(1).deptno is null then
   RAISE_APPLICATION_ERROR (-2021,
        'You have failed to enter
          a department number');
end if;
open a;
fetch a into a_var;
close a;
insert into emp
     (empno, ename, job, mgr,
      hiredate, sal, comm, deptno)
values
     (dmlset(1).empno,
      upper(dmlset(1).ename),
      upper(dmlset(1).job),
      dmlset(1).mgr,
      dmlset(1).hiredate,
      dmlset(1).sal,
      dmlset(1).comm,
      dmlset(1).deptno);
end;
procedure employee_record_update
  (dmlset in out employee_plsql_table)
is
begin
update emp
    set ename = upper(dmlset(1).ename),
        job = dmlset(1).job,
```

10

```
                mgr = dmlset(1).mgr,
                hiredate = dmlset(1).hiredate,
                sal = dmlset(1).sal,
                comm = dmlset(1).comm,
                deptno = dmlset(1).deptno
        where empno = dmlset(1).empno;
        end;
       procedure employee_record_delete
          (dmlset in out employee_plsql_table)
       is
        begin
          delete from emp
          where empno = dmlset(1).empno;
        end;
      END;
      /
```

Creating and Using a Stored Procedure to Query Records in a Data Block

After the PL/SQL package has been developed, the data block can be created using the Data Block Wizard. The first wizard page is the Type page as shown in Figure 10-9. It has two radio buttons—Table or View and Stored Procedure. You must click the Stored Procedure radio button. This sets the wizard to prompt you for the various procedures that perform your data block transactions.

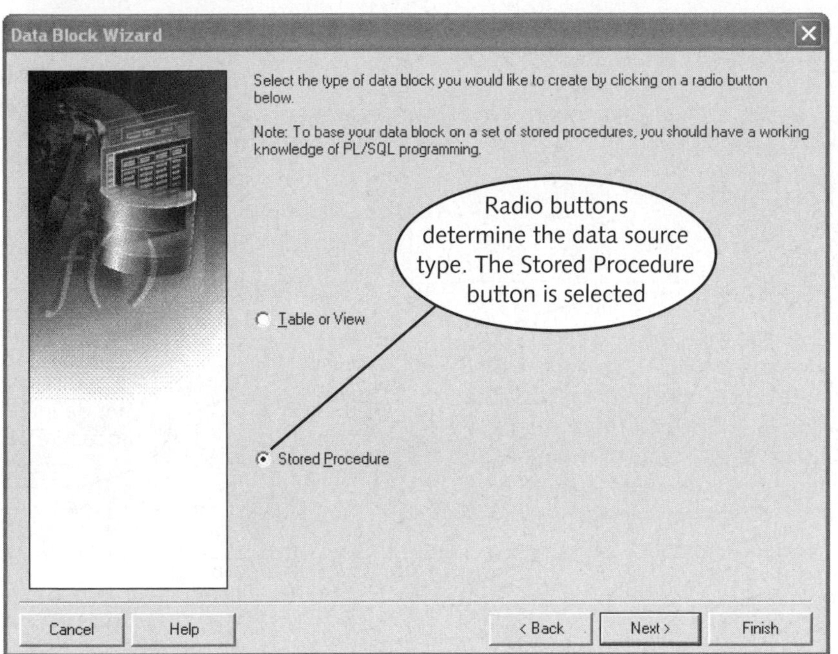

Figure 10-9 Data Block Wizard Type page

Clicking the Next button on the Type page causes the Query page, depicted in Figure 10-10, to appear. This page is used to associate the query package procedure to the data block. In this example, the procedure is named EMPLOYEE_OBJECTS.EMPLOYEE_QUERY. To enter the procedure into this page (and the remainder of the procedure association pages) you would perform the following steps, referring to Figure 10-10 when necessary:

1. Enter the name of the package and procedure (i.e., EMPLOYEE_OBJECTS.EMPLOYEE_QUERY) into the Procedure text item.
2. Click the Refresh button. If Forms Builder locates the procedure, it populates the Available Columns pick list. If it cannot find the procedure, it does not populate the drop-down list, and you should check the spelling of the name you entered.
3. Move the items from the Available Columns drop-down list to the Database Items drop-down list. The moved items are added to the data block.
4. At the bottom of the page are the Argument Name, Type, and Value lists. The latter two are not updateable and are the name and type of the procedure parameters. The Value item is updateable and is used to enter a default value that is supplied to the procedure. This field is generally not populated.

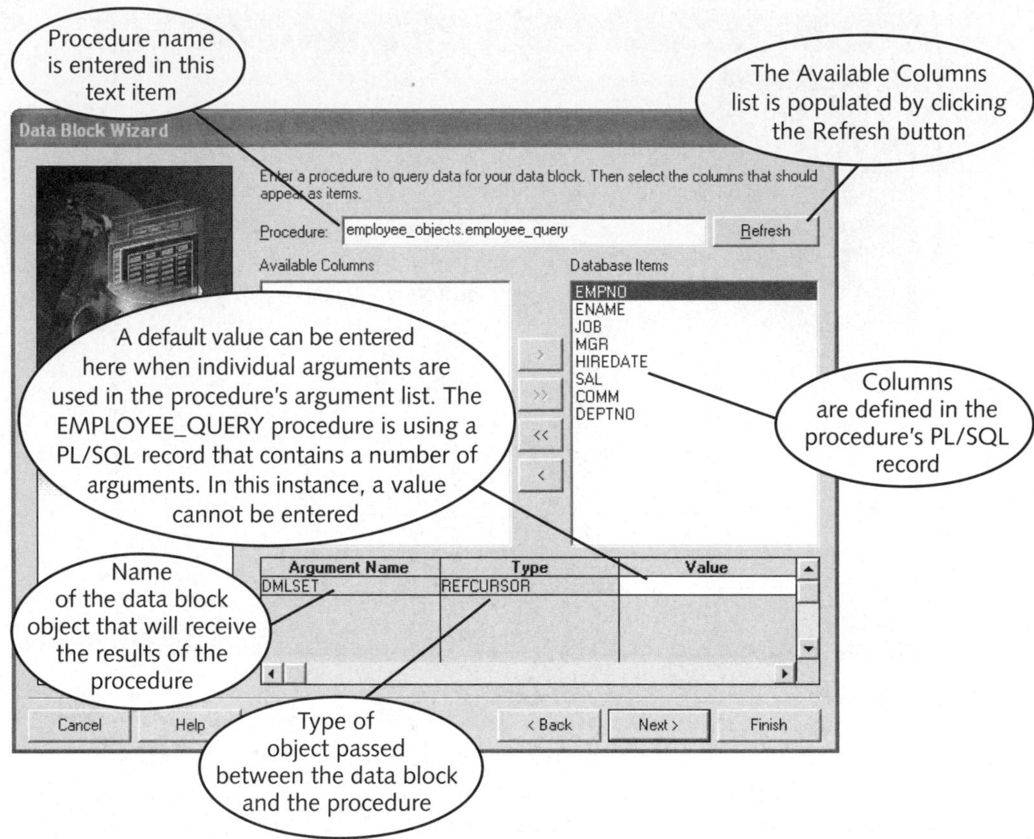

Figure 10-10 Data Block Wizard Query page

The next four pages in the wizard are the Insert, Update, Delete, and Lock pages. They are used to associate procedures to the data block. Figure 10-11 displays the Insert page, which operates like the Query page. You must enter the procedure name and click the Refresh button. If the procedure is found, the PL/SQL attributes are displayed in the list. You may also enter default values into the Value text items.

After associating the procedures to the various pages, the wizard is complete and the data block is created. You can then open the Layout Wizard and format the data block. When you finish the formatting, the form can be executed and used in a way similar to the use of a data block based on a table.

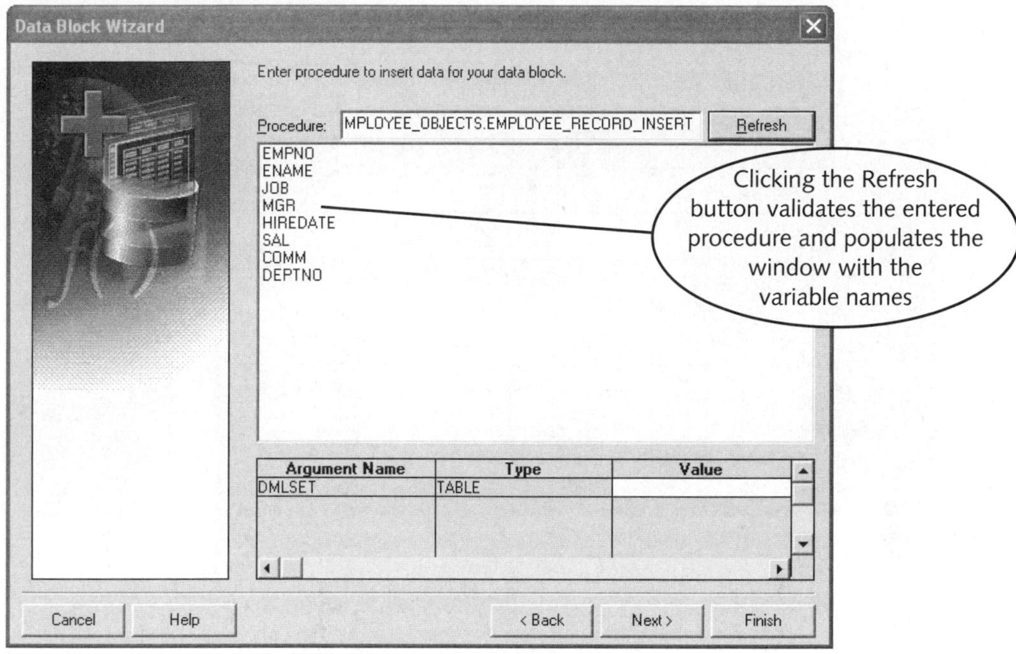

Figure 10-11 Data Block Wizard Insert page

After creating a data block, you can use the data block's Property Palette to add procedures to it. There are five types of procedures that can be associated to the form: Query, Lock, Insert, Update, and Delete. Each of these procedure types has the following three properties:

- **Name**: Identifies the procedure.
- **Columns**: Identifies the items or columns that comprise the PL/SQL record transferred between the data block and the procedure. Each item also has text items for the entry of data type, length, precision, and scale specified. Figure 10-12 illustrates the dialog box used to set these columns.
- **Arguments**: Identifies the device (PL/SQL table, REF cursor) used to transfer the values between the data block and the procedure. Each argument has a Type, Type Name, Mode (i.e., In, Out, In Out), and Value attribute. Figure 10-13 illustrates the dialog box used to set these columns.

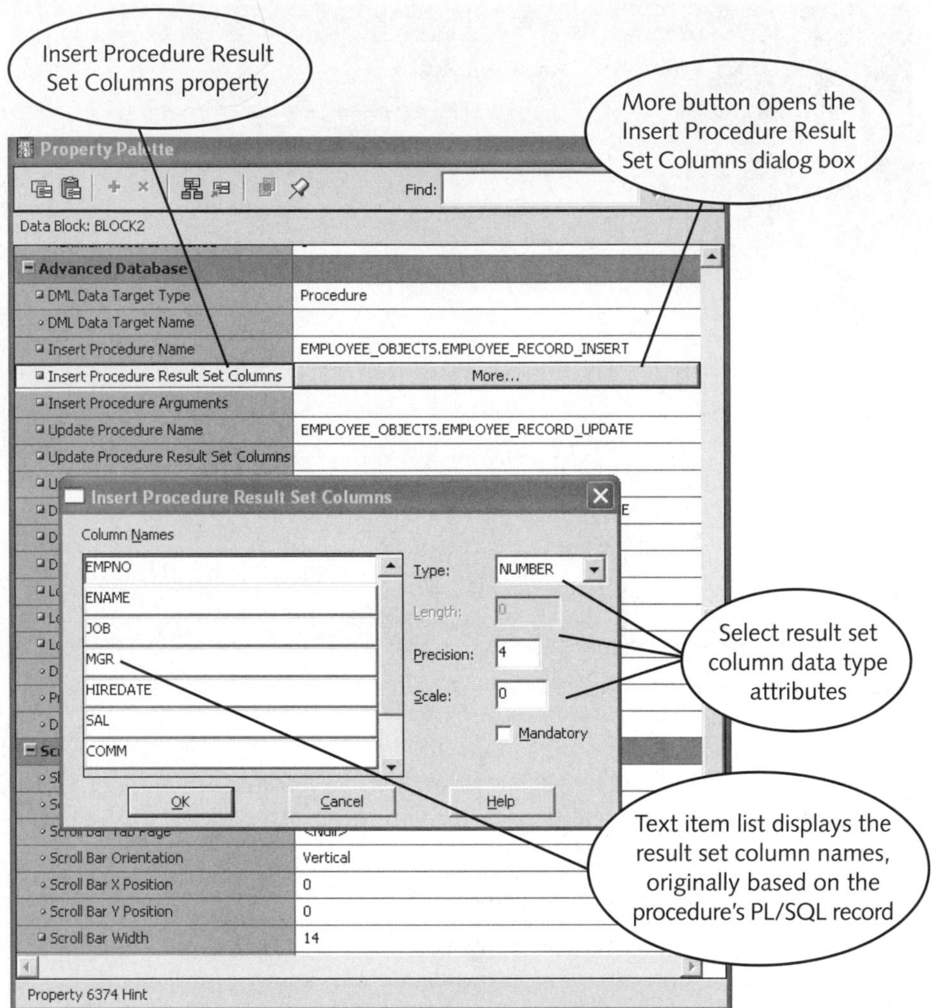

Figure 10-12 Insert Procedure Result Set Columns dialog box used to set column type properties

As practice, create a data block based on procedures using the scripts in the previous section. To accomplish this task, perform the following steps:

1. Open SQL*Plus and create the **EMPLOYEE_OBJECTS** package specification (Listing 10-4) and package body (Listing 10-5).
2. Open the Object Navigator and create a new form module.
3. Open the Data Block Wizard.

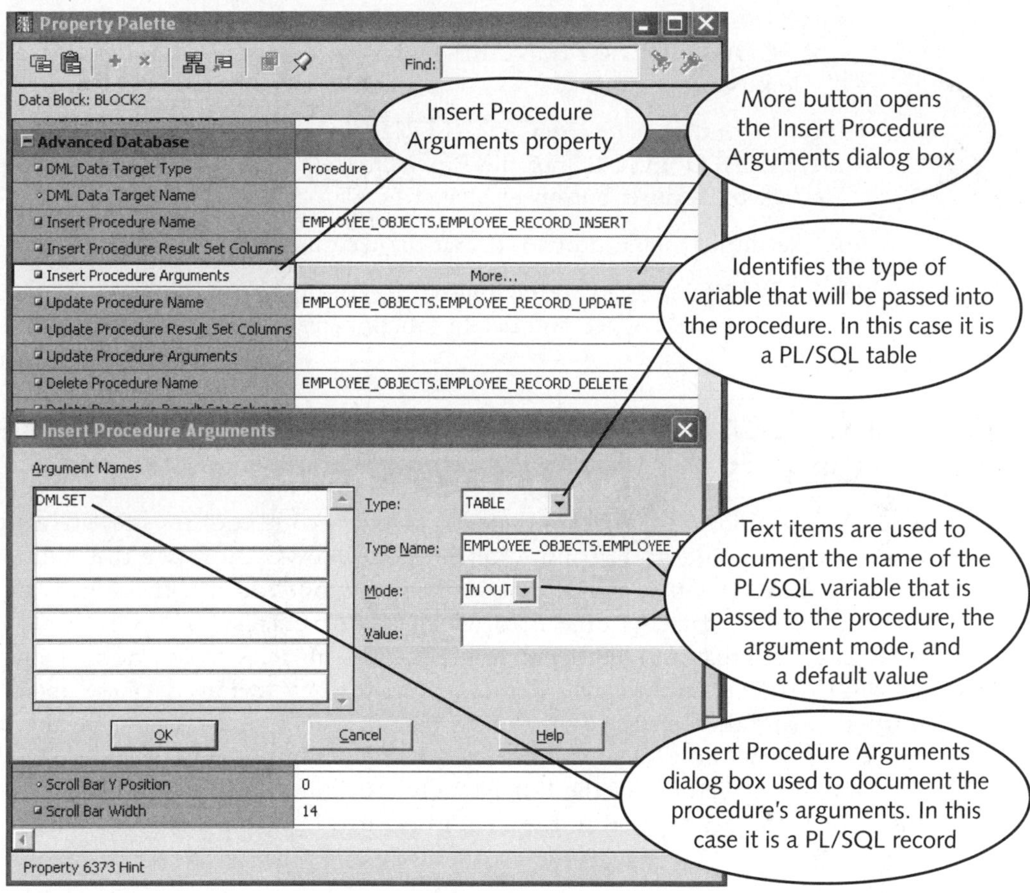

Figure 10-13 Insert Procedure Arguments dialog box used to set column type properties

4. Select the **Stored Procedure** radio button on the Type page. Click **Next**.
5. On the Query page, enter **EMPLOYEE_OBJECTS.EMPLOYEE_QUERY** into the Procedure text box. Click the **Refresh** button. Move all of the columns from the Available Columns drop-down list to the Database Items drop-down list. Click **Next**.
6. On the Insert page, enter **EMPLOYEE_OBJECTS.EMPLOYEE_RECORD_INSERT** into the Procedure text box. Click the **Refresh** button. Click **Next**.
7. On the Update page, enter **EMPLOYEE_OBJECTS.EMPLOYEE_RECORD_UPDATE** into the Procedure text box. Click the **Refresh** button. Click **Next**.

10

8. On the Delete page, enter **EMPLOYEE_OBJECTS.EMPLOYEE_RECORD_DELETE** into the Procedure text box. Click the **Refresh** button. Click **Next**.
9. On the Lock page, enter **EMPLOYEE_OBJECTS.EMPLOYEE_RECORD_LOCK** into the Procedure text box. Click the **Refresh** button. Click the **Finish** button to create the data block.
10. Use the Layout Editor to format the data block.
11. Save the form as **practice1004.fmb.** Run the form and test the data block's query, insert, update, and delete functionality.

Using the Object Navigator to View, Create, and Modify Database Objects

The Object Navigator Database Objects node is a good tool for identifying and maintaining database objects. Expansion of this node allows you to see the additional nodes for the Oracle IDs that are part of your installation. You can investigate any of these nodes to see the database objects to which you have access. The Oracle ID nodes can be expanded so that stored program units, PL/SQL libraries, tables, views, and types nodes are displayed. You can also expand these nodes to view various database objects. You can further expand the objects to see the database triggers assigned to a table, the Instead-Of triggers associated to a view, and the columns that comprise a table. Figure 10-14 depicts the Object Navigator with the Database Objects node expanded so that you can see the Instead-Of trigger assigned to the EMPLOYEE_VIEW that was previously discussed.

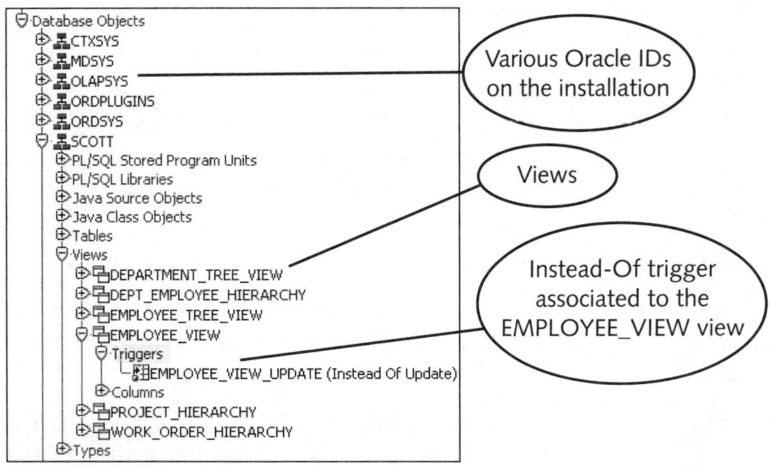

Figure 10-14 Expanded Database Objects node

The Database Objects node enables you to avoid having to log on to SQL*Plus and to issue DESCRIBE commands to identify columns and data types. This saves you time developing forms. The Object Navigator is also a useful tool for creating and maintaining stored procedures. Double-clicking a stored item opens the PL/SQL Editor, which is displayed in Figure 10-15. You can use the editor to modify the PL/SQL object. Notice that the script displayed in Figure 10-15 does not contain the CREATE command that usually precedes the statement. It is not needed because the Save button at the top of the editor compiles and saves the procedure in the database.

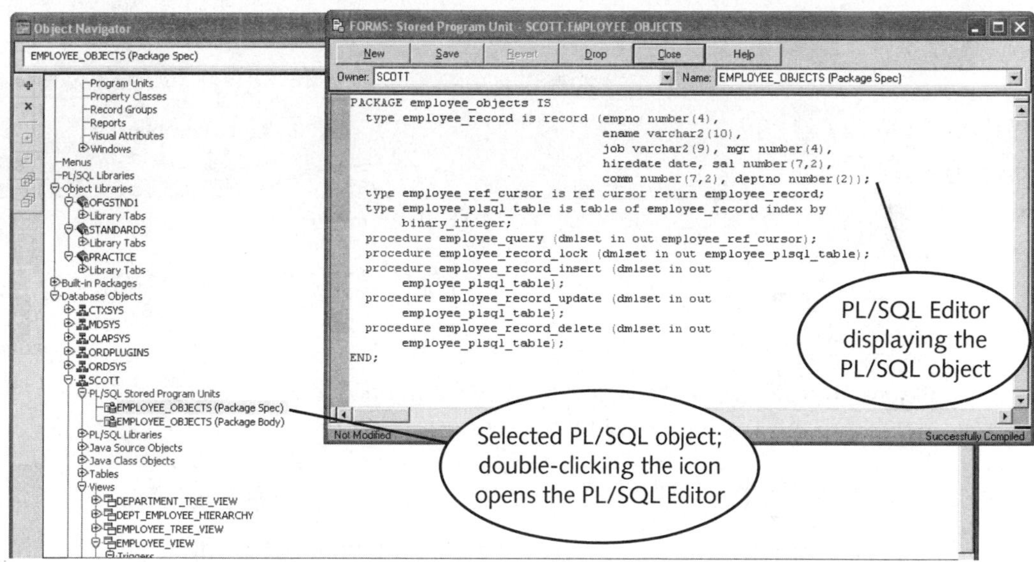

Figure 10-15 PL/SQL Editor displaying the EMPLOYEE_OBJECTS package specification

If the procedure does not compile, errors are displayed at the bottom of the editor. If you want to save the procedure without compiling it, click the Close button. This closes the dialog and saves the procedure in an uncompiled state. Uncompiled procedures can be identified in the Object Navigator by the asterisk appearing to the right of the procedure name as shown in Figure 10-16.

When you need to create database objects even if they are not to be used in a form, the Object Navigator is an effective PL/SQL tool. You will find it a much more effective tool than to create the PL/SQL objects in SQL*Plus.

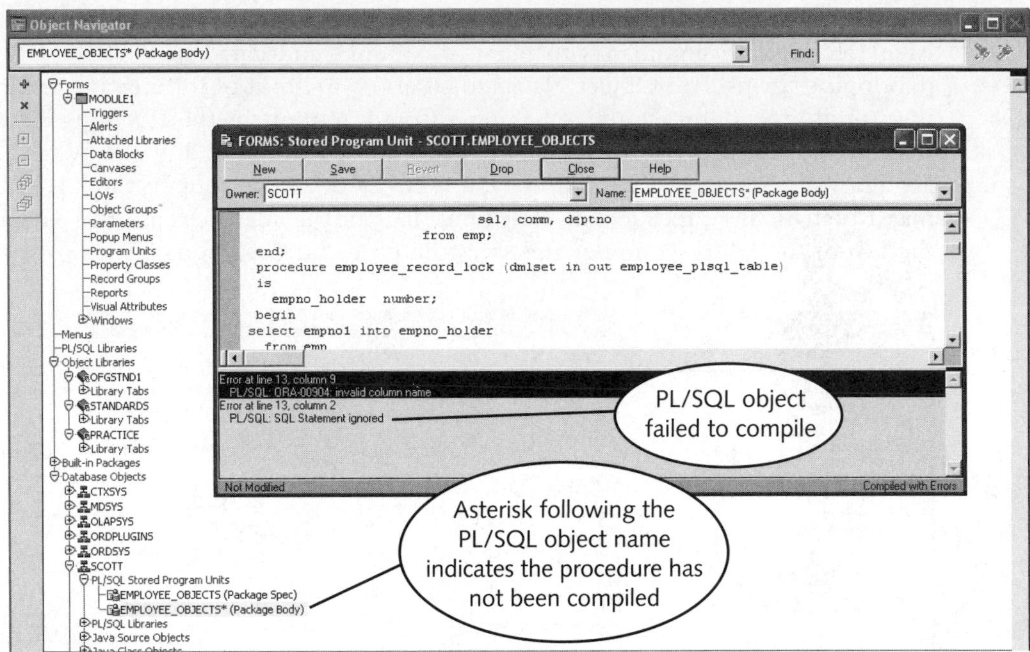

Figure 10-16 Object Navigator displaying an uncompiled procedure

Debugging a Form Manually or with Forms Debugger

As you develop your forms, you can make mistakes that result in your forms not operating as expected. Two different types of errors can occur in an application: A value was not calculated correctly, or the application did not behave as you thought it would. Incorrect code or logic, triggers that failed to fire, or numerous other things cause these errors. When the errors occur, it is your job as a developer to correct the problems. The process of identifying errors and correcting them is called **debugging**.

Regardless of the development tool, debugging is a four-step process:

1. Develop a theory on the cause for the incorrect action or value.
2. Develop a test that proves or disproves the theory. This test should consist of checking values or behaviors that you expect to happen.
3. Perform the test and compare the results to your expected results.
4. If the results prove your theory, correct the condition. If the results do not, return to Step 1.

In the debugging process, developers commonly set up a message that displays at specific times as the code runs. For example, you may have a theory that a trigger is not firing during a procedure. To test your theory, place a message in the trigger, and if the message displays, the trigger has fired. If the message does not display, you can develop another theory for why it didn't fire.

A common problem is failure to enter an IF-THEN construct. A message can be displayed before the construct displaying the IF-THEN evaluation values. This helps you determine whether your code produced a value that can be evaluated in the IF-THEN construct. Perhaps the variable was not populated or an unexpected value was computed. Placing messages in strategic positions can help you determine the flow of the processing steps and the values of variables at these key positions. This is an effective and simple tool for debugging your form.

The Message built-in procedure is the tool of choice, because it sends messages to the status line. The following is a template of several messages that display the evaluation values before entry into an IF-THEN construct. The template also displays text indicating that the application has entered the construct. It typifies the use of messages to debug an application. In addition, Figure 10-17 depicts a form that is displaying the second message indicating that the statements in the IF-THEN construct were executed.


```
Message ('1'||security_value);
If security_value != 'Y' then
      Message ('2 Entered the if construct')
      Show_alert('generic');
```

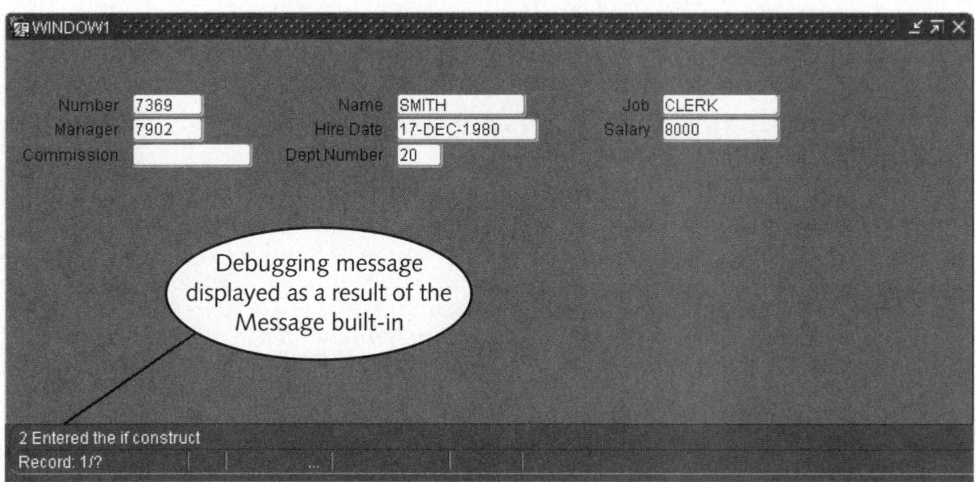

Figure 10-17 Form displaying a debugging message on the status line

The messages have several purposes:

- The first message displays the SECURITY_VALUE value. The developer can determine whether the value is correct or not. The literal "1" was placed at the beginning in the event that SECURITY_VALUE contained a NULL value. The developer would not see the message in this event, because a NULL is blank and the Message built-in does not display NULL values.
- The second message indicates that the application entered the construct.

You will find that using the Message built-in is simple and helpful.

Forms Debugger

Forms Builder has a tool that can be used to debug forms. It is a sophisticated tool that performs the same functions as the message procedure discussed in the previous section. The tool is called Forms Debugger, and it allows you to perform the powerful procedures in the list that follows:

- You can stop the processing at a specific point or statement in the application. At that point, you can inspect the values of all system variables, global variables, and variables that exist within the current trigger or PL/SQL script.
- You can step through the code procedure statement by statement. This helps you identify the flow of the application and to inspect the values as you change steps.
- You can view the code statements currently being executed while simultaneously viewing the form.
- You can change the value of any variable during the debugging process.

Forms Builder Debug Console Window

The Forms Builder Debug Console window is the debugging tool. This window can be opened by:

- Adding a breakpoint to a trigger statement and executing the form using the Run Form Debug tool.
- Adding a breakpoint to a trigger statement and clicking the Debug/Debug Module menu selection.
- Clicking the Debug/Debug Console menu selection.

Forms Debugger was modified with the 9*i* version to make it easier to use. The following section applies to version 9*i* but not to version 6*i*.

The first two items in the preceding bulleted list display the console automatically when a breakpoint is encountered. A **breakpoint** is a designation that tells Forms Builder to halt execution of the form and display the Debug Console window, which can be displayed at any time. No information is displayed in the Debug Console window until the form is suspended due to a breakpoint.

The Debug Console window is depicted in Figure 10-18. The console is actually a series of dialog boxes that display information about the current form. Figure 10-18 illustrates the Debug Console and five of the available debug windows. Four of the windows, Form Values, Global/System Variables, Breakpoints, and Variables are placed (or docked) inside the Debug Console window. The fifth, Stack, is undocked and is a dialog window of its own. The various debug windows can be docked and undocked by clicking the Dock/Undock tool in the top-right corner of the window.

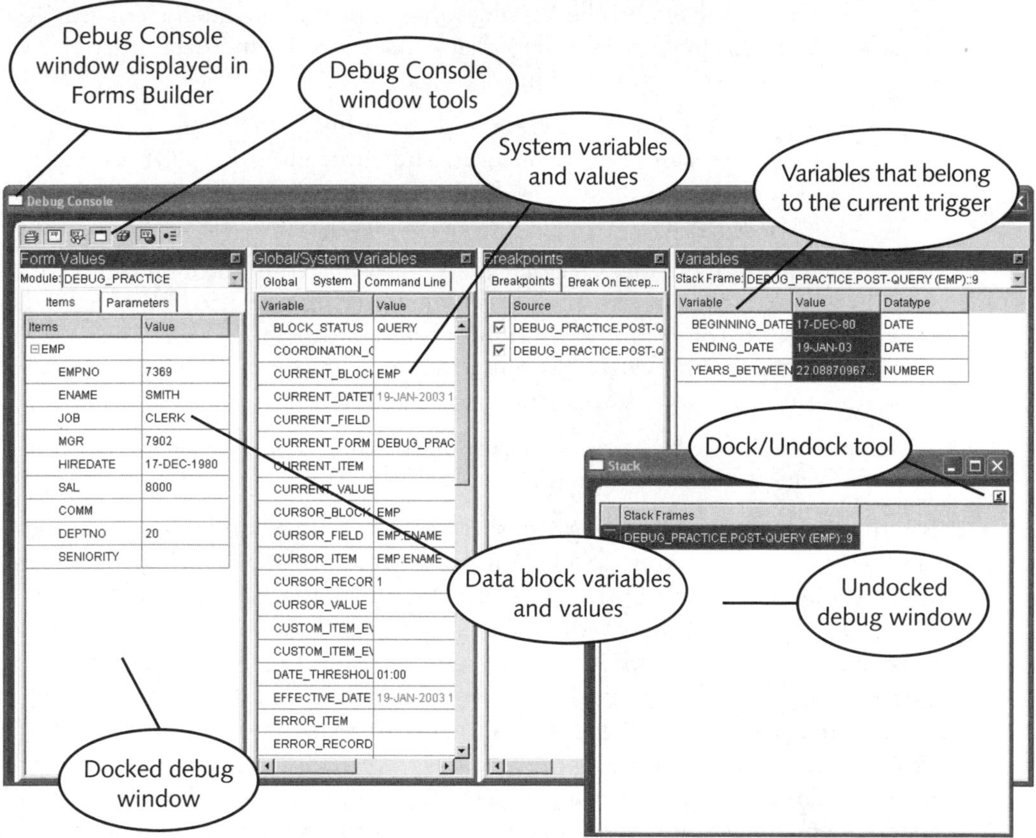

Figure 10-18 Forms Builder Debug Console window

The following list describes the seven different types of debug windows that can be opened in the Debug Console window:

- **Form Values**: Displays the data block items and their current values. These can also be modified by overtyping. This window has tabs at the top. A second tab page exists for form parameters.
- **Global/System Variables**: Contains three tab pages. The pages show global, system, and command-line variables along with their current values. The values can be overtyped.
- **Breakpoints**: Contains two tab pages. The first shows all active breakpoints, which can be enabled and disabled by checking and unchecking the check box. The Break On Exceptions dialog displays various database exception errors. If the check box is checked, the indicated error occurred.
- **Variables**: Shows the variables that exist within the current PL/SQL objects. The window displays the variable name, value, and data type. The value can be modified by overtyping it.
- **Stack**: Displays the current and subordinate PL/SQL objects, such as a trigger or stored program unit. The controlling PL/SQL object is at the top of the list, and the PL/SQL objects that can be called are below the controlling object.
- **Watch**: Contains variables that you want to monitor through the debugging session as the PL/SQL statements are executed. You may add a variable to this window by right-clicking your mouse button over a target variable. This causes a popup menu to appear with an Add to Watch option. Select the option.
- **PL/SQL Packages**: Displays the variables and associated values in PL/SQL packages used by the form.

Before you can use the Debug Console and it's various windows and settings, you must add a breakpoint to your form. This causes the module to halt processing, opens the Debug Console in the Forms Builder IDE, opens the PL/SQL Editor for the current PL/SQL object, and allows you to begin stepping through the various statements while inspecting variables and logic. You can add breakpoints to any PL/SQL script by opening the PL/SQL Editor and double-clicking the gray vertical area to the left of a statement. A red circle appears in the gray area indicating a breakpoint has been set for that statement. You should note that a breakpoint can be placed only on a statement. The breakpoints can be added or removed from a PL/SQL script whenever the Forms Builder IDE is open. Remember that you must add at least one breakpoint to the module or you cannot suspend the module for debugging.

Figure 10-19 illustrates a typical debugging session. The actual form is open in the Web browser but is not displayed in the figure. A query has just been performed and a Post-Query trigger that calculates the number of years between an employee's hiring date (HIREDATE) and the current date is executing. Note the following:

- The Object Navigator is displayed, allowing you to view and inspect any form component.
- The PL/SQL Editor is open and displaying the source code of the Post-Query trigger.
- A breakpoint was added to the Post-Query trigger (a red circle appears in the left area of the editor). This breakpoint is the reason the processing was halted and the Debug Console displayed.
- Below the breakpoint is a right-pointing arrow. This is the Next Statement Indicator. This indicator indicates that the next step that is to be performed is the assignment of a value to the SENIORITY data item in the EMP data block. This step has not yet been performed.
- The Debug Console window is open and displaying the Form Values window and the Variables window.
- The Form Values window is displaying the values of the current EMP data block record. These values were just returned by the latest fetch against the database. Notice that the SENIORITY data block item has not been populated. This has not occurred because the last statement in the Post-Query trigger has not been executed.
- The Variables window is displaying the variables that were defined in the PL/SQL editor (BEGINNING_DATE, ENDING_DATE, and YEARS_BETWEEN).
- The BEGINNING_DATE value is the same as the HIREDATE value in the Form Values window. This indicates that the statement that populated the BEGINNING_DATE value worked correctly.
- The ENDING_DATE value is the same as the current date (19-JAN-03) indicating that the statement that populated that variable worked correctly.
- On the Forms Builder toolbar are several tools, which are described later in this section. The Step Into tool was used to execute the next statement and move the Next Statement Indicator to the next statement. Clicking this tool at this time will cause the SENIORITY value to be computed and the item populated, terminating the trigger.

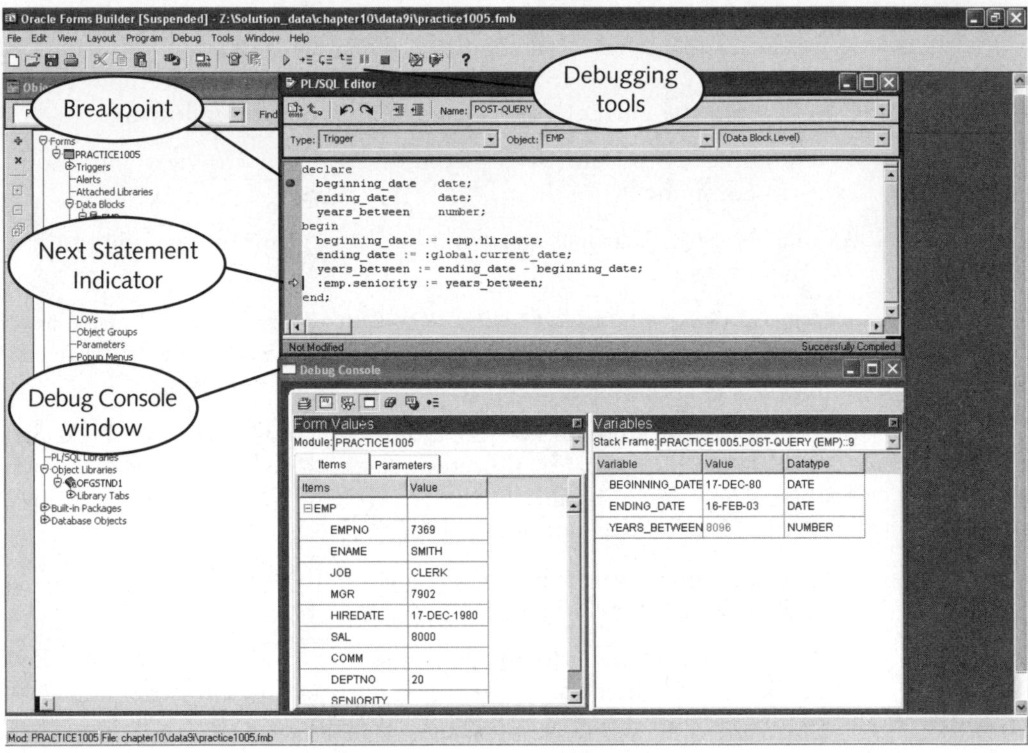

Figure 10-19 Forms Builder IDE and debugging tools displaying a Post-Query trigger

As shown in Figure 10-20, the Forms Builder menu bar holds several tools that are used to debug the form. The tools are enabled and used to control the execution of statements after the form has been halted due to a breakpoint. The following list outlines the functions of these tools:

- **Go**: Terminates the step commands and executes the form beginning with the next statement. The form continues to be executed until a breakpoint is encountered.
- **Step Into**: Executes the current statement and moves the Next Statement Indicator to the next statement. If the next statement is a call to another procedure, Forms Debugger opens and displays the called procedure.
- **Step Over**: Executes the current statement and moves to the next statement in the current procedure. If the next statement is a call to another procedure, Forms Debugger steps over all statements in the called procedure and moves to the next statement in the calling procedure.

- **Step Out**: Moves from statements in a called procedure to the next statement in the calling procedure.
- **Pause**: Stops execution of statements at the current statement.
- **Stop**: Terminates the debugging and also terminates execution of the form.

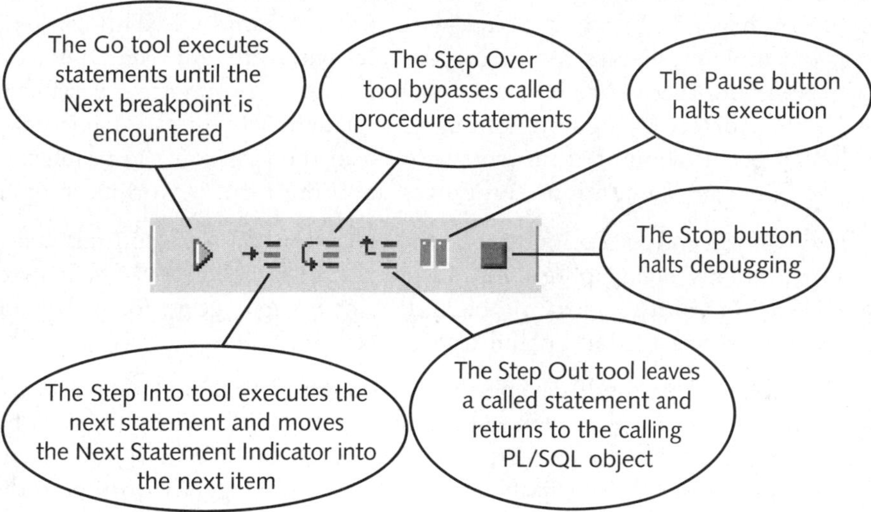

Figure 10-20 Debugger tools

10

Debugging the Form Using the Debug Console Windows

Debugging a form using the Debug Console, in general, is similar to the method for debugging a form with messages that was previously discussed. You must first develop a theory for the form's incorrect results or actions and then test this theory. You use the debugging tool only when you have deduced a possible cause for the problem and are ready to test. The tool does not help you deduce the problem; it simply helps you test to determine whether your deduction is correct.

After identifying the possible cause of an error, you should develop a test case consisting of initial values and expected results. At this point, you can use the debugging tools. The first step is to place a breakpoint as close to the potential problem script as possible. This will save you time by not having to step through many lines of PL/SQL code. If you are having several problems, you may want to add several breakpoints at key statements.

After placing the breakpoints into the form, open the form using the Debug Module menu option or the Run Form Debug tool. When the breakpoint is encountered, you should inspect the values of your target procedure using the Debug Console window and compare these values to those you identified in your test case. If they match the values, you can continue executing statements. If they are incorrect, you have made a mistake in your test case or you have not placed the breakpoint in the proper position, and you must terminate the debugging and evaluate the test case or change the position of the breakpoint.

If the form variables match your test values, execute procedures using the Step tools, following the flow of the statement execution and the variable values. If the flow is not as expected, you have identified a problem with your program logic. This can be caused by a variety of problems, such as comparing variables with different data types, comparing a variable against another variable that is null, or comparing the wrong variables. If a variable value is incorrect, by stepping through the statements you can determine the exact point the value was computed incorrectly. You can then correct the problem or enter a modified value. You can continue this process until the form is working properly.

The ability to suspend execution, watch the execution of steps, and inspect values can help you to quickly debug programs. However, it does not check for incorrect syntax and does not tell you the actual problem. Part of being a good form developer is the ability to hypothesize a situation and test for the conclusion.

As practice, create a Form style data block based on the EMP table. Add a display value that calculates the number of years between the hire date (HIREDATE) and a global variable that has the value of the current date (SYSDATE). Create a When-New-Form-Instance trigger to populate the global variable, and a Post-Query trigger to compute the number of years for each employee displayed in the data block. Add a breakpoint to the Post-Query trigger that suspends execution. Step through the statements and inspect the values. After stepping through the trigger the first time, modify the Post-Query trigger to divide the number of days by 12. Compare the variable values again. To accomplish these tasks, perform the following steps:

1. Create a new form module. Create a data block based on the EMP table. The form should display one record and have a Form style.
2. Open the Layout Editor and add a display item to the form.
3. Double-click the **item** to open its Property Palette and set the following properties:

   Name: **SENIORITY**

   Data Type: **NUMBER**

   Database Item: **NO**

   Prompt: **SENIORITY**
4. In the Layout Editor, double-click the **EMPNO** item. Set the Required property to **NO**.
5. Create a Post-Query trigger under the EMP data block. Use the script depicted in Figure 10-21. Add a breakpoint next to the BEGINNING_DATE variable declaration by double-clicking the vertical gray bar to the left of the statement as depicted in Figure 10-21.

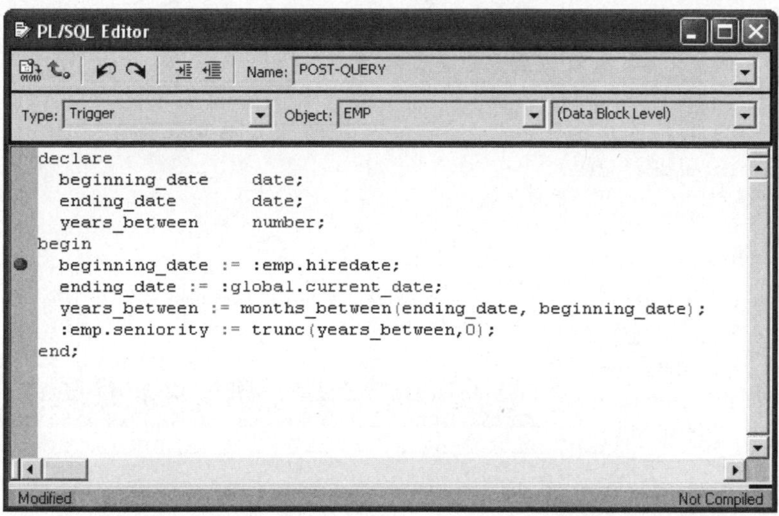

Figure 10-21 Post-Query trigger

6. Click the **Compile PL/SQL Code** button and close the editor.
7. The purpose of this step is to add a global variable to the form, so that it can be depicted in the Forms Debugger console later in the practice. Select the form-level **Triggers** node and click the **Create** tool. Create a When-New-Form-Instance trigger and add the following script to the trigger:

```
:global.current_date := sysdate;
```

8. Save the form as **practice1005.fmb** and execute the form. Execute a query without entering any selection criteria. The form does not return records because it was suspended during the execution of the Post-Query trigger.
9. Open Forms Builder. The Debug Console should be displayed. The Stack window should also be open and displaying a reference to the Post-Query trigger, as shown in Figure 10-22.
10. Click the **Dock** button in the Stack window.
11. Click and dock the **Variables** window.
12. Click and dock the **Form Values** window. It should display a node for the EMP data block. Expand the **EMP** node displaying its data block items and current values.

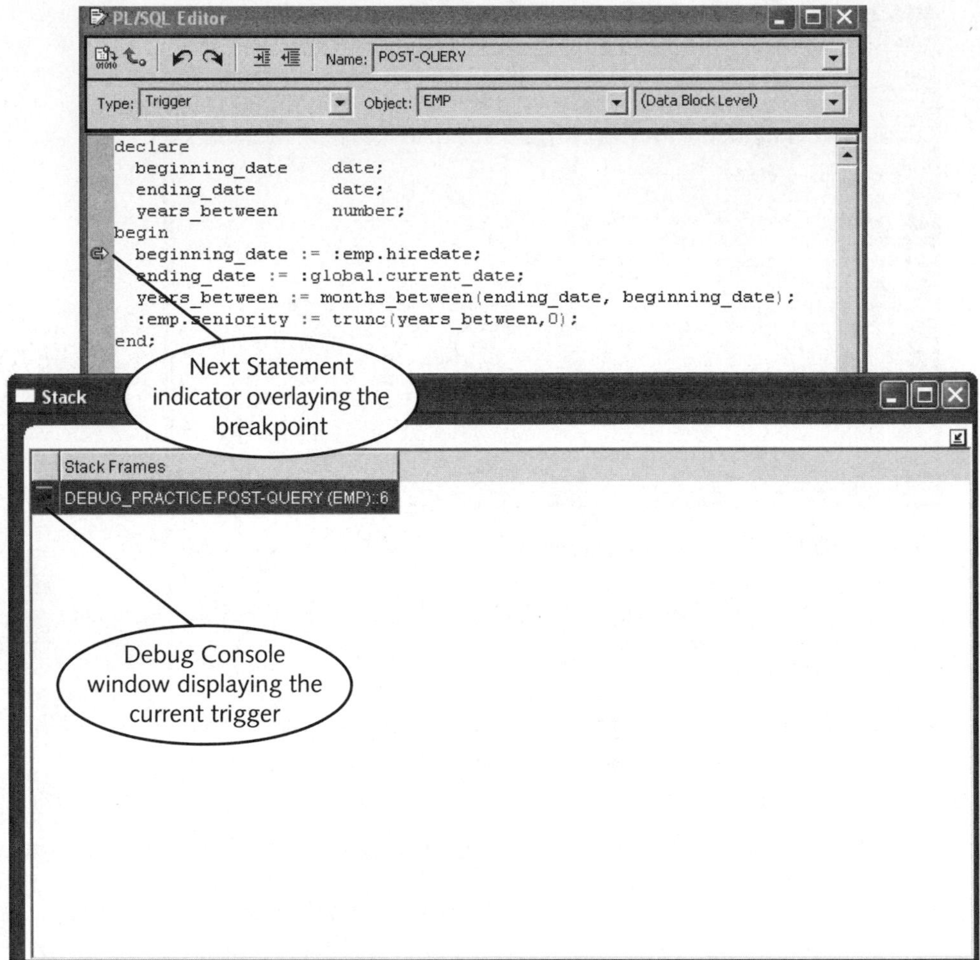

Figure 10-22 A debug window (Stack) immediately after the breakpoint is encountered

13. Click and dock the **Global/System Variables** window. It should display the CURRENT_DATE global variable populated by the When-New-Form-Instance trigger. Figure 10-23 illustrates the Debug Console window after steps 10 through13 have been performed.
14. Arrange the Debug Console and PL/SQL Editor according to Figure 10-23.
15. Notice that the BEGINNING_DATE variable does not have a value. Click the **Step Into** tool. Notice that it now has a value. The Next Statement indicator should be pointing at the ENDING_DATE assignment statement.
16. Notice that the ENDING_DATE variable does not have a value. Click the **Step Into** tool. Notice that the Next Statement indicator moved to the next statement and the ENDING_DATE variable now has the current date as a value.

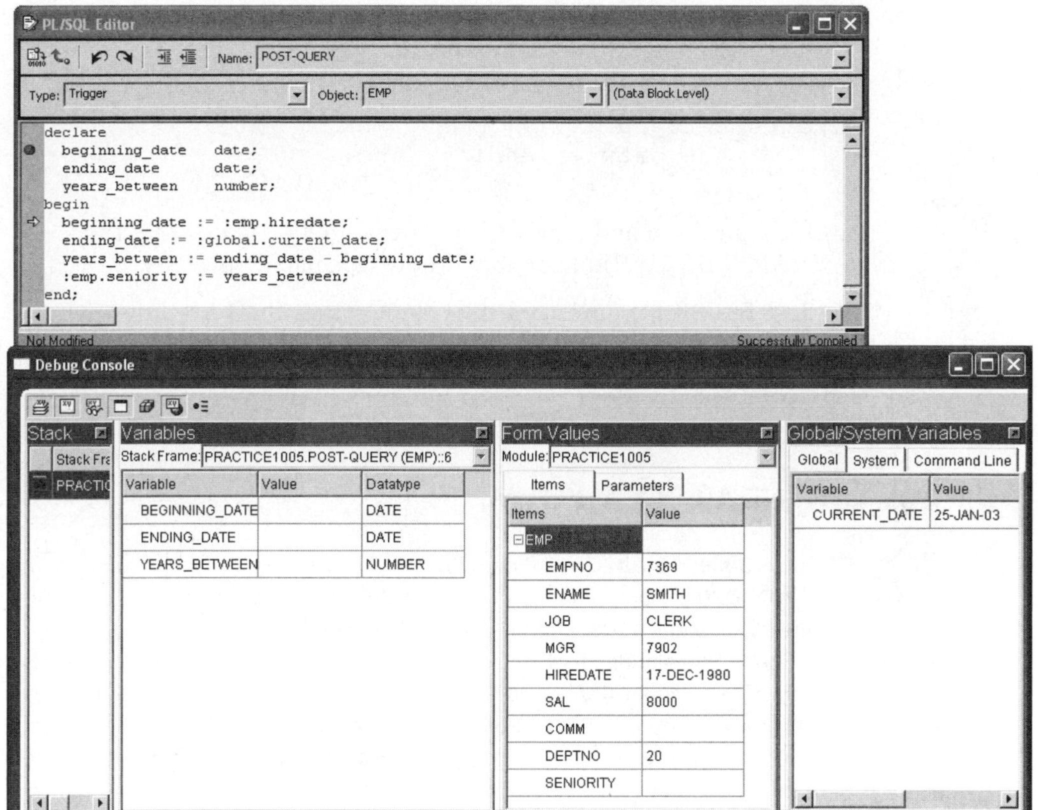

Figure 10-23 Debug Console window after debug windows have been docked

17. Notice that the YEARS_BETWEEN variable does not have a value. Click the **Step Into** tool. Notice that the YEARS_BETWEEN value has been calculated and is greater than 260. This is an incorrect calculation caused by the failure to divide the number of months by 12. This is where the error has occurred.
18. Open the form in the Web browser. Notice that it is in a suspended state and has not displayed the first record. Click the **Go** button in Forms Builder. This causes the form to begin executing statements until it reaches the next breakpoint.
19. Open the form again in the Web browser. Notice that the first record is displayed and the form is displaying the incorrect SENIORITY value. Click the **Next Record** tool. This causes the Post-Query trigger to be fired again. Because the breakpoint is still in this script, the statements are halted. Open Forms Builder. Notice that the Next Statement Indicator is displayed over the breakpoint.

20. Click the **Stop** tool. Close the form and Web browser. Modify the Post-Query script dividing the months between by 12. The statement should appear as shown in the following code segment:

```
Years_between :=
   months_between(ending_date,
                  beginning_date)/12;
```

21. Open the form and repeat steps 9 through 17. Notice that the YEARS_BETWEEN variable is now calculated correctly.
22. Click the **Stop** button and close the form in the Web browser.
23. As an optional practice, run the form in Debug mode and modify the variable in the Debug Console window.

Adding a Calendar to a Form

Form Builder 6*i*, but not Forms Builder 9*i*, has included a package in the **STNDRD20.olb** object library that allows the form operator to open a calendar and select a date. The selected date is then added to a text item. Figure 10-24 illustrates a calendar that returns the selected date into the Hire Date text item. The calendar displays the dates in the form of a calendar and has move buttons. The operator can scroll through the calendar one day or one month at a time. The buttons with the single arrows (> and <) move the selected date forward and backward by one day. The double-arrow buttons (>> and <<) move the selected date forward and backward by one month.

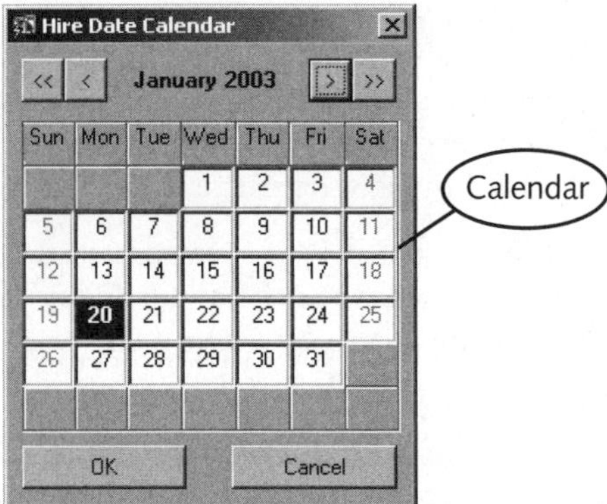

Figure 10-24 Hire Date calendar in Form Builder 6*i*

Calendar Components

To add a calendar(s) to your form, you must add the two necessary components that are outlined in the following list:

- **Calendar object group**: This object contains the data blocks, buttons, and canvases that are needed to display the calendar. This object group is one of the selections in the **STNDRD20.olb** object library.
- **Calendar.pll**: This is a PL/SQL library that provides the calendar mechanics.

When the CALENDAR object group is moved to the form, a large number of form objects are added to the form. If you want to change the default format of the calendar, the objects in the list that follows can be modified:

- Control block named DATE_CONTROL_BLOCK that holds the buttons.
- Control block named DATE_BUTTON_BLOCK that has a button for each day of the month.
- Content canvas named DATE_LOV_CANVAS that displays the calendar.
- Visual attribute named DATE_NORMAL_VA that formats dates that are not selected.
- Visual attribute named DATE_SELECTED_VA that formats the selected date.
- Visual attribute named DATE_WEEKEND_VA that formats the weekend dates.

The Calendar PL/SQL library has a package called Date_lov with procedures that display the calendar and perform other actions. Especially useful is the procedure GET_DATE. This procedure can be placed in a When-Button-Clicked or Key-Listval trigger to display the calendar. The list that follows contains the ten parameters used by this procedure:

- **Calendar date**: The date displayed and selected when the calendar is displayed.
- **Form item**: The form item that receives the selected value.
- **X position**: The horizontal position of the calendar's top-left corner.
- **Y position**: The vertical position of the calendar's top-left corner.
- **Window title**: The title that appears on the calendar.
- **OK button label**: The text that is displayed on the OK button.
- **Cancel button**: The text that is displayed on the Cancel button.
- **Weekend**: Determines whether the weekend dates are colored differently. Boolean values TRUE and FALSE are used in this setting.

- **Autoconfirm**: Causes the date to be sent to the associated form item each time a date is selected. Boolean values TRUE and FALSE are used in this setting.
- **Autoskip**: Causes the input focus to shift to the next navigable item when the calendar is closed. Boolean values TRUE and FALSE are used in this setting.

The following is a template for the GET_DATE procedure that displays the calendar:

```
Date_lov.get_date(calendar date,
                  form item,
                  X position,
                  Y position,
                  Window title,
                  ok button text,
                  cancel button text,
                  Weekend,
                  autoconfirm,
                  autoskip);
```

Creating the Calendar

Creating the calendar is relatively easy compared to many of the tasks that you have seen in this book. To create a calendar you would follow these steps:

1. Locate the CALENDAR.PLL PL/SQL library on your system or on the data disk and attach it to the form. This library is located in the **\tools\devdemo\forms** directory or on the student data disk. If you use the library from the data disk, copy it to a directory on your computer by following these steps:
   a. Select the form Attached Libraries object. Click the Create tool; the Attach Library dialog box displays.
   b. Use the Browse button to open a PL/SQL Library file to locate the **calendar.pll** file and populate the Library text item. Click the Attach button when finished.
   c. An alert displays asking if you want to remove the path from the library. Select the NO option.
2. Find the STRNDRD20, which is located in the Object Libraries node if you used the STRNDRD20 in previous lessons. If it is not there, locate the library and attach it to this node. Open the STRNDRD20 object library in the Object Navigator and locate the CALENDAR object group. Move the CALENDAR object group to the Object Groups node in your form.
3. Format the calendar components.
4. Create a trigger associated to a button, item, or menu to open the calendar. Use the DATE_LOV.GET_DATE procedure as the trigger script.

As practice, add a calendar to the hire date (HIREDATE) item in the form you created in the last practice session. The calendar should be opened by clicking the List of Values function key associated to the HIREDATE item. To accomplish these tasks, perform the following steps:

1. Open the practice form **practice1005.fmb** created in the last practice.
2. Perform the first three steps for creating a calendar from the previous list of steps.
3. Open the Object Navigator and locate the HIREDATE item. Add a Key-Listval trigger to the item by using the following script:

```
date_lov.get_date(sysdate,
                  'emp.hiredate',
                   0, 0,
                  'Hire Date Calendar',
                  'OK', 'Cancel',
                  TRUE, TRUE, FALSE);
```

4. Save the form as **practice1006.fmb.** Open the form and see if the calendar opens when you click the List of Values function key.

WHERE YOU ARE AND WHERE YOU'RE GOING

This chapter completes your study of the most commonly used form features. At this point, you should have the skill to develop a form. The next chapter discusses the use of Oracle's object-oriented database components. With the advent of Oracle8, the database gained object-oriented features such as varrays and nested tables. The next chapter covers the use of these types of objects in a form.

CHAPTER SUMMARY

- A single table seldom has all of the attributes that should be displayed on a data block row. Generally, descriptive information is needed about the attributes.
- Normalized databases generally contain many descriptive tables used to provide information about codes and other associated values.
- Operators can have difficulty interpreting normalized databases without the addition of descriptive data.
- Descriptive information is often brought into a form by using a Post-Query trigger.
- Using a complex view as the data source is another way of bringing descriptive values into a form.
- A From Clause query is another way to bring descriptive values into a form.
- The Post-Query trigger method can have performance problems because of the number of times the form must go to the database for values.

- Descriptive values cannot be used as filter arguments when retrieved from a Post-Query trigger.
- The disadvantages of using a view as a data source include two factors: the view may be dropped, inadvertently causing the disablement of the form; and large numbers of views clutter a database.
- The From Clause query method has the advantage of containing the SELECT statement in the form.
- The Data Block Wizard cannot be used if a From Clause query is the data source.
- A From Clause query is created by setting the Query Data Source Type property to FROM CLAUSE QUERY and adding a SELECT statement to the Query Data Source Name property.
- On-type triggers replace normal form transactions. They can be used to replace the form's LOCK, INSERT, UPDATE, and DELETE statements.
- The Locking Mode property controls when the form locks a database record. The AUTOMATIC and IMMEDIATE settings cause locking to occur as the operator modifies a value. The DELAYED setting occurs when the form actually sends the transaction to the database.
- Whenever you use a From Clause query or view as a data source and intend to issue DML statements from the data block, you must provide for record locking. If you don't, Forms Builder issues an error message.
- You may use an Instead-Of trigger to update complex views. Oracle executes the code in the trigger rather than the statement that fired the trigger.
- Database triggers fire as the result of a database transaction. If a database trigger exists in a data block table, errors can occur if a data block record is modified a second time.
- When updating a table through a view using an Instead-Of trigger, the Key Mode property must be set to UPDATEABLE.
- The data block Query, Insert, Update, Delete, and Lock functions can be produced by stored procedures.
- Placing procedures and functions that affect specific data entities into a package supports the object-oriented concepts of encapsulation and inheritance.
- A REF cursor is a reference to an area of memory that contains the results of a SELECT statement.
- A cursor variable is a set of records returned by a SELECT statement.
- A PL/SQL table is a series of PL/SQL records that have a binary index value.
- REF cursors are used to transfer the results of a SELECT statement from a stored procedure to a form.

- The Data Block Wizard can be used to associate the data block to the stored procedures that perform the query and DML operations.
- The Database Objects node of the Object Navigator can be used to view all database objects. It can also be used to create stored procedures.
- An asterisk appears to the right of the names of uncompiled stored procedures.
- Forms Debugger can be used to troubleshoot your forms. It is opened by selecting the Run Form Debug toolbar tool.
- Applications are debugged by checking values at specific times and observing how the application operates.
- The Message built-in is a tool that is easy to use when debugging a form. Because it can output a message and value at specific times, it enables the developer to determine what is happening during processing.
- Forms Debugger allows the developer to stop the application processing at a specific place that is called a breakpoint.
- When Forms Debugger suspends an application, the developer can execute statements line by line.
- At any point when an application is suspended, the developer can inspect and change global variable, system variable, or stack variable values.
- Oracle has provided a Calendar class in Form Builder 6*i* that can be used to display a calendar in the form.
- The STRNDRD20 object library and the **calendar.pll** PL/SQL library contain the needed components to add a calendar to your form.

Review Questions

1. Match the following terms that have appeared in this chapter with their descriptions:

a. Encapsulation	________	A database trigger that fires as a result of a DML transaction against a view trigger.
b. Date_lov	________	Triggers that replace a form transaction such as an INSERT statement.
c. On-type triggers	________	A reference to an area of memory that contains the results of a SELECT statement. Used to transfer records from a procedure to a form.
d. View	________	An object-oriented concept whereby multiple forms use a common object.

e. * on the right	______________	Forms Debugger buttons that allow the developer to execute statements one at a time.
f. Breakpoint	______________	A data block property that determines when the form locks a database record.
g. FRM-40654: Record has been updated by another user	______________	An object-oriented concept whereby data and the programs that affect it are placed in the same object.
h. Business rules	______________	A data block property that allows the data block to modify a view.
i. REF cursor	______________	A data block property used to document the SELECT statement that is used as a data source.
j. From Clause query	______________	An object-oriented term that represents the programs that modify a specific set of data.
k. Instead-Of trigger	______________	A symbol that indicates that a stored procedure is not compiled.
l. Message built-in	______________	A database object that contains the header information of a set of procedures, functions, and other PL/SQ objects.
m. Step buttons	______________	A data block property value that causes the data block to use a SELECT statement contained within the form as a data source.
n. Locking mode	______________	Programming that enforces the procedures or practices of a company.
o. Query Data Source Name	______________	This stops the form processing to allow the developer to inspect and change values in the application.
p. Package specification	______________	An error that occurs when you attempt to modify a record that has been modified by a database trigger.
q. Stack variables	______________	This allows Forms Debugger to evaluate and react to a specific form condition.
r. Key Mode	______________	A data block property that determines the type of data source used by the block.
s. Debug triggers	______________	Variables that reside in the form trigger and can be inspected in Forms Debugger.

t. Query Data Source Type	________	A PL/SQL object used to transfer a form record to a stored procedure.
u. Inheritance	________	A package procedure that displays a calendar.
v. PL/SQL records	________	A built-in used to display debugging information.
w. Methods	________	A PL/SQL object that consists of a set of attributes, such as those contained in a data block record.
x. PL/SQL tables	________	A SELECT statement that resides in the database and produces a virtual table when it is called.

2. Why do data blocks seldom contain only the items that are stored in a single table?
3. What are the advantages and disadvantages of using a Post-Query trigger to retrieve descriptive values to the data block?
4. What are the advantages and disadvantages of using a view to retrieve descriptive values to the data block?
5. What are the advantages and disadvantages of using a From Clause query to retrieve descriptive values to the data block?
6. What are the advantages and disadvantages of using stored procedures to perform database modifications?
7. What clause do you add to the SELECT statement to lock a record and prevent it from being modified by another user?
8. If you are going to base your data block on a From Clause query and want to perform DML operations, what triggers do you need to add to the data block?
9. What is the purpose of the Key Mode property?
10. Explain what tools you have available to debug a program regardless of the software product you use.
11. Using Forms Builder, how can you determine that a stored procedure has not been compiled? How can you compile the stored procedure?
12. You are developing a form using a trigger to perform a calculation. The trigger is designed to count the number of employees, by department, that have a commission (COMM) greater than 100 and the number of employees with a commission less than 100. The trigger is to then populate two items in the form. When the form is executed, the items are not populated. The following is the troublesome script:

```
Declare
       Comm_high          number;
       Comm_low           number;
       Cursor a is select * from emp
                Where deptno = :dept.deptno;
       A_var   a%rowtype;
```

```
Begin
        Open a;
        Fetch a into a_var;
        While a % found loop
                If a_var.comm > 100 then
                    Comm_high := comm_high + 1;
                Else
                    Comm_low := comm_low + 1;
                End if;
                Fetch a into a_var;
        End loop;
        Close a;
        :dept.high_commissions := comm_high;
        :dept.low_commissions := comm_low;
End;
```

You are not sure if the WHILE loop is executing. You are also not sure what values are computed. Where would you place the Message built-ins to determine whether the loop is being executed and what values are being computed?

13. Explain the procedure you would follow to inspect your application variables as the form is executed.
14. How can you determine whether a breakpoint has been added to your form?
15. Which two libraries are needed to create a calendar?
16. What tools would you use to change the color of the dates in a calendar? How can you ensure that the weekends have a different color than the weekdays?

Exam Review Questions

1. Which data block property value setting causes the data block to act as if it were based on a view?
   a. VIEW QUERY
   b. DYNAMIC VIEW
   c. FROM CLAUSE QUERY
   d. TABLE QUERY
2. Identify three benefits of a From Clause query?
   a. Permanently creates a dynamic view
   b. Reduces the DBA or DA work
   c. Points to a server-side cursor variable
   d. Enhances developer productivity
   e. Points to a server-side dynamic view
   f. Performs complex functions within the database

3. Which is a reason to use a stored procedure in a data block?
   a. The SELECT statement can be specified at runtime.
   b. It reduces the DBA or DA work.
   c. It performs validation within the database.
   d. It performs DML on the client side.
4. You created a form based on a From Clause query. Which type of operation can this data block perform?
   a. DDL
   b. DML
   c. DDL and query
   d. Query
   e. DML and query
5. You have a form with a data block that will be populated by a table that is determined at runtime. Which data source type should be used for this form?
   a. Varray
   b. Nested table
   c. Database table or view
   d. Stored procedure

Hands-on Assignments

1. In this assignment, you create a complex view and use it as the data source of the data block. The view is a join of the DEPT and EMP tables because the data block requires some computed values. In addition, you use Instead-Of triggers to do the following:
   - Insert records into both the DEPT and EMP tables
   - Update values in both the DEPT and EMP tables
   - Delete values from the EMP table

   Perform the following steps:

   a. Open SQL*Plus and create the view displayed in Listing 10-6.

Listing 10-6 DEPARTMENT EMPLOYEES view

```
create or replace view
   department_employees as
   select dept.rowid dept_rowid,
          dept.deptno dept_deptno,
          dept.dname,
```

```
              department_salaries,
              emp.rowid emp_rowid,
              emp.empno, emp.ename,
              emp.hiredate, emp.sal,
              emp.comm, emp.mgr, emp.job,
              emp.deptno emp_deptno
       from dept, emp,
         (select deptno,
            sum(nvl(sal,0)) department_salaries
           from emp
           group by deptno) dept_sal
      where dept.deptno = emp.deptno
        and dept.deptno = dept_sal.deptno;
```

b. Open the Object Navigator and create a new form module.

c. Create a data block based on the DEPARTMENT_EMPLOYEES view. You can locate this view by clicking the **Views** option in the Table dialog box that is opened from the Data Block Wizard Table page. The form should be Tabular and contain 15 rows. Do not display the EMP_DEPTNO, EMP_ROWID, and DEPT_ROWID columns because this is redundant information or needed only for application processing. The form should look similar to Figure 10-25.

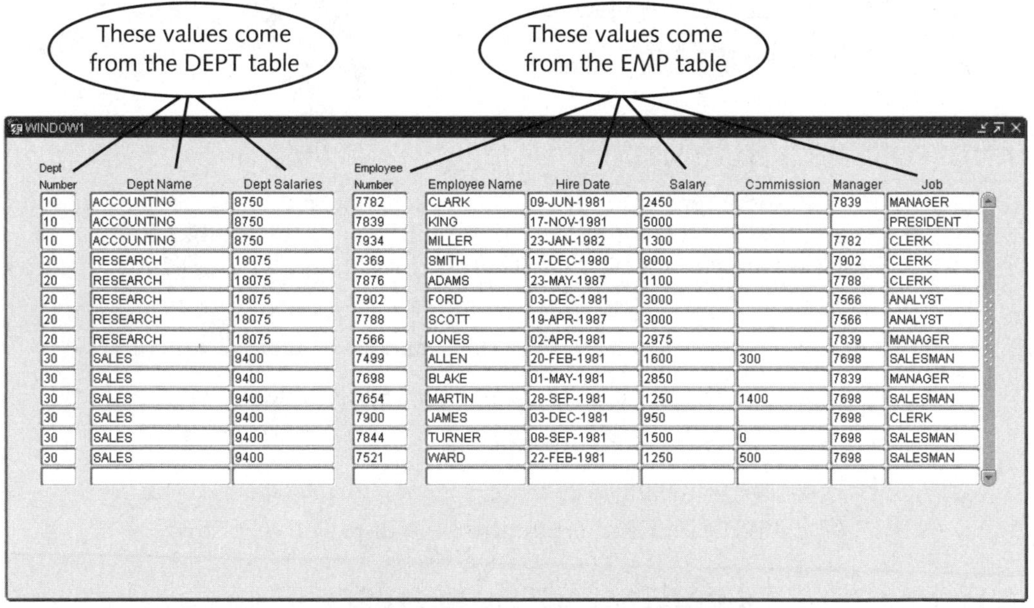

Dept Number	Dept Name	Dept Salaries	Employee Number	Employee Name	Hire Date	Salary	Commission	Manager	Job
10	ACCOUNTING	8750	7782	CLARK	09-JUN-1981	2450		7839	MANAGER
10	ACCOUNTING	8750	7839	KING	17-NOV-1981	5000			PRESIDENT
10	ACCOUNTING	8750	7934	MILLER	23-JAN-1982	1300		7782	CLERK
20	RESEARCH	18075	7369	SMITH	17-DEC-1980	8000		7902	CLERK
20	RESEARCH	18075	7876	ADAMS	23-MAY-1987	1100		7788	CLERK
20	RESEARCH	18075	7902	FORD	03-DEC-1981	3000		7566	ANALYST
20	RESEARCH	18075	7788	SCOTT	19-APR-1987	3000		7566	ANALYST
20	RESEARCH	18075	7566	JONES	02-APR-1981	2975		7839	MANAGER
30	SALES	9400	7499	ALLEN	20-FEB-1981	1600	300	7698	SALESMAN
30	SALES	9400	7698	BLAKE	01-MAY-1981	2850		7839	MANAGER
30	SALES	9400	7654	MARTIN	28-SEP-1981	1250	1400	7698	SALESMAN
30	SALES	9400	7900	JAMES	03-DEC-1981	950		7698	CLERK
30	SALES	9400	7844	TURNER	08-SEP-1981	1500	0	7698	SALESMAN
30	SALES	9400	7521	WARD	22-FEB-1981	1250	500	7698	SALESMAN

Figure 10-25 Department_employees form

d. Open the Object Navigator and open a Property Palette for the EMPNO data block item. Set the Required property to **NO** if it is not already set that way.

e. Open a Property Palette for the DEPT_ROWID and EMP_ROWID items. Set the Maximum Length property to **50**.

f. Save the form as **ch10ex01.fmb.** Open the form and execute a query.

g. Place the form into the Enter Query mode. Retrieve all department and employee records for departments that have a total salary greater than 9500. Enter **# > 9500** in the DEPARTMENT_SALARIES data block item. You should note that this query cannot be performed unless a complex view is used.

h. Modify a record. You should receive the following notice:"FRM-40602 – Cannot Insert Into or Update Data in a View". Close the form.

i. Open the Object Navigator. Open a Property Palette for the DEPARTMENT_EMPLOYEES data block. Set the Key Mode property to **UPDATEABLE**. This eliminates the error message encountered in Step h.

j. Open a Property Palette for the DEPT_ROWID and EMP_ROWID items. Set the Primary Key property to **YES**.

k. Open a Property Palette for the EMP_DEPTNO item. Set the Synchronize With Item property to **DEPT_DEPTNO**. This ensures that this item, which is not displayed, always has the same value as the DEPT_DEPTNO for referential integrity.

l. Using SQL*Plus, create three Instead-Of triggers that perform the DML operations using the script in Listing 10-7.

Listing 10-7 Instead-Of trigger

```
create or replace trigger
  department_employees_update
  instead of update on
    department_employees
for each row
BEGIN
-- Updates the department (DEPT)
-- table based on rowid
  update dept set dname = :new.dname
         where rowid = :new.dept_rowid;
-- Checks to see if an
-- employee record had existed
-- If it existed, the EMP_ROWID
-- item would have a value
-- If it did not, then the
-- department record did not
-- have an associated employee.
-- The employee record
-- must then be inserted
-- into the EMP table
if :new.emp_rowid is not null then
  update emp set empno = :new.empno,
                 ename = :new.ename,
                 hiredate = :new.hiredate,
                 sal = :new.sal,
```

```
                        comm = :new.comm,
                        mgr = :new.mgr,
                        job = :new.job,
                        deptno = :new.emp_deptno
          where rowid = :new.emp_rowid;
        else
          insert into emp
            (empno, ename, hiredate,
             sal, comm, mgr, job, deptno)
          values
            (:new.empno, :new.ename,
             :new.hiredate,:new.sal,
             :new.comm, :new.mgr,
             :new.job, :new.dept_deptno);
        end if;
        end;
        /
        create or replace trigger
          department_employees_insert
        instead of insert on
          department_employees
        for each row
        begin
           declare
           -- This cursor check to see
           -- if the department exists
           -- If it doesn't, then this
           -- is a department insert
             cursor a is
                 select * from dept
                 where deptno = :new.dept_deptno;
             a_var    a%rowtype;
           BEGIN
            open a; fetch a into a_var;
           -- Checks to see if a
           -- department was found
            if a%notfound then
             insert into dept
               (deptno, dname)
             values
               (:new.dept_deptno, :new.dname);
             end if;
             close a;
           -- If an employee number is found,
           -- then this
           -- is a new employee insert
             if :new.empno is not null then
               insert into emp
```

```
          (empno, ename, hiredate,
           sal, comm, mgr, job, deptno)
         values
          (:new.empno, :new.ename,
           :new.hiredate,
           :new.sal, :new.comm,
           :new.mgr, :new.job,
           :new.dept_deptno);
      end if;
    end;
end;
/
create or replace trigger
  department_employees_delete
  instead of delete on department_employees
for each row
begin
  -- This check determines whether
  -- to delete the department
  -- record.  If it has an associated
  -- employee, it cannot
  -- be deleted.  If an associated
  -- employee record exists,
  -- that employee record is deleted
  -- The "old" qualifier is used
  -- because "new" values
  -- do not exist for the Delete statement
  if :old.emp_rowid is null then
    delete from dept
    where rowid = :old.dept_rowid;
  else
    delete from emp
    where rowid = :old.emp_rowid;
  end if;
end;
/
```


m. Save and open the form and test the DML operations performed by the Instead-Of triggers. Perform the following steps:

1. Place a row into the **Insert** mode. Add the following:

   Department Number: **88**

   Department Name: **RETURNS**

2. Save the record. Execute a query and see if the department record was saved.
3. Add an employee to the new department record. Update the following items:

   Employee Number: **8888**

   Employee Name: **Adolph**

Hire Date: **18-JAN-2002**

Salary: **5876**

Commission: **56**

Manager: **7521**

Job: **ANALYST**

4. Save the record. Execute a query and see if the department record was saved.
5. This step tests the On-Update trigger. Navigate to the last row and place one row into the **Insert** mode. Add a new employee for the newly created department by entering the following:

   Department Number: **88**

   Employee Number: **9999**

   Employee Name: **NOAH**

   Hire Date: **29-JAN-2002**

   Salary: **6754**

   Commission: **84**

   Manager: **7521**

   Job: **CLERK**
6. Save the record. Execute a query and see if the record was saved.
7. This step tests the On-Delete trigger. Delete each of the two records that you added. Save the changes and execute a query. The employee records should be removed, but the department record remains.
8. Delete the **department 88** record. Save the transaction and perform a query. The record should be deleted.

n. Save the form as **ch10ex01.fmb**.

2. In this assignment, you follow steps to create the same form as in Hands-on Assignment 1. However you use a From Clause query to retrieve the data and On-type triggers to perform the DML transactions. Much of the code in this assignment can be copied from the triggers created in Hands-on Assignment 1.

   a. Open the Object Navigator and create a new form module.

   b. Create a canvas. Name it **MAIN_CANVAS**.

   c. Create a block. Open the new block and set the following properties:

   Name: **DEPARTMENT_EMPLOYEES**

   Database Data Block: **YES**

   Number of Records Displayed: **15**

   Key Mode: **UPDATEABLE**

   Query Data Source Type: **FROM CLAUSE QUERY**

   Query Data Source Name: Use the following SELECT statement (Listing 10-8):

Listing 10-8 SELECT statement used in the Query Data Source Name property

```
select dept.rowid dept_rowid,
       dept.deptno dept_deptno,
       dept.dname,
       department_salaries,
       emp.rowid emp_rowid, emp.empno,
       emp.ename,emp.hiredate,
       emp.sal, emp.comm, emp.mgr,
       emp.job,emp.deptno emp_deptno
  from dept, emp,
     (select deptno,
             sum(sal) department_salaries
      from emp
      group by deptno) dept_sal
 where dept.deptno = emp.deptno
   and dept.deptno = dept_sal.deptno
```

d. Create 13 new items under the data block.

e. Name the items as follows: **DEPT_ROWID**, **DEPT_DEPTNO**, **DNAME**, **DEPARTMENT_SALARIES**, **EMP_ROWID**, **EMPNO**, **ENAME**, **HIREDATE**, **SAL**, **COMM**, **MGR**, **JOB**, and **EMP_DEPTNO**.

10

f. Open multi-item Property Palettes for the items and set the following properties:

   Database Item: **YES**

   Canvas: **MAIN_CANVAS**

g. Open multi-item Property Palettes for the EMP_DEPTNO, DEPT_ROWID, and EMP_ROWID items. Set the following properties:

   Canvas: **NULL**

   Primary Key: **YES** (EMP_ROWID and DEPT_ROWID only)

h. In this step, you set the Data Type and Maximum Length properties for each data block item. The data block properties must conform to the corresponding data source type and length values, as specified in the database. Add an appropriate PROMPT value to each item. The following are the data block items to be modified and the proposed Data Type and Maximum Length property settings:

DEPT_ROWID:	CHAR	50
DEPT_DEPTNO:	NUMBER	2
DNAME:	CHAR	14
DEPARTMENT_SALARIES:	NUMBER	10
EMP_ROWID:	CHAR	50
EMPNO:	NUMBER	4
ENAME:	CHAR	10
HIREDATE:	DATE	
SAL:	NUMBER	7

COMM:	NUMBER	4
MGR:	NUMBER	4
JOB:	CHAR	9
EMP_DEPTNO.:	NUMBER	2

i. Open the Layout Wizard and set the Prompt properties. Open the Layout Editor and format the canvas to look like Figure 10-25.

j. Save the form as ch10ex02.fmb. Open the form and execute a query. It should return records.

k. Open the Object Navigator and create an On-Lock trigger under the DEPARTMENT_EMPLOYEES block. Use the following script:

```
Null;
```

l. Create an On-Insert trigger under the DEPARTMENT_EMPLOYEES block. The script is the same as the DEPARTMENT_EMPLOYEES_INSERT trigger, except that the "NEW" reference is changed to the name of the data block. Use the script in Listing 10-9.

Listing 10-9 On-Insert trigger

```
begin
   declare
   -- This cursor check to
   -- see if the department exists
   -- If it doesn't then this
   -- is a department insert
     cursor a is
       select * from dept
       where deptno = :
         department_employees.dept_deptno;
     a_var   a%rowtype;
   BEGIN
    open a; fetch a into a_var;
   -- Checks to see if a
   -- department was found
    if a%notfound then
    insert into dept
      (deptno, dname)
     values
       (:department_employees.dept_deptno,
        :department_employees.dname);
     end if;
     close a;
   -- If an employee number is found,
   -- then this
   -- is a new employee insert
     if :department_employees.empno
           is not null then
```

```
        insert into emp
         (empno, ename, hiredate,
          sal, comm, mgr, job, deptno)
        values
         (:department_employees.empno,
          :department_employees.ename,
          :department_employees.hiredate,
          :department_employees.sal,
          :department_employees.comm,
          :department_employees.mgr,
          :department_employees.job,
          :department_employees.dept_deptno);
      end if;
    end;
end;
```

m. Create an On-Update trigger under the DEPARTMENT_EMPLOYEES block. The script is the same as the DEPARTMENT_EMPLOYEE_UPDATE trigger, except that the "NEW" and "OLD" references are changed to the name of the data block. Listing 10-10 contains the script.

Listing 10-10 On-update trigger

```
BEGIN
-- Updates the department (DEPT)
-- table based on rowid
  update dept set
    dname = :department_employees.dname
  where rowid = :department_employees.dept_rowid;
-- Checks to see if an employee
-- record had existed
-- If it existed, the EMP_ROWID item
-- would have a value
-- If it did not, then the department
-- record did not
-- have an associated employee.
-- The employee record
-- must then be inserted into the EMP table
if :department_employees.emp_rowid
    is not null then
  update emp set
    empno = :department_employees.empno,
    ename = :department_employees.ename,
    hiredate = :department_employees.hiredate,
    sal =:department_employees.sal,
    comm = :department_employees.comm,
    mgr = :department_employees.mgr,
    job = :department_employees.job,
    deptno = :department_employees.emp_deptno
```

```
    where rowid = :department_employees.emp_rowid;
  else
    insert into emp
      (empno, ename, hiredate,
       sal, comm, mgr, job, deptno)
    values
      (:department_employees.empno,
       :department_employees.ename,
       :department_employees.hiredate,
       :department_employees.sal,
       :department_employees.comm,
       :department_employees.mgr,
       :department_employees.job,
       :department_employees.dept_deptno);
  end if;
  end;
```

n. Create an On-Delete trigger under the DEPARTMENT_EMPLOYEES block. The script is the same as the DEPARTMENT_EMPLOYEE_UPDATE trigger, except that the "NEW" and "OLD" references are changed to the name of the data block. Listing 10-11 contains the script.

Listing 10-11 On-Delete trigger

```
begin
  -- This check determines whether to delete the department
  -- record.  If it has an associated employee, it cannot
  -- be deleted.  If an associated employee record exists
  -- that employee record is deleted
  -- The "old" qualifier is used here because "new" values
  -- do not exist for the Delete statement
  if :department_employees.emp_rowid is null then
    delete from dept
    where rowid = :department_employees.dept_rowid;
  else
    delete from emp
    where rowid = :department_employees.emp_rowid;
  end if;
end;
```

o. Save and open the form and test the triggers. Perform Hands-on Assignment 1, Step k tests.

3. In this assignment, you create the same form. However, you use stored procedures to perform the query and DML operations. Much of the code in this assignment can be copied from the triggers created in Hands-on Assignment 1. Perform the following:

   a. Open the Object Navigator and expand the Database Objects node.

b. Locate your ID (i.e., Scott). Expand your ID, displaying the various database objects you own.

c. Select the PL/SQL **Stored Program Units** node and click the **Create** tool on the toolbar.

d. The New Program Unit dialog box opens. Select the **Package Spec** radio button and name the object **DEPT_EMP_PACKAGE**.

e. The PL/SQL window opens. Use the script in Listing 10-12.

Listing 10-12 DEPT_EMP_PACKAGE package specification

```
PACKAGE dept_emp_package IS
  type dept_emp_record is record
       (dept_rowid char(18),
        dept_deptno dept.deptno%type,
        dname dept.dname%type,
        department_salaries number,
        emp_rowid char(18),
        empno emp.empno%type,
        ename emp.ename%type,
        hiredate emp.hiredate%type,
        sal emp.sal%type,
        comm emp.comm%type,
        mgr emp.mgr%type,
        job emp.job%type,
        emp_deptno emp.deptno%type);
  type dept_emp_ref_cursor is
     ref cursor return dept_emp_record;
  type dept_emp_table is
     table of dept_emp_record
       index by binary_integer;
  procedure dept_emp_query
    (dmlset in out dept_emp_ref_cursor);
  procedure dept_emp_lock
    (dmlset in out dept_emp_table);
  procedure dept_emp_insert
    (dmlset in out dept_emp_table);
  procedure dept_emp_update
    (dmlset in out dept_emp_table);
  procedure dept_emp_delete
    (dmlset in out dept_emp_table);
END;
```

f. Compile and save the package specification. Create another Stored Program Unit object. This is the DEPT_EMP_PACKAGE package body. Use the script in Listing 10-13.

10

Listing 10-13 DEPT_EMP_PACKAGE package body

```
PACKAGE BODY dept_emp_package IS
 procedure dept_emp_query (dmlset in out dept_emp_ref_cursor)
 is
 begin
      open dmlset for
         select dept.rowid dept_rowid,
              dept.deptno dept_deptno, dept.dname,
         department_salaries, emp.rowid emp_rowid,
         emp.empno, emp.ename,
         emp.hiredate, emp.sal, emp.comm,
         emp.mgr, emp.job,
         emp.deptno emp_deptno
      from dept, emp,
         (select deptno, sum(sal) department_salaries
          from emp
          group by deptno) dept_sal
          where dept.deptno = emp.deptno(+)
          and dept.deptno = dept_sal.deptno(+);
 end;
 procedure dept_emp_lock (dmlset in out dept_emp_table)
 is
 begin
      null;
 end;
 procedure dept_emp_insert (dmlset in out dept_emp_table)
 is
   cursor a is select * from dept
         where deptno = dmlset(1).dept_deptno;
   a_var   a%rowtype;
 BEGIN
   open a; fetch a into a_var;
   if a%notfound then
     insert into dept
       (deptno, dname)
     values
       (dmlset(1).dept_deptno, dmlset(1).dname);
   end if;
   close a;
   if dmlset(1).empno is not null then
     insert into emp
      (empno, ename, hiredate,
       sal, comm, mgr, job, deptno)
     values
      (dmlset(1).empno, dmlset(1).ename, dmlset(1).hiredate,
       dmlset(1).sal, dmlset(1).comm, dmlset(1).mgr,
       dmlset(1).job, dmlset(1).dept_deptno);
   end if;
 end;
 procedure dept_emp_update (dmlset in out dept_emp_table)
```

```
  is
  begin
    update dept set dname = dmlset(1).dname
      where rowid = dmlset(1).dept_rowid;
    if dmlset(1).emp_rowid is not null then
      update emp set empno = dmlset(1).empno,
            ename = dmlset(1).ename,
            hiredate = dmlset(1).hiredate,
            sal = dmlset(1).sal,
            comm = dmlset(1).comm,
            mgr = dmlset(1).mgr,
            job = dmlset(1).job,
            deptno = dmlset(1).emp_deptno
      where rowid = dmlset(1).emp_rowid;
    else
      insert into emp
       (empno, ename, hiredate,
        sal, comm, mgr, job, deptno)
      values
       (dmlset(1).empno, dmlset(1).ename, dmlset(1).hiredate,
        dmlset(1).sal, dmlset(1).comm, dmlset(1).mgr,
        dmlset(1).job, dmlset(1).dept_deptno);
    end if;
  end;
  procedure dept_emp_delete (dmlset in out dept_emp_table)
  is
  begin
    if dmlset(1).emp_rowid is null then
      delete from dept
      where rowid = dmlset(1).dept_rowid;
    else
      delete from emp
      where rowid = dmlset(1).emp_rowid;
    end if;
  end;
 END;
```

g. Open the Object Navigator and create a new form module.

h. Open the Data Block Wizard. On the Type page, select the **Stored Procedure** radio button. Click **Next**.

i. On the Query page, enter **DEPT_EMP_PACKAGE.DEPT_EMP_QUERY** in the Procedure text item.

j. Click the **Refresh** button to populate the Available Columns drop-down list.

k. Move all of the available columns to the Database Items drop-down list. Click **Next**.

l. On the Insert page, enter **DEPT_EMP_PACKAGE.DEPT_EMP_INSERT** in the Procedure text item.

m. Click the **Refresh** button to ensure your entry was correct. Click **Next**.

n. On the Update page, enter **DEPT_EMP_PACKAGE.DEPT_EMP_UPDATE** in the Procedure text item.

o. Click the **Refresh** button to ensure that your entry was correct. Click **Next**.

p. On the Delete page, enter **DEPT_EMP_PACKAGE.DEPT_EMP_DELETE** in the Procedure text item.

q. Click the **Refresh** button to ensure that your entry was correct. Click **Next**.

r. On the Lock page, enter **DEPT_EMP_PACKAGE.DEPT_EMP_LOCK** in the Procedure text item.

s. Click the **Refresh** button to ensure that your entry was correct. Click **Next**.

t. Complete the wizard and open the Layout Wizard. Create a Tabular style layout with 15 records. The DEPT_ROWID, EMP_ROWID, and EMP_DEPTNO items should not be displayed.

u. Save the form as **ch10ex03.fmb.** Open the form and test the triggers. Perform Hands-on Assignment 1, Step k tests.

4. In this assignment, you debug a form using the Message built-in. In the Review Question section, Question 12 requested that you identify places in a Post-Query trigger in which you should add the Message built-in to determine whether a WHILE loop was being executed. This assignment consists of placing the messages into the script and determining the problem. To accomplish these tasks, perform the following steps:

   a. Open the Object Navigator and create a new form module.

   b. Create a data block using the DEPT table. The style of the data block should be Tabular and display 10 records.

   c. Open the Layout Editor and add two display items to the canvas.

   d. Open a Property Palette for the first display item. Set the following properties:

      Name: **HIGH_COMMISSIONS**

      Data Type: **NUMBER**

      Database Item: **NO**

      Prompt: **COMMISSION > 100**

   e. Open a Property Palette for the second display item. Set the following properties:

      Name: **LOW_COMMISSIONS**

      Data Type: **NUMBER**

      Database Item: **NO**

      Prompt: **COMMISSION < 100**

   f. Open the Object Navigator and create a Post-Query trigger under the DEPT block. Use the Listing 10-14 script. It is the same script as in Review Question 12.

Listing 10-14 Post-Query trigger

```
Declare
        Comm_high       number;
        Comm_low        number;
        Cursor a is select * from emp
                 Where deptno = :dept.deptno;
        A_var    a%rowtype;
Begin
        Open a;
        Fetch a into a_var;
        While a % found loop
                If a_var.comm > 100 then
                   Comm_high := comm_high + 1;
                Else
                   Comm_low := comm_low + 1;
                End if;
                Fetch a into a_var;
        End loop;
        Close a;
        :dept.high_commissions := comm_high;
        :dept.low_commissions := comm_low;
End;
```


g. Save the form as **ch10ex04.fmb.** Operate the form and verify that the LOW_COMMISSIONS and HIGH_COMMISSIONS items are not populated.

h. Open a PL/SQL Editor for the Post-Query trigger.

i. You must determine if the trigger is firing. Place the following statement after the Begin keyword:

```
Message ('Trigger has fired');
```

j. You must determine if the application has entered the WHILE loop. Place the following statement after the Loop keyword:

```
Message ('Entered the while loop');
```

k. You must determine if the application can enter the IF-THEN-ELSE construct. Place the following script immediately after the Then keyword:

```
Message ('Entered the first part of the If statement,
                  High comm is '||comm_high);
```

l. You must determine if the application can enter the ELSE section of the IF-THEN-ELSE construct. Place the following script immediately after the Else keyword:

```
Message ('Entered the second part of the If statement,
Low Comm is '||comm_low);
```

m. Save and open the form. Place the form into the Enter Query mode. Enter **40** into the DEPTNO item. Department 40 has only one employee. This minimizes the number of records that will be displayed and the number of messages you see. Execute the query and watch the messages.

n. You should see the following messages. The first two will be displayed in alerts requiring your acknowledgement. The final will appear on the status line.

   TRIGGER HAS FIRED

   ENTERED THE WHILE LOOP

   ENTERED THE SECOND PART OF THE IF STATEMENT, LOW COMM IS

o. By analyzing the messages, you know that the trigger was fired, the WHILE loop was executed, and the condition in the IF-THEN-ELSE construction was evaluated and found to be false, and the ELSE statements were executed. The last message was supposed to have the value of COMM_LOW concatenated to the end of the message. Because this value is missing, you know that the value of COMM_LOW is NULL. This indicates a problem with the calculation. On looking at the calculation, you realize that the COMM_HIGH and COMM_LOW variables have never been initialized to 0. Oracle cannot perform a calculation using NULL values. If the COMM_HIGH and COMM_LOW variables are initialized in the DECLARE statement, the problem is fixed.

p. Change the COMM_HIGH and COMM_LOW declare statements, so that they are assigned a value of **0** at declaration (i.e., COMM_HIGH number := 0).

q. Execute the **form** and determine if the problem has been fixed. Delete the Message statements in the Post-Query trigger and save the form for the next assignment.

5. In this assignment, you perform the same analysis as in Hands-on Assignment 4 using the Forms Debugger rather than the Message built-in.

   a. Open form module **ch10ex04.fmb**.

   b. Open the Object Navigator and locate the Post-Query trigger. It will be located on the Triggers node under the DEPT data block. Double-click its **icon** to open the PL/SQL Editor.

   c. Add a **breakpoint** in the left gray bar on the same row as the "Open a;" statement. Close the PL/SQL Editor.

   d. Run the form by clicking the **Run Form Debug** tool.

   e. Execute a query on the form. This causes the Debug Console to appear in Forms Builder. The Next statement Indicator should be positioned over the breakpoint, which is placed on the "Open a;" row.

f. Open the **Variables** window. Expand the A_VAR PL/SQL record so that you can see all of the record's variables and values. Notice that none of the variables has a value at this time.

g. Arrange the windows so that the PL/SQL Editor and the Post-Query trigger are displayed above the Debug Console in Debug mode.

h. Click the **Step Into** tool. Notice that the Next Statement Indicator moves above the breakpoint to the "Cursor a" row. This is caused by executing the "Open a;" statement which is populating the cursor. It is showing the actual statement that is to be performed.

i. Click the **Step Into** tool and the Next Statement Indicator moves to the FETCH statement row. Notice that none of the variables have been populated at this time.

j. Click the **Step Into** tool. The Next Statement Indicator moves to the WHILE A%FOUND statement. Notice that the A_VAR PL/SQL variables have now been populated. You should especially notice the value of the COMM variable. If it is blank or NULL, the ELSE statement will be executed, because a NULL value cannot be evaluated with an equal operator (=). If it is not NULL, either the COMM_HIGH and COMM_LOW variables will be populated.

k. Click the **Step Into** tool several times until the Next Statement Indicator is on the second FETCH statement. Review the value of the COMM_HIGH and COMM_LOW variables as you step through the IF-THEN-ELSE structure. Notice that they are NULL.

l. At this point, either the COMM_HIGH or COMM_LOW values should have a value of 1. Use the following to determine which variable should have been populated:

- If the COMM value is NULL, the ELSE statement was executed and the COMM_LOW variable should be 1.
- If the COMM value is less that 100, the ELSE statement was executed and the COMM_LOW variable should be 1.
- If the COMM value is greater than 100, the IF statement was executed and the COMM_HIGH variable should be 1.

m. Review the COMM_LOW and COMM_HIGH variables. Notice that they are blank. This is incorrect and indicates that something is wrong with either the COMM_LOW or COMM_HIGH statements. In Step k, you should have determined that the values of COMM_HIGH and COMM_LOW were blank or NULL. In PL/SQL, a NULL value used in a calculation always results in NULL. Thus, the values of COMM_HIGH and COMM_LOW must be NULL because their initial values were NULL. This is the cause of the missing value problem. To solve the problem, you must initialize the COMM_HIGH and COMM_LOW variables with 0.

n. Click the **Stop** tool to terminate the debugging action.

o. Open the Object Navigator and open a PL/SQL Editor for the Post-Query trigger. Change the COMM_HIGH and COMM_LOW variable declarations to the following:

```
Comm_high          number := 0;
Comm_low           number := 0;
```

p. Repeat steps d through g. Notice that the COMM_HIGH and COMM_LOW variables now have values. Continue the debugging and notice that the COMM_HIGH and COMM_LOW values are populated correctly.

q. Save the form.

CASE PROJECT: GREAT STATE ELECTRIC BUDGETING SYSTEM

You essentially completed the Budgeting system in the Chapter 9 Case Project. At this point in the system development life cycle, you actually begin unit testing. Programmers perform unit testing by exercising the forms to find problems that exist in the forms. When the unit testing is complete, the applications are sent to a stakeholder for a system test. This system testing is performed in the Chapter 11 Case Project.

In this Case Project, your first task is to unit test the various tab pages in the application. Determine if the screens are the proper size, whether projects can be reassigned to an engineer, whether buttons work, or whether popup menus are displayed. Try to manipulate the forms in ways you would never expect a user would do. An old programmer's axiom is "You can't make a system foolproof because fools are so ingenious." At this step, you need to be a fool and do something ingenious.

Defects exist in the application, and you should try to identify as many as you can. Most of the defects are minor, but there is one glaring problem that you correct in this chapter's Case study. When you are finished with your unit test, perform the remaining steps in this section to correct the major defect that you probably have identified.

One major problem with the application is on the WORK_ORDERS tab page. The WORK_ORDER_DATA data block displays work orders and work order costs. One of the functions on this screen is to assign and approve the work order. If you have attempted to perform these functions, you noticed the error message: FRM-40501. This error message is generated because the data block is based on a From Clause query, and On-type triggers have not been defined for the data block. In this Case Project, you create the triggers that allow you to update values in this data block. You also create triggers that inform the user that he cannot add or delete a work order from this block. Perform the following steps:

a. Open the Budgeting application. Locate the WORK_ORDER_DATA data block in the Object Navigator.

b. Create an On-Update trigger for the WORK_ORDER_DATA data block. Use the Listing 10-15 On-Update trigger script.

Listing 10-15 On-Update trigger

```
begin
  update work_orders set
    wo_description =
     :work_order_data.wo_description,
    wo_location =
     :work_order_data.wo_location,
    assigned_to =
     :work_order_data.assigned_to,
    approved_by =
     :work_order_data.approved_by
  where work_order_id =
     :work_order_data.work_order_id;
exception
     when others then
       bell;
       message ('You were not able
                 to update the record.
                 Try again or contact
                 a DBA');
end;
```


c. Create an On-Lock trigger for the WORK_ORDER_DATA data block. Use the Listing 10-16 script.

Listing 10-16 On-Lock trigger script

```
declare
   wo  work_orders.work_order_id%type;
begin
   select work_order_id
     into wo
   from work_orders
   where work_order_id =
          :work_order_data.work_order_id
   for update;
 exception
   when others then
     bell;
     message ('You are not able to
              lock the record.  Try
              again or call a DBA');
end;
```

d. Create a Pre-Insert trigger for the WORK_ORDER_DATA data block that notifies the user that he cannot add records using this data block. Use the Listing 10-17 script.

Listing 10-17 Pre-Insert trigger script

```
declare
     alert_button      number;
begin
     set_alert_property('generic',
                         alert_message_text,
                        'You may only
                         insert work orders
                         on the project tab page');
     alert_button := show_alert('generic');
     raise form_trigger_failure;
end;
```

e. Create a Pre-Delete trigger for the WORK_ORDER_DATA data block that notifies the user that a work order cannot be deleted. Use the Listing 10-18 script.

Listing 10-18 Pre-Delete trigger script

```
declare
  alert_button      number;
begin
  set_alert_property
        ('generic',
         alert_message_text,
         'You may not
          delete work orders from the system');
  alert_button := show_alert('generic');
end;
```

f. Create an Alert object. Open a Property Palette for the object and set the following properties:

   Name : **GENERIC**

   Title: **ERROR MESSAGE**

   Button 2 Label: **BLANK**

g. The WORK_ORDER_DATA data block PROJECT_ID and WORK_ORDER_ID items are text items. This allows the user to enter values into the items even though the On-Update trigger does not modify the values. It is more professional if a user can never tab into these items. Change the Item Type property to **DISPLAY ITEM** for the PROJECT_ID and WORK_ORDER_ID items in the WORK_ORDER_DATA data block.

h. Save the form. Execute the form and test the triggers that you added to the WORK_ORDER_DATA data block.

CHAPTER

11

USING FORMS WITH AN OBJECT DATABASE, ON THE WEB, AND WITH JAVA

In this chapter you will:

- Learn the basics of Oracle's object-oriented technology and use this technology in an Oracle form
- Use object tables and REF columns in a form
- Learn the basics of the Oracle Forms Server
- Practice various Web design techniques
- Use Java with forms and bean areas to display Java controls
- Use Java classes in your forms

As the roadmap (Figure 11-1) shows, this is the last chapter. In this chapter, you receive an overview of Oracle object technology that was first implemented with the release of the Oracle8 database. You learn to create objects, embed them into tables, and modify the object values in a form. The chapter also discusses Web performance and format considerations and concludes with an explanation of using Java in a form.

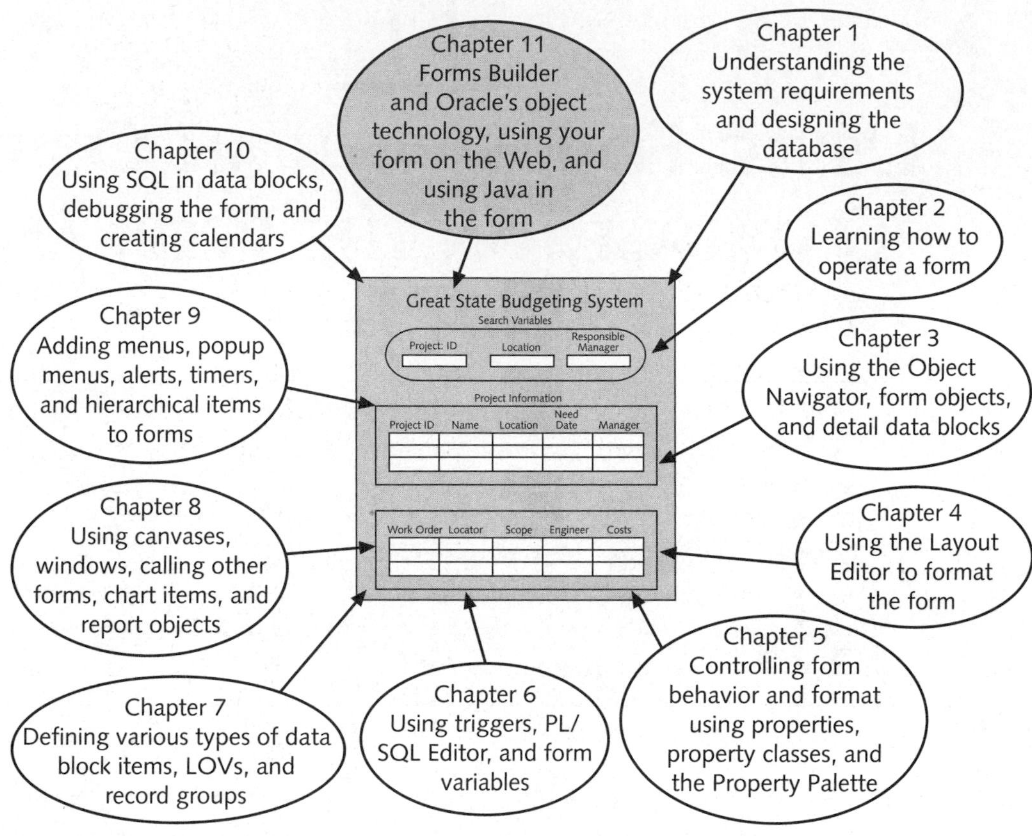

Figure 11-1 Roadmap

USING ORACLE'S OBJECT-ORIENTED TECHNOLOGY IN A FORM

Chapter 10 presented the use of packages to hold the variables, cursors, and procedures that access data. Placing the objects into a package supports the concept of encapsulation. Using the same objects in many different forms is a concept named inheritance. The Oracle database also has additional object-oriented features that affect the storage and use of data. The Oracle database allows you to define **abstract data types (ADTs)**, which are sets of related variables that can be used to store data. The beauty of ADTs is that the same ADT can be embedded into multiple tables, thereby eliminating the need to continually identify the same sets of attributes for each new system.

To illustrate, Oracle has a special type declaration that creates an object. An **object** is a set of related attributes that describe something. The attributes street number, city, state, and zip code describe an address. You can create an ADDRESS ADT containing these attributes and use it in many other objects. For example, the same ADDRESS ADT can be used in a customer, faculty, vendor, or student entity or table because they all require the same address variables. ADTs are in reality building blocks. A developer identifies an object (ADT) and the attributes that describe the object (ADDRESS). The developer can then use different objects to create higher-level objects.

Figure 11-2 illustrates this concept. The figure depicts four different objects, as follows, each of which can be defined as an object type in an Oracle database:

- **PERSON**: A collection of attributes that describe a person (last name, first name, birth date, Social Security number, and gender).
- **ADDRESS**: A collection of attributes that describe an address (street, city, state, and zip code).
- **FACULTY_MEMBER**: A higher-level object that contains attributes unique to a faculty member, such as faculty ID and college. This object also inherits the attributes from the PERSON and ADDRESS objects.
- **CUSTOMER**: A higher-level object that contains attributes that are unique to a customer, such as customer ID and credit limits. This object also inherits the attributes from the PERSON and ADDRESS objects.

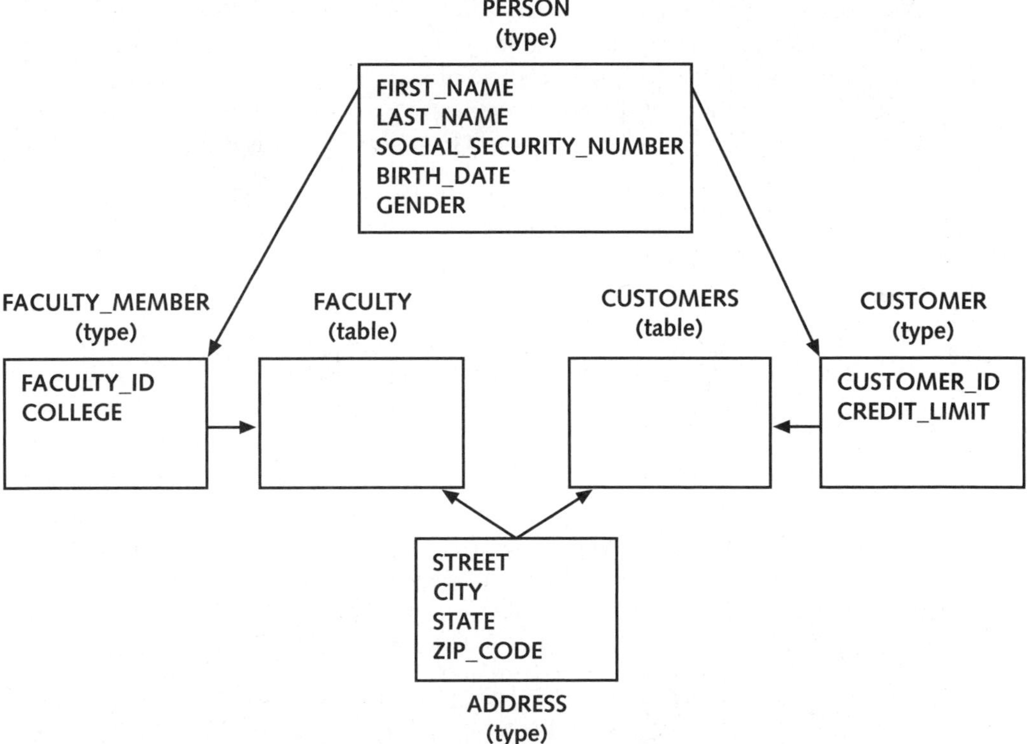

Figure 11-2 Object diagram describing relationships between PERSON, ADDRESS, FACULTY_MEMBER, and CUSTOMER objects

The diagram illustrates how higher-level objects can be developed using lower-level objects. You should also notice that the higher-level objects FACULTY_MEMBER and CUSTOMER use the same lower-level components. This feature is called inheritance. **Inheritance** allows for reusability, which enables you as the developer to design once and use often. That is one of the main benefits of Oracle's objects. A second feature is that changes made to an object propagate through all the higher objects that use the lower-level objects. For example, if a county attribute is added to the ADDRESS object, the county attribute is available to the CUSTOMER and FACULTY_MEMBER objects.

Notice that the diagram also depicts tables. The types must eventually be assigned to a table record in order for Oracle to save values. As in the case of Figure 11-2, the ADTs or object types are simply definitions or declarations. They do not have the ability to store data. When the ADT is associated to a table record, the ADT attributes are added to the table record and the attributes are available for the storage of the values as a part of the table record.

You should also notice that the PERSON type was associated to other object types, whereas the ADDRESS type was associated to tables, because the PERSON type attributes are unique to the FACULTY_MEMBER and CUSTOMER objects. However, the ADDRESS attributes may repeat. A FACULTY_MEMBER or CUSTOMER may have several addresses (for example, regular address or summer home). To save multiple occurrences of the object type attributes, the object type must exist in its own table that allows multiple occurrences of the type to repeat. The repeating types are associated to the parent record by a special value called a REF column that is discussed later in this chapter.

In the previous example, you saw the use of an object type (PERSON) and an object table (CUSTOMERS). There are several other ADTs, but only the object type and object table are supported by Forms Builder. The different types of ADTs are listed as follows:

- **Object type**: A definition of a set of related attributes, such as an address or the attributes that describe an employee
- **Varrays**: An array of values
- **Object table**: A table of objects that contains a pointer to a record in another table
- **Nested table**: A table of objects that are nested inside another table

Object Types

The basic object-oriented component is an object type. An **object type** is a set of columns that can be used in various other components (Refer to Figure 11-2). The benefit of including a type in another object, such as a table, is that if the type changes, all tables that use the type also change. The developer does not have to locate and modify each table independently. (Modifying a type is demonstrated in Hands-on Assignment 3 at the end of this chapter.)

Object types are easy to create. The syntax is the same as the PL/SQL type declarations for a PL/SQL record or table that you encountered in Chapter 10. Listing 11-1 is an object type definition for an ADDRESS object.

Listing 11-1 Object type definition

```
Create or replace type address as object
(street   varchar2(20),
City      varchar2(20),
State     char(2),
Zip_code varchar2(5));
/
```

After the object type has been created, you can embed it into a table. To illustrate, the Listing 11-2 script creates FACULTY and STUDENT tables, both of which use the ADDRESS object type in their attributes. This demonstrates the inheritance value of the object type.

Listing 11-2 CREATE TABLE statements using the ADDRESS object type

```
Create table faculty
(faculty_id              number primary key,
 name                    varchar2(20),
 employment_date         date,
 faculty_address         address);
Create table student
(student_id             number primary key,
 student_name           varchar2(20),
 enrollment_date        date,
 advisor                number references faculty,
 student_address        address);
```


Using the Object Type in a Form

Accessing and using the object type within SQL and PL/SQL can be difficult. You generally have to create a procedure that has a PL/SQL record based on the type. The procedure then brings the values into this record using a cursor. However, Forms Builder makes it easier to use object types. You can use the Data Block Wizard to create the data block. The Data Block Wizard treats the object type variables exactly the same as any other table variable and also creates a data block item for the variable. It also creates the SELECT, INSERT, UPDATE, and DELETE statements that can be used to modify the values.

To illustrate, Figure 11-3 depicts the Data Block Wizard Table page. The FACULTY table is selected on the page. Notice the FACULTY_ADDRESS attribute. This is the table attribute based on the object type. It has an expansion tool on its left. The tool allows you to expand the FACULTY_ADDRESS attribute and select as many of the object type attributes as you need by simply moving them to the Database Items Items list. This is really no different than creating a normal data block based on a table.

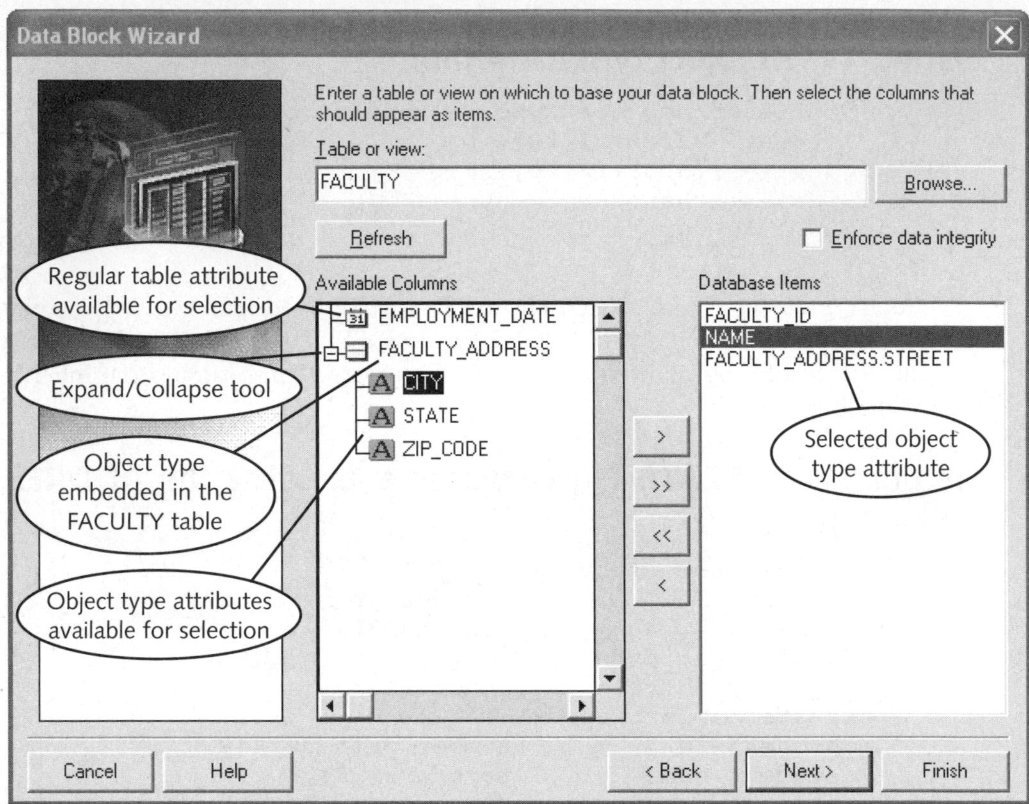

Figure 11-3 Data Block Wizard Table page displaying object type attributes

The Layout Editor also treats the object type attributes like any other attribute and attempts to create an item for each attribute in the data block. Figure 11-4 shows the Layout Wizard's Items page. Notice that the object type attributes are displayed.

After the form is created, you can perform all the normal operations on the object type attributes. You will not even know that variables in the table are from an inherited object. Figure 11-5 depicts a form displaying a data block based on the FACULTY table.

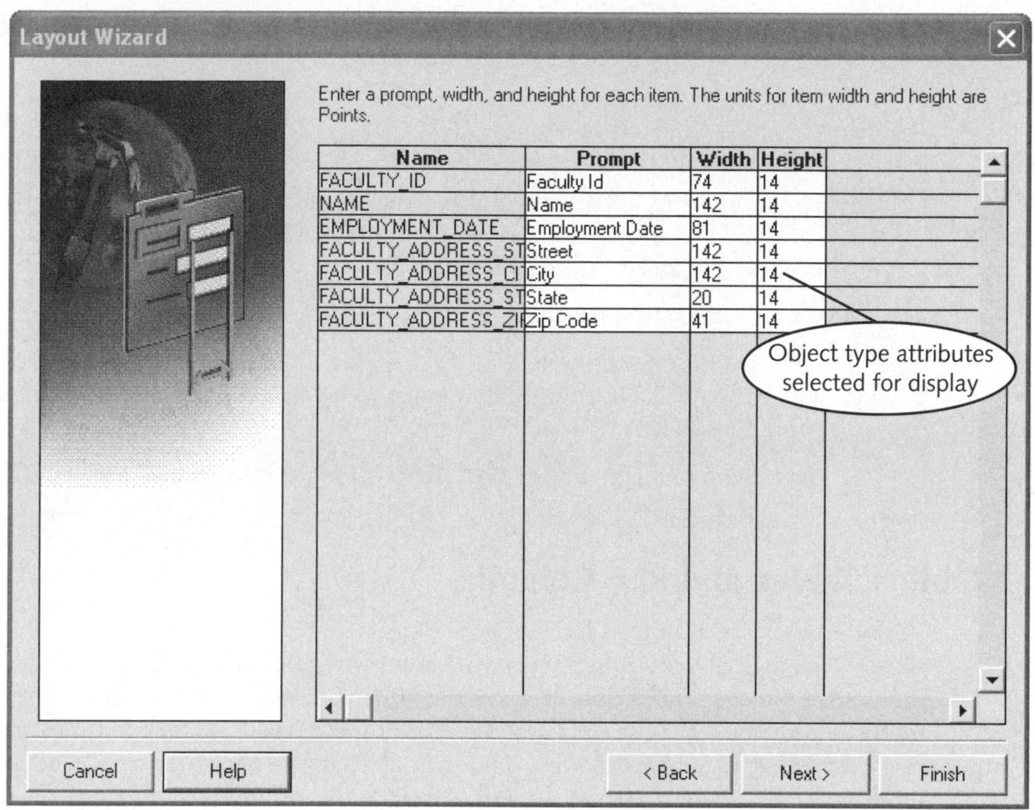

Figure 11-4 Layout Editor Items page listing object type attributes

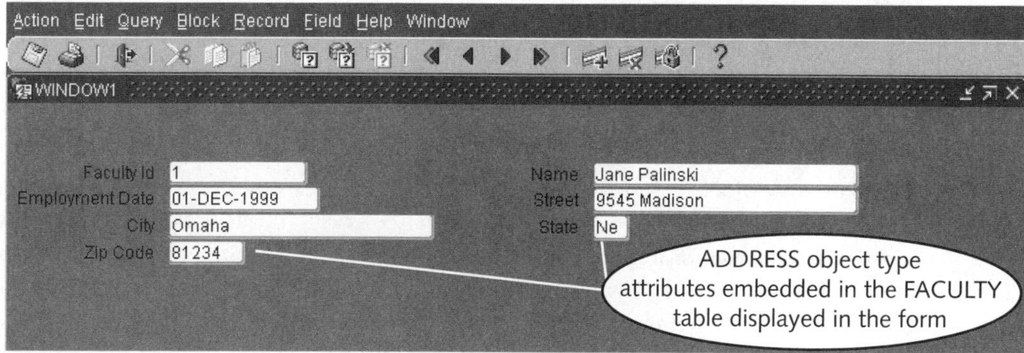

Figure 11-5 Form used to modify the FACULTY table

11

As practice, create the same form shown in Figure 11-5 using the FACULTY table. To accomplish this task, perform the following steps:

1. Log on to SQL*Plus.
2. Create the ADDRESS object type by using the code shown in Listing 11-1.
3. Create the FACULTY table using the top portion of the code shown in Listing 11-2. Note that this listing contains Create statements for both FACULTY and STUDENT tables. Do not create the STUDENT table.
4. Open Forms Builder and create a new form module.
5. Create a new data block. Use the FACULTY table as the data source. Select all of the Available Items. The form should have one record and the style should be Form.
6. Save the form as **practice1101.fmb**. Open the form and test it by adding records, performing a query, and updating an existing value.

Object Tables and REF Columns

In the previous section, you learned how objects are embedded into tables. It is also possible to create a table of object types with rows that reference other tables. The benefit of this is that all common attributes are in the same database object rather than spread across multiple database tables, as they are when the object type is embedded into many tables. For example, if all student, faculty, vendor, and employee addresses are placed into a common table, this table can be analyzed independently of any of the parent objects. This is much easier than having to identify the various tables that contain the attributes and writing unioned SELECT statements that combine the records from the different tables.

To create an object table and relate the table to another table, you would perform the following steps:

1. Define an object type including a REF column.
2. Create a table of the object type.

To relate an object table record to a record in another table, a reference must be included that points to the related record. This reference is called a REF column. A **REF column** is an attribute that stores the object ID of the related record. The object ID is a pointer to the related record's database location. When Oracle encounters the REF column, Oracle can identify the exact location of the matching record without even knowing the name of the table. This is somewhat similar to joining tables, except that the REF column contains a rowid rather than a value that is a primary key in another table. Oracle can locate the record without having to perform the processing needed to join records. This processing essentially consists of locating the matching record. Knowing the rowid of a record allows Oracle to directly retrieve the record. Locating a record based on a rowid is the fastest retrieval method.

The scripts in Listing 11-3 illustrate the creation of a number of the objects depicted in Figure 11-2. As you examine Listing 11-3, study the statements that create the following object types and tables:

- **PERSON** (object type): Contains attributes that describe a typical person.
- **FACULTY_MEMBER** (object type): Contains attributes that describe a typical member of the faculty. Because a faculty member is also a person, the PERSON object type is embedded in this type allowing the FACULTY_MEMBER object to inherit the PERSON attributes.
- **CUSTOMER** (object type): Contains attributes that describe a typical customer. Because a customer is also a person, the PERSON object type is embedded in this type allowing the CUSTOMER object to inherit the PERSON attributes.
- **FACULTY** (table): Composed of records based on the FACULTY_MEMBER object type.
- **CUSTOMERS** (table): Composed of records based on the CUSTOMER object type.
- **ADDRESS** (object type): Contains attributes typical of an address. The ADDRESS object contains two REF columns. The REF column FACULTY_REF will contain the rowid of a record based on the FACULTY_MEMBER object. The REF column CUSTOMER_REF will contain the rowid of a record based on the CUSTOMER object. The ADDRESS can be associated to either the FACULTY or CUSTOMERS table.
- **ADDRESSES** (table): Contains records based on the ADDRESS object type.

You should note that an object can only reference another object. The object types are placed into tables so that they can be used to store data and to be used in a form.

Listing 11-3 Object scripts

```
create or replace type person as object
  (first_name          varchar2(20),
   last_name           varchar2(20),
   social_security_number   varchar2(11),
   birth_date          date,
   gender              char(1));
```

```
/
create or replace type faculty_member as object
  (faculty_id           number,
   college         varchar2(20),
   person_attributes person);
/
create or replace type customer as object
   (customer_id       number,
    credit_limit      varchar2(20),
    person_attributes  person);
/
create table faculty of faculty_member;
create table customers of customer;
Create or replace type address as object
    (street             varchar2(20),
     city               varchar2(20),
     state              char(2),
     Zip_code           varchar2(5)
     faculty_ref        ref faculty_member,
     customer_ref       ref customer);
/
create table addresses of address;
```

USING OBJECT TABLES AND REF COLUMNS IN A FORM

Object types and tables can be used in a form in a manner similar to using normal related tables that we have seen throughout this book. Rather than using related primary and foreign key values in a master-detail block, the form uses an object ID (rowid) and REF column to relate records from the two blocks.

The Data Block Wizard Table page displays object tables in the same manner it displays regular tables. Figure 11-6 depicts the Tables dialog box. It lists the FACULTY object table with other database tables. These tables can be selected for the data block as the figure illustrates.

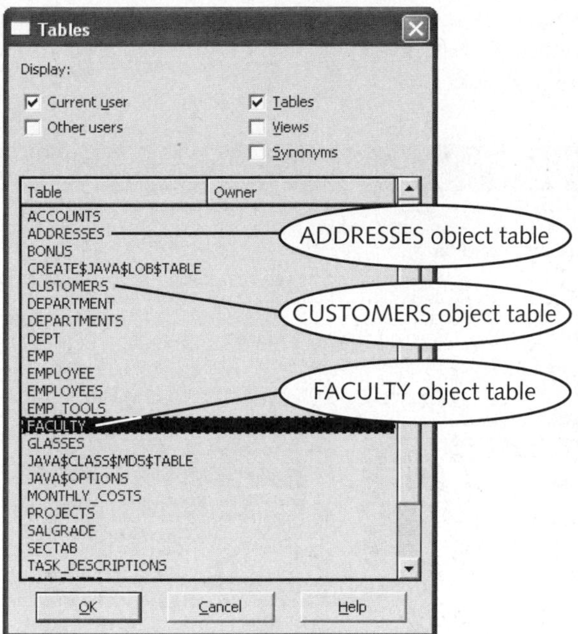

Figure 11-6 Tables dialog box with the FACULTY object table highlighted

11

Using the Data Block Wizard and Layout Wizard, you can create and format object table data blocks exactly as you create and format tables. Differences occur when the second or detail data block is added to the form, because this requires that a relationship be created based on the REF column instead of the primary or foreign key JOIN columns. When you create the detail data block using an object table, you will notice that two REF columns are displayed in the Available Items list on the Data Block Wizard Table page. One of the REF columns, called a REF lookup column, is preceded by an Expand/Collapse tool. Expanding the REF lookup column displays the referenced table's attributes. For example, if the ADDRESSES table columns are displayed on the Data Block Wizard Table page, two FACULTY_REF REF columns will be displayed. Expanding the FACULTY_REF REF lookup column displays the FACULTY table's attributes. The other FACULTY_REF REF column is the actual attribute that contains the pointer to the FACULTY table record. You can move any REF lookup column attributes to the Database Items list. This allows you to display the referenced object's (FACULTY) attributes along with the new data block's (ADDRESSES) attributes. The referenced attributes from the FACULTY table cannot be modified in the data block. The values are displayed so that the form operator knows which parent object is related to the data block's object attributes.

In the case of Figure 11-7, displaying the related FACULTY attributes in the form along with the ADDRESSES attributes identifies the faculty member related to the address, thereby giving meaning to the address set of attributes.

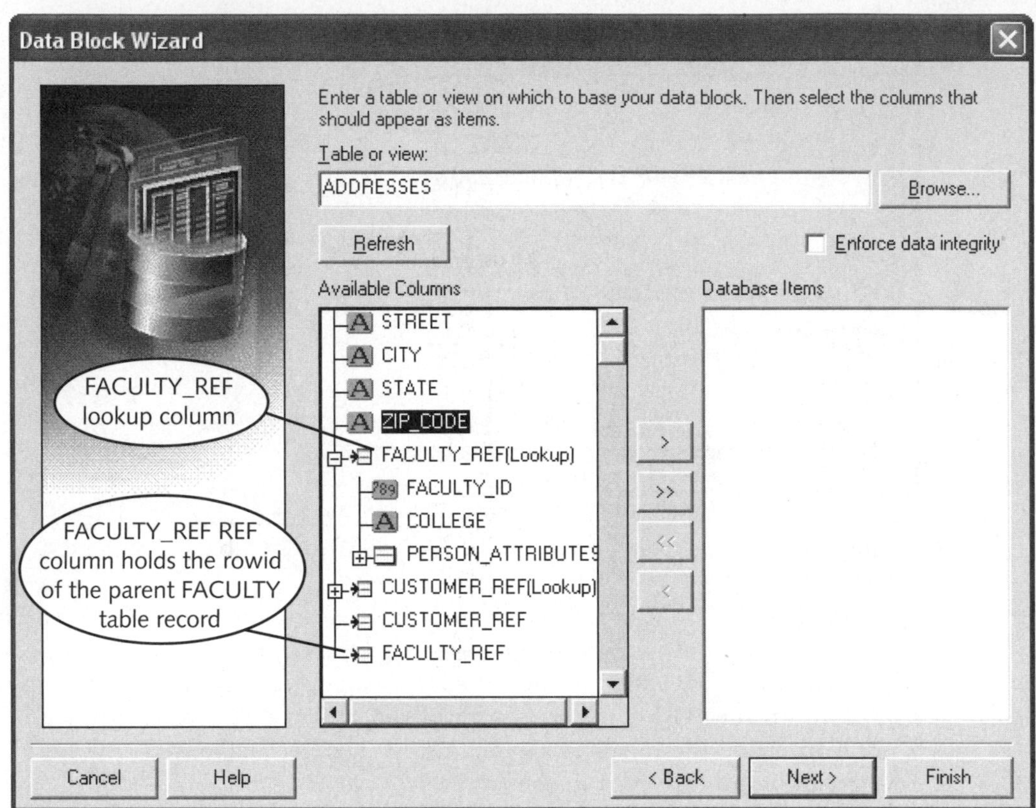

Figure 11-7 Table page displaying dual REF column listings in the Available Columns list box

If the operator wants to modify the referenced object's attributes along with the referencing object's attributes, a master-detail relationship is needed. A master data block containing the referenced object (FACULTY) is needed, along with a detail block for the referencing object (ADDRESSES). When an object table is used as the detail block, the REF lookup column attributes should not be selected, because the needed attributes are already displayed in the master block. Figure 11-7 illustrates the Data Block Wizard Table page with the double reference.

The Master-Detail page of the Data Block Wizard follows the Table page. This page is normally used to set a relation between two tables using primary and foreign keys. When object tables are used, however, the page allows you to set the relationship between the two objects (in this case, FACULTY and ADDRESSES). To set up a relationship between objects using the Master-Detail page, you would perform the following steps:

1. On the Master-Detail Data Block Wizard page, check the Auto-join data blocks check box.
2. Click the Create Relationship button on the Master-Detail page. This opens the Data Blocks dialog box depicted in Figure 11-8.

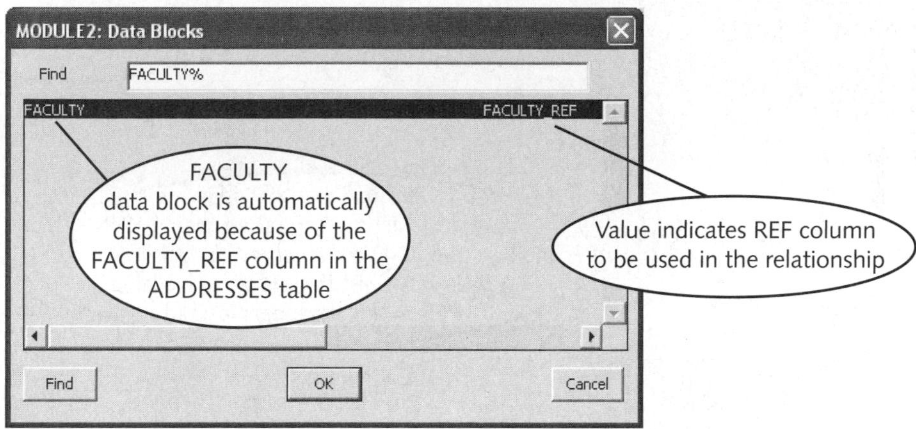

Figure 11-8 Data Blocks dialog box displaying the FACULTY data block

3. The Data Blocks dialog box displays all of the eligible master data blocks along with the reference to the object. Select the appropriate master data block.
4. The selected data block is displayed in the Master Data Blocks list. In addition, a Detail Item drop-down list appears. The object reference appears in the drop-down list as shown in Figure 11-9.

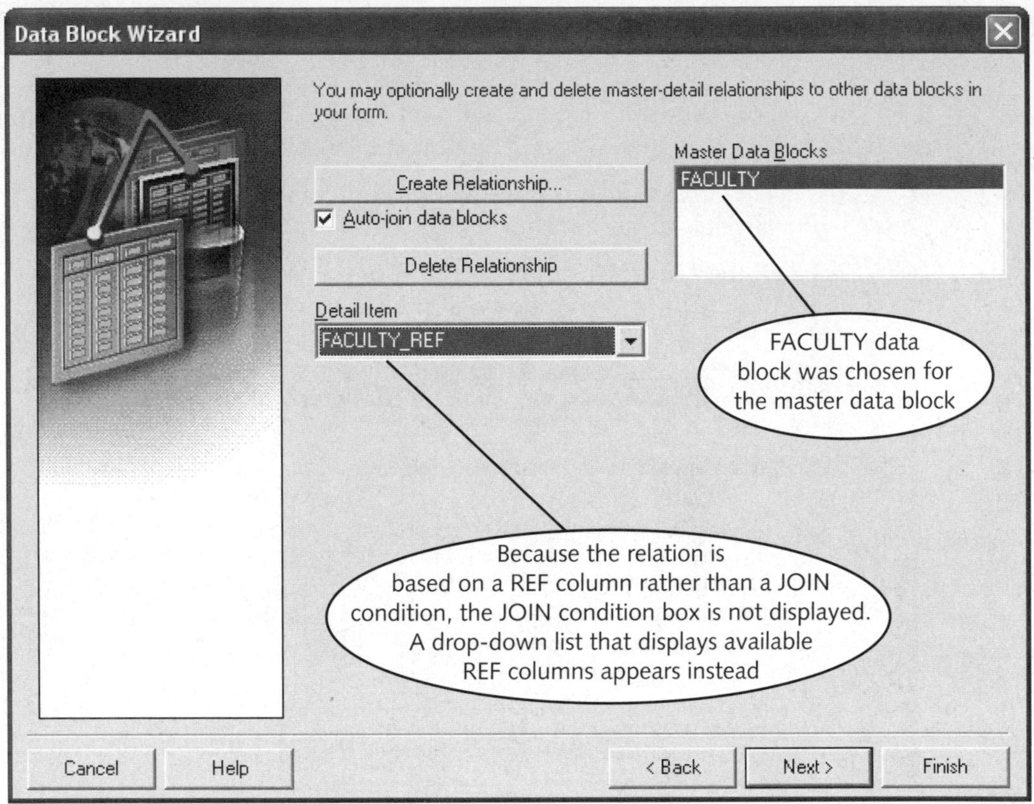

Figure 11-9 Master-Detail page after the master data block has been selected

5. Continue using the Data Block Wizard and the Layout Wizard to create and format the data block.

Figure 11-10 illustrates a completed master-detail form using the FACULTY and ADDRESSES object tables. The form can be used to modify both FACULTY and ADDRESS values.

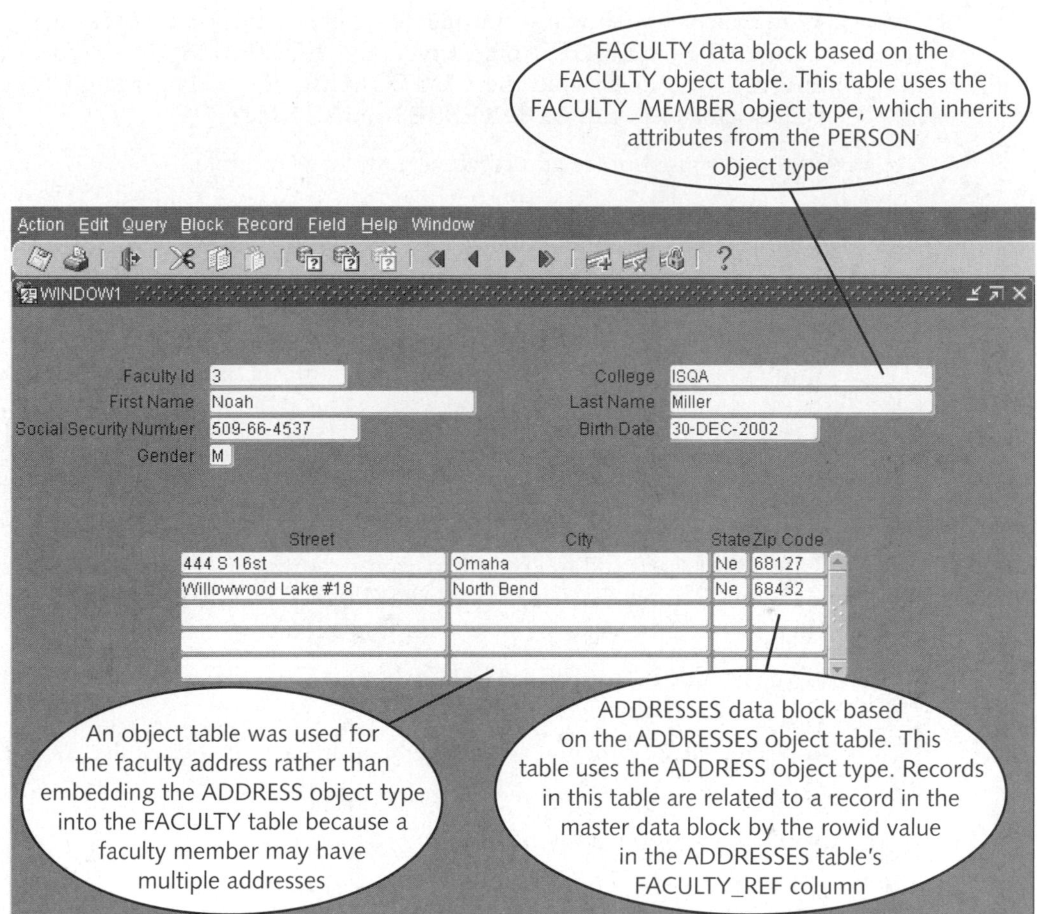

Figure 11-10 Master-detail form using the FACULTY and ADDRESSES object tables

As practice, create the FACULTY-ADDRESS master-detail form depicted in Figure 11-10 by performing the following steps:

1. Log on to SQL*Plus. Delete the **FACULTY** table and the **ADDRESS** object type created in the previous practice by executing these statements:

   ```
   Drop table faculty;
   Drop type address;
   ```

   When attempting to drop the Address object type, you may encounter the following error message: "ORA-02303: Cannot drop or replace a type with type or table dependencies." This might happen because you have created the Student table in the previous practice. If so, delete this table using the "Drop table student;" statement and reexecute the "Drop type address;" statement.

2. Using the script shown in Listing 11-3, create the **PERSON** object type, the **FACULTY_MEMBER** object type, the **ADDRESS** object type, the **FACULTY** object table, the **CUSTOMER** object type, the **CUSTOMERS** object table, and the **ADDRESSES** object table.
3. Open Forms Builder and create a new form module.
4. Create a data block based on the FACULTY object table. The block should have a form layout, and one record should be displayed.
5. Create a second data block based on the ADDRESSES object table.
6. On the Data Block Wizard Table page, select the **FACULTY_REF** REF column along with the **ADDRESSES** attributes. Do not select the REF lookup column or any of its attributes.
7. On the Master-Detail page, click the **Create Relationships** button. Select the **FACULTY** table. The FACULTY_REF item should appear in the Detail Item drop-down list box.
8. Click **Next** and follow the normal procedures for creating and formatting a data block using the remaining Data Block Wizard and Layout Wizard pages. The layout should Form style with four records.
9. Save the form as **practice1102.fmb**. Open the form and test it by performing these functions:
   - Add a faculty member and several addresses for the faculty member.
   - Perform a query and return the inserted record.
   - Update and save the record.
10. Close the form.

FORMS BUILDER AND THE WEB

The major portion of this book has dealt with designing and creating a form using Forms Builder. You learned how to use the Data Block Wizard and Layout Wizard, how to create different types of items, how to create and write PL/SQL for the form, and how to perform a multitude of other techniques. These tools apply to both Form Builder 6*i* and the new Forms Builder 9*i*. The majority of the subjects discussed apply to a form's deployment in either a client-server (Form Builder 6*i*) environment or on the Web (Form Builder 6*i* or Forms Builder 9*i*).

This section reviews the Oracle Forms Web environment and discusses a number of topics that pertain specifically to the use of the form on the Web.

Oracle Forms Server

Forms Server deploys Web forms created by Forms Builder. For work with this text, you have been using a development version of Forms Server that is located on your PC. This version is not intended for production. When your form is used in production, Forms Server will reside on a production server whose primary role is to present applications and perform database calls. The production version of Forms Server resides on the middle tier of a three-tiered environment, as depicted in Figure 11-11.

- **Client tier (front-end tier)**: On this tier, the operator interacts with the application through a Web browser, such as Internet Explorer or Netscape. The form resides within the Web browser as an applet. (An applet is a program that executes from within another application instead of directly from the operating system.)
- **Middle tier (application tier)**: This tier contains the **.fmx** form file as well as the server software. A portion of this software is a listener that watches for requests. When the listener encounters a request, it serves up the application to the Web browser. Forms Server resides in this tier and serves up the form by changing it into an applet and sending it to the browser. Forms Server Runtime maintains the connection to the database and runs the various form objects.
- **Database tier (back-end tier)**: This tier contains the Oracle database. It receives requests for data from the application tier and sends them to Forms Server on the middle tier.

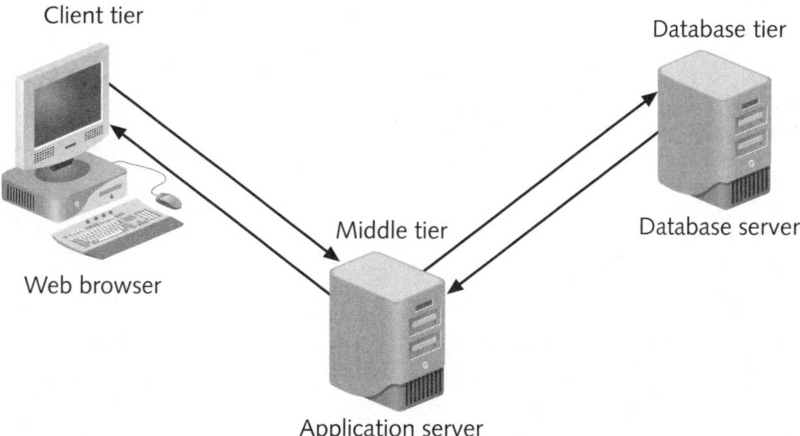

Figure 11-11 Three-tiered environment of Forms Server

To view a form in a browser, you need a Java environment (Java Virtual Machine [JVM]). The Java environment paints the forms and interacts with the operator. JInitiator is the JVM that performs this task. It is a special version of the JVM, which can run on both Nestscape and Internet Explorer browsers. When an operator requests its initial form from Forms Server, JInitiator is downloaded to the client and installed as a plug-in to the browser.

This configuration allows Forms Server to maintain a state over the Web. A **state** is an active connection whereby the server is aware of or has retained information about previous requests. Using Forms Server, the application on the server communicates with the applet and with the database. Maintaining a consistent connection within a session is often needed for complex procedures. Normal Web transactions are stateless, which means that every request is discrete.

WEB DESIGN TECHNIQUES

The form that you design on the Web looks and operates much as it does in the client-server environment; however, there are some differences. One of the first considerations is performance. Web applications imply a thin client, which means that the client has little power and performs minimal work. Most of the work is performed on the server and sent to the client for display in the Web browser. That means that you should evaluate resources and bandwidth, especially for Internet (versus intranet) applications. The following is a list of precautions:

- Limit the number of images, because they are often large and require time to download.
- Avoid roundtrips to the database server. This means that it may be better to retrieve more records into the data block initially than to perform incremental queries.
- If you have an image that is displayed in multiple forms, download the image in the initial form. The image is cached locally in the browser instead of being downloaded repeatedly.
- Avoid multimedia items because they are generally large.
- Perform validation at the highest level possible. Use When-Validate-Record triggers rather than When-Validate-Item triggers. This reduces network traffic by reducing the number of triggers that are fired.
- Use the Prompt property rather than boilerplate text entered by the Layout editor text tool to describe your items. Prompts entered into the Prompt property are retrieved as part of an item rather than as separate items.
- Avoid using mouse triggers, because each time a mouse trigger is fired, the Web browser form must communicate with Forms Server.
- Only display items that are needed, and don't populate all the canvases at one time. Some canvases may be displayed only occasionally. Avoid downloading data for these canvases.
- Avoid using repeating timers. Each time the timer is fired, a roundtrip occurs to Forms Server.

Fonts

Fonts can cause a problem in your forms because they are seldom supported across all platforms. When Forms Builder encounters a font that is not available, it attempts to use a similar font. When a form is executed, Forms Server identifies a Java font. Table 11-1 lists equivalent fonts. If you use these fonts in designing your forms, you minimize differences between design and production.

Table 11-1 Java font equivalents

Java	Windows	X Windows
Dialog	MS Sans Serif	B&h-lucida
Dialog	MS Sans Serif	B&h-lucidatypewriter
MonoSpaced	Courier New	Adobe-courier
SansSerif	Arial	Adobe-helvetica
Serif	Times New Roman	Adobe-times
Symbol	Wingdings	Itc-zapfdingbats

Oracle recommends MS Sans Serif size 9 as your default font, because it is equivalent to Dialog.

Supported and Unsupported Features

Be careful that applications that are run through a Web browser do not require functionality that does not exist. Table 11-2 describes features that you should carefully consider.

Table 11-2 Limitations of Web browser applications

Feature	Limitations
Active X, OCX, OLE, DDE, VBX	Non-Oracle controls are not supported by Forms Server. Use a JavaBean to mimic this functionality.
Iconic button	Icons can be displayed in the form. However, the button icons must be **gif** or **jpg** files and must reside in the same directory as the HTML page.
When-Mouse-Enter/Leave/Move triggers	This is not supported, because it causes a network roundtrip.
Magic menu item	Normal Cut, Copy, and Paste menu items do not work. However, CTRL+X, CTRL+C, and CTRL+V do work.
Sound items	This is not supported.
WIN_API built-ins and calls to Windows DDls	Windows specific calls should be avoided, because Forms Server may not reside on a Windows machine.

Formsweb.cfg File

The **formsweb.cfg** file controls a number of different Web features. In Chapter 4, you saw that it controlled the size of the applet area in which the form is displayed on the Web page. This file has other characteristics that you can control. The following is a code snippet from the file:

```
#   3)  Values for the Forms applet parameters:
#
serverURL=/forms90/l90servlet
codebase=/forms90/java
imageBase=DocumentBase
width=600
height=550
separateFrame=False
splashScreen=
background=
lockAndFeel=generic
colorScheme=teal
logo=
formsMessageListener=
recordFileName=
```

LookAndFeel and ColorScheme Settings

In this section, you learn more about elements of the **formsweb.cfg** file. The LookAndFeel setting determines the form's appearance. The options are ORACLE and GENERIC. The ORACLE look, shown in Figure 11-12, is the default and operates when the ORACLE option is selected. The form window Minimize and Maximize sizing tools are depicted with arrows rather than the normal Windows icons (see Figure 11-13). Another difference is that the ORACLE form appears flat rather than raised. Figures 11-12 and 11-13 contrast the same form using the ORACLE setting and the GENERIC setting, respectively.

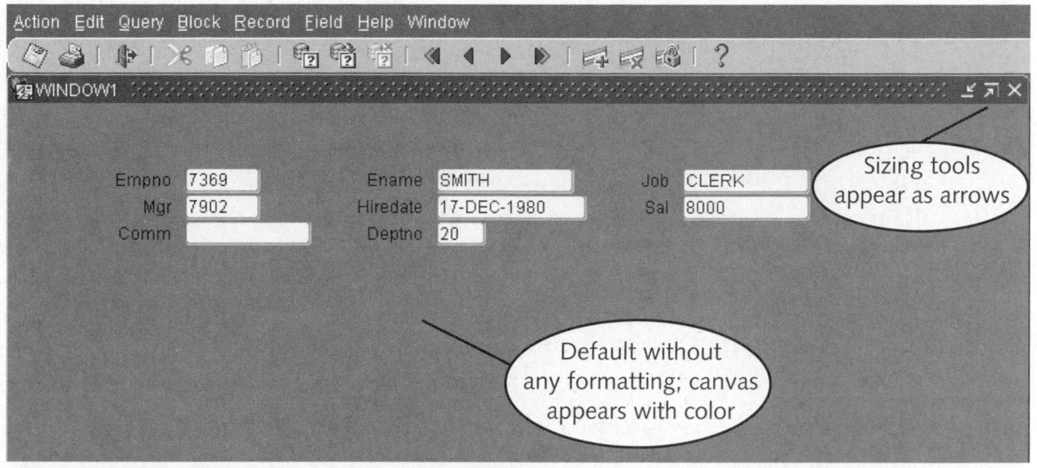

Figure 11-12 EMP form using the ORACLE LookAndFeel setting

The ColorScheme setting determines the color of the header bars, buttons, form title, and menu. Options are TEAL, RED, KHAKI, TITANIUM, BLUE, OLIVE, and PURPLE.

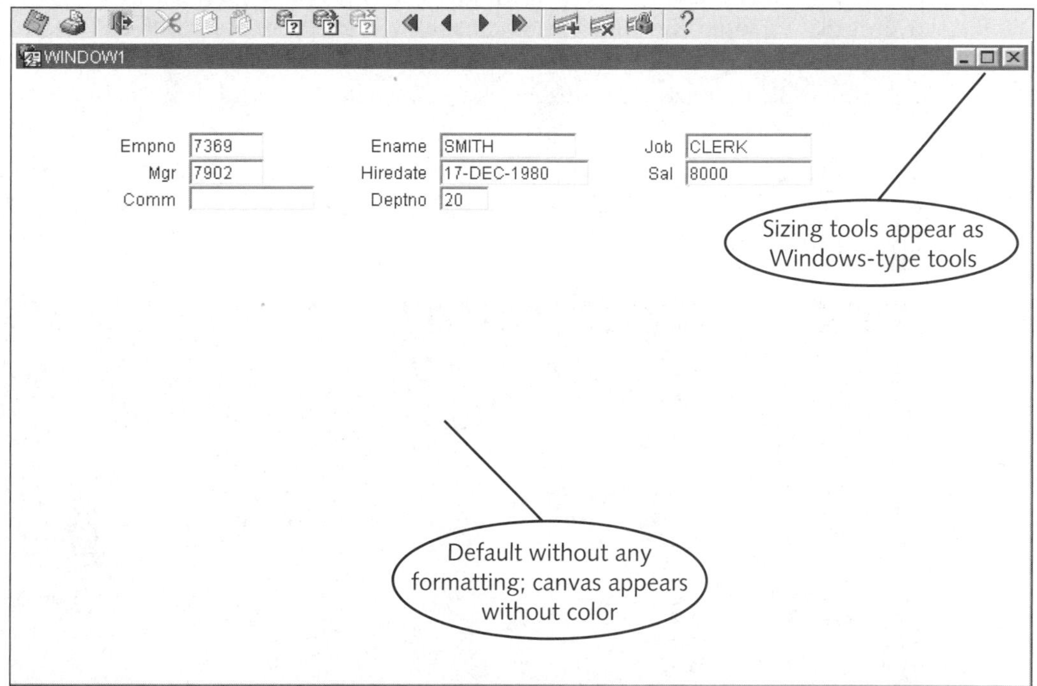

Figure 11-13 EMP form using the GENERIC LookAndFeel setting

USING JAVA WITH FORMS

With the development of the Java language and Oracle's move to the Web, Oracle is increasingly using the Java language and classes in its products. Oracle Developer 2000, which was released five years ago, did not support Java. The successor versions of Developer 2000, Form Builder 6*i* and Forms Builder 9*i*, allow you to use Java classes wrapped in PL/SQL in the form. You may have noticed that Oracle has chosen to display its forms on the Web inside of a Java applet. The applet is sent to the Web browser, and the form window is displayed within the Java applet area. The advent of the Oracle8 database made it possible to create Java classes and store them in the Oracle database. These classes are wrapped in PL/SQL objects. Oracle feels (or hopes) that Java will be the language of the Web, because Java is a strong and open language. Although it is still far easier to use PL/SQL and form components, it is possible to use Java in your forms. The following sections include some simple examples.

Using Bean Areas to Display Java Controls

A **bean area** is a data block item type that is used to display a JavaBean. JavaBeans are often graphic objects, such as a hover button, check box, or an animated graphic, such as a juggler juggling beans. Forms Builder does not have the tools to create these types of objects, nor does the PL/SQL language have the capacity to create them. However, Forms Builder allows you to use controls or animated objects created in Java using JDeveloper, JBuilder, or the Java Development Kit (JDK) and drop them into a bean area item in the form.

Figure 11-14 illustrates a JavaBean that was dropped into a bean area item. It is a sample JavaBean provided by Sun, the developer of Java, that consists of Duke the Juggler juggling beans.

Figure 11-14 Bean area item displaying a JavaBean

Adding Duke the Juggler to a Form with Forms Builder 9*i*

This section describes how to use Forms Builder 9*i* to add a JavaBean consisting of an animation of Duke the Juggler to a form. After reading this section, you may want to repeat the steps and create a form using the JavaBean. Duke the Juggler is used in a JavaBean tutorial developed by Sun. The class containing Duke is part of Sun's Beans Development Kit (BDK), which can be downloaded: *http://java.sun.com/products/javabeans/software/bdk_download.html.* You do not have to download this software, because it is provided in the **juggler.jar** file included with the student files accompanying this book. The **juggler.jar** file contains all the **gifs** and other items needed. It is the JavaBean that will be executed in the form. The **juggler.jar** file is a Java archive file developed by Roger Garfoot, a top-notch Java developer. He added the freely available components to the java archive **(jar)** file.

To add a JavaBean to a bean area, a JavaBean wrapper must be created. This must be done outside Forms Builder in a Java development product. JDeveloper was chosen, because it is an Oracle product and comes bundled with Oracle's Developer suite. If you want to perform the following practice that consists of adding a Duke the Juggler JavaBean to a bean area item, use JDeveloper. The following steps walk you through the creation of a **Jar** file that can be used by the form:

1. Locate the following files from the student files:
   - **juggler.jar**: The actual JavaBean that contains the Duke the Juggler components.
   - **JugglerWrapper.java**: An example of an Oracle wrapper. This is a slightly modified version of the wrapper contained in the "The Container/Wrapper for the Juggler JavaBean" section available through the Forms Builder Help Navigator. This section can be located under Bean Area / Including a Javabean and Custom Controls.
2. Save the files in the **c:\juggler** directory. You may use a different directory, but be sure to replace **c:\juggler** references with your own custom name in the following steps.
3. In this series of steps, you create a new JDeveloper workspace and project:
   a. Open JDeveloper. It should appear similar to Figure 11-15.
   b. This step is performed to remove other workspaces that may confuse you. If there are workspace objects under the Workspaces node, select the workspace and use the **File/Remove From IDE** menu option to remove the workspaces. You may also use the **Ctrl + Delete** keys.

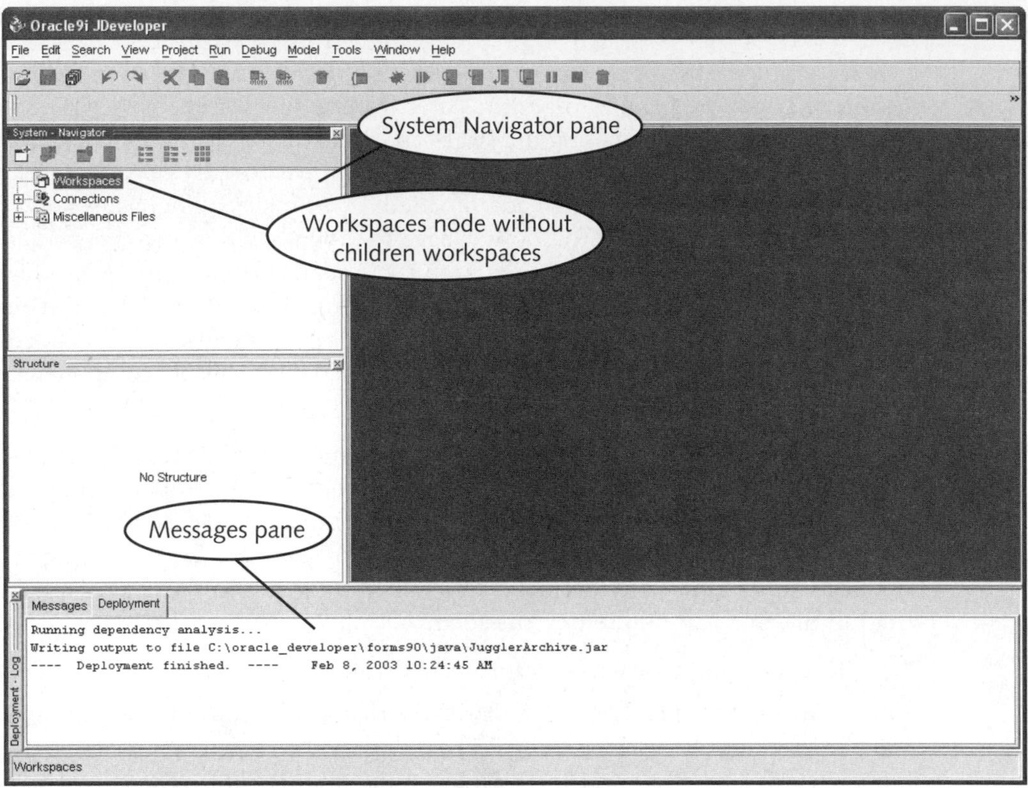

Figure 11-15 Oracle9*i* JDeveloper IDE

c. Create a new workspace by selecting the **File/New** menu option. A New dialog box opens (see Figure 11-16). Select the **Projects/Workspace** option and click **OK**.

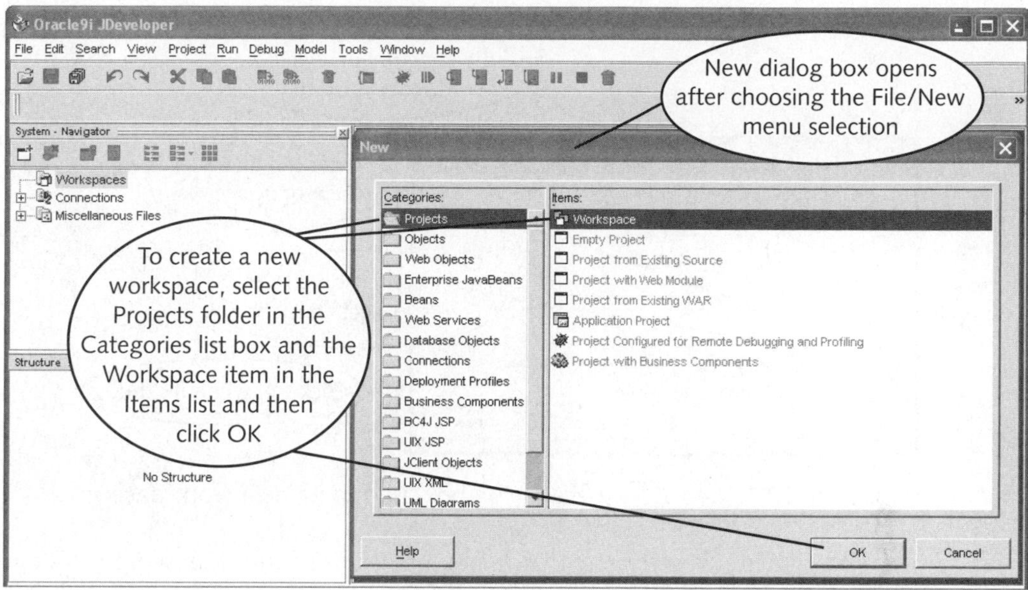

Figure 11-16 New dialog box used to create a new workspace and project

d. The New Workspace dialog box opens.

Throughout this book, the typeface convention for values is to use all capital letters. For this section of the book, however, case restriction is very important, and therefore this typeface convention will be ignored for the remainder of this section.

e. Enter the following values and perform the following operations as shown in Figure 11-17:

- Directory Name: **c:\juggler**
- File Name: **juggler.jws**
- Check the **Add a New Empty Project** check box if necessary
- Click **OK**.

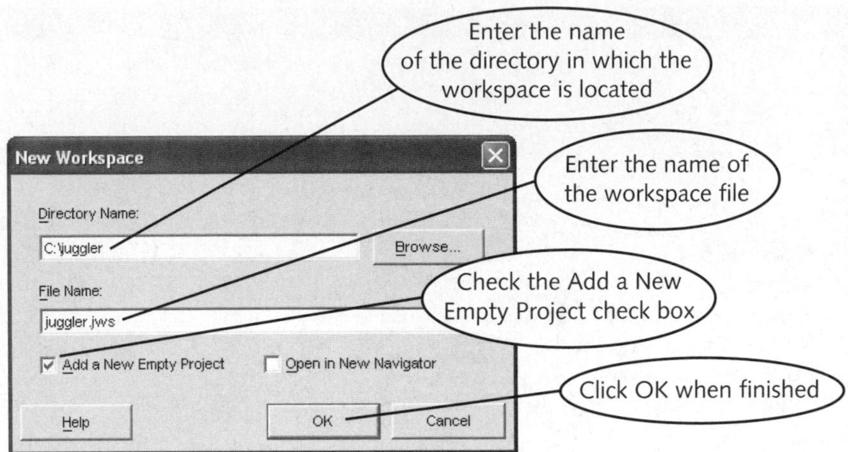

Figure 11-17 New Workspace dialog box used to name a workspace

f. The New Project dialog box opens. Enter the following values and perform the following operations, as shown in Figure 11-18:

- Directory Name: **c:\juggler\juggler_project**
- File Name: **juggler.jpr**
- Click **OK**.

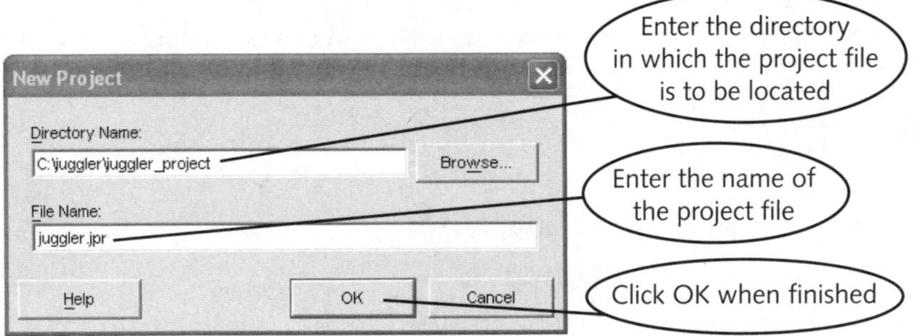

Figure 11-18 New Project dialog box used to name a project

g. At this point, the JDeveloper System Navigator should display the **juggler.jws** workspace and the **juggler.jpr** project (see Figure 11-19). Select the **File/Save** menu option.

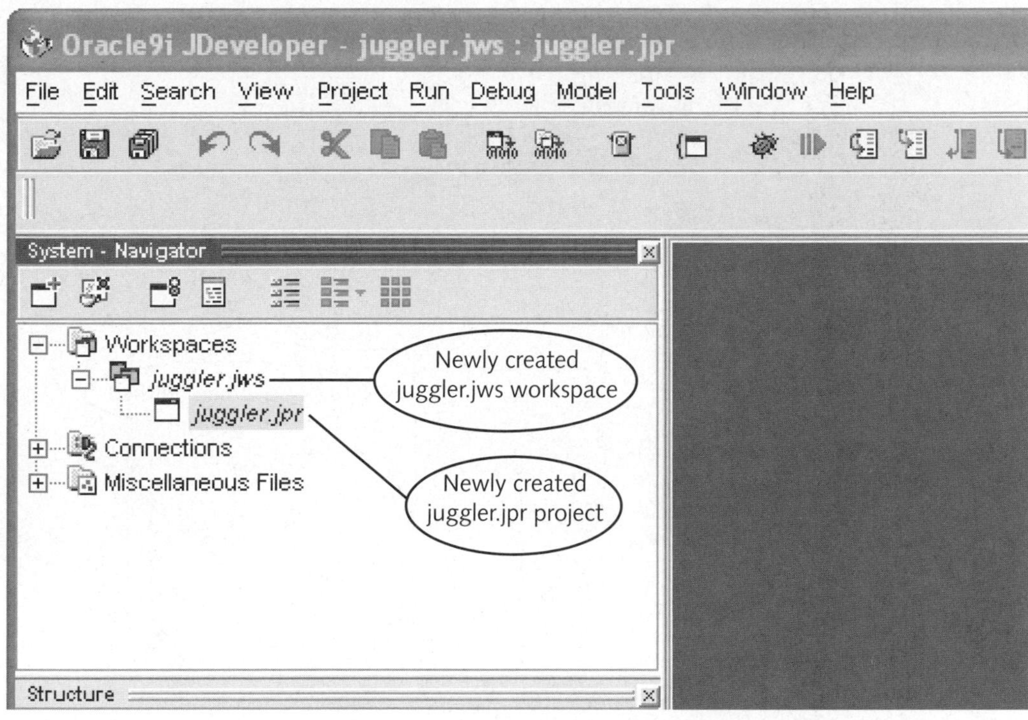

Figure 11-19 JDeveloper System Navigator displaying the new workspace and project

4. The next step is to create the class that will be displayed in the form. Select the **juggler.jpr** object in the System Navigator window. Select the **File/New** menu option to open the New dialog box. Select the **Objects/Class** options as they appear in Figure 11-20. Click **OK**.

   a. The New Class dialog box opens. Enter the following values and perform the following operations, as shown in Figure 11-21:

      - Name: **JugglerWrapper**
      - Package: **beans** (Enter **beans** to match the package name placed in the JugglerWrapper file provided with the student files.)
      - Click **OK**.

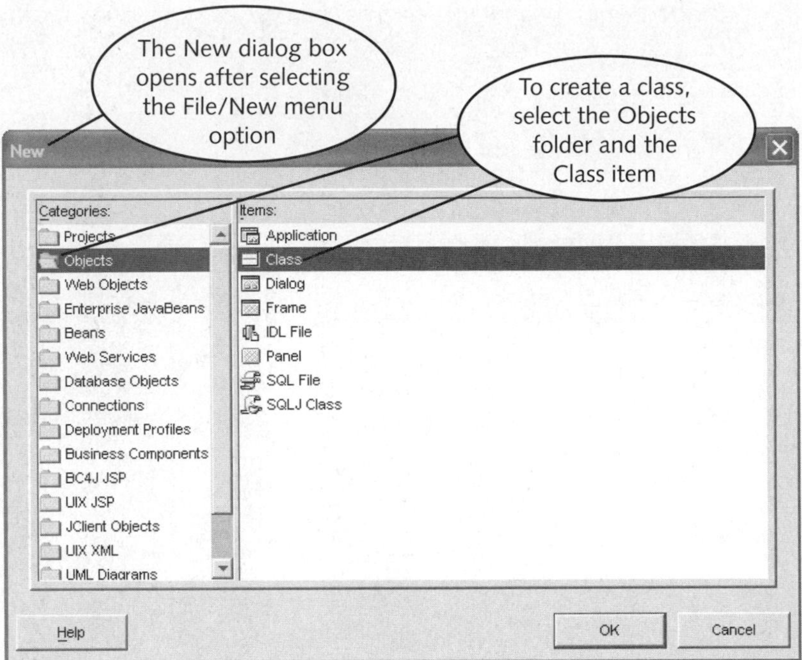

Figure 11-20 New dialog box displaying the Objects/Class options

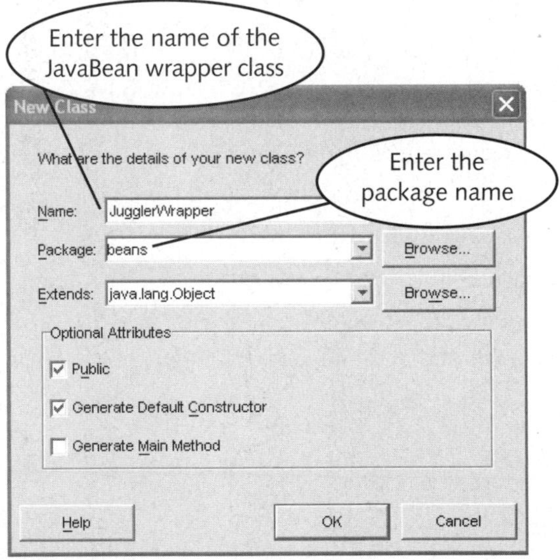

Figure 11-21 New Class dialog box used to name and create a new class

b. The JDeveloper IDE appears, which should look similar to Figure 11-22. On the top right is the code window for the newly created JugglerWrapper class. The window contains default code that must be replaced by the code in the **JugglerWrapper.java** file provided with the student files. Open the **JugglerWrapper.java** file located in the **c:\juggler** directory in a text editor. Copy the contents and paste the script into the newly created JDeveloper JugglerWrapper class in JDeveloper. Be sure to replace all of the default script in the code window. Click the **Save** tool.

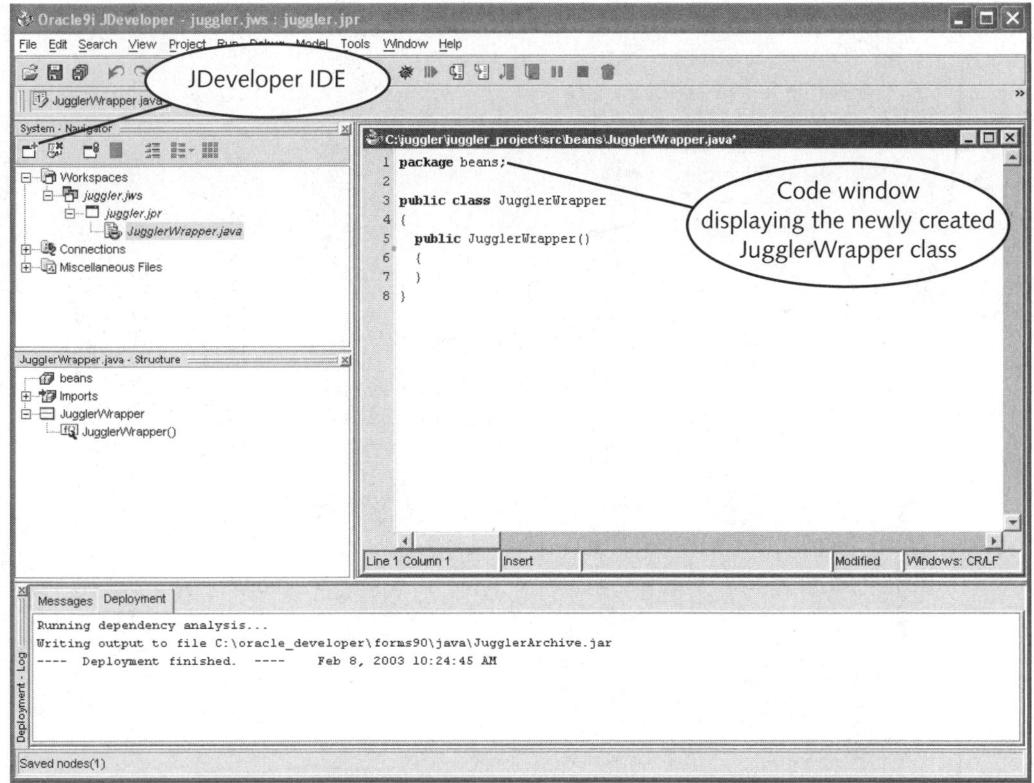

Figure 11-22 JDeveloper code window displaying the default script for the newly created JugglerWrapper class file

5. In this step, you must create and add libraries to the project. These libraries are necessary to execute the JavaBean. You will add the following:
   - **juggler.jar**: This file is the actual JavaBean. You will create a library named "juggler" that contains this archive.
   - **Oracle Forms**: This library contains the component referenced in the JugglerWrapper class file.

11

To create and add these libraries, perform the following steps:

a. Select the **Project/Project Settings** menu item to open the Project Settings dialog box depicted in Figure 11-23. The Libraries node is selected and the Libraries settings are displayed. If the Libraries settings are not displayed, double-click the **Libraries** node. The Oracle Forms library is displayed in the Available Libraries list. Move this **library** to the Selected Libraries node by selecting the **Oracle Forms** library and clicking the **Move** button.

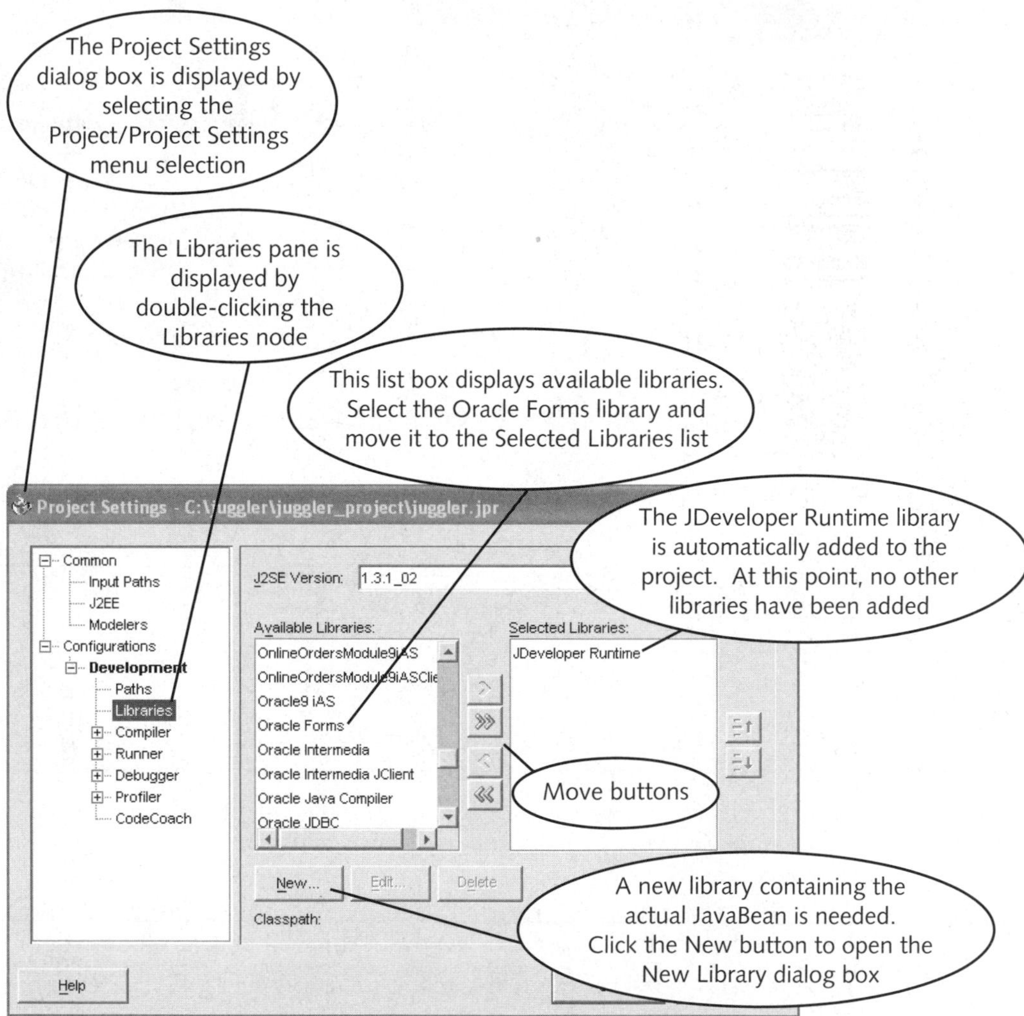

Figure 11-23 Project Settings dialog box used to add and create new libraries

b. In this step, you create a library that contains the **juggler.jar** file. Click the **New** button in the Project Settings dialog box. The New Library dialog box opens. Enter the following values and perform the following operations, as shown in Figure 11-24:
   - Library Name: **juggler**
   - Class Path: **c:\juggler\juggler.jar**
   - Click **OK**.

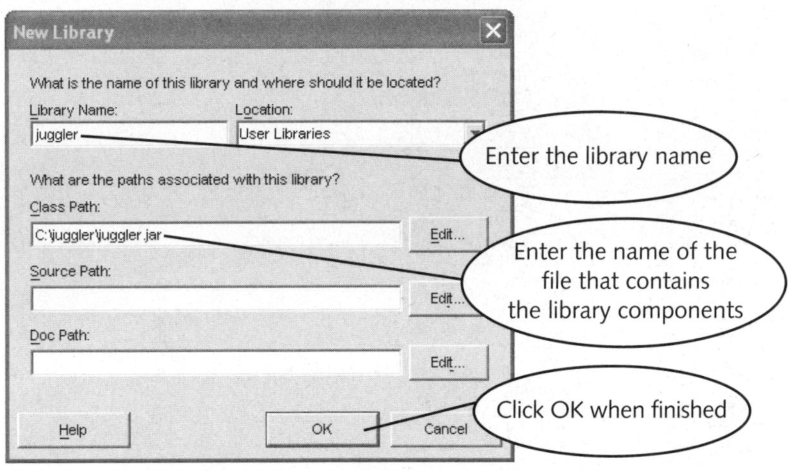

Figure 11-24 New Library dialog box after the juggler library settings have been entered

c. If you performed the previous step correctly, the following libraries should appear in the Selected Libraries list: JDeveloper Runtime, Oracle Forms, and juggler.

d. Click **OK**. Save the file.

e. At this point, you should compile the file to ensure that all components are correct. To compile the file, click the **Build Project** button. If the compilation occurred, your IDE should appear similar to Figure 11-25.

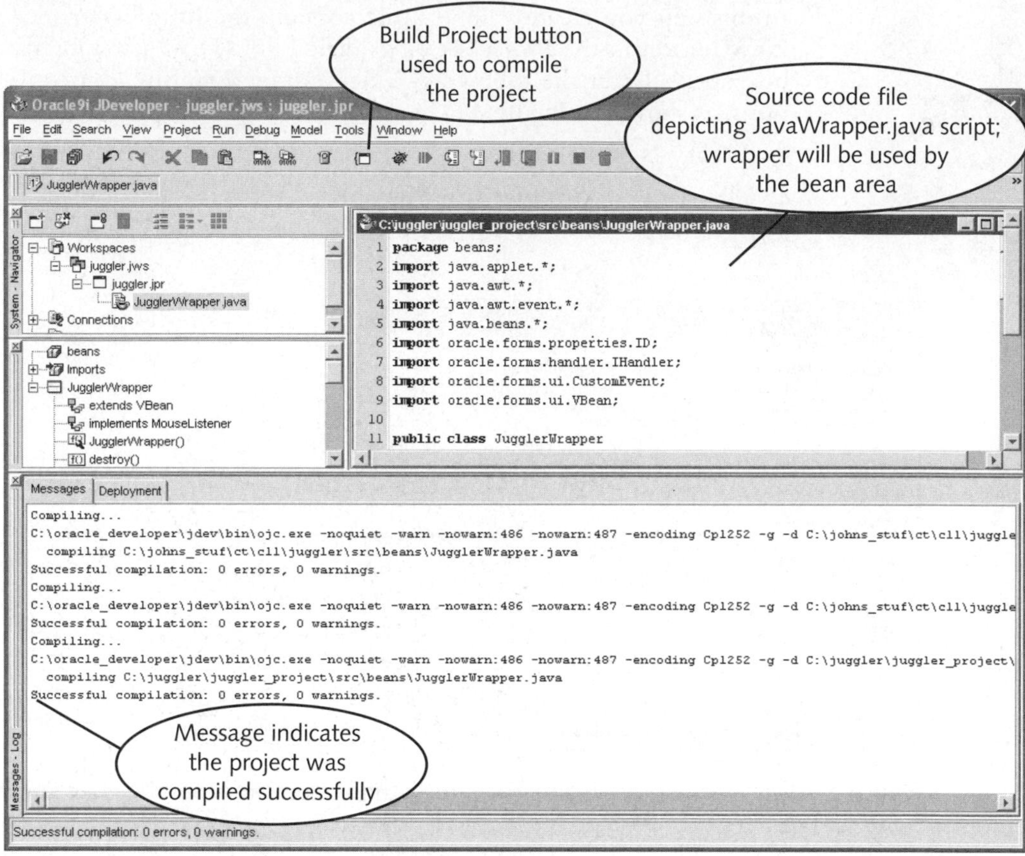

Figure 11-25 JDeveloper IDE after the juggler.jpr project has been compiled

6. In this step, you create a deployment vessel, which is a simple archive file, and place this file into a location where Forms Server can locate the file. Click the **File/New** menu option to open the New dialog box. Select the **Deployment Profiles/JAR File – Simple Archive** settings depicted in Figure 11-26. Click **OK**.

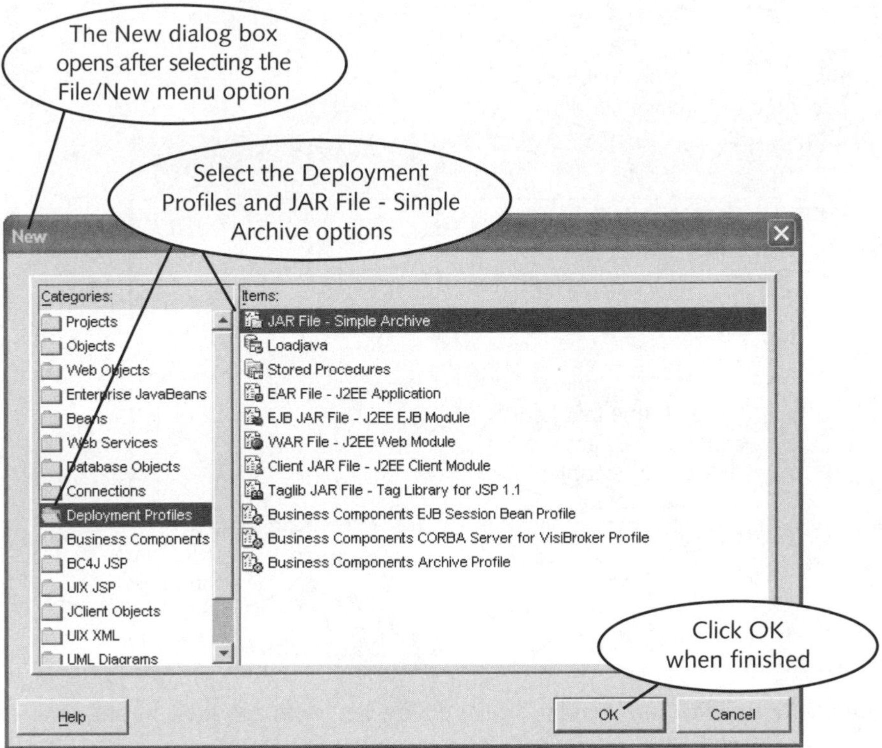

Figure 11-26 New dialog box with the Deployment Profiles/JAR File – Simple Archive settings selected

a. The Save Deployment Profile dialog box opens. Enter the following save settings, as shown in Figure 11-27, into the Location and File Name text boxes. Then click the **Save** button:

- Location: **c:\juggler\juggler_project**
- File Name: **JugglerArchive.deploy**

b. The JAR Deployment Profile Settings dialog box opens . Double-click the **Dependency Analyzer** node to display the libraries. Check the **juggler.jar** check box, as shown in Figure 11-28. Click **OK**. You are returned to the JDeveloper IDE. Click the **Save** tool. The **JugglerArchive.deploy** file is listed under the juggler.jpr project node.

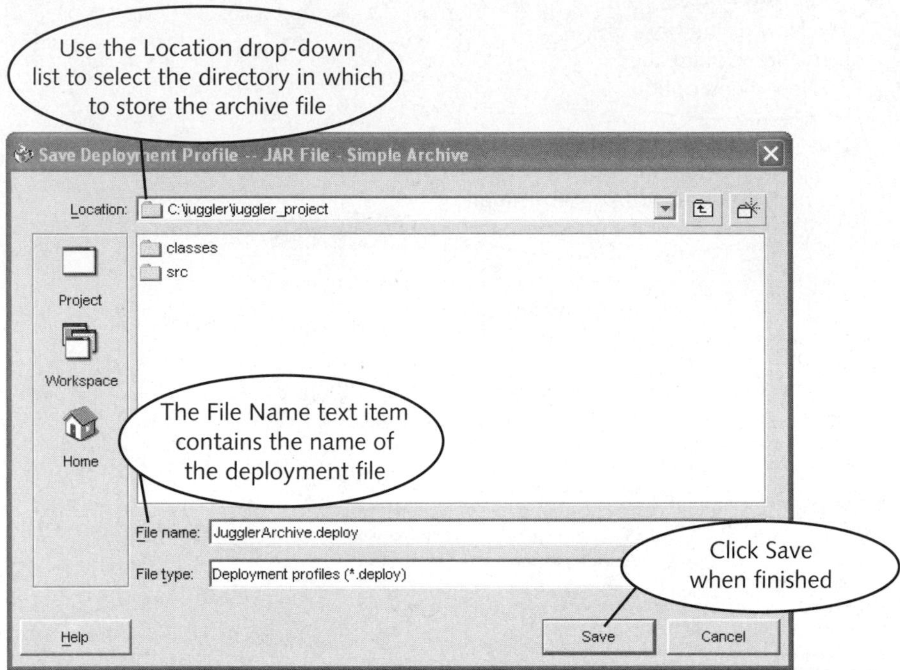

Figure 11-27 Save Deployment Profile dialog box with the save setting entered

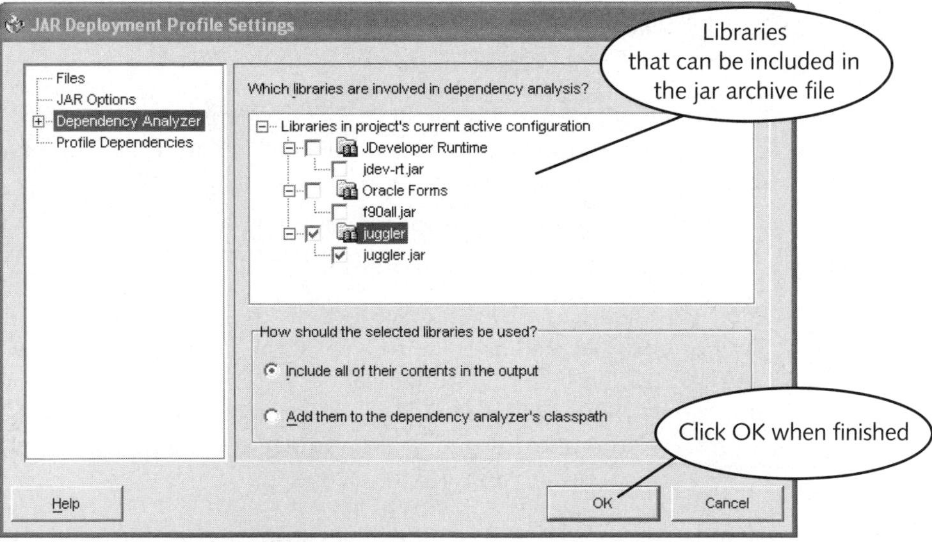

Figure 11-28 JAR Deployment Profile Settings dialog box displaying the libraries

7. In this step, you deploy the **JugglerArchive.jar** file. To start this process, select the **JugglerArchive.deploy** file node in the System – Navigator window. Click the **Right-mouse** button to open a popup menu (see Figure 11-29) that displays a Deploy to pop menu option. Select this option to open the Deploy to Java Archive (JAR) File dialog box.

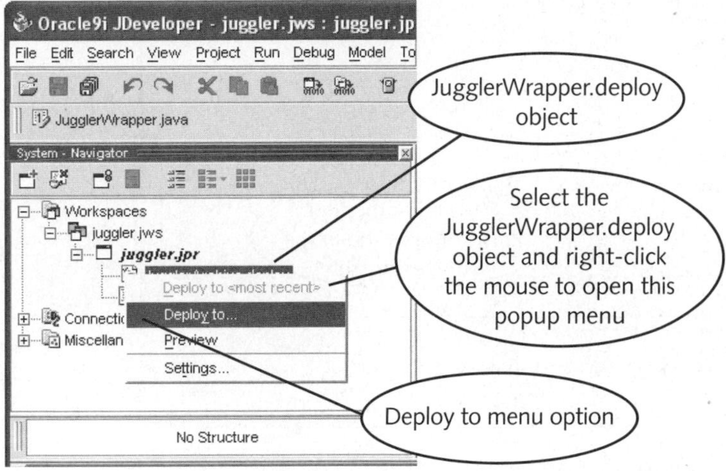

Figure 11-29 JDeveloper IDE displaying the Deploy to popup menu option

a. The **jar** file must be deployed to the directory used by Forms Server. In production, your server administrator will move the **jar** file into the appropriate directory used by the Oracle9iAS Forms Server. For test and practice, you should move the file into the Forms Builder directory. The name of the root directory depends on the name that was used when Forms Builder was installed. For the directories used for this book, it is named **oracle_directory**. You must review your installation to determine the name. After determining the Forms Builder installation directory name, you must place the file in the **\forms90\java directory**. This is depicted in Figure 11-30.

b. At this point, you have completed your work in JDeveloper. You can save the project and close the product.

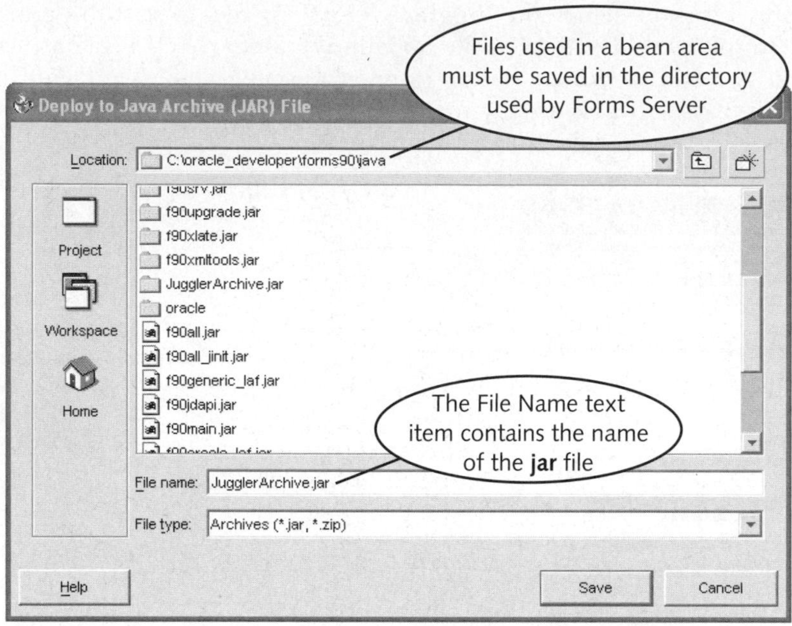

Figure 11-30 Deploy to Java Archive (JAR) File dialog box

8. In this step, you create a Java bean area in a form and associate it to the appropriate class. Perform the following steps to create a simple form that displays Duke the Juggler:

   a. Open Forms Builder and create a new form module.

   b. Select the **Data Blocks** node and click the **Create** tool. In the New Data Block dialog box, select the **Build A New Data Block Manually** radio button and click **OK**. This creates a new control block in which to place the bean area.

   c. Select the **Canvases** node and click the **Create** tool. A canvas object is created. Double-click the icon for this canvas to open the Layout Editor displaying this canvas.

   d. Select and activate the **Bean Area** tool in the Layout Editor. Locate a place on the canvas and click the **Left Mouse** button. Hold the button while dragging the mouse until a bean area is sized to your needs.

   e. Double-click the **bean area** to open its Property Palette. Locate the Implementation Class property and enter **beans.JugglerWrapper**. This is the name of the package and the wrapper class. After entering the Implementation Class property, an error message displays. Ignore this message. Figure 11-31 depicts a bean area, the Property Palette for the area, the Implementation Class property value, and the error message.

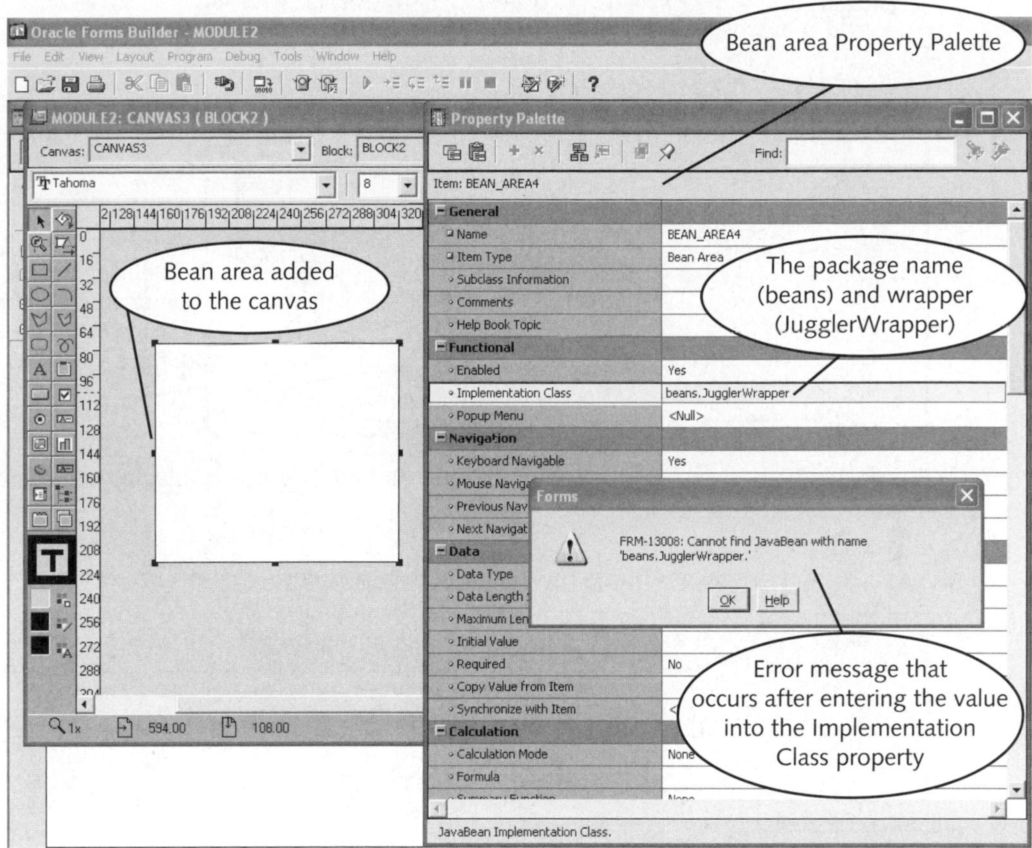

Figure 11-31 Forms Builder IDE displaying a bean area, the bean area Property Palette, and error message

9. In this step, you set a Runtime/Preferences setting to tell Forms Server to download the **JugglerArchive.jar** file when it sends the form module to the Web browser. Select the **Runtime/Preferences** menu option to open the Preferences dialog box. Click the **Runtime** tab. Add **?config=juggler** to the end of the Application Server URL, as depicted in Figure 11-32. Click **OK** when you are finished. Save the module.

10. The last step in setting up Oracle to run the JavaBean is to add a reference to the JavaBean archive in the **formsweb.cfg** file. When the form is used in production, this modification will be made to this file, which is located on the middle tier. Because you are using Forms Builder, this file is located on your machine in the **\forms90\server** directory in your Oracle Developer root directory. At the end of the file, add the following code:

```
[juggler]
IE=JInitiator
archive_jini=f90all.jar, JugglerArchive.jar
```

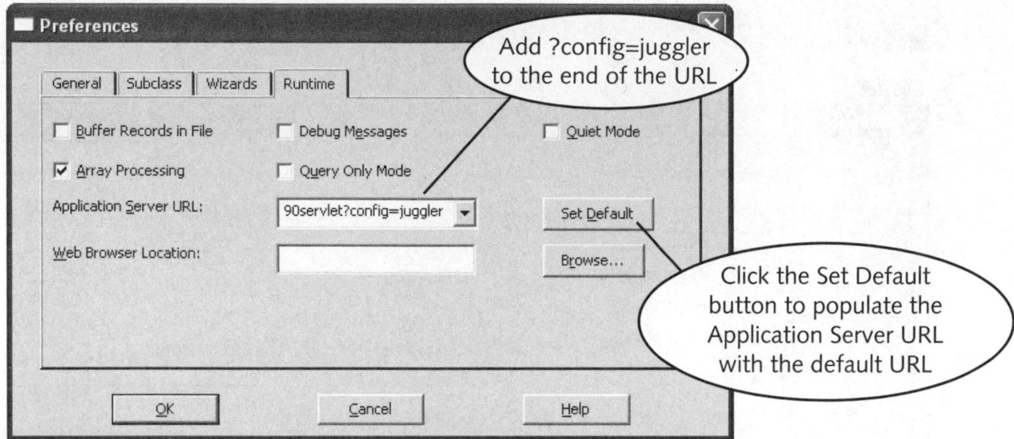

Figure 11-32 Forms Builder Runtime Preferences dialog box displaying the Runtime tab settings

The **formsweb.cfg** file and the code are depicted in Figure 11-33.

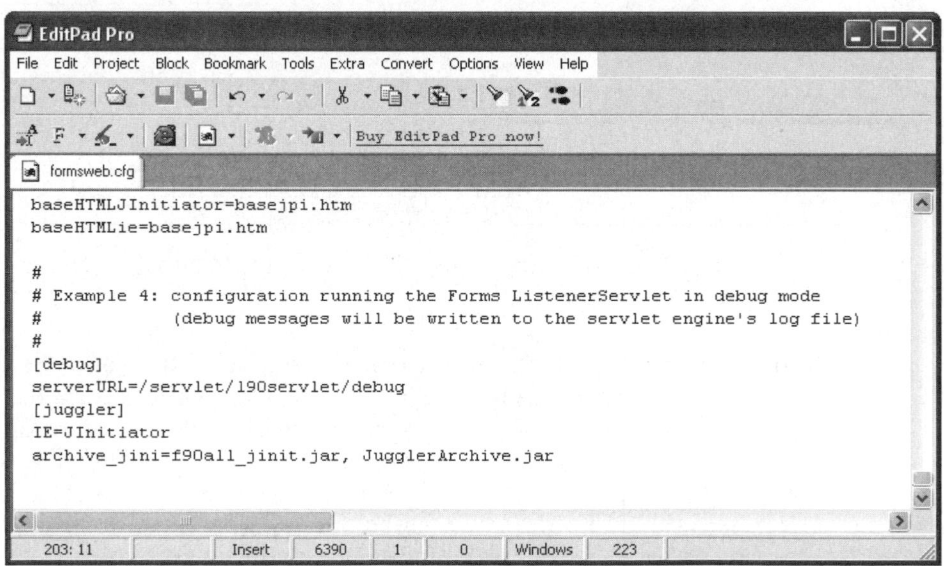

Figure 11-33 Text editor displaying the juggler reference in the **formsweb.cfg** file

11. Execute the form to display Duke the Juggler juggling a set of beans.

Using Java Classes in Your Forms

Oracle allows you to use Java classes within forms. These Java classes are stored in the database and called by the form. If you know the Java language, it is fairly easy to load Java classes into the database and use them within your form. The classes can be created using Oracle's JDeveloper or a comparable product. The following steps give you practice with Java command lines:

1. Create the Java source code file. Listing 11-4 can be used as the source of the code file. Remember that case restriction is very important in Java. The script in Listing 11-4 creates a random number generator class that can be used in your form. Save thc file as **RandomNumberGenerator.java**.

Listing 11-4 Java random number generator class

```
import java.util.Random;
public class RandomNumberGenerator {
 public RandomNumberGenerator () {
 }
 public static int getRandomInteger() {
  Random random = new Random();
  return random.nextInt();
 }
}
```


2. To create the Java class file, compile the source code file created in Step 1. This step requires that you have access to the Java development kit. You can use JDeveloper or download the latest version from Sun at *wwws.sun.com/software/java2/download.html*. At the time of this writing, the Java 2 SDK 1.4.1 is the latest product. If you have downloaded JDeveloper, you may already have the Java development kit downloaded. The executable that compiles the Java source code you created in Step 1 is named Javac. You may find the Javac executable in a **\JDK\BIN** directory.

   This step creates a Java class file called RandonNumberGenerator.class. If you are unable to create the class file, you can use one from the student files. Use the following statement to compile the Java class:

   ```
   Javac RandomNumberGenerator.java
   ```

3. Open a DOS window and navigate to the directory that contains the **RandomNumberGenerator.class** file. Upload the class file into the Oracle database by using the following command:

   ```
   Loadjava —user scott/tiger —oci8 —resolve RandomNumber
   Generator.class
   ```

4. Create a PL/SQL wrapper for the class. In this example, the wrapper consists of a PL/SQL function name RANDOM_NUMBER. This step is done in SQL*Plus or Forms Builder in the Object Navigator Database Objects node. Use the following script:

```
Create or replace function random_number
 Return number
As language java
 Name 'RandomNumberGenerator.getRandomInteger ()
return int';
/
```

The class is now ready for use in a form. Hands-on Assignment 1 in this chapter contains an example in which you can practice using the Java class in a form.

What's Next

It is now time for you to use your Oracle Forms Builder skills to benefit yourself and your employers. You now know how to operate the default form. You have learned how to override this default behavior with custom behaviors by redefining function keys and adding triggers. You have seen how to format your form using the Layout Wizard and the Layout Editor. You should also understand that a large part of Oracle form development is setting properties either programmatically or through the Property Palette. You have been exposed to a large variety of form triggers that return data to the form, perform edits, and replace the default DML statements. You have learned to use data blocks to connect to the database and how to override the default block statements using stored procedures. You have also seen how to group sets of applications together using menus and tab pages.

Oracle Forms Builder is an extremely powerful development tool that allows you to quickly develop complex business applications. If you have completed the book's Case Project, you have already completed a major application. Most of the applications that you will build are no more complex than the Case Project Budgeting System. If you understand the concepts in this book and if you have the intuition and talent to design applications, you are ready to build Web applications using Forms Builder.

Chapter Summary

- The Oracle database has object-oriented features.
- The Oracle database allows you to create abstract data types (ADTs), which are variable definitions that can be used within other objects, such as tables.
- ADTs consist of object types, varrays, object tables, and nested tables.
- Forms Builder supports object types and object tables.

- Object types embedded into a table appear on the Data Block Wizard Table page. An expansion tool appears to the left of the object. The tool causes all of the object's attributes to be displayed for selection.
- The Layout Editor treats the object attributes as it does any other item.
- An object table is a table composed of objects. The object table does not have a foreign key to its parent record but relies instead on a pointer to the parent record. This pointer is called a REF column.
- A REF column value consists of a rowid. Locating a record based on a rowid is Oracle's fastest extraction method.
- When using object tables in a form, the join is through the REF column.
- Forms Builder Web forms are used in a three-tier environment consisting of the client, middle, and database tiers.
- The client tier consists of a Web browser and JInitiator.
- JInitiator is an Oracle product that is a Web browser plug-in. It runs the applet sent back from Forms Server, which resides on the middle tier.
- In constrast to most Web applications that are stateless, Forms Server maintains a state throughout the session.
- In Web application development, resources and bandwidth are major performance considerations.
- All fonts used by Forms Builder on the Web are Java fonts. Forms Builder uses the closest equivalent of a Java font to the Windows and X Windows fonts.
- The **formsweb.cfg** file allows you to define a number of format characteristics, including the height and width of the applet area, the type of window used, and a color scheme.
- Forms Builder on the Web does not support most third-party controls. However, it does support Java controls.
- A bean area data item is used to add JavaBeans to the form.
- A Java class wrapper is a PL/SQL-stored procedure that can be used inside a form.

Review Questions

1. Match the following terms that have appeared in this chapter with their descriptions:

a. Front end	________	A table that is comprised of objects.
b. Object table	________	The quickest Oracle access or retrieval path.

c. Bean area	________________	The pointer to a record in another table.
d. Roundtrip	________________	The tier that interacts with the user via the Web browser.
e. Sans Serif size 9	________________	An object table that is embedded in another table. Forms Builder does not support this type of object.
f. Rowid	________________	A configuration file used to set the applet width, height, LookAndFeel, and ColorScheme attributes.
g. Forms Server	________________	The software that coordinates the requests from the Web browser with requests to the database.
h. Nested table	________________	A set of related variables or attributes that can be inherited by a number of other objects.
i. **formsweb.cfg**	________________	The recommended default font for Web-deployed forms.
j. Varray	________________	The database tier.
k. Object type	________________	An attribute that can be set to determine whether the Web form looks like a Windows application or an Oracle application.
l. REF column	________________	A data block item that can display a Java Bean.
m. Color Scheme	________________	A Web browser plug-in that is downloaded the first time an operator accesses a Web form.
n. Back end	________________	The tier that contains the server software that controls the requests from the Web browser.
o. JInitiator	________________	An object that consists of a series of related variables.
p. LookAndFeel	________________	The attribute that determines the color of the applet, headings, and status bar.
q. Middle tier	________________	A request to the middle-tier server that requires return data.

2. What are the benefits of using Oracle's object technology?
3. What are the disadvantages of using Oracle's object technology?

4. Identify the tiers in a three-tiered environment. What are the functions of each tier? What types of software exist on each tier?
5. Four different tables reference the same object table. How many REF columns must the table have?
6. Why do you think Oracle supports Java so strongly in its products?
7. A user called you and said that it takes a long time to download a Web form that you created, but that after the form is displayed, it performs fairly well. The user would like you to speed up the download. What do can you do to improve performance?
8. You have just compiled and executed a form. You notice that the form's window has arrows in the form rather than the normal Windows Minimize and Maximize icons. Why has this occurred?
9. A user called you on the phone about a form that was built by a contractor who is no longer with the company. The user says the form is extremely sluggish and that every time she clicks the mouse button, the form freezes and the hourglass symbol appears. What do you think is happening?
10. A user called you and reported that the standard Cut, Copy, and Paste tools were not on the toolbar. Can you explain to the user why they are not there and suggest some alternatives?
11. What does it mean to wrap a Java class?

Exam Review Questions

1. You are planning to use objects as the data source of your form. What is the first object to be declared?
   a. Object table
   b. Object type
   c. Object varray
   d. REF column
2. Which abstract data types are not supported by Forms Builder? (Pick two.)
   a. Object table
   b. Nested object table
   c. Varray
   d. Object type
3. You have a table that has a REF column. What kind of value goes into the REF column?
   a. Primary key of the related parent record
   b. Foreign key of the related child record
   c. Rowid of the related parent record
   d. Rowid of the related child record

4. You want the form window's sizing tools to appear just like the Windows sizing tools. You must set the LookAndFeel setting to:
   a. WINDOWS
   b. ORACLE
   c. GENERIC
   d. Blank
5. You are using the Forms Builder Data Block Wizard to reset a data block's items. On which page are an object's attributes displayed?
   a. Object page
   b. Type page
   c. Table page
   d. Master-Detail page

HANDS-ON ASSIGNMENTS

1. In this assignment, you create a form that generates a list of random numbers. The operator enters the total population size and the size of the sample. The form then uses a Java class wrapped in a PL/SQL wrapper to generate the list when a button is clicked. To accomplish this, perform the following steps:
   a. Open the Object Navigator and create a new form module.
   b. Create a canvas object and name it **MAIN_CANVAS**.
   c. Create two control blocks. Name them **RANDOM_SAMPLE_PARAMETERS** and **RANDOM_NUMBER_LIST**.
   d. Open a Property Palette for the RANDOM_SAMPLE_PARAMETERS data block and set the Database Data Block to **NO**.
   e. Open a Property Palette for the RANDOM_NUMBER_LIST and set the following properties:
      - Database Data Block: **NO**
      - Number of Records Displayed: **15**
   f. Create an item under the RANDOM_SAMPLE_PARAMETERS data block and set the following properties:
      - Name: **POPULATION_SIZE**
      - Data Type: **NUMBER**
      - Database Item: **NO**
      - Canvas: **MAIN_CANVAS**
      - Prompt: **POPULATION SIZE**

g. Create a second item under the RANDOM_SAMPLE_PARAMETERS data block and set the following properties:
   - Name: **SAMPLE_SIZE**
   - Data Type: **NUMBER**
   - Database Item: **NO**
   - Canvas: **MAIN_CANVAS**
   - Prompt: **SAMPLE SIZE**
h. Create a button item under the RANDOM_SAMPLE_PARAMETERS data block and set the following properties:
   - Name: **GENERATE**
   - Item Type: **PUSH BUTTON**
   - Label: **GENERATE**
   - Canvas: **MAIN_CANVAS**
i. Create an item under the RANDOM_NUMBER_LIST data block and set the following properties:
   - Name: **RANDOM_NUMBERS**
   - Data Type: **CHAR**
   - Database Item: **NO**
   - Canvas: **MAIN_CANVAS**
   - Prompt: **RANDOM NUMBERS**
j. Open the Layout Editor and format the canvas. It should appear similar to Figure 11-34.
k. Create a When-Button-Pressed trigger under the Generate button using the Listing 11-5 script. Notice that it uses the RandomNumberGenerator Java class that is embedded in the Random_number function you created in the Using Java Classes in your Form Practice Session. If you have not successfully compiled the Random_number function, you will not be able to compile the Listing 11-5 When-Button-Pressed trigger. .

11

Listing 11-5 When-Button-Pressed trigger

```
declare
     random_num                    varchar2(100);
     converted_random_num          number;
     pop_size                      number;
     counter                       number := 0;
```

```
begin
      go_block ('random_number_list');
      clear_block;
      while counter < :random_sample_parameters.sample_size
      loop
-- Determines the scale of the population size.
-- Random number must fit
-- within the scale (i.e If the scale is 1000 then
--                                 all random numbers
--                                 must be 1000 or less.
pop_size := to_number(length(to_char
                  (:random_sample_parameters.population_size)));
-- The following statement generates a reandom number based
-- upon the Java class wrapped in the random_number function
     random_num := to_char(abs(random_number));
-- Trims number on the left to ensure the number fits the scale
     converted_random_num :=
            substr(random_num, pop_size * -1,
                  length(random_num));
-- Determines if the random number is above the population size
-- If it is, the number is discarded
         if converted_random_num <=
                       :random_sample_parameters.population_size
then
         :random_number_list.random_numbers :=
                                       converted_random_num;
     next_record;  -- moves to the next data block record
-- Increments the counter
     counter := counter + 1;
   end if;
-- Random numbers are based upon time.
-- This section allows the clock to move
-- changing the random number
     declare
        counter1    number := 0;
     begin
        while counter1 != 15000 loop
            counter1 := counter1 + 1;
        end loop;
     end;
  end loop;
  first_record;
end;
```

l. Save the form as **ch11ex01.fmb**.

m. Execute the form and test it. Enter a population size of **100,000** and a sample size of **60**. It may take half a minute or more to generate the values and return the results to the screen. Figure 11-34 illustrates the completed form.

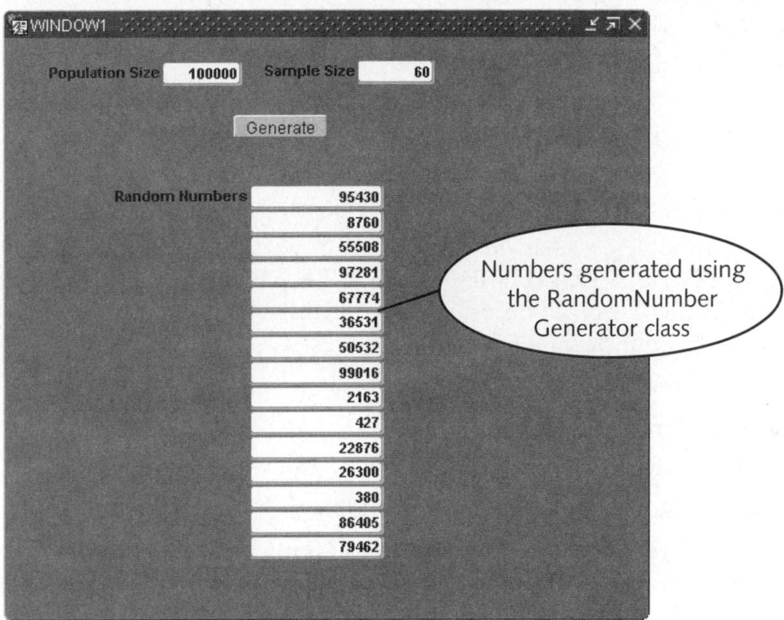

Figure 11-34 Form that generates random numbers using a Java class wrapped in a PL/SQL function

2. In this assignment, you create two tables and embed the ADDRESS object into each of the tables as a type. You then place both tables in one form and verify that both tables are using the same object. To accomplish these tasks, perform the following steps:

   a. Log on to SQL*Plus and create a copy of the EMP table by using the following script:

   ```
   Create table emp2 as select * from emp;
   ```

   b. Add the ADDRESS object to the EMP2 table by using the following script:

   ```
   Alter table emp2 add employee_address address ;
   ```

   c. Using the Listing 11-6 script, create a STUDENT table. If you receive this error, an `ORA-00955:name is already used by an existing object` you may have accidentally created this table in an earlier practice. If so, remove the table from the database using the following command before using Listing 11-6: `Drop table student;`

Listing 11-6 STUDENT CREATE TABLE statement

```
Create table student
(student_id           number primary key,
 student_name         varchar2(20),
 enrollment_date      date,
 student_address      address);
```

d. Create a new form module.

e. Create a data block based on the EMP2 table. Select the **EMPNO**, **ENAME**, **STREET**, **CITY**, **STATE,** and **ZIP_CODE** columns. The layout should be Tabular with 5 records.

f. Create a data block based on the STUDENT table defined earlier in the chapter. This table also has the ADDRESS object embedded in it. Select the **STUDENT_ID**, **STUDENT_NAME**, **STREET**, **CITY**, **STATE,** and **ZIP_CODE** columns. Do not create a relationship between the data blocks. The layout should be Tabular with 5 records.

g. Save this form as **ch11ex02.fmb**.

h. Execute and run the form.

i. Add address information to several of the employees.

j. Add several students along with their addresses.

k. Execute a query in each of the data blocks. This must be done independently, because there is no relationship between the data blocks. Notice that both data blocks have the same address attributes. Figure 11-35 illustrates this form.

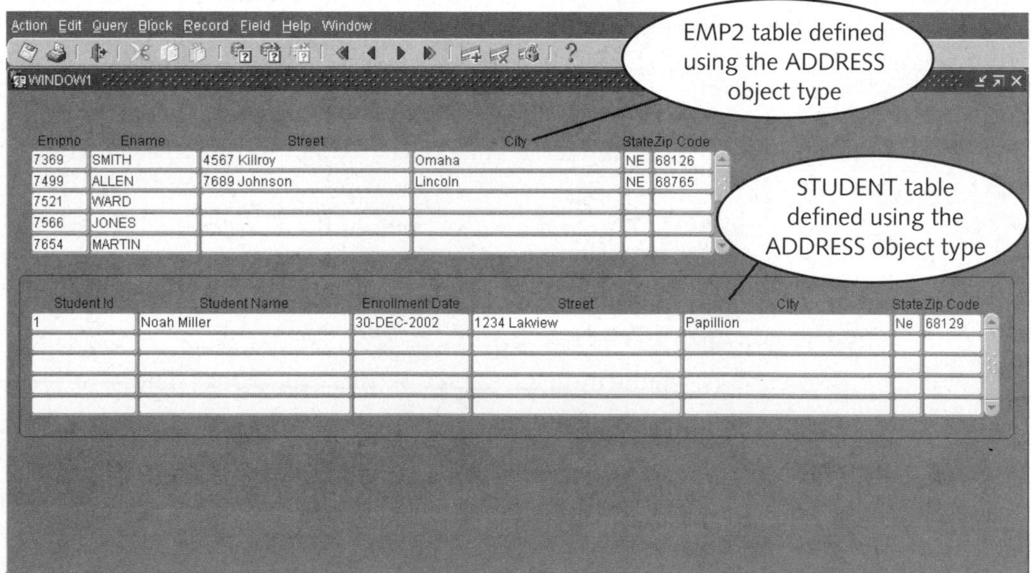

Figure 11-35 EMP2 and STUDENT data blocks containing the ADDRESS object type

Databases older than Oracle9*i* do not support the following statement. In addition, this cannot be done in Form Builder 6*i*.

3. This assignment demonstrates the process that you follow when an object changes or evolves. In this assignment, you add a CELLULAR phone attribute to the ADDRESS_ATTRIBUTES object. This in turn updates all tables that use the object. You use the EMP2 and STUDENT tables. After modifying the object, you use the Data Block Wizard and Layout Wizard to place the new attribute in the form. To accomplish these tasks, perform the following steps:

   a. Log on to SQL*Plus and modify the ADDRESS object by using the following script.

   ```
   Alter type address add attribute cellular varchar2(12)
      Cascade including table data;
   ```

   b. Close and reopen Forms Builder before performing the remaining steps. This resynchronizes Forms Builder with the database change just performed.

   c. Open form module **ch11ex02.fmb**.

   d. Open the Object Navigator and select the **EMP2** data block.

   e. Select the **Tools/Data Block Wizard** menu option.

   f. Click the **Table** tab in the wizard. Notice that the Available Columns list box does not contain the ADDRESS object.

   g. Click the **Refresh** button. The ADDRESS object now displays.

   h. Expand the object and display the CELLULAR attribute. Move it to the Database Items list.

   i. Click the **Finish** button. The CELLULAR attribute has now been added to the data block.

   j. Select the **Tools/Layout Wizard** menu option. On the Data Block page, add **CELLULAR** to the Displayed Items list. Be sure to keep the Tabular style with five records.

   k. Click the **Finish** button.

   l. Repeat steps d through k substituting the STUDENT table.

   m. Save the form as **ch11ex03.fmb**.

   n. You have now added the attribute to both data blocks. The form should look similar to Figure 11-36.

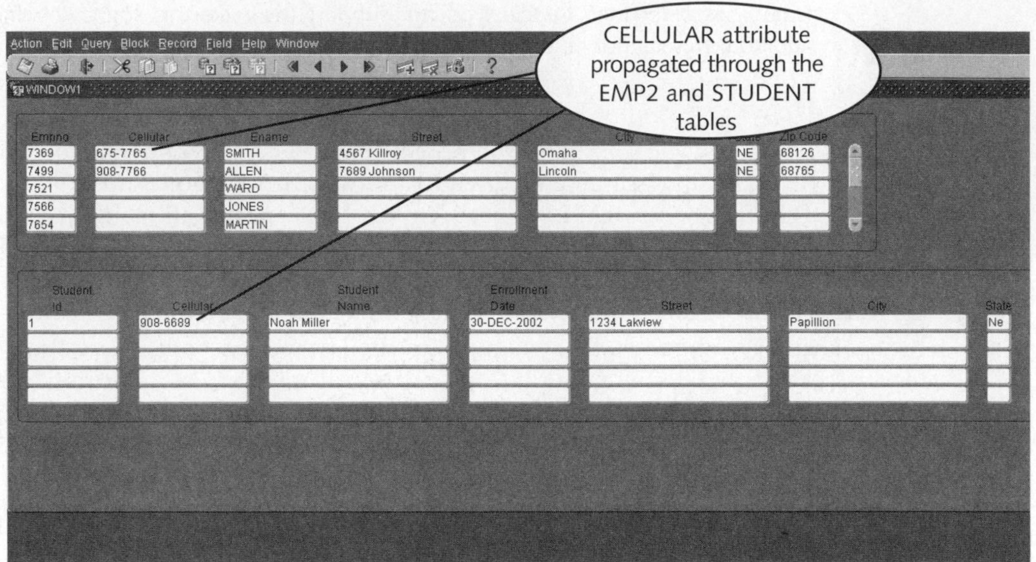

Figure 11-36 Form after the CELLULAR attribute has been added

4. In this assignment, you modify the **formsweb.cfg** file format options. The purpose of this assignment is to help you understand the effect of the setting changes. Perform the following steps:

   a. Open the **formsweb.cfg** file in a text editor, such as EditPad or NotePad. Change the following settings:

      - LookAndFeel: **ORACLE**
      - Width: **1000**

   b. Open Forms Builder and load the module **ch11ex02.fmb**. Run the form, and notice how it looks. Drag the form around the applet area and then close the form.

   c. Reopen the **formsweb.cfg** file in the text editor. Change the **LookAndFeel** setting to **GENERIC**. Save the changes.

   d. Run the **ch11ex02.fmb** form and notice how the form looks. Drag the form around the applet area and then close the form.

   e. Reopen the **formsweb.cfg** file in the text editor. Change the Width setting to **500**. Save the changes.

   f. Run the **ch11ex02.fmb** form and notice that the applet width has changed and a portion of the form is not concealed. Close the form.

   g. Reopen the **formsweb.cfg** file. Change the COLORSCHEME setting to **TITANIUM** or **KHAKI**. Save the changes.

h. Run form **ch11ex02.fmb**. You should see no effect from the last step, because the LookAndFeel setting is GENERIC. Close the form.

i. Reopen the **formsweb.cfg** file. Change the LOOKANDFEEL setting to **ORACLE**. Save the change.

j. Run form **ch11ex02.fmb**. See if the COLORSCHEME setting works now. Close the form when you are finished.

CASE PROJECT: GREAT STATE ELECTRIC BUDGETING SYSTEM

In this chapter, you conduct a system test as the last section of the Case Project. System tests are performed before going into production to prove to the customer that the system performs the functions the customer expects and to obtain formal customer acceptance. A system test is conducted using a test plan that was developed early in the project. It typically consists of many of the scenarios that can occur in day-to-day business, but because this is a case project, the scenarios are limited.

When developing a test plan, it is sensible to begin with a data flow diagram, which depicts the various tasks that the system performs, as well as the data needed and produced by system processes. The test plan for this last section of the Case Project is based on the data flow diagram depicted in Figure 1-12. You may want to review the diagram as you conduct the test.

To conduct the system test, perform the following steps:

1. Open Forms Builder and load the Budgeting Application that you have been working on throughout the book.
2. Open the Object Navigator and locate the Key-Others trigger.
3. Delete the trigger and save the form. This will allow you to tab through the data block items.
4. Run the application. The budgeting process begins when personnel from the Planning department of Great State Electric enter a new project into the system. This is process 1.1 in Figure 1-12, and it occurs on the ADD NEW PROJECTS form.
5. Click the **Add Project** button on the toolbar to open the ADD NEW PROJECTS form and enter the following information:
    - Project ID: **D1000012**
    - Project Name: **BABY BUBBY'S STORAGE FACILITY**
    - Project Need Date: **19-JAN-2003**
    - Project Location: **7834 PINEVIEW ST**
    - Assigned Department ID: **DE**
    - Project Scope: **PROVIDE 3 PHASE UNDERGROUND POWER**

6. Click the **Save** button to save the record.

   The next step is to estimate the project costs (Process 1.2), which consists of a number of subprocesses. In the first of these processes, the Distribution engineering manager assigns the project to an engineer. This occurs in the PROJECTS form.

7. Click the **Close Dialog** button to close the Add New Projects form. Click the **PROJECTS** tab. Using the drop-down list, select **DISTRIBUTION ENGINEERING** as the ASSIGNED DEPARTMENT ID in the Project Search Variables section of the main form. Perform a query by clicking the **Query** button. Scroll through the projects using the scroll bar until you locate project **D1000012**.

   A project is assigned to an engineer when a work order record is created. In this subtask, you create a work order and assign it to the engineer.

8. Make sure the **D1000012** project is selected.

9. Move the insertion point to the **WORK ORDERS** data block ID item. Double-click the mouse to generate a work order ID.

10. Finish populating the work order record by entering the following information:
    - Description: **ADD TRANSFORMER, CABLE, AND PEDESTAL**
    - Location: **4 HOUSES NORTH OF 7832 PINEVIEW ST.**
    - Assign To: **ADOLPH MILLER**

Adolph Miller does not exist. Click the **Employees** tab and add him to the database. Save the employee record. Return to the Projects tab and assign the project to **ADOLPH MILLER**. He should now be displayed on the LOV.

The next process, which also consists of several subprocesses, is to estimate the costs. The first process notifies the engineer that he was assigned a work order that requires an estimate. This process is performed on the Work Orders tab. The engineer places his name in the Assigned To search field and clicks the Query button to display the engineer's work orders. Work orders without calculated costs must be estimated.

11. Select the **Work Orders** tab. Use the LOV to populate the Assigned To search item with Adolph Miller's payroll number. Click the **Query** button to view the work orders that match the selection criteria.

12. Select the **work order** you created in Step 9. Enter a **task** and attempt to save the record. An error should occur.

13. Use your function keys to open the **Database Error** dialog box. A message should indicate that you cannot insert a record with nulls. If you investigate the constraints on the WORK_ORDER_TASKS table, you see that the ASSIGNED_DEPARTMENT_ID field must have a value. Looking at the form,

you should see that the item is not displayed. You have encountered an error (this was intentional to demonstrate that system tests do find errors).

When errors are encountered in a system test, corrections should be made and the test resumed.

14. Make the **ASSIGNED_DEPARTMENT_ID** visible and place it on the WORK_ORDERS tab page so that the user can enter a value. You may also want to add a LOV for the item.
15. Resume the test. Add several tasks and costs to the work order. Next, the project manager approves the work order estimates using the PROJECTS tab page. The manager queries the projects for his department. Projects that have costs but are not approved are marked approved. Retrieve project **D1000012** on the PROJECTS tab page. Approve the work order by placing Matthew Palinski's name into the Approved By item.

You could test more system functions, but the work in this Case Project has given you a feel for system testing. It is also highly likely that you found errors. If you have completed this test and were able to perform the described functions, you have built an actual budgeting system that is similar to an actual system of a functioning organization. You should be proud of yourself and feel confident that you can now build Oracle Form Web-based systems.

Installing Packages and Solving Common Problems

This book was written using three products:

- Oracle9*i* Database Release 2 Enterprise for Windows NT/2000/XP
- Oracle9*i*DS (Developer Suite) Release 2 (9.0.2)
- Oracle6*i* Developer

The examples in this book were created using Oracle9*i*DS Forms Builder. The steps in the practices, assignments, and case project were created in both Oracle6*i* Form Builder and Oracle9*i* Forms Builder. The concepts in this book apply to both products, except in instances that are documented in the later chapters. The main difference between Forms Builder 9*i* and Form Builder 6*i* are:

- Forms Builder 9*i* cannot be used in a client/server environment, whereas Form Builder 6*i* can be used both in a client/server environment and on the Web.
- Reports are executed differently in Forms Builder 9*i*.
- Forms Builder 9*i* does not have all the functionality of Form Builder 6*i*, but it is very close.
- The screens and menus of the two products' integrated development environment (IDE) have slightly different looks but are essentially the same.

Although 9*i* is obviously the most recent release, the application steps in this book were tested both with Form Builder 6*i* and 9*i*, because a large base of 6*i* installations exists. In spite of the fact that Oracle will stop supporting 6*i* in 2004, many companies will continue to use it for a number of years, because they have stable systems, and they prefer to stay in the client/server environment. As a matter of fact, many companies are using unsupported versions 3.0, 4.5, and 5.0 of Form Builder.

Before using this book, you must install the Oracle9*i* database and either the Oracle 6*i* Developer or Oracle 9*i* Developer Suite. You can buy a copy of the Oracle9*i* database from Course Technology as part of the Course Technology Kit for Oracle9*i* Software. Please contact your Course Technology Sales Representative for information about purchasing this CD Kit. The Oracle9*i* Developer Suite comes packaged in the back of this book. These products are also available from Oracle. Please visit the Oracle Web site *at www.oracle.com* for more information about purchasing and downloading these products.

Evaluation copies downloaded from the Oracle Web site were used to test the steps in this book. The following sections of this appendix describe how to download the files from Oracle and install them on your computer.

Downloading the files from *www.oracle.com* is an option if you choose not to purchase the Course Technology Kit for Oracle9i Software. Downloading the files from *www.oracle.com* may or may not be a practical option, depending on the limitations of your system and what type of Internet connection you are working with. If you do purchase the Course Technology Kit, the installation process will be very similar to what you see in this appendix. Specific installation instructions for the kit are available at *www.course.com/cdkit*.

You should note that the Oracle Web site constantly changes. The screens that you actually see during your installation may differ from those illustrated in this appendix. This, however, is only an inconvenience, and it should be relatively easy to obtain evaluation software from Oracle.

The downloadable Oracle9*i* database will consist of three very large zip files. You must unzip or extract the files after they are downloaded. These extracted files are *not* the Oracle9*i* database but rather the files needed to install the database. You need at least 5 gigabytes (GB) of hard disk space for the downloaded zip files, extracted files, and the Oracle9*i* database. Of course, after you have extracted the files, you can delete the zip files, and after you have set up the database, you can delete the extracted files to free up some space.

A second caution involves the speed of your Internet service. If you do not have a fast connection, do not attempt to download the files. Instead, you must purchase the evaluation software from Oracle. Oracle generally charges $39.95 for the database files and $39.95 for the Development Suite and sends them to you on a CD. The evaluation software can be purchased on the Oracle Web site. This eliminates the need for the 5 GB of memory and a fast connection. You will still need 2.86 GB for the Oracle database.

FINDING THE SOFTWARE ON THE ORACLE WEB SITE

To find the software you need, follow these steps:

1. Open your Web browser and display Oracle's main page using this URL: *www.oracle.com*. The page should look similar to Figure A-1.

Figure A-1 Oracle main Web page and the Downloads link

2. Locate and click the **Downloads** link to open the Oracle Technology Network (OTN) Downloads page (see Figure App_A-2). OTN is a free network that Oracle makes available to all interested parties. OTN offers the evaluation software and a massive variety of white papers on various Oracle topics. Membership is required because Oracle wants to keep track of who receives downloads and what papers you view. All Oracle users access this network at one time or another.

3. Click the **registration** link to be stepped through the registration process. When you complete this process, Oracle sends you by e-mail a user ID and password. You can then download products and perform searches.

The Downloads page contains listings for all available Oracle products. You are interested in the Oracle9*i* Database and the Oracle9*i* Developer Suite links that are illustrated in Figure A-2.

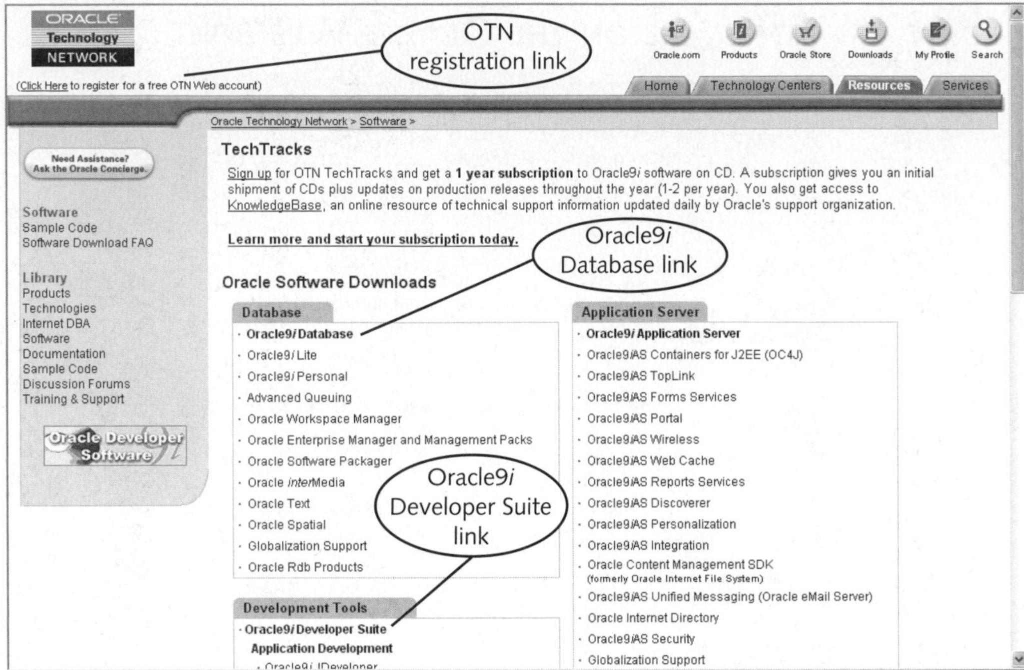

Figure A-2 Oracle Technology Network Downloads page

DOWNLOADING AND UNZIPPING THE ORACLE9*i* DATABASE

To download and unzip the Oracle 9*i* database, follow these steps:

1. Click the **Oracle9*i* Database** link.
2. The Oracle9*i* Database Downloads page appears, as shown in Figure App_A-3. Click the appropriate download link, which is probably the Oracle9*i* Database Release 2 Enterprise/Standard/Personal Edition for Windows NT/2000/XP product.
3. A page with the terms of the Oracle Technology Network Developer License will be displayed. Accept the terms by checking each of the checkboxes and clicking the **I Accept** button. The Download Now page displays, as shown in Figure A-4. Click the **Download Now** button. You are prompted to enter your OTN password and to enter personal information on a series of pages.

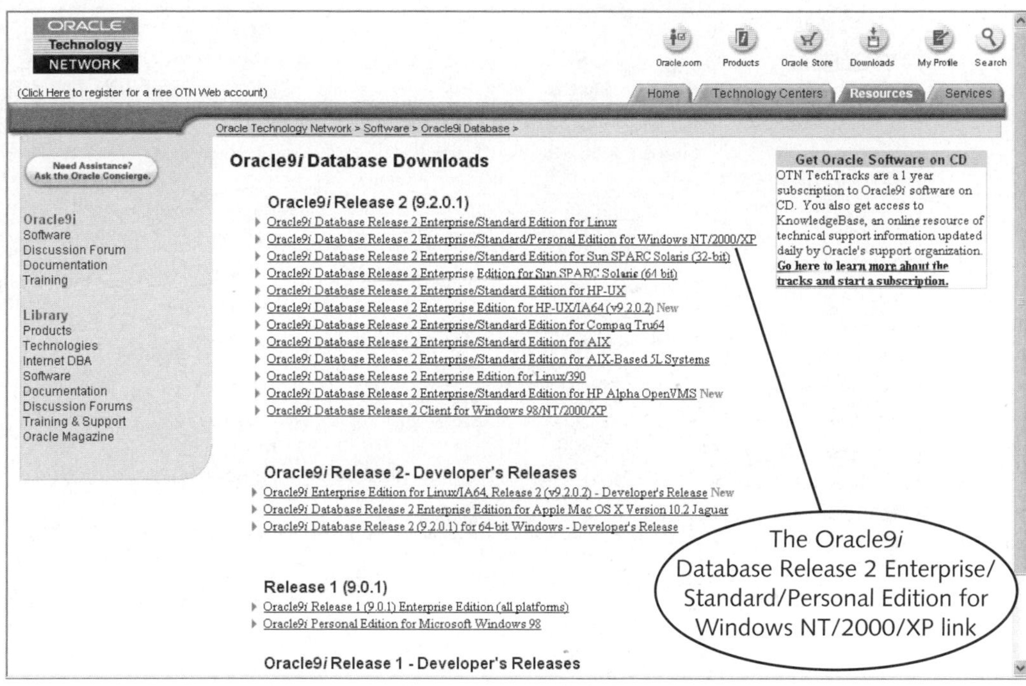

Figure A-3 Oracle9*i* Database Downloads page

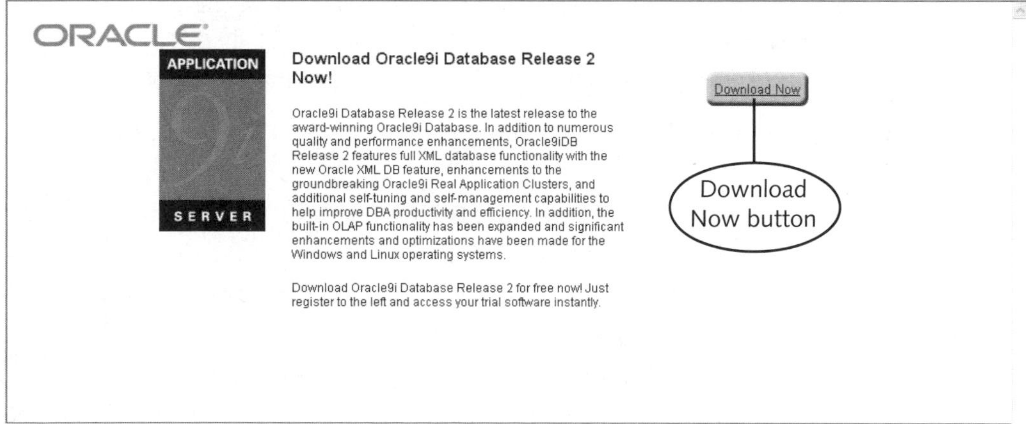

Figure A-4 Download Now page

4. After entering the information, the resulting page displays links to three zip files, as illustrated in Figure A-5. Note the directions on the zip file page. If they differ from the steps that follow in this section, disregard these steps and follow those that Oracle provides.

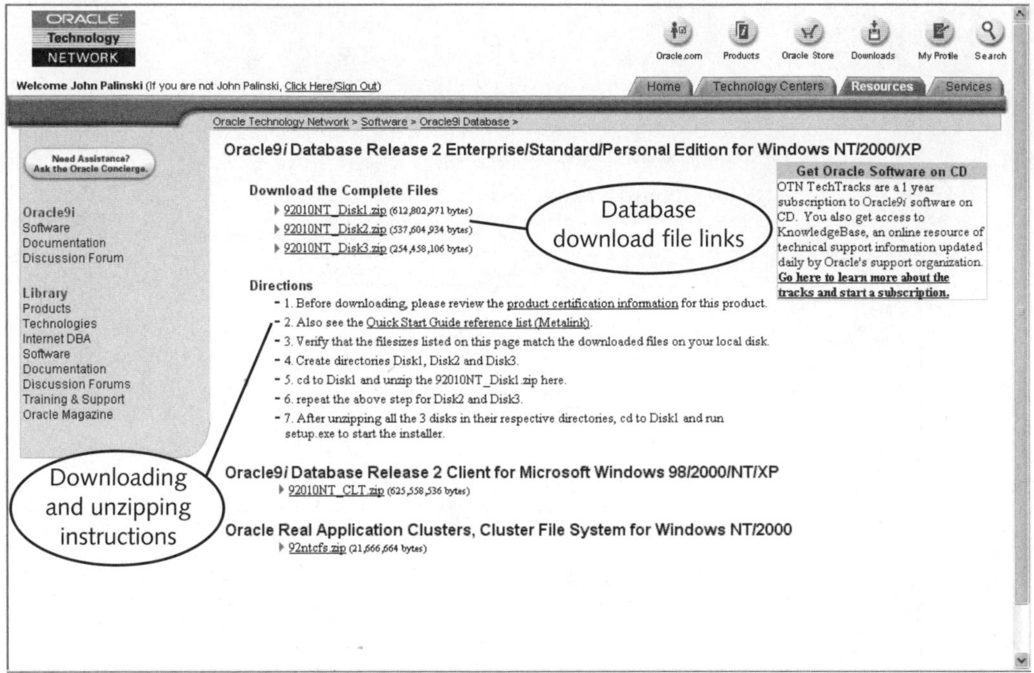

Figure A-5 Zip file page

5. Create three directories on your computer using the following names: **disk1, disk2, disk3**.
6. Download the first zip file named **92010NT_Disk1.zip** into the disk1 directory.
7. Download the second zip file named **92010NT_Disk2.zip** into the disk2 directory.
8. Download the third zip file named **92010NT_Disk3.zip** into the disk3 directory.
9. Extract the **92010NT_Disk1.zip** file into the disk1 directory using WinZip or PKZIP. Both products are available for download and evaluation on the Web.
10. Extract the **92010NT_Disk2.zip** file into the disk2 directory.
11. Extract the **92010NT_Disk3.zip** file into the disk3 directory.

INSTALLING THE ORACLE9*I* DATABASE

To install the Oracle9*i* database, follow these steps:

1. Open Windows Explorer and locate the **setup.exe** file in the disk1 directory shown in Figure A-6. This executable opens the Oracle Universal Installer and begins the database installation. Double-click the **setup.exe** startup file icon.

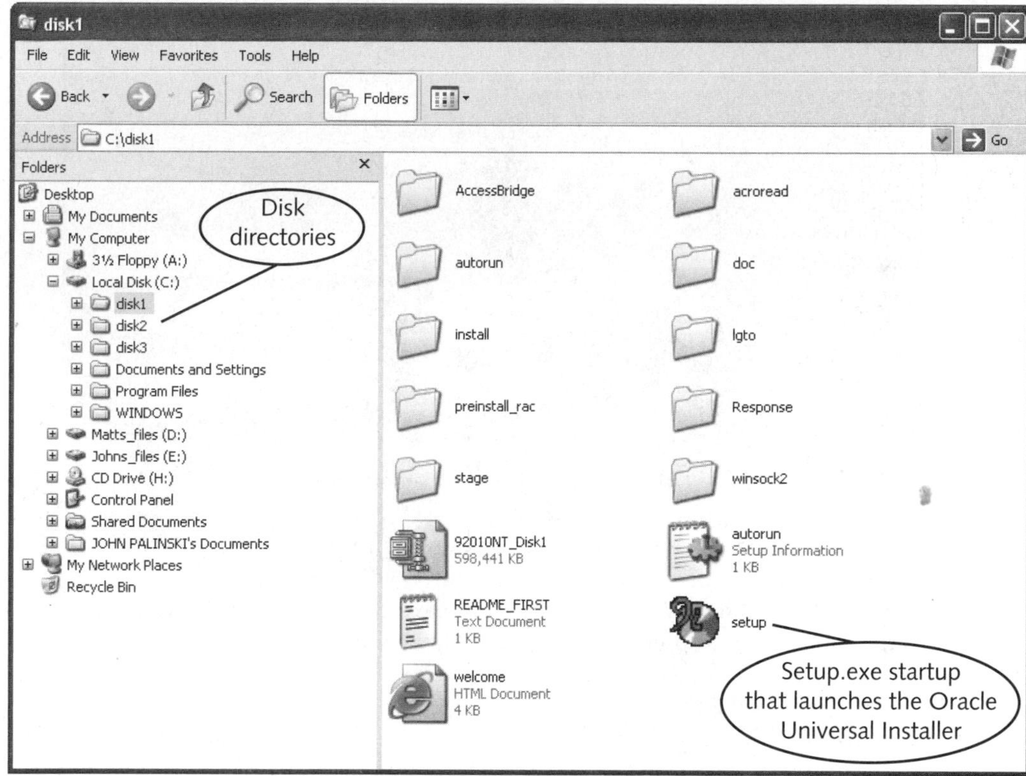

Figure A-6 Windows Explorer displaying the setup.exe file icon

2. Once the Oracle Universal Installer starts, you may see a page asking whether you want to install, deinstall, or browse. Select the Install/Deinstall option. The Oracle Universal Installer Welcome page displays, as shown in Figure A-7. Click **Next**.

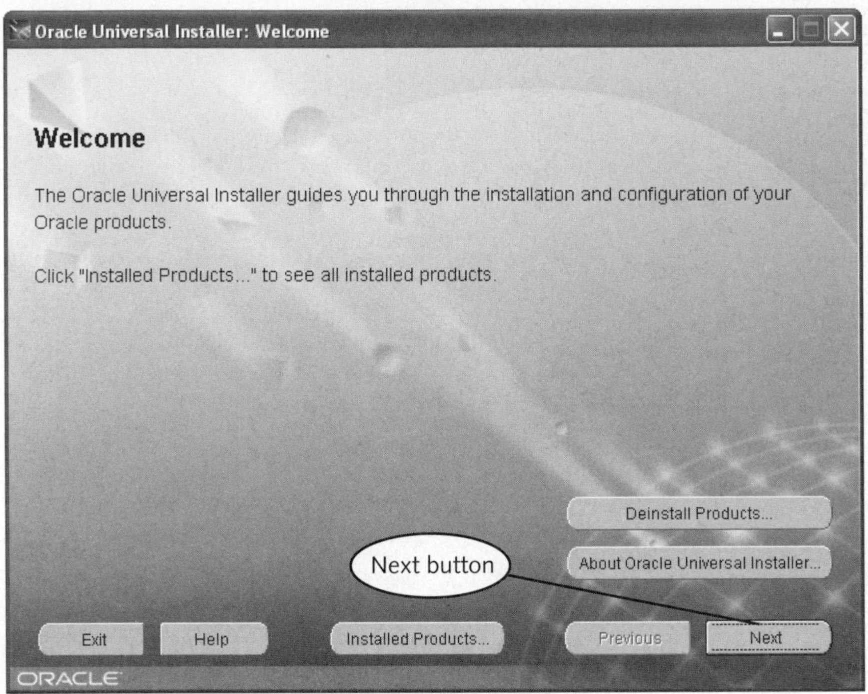

Figure A-7 Oracle Universal Installer Welcome page

3. The File Locations page displays, as shown in Figure A-8. If you have not installed Oracle on your computer, you can accept the default settings. If you have installed Oracle, you may have to change the Destination Name value to another unused Name value. Click **Next**.

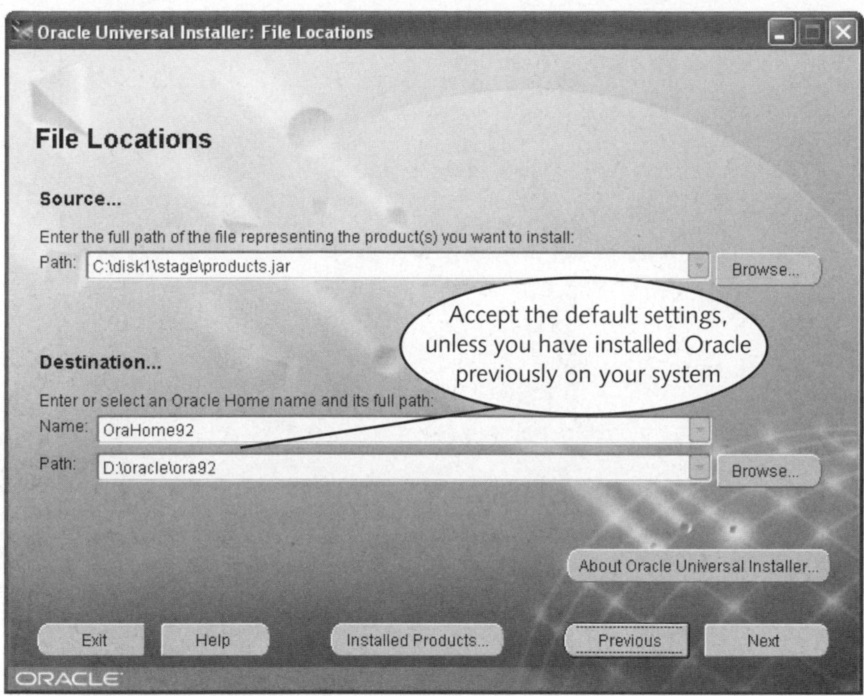

Figure A-8 File Locations page

4. The Available Products page displays, as shown in Figure A-9. If necessary select the **Oracle9*i* Database 9.2.0.1.0** radio button. Click **Next**.

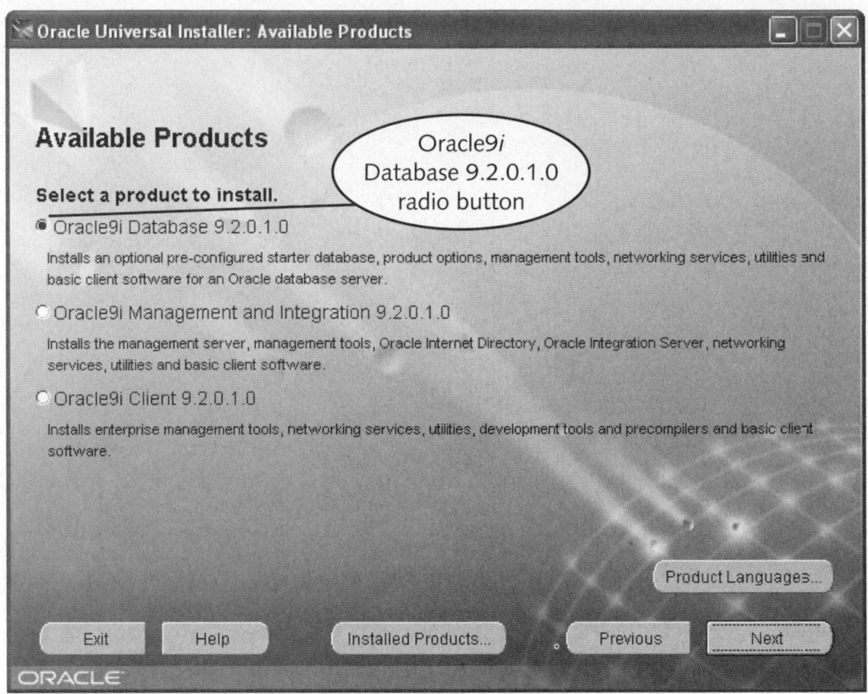

Figure A-9 Available Products page

5. The Installation Types page displays, as shown in Figure A-10. Click the **Enterprise Edition** radio button and then click **Next**.

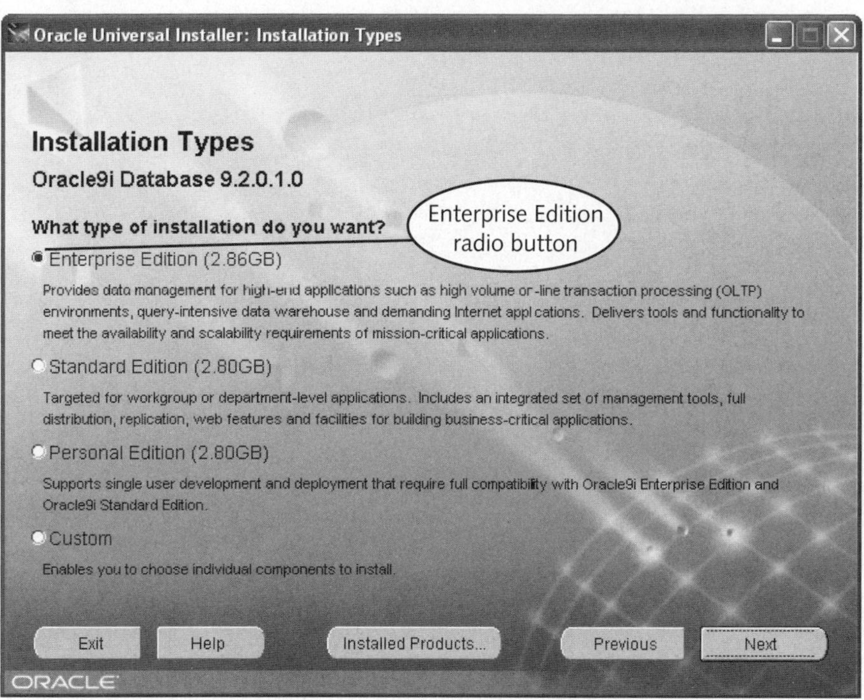

Figure A-10 Installation Types page

6. The Database Configuration page displays, as shown in Figure A-11. Click the **General Purpose** radio button, and then click **Next**.

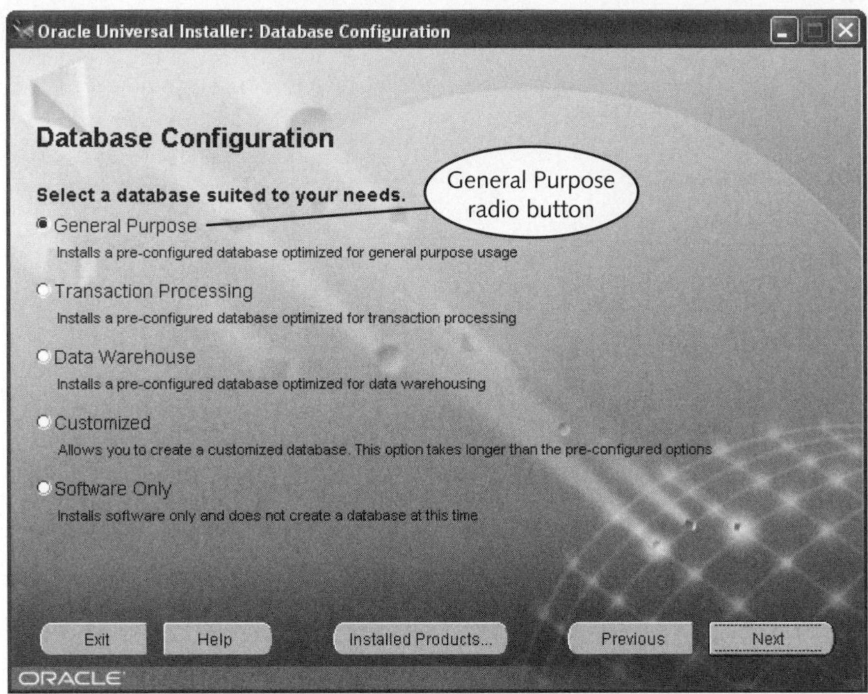

Figure A-11 Database Configuration page

7. The Oracle Services for Microsoft Transaction Server page displays, as shown in Figure A-12. Accept the default port number and click **Next**.

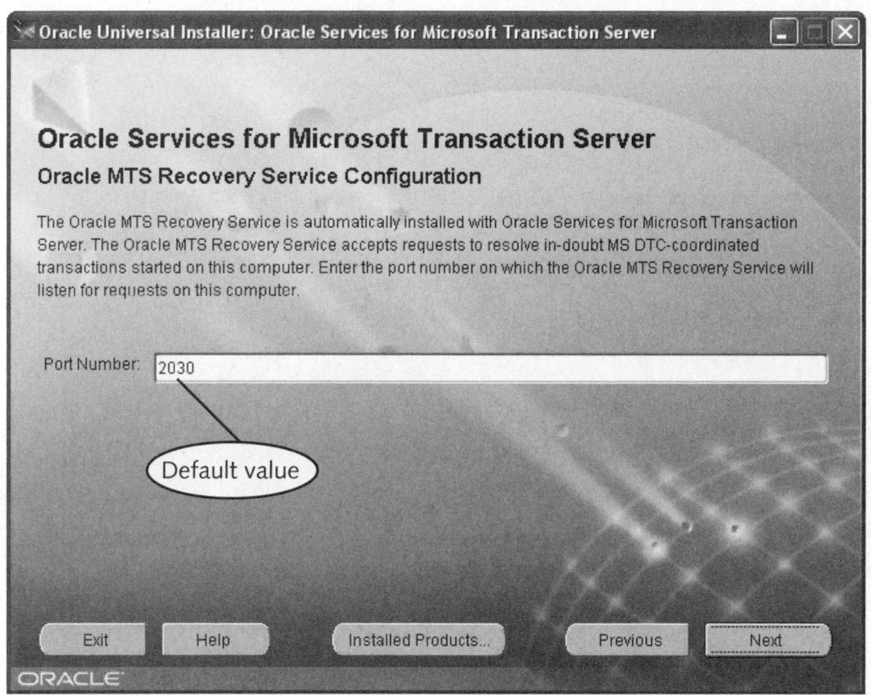

Figure A-12 Oracle Services for Microsoft Transaction Server page

8. The Database Identification page displays, as shown in Figure A-13. For the Global Database Name, enter a name that you are familiar with that does not exceed eight characters. REAL is the first four characters of my consulting company name. The SID (or site ID) text item is automatically populated with up to the first eight characters of the name. Click **Next**.

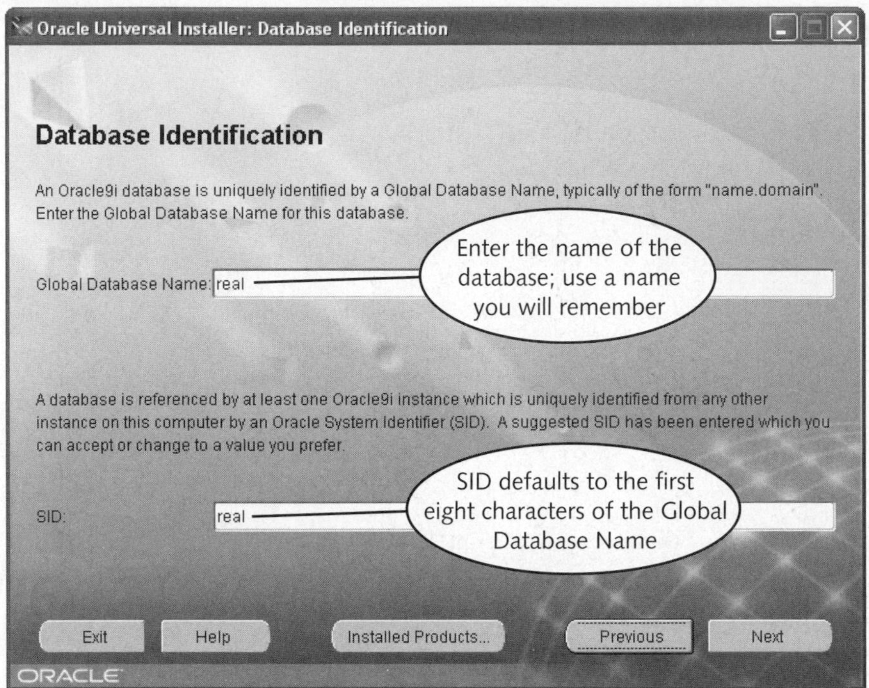

Figure A-13 Database Identification page

9. The Database File Location page displays, as shown in Figure A-14. Accept the defaults and click **Next**.

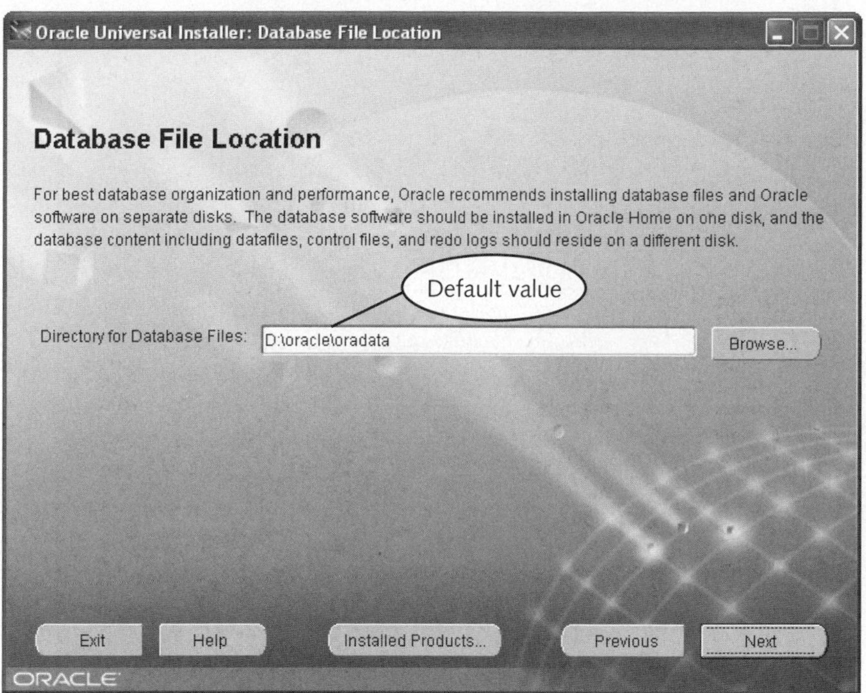

Figure A-14 Database File Location page

10. The Database Character Set page displays, as shown in Figure A-15. Accept the default settings and click **Next**.

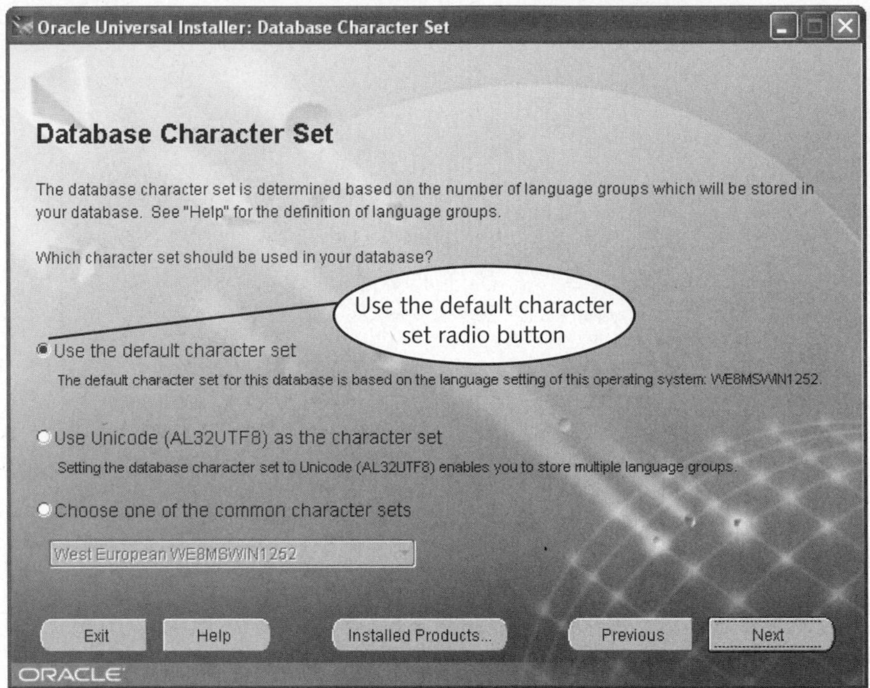

Figure A-15 Database Character Set page

11. The Summary page displays (see Figure A-16), from which the actual installation begins. Click the **Install** button.

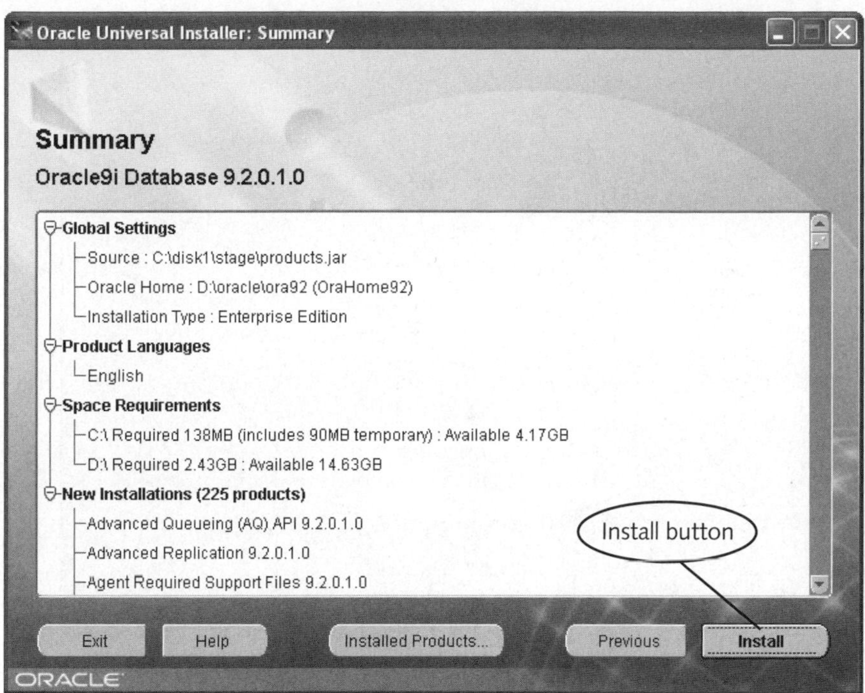

Figure A-16 Summary page

12. The installation takes some time and you can watch its progress on the Install page depicted in Figure A-17.

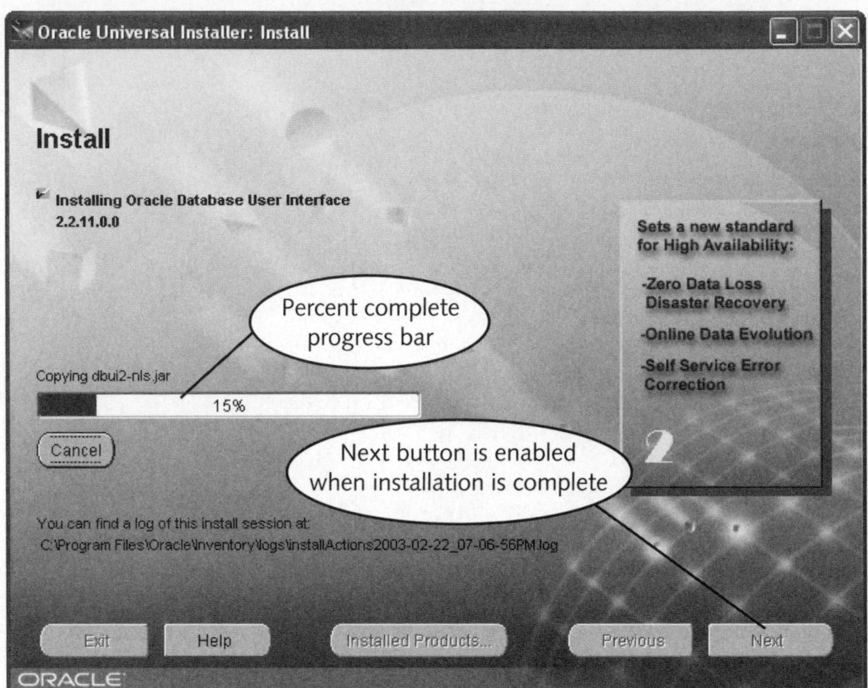

Figure A-17 Install page

13. During the installation, you are prompted to enter passwords for the SYS and SYSTEM IDs, as shown in Figure A-18. These are the master Oracle IDs. Enter names that you will remember, and then click **OK**.

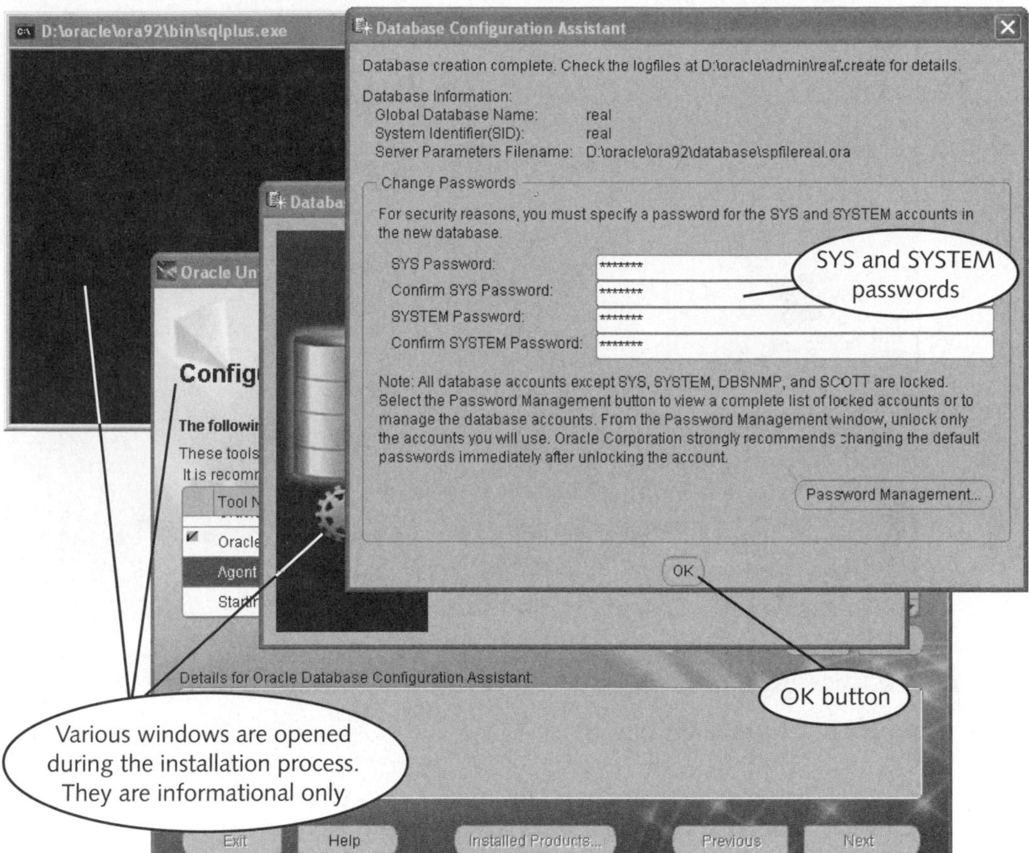

Figure A-18 Database Configuration Assistant page

During the installation process, other screens open, but you don't have to add information to them. When the installation is complete, the End of Installation page displays, as shown in Figure A-19. Click the **Exit** button to close the Oracle Universal Installer. An alert displays asking if you actually want to quit. Select the **Yes** option. If the standalone window of the Oracle Enterprise Manager console displays, close the window.

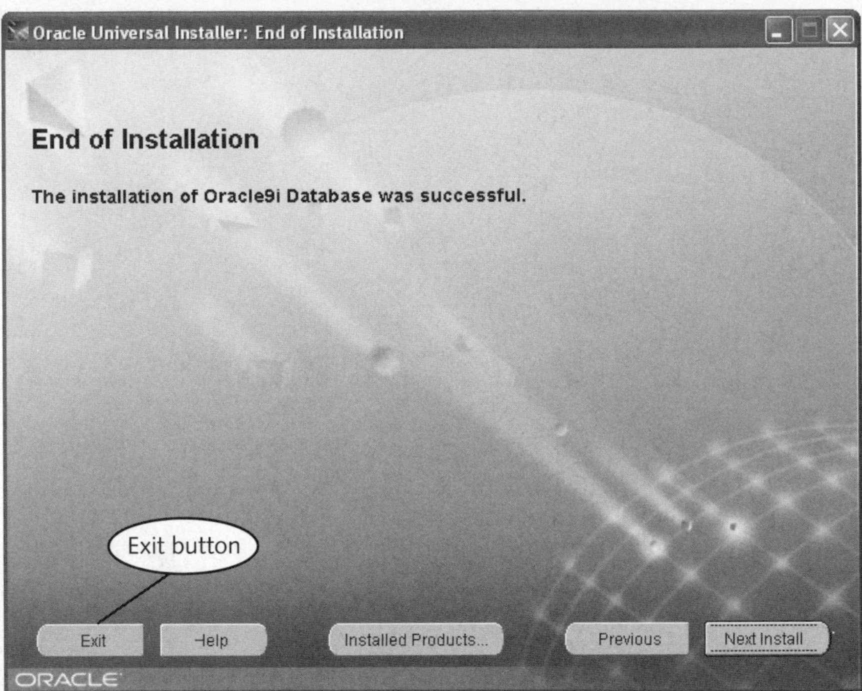

Figure A-19 End of Installation page

14. To test whether the installation was successful, open SQL*Plus. To do so, choose **Start>All Programs>Oracle - OraHome92> Application Development>SQL Plus**, as shown in Figure A-20.

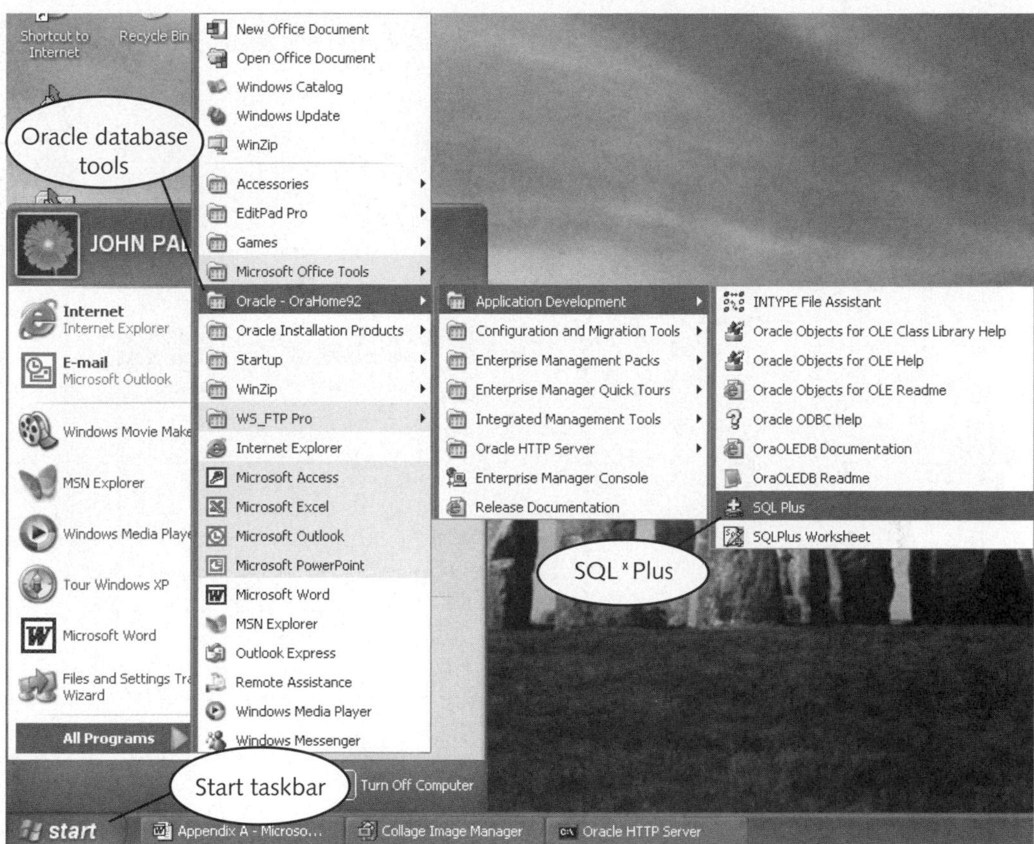

Figure A-20 SQL*Plus menu selection

a. When SQL*Plus opens (see Figure A-21), the Log On dialog box opens prompting for your Oracle user name and password. Enter SCOTT into the User Name text box and TIGER into the Password text box (note that there is no case restriction for the user name and password). Click the **OK** button.

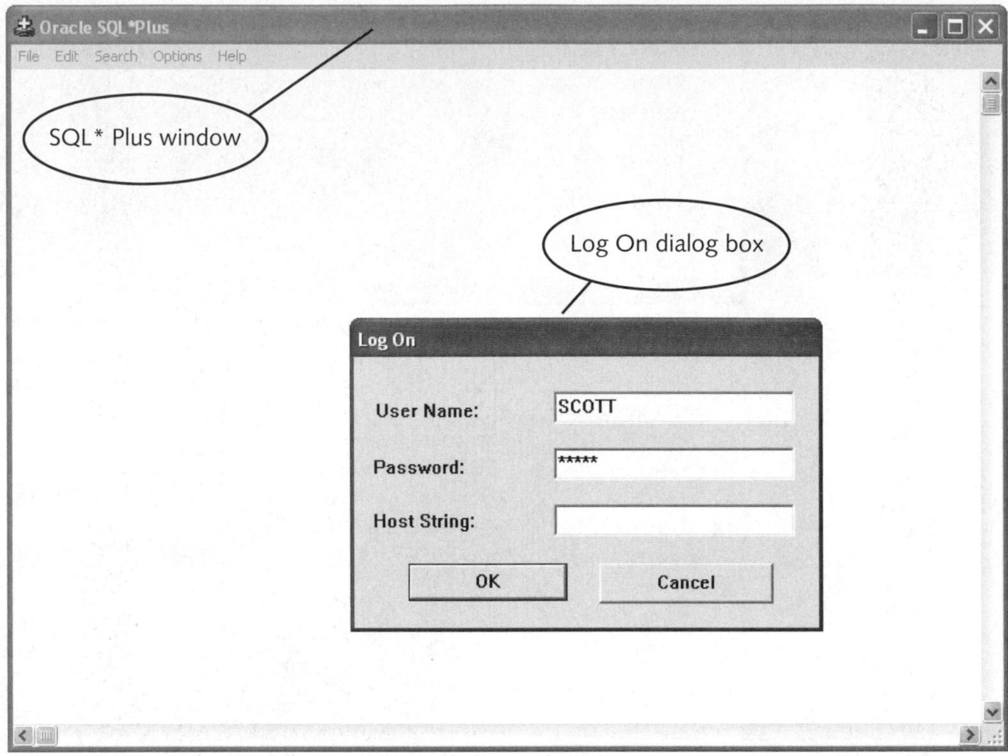

Figure A-21 SQL*Plus Log On dialog box

b. Enter the following SQL statement at the SQL prompt. Click **Enter** when finished.

```
Select * from emp;
```

c. You should see some records scroll by. You have now installed and tested the Oracle9*i* database and have access to the tables needed for this book's practice sessions.

d. Enter **Exit** at the SQL prompt to close SQL*Plus.

15. You can now delete the disk1, disk2, and disk3 directories to recover disk space.

INSTALLING ORACLE9*I* DEVELOPER SUITE

The next toolset to install is the Oracle9*i*Developer Suite that contains Forms Builder 9*i*. The Oracle9*i* Developer Suite (2 CDs) comes packaged with this book. Installation instructions are available at *www.course.com/cdkit.* You may also choose to download the Oracle9*i* Developer Suite from *www.oracle.com*. If you choose that option, you may use the installation instructions that follow. Note that both sets of installations instructions will be very similar, if not identical, so you should have a successful installation of the Oracle9*i* Developer Suite whether you use the instructions provided below, or the instructions found at *www.course.com/cdkit*.

Follow these steps to download and install Oracle9*i* Developer Suite from *www.oracle.com*:

1. Return to the OTN Downloads page illustrated in Figure A-2. Double-click the **Oracle9*i*Developer Suite** link.
2. The Oracle9*i*DS Software Download page displays, as shown in Figure A-22. Notice the link at the bottom of the page to previously released products. Clicking the Oracle Forms and Reports link takes you to a page that allows you to download Oracle Forms Developer 6*i*, the toolset that includes Form Builder 6*i*. The instructions that follow cover Oracle9*i* Developer Suite, so click the **Oracle9*i*DS** link (the Windows link if the product is to be loaded on a Windows operating system).

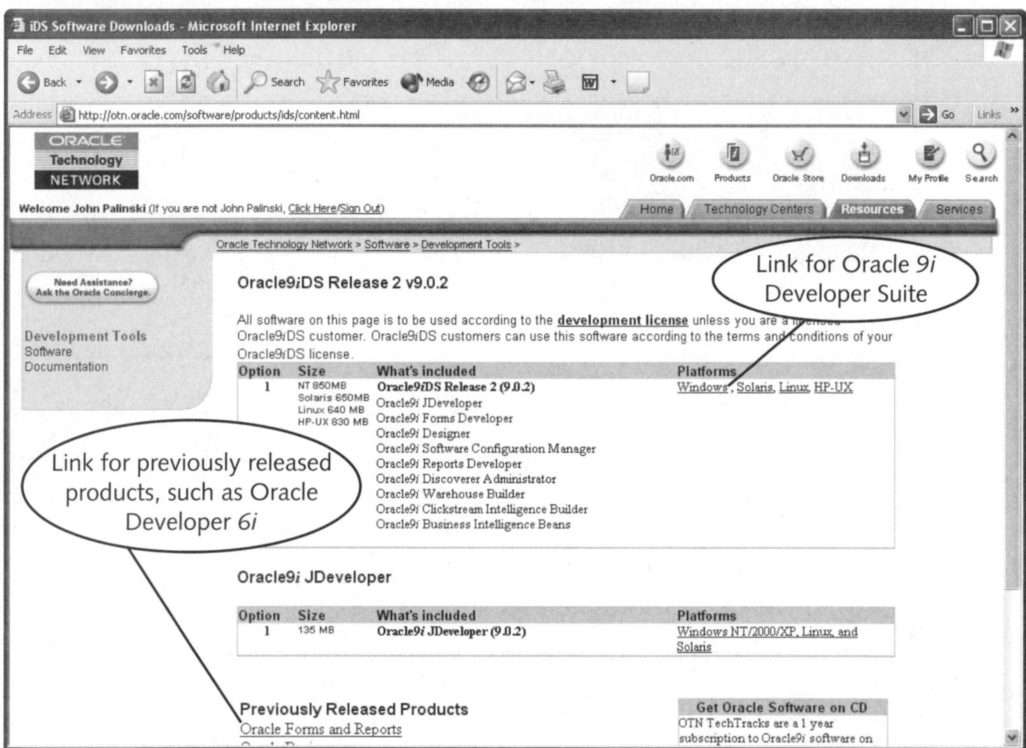

Figure A-22 Oracle9*i*DS Software Download page

3. After you complete an Acceptance screen, you reach the Oracle9*i*DS Download Page for Microsoft Windows page, as shown in Figure A-23. Note that if the instructions that follow differ from the instructions on the screen itself, follow the instructions on the screen.

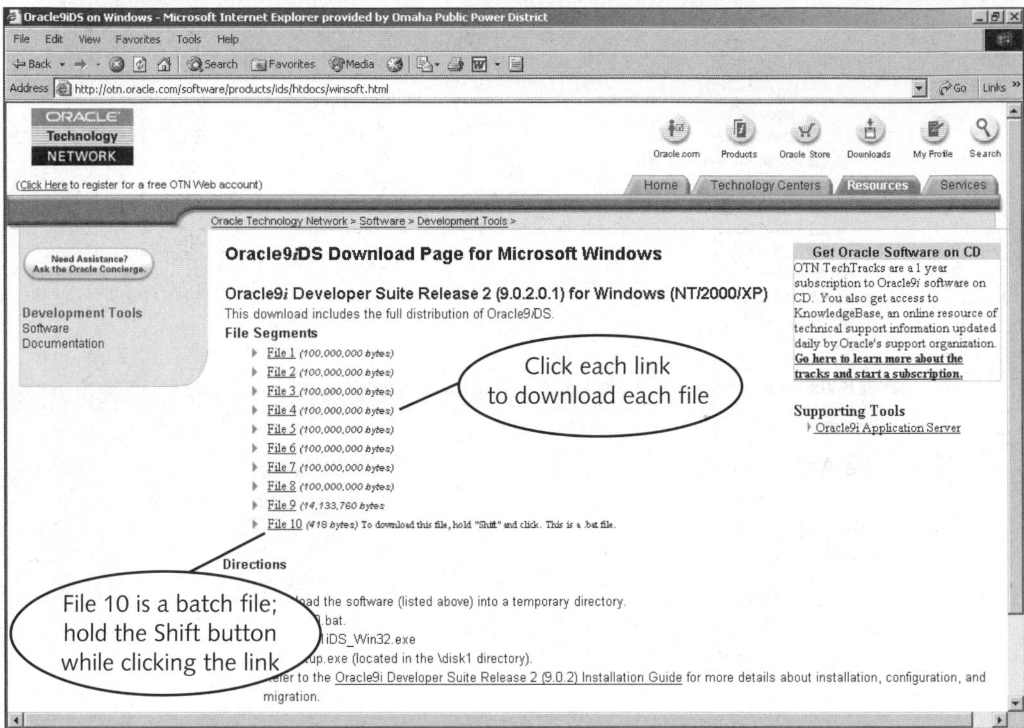

Figure A-23 Oracle9*i*DS Download Page for Microsoft Windows page

a. Because Oracle9*i*DS consists of a variety of products, you must download ten files into a temporary directory. To do so, create a directory named **oracletools** and download the first nine zip files into that directory.

b. The tenth file, which is named **file10**, is a batch file. Hold down the **Shift** key when you click the **File 10** link.

c. Open Windows Explorer, as shown in Figure A-24, and navigate to the **oracletools** directory. Run the file10 batch file by double-clicking the **file name**. This step takes some time.

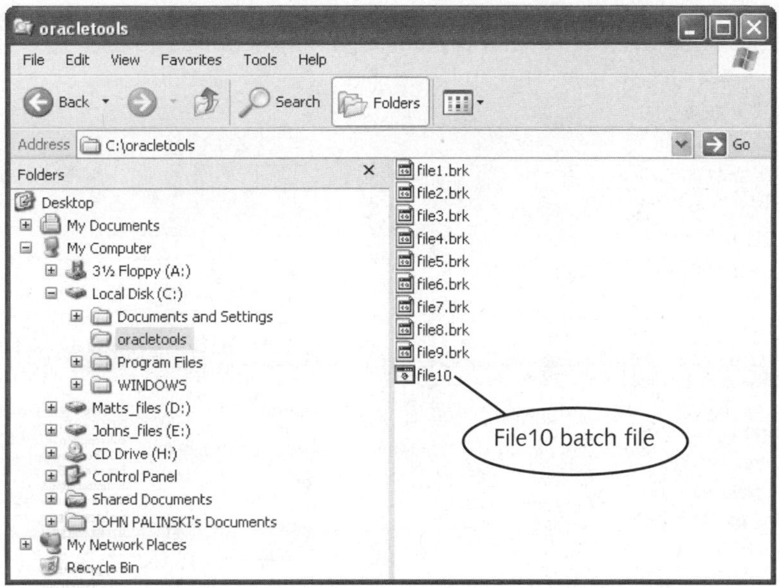

Figure A-24 Windows Explorer displaying the file10 batch file

d. Using Windows Explorer, locate and double-click the **90201iDS_Win32.exe** file, which should be located in the **oracletools** directory. A WinZip Self Extractor dialog box opens, as shown in Figure A-25. Enter **c:\oratools** into the Unzip to folder text box, and click the **Unzip** button. This step takes some time.

The drive letter may vary depending on the setup of your computer.

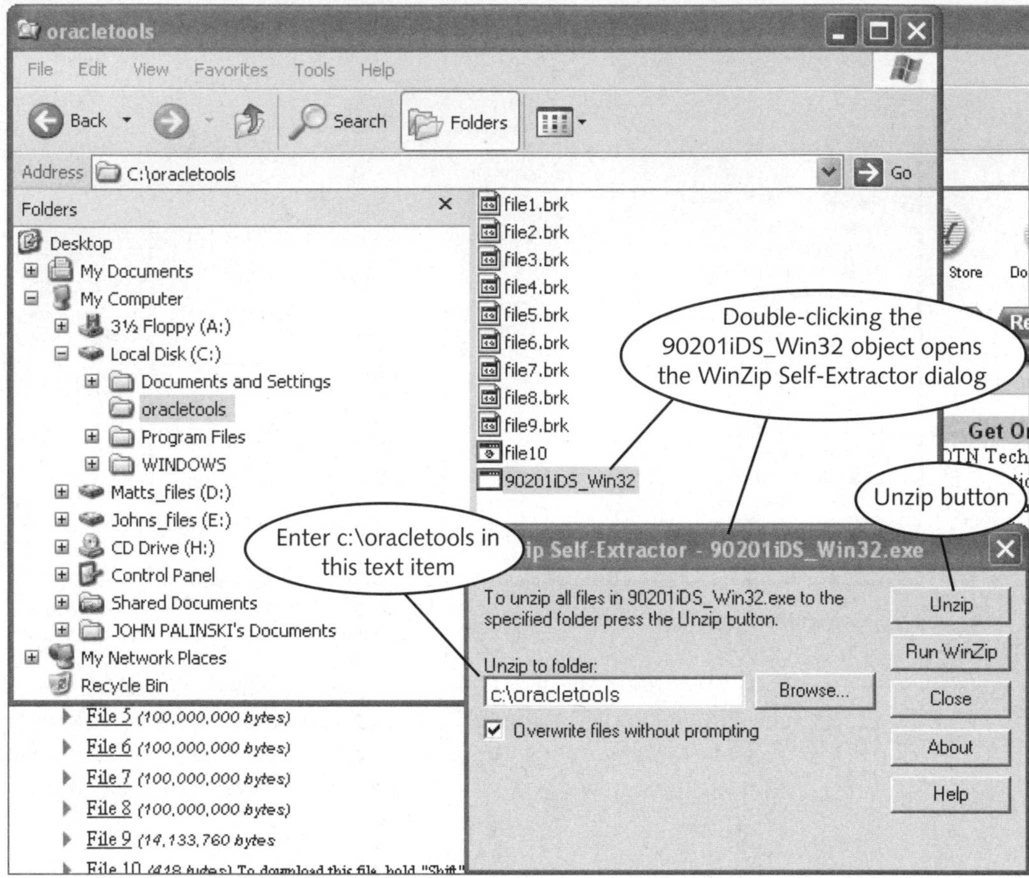

Figure A-25 WinZip Self Extractor dialog box

e. Using Windows Explorer, locate and double-click the **setup.exe** executable in the **\oracletools\Disk1** directory (see Figure A-26).

f. The first page of the Universal Installer is the Welcome dialog box. Click **Next**.

g. Next is the File Locations page, as shown previously in Figure A-8. Set the following:

   Destination Name: **OraHome92a**
   Destination Path: **c:\oracle_toolset**

   Accept the remaining defaults and click **Next**.

h. The Installation Types page displays, as shown in Figure A-27. Click the **Complete** radio button, and then click **Next**.

A

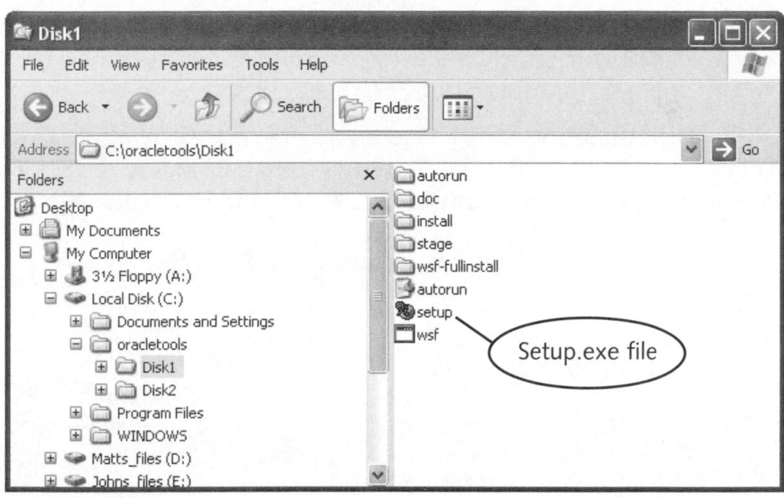

Figure A-26 Windows Explorer displaying the setup.exe executable

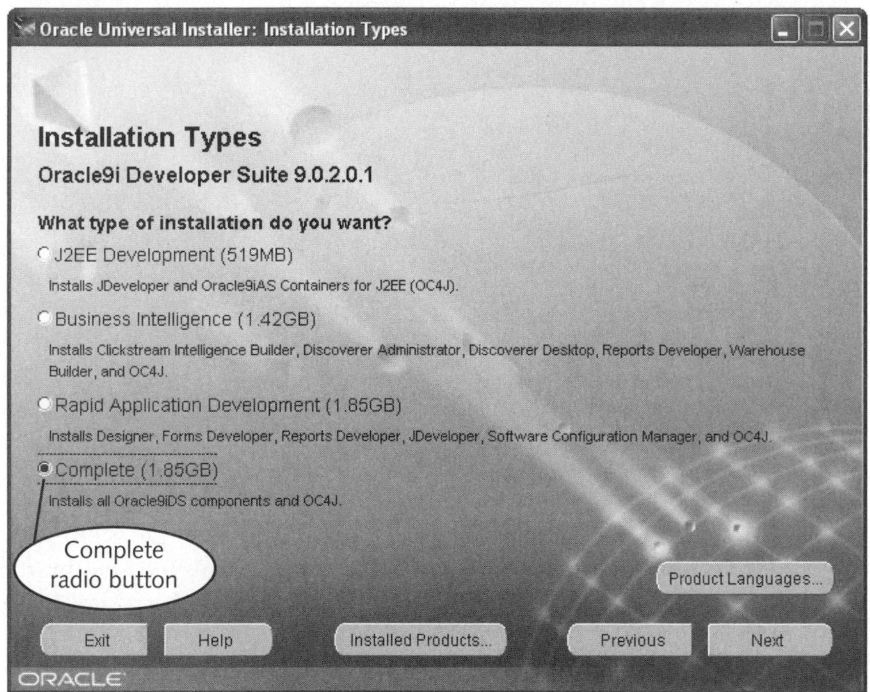

Figure A-27 Installation Types page

i. The Provide Outgoing Mail Server Information page displays. Click **Next** without entering in a value.

j. The Summary page displays. Under the word Summary, the screen displays the installation for Oracle9*i* Developer Suite 9.2.0.1.0. Click the **Install** button to begin the installation.

k. During the installation, which takes some time, the Oracle Net Configuration Assistant: Welcome dialog box displays, as shown in Figure A-28. Check the **Perform typical configuration** check box, and then click **Next**.

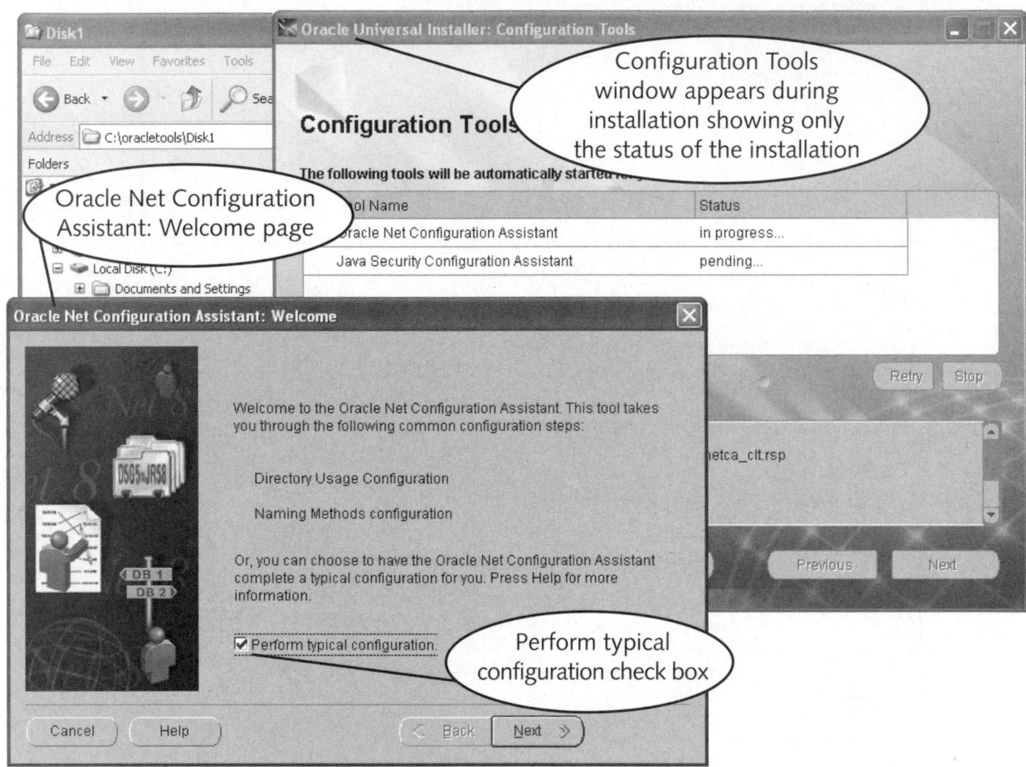

Figure A-28 Oracle Net Configuration Assistant: Welcome dialog box

l. The Welcome dialog box offers you two alternative approaches for a net service name, as shown in Figure A-29. Select the **No** radio button unless you have a service. Selecting No causes the Oracle Universal Installer to step you through the wizard pages to set up the service. Click **Next**.

m. The Net Service Name Configuration, Database Version page displays, as shown in Figure A-30. Because you have just installed Oracle9*i,* if necessary, select the **Oracle 8*i* or later database or service** radio button, and then click **Next**.

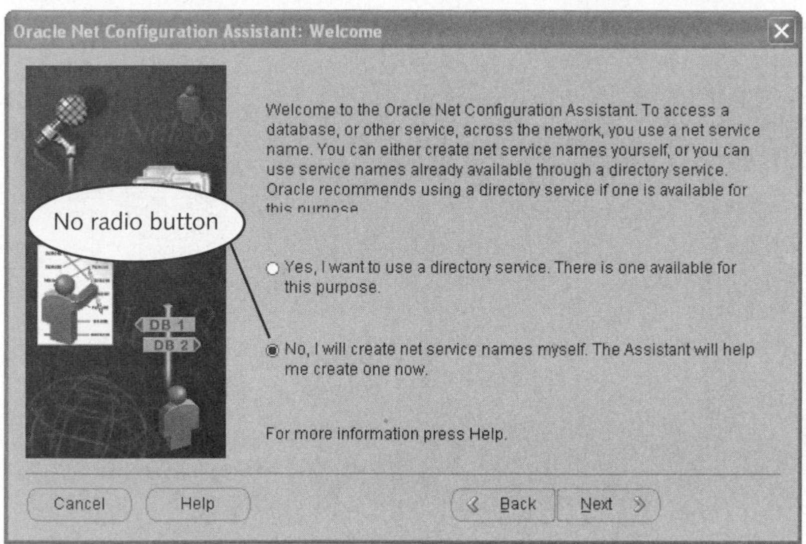

Figure A-29 Oracle Universal Installer prompting for the service name

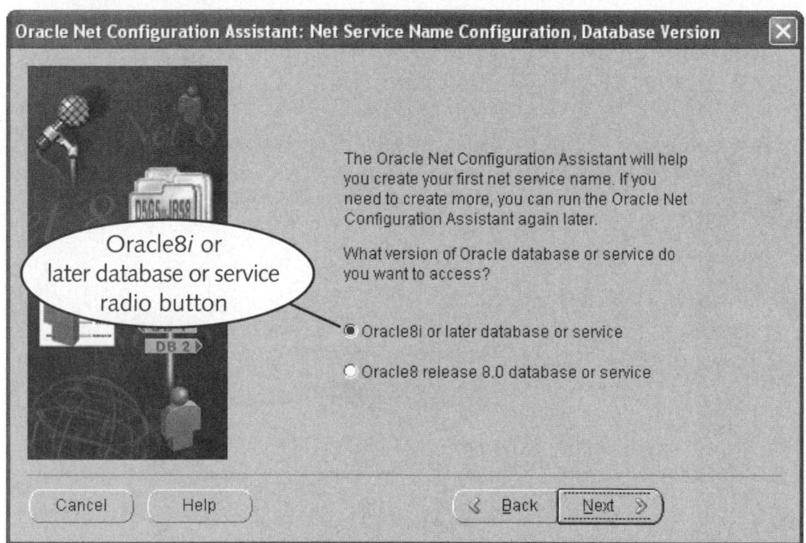

Figure A-30 Net Service Name Configuration, Database Version page

n. The Net Service Name Configuration, Service Name page depicted in Figure A-31 now displays. This value will be the host string used when logging on. Enter the value entered into the Global Database Name text item in Step 8 of the database installation steps (Figure A-13) into the Service Name text item. Figure A-31 shows a value of REAL as the Service Name value. If you used the value of REAL in Step 8, use that value. Otherwise use the value you entered in Step 8. Click **Next**.

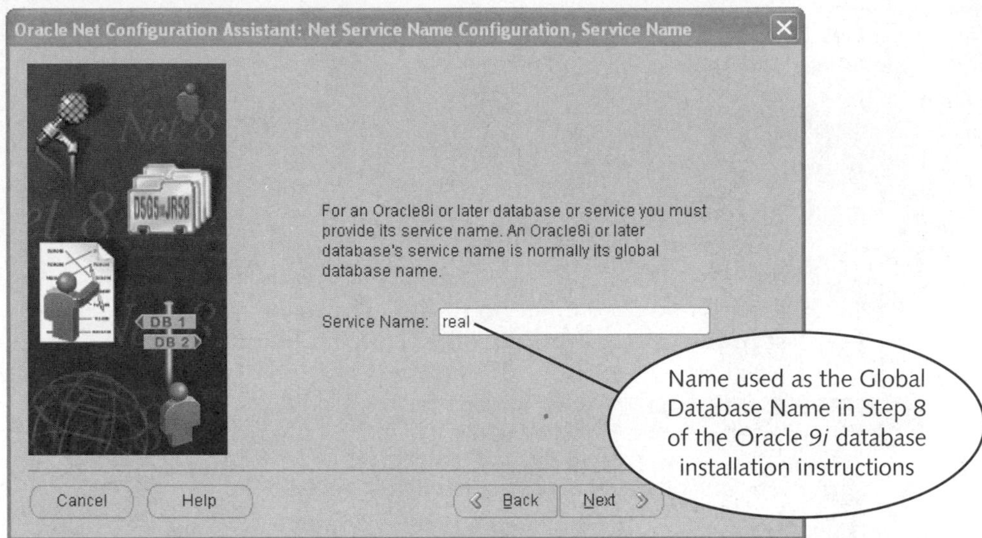

Figure A-31 Net Service Name Configuration, Service Name page

o. The next wizard page is the Net Service Name Configuration, Select Protocols page, as shown in Figure A-32. If necessary, select the **TCP** option, and then click **Next**.

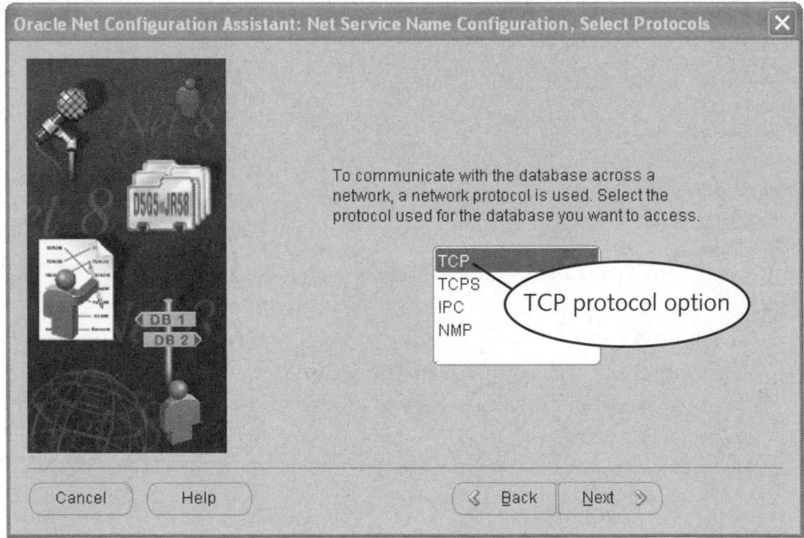

Figure A-32 Net Service Name Configuration, Select Protocols page

p. The Net Service Name Configuration, TCP/IP Protocol page displays, as shown in Figure A-33. Enter the name of your computer into Host name text box. This is the name that was given to your computer when Windows XP was installed. The name in the example is Johns. There are several ways to determine the name of your computer. The first is to open Windows Explorer (see Figure A-34) and locate your computer under the My Network Places node. The second way is to right-click the **My Computer** start-up icon on your desktop, select the **Properties** option on the popup menu, then select the **Computer Name** tab. After entering the name of your computer into the Host name text box, select the **Use the standard port number of 1521** radio button, and then click **Next**.

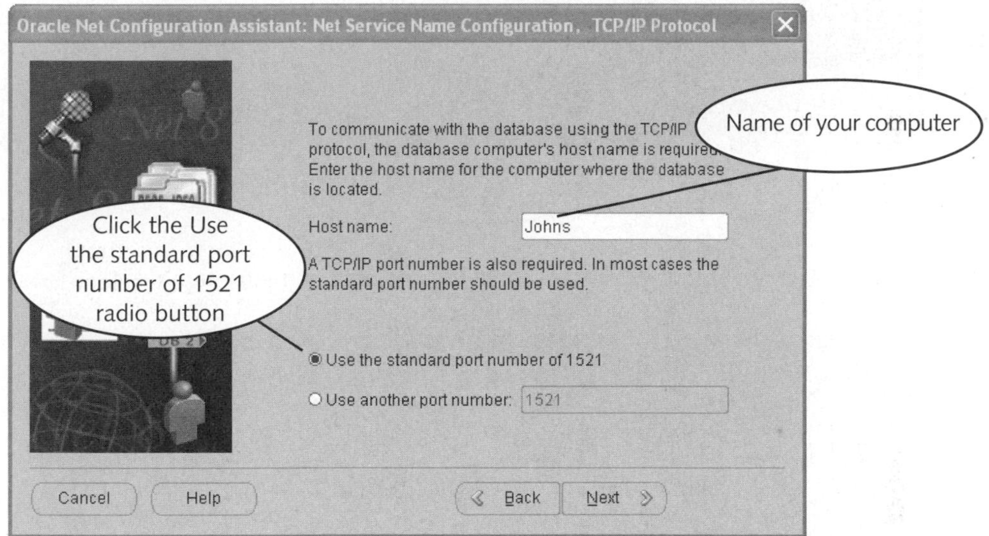

Figure A-33 Net Service Name Configuration, TCP/IP Protocol page

q. The wizard now displays the Net Service Name Configuration, Test page. The purpose of this page is to test the connection. If this test fails, Forms Builder will not be able to connect to the Oracle9*i* database, and you have not set up the configuration properly. Select the **Yes, perform a test** radio button as depicted in Figure A-35, and then click **Next**.

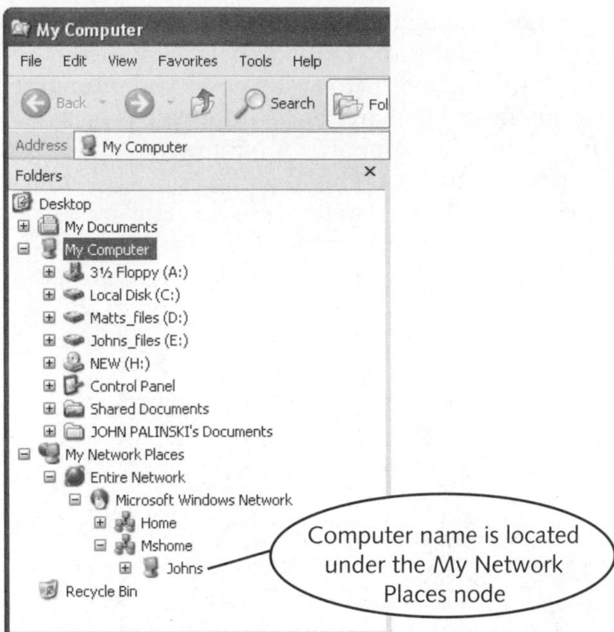

Figure A-34 Windows Explorer displaying the host name or name of the computer

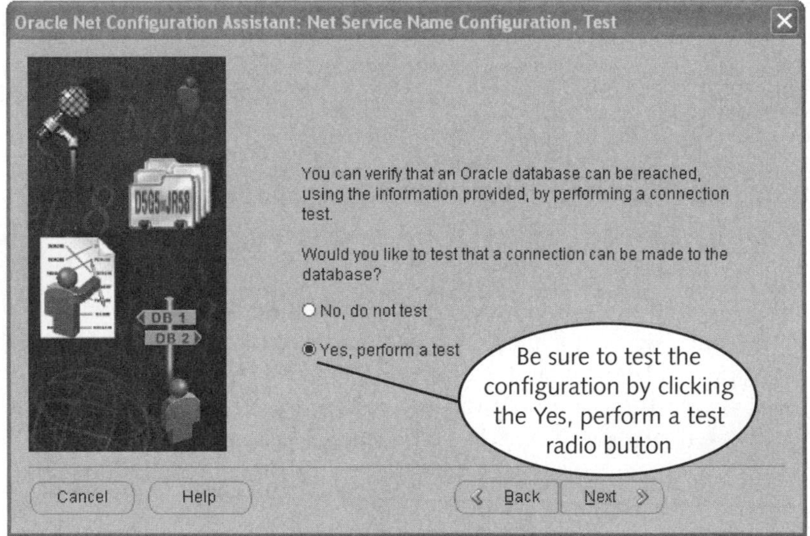

Figure A-35 Net Service Name Configuration, Test page

r. The results of the test are displayed in the Net Service Name Configuration, Connecting page (see Figure A-36). If you have successfully configured the service, the following message displays: Connecting…Test Successful. If you are successful, click **Next**. If you are not successful, use the Back button to check the settings.

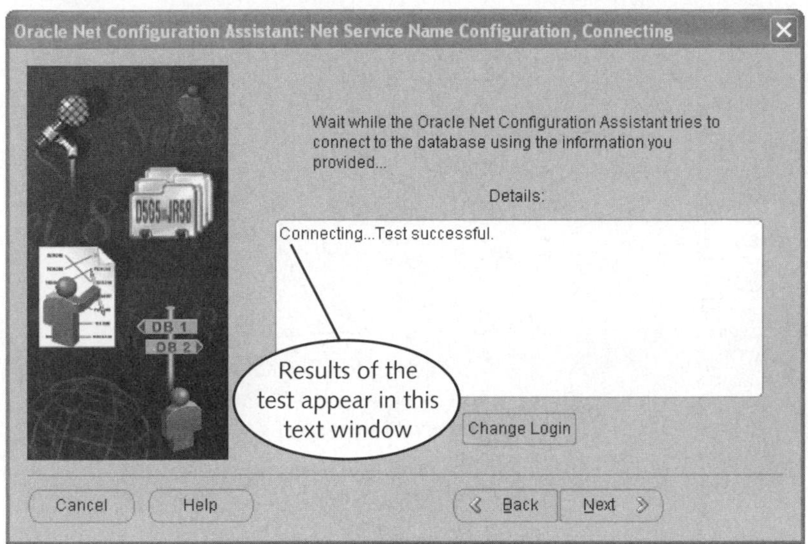

Figure A-36 Net Service Name Configuration, Connecting page

s. The Net Service Name Configuration, Net Service Name page displays, as shown in Figure A-37. Accept the defaults and click **Next**.

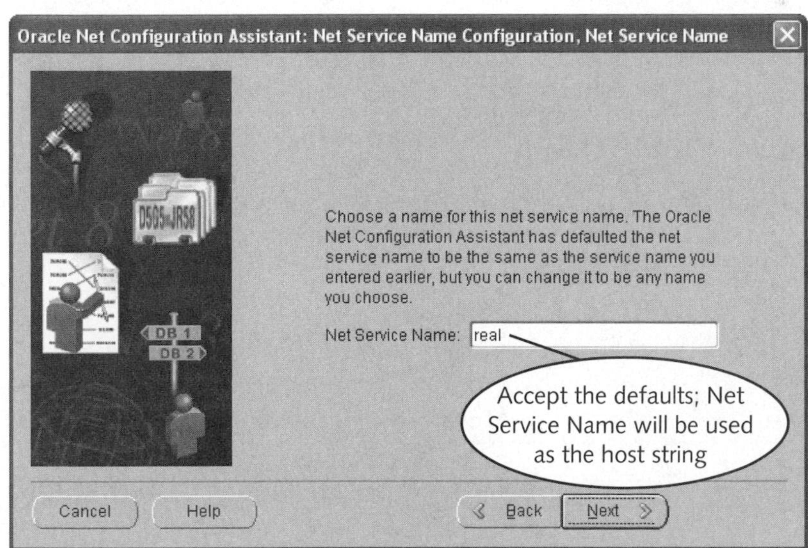

Figure A-37 Net Service Name Configuration, Net Service page

t. The wizard now displays the Net Service Name Configuration, Another Net Service page (see Figure A-38), which allows you to set up another net service name. If necessary, select the **No** radio button, and then click **Next**.

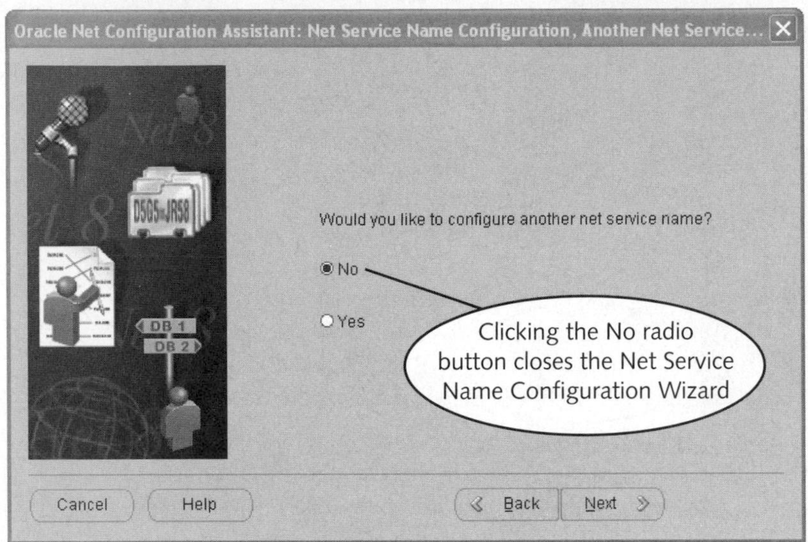

Figure A-38 Net Service Name Configuration, Another Net Service page

u. You now see the Net Service Name Configuration Done page, as shown in Figure A-39. Click **Next** to begin your Oracle Universal Installer exit steps.

If you are installing from the CDs you may have a Done button on this page. In this case, click the Done button and skip the steps that follow.

v. Figure A-40 shows the next page that displays, the Oracle Universal Installer: Oracle Services for Microsoft Transaction Server page. Accept the defaults and click **Next**.

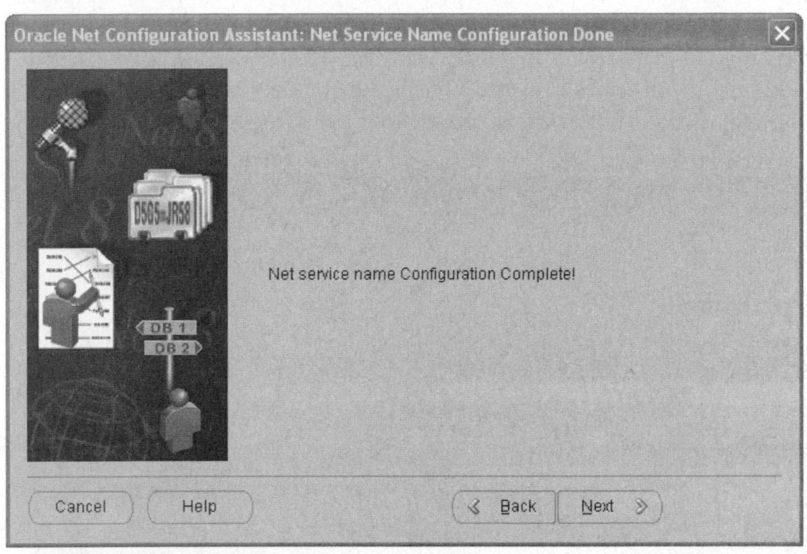

Figure A-39 Net Service Name Configuration Done page

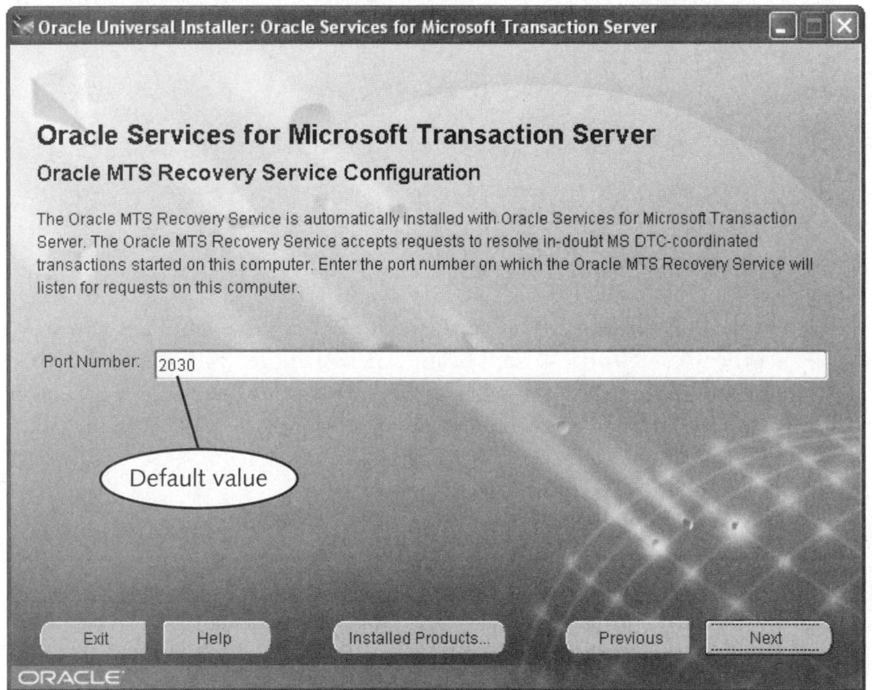

Figure A-40 Oracle Services for Microsoft Transaction Server page

w. The End of Installation page displays, as shown in Figure A-41. You have now completed the installation of the Oracle9*i* Developer Suite. Click the **Exit** button and close the Oracle Universal Installer. An alert window displays to confirm your wish to exit. Click **Yes**.

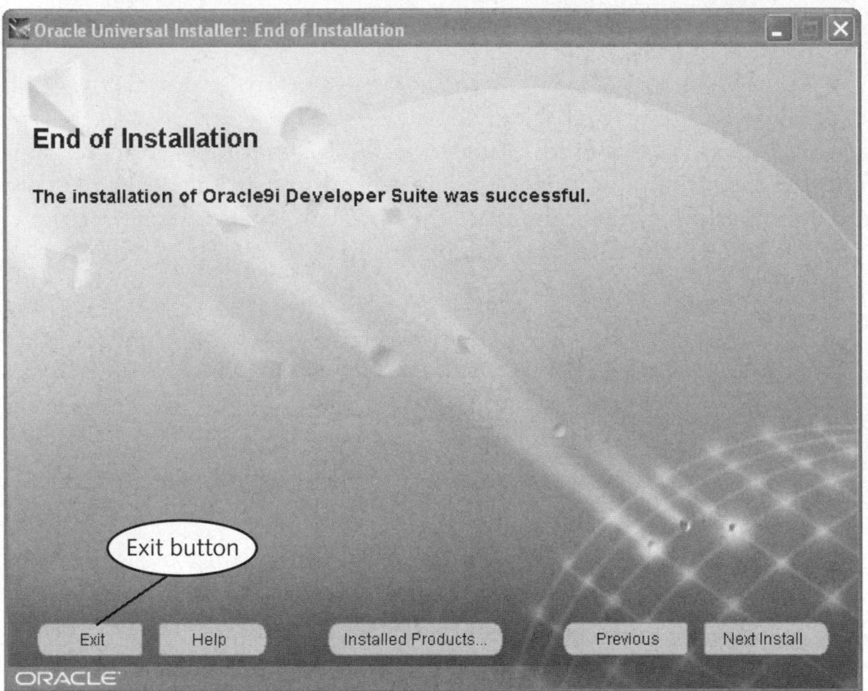

Figure A-41 End of Installation page

x. You can now test Forms Builder and determine whether you can connect to the Oracle9*i* database. Locate Forms Builder on your Start menu. It is probably located as follows: Start>All Programs>Oracle9*i* Developer Suite – Ora92> Forms Developer>Forms Builder.

y. When the Forms Builder IDE is launched, attempt to connect to the Oracle database. Select the **File/Connect** menu option to open a Connect dialog box, and then enter the following:

User Name: **scott**
Password: **tiger**
Host String: **real** (or the Service Name you entered in Step 3n)

If the Connect dialog box disappears, you have connected to the Oracle database and are prepared to perform the lessons in this book. Close Forms Builder.

z. To restore some of your PC's disk space, delete the **oracletools** directory.

COMMON PROBLEMS

Two problems often arise when you are using the Forms Builder IDE. The following sections discuss these problems.

FRM-90928 – Positional parameter after key on command line

The FRM-90928 error often occurs. This indicates a problem with the positional parameter after key on command line. This error, shown in Figure A-42, is displayed when the form is executed from Forms Builder. It displays in the Web browser applet area and prevents the form from displaying. This error occurs when the developer fails to save the form before executing it. To eliminate this problem, save the form before executing it from Forms Builder the first time. You do not have to save it each time you execute the form, only before the first launch.

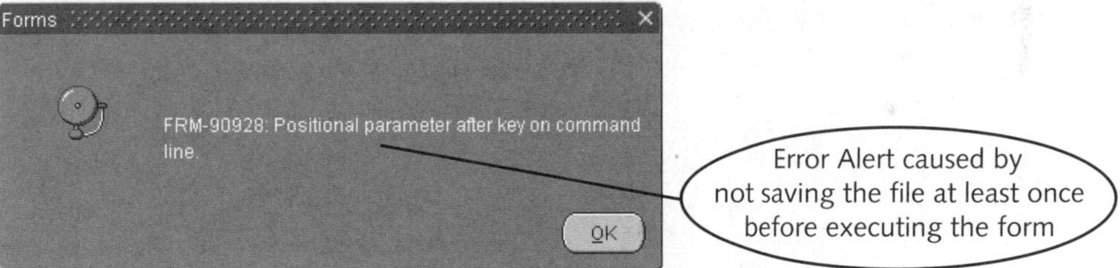

Figure A-42 Alert displaying FRM-90928 – Positional parameter after key on command line

FRM-30087: Unable to create form file

When you launch a form from the Forms Builder IDE, Forms Builder, by default, compiles the form creating a new **.fmx** file. One of the Forms Builder preference settings causes this problem. Occasionally, you get the error message depicted in Figure A-43.

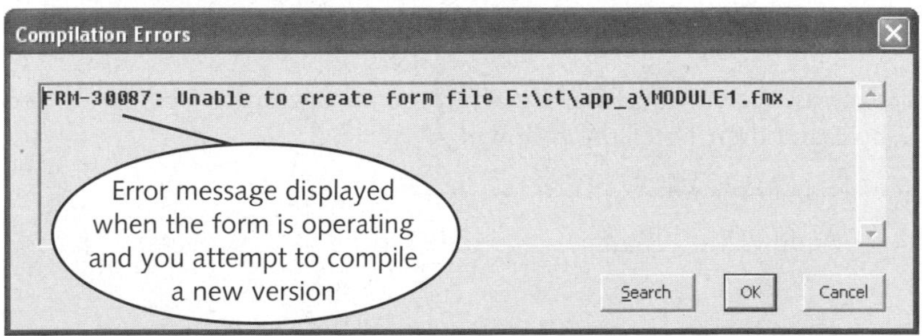

Figure A-43 FRM-30087:Unable to create form file

This error occurs when Forms Builder attempts to create a file while it is running. The Windows operating system prevents the creation of a file that is being executed. Attempting to do so causes the error message. In most cases, you will see that a Web browser window is open displaying the form. You should close the form or the Web browser window. Windows then allows you to create a new **.fmx** file and execute the form.

In rare cases, this error message occurs and all Web browser windows are closed. Windows (or Forms Builder) sometimes fails to clear the application from memory. In these cases, you must open the Windows Task Manager and close the process. Figure A-44 illustrates the Task Manager and the Web form process.

Perform the following steps to close the Forms Builder processes:

1. Open the Windows Task Manager by pressing the **Control + Alt + Delete** keys.
2. Select the **Processes** tab.
3. Select all instances of the **ifweb90.exe** processes. Click the **End Process** button. You are then asked to confirm the termination. Confirm it.

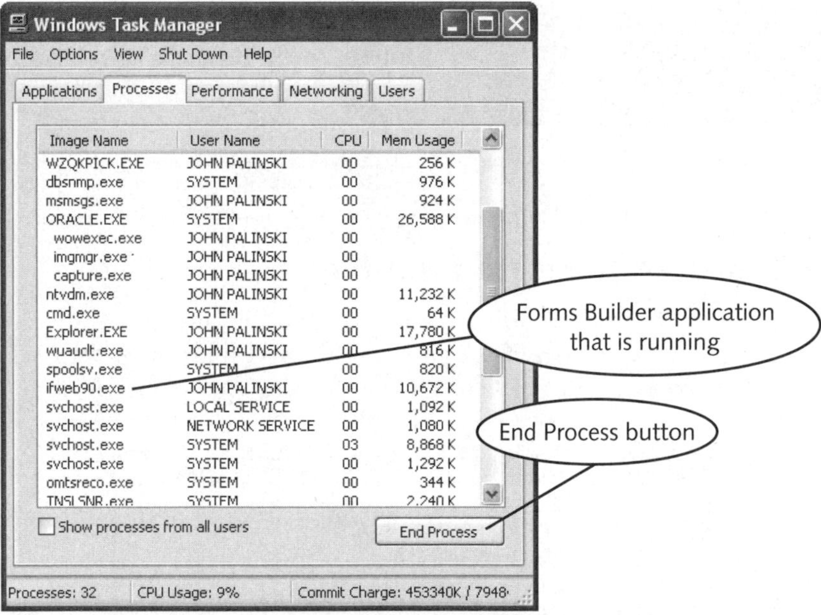

Figure A-44 Windows Task Manager and the Forms Builder process

APPENDIX

B

PROPERTIES

Forms Builder has hundreds of properties ranging from those that control the size of a data block item to those that control the quality of the image displayed. Each object in a form has a set of properties. In fact, even the application has properties. Most of the properties are set using the Property Palette, although some can only be set programmatically using built-ins such as Set_item_property, Set_block_property, or Set_application_property. Some properties, such as Next_item that contains the sequence number of the next item, are not settable. Table B-1 describes Forms Builder's properties. Properties with underscores in their names can be set only by using a built-in. Properties that cannot be modified are described as such.

Table B-1 Description of Forms Builder properties

Name	Object	Description
Access Key	Item (button, check box, and radio button)	Determines the character used as an access key. An access key is essentially a hot key. For example, if a push button were named Query and the property assigned a value of Q, clicking the Alt + Q keys causes the button to be clicked.
Alert Style	Alert	Determines the severity level of the symbol that is displayed in the alert.
Alias	Data block	Sets an alternate name for the data block's data source when it is a table.
Allow Empty Branches	Hierarchical tree item	Determines whether nodes that contain children display the Expand (+) and Collapse (–) symbols. The default value of YES shows the symbol on nodes that do not contain children. A value of NO suppresses the symbols.
Allow Expansion	Frame	Determines whether the frame can be expanded when the objects are larger than the frame.
Allow Multi-Line Prompts	Frame	Determines where Forms Builder can split a prompt into multiple lines.
Allow Start-Attached Prompts	Frame	Determines whether you can attach a prompt to the item's start edge.
Allow Top-Attached Prompts	Frame	Determines whether you can attach a prompt to the item's top edge.

Table B-1 Description of Forms Builder properties (continued)

Name	Object	Description
Arrow Style	Graphic line	Determines the arrow style. Values are NONE, START, END, BOTH ENDS, MIDDLE TO START, and MIDDLE TO END.
Automatic Column Width	LOV	Determines whether the LOV column width is automatically set based on whichever is greater—the Display Width property or the Column Title property.
Automatic Display	LOV	Displays an item's associated LOV when the operator tabs into the item. The default value of NO suppresses the display.
Automatic Position	LOV	Positions the LOV close to the item associated to the LOV.
Automatic Query	Relation	Determines how a detail data block is populated. This property works in conjunction with the Deferred property. If Deferred is set to YES and Automatic Query is set to YES, Forms Builder defers the population of the detail block until the operator navigates to the data block. If the default is YES and Deferred is set to NO, Forms Builder automatically populates the detail data block.
Automatic Refresh	LOV	Determines when a LOV is populated. Setting this property to YES populates the LOV each time the LOV opens.
Automatic Select	LOV	Setting this property to YES causes the LOV to select the value for the item when the value list is reduced to a single value.
Automatic Skip	Item and LOV	Moves the insertion point to the next navigable item without tabbing when the item length has been reached.
Background Color	Canvas, item (radio button), tab page, and canvas	Determines the color of the object's background.
Border Bevel	Item (chart, image, custom, text) and canvas (stacked)	Determines the look of the object's border. Options are RAISED, LOWERED, INSET, OUTSET, and NONE.
Bottom Title	Editor	Contains the name that appears at the bottom of the editor.
Bounding Box Scaleable	Graphic text	Determines whether the object's bounding or enclosing box should be scaled when the text object is rescaled.

Table B-1 Description of Forms Builder properties (continued)

Name	Object	Description
Builtin Date Format	Application	Determines the format mask used in converting a data value to or from a string when the string is not visible.
Button 1 Label	Alert	Contains text that is displayed on the default button. This property must have a value. If this button is clicked, a value represented by the numeric constant ALERT_BUTTON1 is returned to the calling function.
Button 2 Label	Alert	Contains text that is displayed on a second button. If a value is not placed in this property, the button is not displayed. If this button is clicked, a value represented by the numeric constant ALERT_BUTTON2 is returned to the calling function.
Button 3 Label	Alert	Contains text that is displayed on a third button. If a value is not placed in this property, the button is not displayed. If this button is clicked, a value represented by the numeric constant ALERT_BUTTON3 is returned to the calling function.
Calculation Mode	Item	Determines how the item's value will be computed. Values are FORMULA and SUMMARY.
Calling Form	Application	Determines the name of the calling form.
Canvas	Item	Determines the canvas on which the item is displayed. The item will not be displayed if a NULL value is specified.
Canvas Type	Canvas	Determines the type of canvas.
Cap Style	Graphic	Determines the graphic edge of the object. Values are BUTT, ROUND, and PROJECTING.
Case Insensitive Query	Item	Setting this property to YES causes Forms Builder to return matching records regardless of the case of the search criteria. It is recommended that this property be set to YES.
Case Restriction	Item	Determines the case of the text.
Character Cell Height	Module	Determines the height of a character cell when the coordinate system is Real.
Character Cell Width	Module	Determines the width of a character cell when the coordinate system is Real.
Chart Subtype	Item (chart)	Identifies a variation of the type of the chart.

Table B-1 Description of Forms Builder properties (continued)

Name	Object	Description
Chart Type	Item (chart)	Identifies the type of chart item. Values are COLUMN, PIE, BAR, TABLE, LINE, SCATTER, MIXED, HIGH-LOW, DOUBLE-Y, and GANTT.
Check Box Mapping of Other Values	Item (check box)	Determines how values that do not match the predefined CHECKED and UNCHECKED are displayed. Values are: NOT ALLOWED, CHECKED, and UNCHECKED.
Checked	Menu item	Determines the state of a checked or radio-style menu item. Values are CHECKED or UNCHECKED.
Clip Height	Graphic image	Determines the height of a cropped image.
Clip Width	Graphic image	Determines the width of a cropped image.
Clip X Position	Graphic image	Determines how much to clip from the left side of the image.
Clip Y Position	Graphic image	Determines how much to clip from the top of the image.
Close Allowed	Window	Determines whether the window manager CLOSE command is enabled or disabled. The default is YES.
Closed	Window	Enables or disables the window manager-specific CLOSE command. The CLOSE command is available by double-clicking the Close box in the top-left corner of the window.
Column Mapping Properties	LOV	Is a property group that has values for the column name, column title, display width, and return item.
Column Name	Item	Represents the item in any SQL statement that Forms Builder generates. If this value is blank, Forms Builder uses the item's name in the SQL statements. This property is used only if the item name does not match a database column name.
Column Specifications	Record group	Is a property group used to record the column name, column value, data type, and length of the column.
Column Title	LOV	Contains the heading used for the target LOV column.
Column Value	Record group	Contains the value of the specified record group column.

Table B-1 Description of Forms Builder properties (continued)

Name	Object	Description
Command Text	Menu item	Contains the executed script for the associated menu item. The script is determined by the menu item's Command Type property.
Command Type	Menu item	Determines the type of script executed when the menu item is selected. Values are NULL (used for separators), MENU (calls a submenu), and PL/SQL (executes PL/SQL statements).
Comments	All objects	Contains the general text that pertains to the object.
Communication Mode	Chart and reports	Determines the communication mode. Values are SYNCHRONOUS and ASYNCHRONOUS. Synchronous specifies that control returns to the calling object after the product has finished. Asynchronous means control is returned immediately.
Compression Quality	Image item	Determines the degree of compression applied to images read into a form. Values are NONE, MINIMUM, LOW, MEDIUM, HIGH, and MAXIMUM.
Conceal Data	Item (text)	Hides the characters entered into the text item. Values are YES and NO.
Connect String	Application	Identifies the SQL*NET connect string.
Console Window	Form	Determines the name of the window displaying the Forms Builder console. The console includes the status and message lines and is displayed at the bottom of the window.
Coordination	Relation	Determines how and when the detail block is populated.
Coordinate System	Form	Determines whether the object size and position are interpreted as character cell values or real units.
Coordination Status	Relation	Contains the coordination status of the block in respect to its master block. Values are COORDINATED and NON_COORDINATED.
Copy Value From Item	Item (all except buttons, chart items, and image items)	Causes a target item's value to be copied into the current item.
Current Form	Application	Identifies the name of the **.fmx** file that is being executed.
Current Form Name	Application	Identifies the name of the current form.

Table B-1 Description of Forms Builder properties (continued)

Name	Object	Description
Current Record	Block	Identifies the number of the record in the block's result set.
Current Record Visual Attribute Group	Block, form, and item	Determines the visual attribute for the current record.
Current_row_ background_color	Block, form, and item	Determines the color of the object's background. This property is set programmatically.
Current_row _fill_pattern	Block, form, and item	Determines the fill pattern of the object. This property is set programmatically.
Current_row_font_name	Block, form, and item	Determines the font of the object. This property is set programmatically.
Current_row_font_spacing	Block, form, and item	Determines the amount of space between characters. This property is set programmatically.
Current_row_font_style	Block, form, and item	Determines the style of the font. This property is set programmatically.
Current_row_font_weight	Block, form, and item	Determines the weight (boldness) of the font. This property is set programmatically.
Current_row_ foreground_color	Block, form, and item	Determines the color of the object's foreground features, such as text. This property is set programmatically.
Cursor_style	Application	Determines the look of the mouse cursor. Values are BUSY, CROSSHAIR, DEFAULT, HELP, and INSERTION. This property is set programmatically.
Custom Spacing	Graphic text	Determines the text object's custom spacing.
Dash Style	Graphic physical	Determines the style of the object. Values are SOLID, DOTTED, DASHED, DASH, DOT, DOUBLE DOT, LONG DASH, and DASH DOUBLE DOT.
Data Query	Hierarchical tree item	Contains the SELECT statement that is used to supply data to the tree. If the Record Group property is populated, this property should not be filled in.
Database Block	Block	Determines whether the block can be used to access the database. If the value is YES, the data block can access the database.

Table B-1 Description of Forms Builder properties (continued)

Name	Object	Description
Database Item	Item	Determines whether the item is associated to the data block's data source. If this value is set to YES, Forms Builder attempts to use the item name in any SQL statement issued by the data block. If the value is set to NO, Forms Builder does not add the item to the SQL statement. Data blocks can and do have items that are not associated to the data source. Failure to set this property correctly causes a form error when the form executes an SQL statement.
Database Value	Items (all except buttons, chart items, and image items)	Returns the value that was originally fetched from the database. If a value was updated and committed, it returns the value that was committed.
Data Length Semantics	Item	Specifies the semantics of the Maximum Length and Query Length properties.
Datetime_local_tz	Application	Sets the local time zone region for DATETIME items.
Datetime_server_tz	Application	Sets the server time zone for Datetime items.
Default Alert Button	Alert	Determines the default Alert button.
Default Button	Item (button)	Identifies the default button.
Default Font Scaling	Module	Determines that the font indicated for use in a form defaults to the relative character scale of the display device in use.
Defer Required Enforcement	Form	Determines whether items that have the Required property set to TRUE are to defer enforcement until the record is validated.
Deferred	Relation	Determines how a detail data block is populated. This property works in conjunction with the Automatic Query property. If Deferred is set to YES and Automatic Query is set to YES, Forms Builder defers the population of the detail block until the operator navigates to the data block. If the default is set to YES and Deferred is set to NO, Forms Builder automatically populates the data block.
Delete Allowed	Block	Determines whether the record can be deleted.

Table B-1 Description of Forms Builder properties (continued)

Name	Object	Description
Delete Record Behavior	Relation	Determines how the deletion of a record in the master block affects the detail block. Values are NON-ISOLATED (prevents the deletion of the master record when the detail exists), ISOLATED (allows the master record to be deleted even though there is a detail record), and CASCADING (deletes the detail records along with the master records). NON-ISOLATED is the default.
Delete Procedure Arguments	Block	Determines the names, data types, and values of the arguments used by the procedure that replaces a block's normal delete operation.
Delete Procedure Name	Block	Specifies the name of the procedure that replaces a block's normal delete operation.
Delete Procedure Result Set Columns	Block	Determines the names and data types of the result set columns that are associated to the procedure that replaces a block's normal delete operation.
Detail Block	Relation	Identifies the name of the detail block.
Detail Reference Item	Relation	Determines the REF item in the relation's detail data block.
Direction	All objects	Determines the layout direction for bi-directional objects.
Display Hint Automatically	Item (all except chart, display, and custom)	Determines when the Hint property value associated to the item is displayed. A value of YES displays the Hint value when the item receives the input focus. A value of NO displays the Hint value when the HELP command is issued.
Display in 'Keyboard Help'	Trigger	Determines whether a key trigger description is displayed in the Keys help screen.
Display Quality	Item (image)	Sets the quality level of the image. The higher the quality, the more performance is degraded. Values are HIGH, MEDIUM, and LOW.
Display Width	Application	Specifies the width of the display device when used for an application. When used for a LOV, it sets the width of the associated LOV column.
Display Without Privilege	Menu item	Specifies whether the menu item is displayed when the form operator does not have the privileges to select the option.

Table B-1 Description of Forms Builder properties (continued)

Name	Object	Description
Distance Between Records	Frame and item	Determines the amount of space between records. If the item has a value of 0, it will use the frame's property value.
Dither	Item (image)	Determines whether the image is dithered. Dithering consists of substituting a Forms Builder color for that specified in the image.
DML Array Size	Block	Determines the maximum array size when performing INSERT, UPDATE, and DELETE statements. A larger size reduces network traffic but increases memory use. The best size is one that matches the number of records modified in one transaction.
DML Data Target Name	Block	Determines the name of the target database object used in DML statements.
DML Data Target Type	Block	Determines the type of object the data block will reference when attempting to issue a DML operation. Values are TABLE (Forms Builder issues normal INSERT, UPDATE, and DELETE statements), PROCEDURE (Forms Builder uses the procedure for the DML), and Transactional trigger.
DML Returning Value	Block	Determines whether Forms should use the new or old behavior when updating client-side data. A value of YES causes the behavior used with the release of 6*i* to be used. A value of NO causes Forms Builder to use 5.0 behavior.
Edge Background Color	Graphic font and color	Determines the color of the object's edge.
Edge Foreground Color	Graphic font and color	Determines the foreground color of the object's edge.
Edge Pattern	Graphic font and color	Determines the fill pattern of the object's edge.
Editor	Item (text)	Determines the editor displayed by the text item.
Editor X Position	Item (text)	Determines the X position of the top-left corner of the editor.
Editor Y Position	Item (text)	Determines the Y position of the top-left corner of the editor.
Enabled	Item and menu Item	Specifies whether the operator can use the mouse to manipulate the item.
End Angle	Graphic arc	Determines the ending angle of the arc using the horizontal axis as the origin.

Table B-1 Description of Forms Builder properties (continued)

Name	Object	Description
Enforce Column Security	Block	Determines whether Forms Builder should enforce update privileges on a column-by-column basis. If the value is set to YES, Forms Builder will enforce the privileges defined in the database for the operator.
Enforce Primary Key	Block	Specifies that all records in the data block must have a unique key value.
Enterable	Block	Determines whether the block is enterable.
Error_date_format	Application	Specifies the current error date used in runtime error processing. This property is set programmatically.
Error_datetime_format	Application	Specifies the default format mask for run-time error processing. This property is set programmatically.
Execution Hierarchy	Trigger	Determines how the current trigger code executes when a trigger of the same name exists at a higher level. Values are OVERRIDE, BEFORE, and AFTER.
Execution Mode	Item (chart) and Reports	Determines whether the object is run in Batch or Runtime mode. Batch mode runs the object without user interaction. Runtime mode enables user interaction.
Filename	Form and Reports	Determines the name of the file in which the named object is stored.
Fill	Graphic arc	Determines the fill shape of the arc. Values are PIE and CHORD.
Fill_Pattern	Canvas, item, tab page, radio button, and window	Determines the pattern used in the object. This property is set programmatically.
Filter Before Display	LOV	Determines whether the LOV will prompt the operator for selection criteria before populating the LOV.
Fire in Enter-Query Mode	Trigger	Determines whether the trigger can be fired in the Enter Query mode as well as in the Normal mode.
First_block	Form	Determines that the block is the first block in the form. This property is not settable.
First_detail_relation	Block	Identifies the name of the first master-detail block relation for a detail data block. This property is not settable.
First_item	Block	Identifies the first item in the current block. This property is not settable.

Table B-1 Description of Forms Builder properties (continued)

Name	Object	Description
First_master_relation	Block	Identifies the first master-detail block relation in which the given block is the master block. This property is not settable.
First Navigation Block	Module	Determines the first block in which Forms Builder should navigate when the form is launched.
Fixed Bounding Box	Graphic text	Determines whether the object's enclosing or bounding box should remain a fixed size.
Flag_user_value_too_long	Application	Determines how a user-entered value that exceeds the Maximum Length property value is handled. This property is set programmatically.
Font_name	Canvas, item, tab page, radio button, and window	Determines the font used by the object. This property is set programmatically.
Font_size	Canvas, item, tab page, radio button, and window	Determines the size of the font in points. This property is set programmatically.
Font_spacing	Canvas, item, tab page, radio button, and window	Determines the width of the font. This property is set programmatically.
Font_style	Canvas, item, tab page, radio button, and window	Determines the style of the font. This property is set programmatically.
Font_weight	Canvas, item, tab page, radio button, and window	Determines the weight of the font. This property is set programmatically.
Foreground_color	Canvas, item, tab page, radio button, and window	Determines the color of the object's foreground (text). This property is set programmatically.
Form Horizontal Toolbar Canvas	Form	Identifies the canvas used as a horizontal toolbar.
Form Vertical Toolbar Canvas	Form	Identifies the canvas used as a vertical toolbar.
Form_name	Form	Identifies the name of the form. This property is not settable.
Format Mask	Item	Determines how the item's value is displayed and entered.
Formula	Item	Contains the formula used to compute the item's value.

Table B-1 Description of Forms Builder properties (continued)

Name	Object	Description
Frame Alignment	Frame	Determines how items are aligned. This property is only valid for Form layout styles. Values are START, END, CENTER, FILL, and COLUMN. COLUMN places the items into a set of columns. FILL spaces each item equally apart on a row. START essentially left-justifies items on a row. END right-justifies items on a row. CENTER causes the row items to be center-justified.
Frame Title	Frame	Contains the frame's title.
Frame Title Alignment	Frame	Determines the alignment of the frame title. Values are START, END, and CENTER.
Frame Title Background Color	Frame	Determines the background color of the title.
Frame Title Font Name	Frame	Determines the font used by the frame title.
Frame Title Font Size	Frame	Determines the size of the font used by the frame title.
Frame Title Font Spacing	Frame	Determines the space between the characters in the font.
Frame Title Font Style	Frame	Determines the style of the frame title.
Frame Title Font Weight	Frame	Determines the weight of the frame title.
Frame Title Foreground Color	Frame	Determines the color of the frame foreground (text).
Frame Title Offset	Frame	Determines the distance between the frame and its title.
Frame Title Reading Order	Frame	Determines the reading order of the frame title. Values are DEFAULT, LEFT-TO-RIGHT, and RIGHT-TO-LEFT.
Frame Title Spacing	Frame	Determines the amount of space on either side of the frame title.
Frame Title Visual Attribute Group	Frame	Determines the visual attribute group that is used to set frame format properties.
Graphics Type	Graphics general	Determines the type of graphic object. Values are ARC, CHART, GROUP, IMAGE, POLYGON, RECTANGLE, ROUNDED RECTANGLE, SYMBOL, and TEXT.
Group_name	LOV	Determines the name of the LOV's record group. This property is set programmatically.
Hide on Exit	Window	Determines whether the window is hidden when the operator navigates from the window. This property is only used for non-modal windows.

Table B-1 Description of Forms Builder properties (continued)

Name	Object	Description
Highest Allowed Value	Item	Sets a high range value for the item. Forms Builder prevents the entry of a value that is less than this setting.
Hint	Item (all except chart items, display items, and custom items)	Determines the text that is displayed on the message line of the window.
Horizontal Justification	Graphic text	Determines the horizontal justification of the object. Values are LEFT, RIGHT, CENTER, START, and END.
Horizontal Margin	Frame	Determines the distance between the frame's left and right borders and the objects within the frame.
Horizontal Object Offset	Frame	Determines the horizontal distance between frame objects.
Horizontal Origin	Graphic text	Determines the horizontal position of the object relative to its origin point.
Horizontal Toolbar Canvas	Window	Contains the name of the horizontal toolbar canvas displayed within the window.
Icon Filename	Window	Contains the name of the icon file used when the window is minimized.
Icon in Menu	Menu item	Determines that an icon will be displayed adjacent to the menu item. Values are YES and NO.
Iconic	Item (button)	Determines whether the button will display an icon.
Image Depth	Item (image)	Determines the image depth setting applied to images. Values are ORIGINAL, MONOCHROME, GRAY, LUT (lookup table), and RGB (red, green, blue).
Image Format	Item (image)	Determines the format of the image stored in the database. Values are BMP, CALS, GIF, JFIF, PICT, RAS, TIFF, and TPIC.
Implementation Class	Item (bean area, check box, list item, push button, radio group, and text item)	Identifies the class name of the JavaBean used by the item.
Include REF Item	Block	Creates a hidden item called REF for the block. The item is used to coordinate records between a master and detail data block.
Inherit Menu	Window	Determines whether the window can use the same menu as the calling window.

Table B-1 Description of Forms Builder properties (continued)

Name	Object	Description
Initial Keyboard State	Item (display and text)	Sets the keyboard to generate Local or Roman characters. Values are DEFAULT, LOCAL, and ROMAN.
Initial Menu	Module	Determines the name of the menu used by the module as the main menu when the form is launched.
Initial Value	Item	Sets a default value for the item. This value is normally blank.
Insert Allowed	Item	Prevents the operator from entering a value into the item when the data block is in the Insert mode.
Insert Procedure Arguments	Block	Determines the names, data types, and values of the arguments used by the procedure that replaces a block's normal insert operation.
Insert Procedure Name	Block	Specifies the name of the procedure that replaces a block's normal insert operation.
Insert Procedure Result Set Columns	Block	Determines the names and data types of the result set columns that are associated to the procedure that replaces a block's normal insert operation.
Interaction Mode	Module	Determines how a user interacts with a form during a query. The value BLOCKING prevents the operator from resizing or interacting with the form until the records have been fetched to the data block. NON-BLOCKING is useful when you expect the query to be long, and you want the operator to be able to cancel the query.
Isolation Mode	Module	Determines whether transactions in a session are serializable. If the value SERIALIZABLE is set, the operator sees a constant view of the database regardless of updates performed by other users.
Item_is_valid	Item	Determines whether an item is marked as valid. This property is set programmatically.
Item Roles	Menu item	Determines which database roles can select the menu item.
Item Tab Page	Item	Determines the tab page on which the item is displayed.

Table B-1 Description of Forms Builder properties (continued)

Name	Object	Description
Item Type	Item	Determines the type of item. Values are BEAN AREA, CHART ITEM, CHECK BOX, DISPLAY ITEM, HIERARCHICAL TREE, IMAGE, LIST ITEM, PUSH BUTTON, RADIO GROUP, TEXT ITEM, and USER AREA.
Join Condition	Relation	Contains the relationship that links a detail block with a master block.
Join Style	Graphic and physical	Determines the join style of the object. Values are MITRE, BEVEL, and ROUND.
Justification	Item (display and text)	Determines the text justification used in the item. Values are CENTER, END, LEFT, RIGHT, and START.
Keep Cursor Position	Item	Determines that the cursor will return to the same position in a value on re-entry.
Key Mode	Block	Determines how Forms Builder identifies a row in the database. Values are AUTOMATIC (uses the rowid), NON-UPDATEABLE (does not use the primary key in issued UPDATE statements), UNIQUE (causes Forms Builder to use rowid constructs to identify unique rows in the database), and UPDATEABLE (allows Forms Builder to issue UPDATE statements that include the primary key).
Keyboard Accelerator	Menu item	Determines a function key that can be associated to the menu item. The function key can be used in place of the menu selection.
Keyboard Help Description	Trigger	Determines the key trigger descriptions displayed in the runtime Keys help screen. This can only be used if the Display Keyboard Help property is set to YES.
Keyboard Navigable	Item (all except chart and display)	Determines whether the user can move into the item by tabbing.
Keyboard State	Item	Determines supported keyboards states. Values are ANY, ROMAN ONLY, or LOCAL ONLY.
Label	Frame	Specifies the data block affected by the frame.
Last_block	Module	Identifies the name of the block with the highest sequence number.
Last_item	Block	Identifies the name of the item with the highest sequence number in the target block.

Table B-1 Description of Forms Builder properties (continued)

Name	Object	Description
Last_query	Block	Identifies the SQL statement for the last query executed by the specified block.
Layout Data Block	Frame	Determines the name of the data block to which the frame is associated.
Layout Style	Frame	Determines the type of layout: Form or Tabular.
Line Spacing	Graphic text	Determines the line spacing for the text object. Values are SINGLE, ONE-AND-A-HALF, DOUBLE, and CUSTOM.
Line Width	Graphic physical	Determines the width of the object's edge.
List of Values	Item (text)	Identifies the LOV attached to the item.
List Style	Item (list)	Determines the type of list. Values are POPLIST, COMBO BOX, and TLIST.
List X Position	Item (text)	Determines the X coordinate of the top-left corner of the LOV.
List Y Position	Item (text)	Determines the Y coordinate of the top-left corner of the LOV.
Lock Procedure Arguments	Block	Determines the names, data types, and values of the arguments used by the procedure that replaces a block's normal lock operation.
Lock Procedure Name	Block	Determines the name of the procedure that replaces a block's normal lock operation.
Lock Procedure Result Set	Block	Determines the names and data types of the result set columns that are associated to the procedure that replaces a block's normal lock operation.
Lock Record	Item (text)	Determines whether Forms Builder should lock the database row that corresponds to the item's row when the item is modified.
Locking Mode	Block	Determines when Forms Builder locks the database record. Values are AUTOMATIC, IMMEDIATE, and DELAYED.
Lowest Allowed Value	Item	Sets a low range value for the value. Forms Builder prevents the entry of a value that is lower than this setting.
Magic Item	Menu item	Determines that the menu item launches an operating system function such as CUT or COPY.
Main Menu	Menu module	Specifies the name of the menu that is to be the main or starting menu.

Table B-1 Description of Forms Builder properties (continued)

Name	Object	Description
Mapping of Other Values	Item (list and radio group)	Determines how values not defined in the list or radio group are handled.
Maximize Allowed	Window	Determines whether the window can be maximized.
Maximum Length	Item (all except buttons, images, and charts)	Determines the maximum length of the data value stored in the item.
Maximum Objects Per Line	Frame	Determines the maximum number of data block items that are displayed on a row within the frame. The property is only valid when the Frame Style property is set to FORM.
Maximum Query Time	Form and block	When used in conjunction with the Query All Records property, aborts a query when the elapsed time of the query exceeds the value of the property.
Maximum Records Fetched	Form and block	Determines the number of records fetched by a query before the query is aborted.
Menu Directory	Menu module	Determines in which directory Forms Builder should look for the **.mmx** runtime menu file. This property is used when Forms Builder is to locate the menu's runfile in the database.
Menu Filename	Menu module	Determines the name of the **.mmx** runtime menu file Forms Builder should use at startup. This property is used when Forms Builder is to locate the menu's runfile in the database.
Menu Item Code	Menu item	Holds the PL/SQL statements for the menu item.
Menu Item Radio Group	Menu item	Contains the name of the radio group to which the current radio menu item belongs.
Menu Item Type	Menu item	Determines the type of menu item. Values are PLAIN, CHECK, MAGIC, RADIO, and SEPARATOR.
Menu Module	Module	Identifies the name of the menu used with the form.
Menu Role	Module	Determines the database role that Forms Builder should use for security with the menu.
Menu Style	Module	Determines the menu display style. Value are PULL-DOWN and BAR.

Table B-1 Description of Forms Builder properties (continued)

Name	Object	Description
Message	Alert	Contains the text that is displayed in the body of the alert.
Minimize Allowed	Window	Determines whether the window can be minimized.
Minimized Title	Window	Determines the text displayed when the window is minimized.
Modal	Window	Determines whether the window is modal. Modal dialog boxes require the user to dismiss or close the window before proceeding.
Module_nls_lang	Form	Determines the complete current value of the NLS_LANG environment variable defined for the form. This property is not settable.
Mouse Navigate	Item (button, check box, list item, and radio group)	Determines whether Forms Builder navigates to the item when the end user activates the item with the mouse.
Mouse Navigation Limit	Form	Specifies how far outside the current item the user can navigate using a mouse. Values are FORM, BLOCK, RECORD, and ITEM.
Move Allowed	Window	Allows the window to be moved manually or programmatically.
Multi-Line	Item (text)	Specifies whether the text item is a single-line or multi-line editing region.
Multi-Selection	Hierarchical tree item	Determines whether the user can select multiple items while holding down the Shift button. A value of NO disables this function. A value of YES allows multi-selection.
Name	All form objects	Identifies the object name.
Navigation Style	Block	Determines what occurs when the operator tabs from the last item in a record. Values are SAME RECORD, CHANGE RECORD, and CHANGE BLOCK.
NextBlock	Block	Determines the name of the block with the next higher sequence number. This property is not settable.
Next_detail_relation	Relation	Identifies the name of the relation that uses the same detail block as the specified relation.
Next_item	Item	Identifies the name of the item with the next higher sequence number. This property is not settable.

Table B-1 Description of Forms Builder properties (continued)

Name	Object	Description
Next_master_relation	Relations	Contains the name of the next relation that has the same master block as the specified relation. This property is not settable.
Next Navigation Block	Block	Determines the name of the next block that will receive the input focus.
Next Navigation Item	Item	Determines the name of the next item that will receive the input focus.
Number of Items Displayed	Item	Determines the number of items that are displayed in the data block. A value of 0 causes Forms Builder to use the block's setting. Other values supercede the block's setting.
Number of Records Buffered	Block	Determines the number of records placed into memory during a query.
Number of Records Displayed	Item	Determines how many items can be displayed. This item is normally set to 0, which specifies that the item should use the data block setting. Changing this setting overrides the data block setting.
Onetime_where	Form and block	Sets a one-time Where clause for the block. It will override the existing Where clause and can only be used for the next query.
Operating System	Application	Determines the name of the current operating system.
Optimizer Hint	Block	Contains a hint that can be added to the SELECT statement that is issued by the block.
Order By Clause	Block	Determines the order in which records are displayed by the block.
Other Reports Parameters	Reports	Contains a list of parameters to pass to the called report module.
Parameter Data Type	Forms Builder	Determines the kinds of values Forms Builder allows as input and how Forms Builder displays those values.
Parameter Initial Value	Forms Builder	Determines the value assigned to the parameter at form startup.
Password	Application	Contains the password of the current user. This property is not settable.
PL/SQL_date_format	Application	Sets the format mask for converting date values when executing PL/SQL.
PL/SQL Library Location	PL/SQL library	Identifies the location of the attached PL/SQL library.

Table B-1 Description of Forms Builder properties (continued)

Name	Object	Description
PL/SQL Library Source	PL/SQL library	Identifies the source of the PL/SQL library. Values are FILE or DATABASE.This is a display-only property.
Popup Menu	Canvas and item	Identifies the popup menu attached to the object.
Precompute Summaries	Block	Causes the value of any summarized item to be computed before the query is issued.
Prevent Masterless Operations	Relation	Determines whether the operator can perform a query or insert records on a detail block. A value of YES prevents a record from being inserted into the data block when a corresponding master record does not exist. It also prevents a query from occurring on the detail block if a master record does not exist.
PreviousBlock	Block	Identifies the block with the next lower sequence number. This property is not settable.
Previous_item	Item	Identifies the item with the next lower sequence number in the block.
Previous Navigation Block	Block	Identifies the block that precedes the current block in the navigation order.
Previous Navigation Item	Item	Identifies the item that precedes the current item in the tabbing order.
Primary Canvas	Window	Identifies the default canvas that is displayed when the window is opened.
Primary Key	Item	Notifies Forms Builder that the item is the primary key. Forms Builder then checks the database to ensure that the value is unique before issuing an SQL statement. At least one column in the data block must have this value set to YES.
Program Unit Text	Program unit	Contains the program unit's PL/SQL code.
Prompt	Item	Contains the text displayed in the item's prompt.
Prompt Alignment	Item	Determines how the prompt is aligned along the item's edge. Values are START, END, and CENTER.
Prompt Alignment Offset	Item	Determines the prompt's alignment offset.
Prompt Attachment Edge	Item	Determines to which edge the prompt is attached. Values are START, END, TOP, and BOTTOM.

Table B-1 Description of Forms Builder properties (continued)

Name	Object	Description
Prompt Attachment Offset	Item	Determines the distance between the item and its prompt.
Prompt Display Style	Item	Determines the prompt's display style. This property is set programmatically.
Prompt Justification	Item	Determines the justification of the prompt. Values are LEFT, RIGHT, CENTER, START, and END.
Prompt Reading Order	Item	Determines the prompt's reading order. Values are DEFAULT, LEFT TO RIGHT, and RIGHT TO LEFT.
Prompt Visual Attribute Group	Item	Determines the visual attribute used by the prompt for its formatting values.
Prompt_background_color	Item (radio button)	Determines the color of the object's background. This property is set programmatically.
Prompt_fill_pattern	Item (radio button)	Determines the fill pattern of the prompt. This property is set programmatically.
Prompt_font_name	Item (radio button)	Determines the font used by the prompt. This property is set programmatically.
Prompt_font_size	Item (radio button)	Determines the size of the font. This property is set programmatically.
Prompt_font_spacing	Item (radio button)	Determines the spacing of the characters in the prompt. This property is set programmatically.
Prompt_font_style	Item (radio button)	Determines the style of the prompt's font. This property is set programmatically.
Prompt_font_weight	Item (radio button)	Determines the weight of the font used by the prompt. This property is set programmatically.
Prompt_foreground_color	Item (radio button)	Determines the color of the object's prompt foreground. This property is set programmatically.
Property Class	All objects	Identifies the property class used by the object for property settings.
Query All Records	Block	Determines whether all records should be fetched into the data block when the query is executed. A value of YES offers greater scrolling ability but takes longer to return the initial records.

Table B-1 Description of Forms Builder properties (continued)

Name	Object	Description
Query Allowed	Item	Determines whether the item can be used to enter search criteria when the data block is in the Enter Query mode. It is recommended that only the items logically used to filter records have a value of YES. The remainder of the items should be set to NO. This prevents excessive tabbing by the operator.
Query Array Size	Block	Determines the maximum number of records Forms Builder should fetch at one time.
Query Data Source Arguments	Block	Determines the names, data types, and values of the arguments used by the procedure that replaces a block's normal insert operation.
Query Data Source Columns	Block	Identifies the name of the procedure that replaces a block's normal insert operation.
Query Data Source Name	Block	Determines the names and data types of the result set columns that are associated to the procedure that replaces a block's normal insert operation.
Query Data Source Type	Block	Determines the query data source of the block. Values are TABLE, PROCEDURE, TRANSACTIONAL TRIGGER, and FROM CLAUSE QUERY.
Query_hits	Block	Determines the number of records identified in a Count_query operation. This property is set programmatically and is included for applications that use non-Oracle data sources.
Query Length	Item	Determines the number of characters the operator may place into the item when the data block is in the Enter Query mode. If the value is set to the default of 0, Forms Builder makes this the same length as the Maximum Length property. If this property has any other value, Forms Builder does not allow you to set it, unless the value is the same or greater than the Maximum Length property.
Query Name	Reports	Identifies the name of the query in the report with which to associate the form's block.
Query Only	Item	Setting this value to YES disables the item from being used to enter search values.

Table B-1 Description of Forms Builder properties (continued)

Name	Object	Description
Query_options	Block	Determines the type of query operation that would be performed by default if the default processing were not circumvented. This property is included for applications that use non-Oracle data sources. This property is not settable.
Radio Button Value	Item (radio button)	Identifies the values associated with a specific radio button.
Raise On Entry	Canvas	Brings the canvas forward whenever the operator navigates to the canvas. The default is NO. This property is seldom used.
Reading Order	Item (display and text)	Specifies the reading order for groups of words in the same language within a single text item. This property allows you to control the display of bilingual text items.
Real Unit	Module	Determines the unit of measure used by the form when the Coordinate System property is set to REAL. Values are CENTIMETER, INCH, PIXCELS, POINTS, and DECIPOINTS.
Record Group	Hierarchical tree item	Determines whether the user can select multiple items while holding down the Shift key. A value of NO disables this function. A value of YES allows multi-selection.
Record Group Fetch Size	Record group	Determines the size of the records to be fetched. A large value reduces the number of fetches required to populate the record group.
Record Group Query	Record group	Contains the SELECT statement used by the record group.
Record Group Type	Record group	Determines the type of data source used by the record group. Values are STATIC and QUERY.
Record Orientation	Block	Specifies the orientation of records in the block. Values are HORIZONTAL and VERTICAL.
Records_to_fetch	Block	Returns the number of records Forms Builder expects an On-Fetch trigger to fetch.
Relation Type	Relations	Determines the type of link between a master and detail block. Values are JOIN and REF.
Rendered	Item (text and display)	Determines whether the item is displayed as a rendered object when it does not have focus.

Table B-1 Description of Forms Builder properties (continued)

Name	Object	Description
Report Destination Format	Reports	Identifies the format of the report output. Values are PDF, HTML, HTMLCSS, HTMLCSSIE, RTF, and DELIMITED.
Report Destination Name	Reports	Identifies the name of the report's destination.
Report Destination Type	Reports	Identifies the destination of the report output. Values are FILE, INTEROFFICE, MAIL, PREVIEW, PRINTER, and SCREEN.
Report Server	Reports	Identifies the Report Server against which you can run the report.
Required	Item	Prevents the operator from navigating from the item unless a value is entered. If the related database item has a NOT NULL constraint, this property value is set to YES by default. It is recommended that this property always be set to NO, because the operator may not want to enter a value into the item, especially when the data block is in the Enter Query mode.
Resize Allowed	Window	Determines whether the window can be resized.
Rotation Angle	Graphics physical	Determines the graphic object's rotation angle.
Runtime Compatibility Mode	Forms Builder	Determines the Forms Builder version with which the current form's runtime behavior is compatible.
Savepoint Mode	Module	Determines whether Forms Builder should issue savepoints during a session. This property is used for applications that use non-Oracle data sources.
Savepoint Name	Application	Determines the name of the savepoint Forms Builder is expecting to be set or rolled back to. This property is settable.
Scroll Bar Alignment	Frame	Determines whether the scroll bar is displayed at the start or end of the frame.
Scroll Bar Canvas	Block	Determines the canvas on which the scroll bar is displayed.
Scroll Bar Height	Block and item	Determines the height of the scroll bar.
Scroll Bar Tab Page	Block	Determines the tab page on which the scroll bar is displayed.
Scroll Bar Width	Block and item	Determines the width of the scroll bar.

Table B-1 Description of Forms Builder properties (continued)

Name	Object	Description
Share Library With Form	Menus	Determines whether forms that have identical libraries attached can share library package data.
Show Horizontal Scroll Bar	Window	Determines whether the window has a horizontal scroll bar when the canvas is larger than the window.
Show Lines	Hierarchical tree item	Determines whether a line links the tree nodes. Set the value to YES to display the lines, and to NO to suppress the lines.
Show Palette	Item (Image)	Specifies whether an image-manipulation palette is displayed next to the image. The palette has three tools: Zoom, Pan, and Rotate.
Show Scroll Bar	Block	Determines whether the scroll bar is displayed on the canvas specified by the Scroll Bar Canvas property.
Show Symbols	Hierarchical tree item	Determines whether the nodes can be expanded and collapsed. A value of NO disables the functionality, and a value of YES enables it. When the NO value is selected, the tree is fully expanded.
Show Vertical Scroll Bar	Window	Determines whether the window has a vertical scroll bar when the canvas is larger than the window.
Shrinkwrap	Frame	Determines whether blank space should be removed from the frame placing the items in the smallest possible area. When this property is set to YES, you will not be able to resize the frame, because Forms Builder will automatically reduce the frame.
Single Object Alignment	Frame	Determines whether empty space surrounding a frame object is used. This setting is only used when the Layout Style property is set to FORM.
Single Record		Determines the maximum number of items than can appear on each line. The default value is 0, which means there is no maximum.
Size	Canvas	Determines the width and height of the canvas. This property is set programmatically.
Sizing Style	Item (image)	Specifies the display style of the image when it does not match the size of the image item. Values are CROP (clip a portion) and ADJUST (change the size of the image).

Table B-1 Description of Forms Builder properties (continued)

Name	Object	Description
SSO USERID	Application	Identifies a string containing the Single Sign On user ID. This property is not settable.
Start Angle	Graphic arc	Determines the starting angle of the arc, using the horizontal axis as an origin.
Start Prompt Alignment	Frame	Determines how an item's prompt is aligned to the horizontal edge.The property is only used if the Layout Style property is set to FORM.
Start Prompt Offset	Frame	Determines the distance between the prompt and its related item. The property is only used when the Start Prompt Alignment property is set to START.
Startup Code	Menu module	Determines the optional PL/SQL code Forms Builder executes when the menu module is first executed.
Status	Record	Determines the status of the indicated record. Values are NEW, CHANGED, QUERY, and INSERT. This property is set programmatically.
Subclass Information	All objects	Identifies a linked form object or a property class that is used by the object for property settings.
Submenu Name	Menu item	Determines the name of the submenu associated to a main menu.
Summarized Block	Item	Identifies the block that contains the item that is used as the source of the aggregate value.
Summarized Item	Item	Identifies the item that is used as the source of the aggregate value.
Summary Function	Item	Determines the type of summary value that will be calculated for the item. Values are AVG, COUNT, MAX, MIN, STDDEV, SUM, and VARIANCE.
Synchronize With Item	All objects	Causes the target item to always have the same value as the referenced item and vice versa.
Tab Attachment Edge	Canvas	Determines the location of the tabs attached to the canvas.
Tab Page	Item	Identifies the page on which the item is located.
Tab Page X Offset	Canvas	Determines the distance between the left edge of the tab page and the left edge of the tab canvas.

Table B-1 Description of Forms Builder properties (continued)

Name	Object	Description
Tab Page Y Offset	Canvas	Determines the distance between the top edge of the tab page and the top edge of the tab canvas.
Tab Style	Canvas	Determines the style of the tab canvas' tabs.
Tear-Off Menu	Menu	Determines whether the menu can be moved.
Timer_name	Application	Identifies the name of the most recently expired timer.
Title	Alert and Window	Identifies the name that appears in the alert or window.
Tooltip	Item	Contains the Tooltip message.
Tooltip Background Color	Item	Determines the background color of the Tooltip.
Tooltip Fill Pattern	Item	Determines the fill pattern used by the Tooltip.
Tooltip Font Name	Item	Determines the name of the Tooltip font.
Tooltip Font Size	Item	Determines the size of the Tooltip font.
Tooltip Font Spacing	Item	Determines the space between the Tooltip characters.
Tooltip Font Weight	Item	Determines the font weight of the Tooltip.
Tooltip Foreground Color	Item	Determines the color of the Tooltip foreground (text).
Tooltip Visual Attribute Group	Item	Identifies the visual attribute used by the Tooltip.
Top Prompt Alignment	Frame	Determines the alignment of the top prompt with the item's top edge. Values are CENTER, END, and START.
Top Prompt Offset	Frame	Determines the distance between the item and its prompt when the Top Prompt Alignment property is set to TOP.
Top Record	Block	Determines the record number of the topmost record displayed in the block. This property is not settable.
Top Title	Editor	Contains a title displayed in the editor window. The length cannot be greater than 72 characters.
Topmost Tab Page	Canvas (tab)	Identifies the topmost page in the tab canvas.
Transactional Triggers	Block	Determines that the block is a transaction control block. This property is used when the form is used against non-Oracle data sources.

Table B-1 Description of Forms Builder properties (continued)

Name	Object	Description
Trigger Style	Trigger	Determines whether the trigger is a PL/SQL trigger or a V2-style used in an early version of Forms Builder.Oracle recommends the use of PL/SQL.
Trigger Text	Trigger	Contains the PL/SQL code executed when the trigger fires.
Trigger Type	Trigger	Determines whether the trigger is built in or user named.
Update Allowed	Item	Prevents the item from being modified when the data block is in the Normal mode.
Update Changed Columns Only	Block	Causes only the columns that have a modified value to be included in the UPDATE statement created by the data block.
Update_column	Item	Determines whether a column can be updated. This property is set programmatically.
Update Commit	Item (chart)	Determines whether a chart item is updated to reflect changes made when committing records.
Update Layout	Frame	Controls when the data block is updated as a result of a frame property change. Values are AUTOMATICALLY (update occurs after every change), MANUALLY (update occurs only after clicking the Update Layout tool in the Layout Editor), and LOCKED (the layout cannot be changed).
Update Only If Null	Item	Prevents the item from being modified if the item contains a value.
Update_permission	Item (all except buttons and charts)	Changing this property to NO sets the Update only If Null and Update Allowed properties to NO. It also specifies that the column should not be included in any UPDATE statement issued by the block. This property is set programmatically.
Update Procedure Arguments	Item	Prevents the operator from entering a value into the item when the data block is in the Insert mode.
Update Procedure Name	Block	Determines the names, data types, and values of the arguments used by the procedure that replaces a block's normal insert operation.

Table B-1 Description of Forms Builder properties (continued)

Name	Object	Description
Update Result Set	Block	Identifies the name of the procedure that replaces a block's normal Update operation.
Update Query	Block	Determines the names and data types of the result set columns that are associated to the procedure that replaces a block's normal Update operation.
Use 3D Controls	Form	Determines whether Forms Builder displays items with a three-dimensional, beveled look.
Use Security	Menu module	Instructs Forms Builder to enforce the security schema defined for the menu.
User Interface	Application	Determines the name of the user interface in use. Values are BLOCKMODE, CHARMODE, MACINTOSH, MOTIF, MSWINDOWS, MSWINDOWS32, PM, WIN32COMMON, WEB, and X.
User NLS Date Format	Application	Obtains the current NLS date format mask. This property is not settable.
User NLS Lang	Application	Determines the value of the NLS_LANG environment variable used in the current session. This property is not settable.
Username	Application	Contains the Oracle ID name of the current operator. It property is not settable.
Validate From List	Item (text)	Determines whether values entered in the item should be validated against values in an attached LOV.
Validation	Module	Determines whether validation processing is enabled.
Validation Unit	Module	Determines the scope of form validation. It specifies the maximum amount of data the operator can enter before Forms Builder initiates validation.
Value When Checked	Check box	Determines what value causes the box to be checked.
Value When Unchecked	Check box	Determines what value causes the box to be unchecked.
Vertical Fill	Frame	Determines the empty space surrounding an object. This property is used in conjunction with the Layout Style property when it is set to FORM. Values are YES and NO.
Vertical Justification	Graphic text	Determines the vertical justification of the test. Values are BOTTOM, CENTER, and TOP.

Table B-1 Description of Forms Builder properties (continued)

Name	Object	Description
Vertical Margin	Frame	Determines the distance between the frame's bottom and top borders and the objects within the frame.
Vertical Object Offset	Frame	Determines the vertical distance between frame objects.
Vertical Origin	Graphic text	Determines the vertical position of the text relative to its origin. Values are BOTTOM, CENTER, and TOP.
Vertical Toolbar Canvas	Window	The name of the vertical toolbar canvas displayed within the window.
Viewport Height	Canvas	Determines the height of the stacked canvas.
Viewport Width	Canvas	Determines the width of the stacked canvas.
Viewport X Position	Canvas	Determines the stacked canvas's top-left-corner X coordinate relative to the window. This property can be set programmatically.
Viewport X Position on Canvas	Canvas	Determines the X location of the canvas's top-left edge within the window or view. A setting of 10 causes the canvas to be displayed 10 points to the right of the window's left edge. This property is only relevant for stacked canvases.
Viewport Y Position	Canvas	Determines the stacked canvas's top-left-corner Y coordinate relative to the window. This property can be set programmatically.
Viewport Y Position on Canvas	Canvas	Determines the Y location of the canvas's top-left corner within the window or view. A setting of 10 causes the canvas to be displayed 10 points to the right of the window's left edge. This property is only relevant for stacked canvases.
Visible	Canvas, item, and tab page	Determines whether the item can be seen when the form is displayed.
Visual Attribute	Canvas, item, tab page, and radio button	Determines the visual attribute group for the object.
Visual Attribute Group	All displayed items	Associates a visual attribute group object to the item.
Visual Attribute Type	Visual attribute group	Determines the type of visual attribute group. Values are COMMON, PROMPT, and TITLE.
Where Clause	Block	Contains SELECT statement arguments that filter the records returned to the data block.

Table B-1 Description of Forms Builder properties (continued)

Name	Object	Description
Window	Canvas	Identifies the window that displays the canvas.
Window State	Window	Determines the state of the current window. Values are NORMAL, MINIMIZE, and MAXIMIZE.
Window Style	Window	Identifies the window. Values are DOCUMENT and DIALOG. Document windows remain within the application window. If the operator resizes the window, a document window is clipped. A dialog window is free floating and can even be moved outside the window if it is defined as Movable. If a dialog window is resized, the window is not clipped.
Wrap Style	Editor and item (text)	Determines where the displayed text will wrap when it exceeds the width of the item or editor. Values are NONE, CHARACTER (wraps on individual characters), and WORD (moves complete words to the next line).
Wrap Text	Graphic text	Determines whether the text in a text object wraps to the next line to fit within the enclosing or bounding box.
X Corner Radius	Graphic round rectangle	Determines the horizontal rounding of the corners of a rounded rectangle.
X Position	Canvas, editor, item, LOV, and window	Determines the X position of the top-left corner of the object.
Y Corner Radius	Graphic round rectangle	Determines the vertical rounding of the corners of a rounded rectangle.
Y Position	Canvas, editor, item, LOV, and window	Determines the Y position of the top-left corner of the object.

APPENDIX

C

SYSTEM VARIABLES

Table C-1 supplies a description of system variables, which you can use to determine information about a form while it is in operation. For example, you can determine in which block the input focus is located, whether the current record has been changed, and whether the current record is the last record in the data block. You can also use system variables to suppress messages. System variables are always qualified by a system keyword. The following system variable example is used in a statement to suppress all Forms Builder messages:

```
:system.message_level := '25';
```

Table C-1 System variable descriptions

Variable name	Description
Block_status	A read-only variable that identifies the status of the current block. Values are: ■ QUERY: indicates that records were returned from the database ■ NEW: indicates that only new records are in the data block ■ CHANGED: indicates that at least one record was modified
Coordination_operation	A read-only variable used with the Master_block variable to help the On-Clear-Details trigger identify the type of coordination-causing operation that fired the On-Clear-Details trigger.
Current_block	A read-only variable that identifies the block that contains the input focus. If the input focus has not moved to a data block, as is the case when a Pre-Form trigger is fired, the value will be NULL.
Current_datetime	A read-only variable that identifies the operating system date and time. It will be displayed using the default Oracle date picture.
Current_form	A read-only variable that identifies the name of the current form module.
Current_item	A read-only variable that identifies the name of the block and item in which the input focus resides.
Current_value	A read-only variable that identifies the value of the item in which the input focus resides.
Cursor_block	A read-only variable that identifies the data block in which the cursor resides. If the cursor does not reside in a data block, as is the case when a Pre-Form trigger is fired, the value will be NULL.
Cursor_item	A read-only variable that identifies the block and item in which the input focus resides.
Cursor_record	A read-only variable that identifies the number of the data block record in which the input focus resides. This value is a character string.
Cursor_value	A read-only variable that identifies the value of the item in which the cursor resides. This value is always a character string.
Date_threshold	An updateable value that represents the database requery threshold. This variable, along with the variables $$DBDATE$$, $$DBDATETIME$$, and $$DBTIME$$, controls how often Forms Builder synchronizes the database date with the RDBMS.
Effective_date	An updateable value that represents the effective database data. The value must always use the default Oracle data picture.
Event_window	A read-only variable that identifies the last window that was affected by an action that caused a window event trigger to fire.
Form_status	A read-only variable that identifies the status of the current form. Values are: ■ QUERY: indicates that records were returned from the database ■ NEW: indicates that only new records are in the data block ■ CHANGED: indicates that at least one record was modified

Table C-1 System variable descriptions (continued)

Variable name	Description
Last_query	A read-only variable that identifies the SELECT statement most recently executed by Forms Builder.
Last_record	A read-only variable that identifies whether the current record is the last record in the data block. A value of TRUE indicates the record is the last, and FALSE indicates it is not.
Master_block	A read-only variable that is used with the Coordination_operation variable to help the On-Clear-Details trigger identify the type of coordination-causing operation that fired the On-Clear-Details trigger.
Message_level	An updateable value that suppresses nonfatal form messages. Values can range between 0 and 25. A value of 0 notifies Forms Builder not to suppress any message.
Mode	A read-only variable that identifies the mode of the current block. Values are: ■ NORMAL: indicates that the form is displaying records or is avail able to add records ■ ENTER QUERY: indicates that the data block is prompting for the entry of selection criteria ■ QUERY: indicates that the data block is in the process of fetching records to the form
Mouse_button_pressed	A read-only variable that identifies the number of the button that was clicked. A value of 1 indicates the left button, 2 the middle button, and 3 the right button.
Mouse_button_shift_state	A read-only variable that identifies the auxiliary key that was pressed during a click. Values returned by this variable are: ■ SHIFT+ (The Shift key was pressed.) ■ CTRL+ (The Control key was pressed.) ■ ALT+ (The Alt key was pressed.) ■ SHIFT+CONTROL+ (The Shift and Control keys were pressed.)
Mouse_item	A read-only variable that identifies the name of the block and item that received the mouse click.
Mouse_canvas	A read-only variable that identifies the name of the canvas that received the mouse click.
Mouse_x_pos	A read-only variable that identifies the X coordinate of the mouse's current position in the form. It uses the same unit of measure as that used by the form.
Mouse_y_pos	A read-only variable that identifies the Y coordinate of the mouse's current position in the form. It uses the same unit of measure as that used by the form.
Mouse_record	A read-only variable that identifies the record number of the record that received the mouse click.

Table C-1 System variable descriptions (continued)

Variable name	Description
Mouse_record_offset	A read-only variable that identifies the offset from the first visible record from the top of the data block. For example, if the clicked record is the fourth from the top, the value of the variable is 4.
Record_status	A read-only variable that identifies the status of the current record. Values are: ■ CHANGED: indicates that the record was modified ■ INSERT: indicates that the record has a value and does not exist in the database ■ NEW: indicates that the record does not have a value ■ QUERY: indicates that the record can be used to enter search criteria
Suppress_working	Updateable variable suppresses the "Working…" message seen during runtime. A value of TRUE causes Forms Builder to suppress the message. A value of FALSE allows the message.
Tab_new_page	A read-only variable that identifies the tab page to which navigation occurred.
Tab_previous_page	A read-only variable that identifies the table page from which navigation occurred.
Trigger_block	A read-only variable that identifies the block on which the currently fired trigger is located.
Trigger_item	A read-only variable that identifies the block and item on which the currently fired trigger is located.
Trigger_record	A read-only variable that identifies the number of the record that Forms Builder is processing. This value is the current physical order in the block's list of records.

APPENDIX

D

TRIGGERS

Triggers are form objects that contain executable statements and can be used to execute PL/SQL statements, database functions and procedures, Oracle form built-ins, SELECT statements, and DML statements. Triggers are executed or fired based on a specific event, which is generally denoted in the trigger's name. A trigger is always associated to another form object, which can be the form itself, a block, or an item. The associated object determines the trigger's scope. A trigger associated to the form can be fired as a result of a particular action that occurs on the entire form. A trigger associated to an item has the smallest scope, because it can be fired based only on a specific action on the item.

Triggers also have a number of limitations. Some triggers cannot be fired when the form is in the Enter Query mode, and others cannot fire restricted built-ins. In addition, certain triggers cannot execute restricted built-ins, because the trigger is fired as the result of navigation. Some built-ins cannot fire when navigation is occurring.

Table D-1 lists the form triggers. Beneath the name of most triggers is the scope declaration, which indicates at what level the trigger can be established. The table also identifies the types of commands that can be used in the trigger and supplies a brief description of the trigger.

Table D-1 Form triggers

Trigger name	Enter Query mode	Commands allowed	Description
Delete-Procedure	Not applicable	Not applicable	Associated to a stored procedure and fired when a delete is to be performed.
Insert-Procedure	Not applicable	Not applicable	Associated to a stored procedure and fired when an insert is to be performed.
Key-Fn (form, block, or item)	Yes	SELECT statements, restricted built-ins, and unrestricted built-ins	A series of triggers attached to F0 through F9 keys. These triggers are fired when the designated key is pressed.
Key-Others (form, block, or item)	Yes	SELECT statements, restricted built-ins, and unrestricted built-ins	Fired when an operator presses a function key that does not have an associated Key-Fn trigger.
Lock-Procedure	Not applicable	Not applicable	Associated to a stored procedure and fired when a database lock is to be performed.
On-Check-Delete-Master (form or block)	No	Any command, unrestricted built-ins, and restricted built-ins	Fired when there is an attempt to delete a record in a master block.
On-Check-Unique (form or block)	No	SELECT statement and unrestricted built-ins	Fired during a commit operation to ensure that the primary key data block items are unique.
On-Clear-Details (form or block)	No	Any command, unrestricted built-ins, and restricted built-ins	Fired during a master-detail data block coordination event.
On-Close (form)	No	SELECT statements, PL/SQL, and unrestricted built-ins	Fired when a query is closed.
On-Column-Security (form or block)	No	SELECT statements, PL/SQL, and unrestricted built-ins	Fired when Forms Builder enforces column security. This consists of a database procedure that ensures that an operator has update privileges.

Table D-1 Form triggers (continued)

Trigger name	Enter Query mode	Commands allowed	Description
On-Commit (form)	No	SELECT statements, PL/SQL, and unrestricted built-ins	Fired when Forms Builder issues a COMMIT statement to the database.
On-Count (form or block)	Yes	SELECT statements, PL/SQL, and unrestricted built-ins	Fired when Forms Builder performs a Count Query process that determines the number of records retrieved by the query.
On-Delete (form or block)	No	SELECT statements, DML statements, and unrestricted built-ins	Fired when a delete transaction occurs. It replaces the default data block delete processing.
On-Error (form, block, or item)	Yes	SELECT statements and unrestricted built-ins	Fired to replace Forms Builder error messages.
On-Fetch (form or block)	No	SELECT statements, PL/SQL, and unrestricted built-ins	Fired when a query is first opened and records are fetched to the screen.
On-Insert (form or block)	No	SELECT statements, DML statements, and unrestricted built-ins	Fired to replace Insert statements issued by the data block.
On-Lock (form or block)	No	SELECT statements and unrestricted built-ins	Fired when Forms Developer attempts to lock a record.
On-Logon (form)	No	Unrestricted built-ins	Fired during the initial Oracle logon sequence.
On-Logout (form)	No	SELECT statements and unrestricted built-ins	Fired when Forms Builder begins to log out.
On-Message (form, block, or item)	Yes	SELECT statements and unrestricted built-ins	Fired to replace messages sent by Forms Builder.
On-Populate-Details (form or block)	No	SELECT statements, PL/SQL, unrestricted built-ins, and restricted built-ins	Fired when Forms Builder populates the detail data block.
On-Rollback (form)	No	SELECT statements, PL/SQL, and unrestricted built-ins	Fired when Forms Builder issues a ROLLBACK statement.

Table D-1 Form triggers (continued)

Trigger name	Enter Query mode	Commands allowed	Description
On-Savepoint (form)	No	SELECT statements, PL/SQL, and unrestricted built-ins	Fired when Forms Builder issues a Savepoint statement. This happens when the form starts up or at the start of each Post and Commit Transactions process.
On-Select (form or block)	No	SELECT statements, PL/SQL, and unrestricted built-ins	Fired to replace SELECT statements issued by the data block.
On-Sequence-Number (form, block, or item)	No	SELECT statements and unrestricted built-ins	Fired to replace the action that occurs when Forms Builder attempts to get a value from a sequence object.
On-Update (form or block)	No	SELECT statements, DML statements, and unrestricted built-ins	Fired to replace an Update statement issued by the form.
Post-Block (form or block)	No	SELECT statements and unrestricted built-ins	Fired when the input focus leaves a data block.
Post-Change (form, block, or item)	No	SELECT statements and unrestricted built-ins	Fired after a data block value is changed and the validation process occurs.
Post-Database-Commit (form)	No	SELECT statements, DML statements, and unrestricted built-ins	Fired after a database commit has occurred.
Post-Delete (form or block)	No	SELECT statements, DML statements, and unrestricted built-ins	Fired once for each row deleted from a table.
Post-Form (form)	No	SELECT statements and unrestricted built-ins	Fired when an operator exits the form.
Post-Forms-Commit (form)	No	SELECT statements, DML statements, and unrestricted built-ins	Fired during the Post and Commit Transactions process.

Table D-1 Form triggers (continued)

Trigger name	Enter Query mode	Commands allowed	Description
Post-Insert (form or block)	No	SELECT statements, DML statements, and unrestricted built-ins	Fired once for each record inserted into a table.
Post-Logon (form)	No	SELECT statements and unrestricted built-ins	Fired after the logon procedure is completed.
Post-Logout (form)	No	SELECT statements and unrestricted built-ins	Fired after Forms Builder logs out of Oracle.
Post-Query (form or block)	No	SELECT statements and unrestricted built-ins	Fired after each record is fetched to the data block.
Post-Record (form or block)	No	SELECT statements and unrestricted built-ins	Fired when an operator moves from a record.
Post-Select (form or block)	No	SELECT statements and unrestricted built-ins	Fired after a data block executes a select statement and before records are fetched to the data block.
Post-Text-Item (form, block, or item)	No	SELECT statements and unrestricted built-ins	Fired when the input focus leaves an item.
Post-Update (form or block)	No	SELECT statements, DML statements, unrestricted function codes, and unrestricted built-ins	Fired after each record is updated.
Pre-Block (block)	No	SELECT statements and unrestricted built-ins	Fired during navigation into another block.
Pre-Commit (form)	No	SELECT statements, DML statements, and unrestricted built-ins	Fired before a COMMIT statement is issued.
Pre-Delete (form or block)	No	SELECT statements, DML statements, and unrestricted built-ins	Fired before a row is deleted.

Table D-1 Form triggers (continued)

Trigger name	Enter Query mode	Commands allowed	Description
Pre-Form (form)	No	SELECT statements and unrestricted built-ins	Fired before the input focus moves into a new form.
Pre-Insert (form or block)	No	SELECT statements, DML statements, and unrestricted built-ins	Fired before a record is inserted into a table.
Pre-Logon (form)	No	SELECT statements and unrestricted built-ins	Fired before Forms Builder attempts to log on to Oracle.
Pre-Popup-Menu (popup menu)	Yes	SELECT statements, restricted built-ins, and unrestricted built-ins	Fired before a popup menu is displayed.
Pre-Query (form or block)	No	SELECT statements and unrestricted built-ins	Fired before a SELECT statement is issued.
Pre-Record (form or block)	No	SELECT statements and unrestricted built-ins	Fired during navigation to another record.
Pre-Select (form or block)	No	SELECT statements and unrestricted built-ins	Fired after a SELECT statement has been constructed but before it is issued.
Pre-Text-Item (form, block, or item)	No	SELECT statement and unrestricted built-ins	Fired before entry into an item.
Pre-Update (form or block)	No	SELECT statements, DML statements, and unrestricted built-ins	Fired before a record is updated.
Query-Procedure	Not applicable	Not applicable	Associated to a stored procedure and fired when a query is to be performed.
Update-Procedure	Not applicable	Not applicable	Associated to a stored procedure and fired when an update is to be performed.
When-Button-Pressed (form, block, or item)	Yes	SELECT statements, unrestricted built-ins, and restricted built-ins	Fired when a button item is clicked.

Table D-1 Form triggers (continued)

Trigger name	Enter Query mode	Commands allowed	Description
When-Checkbox-Changed (form, block, or item)	Yes	SELECT statements unrestricted built-ins, and restricted built-ins	Fired when an operator modifies a check box.
When-Clear-Block (form or block)	Yes	SELECT statements and unrestricted built-ins	Fired before Forms Builder clears a block of records.
When-Create-Record (form or block)	No	SELECT statements and unrestricted built-ins	Fired when Forms Builder creates a new record.
When-Database-Record (form or block)	No	SELECT statements and unrestricted built-ins	Fired when a record is marked for insert or update. This generally occurs when an operator modifies a value.
When-Form-Navigate (form)	No	Unrestricted built-ins and restricted built-ins	Fired when navigation occurs in the form.
When-Image-Activated (form, block, or item)	No	SELECT statements and unrestricted built-ins	Fired when an operator uses the mouse to single-click or double-click an image item.
When-Image Pressed (form, block, or item)	Yes	SELECT statements, unrestricted built-ins, and restricted built-ins	Fired when an operator clicks or double-clicks an image item.
When-List-Activated (form, block, or item)	Yes	SELECT statements, unrestricted built-ins, and restricted built-ins	Fired when an operator double-clicks a list item.
When-List-Changed (form, block, or item)	Yes	SELECT statements, unrestricted built-ins, and restricted built-ins	Fired when an operator selects a different list item.
When-Mouse-Click (form, block, or item)	Yes	SELECT statements, unrestricted built-ins, and restricted built-ins	Fired when the mouse is clicked.
When-Mouse-DoubleClick (form, block, or item)	Yes	SELECT statements, unrestricted built-ins, and restricted built-ins	Fired when the mouse is double-clicked.

Table D-1 Form triggers (continued)

Trigger name	Enter Query mode	Commands allowed	Description
When-Mouse-Down (form, block, or item)	Yes	SELECT statements, unrestricted built-ins, and restricted built-ins	Fired when an operator clicks the mouse button.
When-Mouse-Enter (form, block, or item)	Yes	SELECT statements, unrestricted built-ins, and restricted built-ins	Fired when the mouse enters an item or canvas.
When-Mouse-Leave (form, block, or item)	Yes	SELECT statements, unrestricted built-ins, and restricted built-ins	Fired when the mouse leaves an item or canvas.
When-Mouse-Move (form, block, or item)	Yes	SELECT statements, unrestricted built-ins, and restricted built-ins	Fired each time the mouse moves.
When-Mouse-Up (Form, block, or item)	Yes	SELECT statements, unrestricted built-ins, and restricted built-ins	Fired each time an operator releases the mouse button.
When-New-Block-Instance (form or block)	No	SELECT statements, unrestricted built-ins, and restricted built-ins	Fired when the input focus moves to a different block.
When-New-Form-Instance (form)	No	SELECT statements, unrestricted built-ins, and restricted built-ins	Fired when Forms Builder navigates into a form for the first time.
When-New-Item-Instance (form, block, or item)	Yes	SELECT statements, restricted built-ins, and unrestricted built-ins	Fired when the input focus moves into an item.
When-New-Record-Instance (form or block)	Yes	SELECT statements, unrestricted built-ins, and restricted built-ins	Fired when the input focus enters a different record.
When-Radio-Changed (form, block, or item)	Yes	SELECT statements, unrestricted built-ins, and restricted built-ins	Fired when a different radio button is selected.
When-Remove-Record (form or block)	No	SELECT statements and unrestricted built-ins	Fired when a record is cleared or removed.

Table D-1 Form triggers (continued)

Trigger name	Enter Query mode	Commands allowed	Description
When-Tab-Page-Changed (form)	No	Unrestricted built-ins and restricted built-ins	Fired when an operator navigates from one tab page to another.
When-Timer-Expired (form)	Yes	SELECT statements, unrestricted built-ins, and restricted built-ins	Fired when a timer terminates.
When-Validate-Item (form, block, or item)	No	SELECT statements and unrestricted built-ins	Fired during an item validation process.
When-Validate-Record (form or block)	No	SELECT statements and unrestricted built-ins	Fired as the final part of the record validation process.
When-Window-Activated (form)	Yes	SELECT statements, unrestricted built-ins, and restricted built-ins	Fired when a window is activated at form startup or whenever a different window is given focus.
When-Window-Closed (form)	Yes	SELECT statements, unrestricted built-ins, and restricted built-ins	Fired when an operator uses the CLOSE command to close a window.
When-Window-Deactivated (form)	Yes	SELECT statements, unrestricted built-ins, and restricted built-ins	Fired when a window is deactivated by an operator who changes the input focus to another window.
When-Window-Resized (form)	Yes	SELECT statements, unrestricted built-ins, and restricted built-ins	Fired when the window is resized.

APPENDIX

E

BUILT-IN SUBPROGRAMS

Built-in subprograms are procedures and functions created by Oracle that can be added to your form. The built-ins perform a variety of tasks, such as placing the form into the Enter Query mode, setting object properties, and displaying error messages. Built-ins are placed into PL/SQL code blocks that reside in a trigger. Table E-1 describes the built-ins available in Forms Builder 9*i* and whether restrictions apply. The following two restrictions that can affect the use of the built-ins are included in the table.

- Fired In the Query Mode — Indicates whether the trigger can be fired when the data block is in the Enter Query mode. A value of YES indicates that the trigger can be fired in this mode. A value of NO indicates that the trigger cannot be fired in the Enter Query mode.
- Restricted Procedure — Indicates whether the built-in can be used in a trigger that is fired as a result of navigation. Restricted procedures cannot be fired by these types of triggers. Built-ins with a value of YES in this column are Restricted procedures and cannot be used in triggers fired during navigation. Built-ins with a value of NO can be used in any trigger.

Table E-1 is designed as a handy reference for learning about and using built-ins. If you need a built-in to perform a specific function, use this table to find the function. Most of these built-ins take arguments and have options. In addition, many of the built-ins are overloaded. This means that there are multiple versions of the same named procedure. Before using these built-ins, you may want to check the Forms Builder On-Line Help.

Table E-1 Forms Builder built-ins

Name	Fired in the Query mode	Restricted procedure	Description
Abort_query	Yes	No	Terminates a query that is open in the current block.
Add_group_column	Yes	No	Adds a column to a target record group.
Add_group_row	Yes	No	Adds a row to a target record group.
Add_list_element	Yes	No	Adds an element to a list item.
Add_parameter	Yes	No	Adds a parameter to a parameter list.
Add_tree_data	No	No	Adds data to the hierarchical tree item under the target node.
Add_tree_node	No	No	Adds a data element to a hierarchical tree item.
Adjust_tz	Yes	No	Modifies a date from one time zone to another.
Bell	Yes	No	Causes a bell to sound.
Call_form	Yes	No	Runs the target form. The calling form remains open and the operator is returned to this form when the called form is closed.
Call_input	No	Yes	Accepts and processes function key input from the end user.
Cancel_report_object	Yes	No	Cancels long-running asynchronous reports.
Checkbox_checked	Yes	No	Returns a Boolean value indicating the state of a check box.
Check_record_uniqueness	Yes	No	Starts the default Forms Builder processing for checking the primary key uniqueness of a record.
Clear_block	No	Yes	Causes Forms Builder to remove all records from the current block.
Clear_eol	Yes	Yes	Removes the text in a text item from the current cursor position to the end of the line.
Clear_form	No	Yes	Causes Forms Builder to remove all records from a form.
Clear_item	Yes	Yes	Removes the value from the current text item.
Clear_message	Yes	Yes	Deletes the current message from the message area.
Clear_record	Yes	Yes	Causes Forms Builder to remove records from the data block without validating the records.

Table E-1 Forms Builder built-ins (continued)

Name	Fired in the Query mode	Restricted procedure	Description
Close_form	No	Yes	Closes the target form.
Commit_form	No	Yes	Causes Forms Builder to make permanent the changes in the database. This makes the database record the same as the Forms record.
Convert_other_value	Yes	Yes	Changes the current value of a check box, radio group, or list item to the value associated with the current check box state.
Copy	Yes	No	Replicates a value from one target item to another target item.
Copy_report_object_output	Yes	No	Replicates the output of a report to a file.
Copy_region	Yes	Yes	Replicates the selected text item or image item region and stores it in the clipboard.
Count_query	Yes	Yes	Performs the default Forms Builder processing for identifying the number of rows that a query will retrieve for the current block.
Create_group	Yes	No	Creates a non-query record group that has no columns and rows.
Create_group_from_query	Yes	No	Creates a record group based on the columns in a target SELECT statement.
Create_parameter_list	Yes	No	Creates a blank parameter list.
Create_queried_record	No	Yes	Creates a record on the block's waiting list. A waiting list is an intermediary buffer that contains records that have been fetched from the data source but have not yet been placed on the block's list of active records.
Create_record	No	Yes	Creates a new record in the current record. The record will be placed immediately after the current record.
Create_timer	Yes	No	Creates a new timer with a target name.
Create_var	Yes	No	Creates an unnamed and empty variant.
Cut_region	Yes	Yes	Removes a selected region of a text item or an image item from the screen and stores it in the clipboard.

E

Table E-1 Forms Builder built-ins (continued)

Name	Fired in the Query mode	Restricted procedure	Description
Dbms_error_code	Yes	No	Returns the error number of the last database error.
Dbms_error_text	Yes	No	Returns the error number and error text of the last database error.
Default_value	Yes	No	Populates a target variable with a value when it is NULL.
Delete_group	Yes	No	Deletes a programmatically created record group.
Delete_group_row	Yes	No	Deletes a target row in a specified record group.
Delete_list_element	Yes	No	Deletes an element from a list item.
Delete_parameter	Yes	No	Deletes a target parameter from the parameter list.
Delete_record	No	Yes	Deletes the current record from the block and marks it for deletion in the database.
Delete_timer	Yes	No	Deletes a target timer from the form.
Delete_tree_node	No	No	Removes a target data element from a hierarchical tree item.
Destroy_parameter_list	Yes	No	Deletes a programmatically created parameter list along with its parameters.
Destroy_variant	Yes	No	Destroys a variant that was created by the Create_var function.
Display_error	Yes	No	Displays the Display Error screen if a logged error occurs.
Display_item	Yes	No	Modifies an item's appearance. It is maintained for backward compatibility. The Set_item_instance_property built-in should be used instead.
Do_key	Yes	No	Fires the key trigger that corresponds to the specified built-in subprogram.
Down	No	Yes	Moves the input focus to the record with the next higher sequence number.
Dummy_reference	Yes	No	Provides a mechanism for coding an explicit reference to a bind variable that otherwise would be referred to only indirectly in a formula.
Duplicate_item	No	Yes	Populates the current item with the same values as the corresponding item in the previous record.

Table E-1 Forms Builder built-ins (continued)

Name	Fired in the Query mode	Restricted procedure	Description
Duplicate_record	No	Yes	Populates the current record's items with the same values as the items in the previous record.
Edit_textitem	Yes	No	Invokes the Runform item editor for the current text item.
Enforce_column_security	Yes	No	Executes default processing for checking column security on a database column.
Enter	Yes	No	Validates data in the current validation unit.
Enter_query	Yes	No	Places the data block into the Enter Query mode.
Erase	Yes	No	Deletes a target global variable.
Error_code	Yes	No	Returns the error number of the Forms Builder error.
Error_text	Yes	No	Returns the message text of the Forms Builder error.
Error_type	Yes	No	Returns the message type for the most recently performed action.
Execute_query	Yes	Yes	Executes the query and fetches the records to the data block by placing the form into the Execute Query mode.
Execute_trigger	Yes	Yes	Fires the target trigger.
Exit_form	Yes	Yes	Closes the form when the form is in the Normal mode. Places the form into the Normal mode when the form is in the Enter Query mode.
Fetch_records	No	Yes	Initiates the default Forms Builder processing for fetching records that have been identified by SELECT statement processing.
Find_alert	Yes	No	Returns the ID of the named alert.
Find_block	Yes	No	Returns the ID of the named block.
Find_canvas	Yes	No	Returns the ID of the named canvas.
Find_column	Yes	No	Returns the group column ID of the named column.
Find_editor	Yes	No	Returns the editor ID of the named editor.
Find_form	Yes	No	Returns the form ID of the named form.

Table E-1 Forms Builder built-ins (continued)

Name	Fired in the Query mode	Restricted procedure	Description
Find_group	Yes	No	Returns the group ID of the named record group.
Find_item	Yes	No	Returns the item ID of the named data block item.
Find_lov	Yes	No	Returns the LOV ID of the named data block item.
Find_menu_item	Yes	No	Returns the menu item ID of the named menu item.
Find_relation	Yes	No	Returns the relation ID of the named relation.
Find_report_object	Yes	No	Returns the ID of the named report object.
Find_tab_page	Yes	No	Returns the ID of the named tab page.
Find_timer	Yes	No	Returns the timer ID of a target timer name.
Find_tree_node	No	No	Identifies the next node in the tree whose label matches the target string.
Find_va	Yes	No	Returns the visual attribute ID of a target visual attribute name.
Find_view	Yes	No	Returns the view ID of a target view name.
Find_window	Yes	No	Returns the window ID of a target window name.
First_record	No	Yes	Navigates to the first record in a data block.
Form_failure	Yes	No	Returns a value representing the outcome of a recent form action. Values are TRUE (failure) and FALSE (success, failure).
Form_fatal	Yes	No	Returns a value representing the outcome of a recent form action. Values are TRUE (fatal error) and FALSE (success, failure).
Form_success	Yes	No	Returns a Boolean value representing the success of the last form action. Values are TRUE (success) and FALSE (failure, fatal error).
Forms_ddl	Yes	No	Issues dynamic SQL, PL/SQL, and DDL statements.

Table E-1 Forms Builder built-ins (continued)

Name	Fired in the Query mode	Restricted procedure	Description
Generate_sequence_number	Yes	No	Initiates the default Forms Builder processing for generating a unique sequence number when a record is created.
Get_application_property	Yes	No	Determines a property value for the current form.
Get_block_property	Yes	No	Determines a property value for a target data block.
Get_canvas_property	Yes	No	Determines a property value for a target canvas.
Get_file_name	Yes	No	Displays the standard Open File dialog box.
Get_form_property	Yes	No	Determines the property value of a target form.
Get_group_char_cell	Yes	No	Determines the varchar2 or long value for a record group cell. The returned value is based on a row and column value.
Get_group_date_cell	Yes	No	Determines the date value for a record group cell. The returned value is based on a row and column value.
Get_group_number_cell	Yes	No	Determines the numeric value for a record group cell. The returned value is based on a row and column value.
Get_group_record_number	Yes	No	Returns the first record number in the record group that has a column value equal to a specific parameter.
Get_group_row_count	Yes	No	Returns the number of rows in a record group.
Get_group_selection	Yes	No	Returns the sequence number of a selected record group row.
Get_group_selection_count	Yes	No	Returns the number of selected rows in a record group.
Get_item_instance_property	Yes	No	Returns a property value for the specific instance of an item.
Get_item_property	Yes	No	Returns the property value of a target data block item.
Get_list_element_count	Yes	No	Returns the number of elements in a target list item.
Get_list_element_label	Yes	No	Returns a label value for a target list item element.

Table E-1 Forms Builder built-ins (continued)

Name	Fired in the Query mode	Restricted procedure	Description
Get_list_element_value	Yes	No	Returns a value for a target list item element.
Get_lov_property	Yes	No	Returns a property value for a target LOV.
Get_menu_item_property	Yes	No	Returns the value of a target menu item property.
Get_message	Yes	No	Returns the current message.
Get_parameter_attr	Yes	No	Returns the current value and type of parameter for an indicated parameter.
Get_parameter_list	Yes	No	Returns a parameter list ID for the target parameter form name.
Get_radio_button_property	Yes	No	Returns a target radio button's property value.
Get_record_property	Yes	No	Returns a property value for a target record.
Get_relation_property	Yes	No	Returns the value of the target relation property.
Get_report_object_property	Yes	No	Returns the report object property values.
Get_tab_page_property	Yes	No	Returns a property value of the target tab page.
Get_tree_node_parent	No	No	Returns the parent of the target node.
Get_tree_node_property	No	No	Returns the value of the target hierarchical tree item property.
Get_tree_property	No	No	Returns the value of the target hierarchical tree item.
Get_tree_selection	No	No	Returns the data node for the selection.
Get_va_property	Yes	No	Returns the value of a visual attribute property.
Get_var_bounds	Yes	No	Returns the bounds of the OLE variant's array.
Get_var_dims	Yes	No	Identifies whether an OLE variant is an array and returns the dimensions of the array.
Get_var_type	Yes	No	Returns the type of OLE variant.
Get_view_property	Yes	No	Returns the value of the indicated view property.
Get_window_property	Yes	No	Returns the value of the indicated window property.

Table E-1 Forms Builder built-ins (continued)

Name	Fired in the Query mode	Restricted procedure	Description
Go_block	No	Yes	Navigates to the targeted data block.
Go_form	No	Yes	Navigates to the specified form in a multiple-form application.
Go_item	Yes	Yes	Navigates to the target item.
Go_record	No	Yes	Navigates to the record specified by the record number.
Help	Yes	Yes	Displays the current item's hint message on the status line.
Hide_view	Yes	No	Hides the target canvas.
Hide_window	Yes	No	Hides the target window.
Host	Yes	No	Launches and runs an operating system command.
Id_null	Yes	No	Returns a Boolean value indicating that the object ID is available.
Image_scroll	Yes	No	Scrolls the image item as close to the specified offset X and Y coordinates as possible.
Image_zoom	Yes	No	Changes the amount of the image that is displayed in the image item. This makes the image objects appear larger or smaller.
Insert_record	No	Yes	Inserts the current record into the database when called from an On-Insert trigger.
Issue_rollback	No	Yes	Initiates the default processing for rolling back transactions to the indicated savepoint when called from an On-Rollback trigger.
Issue_savepoint	No	Yes	Initiates the default processing for issuing a savepoint when called from an On-Savepoint trigger.
Last_record	No	Yes	Navigates to the last of the data block's records.
List_values	No	Yes	Displays the LOV for the current item.
Lock_record	No	Yes	Tries to lock the database table row that corresponds to the current record.
Logon	Yes	No	Logs the application session with Oracle using the supplied user name and password.

Table E-1 Forms Builder built-ins (continued)

Name	Fired in the Query mode	Restricted procedure	Description
Logon_screen	Yes	No	Displays the Forms Builder logon screen, which prompts for a valid user name, password, and host string.
Logout	Yes	No	Disconnects the application from Oracle.
Message	Yes	No	Displays the indicated text on the message line.
Message_code	Yes	No	Returns the identifying number of the last message displayed by Forms Builder.
Message_text	Yes	No	Returns the message most recently generated by Forms Builder.
Message_type	Yes	No	Returns the type of message generated most recently by Forms Builder. Values are FRM (Forms Builder), ORA (Oracle message), and NULL (no message has been issued).
Move_window	Yes	No	Changes the location of a target window based upon new X and Y coordinate values.
Name_in	Yes	No	Returns the value of the indicated variable.
New_form	No	Yes	Opens a target form that closes the current form.
Next_block	No	Yes	Navigates to the first navigable item in the data block with the next highest sequence number.
Next_form	No	Yes	Navigates to the form with the next highest sequence number in a multiple-form application.
Next_item	No	Yes	Navigates to the navigable item with the next highest sequence number.
Next_key	Yes	Yes	Navigates to the primary key item with the next highest sequence number.
Next_record	No	Yes	Navigates to the first navigable item in the data block record that has the next highest sequence number.
Next_set	No	Yes	Fetches another set of records from the database and places the input focus into the first record of the set.

Table E-1 Forms Builder built-ins (continued)

Name	Fired in the Query mode	Restricted procedure	Description
Open_form	No	Yes	Opens the target form leaving the current form open.
Paste_region	Yes	Yes	Pastes the clipboard contents into the selected area.
Pause	Yes	No	Halts processing until a user presses a function key.
Populate_group	Yes	No	Populates a record group using the query associated with the record group.
Populate_group_with_query	Yes	No	Populates a record group with the data set returned by a SELECT statement.
Populate_group_from_tree	No	No	Populates a record group with data from a hierarchical tree item.
Populate_list	Yes	No	Deletes the contents of a current list and replaces the contents with the values from a record group.
Populate_tree	No	Yes	Removes the values in a hierarchical tree item and replaces the contents with a data set from a record group or SELECT statement generated by the Recordgroup or Querytext properties.
Post	No	Yes	Sends form data to the database but does not perform a commit.
Previous_block	No	Yes	Moves to the first navigable item in the block with the next lower sequence number.
Previous_form	No	Yes	Moves to the form with the next lower sequence number.
Previous_item	Yes	No	Moves to the item in the current record that has the next lower sequence number.
Previous_record	No	Yes	Moves the input focus to a navigable item in a data block record that has the next lower sequence number.
Print	Yes	No	Writes the current window to a printer or file.
Read_image_file	Yes	No	Reads an image file and places the image into an image item.

Table E-1 Forms Builder built-ins (continued)

Name	Fired in the Query mode	Restricted procedure	Description
Recalculate	Yes	No	Marks a target formula calculated item in each block record for recalculation. The actual recalculation occurs sometime after the item is marked and before the new value is referenced.
Redisplay	Yes	No	Clears system messages by redrawing the screen.
Replace_content_view	Yes	No	Replaces the content canvas displayed in the target window with another content canvas.
Replace_menu	Yes	No	Replaces the current menu with another menu.
Report_object_status	Yes	No	Determines the report status of a report launched using the Run_report_object built-in.
Reset_group_selection	Yes	No	Deselects selected rows in a target group.
Resize_window	Yes	No	Modifies the height and width properties of a target window.
Retrieve_list			Retrieves and places a current list into a target record group. The record group must have a two-column structure.
Run_product	Yes	No	Launches the Graphics product and specifies the name of the Graphics module to be run. In older versions of Forms Builder, this built-in can be also used to call reports. This is not the case in Forms Builder 9*i*.
Scroll_down	No	Yes	Changes the records displayed in the data block when the data block has more records than can be displayed at one time. Records hidden above the current set will be displayed.
Scroll_up	No	Yes	Changes the records displayed in the data block when the data block has more records than can be displayed at one time. Records hidden below the current set will be displayed.
Scroll_view	Yes	No	Changes the position of the view on a canvas by modifying the Viewport X Position on Canvas and Viewport Y Position on Canvas properties.

Table E-1 Forms Builder built-ins (continued)

Name	Fired in the Query mode	Restricted procedure	Description
Select_all	Yes	Yes	Selects the text in a current item for cutting and pasting.
Select_records	No	Yes	Initiates default Forms Builder Select processing. Used primarily when using non-Oracle databases.
Set_alert_property	Yes	No	Sets the message text for a target alert.
Set_alert_button_property	Yes	No	Sets the button label for a target alert.
Set_application_property	Yes	No	Sets a property for the current application.
Set_block_property	Yes	No	Sets a property for a target data block.
Set_canvas_property	Yes	No	Sets a property for a target canvas.
Set_custom_property	Yes	No	Sets the value of a user-defined property in a Java-pluggable component.
Set_form_property	Yes	No	Sets a property for a target form.
Set_group_char_cell	Yes	No	Sets the value of a char record group cell value. The cell is determined by row and column parameters.
Set_group_date_cell	Yes	No	Sets the value of a date record group cell value. The cell is determined by row and column parameters.
Set_group_number_cell	Yes	No	Sets the value of a numeric record group cell value. The cell is determined by row and column parameters.
Set_group_selection	Yes	No	Marks a target row in a record group for subsequent programmatic row operations.
Set_item_instance_property	Yes	No	Sets an item property. This property affects only a specific instance of the item on the data block.
Set_item_property	Yes	No	Sets an item property. This built-in affects all instances of the item on the data block.
Set_lov_column_property	Yes	No	Sets a target LOV column property.
Set_lov_property	Yes	No	Sets a target LOV property.
Set_menu_item_property	Yes	No	Sets a target menu item property.
Set_parameter_attr	Yes	No	Modifies a parameter in a target parameter list.
Set_radio_button_property	Yes	No	Modifies a radio button property.
Set_record_property	Yes	No	Modifies a record property value.

Table E-1 Forms Builder built-ins (continued)

Name	Fired in the Query mode	Restricted procedure	Description
Set_relation_property	Yes	No	Modifies a relation property value.
Set_report_object_property	Yes	No	Modifies a report property value.
Set_tab_page_property	Yes	No	Sets a property for a target tab page.
Set_timer	Yes	No	Modifies settings for a running timer.
Set_tree_node_property	No	Yes	Sets the state (expanded/collapsed) of a branch node for a target hierarchical item.
Set_tree_property	No	Yes	Sets a specified property for a target hierarchical tree item.
Set_tree_selection	No	No	Causes the selection of a single node.
Set_va_property	Yes	No	Sets a specified property for a target visual attribute.
Set_view_property	Yes	No	Sets a specified property for a target view.
Set_window_property	Yes	No	Sets a specified property for a target window.
Show_alert	Yes	No	Displays the target alert and returns a number value indicating the button that was pressed in the alert.
Show_editor	Yes	No	Displays the target editor.
Show_keys	Yes	No	Opens and displays the Keys screen.
Show_lov	Yes	No	Displays the target LOV and returns a value of TRUE if the operator selects a value.
Show_view	Yes	No	Displays the target canvas. If it is displayed, it will raise the canvas above any other opened canvas.
Show_window	Yes	No	Displays the target window.
Synchronize	Yes	No	Synchronizes the display's screen with the internal state of the form.
Unset_group_selection	Yes	No	Removes the mark from the target row in the selected record group.
Up	No	Yes	Moves to the record with the next lowest data block record sequence number.
Update_chart	Yes	No	Causes a chart item to be updated.

Table E-1 Forms Builder built-ins (continued)

Name	Fired in the Query mode	Restricted procedure	Description
Update_record	No	Yes	Launches the default Forms Builder processing for updating a database record during the Post and Commit Transactions process. This built-in is used primarily for non-Oracle data sources.
User_exit	Yes	No	Calls the named user exit.
Validate	Yes	No	Causes Forms Developer to immediately execute validation processing.
Web.Show_document	Yes	No	Displays a Web document for a specific URL in a specified Web browser window.
Write_image_file	Yes	No	Writes an image to a file from a Forms Developer image item.

Glossary

ADT — *See* abstract data type.

Abstract data type — A data type developed by Oracle that essentially consists of a template of a series of columns. The abstract data types are used to define a PL/SQL record, as the data type of a column in a table, or as an array of values. An abstract data type is an object-oriented database device.

Alert — A form module object or component. It is a modal dialog box that notifies or alerts the form operator of an event.

Application tier — The middle tier in a three-tier architecture, which contains the applications. It also synchronizes the database calls and the Web browser requests. For Oracle Developer systems, it is the Oracle9*i* Application Server. It is also called the middle tier.

Associative entity — An entity relationship drawing symbol that relates one entity with another entity. An associative entity is also called a gerund and relates two other entities that are in a many-to-many relationship. For example, Courses Taken is an associative entity that relates the entity Courses with the entity Students. An associative entity is needed, because the relationship between Courses and Students is a many-to-many relationship. A student can take many courses and a course can have many students. Associative entities often have data attributes of their own. The Courses Taken entity would have the student's grade as an attribute that describes the course that was taken.

Attached library — A file containing PL/SQL objects. This file or library can be attached to a form module allowing the module to use portions of the library.

Back end tier — The database tier in a three-tier architecture. It is the tier called by the Application Server on the Application tier.

Bean area — A data block item that displays the output of a JavaBean.

Breakpoint — A function that causes Forms Builder to suspend execution of a form during Debug mode. It allows the developer to inspect variables and to execute statements a line at a time. Breakpoints are added in the left margin of the PL/SQL Editor.

Built-in subprogram — Functions and procedures developed by Oracle that are used inside triggers to perform actions such as placing the form into the query mode, displaying an alert, or setting a property programmatically.

Business rules — Rules that affect data values, for example, the rule that a work order must have a parent project.

Calculated item — A data block item that receives its value based on a summarization of another data block column or a formula contained in its Formula property.

Calendar.pll — The PL/SQL library that must be attached to the form to create a calendar that is callable from a data block item.

Canvas — A form module graphic object. All items and graphics that are displayed must be placed on a canvas.

Cardinality — An entity relationship concept that identifies the number of related entity instances that can occur. For example, a project can have many related work orders, but a work order can have only one related project. The cardinality of this relationship is one-to-many.

CASE — Acronym for computer aided software engineering. CASE implies the use of software packages such as Oracle's Designer9*i*. These tools allow the developer to create data flow diagrams, entity relationship diagrams, data schema diagrams, DDL statements, and to generate the default form module.

Client tier — The tier accessed by the user in a three-tier architecture, for example, the Web browser containing the form. Also called the Front End tier.

Code management — Procedures that comprise the rules for placing code into production. This can consist of a code librarian or tools used to check out code.

Column — An attribute or named value that is stored in a table. WORK ORDER NUMBER is an example of a column that is stored in the WORK ORDERS table.

Combo Box — A type of data block list item. Combo boxes automatically select the first element that matches the entered combo box characters.

Composite key — A primary key that comprises two or more columns. A related child table such as COURSES TAKEN (by a student) is representative of a table containing a composite key (STUDENT ID and COURSE ID).

Connect string — A value that identifies the Oracle installation to which the operator wants to connect. This value is generally needed when logging on to a database not located on your computer.

Content canvas — A type of canvas used by the form. It is a base or main canvas.

Control block — A data block that is not associated to a data source.

Coordination-type toggle trigger — A trigger that allows the operator to dynamically change a relation's Deferred and Automatic Query properties, which determine when a detail block is populated.

Cursor — A PL/SQL component that consists of a named area of memory that temporarily stores the results of a SELECT statement for later processing by the PL/SQL code block.

Cursor variable — A variable consisting of a series of PL/SQL records that store a SELECT statement's result set. The variable is the tool that passes the result set to another PL/SQL procedure.

Data block — A form module component that contains items that hold data values. Data blocks are generally associated with a database table and its columns.

Data definition language — A language that defines data and its relationships to other data.

Data flow diagram — A data flow diagram that represents the data elements that are moving into or out of a process.

Data manipulation language — A subset of the structured query language (SQL) that is used to modify the data within the table. The language uses INSERT, UPDATE, and DELETE statements.

Data Stores — A data flow diagram object that represents data at rest.

Database schema — The design of the database. It consists of the tables, columns, keys, relationships, and data types.

DDL — *See* data definition language.

Detail data block — The data block that displays the child records in a one-to-many or one-to-one relationship. Detail data blocks have their foreign key items populated using the Copy Value From property referencing the primary key in a master or coordinating block.

DFD — *See* data flow diagram.

Directory — A special application consisting of a control block used to enter selection criteria and a multiple item block that displays records that match the entered search values. The benefit of this style of application is that the search values are always displayed.

Display item — A data block item that cannot be modified.

DML — *See* data manipulation language.

Editor — A text area that can be launched from a form item or a property setting area in Forms Builder. They are used to enter lengthy values.

Encapsulation — An object-oriented concept in which data and the methods that affect the data are bound together. Oracle Packages are a method of binding many PL/SQL objects together into one object.

Entity — A data modeling object. An entity is something about which data is kept. Identifying entities is the first task in designing the tables that comprise a database.

Entity relationship drawing — A data modeling tool that represents entities, the attributes that describe an entity instance, and the relationships between entities.

ERD — *See* entity relationship drawing.

External entity — A data flow diagram symbol that identifies the sources of system input and the receivers of the system's output.

FMB file extension — A group of characters that identify the form binary source files used in the Forms Builder IDE.

FMX file extension — A group of characters that identify the form source code file actually executed by Forms Builder runtime.

Foreign key — A column in a related or child table that is a primary key value in the other related table. It is used to relate the record to a record in the parent table.

Formsweb.cfg — A server file that is used to configure the applet that displays the form in the Web browser.

From clause query — A data block property (Query Data Source Type) value that indicates the block's data source is a SELECT statement entered into the Query Data Source Name property.

Front end tier — The tier accessed by the user in a three-tier architecture. The Web browser containing the form is representative of this tier.

Function — PL/SQL code block that is stored in the database. The code block always returns a value to the calling statement.

Gerund — *See* associative entity.

Global variable — A variable that is defined during the session and stays in memory until the session is closed or deleted. The variable values can be passed from one form to another.

Grab handle — Graphic symbols that appear around an object in the Layout Editor when the object is selected. They allow the developer to resize the object.

Grid — A pattern of points that underlay the canvas in the Layout Editor work area and are used to align objects. The snap-to-grid option causes a canvas object to always move to the closest grid point.

Hierarchical tree item — A data block item that stores the results of a SELECT statement in a hierarchical framework or nodes. It allows the operator to easily navigate through the data.

Horizontal toolbar canvas — A type of canvas that is displayed at the top of the Forms runtime area or at the top of the form window. It displays a series of buttons that perform tasks. The buttons are often iconic.

ICO file extension — A file extension for files used as icons on a button.

Iconic button — A type of data block push button that has an associated icon file. The icon file is displayed on top of the button.

Identifier — A data modeling concept. It is an entity attribute that makes an instance of the entity unique from all other instances of the entity.

Inheritance — An object-oriented concept whereby a higher level object can inherit the attributes and behaviors of lower level object. A higher-level object, such as a faculty member, can inherit address attributes from a lower-level address object.

In-line view — A SELECT statement that is embedded into a SELECT statement From clause. It operates like a view except that it is not defined in the database.

Input focus — The current position on the screen where the operator can enter a value.

Insertion point — *See* input focus.

Instance — An occurrence of an entity. For example, John Palinski is an instance of the entity Author.

Instead-of trigger — A database trigger that is associated with a view. When DML statements are executed against the view, the Instead-Of trigger is fired replacing the original DML statement.

Layout Editor — A major Forms Builder tool used to format a form's canvases.

Library tab — One of the tabs in an Object library.

List item — A data block item that consists of a series of elements displayed on a list. There are three types of list items: pick list, Tlist, and combo box.

LOV — A popup dialog box that displays a dynamic or static list of values. LOVs are used to populate and validate item values.

Magic menu item — A menu item that executes an operating system function such as cut, paste, or copy.

Master data block — The controlling block in a two-block relationship. The primary key value from this data block is passed to the detail block to ensure it displays records that pertain to the selected master data block record.

Master-detail layout — A data block format style that consists of two data blocks displaying a record in the master data block and a series of related child records in a detail data block. This style relates to tables that are related in a one-to-many relationship.

Menudefs.mmb — An Oracle supplied menu module that replicates the Default&smartbar toolbar used on default forms. It can be modified to suit your needs.

Methods — An object-oriented component that consists of the programs that affect a specific set of attributes.

Middle tier — The middle tier in a three-tier architecture. It contains the applications and synchronizes the database calls and the Web browser requests. For Oracle Developer systems, it is the Oracle 9*i* Application Server. It is also called the application tier.

MMB file extension — A set of characters that identifies the menu binary source files used in the Forms Builder IDE.

MMX file extension — Identifies the menu source code file actually executed by Forms Builder runtime.

Modes (form) — The various form operating modes that include the following: Enter Query mode, which occurs when the form is prompting the operator for search or filter values; Query mode, which occurs when the form is retrieving records to the data block; and Normal mode, which occurs when the data block is displaying records or is available for adding records.

Module — The term that Forms Builder uses for a file.

Non-base table blocks — *See* control block.

Not null — A database column constraint that requires the target item to always contain a value.

Object — An object-oriented concept and term. It is a set of attributes that represent or model a thing, such as a student, car, address, or building. An object also consists of the methods that affect its attributes.

Object group — A form component that combines a series of other form module components. The group is used to copy its components into another form as one set of components rather than as individual components.

Object Navigator — The main Forms Builder tool that displays various Forms Builder modules in a hierarchy. The modules can be expanded, exposing the various module components. It can be used to locate, add, update, and delete any module component.

Object privileges — A class of database privileges that consists of the ability to insert, update, and delete table records. It also consists of the privilege to execute PL/SQL stored procedures.

Object type — A database declaration that consists of a series of attributes that describe an object.

Object library — A Forms Builder module that stores forms and menu components for reuse in other modules.

OLB extension — A set of characters that identifies an object library file.

Ordinality — A data modeling characteristic that identifies whether a related entity instance is mandatory. For example, it is mandatory that Courses Taken entity instances have related Courses entity instances. However, it is not mandatory for a Courses entity to have a related Courses Taken entity.

Overloaded — A programming concept whereby multiple database code objects have exactly the same name but are differentiated by the objects argument list.

Package — A PL/SQL construct that is used to group PL/SQL components such as cursors, functions, and procedures.

Package body — The package component that contains the actual PL/SQL objects along with their code blocks.

Package specification — The package component that contains the PL/SQL header sections. Objects identified in this section can be referenced by objects outside the package.

Parameter — A form variable that can receive a value from outside the form session.

PL/SQL — An Oracle proprietary programming language.

PL/SQL Editor — One of the main Forms Builder IDE tools that is used to document and compile PL/SQL code blocks that are used by the form or stored in the database.

PL/SQL record — A PL/SQL construct that consists of a series of variables. This construct can store one instance of the variable set. PL/SQL records are often used to store the values from a single database record.

PL/SQL table — A PL/SQL construct that comprises one or more PL/SQL records.

Poplist — A type of data block list item that displays a drop-down list when launched.

Popup menu — A form object that consists of a menu that appears adjacent to the insertion point when the right mouse button is pressed.

Primary key — A column(s) that contains values that make each record distinct from other records in the table.

Procedure — A PL/SQL object consisting of a PL/SQL code block that can be called from a trigger. A procedure can be stored in the database or within the form.

Program unit — A form object node used to group functions, procedures, package specifications, and package bodies defined within the form module.

Prompt — Text that precedes a data block item and is used to describe or give meaning to the value within the item.

Property class — A form object that consists of a set of properties and property values. The property values are inherited by any object associated to the property class via the Subclass Information property.

Property palette — A Forms Builder IDE tool used to set form object property values.

Prototype — A quickly developed application that does not contain all of the features of the final application. Its purpose is to offer users an evaluation glimpse of the application early in the development phase. Prototypes are not generally perfected until the final application is ready.

RAD — Rapid application development. A methodology that shortens the system development life cycle by eliminating some of the life cycle steps.

Radio group button — A radio group child object that consists of a button that represents a specific value when pressed. Radio group buttons are grouped together. Each button represents the distinct value of the item.

Radio group — A type of data block item. It is the parent object of a series of radio buttons that comprise the item's possible value.

REF cursor — A pointer to a record in an object table. Object tables do not contain foreign keys, thus the need for a pointer to the record.

Regular entity — A data modeling symbol for an entity that can have an instance regardless of the existence of a related entity instance. The Student entity is an example of a regular entity. It does not need a different entity instance to be created for its existence. It compares to the Courses Taken entity, which needs a Student entity instance to be created before it can exist.

Relation — A form module object that determines how master-detail data blocks relate and their behavior.

Reports — A form module object that contains settings for the execution of an Oracle report module.

Restricted built-in subprogram — An Oracle-developed procedure or function that cannot be executed in a trigger that is fired as a result of navigation.

Reusability — A programming concept whereby components are reused. This concept is supported by the object groups, object libraries, procedures, and functions available in forms.

Role — A database security object. It consists of a set of object and system privileges that can be assigned to a user. Roles are used in menus to determine which item can be pressed.

Rowid — The Oracle unique record identifier.

Ruler — A feature of the Layout Editor. It measures the size of the canvas in various measurements.

Same record navigation — A style of navigation whereby the input focus returns to the first navigable record item after tabbing from the last item in the record.

SELECT statement — The SQL command or statement used to retrieve records or values from the database.

Sink — A data flow diagram symbol indicating the receiver of system output.

SmartClasses — A designation that can be placed on a property class stored in an object library. Placing this designation on the property class will cause its components to appear under the SmartClasses menu item when the right mouse button is clicked on the Object Navigator.

Source — A data flow diagram symbol indicating the sender of system input.

SQL — *See* Structured Query Language.

Sqlcode — An Oracle built-in that returns the number of the last database error.

Sqlerrm — An Oracle built-in that returns text that describes the last database error.

Stacked canvas — A canvas type that can overlay a stacked canvas. It is generally used as the canvas for a dialog box that is displayed in a form.

State — An active connection whereby the server is aware or has retained information about previous requests from the client.

Stndrd20.olb — A default object library supplied with Form Builder 6i that contains form components for wizards, calendars and other custom tools.

Stored procedure — A PL/SQL code block that has a name and is stored in the database.

Structured Query Language — The language used to interact with a relational database. It can be used to retrieve and maintain records as well as maintain the database objects that store the records.

Subclass — A form object property that associates the object to a property class or another object. Whenever the associated object has a property value change, the modification is propagated to the object when it is recompiled.

Synonym — Another name for a database object such as a table. It can mask the complexity caused by using objects on many different Oracle installations.

System privileges — Privileges that allow the developer to perform database maintenance such as creating tables, establishing user IDs, and granti-ng privileges.

System variable — A form variable that indicates a characteristic of the form or controls a behavior of the form. For example, the MESSAGE_LEVEL variable can suppress the issuance of error messages.

Tab canvas — A type of canvas that consists of a series of pages that overlay each other. Only the current page and each page's tab are displayed.

Tab page — A stacked canvas with a tab that is displayed on a tab canvas.

Table — A database object that is used to store values. It consists of records that have a series of named columns that store the values.

Text item — A data block item type that is used to enter, display, modify, or delete a value.

Timer — A form programming tool that fires a triggering event when the timer has expired.

Tlist — A data block list item type, which consists of two scroll tools that allow the user to scroll through a value list displaying one value at a time.

Tooltip — Text that appears when the cursor is placed over an item.

Trigger — A form module object that contains a PL/SQL code block. The code block is executed as the result of a specific event.

Triggering event — An event that causes a trigger to be fired. Examples of triggering events are the opening of a new form, pressing a button, or retrieving a record to the data block.

Unrestricted built-in subprogram — An Oracle-developed procedure or function that can be executed by a trigger.

Vertical toolbar canvas — A type of canvas that is displayed at the side of the Forms runtime area or at the side of the form window. It displays a series of buttons that perform tasks. These buttons are often iconic.

View — A SELECT statement that is stored in the database. When the view is called, the SELECT statement is executed and the result set is sent to the calling object.

Visual attributes — A form module component that contains format properties. Visual attributes are assigned to various other form objects. They allow the developer to set many form component properties with little effort.

Weak entity — A data modeling symbol that identifies an entity that cannot exist without a parent entity. Weak entities generally represent repeating sets of values that are stored in related child tables.

Where clause — One of the clauses in an SQL statement (select, update, delete) that identify the records to be retrieved, updated, or deleted.

Wild-card symbol — Two symbols used in an SQL statement's Where clause to cause Oracle to ignore strings of characters when evaluating database values that determine whether the record is retrieved. The '%' symbol tells Oracle to ignore characters in the relative position of the symbol. The '_' symbol tells Oracle to ignore characters that are in the same position as the symbol.

Window — A form module component that displays the canvas.

Index

A

B

C

G

N

O

P

U

V

W

ORACLE SOFTWARE LICENSE AGREEMENT

YOU SHOULD CAREFULLY READ THE FOLLOWING TERMS AND CONDITIONS BEFORE BREAKING THE SEAL ON THE DISC ENVELOPE. AMONG OTHER THINGS, THIS AGREEMENT LICENSES THE ENCLOSED SOFTWARE TO YOU AND CONTAINS WARRANTY AND LIABILITY DISCLAIMERS. BY USING THE DISC AND/OR INSTALLING THE SOFTWARE, YOU ARE ACCEPTING AND AGREEING TO THE TERMS AND CONDITIONS OF THIS AGREEMENT. IF YOU DO NOT AGREE TO THE TERMS OF THIS AGREEMENT, DO NOT BREAK THE SEAL OR USE THE DISC. YOU SHOULD PROMPTLY RETURN THE PACKAGE UNOPENED.

LICENSE: ORACLE CORPORATION ("ORACLE") GRANTS END USER ("YOU" OR "YOUR") A NON-EXCLUSIVE, NON-TRANSFERABLE DEVELOPMENT ONLY LIMITED USE LICENSE TO USE THE ENCLOSED SOFTWARE AND DOCUMENTATION ("SOFTWARE") SUBJECT TO THE TERMS AND CONDITIONS, INCLUDING USE RESTRICTIONS, SPECIFIED BELOW.

You shall have the right to use the Software (a) only in object code form, (b) for development purposes only in the indicated operating environment for a single developer (one person) on a single computer, (c) solely with the publication with which the Software is included, and (d) solely for Your personal use and as a single user.

You are prohibited from and shall not (a) transfer, sell, sublicense, assign or otherwise convey the Software, (b) timeshare, rent or market the Software, (c) use the Software for or as part of a service bureau, (d) distribute the Software in whole or in part, (e) use the Programs for or as part of any third party training or as part of any classroom training, and/or (f) use the Programs for any other use not expressly permitted by this Agreement. Any attempt to transfer, sell, sublicense, assign or otherwise convey any of the rights, duties or obligations hereunder is void. You are prohibited from and shall not use the Software for internal data processing operations, processing data of a third party or for any commercial or production use. If You desire to use the Software for any use other than the development use allowed under this Agreement, You must contact Oracle, or an authorized Oracle reseller, to obtain the appropriate licenses. You are prohibited from and shall not cause or permit the reverse engineering, disassembly, decompilation, modification or creation of derivative works based on the Software. You are prohibited from and shall not copy or duplicate the Software except as follows: You may make one copy of the Software in machine-readable form solely for back-up purposes. No other copies shall be made without Oracle's prior written consent. You are prohibited from and shall not: (a) remove any product identification, copyright notices, or other notices or proprietary restrictions from the Software, or (b) run any benchmark tests with or of the Software. This Agreement does not authorize You to use any Oracle name, trademark or logo.

COPYRIGHT/OWNERSHIP OF SOFTWARE: The Software is the confidential and proprietary product of Oracle and is protected by copyright and other intellectual property laws. You acquire only the right to use the Software and do not acquire any rights, express or implied, in the Software or media containing the Software other than those specified in this Agreement. Oracle, or its licensor, shall at all times, including but not limited to after termination of this Agreement, retain all rights, title, and interest, including intellectual property rights, in the Software and media.

WARRANTY DISCLAIMER: THE SOFTWARE IS PROVIDED "AS IS" AND ORACLE SPECIFICALLY DISCLAIMS ALL WARRANTIES OF ANY KIND, EITHER EXPRESS OR IMPLIED, INCLUDING, BUT NOT LIMITED TO, THE IMPLIED WARRANTIES OF MERCHANTABILITY, SATISFACTORY QUALITY AND FITNESS FOR A PARTICULAR PURPOSE. ORACLE DOES NOT WARRANT, GUARANTEE OR MAKE ANY REPRESENTATIONS REGARDING THE USE, OR THE RESULTS OF THE USE, OF THE SOFTWARE IN TERMS OF CORRECTNESS, ACCURACY, RELIABILITY, CURRENTNESS OR OTHERWISE, AND DOES NOT WARRANT THAT THE OPERATION OF THE SOFTWARE WILL BE UNINTERRUPTED OR ERROR FREE. ORACLE EXPRESSLY DISCLAIMS ALL WARRANTIES NOT STATED HEREIN, NO ORAL OR WRITTEN INFORMATION OR ADVICE GIVEN BY ORACLE OR OTHERS SHALL CREATE A WARRANTY OR IN ANY WAY INCREASE THE SCOPE OF THIS LICENSE, AND YOU MAY NOT RELY ON ANY SUCH INFORMATION OR ADVICE.

LIMITATION OF LIABILITY: IN NO EVENT SHALL ORACLE BE LIABLE FOR ANY DIRECT, INDIRECT, INCIDENTAL, SPECIAL OR CONSEQUENTIAL DAMAGES, OR DAMAGES FOR LOSS OF PROFITS, REVENUE, DATA OR DATA USE, INCURRED BY YOU OR ANY THIRD PARTY, WHETHER IN AN ACTION IN CONTRACT OR TORT, EVEN IF ORACLE HAS BEEN ADVISED OF THE POSSIBILITY OF SUCH DAMAGES. SOME JURISDICTIONS DO NOT ALLOW THE EXCLUSION OF IMPLIED WARRANTIES OR LIMITATION OR EXCLUSION OF LIABILITY FOR INCIDENTAL OR CONSEQUENTIAL DAMAGES SO THE ABOVE EXCLUSIONS AND LIMITATION MAY NOT APPLY TO YOU.

TERMINATION: You may terminate this license at any time by discontinuing use of and destroying the Software together with any copies in any form. This license will also terminate if You fail to comply with any term or condition of this Agreement. Upon termination of the license, You agree to discontinue use of and destroy the Software together with any copies in any form. The Warranty Disclaimer, Limitation of Liability and Export Administration sections of this Agreement shall survive termination of this Agreement.

NO TECHNICAL SUPPORT: Oracle is not obligated to provide and this Agreement does not entitle You to any updates or upgrades to, or any technical support or phone support for, the Software.

EXPORT ADMINISTRATION: You acknowledge that the Software, including technical data, is subject to United States export control laws, including the United States Export Administration Act and its associated regulations, and may be subject to export or import regulations in other countries. You agree to comply fully with all laws and regulations of the United States and other countries ("Export Laws") to assure that neither the Software, nor any direct products thereof, are (a) exported, directly or indirectly, in violation of Export Laws, either to countries or nationals that are subject to United States export restrictions or to any end user who has been prohibited from participating in the Unites States export transactions by any federal agency of the United States government; or (b) intended to be used for any purposes prohibited by the Export Laws, including, without limitation, nuclear, chemical or biological weapons proliferation. You acknowledge that the Software may include technical data subject to export and re-export restrictions imposed by United States law.

RESTRICTED RIGHTS: The Software is provided with Restricted Rights. Use, duplication or disclosure of the Software by the United State government is subject to the restrictions set forth in the Rights in Technical Data and Computer Software Clauses in DFARS 252.227-7013(c)(1)(ii) and FAR 52.227-19(c)(2) as applicable. Manufacturer is Oracle Corporation, 500 Oracle Parkway, Redwood City, CA 94065.

MISCELLANEOUS: This Agreement and all related actions thereto shall be governed by California law. Oracle may audit Your use of the Software. If any provision of this Agreement is held to be invalid or unenforceable, the remaining provisions of this Agreement will remain in full force.

YOU ACKNOWLEDGE THAT YOU HAVE READ THIS AGREEMENT, UNDERSTAND IT, AND AGREE TO BE BOUND BY ITS TERMS AND CONDITIONS. YOU FURTHER AGREE THAT IT IS THE COMPLETE AND EXCLUSIVE STATEMENT OF THE AGREEMENT BETWEEN ORACLE AND YOU.

The two CDs attached to the back cover of this text include Oracle9*i* Developer Suite, Release 9.0.2.0.1, for Microsoft Windows NT, Microsoft Windows 2000, and Microsoft Windows XP.

For complete installation instructions, go to *www.course.com/cdkit*

MUST REGISTER FOR ORACLE TECHNOLOGY NETWORK

Oracle Technology Network puts you in touch with the online community behind the software that powers the internet. Download the latest development programs and sample code. Engage in discussions with the web's leading technologists. Keep connected with the latest insights and resources you need to stay ahead. Membership is FREE, and so is the latest development software. Before proceeding to use the software, **you must join OTN today at** *http://www.otn.oracle.com/books*. Once you join OTN, you agree that Oracle may contact you for marketing purposes. You also agree that any information you provide Oracle may be used for marketing purposes.